FEDERAL RULES OF EVIDENCE FOR UNITED STATES COURTS AND MAGISTRATES

With Amendments Effective
December 1, 1991

Including
Notes by the Federal Judicial Center
Pertinent Advisory Committee Notes
Relevant Legislative History
References to McCormick on Evidence, 4th
also

EMERGING PROBLEMS UNDER THE RULES

RULES FLOW CHART

ELECTRONIC RESEARCH IN EVIDENCE

WEST PUBLISHING CO.
ST. PAUL, MINN., 1992

ISBN 0–314–01074–2

INTRODUCTION
FEDERAL RULES OF EVIDENCE

Introduction[1]

This Pamphlet consists of the Federal Rules of Evidence and materials designed to aid in understanding, construing, and applying them.

Chief Justice Warren in 1965 appointed an advisory committee to draft rules of evidence for the federal courts. The committee's Preliminary Draft was published and circulated for comment in 1969. 46 F.R.D. 161. A Revised Draft was circulated in 1971. 51 F.R.D. 315. In 1972, the Supreme Court prescribed Federal Rules of Evidence, to be effective July 1, 1973. 56 F.R.D. 183. Justice Douglas dissented. Pursuant to the various enabling acts, Chief Justice Burger transmitted the rules to the Congress, which suspended the rules pending further study by the Congress. P.L. 93–12. After extensive study, the Congress enacted the rules into law with various amendments, to become effective July 1, 1975. P.L. 93–595, approved January 2, 1975, 88 Stat. 1926. The occasional amendments and additions that have since been made are reflected in the rules as here presented.

Thus the Federal Rules of Evidence are the product of both the rulemaking process established by the Supreme Court and the legislative process of the Congress. Of at least equal importance is the vast collection of common law precedents, with occasional statutes, that constituted the background against which the rules were evolved. It can be seen that each of these sources must be taken into consideration in reaching understanding of the rules.

The rules are in final analysis legislative in nature, and problems of their effect are problems of statutory interpretation. Questions whether interpretive inquiry should be directed to ascertaining the intent of the legislature or the meaning to its audience tend to be minimal, since the rules are directed to a skilled professional audience in the main, in contrast to, say, a criminal statute directed to the public generally. With the rules,

1. This introductory material was prepared by the late Professor Edward W. Cleary, Reporter to the Advisory Committee for the Federal Rules of Evidence. For a more detailed discussion, see Cleary, Preliminary Notes on Reading the Rules of Evidence, 57 Neb.L.Rev. 908 (1978).

intent and meaning tend to come together, with the same interpretive materials relevant to both. The basic relevant interpretive materials are the common law background and the legislative history, with the most significant aspects of the latter consisting of the Advisory Committee's Notes and various congressional reports and debates, briefly described below.

References to McCormick Text. The first item after each federal rule in the Pamphlet is a heading "Section References, McCormick 4th ed." [It should be noted that these references will differ somewhat from those of McCormick 1st Edition utilized in the Advisory Committee Notes following each rule.] Under it are the numbers of the text sections where the rule is mentioned or discussed, with the discussions more in depth shown in italics. Judicial decisions and other authorities construing the rule will be found in the listed sections. Any differences between the federal rule and the revised Uniform rule are pointed out in the text. Sections where the background and current posture of the common law are set forth and evaluated will be found near, usually preceding, sections discussing the rule.

Rules Prescribed by the Supreme Court. These rules were transmitted by the Court to the Congress, carried the prestige of the Court, and were the Court's exercise of the rulemaking powers granted by the various enabling acts. They constitute the framework and to a large extent also the particulars of the rules enacted by the Congress. Whether and how a Court's rule was amended by the Congress is described in the *Note by Federal Judicial Center* following each rule in the Pamphlet.

Advisory Committee's Notes. The Notes supported and explained the rules, were circulated with them, and were transmitted to the Congress with the rules. The involved congressional committees and subcommittees were thoroughly familiar with the Notes, and except where changes were made in the rules the Notes should be taken as the equivalent of a congressional committee report as representing the thinking of the Congress. The pertinent Note, or portion thereof, is set forth in the Pamphlet for each rule. Where the Congress returned to an earlier version of the rule, the Note is the one that corresponds to that version. Portions no longer relevant because of congressional changes in the rule are omitted.

Congressional Materials. The House took the lead in congressional consideration of the rules. Accordingly, in the Pamphlet any pertinent portion of the *Report of the House Committee on the*

Judiciary is the first of the congressional materials under each rule. Senate consideration of the rules chronologically followed that of the House, and as a result any pertinent portion of the *Report of the Senate Committee on the Judiciary* is located under each rule in the Pamphlet after that of the House committee. Where House and Senate passed differing versions of a rule, the difference was resolved by conference, and the *Conference Report* generally concludes the congressional materials. In some instances other congressional materials which are authoritative and helpful are, however, also included.

Some General Observations

Questions as to what a rule really means present probably the most basic problem of interpretation. The language of the rule itself should be taken as the prime source of meaning, read in the light of such context as may be relevant. The most relevant context will often be legislative history, which on occasion may even override an apparently plain and unmistakable meaning of the words of the rule.[2] The result may be startling, as when the Court of Appeals for the District of Columbia Circuit concluded that a conviction for attempted burglary used for impeachment under Rule 609(a) did not involve dishonesty as the language was used in the rule.[3] Yet the opposite conclusion would have been most difficult to reach in view of the legislative history of the rule.[4]

No common law of evidence in principle remains under the rules. "All relevant evidence is admissible except as otherwise provided. . . ."[5] In reality, of course, the common law remains as a source of guidance in identifying problems and suggesting solutions, within the confines of the rules.

A recurring question is that of the extent to which the application of the rules may be extended beyond their express provisions. Some explicit authorizations to courts to invent and create are found, as for example the provision of Rule 501 that privileges "shall be governed by the principles of the common law as they

2. The manner of exercise of its legislative powers by the Congress as spelled out in the Constitution is the passing of bills and obtaining the President's approval or overriding his veto. U.S. Const. art. 1 § 7. While this may suggest the irrelevance of legislative history, in the British tradition, the American commitment is contrary, and it can scarcely be denied that the reasoning of those involved is a helpful source of illumination, without having the authority of law.

3. United States v. Smith, 551 F.2d 348 (D.C.Cir.1976).

4. Id. at 362.

5. Fed.R.Evid. 402.

may be interpreted by the courts of the United States in the light of reason and experience," and the provisions of Rules 803(24) and 804(b)(5) for the restricted admission of hearsay statements not falling within an enumerated exception. A somewhat tighter rein is kept on the judiciary by the rules that obviously contemplate a measure of invention but only within the confines of a stated principle, as in Rule 404(b) where illustrations are given of purposes for which evidence of other crimes may be admitted.

With regard to the more particularized rules, how should parallel situations be treated? Should the rule be regarded as occuping the field exclusively, or should it be extended by analogy to related situations? The answer lies in the purpose of the rule: if the additional situation presents the same problem as that with which the rule was designed to deal, application of the rule is appropriate. For example, under Rule 801(d)(1)(C) an out-of-court identification statement made after viewing a photograph has been held to be governed by the nonhearsay rule specifically applicable to statements made after viewing the accused in person.[6] Or again, the prohibition against testimony by the judge in the trial over which he is presiding, in Rule 605, was extended to preclude testimony by his clerk.[7]

Not to be confused with the foregoing is the judicial engrafting onto a rule of a requirement not set forth in the rule and not supported by legislative history or other relevant context. An example is the engrafting of a requirement that other crimes as proof of intent under Rule 404(b) be proved by clear and convincing evidence, although no such provision is found in the rule.[8]

Rule 102 provides:

> These rules shall be construed to secure fairness in administration, elimination of unjustifiable expense and delay, and promotion of growth and development of the law of evidence to the end that the truth may be ascertained and proceedings justly determined.

Entitled "Purpose and Construction," the rule sets a high standard for approaching problems of application and meaning but furnishes small guidance to solving particular questions. The most important aspect of the rule may well be its implicit recogni-

6. United States v. Lewis, 565 F.2d 1248 (2d Cir.1977), cert. denied 435 U.S. 973.

7. Kennedy v. Great Atlantic & Pacific Tea Co., 551 F.2d 593 (5th Cir.1977), rehearing denied 554 F.2d 475.

8. United States v. Beechum, 555 F.2d 487 (5th Cir.1977). The panel decision was overturned in banc. 582 F.2d 898, cert. denied 440 U.S. 920.

tion that the rules do not, and cannot, resolve in specific terms a very large proportion of evidentiary uncertainties that may arise, and that solutions must be reached through application of accepted principles of statutory construction.

*

TABLE OF CONTENTS

TABLE OF CONTENTS

TABLE OF CONTENTS

*

FEDERAL RULES OF EVIDENCE FOR UNITED STATES COURTS AND MAGISTRATES *

PUBLIC LAW 93–595; 88 STAT. 1926

Approved Jan. 2, 1975

[H.R. 5463]

An Act to establish rules of evidence for certain courts and proceedings.

Be it enacted by the Senate and House of Representatives of the United States of America in Congress assembled, That:

The following rules shall take effect on the one hundred and eightieth day beginning after the date of the enactment of this Act. These rules apply to actions, cases, and proceedings brought after the rules take effect. These rules also apply to further procedure in actions, cases, and proceedings then pending, except to the extent that application of the rules would not be feasible, or would work injustice, in which event former evidentiary principles apply.

ORDER OF APRIL 30, 1979

1. That Rule 410 of the Federal Rules of Evidence be, and it hereby is, amended to read as follows:

[See amendment made thereby following Rule 410, post.]

2. That the foregoing amendment to the Federal Rules of Evidence shall take effect on November 1, 1979, and shall be applicable to all proceedings then pending except to the extent that in the opinion of the court the application of the amended rule in a particular proceeding would not be feasible or would work injustice.

3. That THE CHIEF JUSTICE be, and he hereby is, authorized to transmit to the Congress the foregoing amendment to the Federal Rules of Evidence in accordance with the provisions of 28 U.S.C. § 2076.

CONGRESSIONAL ACTION ON AMENDMENT PROPOSED APRIL 30, 1979

Pub.L. 96–42, July 31, 1979, 93 Stat. 326, provided that the amendment proposed and transmitted to the Federal Rules of Evidence

* References to sections of *McCormick on Evidence*, 4th ed. follow the text of each Rule. The more important section references are printed in italic.

affecting rule 410, shall not take effect until Dec. 1, 1980, or until and then only to the extent approved by Act of Congress, whichever is earlier.

ORDER OF MARCH 2, 1987

1. That the Federal Rules of Evidence be, and they hereby are, amended by including therein amendments to Rules 101, 104, 106, 404, 405, 411, 602, 603, 604, 606, 607, 608, 609, 610, 611, 612, 613, 615, 701, 703, 705, 706, 801, 803, 804, 806, 902, 1004, 1007 and 1101, as hereinafter set forth:

[See amendments made thereby under respective rules, post.]

2. That the foregoing changes in the Federal Rules of Evidence shall take effect on October 1, 1987.

3. That THE CHIEF JUSTICE be, and he hereby is, authorized to transmit to the Congress the foregoing changes in the rules of evidence in accordance with the provisions of Section 2076 of Title 28, United States Code.

ORDER OF APRIL 25, 1988

1. That the Federal Rules of Evidence be, and they hereby are, amended by including therein amendments to Rules 101, 602, 608, 613, 615, 902, and 1101, as hereinafter set forth:

[See amendments made thereby under respective rules, post.]

2. That the foregoing changes in the Federal Rules of Evidence shall take effect on November 1, 1988.

3. That THE CHIEF JUSTICE be, and he hereby is, authorized to transmit to the Congress the foregoing changes in the rules of evidence in accordance with the provisions of Section 2076 of Title 28, United States Code.

ORDER OF JANUARY 26, 1990

1. That the Federal Rules of Evidence be, and they hereby are, amended by including therein amendments to Rule 609(a)(1) and (2), as hereinafter set forth:

[See amendment made thereby, post].

2. That the foregoing changes in the Federal Rules of Evidence shall take effect on December 1, 1990.

3. That THE CHIEF JUSTICE be, and he hereby is, authorized to transmit to the Congress the foregoing changes in the rules of evidence in accordance with the provisions of Section 2074 of Title 28, United States Code.

ORDER OF APRIL 30, 1991

1. That the Federal Rules of Evidence for the United States District Courts be, and they hereby are, amended by including therein amendments to Evidence Rules 404(b) and 1102.

[See amendments made thereby under respective rules, post.]

2. That the foregoing amendments to the Federal Rules of Evidence shall take effect on December 1, 1991, and shall govern in all proceedings thereafter commenced and, insofar as just and practicable, all proceedings then pending.

3. That THE CHIEF JUSTICE be, and he hereby is, authorized to transmit to the Congress the foregoing amendments to the Federal Rules of Evidence in accordance with the provisions of Section 2072 of Title 28, United States Code.

ARTICLE I. GENERAL PROVISIONS

Rule 101. Scope

These rules govern proceedings in the courts of the United States and before United States bankruptcy judges and United States magistrates, to the extent and with the exceptions stated in rule 1101.

(As amended Mar. 2, 1987, eff. Oct. 1, 1987; Apr. 25, 1988, eff. Nov. 1, 1988.)

Note by Federal Judicial Center

The rule enacted by the Congress is the rule prescribed by the Supreme Court without change.

Advisory Committee's Note

56 F.R.D. 183, 194

Rule 1101 specifies in detail the courts, proceedings, questions, and stages of proceedings to which the rules apply in whole or in part.

1987 Amendment. United States bankruptcy judges are added to conform this rule with Rule 1101(b) and Bankruptcy Rule 9017.

1988 Amendment. The amendment is technical. No substantive change is intended.

Rule 102. Purpose and Construction

These rules shall be construed to secure fairness in administration, elimination of unjustifiable expense and delay, and promotion of growth and development of the law of evidence to the end that the truth may be ascertained and proceedings justly determined.

Section references, McCormick 4th ed.

§ 60

Note by Federal Judicial Center

The rule enacted by the Congress is the rule prescribed by the Supreme Court without change.

Advisory Committee's Note

56 F.R.D. 183, 194

For similar provisions see Rule 2 of the Federal Rules of Criminal Procedure, Rule 1 of the Federal Rules of Civil Procedure, California Evidence Code § 2, and New Jersey Evidence Rule 5.

Rule 103. Rulings on Evidence

(a) Effect of erroneous ruling. Error may not be predicated upon a ruling which admits or excludes evidence unless a substantial right of the party is affected, and

(1) Objection. In case the ruling is one admitting evidence, a timely objection or motion to strike appears of record, stating the specific ground of objection, if the specific ground was not apparent from the context; or

(2) Offer of proof. In case the ruling is one excluding evidence, the substance of the evidence was made known to the court by offer or was apparent from the context within which questions were asked.

(b) Record of offer and ruling. The court may add any other or further statement which shows the character of the evidence, the form in which it was offered, the objection made, and the ruling thereon. It may direct the making of an offer in question and answer form.

(c) Hearing of jury. In jury cases, proceedings shall be conducted, to the extent practicable, so as to prevent inadmissible evidence from being suggested to the jury by any means, such as making statements or offers of proof or asking questions in the hearing of the jury.

(d) Plain error. Nothing in this rule precludes taking notice of plain errors affecting substantial rights although they were not brought to the attention of the court.

Section references, McCormick 4th ed.

Generally § *51,* § *52,* § 58.

(a). § 183

(1). § *52,* § 55, § 73

(2). § *51,* § *52*

(b). § *51,* § *58*

(c). § *51,* § *52,* § 190

(d). § *52,* § 55

Note by Federal Judicial Center

The rule enacted by the Congress is the rule prescribed by the Supreme Court, amended by substituting "court" in place of "judge," with appropriate pronominal change.

Advisory Committee's Note

56 F.R.D. 183, 195

Subdivision (a) states the law as generally accepted today. Rulings on evidence cannot be assigned as error unless (1) a substantial right is affected, and (2) the nature of the error was called to the attention of the judge, so as to alert him to the proper course of action and enable opposing counsel to take proper corrective measures. The objection and the offer of proof are the techniques for accomplishing these objectives. For similar provisions see Uniform Rules 4 and 5; California Evidence Code §§ 353 and 354; Kansas Code of Civil Procedure §§ 60–404 and 60–405. The rule does not purport to change the law with respect to harmless error. See 28 USC § 2111, F.R.Civ.P. 61, F.R.Crim.P. 52, and decisions construing them. The status of constitutional error as harmless or not is treated in Chapman v. California, 386 U.S. 18, 87 S.Ct. 824, 17 L.Ed.2d 705 (1967), reh. denied id. 987, 87 S.Ct. 1283, 18 L.Ed.2d 241.

Subdivision (b). The first sentence is the third sentence of Rule 43(c) of the Federal Rules of Civil Procedure [1] virtually verbatim. Its purpose is to

1. Rule 43(c) of the Federal Rules of Civil Procedure was deleted by order of the Supreme Court entered on November 20, 1972, 93 S.Ct. 3073, 3075, 3076, 3077, 34 L.Ed.2d

reproduce for an appellate court, insofar as possible, a true reflection of what occurred in the trial court. The second sentence is in part derived from the final sentence of Rule 43(c).[1] It is designed to resolve doubts as to what testimony the witness would have in fact given, and, in nonjury cases, to provide the appellate court with material for a possible final disposition of the case in the event of reversal of a ruling which excluded evidence. See 5 Moore's Federal Practice § 43.11 (2d ed. 1968). Application is made discretionary in view of the practical impossibility of formulating a satisfactory rule in mandatory terms.

Subdivision (c). This subdivision proceeds on the supposition that a ruling which excludes evidence in a jury case is likely to be a pointless procedure if the excluded evidence nevertheless comes to the attention of the jury. Bruton v. United States, 389 U.S. 818, 88 S.Ct. 126, 19 L.Ed.2d 70 (1968). Rule 43(c) of the Federal Rules of Civil Procedure[1] provides: "The court may require the offer to be made out of the hearing of the jury." In re McConnell, 370 U.S. 230, 82 S.Ct. 1288, 8 L.Ed.2d 434 (1962), left some doubt whether questions on which an offer is based must first be asked in the presence of the jury. The subdivision answers in the negative. The judge can foreclose a particular line of testimony and counsel can protect his record without a series of questions before the jury, designed at best to waste time and at worst "to waft into the jury box" the very matter sought to be excluded.

Subdivision (d). This wording of the plain error principle is from Rule 52(b) of the Federal Rules of Criminal Procedure. While judicial unwillingness to be constricted by mechanical breakdowns of the adversary system has been more pronounced in criminal cases, there is no scarcity of decisions to the same effect in civil cases. In general, see Campbell, Extent to Which Courts of Review Will Consider Questions Not Properly Raised and Preserved, 7 Wis.L.Rev. 91, 160 (1932); Vestal, Sua Sponte Consideration in Appellate Review, 27 Fordham L.Rev. 477 (1958–59); 64 Harv.L.Rev. 652 (1951). In the nature of things the application of the plain error rule will be more likely with respect to the admission of evidence than to exclusion, since failure to comply with normal requirements of offers of proof is likely to produce a record which simply does not disclose the error.

Rule 104. Preliminary Questions

(a) Questions of admissibility generally. Preliminary questions concerning the qualification of a person to be a witness, the existence of a privilege, or the admissibility of evidence shall be determined by the court, subject to the provisions of subdivision (b). In making its determination it is not bound by the rules of evidence except those with respect to privileges.

(b) Relevancy conditioned on fact. When the relevancy of evidence depends upon the fulfillment of a condition of fact, the court shall admit it upon, or subject to, the introduction of evidence sufficient to support a finding of the fulfillment of the condition.

lxv, ccv, ccviii, which action was affirmed by the Congress in P.L. 93–595 § 3 (January 2, 1975).—Federal Judicial Center.

(c) Hearing of jury. Hearings on the admissibility of confessions shall in all cases be conducted out of the hearing of the jury. Hearings on other preliminary matters shall be so conducted when the interests of justice require, or when an accused is a witness and so requests.

(d) Testimony by accused. The accused does not, by testifying upon a preliminary matter, become subject to cross-examination as to other issues in the case.

(e) Weight and credibility. This rule does not limit the right of a party to introduce before the jury evidence relevant to weight or credibility.

(As amended Mar. 2, 1987, eff. Oct. 1, 1987.)

Section references, McCormick 4th ed.

Generally § 15, § 53

(a). § *53,* § 68, § 70, § *227*

(b). § *10,* § *53,* § 54, § 58, § *227*

(c). § *52,* § *53,* § *162*

(d). § *53*

(e). § *53*

Note by Federal Judicial Center

The rule enacted by the Congress is the rule prescribed by the Supreme Court, amended by substituting "court" in place of "judge," with appropriate pronominal change, and by adding to subdivision (c) the concluding phrase, "or when an accused is a witness, if he so requests."[1]

Advisory Committee's Note

56 F.R.D. 183, 196

Subdivision (a). The applicability of a particular rule of evidence often depends upon the existence of a condition. Is the alleged expert a qualified physician? Is a witness whose former testimony is offered unavailable? Was a stranger present during a conversation between attorney and client? In each instance the admissibility of evidence will turn upon the answer to the question of the existence of the condition. Accepted practice, incorporated in the rule, places on the judge the responsibility for these determinations. McCormick § 53; Morgan, Basic Problems of Evidence 45–50 (1962).

To the extent that these inquiries are factual, the judge acts as a trier of fact. Often, however, rulings on evidence call for an evaluation in terms of a legally set standard. Thus when a hearsay statement is offered as a declaration against interest, a decision must be made whether it possesses the required against-interest characteristics. These decisions, too, are made by the judge.

1. The effect of the amendment was to restore language included in the 1971 Revised Draft of the Proposed Rules but deleted before the rules were presented to and prescribed by the Supreme Court.—Federal Judicial Center.

In view of these considerations, this subdivision refers to preliminary requirements generally by the broad term "questions," without attempt at specification.

This subdivision is of general application. It must, however, be read as subject to the special provisions for "conditional relevancy" in subdivision (b) and those for confessions in subdivision (c).

If the question is factual in nature, the judge will of necessity receive evidence pro and con on the issue. The rule provides that the rules of evidence in general do not apply to this process. McCormick § 53, p. 123, n. 8, points out that the authorities are "scattered and inconclusive," and observes:

> "Should the exclusionary law of evidence, 'the child of the jury system' in Thayer's phrase, be applied to this hearing before the judge? Sound sense backs the view that it should not, and that the judge should be empowered to hear any relevant evidence, such as affidavits or other reliable hearsay."

This view is reinforced by practical necessity in certain situations. An item, offered and objected to, may itself be considered in ruling on admissibility, though not yet admitted in evidence. Thus the content of an asserted declaration against interest must be considered in ruling whether it is against interest. Again, common practice calls for considering the testimony of a witness, particularly a child, in determining competency. Another example is the requirement of Rule 602 dealing with personal knowledge. In the case of hearsay, it is enough, if the declarant "so far as appears [has] had an opportunity to observe the fact declared." McCormick, § 10, p. 19.

If concern is felt over the use of affidavits by the judge in preliminary hearings on admissibility, attention is directed to the many important judicial determinations made on the basis of affidavits. Rule 47 of the Federal Rules of Criminal Procedure provides:

> "An application to the court for an order shall be by motion. . . . It may be supported by affidavit."

The Rules of Civil Procedure are more detailed. Rule 43(e), dealing with motions generally, provides:

> "When a motion is based on facts not appearing of record the court may hear the matter on affidavits presented by the respective parties, but the court may direct that the matter be heard wholly or partly on oral testimony or depositions."

Rule 4(g) provides for proof of service by affidavit. Rule 56 provides in detail for the entry of summary judgment based on affidavits. Affidavits may supply the foundation for temporary restraining orders under Rule 65(b).

The study made for the California Law Revision Commission recommended an amendment to Uniform Rule 2 as follows:

"In the determination of the issue aforesaid [preliminary determination], exclusionary rules shall not apply, subject, however, to Rule 45 and any valid claim of privilege." Tentative Recommendation and a Study Relating to the Uniform Rules of Evidence (Article VIII, Hearsay), Cal.Law Revision Comm'n, Rep., Rec. & Studies, 470 (1962). The proposal was not adopted in the California Evidence Code. The Uniform Rules are likewise silent on the subject.

However, New Jersey Evidence Rule 8(1), dealing with preliminary inquiry by the judge, provides:

"In his determination the rules of evidence shall not apply except for Rule 4 [exclusion on grounds of confusion, etc.] or a valid claim of privilege."

Subdivision (b). In some situations, the relevancy of an item of evidence, in the large sense, depends upon the existence of a particular preliminary fact. Thus when a spoken statement is relied upon to prove notice to X, it is without probative value unless X heard it. Or if a letter purporting to be from Y is relied upon to establish an admission by him, it has no probative value unless Y wrote or authorized it. Relevance in this sense has been labelled "conditional relevancy." Morgan, Basic Problems of Evidence 45–46 (1962). Problems arising in connection with it are to be distinguished from problems of logical relevancy, e.g. evidence in a murder case that accused on the day before purchased a weapon of the kind used in the killing, treated in Rule 401.

If preliminary questions of conditional relevancy were determined solely by the judge, as provided in subdivision (a), the functioning of the jury as a trier of fact would be greatly restricted and in some cases virtually destroyed. These are appropriate questions for juries. Accepted treatment, as provided in the rule, is consistent with that given fact questions generally. The judge makes a preliminary determination whether the foundation evidence is sufficient to support a finding of fulfillment of the condition. If so, the item is admitted. If after all the evidence on the issue is in, pro and con, the jury could reasonably conclude that fulfillment of the condition is not established, the issue is for them. If the evidence is not such as to allow a finding, the judge withdraws the matter from their consideration. Morgan, supra; California Evidence Code § 403; New Jersey Rule 8(2). See also Uniform Rules 19 and 67.

The order of proof here, as generally, is subject to the control of the judge.

Subdivision (c). Preliminary hearings on the admissibility of confessions must be conducted outside the hearing of the jury. See Jackson v. Denno, 378 U.S. 368, 84 S.Ct. 1774, 12 L.Ed.2d 908 (1964).[2] Otherwise, detailed treatment of when preliminary matters should be heard outside the hearing of the jury is not feasible. The procedure is time consuming. Not infrequently the same evidence which is relevant to the issue of establishment of fulfillment of a condition precedent to admissibility is also relevant to weight or credibility, and time is saved by taking foundation proof in the presence of the jury. Much evidence on preliminary questions, though not relevant to jury issues, may be heard by the jury with no adverse effect. A great deal must be left to the discretion of the judge who will act as the interests of justice require.

2. At this point the Advisory Committee's Note to the 1971 Revised Draft contained the sentence, "Also, due regard for the right of an accused not to testify generally in the case requires that he be given an option to testify out of the presence of the jury upon preliminary matters." The statement was deleted in view of the deletion from the rule, mentioned in the preceding footnote.—Federal Judicial Center.

Report of the House Committee on the Judiciary

House Comm. on Judiciary, Fed. Rules of Evidence, H.R.Rep. No. 650, 93d Cong., 1st Sess., p. 15 (1973); 1974 U.S.Code Cong. & Ad. News 7075, 7080

Rule 104(c) as submitted to the Congress provided that hearings on the admissibility of confessions shall be conducted outside the presence of the jury and hearings on all other preliminary matters should be so conducted when the interests of justice require. The Committee amended the Rule to provide that where an accused is a witness as to a preliminary matter, he has the right, upon his request, to be heard outside the jury's presence. Although recognizing that in some cases duplication of evidence would occur and that the procedure could be subject to abuse, the Committee believed that a proper regard for the right of an accused not to testify generally in the case dictates that he be given an option to testify out of the presence of the jury on preliminary matters.

The Committee construes the second sentence of subdivision (c) as applying to civil actions and proceedings as well as to criminal cases, and on this assumption has left the sentence unamended.

Advisory Committee's Note

56 F.R.D. 183, 199

Subdivision (d). The limitation upon cross-examination is designed to encourage participation by the accused in the determination of preliminary matters. He may testify concerning them without exposing himself to cross-examination generally. The provision is necessary because of the breadth of cross-examination [possible] under Rule 611(b).

The rule does not address itself to questions of the subsequent use of testimony given by an accused at a hearing on a preliminary matter. See Walder v. United States, 347 U.S. 62 (1954); Simmons v. United States, 390 U.S. 377 (1968); Harris v. New York, 401 U.S. 222 (1971).

Report of Senate Committee on the Judiciary

Senate Comm. on Judiciary, Fed. Rules of Evidence, S.Rep. No. 1277, 93d Cong., 2d Sess., p. 24 (1974); 1974 U.S.Code Cong. & Ad. News 7051, 7070

Under Rule 104(c) the hearing on a preliminary matter may at times be conducted in front of the jury. Should an accused testify in such a hearing, waiving his privilege against self-incrimination as to the preliminary issue, Rule 104(d) provides that he will not generally be subject to cross-examination as to any other issue. This rule is not, however, intended to immunize the accused from cross-examination where, in testifying about a preliminary issue, he injects other issues into the hearing. If he could not be cross-examined about any issues gratuitously raised by him beyond the scope of the preliminary matters, injustice might result. Accordingly, in order to prevent any such unjust result, the committee intends the rule to be construed to provide that the accused may subject himself to cross-examination as to issues raised by his own testimony upon a preliminary matter before a jury.

Advisory Committee's Note

56 F.R.D. 183, 199

Subdivision (e). For similar provisions see Uniform Rule 8; California Evidence Code § 406; Kansas Code of Civil Procedure § 60–408; New Jersey Evidence Rule 8(1).

1987 Amendment. The amendments are technical. No substantive change is intended.

Rule 105. Limited Admissibility

When evidence which is admissible as to one party or for one purpose but not admissible as to another party or for another purpose is admitted, the court, upon request, shall restrict the evidence to its proper scope and instruct the jury accordingly.

Section references, McCormick 4th ed.

§ 59

Note by Federal Judicial Center

The rule enacted by the Congress is the rule prescribed by the Supreme Court as Rule 106, amended by substituting "court" in place of "judge." Rule 105 as prescribed by the Court, which was deleted from the rules enacted by the Congress, is set forth in the Appendix hereto, together with a statement of the reasons for the deletion.

Advisory Committee's Note

56 F.R.D. 183, 200

A close relationship exists between this rule and Rule 403 which . . . [provides for] exclusion when "probative value is substantially outweighed by the danger of unfair prejudice, confusion of the issues, or misleading the jury." The present rule recognizes the practice of admitting evidence for a limited purpose and instructing the jury accordingly. The availability and effectiveness of this practice must be taken into consideration in reaching a decision whether to exclude for unfair prejudice under Rule 403. In Bruton v. United States, 389 U.S. 818, 88 S.Ct. 126, 19 L.Ed.2d 70 (1968), the Court ruled that a limiting instruction did not effectively protect the accused against the prejudicial effect of admitting in evidence the confession of a codefendant which implicated him. The decision does not, however, bar the use of limited admissibility with an instruction where the risk of prejudice is less serious.

Similar provisions are found in Uniform Rule 6; California Evidence Code § 355; Kansas Code of Civil Procedure § 60–406; New Jersey Evidence Rule 6. The wording of the present rule differs, however, in repelling any implication that limiting or curative instructions are sufficient in all situations.

Report of House Committee on the Judiciary

House Comm. on Judiciary, Fed. Rules of Evidence, H.R.Rep. No. 650, 93d Cong., 1st Sess., p. 6 (1973); 1974 U.S.Code Cong. & Ad. News 7075, 7080

Rule 106 as submitted by the Supreme Court (now Rule 105 in the bill) dealt with the subject of evidence which is admissible as to one party or for one purpose but is not admissible against another party or for another purpose. The Committee adopted this Rule without change on the understanding that it does not affect the authority of a court to order a severance in a multi-defendant case.

Rule 106. Remainder of or Related Writings or Recorded Statements

When a writing or recorded statement or part thereof is introduced by a party, an adverse party may require the introduction at that time of any other part or any other writing or recorded statement which ought in fairness to be considered contemporaneously with it.

(As amended Mar. 2, 1987, eff. Oct. 1, 1987.)

Section references, McCormick 4th ed.

§ 21, § 32, § 47, § *56,* § 57, § 59, § 307

Note by Federal Judicial Center

The rule enacted by the Congress is the rule prescribed by the Supreme Court as Rule 107 without change.

Advisory Committee's Note

56 F.R.D. 183, 201

The rule is an expression of the rule of completeness. McCormick § 56. It is manifested as to depositions in Rule 32(a)(4) of the Federal Rules of Civil Procedure, of which the proposed rule is substantially a restatement.

The rule is based on two considerations. The first is the misleading impression created by taking matters out of context. The second is the inadequacy of repair work when delayed to a point later in the trial. See McCormick § 56; California Evidence Code § 356. The rule does not in any way circumscribe the right of the adversary to develop the matter on cross-examination or as part of his own case.

For practical reasons, the rule is limited to writings and recorded statements and does not apply to conversations.

1987 Amendment. The amendments are technical. No substantive change is intended.

ARTICLE II. JUDICIAL NOTICE

Rule 201. Judicial Notice of Adjudicative Facts

(a) Scope of rule. This rule governs only judicial notice of adjudicative facts.

(b) Kinds of facts. A judicially noticed fact must be one not subject to reasonable dispute in that it is either (1) generally known within the territorial jurisdiction of the trial court or (2) capable of accurate and ready determination by resort to sources whose accuracy cannot reasonably be questioned.

(c) When discretionary. A court may take judicial notice, whether requested or not.

(d) When mandatory. A court shall take judicial notice if requested by a party and supplied with the necessary information.

(e) Opportunity to be heard. A party is entitled upon timely request to an opportunity to be heard as to the propriety of taking judicial notice and the tenor of the matter noticed. In the absence of prior notification, the request may be made after judicial notice has been taken.

(f) Time of taking notice. Judicial notice may be taken at any stage of the proceeding.

(g) Instructing jury. In a civil action or proceeding, the court shall instruct the jury to accept as conclusive any fact judicially noticed. In a criminal case, the court shall instruct the jury that it may, but is not required to, accept as conclusive any fact judicially noticed.

Section references, McCormick 4th ed.

Generally § *328*, § *332*, § *333*

(a). § 331, § *332*, § *334*

(b)(1). § *328*, § 329

(2). § 329, § *330*

(c). § *333*

(d). § *333*

(e). § *334*

(f). § *333*

(g). § *332*

Note by Federal Judicial Center

The rule enacted by the Congress is the rule prescribed by the Supreme Court with the following changes:

In subdivisions (c) and (d) the words "judge or" before "court" were deleted.

Subdivision (g) as it is shown was substituted in place of, "The judge shall instruct the jury to accept as established any facts judicially noticed." The substituted language is from the 1969 Preliminary Draft. 46 F.R.D. 161, 195.

Advisory Committee's Note

56 F.R.D. 183, 201

Subdivision (a). This is the only evidence rule on the subject of judicial notice. It deals only with judicial notice of "adjudicative" facts. No rule deals with judicial notice of "legislative" facts. Judicial notice of matters of foreign law is treated in Rule 44.1 of the Federal Rules of Civil Procedure and Rule 26.1 of the Federal Rules of Criminal Procedure.

The omission of any treatment of legislative facts results from fundamental differences between adjudicative facts and legislative facts. Adjudicative facts are simply the facts of the particular case. Legislative facts, on the other hand, are those which have relevance to legal reasoning and the lawmaking process, whether in the formulation of a legal principle or ruling by a judge or court or in the enactment of a legislative body. The terminology was coined by Professor Kenneth Davis in his article An Approach to Problems of Evidence in the Administrative Process, 55 Harv.L.Rev. 364, 404–407 (1942). The following discussion draws extensively upon his writings. In addition, see the same author's Judicial Notice, 55 Colum.L.Rev. 945 (1955); Administrative Law Treatise, ch. 15 (1958); A System of Judicial Notice Based on Fairness and Convenience, in Perspectives of Law 69 (1964).

The usual method of establishing adjudicative facts is through the introduction of evidence, ordinarily consisting of the testimony of witnesses. If particular facts are outside the area of reasonable controversy, this process is dispensed with as unnecessary. A high degree of indisputability is the essential prerequisite.

Legislative facts are quite different. As Professor Davis says:

> "My opinion is that judge-made law would stop growing if judges, in thinking about questions of law and policy, were forbidden to take into account the facts they believe, as distinguished from facts which are 'clearly . . . within the domain of the indisputable.' Facts most needed in thinking about difficult problems of law and policy have a way of being outside the domain of the clearly indisputable." A System of Judicial Notice Based on Fairness and Convenience, supra, at 82.

An illustration is Hawkins v. United States, 358 U.S. 74, 79 S.Ct. 136, 3 L.Ed.2d 125 (1958), in which the Court refused to discard the common law rule that one spouse could not testify against the other, saying, "Adverse testimony given in criminal proceedings would, we think, be likely to destroy almost any marriage." This conclusion has a large intermixture of fact, but the factual aspect is scarcely "indisputable." See Hutchins and Slesinger, Some Observations on the Law of Evidence—Family Relations, 13 Minn.L.Rev. 675 (1929). If the destructive effect of the giving of adverse testimony by a spouse is not indisputable, should the Court have refrained from considering it in the absence of supporting evidence?

"If the Model Code or the Uniform Rules had been applicable, the Court would have been barred from thinking about the essential factual ingredient of the problems before it, and such a result would be obviously intolerable. What the law needs at its growing points is more, not less, judicial thinking about the factual ingredients of problems of what the law ought to be, and the needed facts are seldom 'clearly' indisputable." Davis, supra, at 83.

Professor Morgan gave the following description of the methodology of determining domestic law:

> "In determining the content or applicability of a rule of domestic law, the judge is unrestricted in his investigation and conclusion. He may reject the propositions of either party or of both parties. He may consult the sources of pertinent data to which they refer, or he may refuse to do so. He may make an independent search for persuasive data or rest content with what he has or what the parties present. . . . [T]he parties do no more than to assist; they control no part of the process." Morgan, Judicial Notice, 57 Harv.L.Rev. 269, 270–271 (1944).

This is the view which should govern judicial access to legislative facts. It renders inappropriate any limitation in the form of indisputability, any formal requirements of notice other than those already inherent in affording opportunity to hear and be heard and exchanging briefs, and any requirement of formal findings at any level. It should, however, leave open the possibility of introducing evidence through regular channels in appropriate situations. See Borden's Farm Products Co. v. Baldwin, 293 U.S. 194, 55 S.Ct. 187, 79 L.Ed. 281 (1934), where the cause was remanded for the taking of evidence as to the economic conditions and trade practices underlying the New York Milk Control Law.

Similar considerations govern the judicial use of non-adjudicative facts in ways other than formulating laws and rules. Thayer described them as a part of the judicial reasoning process.

> "In conducting a process of judicial reasoning, as of other reasoning, not a step can be taken without assuming something which has not been proved; and the capacity to do this with competent judgment and efficiency, is imputed to judges and juries as part of their necessary mental outfit." Thayer, Preliminary Treatise on Evidence 279–280 (1898).

As Professor Davis points out, A System of Judicial Notice Based on Fairness and Convenience, in Perspectives of Law 69, 73 (1964), every case involves the use of hundreds or thousands of non-evidence facts. When a witness in an automobile accident case says "car," everyone, judge and jury included, furnishes, from non-evidence sources within himself, the supplementing information that the "car" is an automobile, not a railroad car, that it is self-propelled, probably by an internal combustion engine, that it may be assumed to have four wheels with pneumatic rubber tires, and so on. The judicial process cannot construct every case from scratch, like Descartes creating a world based on the postulate *Cogito, ergo sum.* These items could not possibly be introduced into evidence, and no one suggests that they be. Nor are they appropriate subjects for any formalized treatment of judicial notice of facts. See Levin and Levy, Persuading the Jury with Facts Not in Evidence: The Fiction-Science Spectrum, 105 U.Pa.L.Rev. 139 (1956).

Another aspect of what Thayer had in mind is the use of non-evidence facts to appraise or assess the adjudicative facts of the case. Pairs of cases from two jurisdictions illustrate this use and also the difference between non-evidence facts thus used and adjudicative facts. In People v. Strook, 347 Ill. 460, 179 N.E. 821 (1932), venue in Cook County had been held not established by testimony that the crime was committed at 7956 South Chicago Avenue, since judicial notice would not be taken that the address was in Chicago. However, the same court subsequently ruled that venue in Cook County was established by testimony that a crime occurred at 8900 South Anthony Avenue, since notice would be taken of the common practice of omitting the name of the city when speaking of local addresses, and the witness was testifying in Chicago. People v. Pride, 16 Ill.2d 82, 156 N.E.2d 551 (1951). And in Hughes v. Vestal, 264 N.C. 500, 142 S.E.2d 361 (1965), the Supreme Court of North Carolina disapproved the trial judge's admission in evidence of a state-published table of automobile stopping distances on the basis of judicial notice, though the court itself had referred to the same table in an earlier case in a "rhetorical and illustrative" way in determining that the defendant could not have stopped her car in time to avoid striking a child who suddenly appeared in the highway and that a nonsuit was properly granted. Ennis v. Dupree, 262 N.C. 224, 136 S.E.2d 702 (1964). See also Brown v. Hale, 263 N.C. 176, 139 S.E.2d 210 (1964); Clayton v. Rimmer, 262 N.C. 302, 136 S.E.2d 562 (1964). It is apparent that this use of non-evidence facts in evaluating the adjudicative facts of the case is not an appropriate subject for a formalized judicial notice treatment.

In view of these considerations, the regulation of judicial notice of facts by the present rule extends only to adjudicative facts.

What, then, are "adjudicative" facts? Davis refers to them as those "which relate to the parties," or more fully:

> "When a court or an agency finds facts concerning the immediate parties—who did what, where, when, how, and with what motive or intent—the court or agency is performing an adjudicative function, and the facts are conveniently called adjudicative facts. . . .
>
> "Stated in other terms, the adjudicative facts are those to which the law is applied in the process of adjudication. They are the facts that normally go to the jury in a jury case. They relate to the parties, their activities, their properties, their businesses." 2 Administrative Law Treatise 353.

Subdivision (b). With respect to judicial notice of adjudicative facts, the tradition has been one of caution in requiring that the matter be beyond reasonable controversy. This tradition of circumspection appears to be soundly based, and no reason to depart from it is apparent. As Professor Davis says:

> "The reason we use trial-type procedure, I think, is that we make the practical judgment, on the basis of experience, that taking evidence, subject to cross-examination and rebuttal, is the best way to resolve controversies involving disputes of adjudicative facts, that is, facts pertaining to the parties. The reason we require a determination on the record is that we think fair procedure in resolving disputes of adjudicative facts calls for giving each party a chance to meet in the appropriate fashion the facts that come to the tribunal's attention, and the appropriate fashion for meeting disputed adjudicative facts includes rebuttal evidence, cross-examination, usually confrontation, and argument (either written or oral or both). The key to a fair trial is opportunity to use the appropriate weapons (rebuttal evidence, cross-examination, and argument) to meet adverse materials that come to the tribunal's attention." A System of Judicial Notice Based on Fairness and Convenience, in Perspectives of Law 69, 93 (1964).

The rule proceeds upon the theory that these considerations call for dispensing with traditional methods of proof only in clear cases. Compare Professor Davis' conclusion that judicial notice should be a matter of convenience, subject to requirements of procedural fairness. Id., 94.

This rule is consistent with Uniform Rule 9(1) and (2) which limit judicial notice of facts to those "so universally known that they cannot reasonably be the subject of dispute," those "so generally known or of such common notoriety within the territorial jurisdiction of the court that they cannot reasonably be the subject of dispute," and those "capable of immediate and accurate determination by resort to easily accessible sources of indisputable accuracy." The traditional textbook treatment has included these general categories (matters of common knowledge, facts capable of verification), McCormick §§ 324, 325, and then has passed on into detailed treatment of such specific topics as facts relating to the personnel and records of the court, id. § 327, and other governmental facts, id. § 328. The California draftsmen, with a background of detailed statutory regulation of judicial notice, followed a somewhat similar pattern. California Evidence Code §§ 451, 452. The Uniform Rules, however, were drafted on the theory that these particular matters are included within the general categories and need no specific mention. This approach is followed in the present rule.

The phrase "propositions of generalized knowledge," found in Uniform Rule 9(1) and (2) is not included in the present rule. It was, it is believed, originally included in Model Code Rules 801 and 802 primarily in order to afford some minimum recognition to the right of the judge in his "legislative" capacity (not acting as the trier of fact) to take judicial notice of very limited categories of generalized knowledge. The limitations thus imposed have been discarded herein as undesirable, unworkable, and contrary to existing practice. What is left, then, to be considered, is the status of a "proposition of generalized knowledge" as an "adjudicative" fact to be noticed judicially and communicated by the judge to the jury. Thus viewed, it is considered to be lacking practical significance. While judges used judicial notice of "propositions of generalized knowledge" in a variety of situations: determining the validity and meaning of statutes, formulating common law rules, deciding whether evidence should be admitted, assessing the sufficiency and effect of evidence, all are essentially nonadjudicative in nature. When judicial notice is seen as a significant vehicle for progress in the law, these are the areas involved, particularly in developing fields of scientific knowledge. See McCormick 712. It is not believed that judges now instruct juries as to "propositions of generalized knowledge" derived from encyclopedias or other sources, or that they are likely to do so, or, indeed, that it is desirable that they do so. There is a vast difference between ruling on the basis of judicial notice that radar evidence of speed is admissible and explaining to the jury its principles and degree of accuracy, or between using a table of stopping distances of automobiles at various speeds in a judicial evaluation of testimony and telling the jury its precise application in the case. For cases raising doubt as to the propriety of the use of medical texts by lay triers of fact in passing on disability claims in administrative proceedings, see Sayers v. Gardner, 380 F.2d 940 (6th Cir.1967); Ross v. Gardner, 365 F.2d 554 (6th Cir.1966); Sosna v. Celebrezze, 234 F.Supp. 289 (E.D.Pa.1964); Glendenning v. Ribicoff, 213 F.Supp. 301 (W.D.Mo.1962).

Subdivisions (c) and (d). Under subdivision (c) the judge has a discretionary authority to take judicial notice, regardless of whether he is so requested by a party. The taking of judicial notice is mandatory, under subdivision (d), only when a party requests it and the necessary information is supplied. This scheme is believed to reflect existing practice. It is simple and workable. It avoids troublesome distinctions in the many situations in which the process of taking judicial notice is not recognized as such.

Compare Uniform Rule 9 making judicial notice of facts universally known mandatory without request, and making judicial notice of facts generally known in the jurisdiction or capable of determination by resort to accurate sources discretionary in the absence of request but mandatory if request is made and the information furnished. But see Uniform Rule 10(3), which directs the judge to decline to take judicial notice if available information fails to convince him that the matter falls clearly within Uniform Rule 9 or is insufficient to enable him to notice it judicially. Substantially the same approach is found in California Evidence Code §§ 451–453 and in New Jersey Evidence Rule 9. In contrast, the present rule treats alike all adjudicative facts which are subject to judicial notice.

Subdivision (e). Basic considerations of procedural fairness demand an opportunity to be heard on the propriety of taking judicial notice and the tenor of the matter noticed. The rule requires the granting of that opportunity upon request. No formal scheme of giving notice is provided. An adversely affected party may learn in advance that judicial notice is in contemplation, either by virtue of being served with a copy of a request by another party under subdivision (d) that judicial notice be taken, or through an advance indication by the judge. Or he may have no advance notice at all. The likelihood of the latter is enhanced by the frequent failure to recognize judicial notice as such. And in the absence of advance notice, a request made after the fact could not in fairness be considered untimely. See the provision for hearing on timely request in the Administrative Procedure Act, 5 U.S.C. § 556(e). See also Revised Model State Administrative Procedure Act (1961), 9C U.L.A. § 10(4) (Supp.1967).

Subdivision (f). In accord with the usual view, judicial notice may be taken at any stage of the proceedings, whether in the trial court or on appeal.

Uniform Rule 12; California Evidence Code § 459; Kansas Rules of Evidence § 60–412; New Jersey Evidence Rule 12; McCormick § 330, p. 712.

Subdivision (g). Much of the controversy about judicial notice has centered upon the question whether evidence should be admitted in disproof of facts of which judicial notice is taken.

The writers have been divided. Favoring admissibility are Thayer, Preliminary Treatise on Evidence 308 (1898); 9 Wigmore § 2567; Davis, A System of Judicial Notice Based on Fairness and Convenience, in Perspectives of Law, 69, 76–77 (1964). Opposing admissibility are Keeffe, Landis and Shaad, Sense and Nonsense about Judicial Notice, 2 Stan.L.Rev. 664, 668 (1950); McNaughton, Judicial Notice—Excerpts Relating to the Morgan-Whitmore Controversy, 14 Vand.L.Rev. 779 (1961); Morgan, Judicial Notice, 57 Harv.L.Rev. 269, 279 (1944); McCormick 710–711. The Model Code and the Uniform Rules are predicated upon indisputability of judicially noticed facts.

The proponents of admitting evidence in disproof have concentrated largely upon legislative facts. Since the present rule deals only with judicial notice of adjudicative facts, arguments directed to legislative facts lose their relevancy.

Report of House Committee on the Judiciary

House Comm. on Judiciary, Fed. Rules of Evidence, H.R.Rep. No. 650, 93d Cong., 1st Sess., p. 6 (1973); 1974 U.S.Code Cong. & Ad.News 7075, 7080

Rule 201(g) as received from the Supreme Court provided that when judicial notice of a fact is taken, the court shall instruct the jury to accept that fact as established. Being of the view that mandatory instruction to a jury in a criminal case to accept as conclusive any fact judicially noticed is inappropriate because contrary to the spirit of the Sixth Amendment right to a jury trial, the Committee adopted the 1969 Advisory Committee draft of this subsection, allowing a mandatory instruction in civil actions and proceedings and a discretionary instruction in criminal cases.

Advisory Committee's Note (Continued)

[The following portion of the Advisory Committee's Note is from the 1969 Preliminary Draft. 46 F.R.D. 161, 204.]

Within its relatively narrow area of adjudicative facts, the rule contemplates there is to be no evidence before the jury in disproof in civil cases. The judge instructs the jury to take judicially noticed facts as conclusive. This position is justified by the undesirable effects of the opposite rule in limiting the rebutting party, though not his opponent, to admissible evidence, in defeating the reasons for judicial notice, and in affecting the substantive law to an extent and in ways largely unforeseeable. Ample protection and flexibility are afforded by the broad provision for opportunity to be heard on request, set forth in subdivision (e).

Criminal cases are treated somewhat differently in the rule. While matters falling within the common fund of information supposed to be possessed by jurors need not be proved, State v. Dunn, 221 Mo. 530, 120 S.W. 1179 (1909), these are not, properly speaking, adjudicative facts but an aspect of legal reasoning. The considerations which underlie the general rule that a verdict cannot be directed against the accused in a criminal case seem to foreclose the judge's directing the jury on the basis of judicial notice to accept as conclusive any adjudicative facts in the case. State v. Main, 91 R.I. 338, 180 A.2d 814 (1962); State v. Lawrence, 120 Utah 323, 234 P.2d 600 (1951). Cf. People v. Mayes, 113 Cal. 618, 45 P. 860 (1896); Ross v. United States, 374 F.2d 97 (8th Cir.1967). However, this view presents no obstacle to the judge's advising the jury as to a matter judicially noticed, if he instructs them that it need not be taken as conclusive.

Note on Judicial Notice of Law (by the Advisory Committee)

56 F.R.D. 183, 207

By rules effective July 1, 1966, the method of invoking the law of a foreign country is covered elsewhere. Rule 44.1 of the Federal Rules of Civil Procedure; Rule 26.1 of the Federal Rules of Criminal Procedure. These two new admirably designed rules are founded upon the assumption that the manner in which law is fed into the judicial process is never a proper concern of the rules of evidence but rather of the rules of procedure. The Advisory Committee on Evidence, believing that this assumption is entirely correct, proposes no evidence rule with respect to judicial notice of law, and suggests that those matters of law which, in addition to foreign-country law, have traditionally been treated as requiring pleading and proof and more recently as the subject of judicial notice be left to the Rules of Civil and Criminal Procedure.

ARTICLE III. PRESUMPTIONS IN CIVIL ACTIONS AND PROCEEDINGS

Rule 301. Presumptions in General in Civil Actions and Proceedings

In all civil actions and proceedings not otherwise provided for by Act of Congress or by these rules, a presumption imposes on the party against whom it is directed the burden of going forward with evidence to rebut or meet the presumption, but does not shift to such party the burden of proof in the sense of the risk of nonpersuasion, which remains throughout the trial upon the party on whom it was originally cast.

Section references, McCormick 4th ed.

§ 336, § 342, § 344

Note by Federal Judicial Center

The bill passed by the House substituted a substantially different rule in place of that prescribed by the Supreme Court. The Senate bill substituted yet a further version, which was accepted by the House, was enacted by the Congress, and is the rule shown above. . . .

Report of Senate Committee on the Judiciary

Senate Comm. on Judiciary, Fed. Rules of Evidence, S.Rep. No. 1277, 93d Cong., 2d Sess., p. 9 (1974); 1974 U.S.Code Cong. & Ad. News 7051, 7055

This rule governs presumptions in civil cases generally. Rule 302 provides for presumptions in cases controlled by State law.

As submitted by the Supreme Court, presumptions governed by this rule were given the effect of placing upon the opposing party the burden of establishing the nonexistence of the presumed fact, once the party invoking the presumption established the basic facts giving rise to it.

Instead of imposing a burden of persuasion on the party against whom the presumption is directed, the House adopted a provision which shifted the burden of going forward with the evidence. They further provided that "even though met with contradicting evidence, a presumption is sufficient evidence of the fact presumed, to be considered by the trier of fact." The effect of the amendment is that presumptions are to be treated as evidence.

The committee feels the House amendment is ill-advised. As the joint committees (the Standing Committee on Practice and Procedure of the Judicial Conference and the Advisory Committee on the Rules of Evidence) stated: "Presumptions are not evidence, but ways of dealing with evidence."[1] This treatment requires juries to perform the task of considering "as evidence" facts upon which they have no direct evidence and which may confuse them in performance of their duties. California had a rule much like that contained in the House amendment. It was sharply criticized by Justice Traynor in Speck v. Sarver[2] and was repealed after 93 troublesome years.[3]

Professor McCormick gives a concise and compelling critique of the presumption as evidence rule:

* * *

"Another solution, formerly more popular than now, is to instruct the jury that the presumption is 'evidence', to be weighed and considered with the testimony in the case. This avoids the danger that the jury may infer that the presumption is conclusive, but it probably means little to the jury, and certainly runs counter to accepted theories of the nature of evidence.[4]"

For these reasons the committee has deleted that provision of the House-passed rule that treats presumptions as evidence. The effect of the rule as adopted by the committee is to make clear that while evidence of facts giving rise to a presumption shifts the burden of coming forward with evidence to rebut or meet the presumption, it does not shift the burden of persuasion on the existence of the presumed facts. The burden of persuasion remains on the

1. Hearings Before the Committee on the Judiciary, United States Senate, H.R. 5463, p. 56.

2. 20 Cal.2d 585, 594, 128 P.2d 16, 21 (1942).

3. Cal.Ev.Code 1965, § 600.

4. McCormick, Evidence, 669 (1954); id. 825 (2d ed. 1972).

party to whom it is allocated under the rules governing the allocation in the first instance.

The court may instruct the jury that they may infer the existence of the presumed fact from proof of the basic facts giving rise to the presumption. However, it would be inappropriate under this rule to instruct the jury that the inference they are to draw is conclusive.

Conference Report

H.R., Fed. Rules of Evidence, Conf.Rep. No. 1597, 93d Cong., 2d Sess., p. 5 (1974); 1974 U.S. Code Cong. & Ad. News 7098, 7099

The House bill provides that a presumption in civil actions and proceedings shifts to the party against whom it is directed the burden of going forward with evidence to meet or rebut it. Even though evidence contradicting the presumption is offered, a presumption is considered sufficient evidence of the presumed fact to be considered by the jury. The Senate amendment provides that a presumption shifts to the party against whom it is directed the burden of going forward with evidence to meet or rebut the presumption, but it does not shift to that party the burden of persuasion on the existence of the presumed fact.

Under the Senate amendment, a presumption is sufficient to get a party past an adverse party's motion to dismiss made at the end of his case-in-chief. If the adverse party offers no evidence contradicting the presumed fact, the court will instruct the jury that if it finds the basic facts, it may presume the existence of the presumed fact. If the adverse party does offer evidence contradicting the presumed fact, the court cannot instruct the jury that it may *presume* the existence of the presumed fact from proof of the basic facts. The court may, however, instruct the jury that it may infer the existence of the presumed fact from proof of the basic facts.

The Conference adopts the Senate amendment.

Rule 302. Applicability of State Law in Civil Actions and Proceedings

In civil actions and proceedings, the effect of a presumption respecting a fact which is an element of a claim or defense as to which State law supplies the rule of decision is determined in accordance with State law.

Section references, McCormick 4th ed.

§ 336, § 344, § 349

Note by Federal Judicial Center

The rule enacted by the Congress is the rule prescribed by the Supreme Court, amended by adding "and proceedings" after "actions."

Advisory Committee's Note

56 F.R.D. 183, 211

A series of Supreme Court decisions in diversity cases leaves no doubt of the relevance of Erie Railroad Co. v. Tompkins, 304 U.S. 64, 58 S.Ct. 817, 82 L.Ed. 1188 (1938), to questions of burden of proof. These decisions are Cities Service Oil Co. v. Dunlap, 308 U.S. 208, 60 S.Ct. 201, 84 L.Ed. 196 (1939), Palmer v. Hoffman, 318 U.S. 109, 63 S.Ct. 477, 87 L.Ed. 645 (1943), and Dick v. New York Life Ins. Co., 359 U.S. 437, 79 S.Ct. 921, 3 L.Ed.2d 935 (1959). They involved burden of proof, respectively, as to status as bona fide purchaser, contributory negligence, and nonaccidental death (suicide) of an insured. In each instance the state rule was held to be applicable. It does not follow, however, that all presumptions in diversity cases are governed by state law. In each case cited, the burden of proof question had to do with a substantive element of the claim or defense. Application of the state law is called for only when the presumption operates upon such an element. Accordingly the rule does not apply state law when the presumption operates upon a lesser aspect of the case, i.e. "tactical" presumptions.

The situations in which the state law is applied have been tagged for convenience in the preceding discussion as "diversity cases." The designation is not a completely accurate one since *Erie* applies to any claim or issue having its source in state law, regardless of the basis of federal jurisdiction, and does not apply to a federal claim or issue, even though jurisdiction is based on diversity. Vestal, Erie R.R. v. Tompkins: A Projection, 48 Iowa L.Rev. 248, 257 (1963); Hart and Wechsler, The Federal Courts and the Federal System, 697 (1953); 1A Moore, Federal Practice ¶ 0.305[3] (2d ed. 1965); Wright, Federal Courts, 217–218 (1963). Hence the rule employs, as appropriately descriptive, the phrase "as to which state law supplies the rule of decision." See A.L.I. Study of the Division of Jurisdiction Between State and Federal Courts, § 2344(c), p. 40, P.F.D. No. 1 (1965).

Presumptions in Criminal Cases

Note by Federal Judicial Center

The rules prescribed by the Supreme Court included Rule 303, Presumptions in Criminal Cases. The rule was not included in the rules enacted by the Congress. . . .

ARTICLE IV. RELEVANCY AND ITS LIMITS

Rule

Rule 401. Definition of "Relevant Evidence"

"Relevant evidence" means evidence having any tendency to make the existence of any fact that is of consequence to the determination of the action more probable or less probable than it would be without the evidence.

Section references, McCormick 4th ed.

§ 39, § 44, § 45, § 47, § 52, § 185, § 196, § 197, § 199, § 200, § 202

Note by Federal Judicial Center

The rule enacted by the Congress is the rule prescribed by the Supreme Court without change.

Advisory Committee's Note

56 F.R.D. 183, 215

Problems of relevancy call for an answer to the question whether an item of evidence, when tested by the processes of legal reasoning, possesses sufficient probative value to justify receiving it in evidence. Thus, assessment of the probative value of evidence that a person purchased a revolver shortly prior to a fatal shooting with which he is charged is a matter of analysis and reasoning.

The variety of relevancy problems is coextensive with the ingenuity of counsel in using circumstantial evidence as a means of proof. An enormous number of cases fall in no set pattern, and this rule is designed as a guide for handling them. On the other hand, some situations recur with sufficient frequency to create patterns susceptible of treatment by specific rules. Rule 404 and those following it are of that variety; they also serve as illustrations of the application of the present rule as limited by the exclusionary principles of Rule 403.

Passing mention should be made of so-called "conditional" relevancy. Morgan, Basic Problems of Evidence 45–46 (1962). In this situation, probative value depends not only upon satisfying the basic requirement of relevancy as described above but also upon the existence of some matter of fact. For example, if evidence of a spoken statement is relied upon to prove notice, probative value is lacking unless the person sought to be charged heard the statement. The problem is one of fact, and the only rules needed are for the purpose of determining the respective functions of judge and jury. See Rules 104(b) and 901. The discussion which follows in the present note is concerned with relevancy generally, not with any particular problem of conditional relevancy.

Relevancy is not an inherent characteristic of any item of evidence but exists only as a relation between an item of evidence and a matter properly provable in the case. Does the item of evidence tend to prove the matter sought to be proved? Whether the relationship exists depends upon principles evolved by experience or science, applied logically to the situation at hand. James, Relevancy, Probability and the Law, 29 Calif.L.Rev. 689, 696, n. 15 (1941), in Selected Writings on Evidence and Trial 610, 615, n. 15 (Fryer ed. 1957). The rule summarizes this relationship as a "tendency to make the existence" of the fact to be proved "more probable or less probable." Compare Uniform Rule 1(2) which states the crux of relevancy as "a tendency in reason," thus perhaps emphasizing unduly the logical process and ignoring the need to draw upon experience or science to validate the general principle upon which relevancy in a particular situation depends.

The standard of probability under the rule is "more . . . probable than it would be without the evidence." Any more stringent requirement is unworkable and unrealistic. As McCormick § 152, p. 317, says, "A brick is not a wall," or, as Falknor, Extrinsic Policies Affecting Admissibility, 10 Rutgers L.Rev. 574, 576 (1956), quotes Professor McBaine, ". . . [I]t is not to be supposed that every witness can make a home run." Dealing with probability in the language of the rule has the added virtue of avoiding confusion between questions of admissibility and questions of the sufficiency of the evidence.

The rule uses the phrase "fact that is of consequence to the determination of the action" to describe the kind of fact to which proof may properly be directed. The language is that of California Evidence Code § 210; it has the advantage of avoiding the loosely used and ambiguous word "material." Tentative Recommendation and a Study Relating to the Uniform Rules of Evidence (Art. I. General Provisions), Cal. Law Revision Comm'n, Rep., Rec. & Studies, 10–11 (1964). The fact to be proved may be ultimate, intermediate, or evidentiary; it matters not, so long as it is of consequence in the determination of the action. Cf. Uniform Rule 1(2) which requires that the evidence relate to a "material" fact.

The fact to which the evidence is directed need not be in dispute. While situations will arise which call for the exclusion of evidence offered to prove a point conceded by the opponent, the ruling should be made on the basis of such considerations as waste of time and undue prejudice (see Rule 403), rather than under any general requirement that evidence is admissible only if directed to matters in dispute. Evidence which is essentially background in nature can scarcely be said to involve disputed matter, yet it is universally offered and admitted as an aid to understanding. Charts, photographs, views of real estate, murder weapons, and many other items of evidence fall in this category. A rule limiting admissibility to evidence directed to a controversial point would invite the exclusion of this helpful evidence, or at least the raising of endless questions over its admission. Cf. California Evidence Code § 210, defining relevant evidence in terms of tendency to prove a disputed fact.

Rule 402. Relevant Evidence Generally Admissible; Irrelevant Evidence Inadmissible

All relevant evidence is admissible, except as otherwise provided by the Constitution of the United States, by Act of Congress, by these rules, or by other rules prescribed by the Supreme Court pursuant to statutory authority. Evidence which is not relevant is not admissible.

Section references, McCormick 4th ed.

§ 44, § 45, § 47, § *184*, § 196, § 197, § 199, § 200, § 202, § *212*

Note by Federal Judicial Center

The rule enacted by the Congress is the rule prescribed by the Supreme Court, with the first sentence amended by substituting "prescribed" in place of "adopted", and by adding at the end thereof the phrase "pursuant to statutory authority."

Advisory Committee's Note

56 F.R.D. 183, 216

The provisions that all relevant evidence is admissible, with certain exceptions, and that evidence which is not relevant is not admissible are "a presupposition involved in the very conception of a rational system of evidence." Thayer, Preliminary Treatise on Evidence 264 (1898). They constitute the foundation upon which the structure of admission and exclusion rests. For similar provisions see California Evidence Code §§ 350, 351. Provisions that all relevant evidence is admissible are found in Uniform Rule 7(f); Kansas Code of Civil Procedure § 60–407(f); and New Jersey Evidence Rule 7(f); but the exclusion of evidence which is not relevant is left to implication.

Not all relevant evidence is admissible. The exclusion of relevant evidence occurs in a variety of situations and may be called for by these rules, by the Rules of Civil and Criminal Procedure, by Bankruptcy Rules, by Act of Congress, or by constitutional considerations.

Succeeding rules in the present article, in response to the demands of particular policies, require the exclusion of evidence despite its relevancy. In addition, Article V recognizes a number of privileges; Article VI imposes limitations upon witnesses and the manner of dealing with them; Article VII specifies requirements with respect to opinions and expert testimony; Article VIII excludes hearsay not falling within an exception; Article IX spells out the handling of authentication and identification; and Article X restricts the manner of proving the contents of writings and recordings.

The Rules of Civil and Criminal Procedure in some instances require the exclusion of relevant evidence. For example, Rules 30(b) and 32(a) (3) of the Rules of Civil Procedure, by imposing requirements of notice and unavailability of the deponent, place limits on the use of relevant depositions. Similarly, Rule 15 of the Rules of Criminal Procedure restricts the use of depositions in criminal cases, even though relevant. And the effective enforcement of the command, originally statutory and now found in Rule 5(a) of the Rules of Criminal Procedure, that an arrested person be taken without unnecessary delay before a commissioner or other similar officer is held to require the exclusion of statements elicited during detention in violation thereof. Mallory v. United States, 354 U.S. 449, 77 S.Ct. 1356, 1 L.Ed.2d 1479 (1957); 18 U.S.C. § 3501(c).

While congressional enactments in the field of evidence have generally tended to expand admissibility beyond the scope of the common law rules, in some particular situations they have restricted the admissibility of relevant evidence. Most of this legislation has consisted of the formulation of a privilege or of a prohibition against disclosure. 8 U.S.C. § 1202(f), records of refusal of visas or permits to enter United States confidential, subject to discretion of Secretary of State to make available to court upon certification of need; 10 U.S.C. § 3693, replacement certificate of honorable discharge from Army not admissible in evidence; 10 U.S.C. § 8693, same as to Air Force; 11 U.S.C. § 25(a)(10), testimony given by bankrupt on his examination not admissible in criminal proceedings against him, except that given in hearing upon objection to discharge; 11 U.S.C. § 205(a), railroad reorganization petition, if dismissed, not admissible in evidence; 11 U.S.C. § 403(a), list of creditors filed with municipal composition plan not an admission; 13 U.S.C. § 9(a), census information confidential, retained copies of reports privileged; 47 U.S.C. § 605, interception and divulgence of wire or radio communications prohibited unless authorized by sender. These statutory provisions would remain undisturbed by the rules.

The rule recognizes but makes no attempt to spell out the constitutional considerations which impose basic limitations upon the admissibility of relevant evidence. Examples are evidence obtained by unlawful search and seizure, Weeks v. United States, 232 U.S. 383, 34 S.Ct. 341, 58 L.Ed. 652 (1914); Katz v. United States, 389 U.S. 347, 88 S.Ct. 507, 19 L.Ed.2d 576 (1967); incriminating statement elicited from an accused in violation of right to counsel, Massiah v. United States, 377 U.S. 201, 84 S.Ct. 1199, 12 L.Ed.2d 246 (1964).

Report of House Committee on the Judiciary

House Comm. on Judiciary, Fed Rules of Evidence, H.R. Rep. No. 650, 93d Cong., 1st Sess., p. 7 (1973); 1974 U.S. Code Cong. & Ad. News 7075, 7081

Rule 402 as submitted to the Congress contained the phrase "or by other rules adopted by the Supreme Court". To accommodate the view that the Congress should not appear to acquiesce in the Court's judgment that it has authority under the existing Rules Enabling Acts to promulgate Rules of Evidence, the Committee amended the above phrase to read "or by other rules prescribed by the Supreme Court pursuant to statutory authority" in this and other Rules where the reference appears.

Rule 403. Exclusion of Relevant Evidence on Grounds of Prejudice, Confusion, or Waste of Time

Although relevant, evidence may be excluded if its probative value is substantially outweighed by the danger of unfair prejudice, confusion of the issues, or misleading the jury, or by considerations of undue delay, waste of time, or needless presentation of cumulative evidence.

Section references, McCormick 4th ed.

§ 7, § 11, § 12, § 13, § 16, § 19, § 26, § 30, § 35, § 36, § 39, § 41, § 42, § 44, § 45, § 47, § 52, § 56, § 57, § 58, § 59, § 185, § 193, § 196, § 197, § 199, § 200, § 202, § 212, § 250, § 255, § 293, § 322

Note by Federal Judicial Center

The rule enacted by the Congress is the rule prescribed by the Supreme Court without change.

Advisory Committee's Note

56 F.R.D. 183, 218

The case law recognizes that certain circumstances call for the exclusion of evidence which is of unquestioned relevance. These circumstances entail risks which range all the way from inducing decision on a purely emotional basis, at one extreme, to nothing more harmful than merely wasting time, at the other extreme. Situations in this area call for balancing the probative value of and need for the evidence against the harm likely to result from its admission. Slough, Relevancy Unraveled, 5 Kan.L.Rev. 1, 12–15 (1956); Trautman, Logical or Legal Relevancy—A Conflict in Theory, 5 Van.L.Rev. 385, 392 (1952); McCormick § 152, pp. 319–321. The rules which follow in this Article are concrete applications evolved for particular situations. However, they reflect the policies underlying the present rule, which is designed as a guide for the handling of situations for which no specific rules have been formulated.

Exclusion for risk of unfair prejudice, confusion of issues, misleading the jury, or waste of time, all find ample support in the authorities. "Unfair prejudice" within its context means an undue tendency to suggest decision on an improper basis, commonly, though not necessarily, an emotional one.

The rule does not enumerate surprise as a ground for exclusion, in this respect following Wigmore's view of the common law. 6 Wigmore § 1849. Cf. McCormick § 152, p. 320, n. 29, listing unfair surprise as a ground for exclusion but stating that it is usually "coupled with the danger of prejudice and confusion of issues." While Uniform Rule 45 incorporates surprise as a ground and is followed in Kansas Code of Civil Procedure § 60–445, surprise is not included in California Evidence Code § 352 or New Jersey Rule 4, though both the latter otherwise substantially embody Uniform Rule 45. While it can scarcely be doubted that claims of unfair surprise may still be justified despite procedural requirements of notice and instrumentalities of discovery, the granting of a continuance is a more appropriate remedy than exclusion of the evidence. Tentative Recommendation and a Study Relating to the Uniform Rules of Evidence (Art. VI. Extrinsic Policies Affecting Admissibility), Cal. Law Revision Comm'n, Rep., Rec. & Studies, 612 (1964). Moreover, the impact of a rule excluding evidence on the ground of surprise would be difficult to estimate.

In reaching a decision whether to exclude on grounds of unfair prejudice, consideration should be given to the probable effectiveness or lack of effectiveness of a limiting instruction. See Rule 106 [105] and Advisory Committee's Note thereunder. The availability of other means of proof may also be an appropriate factor.

Rule 404. Character Evidence Not Admissible to Prove Conduct; Exceptions; Other Crimes

(a) Character evidence generally. Evidence of a person's character or a trait of character is not admissible for the purpose of proving action in conformity therewith on a particular occasion, except:

(1) Character of accused. Evidence of a pertinent trait of character offered by an accused, or by the prosecution to rebut the same;

(2) Character of victim. Evidence of a pertinent trait of character of the victim of the crime offered by an accused,[1] or by the prosecution to rebut the same, or evidence of a character trait of peacefulness of the victim offered by the prosecution in a homicide case to rebut evidence that the victim was the first aggressor;

(3) Character of witness. Evidence of the character of a witness, as provided in rules 607, 608, and 609.

(b) Other crimes, wrongs, or acts. Evidence of other crimes, wrongs, or acts is not admissible to prove the character of a person in order to show action in conformity therewith. It may, however, be admissible for other purposes, such as proof of motive, opportunity, intent, preparation, plan, knowledge, identity, or absence of mistake or accident, provided that upon request by the accused, the prosecution in a criminal case shall provide reasonable notice in advance of trial, or during trial if the court excuses pretrial notice on good cause shown, of the general nature of any such evidence it intends to introduce at trial.

(As amended Mar. 2, 1987, eff. Oct. 1, 1987; Apr. 30, 1991, eff. Dec. 1, 1991.)

Section references, McCormick 4th ed.

Generally, § 189, § 192, § 196, § 197, § 200

(a). § 186, § 187, § 192

(1). § 186, § 187, § 191

(2). § 186, § 193

(3). § 186, § 191

(b). § 59, § 186, § 187, § 190, § 193

Note by Federal Judicial Center

The rule enacted by the Congress is the rule prescribed by the Supreme Court, with the second sentence of subdivision (b) amended by substituting "It may, however, be admissible" in place of "This subdivision does not exclude the evidence when offered."

1. The applicability of this provision in cases of rape or assault with intent to commit rape is greatly circumscribed by Rule 412, infra, added by Act of Congress in 1978.—Ed.

Advisory Committee's Note

56 F.R.D. 183, 219

Subdivision (a). This subdivision deals with the basic question whether character evidence should be admitted. Once the admissibility of character evidence in some form is established under this rule, reference must then be made to Rule 405, which follows, in order to determine the appropriate method of proof. If the character is that of a witness, see Rules 608 and 609 for methods of proof.

Character questions arise in two fundamentally different ways. (1) Character may itself be an element of a crime, claim, or defense. A situation of this kind is commonly referred to as "character in issue." Illustrations are: the chastity of the victim under a statute specifying her chastity as an element of the crime of seduction, or the competency of the driver in an action for negligently entrusting a motor vehicle to an incompetent driver. No problem of the general relevancy of character evidence is involved, and the present rule therefore has no provision on the subject. The only question relates to allowable methods of proof, as to which see Rule 405, immediately following. (2) Character evidence is susceptible of being used for the purpose of suggesting an inference that the person acted on the occasion in question consistently with his character. This use of character is often described as "circumstantial." Illustrations are: evidence of a violent disposition to prove that person was the aggressor in an affray, or evidence of honesty in disproof of a charge of theft. This circumstantial use of character evidence raises questions of relevancy as well as questions of allowable methods of proof.

In most jurisdictions today, the circumstantial use of character is rejected but with important exceptions: (1) an accused may introduce pertinent evidence of good character (often misleadingly described as "putting his character in issue"), in which event the prosecution may rebut with evidence of bad character; (2) an accused may introduce pertinent evidence of the character of the victim, as in support of a claim of self-defense to a charge of homicide or consent in a case of rape,[2] and the prosecution may introduce similar evidence in rebuttal of the character evidence, or, in a homicide case, to rebut a claim that deceased was the first aggressor, however proved; and (3) the character of a witness may be gone into as bearing on his credibility. McCormick §§ 155–161. This pattern is incorporated in the rule. While its basis lies more in history and experience than in logic an underlying justification can fairly be found in terms of the relative presence and absence of prejudice in the various situations. Falknor, Extrinsic Policies Affecting Admissibility, 10 Rutgers L.Rev. 574, 584 (1956); McCormick § 157. In any event, the criminal rule is so deeply imbedded in our jurisprudence as to assume almost constitutional proportions and to override doubts of the basic relevancy of the evidence.

The limitation to pertinent traits of character, rather than character generally, in paragraphs (1) and (2) is in accordance with the prevailing view. McCormick § 158, p. 334. A similar provision in Rule 608, to which reference is made in paragraph (3), limits character evidence respecting witnesses to the trait of truthfulness or untruthfulness.

2. But see Rule 412, infra, added by Act of Congress in 1978.—Ed.

The argument is made that circumstantial use of character ought to be allowed in civil cases to the same extent as in criminal cases, i.e. evidence of good (nonprejudicial) character would be admissible in the first instance, subject to rebuttal by evidence of bad character. Falknor, Extrinsic Policies Affecting Admissibility, 10 Rutgers L.Rev. 574, 581–583 (1956); Tentative Recommendation and a Study Relating to the Uniform Rules of Evidence (Art. VI. Extrinsic Policies Affecting Admissibility), Cal. Law Revision Comm'n, Rep., Rec. & Studies, 657–658 (1964). Uniform Rule 47 goes farther, in that it assumes that character evidence in general satisfies the conditions of relevancy, except as provided in Uniform Rule 48. The difficulty with expanding the use of character evidence in civil cases is set forth by the California Law Revision Commission in its ultimate rejection of Uniform Rule 47, id., 615:

> "Character evidence is of slight probative value and may be very prejudicial. It tends to distract the trier of fact from the main question of what actually happened on the particular occasion. It subtly permits the trier of fact to reward the good man and to punish the bad man because of their respective characters despite what the evidence in the case shows actually happened."

Much of the force of the position of those favoring greater use of character evidence in civil cases is dissipated by their support of Uniform Rule 48 which excludes the evidence in negligence cases, where it could be expected to achieve its maximum usefulness. Moreover, expanding concepts of "character," which seem of necessity to extend into such areas as psychiatric evaluation and psychological testing, coupled with expanded admissibility, would open up such vistas of mental examinations as caused the Court concern in Schlagenhauf v. Holder, 379 U.S. 104, 85 S.Ct. 234, 13 L.Ed.2d 152 (1964). It is believed that those espousing change have not met the burden of persuasion.

Subdivision (b) deals with a specialized but important application of the general rule excluding circumstantial use of character evidence. Consistently with that rule, evidence of other crimes, wrongs, or acts is not admissible to prove character as a basis for suggesting the inference that conduct on a particular occasion was in conformity with it. However, the evidence may be offered for another purpose, such as proof of motive, opportunity, and so on, which does not fall within the prohibition. In this situation the rule does not require that the evidence be excluded. No mechanical solution is offered. The determination must be made whether the danger of undue prejudice outweighs the probative value of the evidence in view of the availability of other means of proof and other factors appropriate for making decisions of this kind under Rule 403. Slough and Knightly, Other Vices, Other Crimes, 41 Iowa L.Rev. 325 (1956).

Report of House Committee on the Judiciary

House Comm. on Judiciary, Fed. Rules of Evidence, H.R. Rep. No. 650, 93d Cong., 1st Sess., p. 7 (1973); 1974 U.S.Code Cong. & Ad. News 7075, 7081

The second sentence of Rule 404(b) as submitted to the Congress began with the words "This subdivision does not exclude the evidence when offered". The Committee amended this language to read "It may, however, be admissible", the words used in the 1971 Advisory Committee draft, on the ground that this formulation properly placed greater emphasis on admissibility than did the final Court version.

Report of Senate Committee on the Judiciary

Senate Comm. on Judiciary, Fed. Rules of Evidence, S. Rep. No. 1277, 93d Cong., 2d Sess., p. 24 (1974); 1974 U.S.Code Cong. & Ad. News 7051, 7071

This rule provides that evidence of other crimes, wrongs, or acts is not admissible to prove character but may be admissible for other specified purposes such as proof of motive.

Although your committee sees no necessity in amending the rule itself, it anticipates that the use of the discretionary word "may" with respect to the admissibility of evidence of crimes, wrongs, or acts is not intended to confer any arbitrary discretion on the trial judge. Rather, it is anticipated that with respect to permissible uses for such evidence, the trial judge may exclude it only on the basis of those considerations set forth in Rule 403, i.e. prejudice, confusion or waste of time.

1987 Amendment. The amendments are technical. No substantive change is intended.

1991 Amendment. Rule 404(b) has emerged as one of the most cited Rules in the Rules of Evidence. And in many criminal cases evidence of an accused's extrinsic acts is viewed as an important asset in the prosecution's case against an accused. Although there are a few reported decisions on use of such evidence by the defense, *see, e.g., United States v. McClure,* 546 F.2d 670 (5th Cir.1990) (acts of informant offered in entrapment defense), the overwhelming number of cases involve introduction of that evidence by the prosecution.

The amendment to Rule 404(b) adds a pretrial notice requirement in criminal cases and is intended to reduce surprise and promote early resolution on the issue of admissibility. The notice requirement thus places Rule 404(b) in the mainstream with notice and disclosure provisions in other rules of evidence. *See, e.g.,* Rule 412 (written motion of intent to offer evidence under rule), Rule 609 (written notice of intent to offer conviction older than 10 years), Rule 803(24) and 804(b)(5) (notice of intent to use residual hearsay exceptions).

The Rule expects that counsel for both the defense and the prosecution will submit the necessary request and information in a reasonable and timely fashion. Other than requiring pretrial notice, no specific time limits are stated in recognition that what constitutes a reasonable request or disclosure will depend largely on the circumstances of each case. *Compare* Fla.Stat.Ann. § 90.404(2)(b) (notice must be given at least 10 days before trial) *with* Tex.R. Evid. 404(b) (no time limit).

Likewise, no specific form of notice is required. The Committee considered and rejected a requirement that the notice satisfy the particularity requirements normally required of language used in a charging instrument. *Cf.* Fla. Stat.Ann. § 90.404(2)(b) (written disclosure must describe uncharged misconduct with particularity required of an indictment or information). Instead, the Committee opted for a generalized notice provision which requires the prosecution to apprise the defense of the general nature of the evidence of extrinsic acts. The Committee does not intend that the amendment will supercede other rules of admissibility or disclosure, such as the Jencks Act, 18 U.S.C. § 3500, et seq. nor require the prosecution to disclose directly or indirectly the names and addresses of its witnesses, something it is currently not required to do under Federal Rule of Criminal Procedure 16.

The amendment requires the prosecution to provide notice, regardless of how it intends to use the extrinsic act evidence at trial, i.e., during its case-in-chief, for impeachment, or for possible rebuttal. The court in its discretion may, under the facts, decide that the particular request or notice was not reasonable, either because of the lack of timeliness or completeness. Because the notice requirement serves as condition precedent to admissibility of 404(b) evidence, the offered evidence is inadmissible if the court decides that the notice requirement has not been met.

Nothing in the amendment precludes the court from requiring the government to provide it with an opportunity to rule *in limine* on 404(b) evidence before it is offered or even mentioned during trial. When ruling *in limine,* the court may require the government to disclose to it the specifics of such evidence which the court must consider in determining admissibility.

The amendment does not extend to evidence of acts which are "intrinsic" to the charged offense, *see United States v. Williams,* 900 F.2d 823 (5th Cir. 1990) (noting distinction between 404(b) evidence and intrinsic offense evidence). Nor is the amendment intended to redefine what evidence would otherwise be admissible under Rule 404(b). Finally, the Committee does not intend through the amendment to affect the role of the court and the jury in considering such evidence. *See United States v. Huddleston,* ___ U.S. ___, 108 S.Ct. 1496 (1988).

Rule 405. Methods of Proving Character

(a) Reputation or opinion. In all cases in which evidence of character or a trait of character of a person is admissible, proof may be made by testimony as to reputation or by testimony in the form of an opinion. On cross-examination, inquiry is allowable into relevant specific instances of conduct.

(b) Specific instances of conduct. In cases in which character or a trait of character of a person is an essential element of a charge, claim, or defense, proof may also be made of specific instances of that person's conduct.

(As amended Mar. 2, 1987, eff. Oct. 1, 1987.)

Section references, McCormick 4th ed.

Generally § 186, § 189, § 191, § 196, § 197, § 206

(a). § 191

(b). § 187

Note by Federal Judicial Center

The rule enacted by the Congress is the rule prescribed by the Supreme Court without change. The bill reported by the House Committee on the Judiciary deleted the provision in subdivision (a) for making proof by testimony in the form of an opinion, but the provision was reinstated on the floor of the House. [120 Cong.Rec. 2370–73 (1974)].

Advisory Committee's Note

56 F.R.D. 183, 222

The rule deals only with allowable methods of proving character, not with the admissibility of character evidence, which is covered in Rule 404.

Of the three methods of proving character provided by the rule, evidence of specific instances of conduct is the most convincing. At the same time it possesses the greatest capacity to arouse prejudice, to confuse, to surprise, and to consume time. Consequently the rule confines the use of evidence of this kind to cases in which character is, in the strict sense, in issue and hence deserving of a searching inquiry. When character is used circumstantially and hence occupies a lesser status in the case, proof may be only by reputation and opinion. These latter methods are also available when character is in issue. This treatment is, with respect to specific instances of conduct and reputation, conventional contemporary common law doctrine. McCormick § 153.

In recognizing opinion as a means of proving character, the rule departs from usual contemporary practice in favor of that of an earlier day. See 7 Wigmore § 1986, pointing out that the earlier practice permitted opinion and arguing strongly for evidence based on personal knowledge and belief as contrasted with "the secondhand, irresponsible product of multiplied guesses and gossip which we term 'reputation'." It seems likely that the persistence of reputation evidence is due to its largely being opinion in disguise. Traditionally character has been regarded primarily in moral overtones of good and bad: chaste, peaceable, truthful, honest. Nevertheless, on occasion nonmoral considerations crop up, as in the case of the incompetent driver, and this seems bound to happen increasingly. If character is defined as the kind of person one is, then account must be taken of varying ways of arriving at the estimate. These may range from the opinion of the employer who has found the man honest to the opinion of the psychiatrist based upon examination and testing. No effective dividing line exists between character and mental capacity, and the latter traditionally has been provable by opinion.

According to the great majority of cases, on cross-examination inquiry is allowable as to whether the reputation witness has heard of particular instances of conduct pertinent to the trait in question. Michelson v. United States, 335 U.S. 469, 69 S.Ct. 213, 93 L.Ed. 168 (1948); Annot., 47 A.L.R.2d 1258. The theory is that, since the reputation witness relates what he has heard, the inquiry tends to shed light on the accuracy of his hearing and reporting. Accordingly, the opinion witness would be asked whether he knew, as well as whether he had heard. The fact is, of course, that these distinctions are of slight if any practical significance, and the second sentence of subdivision (a) eliminates them as a factor in formulating questions. This recognition of the propriety of inquiring into specific instances of conduct does not circumscribe inquiry otherwise into the bases of opinion and reputation testimony.

The express allowance of inquiry into specific instances of conduct on cross-examination in subdivision (a) and the express allowance of it as part of a case in chief when character is actually in issue in subdivision (b) contemplate that testimony of specific instances is not generally permissible on the direct examination of an ordinary opinion witness to character. Similarly as to witnesses to the character of witnesses under Rule 608(b). Opinion testimony on direct in these situations ought in general to correspond to reputation testimony as now given, i.e., be confined to the nature and extent of observation and acquaintance upon which the opinion is based. See Rule 701.

1987 Amendment. The amendment is technical. No substantive change is intended.

Rule 406. Habit; Routine Practice

Evidence of the habit of a person or of the routine practice of an organization, whether corroborated or not and regardless of the presence of eyewitnesses, is relevant to prove that the conduct of the person or organization on a particular occasion was in conformity with the habit or routine practice.

Section references, McCormick 4th ed.

§ 195, § 271

Note by Federal Judicial Center

The rule enacted by the Congress is subdivision (a) of the rule prescribed by the Supreme Court. Subdivision (b) of the Court's rule was deleted for reasons stated in the Report of the House Committee on the Judiciary set forth below.

* * *

Advisory Committee's Note

56 F.R.D. 183, 223

An oft-quoted paragraph, McCormick, § 162, p. 340, describes habit in terms effectively contrasting it with character:

> "Character and habit are close akin. Character is a generalized description of one's disposition, or of one's disposition in respect to a general trait, such as honesty, temperance, or peacefulness. 'Habit,' in modern usage, both lay and psychological, is more specific. It describes one's regular response to a repeated specific situation. If we speak of character for care, we think of the person's tendency to act prudently in all the varying situations of life, in business, family life, in handling automobiles and in walking across the street. A habit, on the other hand, is the person's regular practice of meeting a particular kind of situation with a specific type of conduct, such as the habit of going down a particular stairway two stairs at a time, or of giving the hand-signal for a left turn, or of alighting from railway cars while they are moving. The doing of the habitual acts may become semi-automatic."

Equivalent behavior on the part of a group is designated "routine practice of an organization" in the rule.

Agreement is general that habit evidence is highly persuasive as proof of conduct on a particular occasion. Again quoting McCormick § 162, p. 341:

> "Character may be thought of as the sum of one's habits though doubtless it is more than this. But unquestionably the uniformity of one's response to habit is far greater than the consistency with which one's conduct conforms to character or disposition. Even though character

comes in only exceptionally as evidence of an act, surely any sensible man in investigating whether X did a particular act would be greatly helped in his inquiry by evidence as to whether he was in the habit of doing it."

When disagreement has appeared, its focus has been upon the question what constitutes habit, and the reason for this is readily apparent. The extent to which instances must be multiplied and consistency of behavior maintained in order to rise to the status of habit inevitably gives rise to differences of opinion. Lewan, Rationale of Habit Evidence, 16 Syracuse L.Rev. 39, 49 (1964). While adequacy of sampling and uniformity of response are key factors, precise standards for measuring their sufficiency for evidence purposes cannot be formulated.

The rule is consistent with prevailing views. Much evidence is excluded simply because of failure to achieve the status of habit. Thus, evidence of intemperate "habits" is generally excluded when offered as proof of drunkenness in accident cases, Annot., 46 A.L.R.2d 103, and evidence of other assaults is inadmissible to prove the instant one in a civil assault action, Annot., 66 A.L.R.2d 806. In Levin v. United States, 119 U.S.App.D.C. 156, 338 F.2d 265 (1964), testimony as to the religious "habits" of the accused, offered as tending to prove that he was at home observing the Sabbath rather than out obtaining money through larceny by trick, was held properly excluded:

> "It seems apparent to us that an individual's religious practices would not be the type of activities which would lend themselves to the characterization of 'invariable regularity.' [1 Wigmore 520.] Certainly the very volitional basis of the activity raises serious questions as to its invariable nature, and hence its probative value." Id. at 272.

These rulings are not inconsistent with the trend towards admitting evidence of business transactions between one of the parties and a third person as tending to prove that he made the same bargain or proposal in the litigated situation. Slough, Relevancy Unraveled, 6 Kan.L.Rev. 38–41 (1957). Nor are they inconsistent with such cases as Whittemore v. Lockheed Aircraft Corp., 65 Cal.App. 2d 737, 151 P.2d 670 (1944), upholding the admission of evidence that plaintiff's intestate had on four other occasions flown planes from defendant's factory for delivery to his employer airline, offered to prove that he was piloting rather than a guest on a plane which crashed and killed all on board while en route for delivery.

A considerable body of authority has required that evidence of the routine practice of an organization be corroborated as a condition precedent to its admission in evidence. Slough, Relevancy Unraveled, 5 Kan.L.Rev. 404, 449 (1957). This requirement is specifically rejected by the rule on the ground that it relates to the sufficiency of the evidence rather than admissibility. A similar position is taken in New Jersey Rule 49. The rule also rejects the requirement of the absence of eyewitnesses, sometimes encountered with respect to admitting habit evidence to prove freedom from contributory negligence in wrongful death cases. For comment critical of the requirements see Frank, J., in Cereste v. New York, N.H. & H.R. Co., 231 F.2d 50 (2d Cir.1956), cert. denied 351 U.S. 951, 76 S.Ct. 848, 100 L.Ed. 1475, 10 Vand.L.Rev. 447 (1957); McCormick § 162, p. 342. The omission of the requirement from the California Evidence Code is said to have effected its elimination. Comment, Cal.Ev.Code § 1105.

Report of House Committee on the Judiciary

House Comm. on Judiciary, Fed. Rules of Evidence, H.R. Rep. No. 650, 93d Cong., 1st Sess., p. 5 (1973); 1974 U.S.Code Cong.& Ad. News 7075, 7079

Rule 406 as submitted to Congress contained a subdivision (b) providing that the method of proof of habit or routine practice could be "in the form of an opinion or by specific instances of conduct sufficient in number to warrant a finding that the habit existed or that the practice was routine." The Committee deleted this subdivision believing that the method of proof of habit and routine practice should be left to the courts to deal with on a case-by-case basis. At the same time, the Committee does not intend that its action be construed as sanctioning a general authorization of opinion evidence in this area.

Rule 407. Subsequent Remedial Measures

When, after an event, measures are taken which, if taken previously, would have made the event less likely to occur, evidence of the subsequent measures is not admissible to prove negligence or culpable conduct in connection with the event. This rule does not require the exclusion of evidence of subsequent measures when offered for another purpose, such as proving ownership, control, or feasibility of precautionary measures, if controverted, or impeachment.

Section references, McCormick 4th ed.

§ 267

Note by Federal Judicial Center

The rule enacted by the Congress is the rule prescribed by the Supreme Court without change.

Advisory Committee's Note

56 F.R.D. 183, 225

The rule incorporates conventional doctrine which excludes evidence of subsequent remedial measures as proof of an admission of fault. The rule rests on two grounds. (1) The conduct is not in fact an admission, since the conduct is equally consistent with injury by mere accident or through contributory negligence. Or, as Baron Bramwell put it, the rule rejects the notion that "because the world gets wiser as it gets older, therefore it was foolish before." Hart v. Lancashire & Yorkshire Ry. Co., 21 L.T.R. N.S. 261, 263 (1869). Under a liberal theory of relevancy this ground alone would not support exclusion as the inference is still a possible one. (2) The other, and more impressive, ground for exclusion rests on a social policy of encouraging people to take, or at least not discouraging them from taking, steps in furtherance of added safety. The courts have applied this principle to exclude evidence of subsequent repairs, installation of safety devices, changes in company rules, and discharge of employees, and the language of the present rule is broad enough to encompass all of them. See Falknor, Extrinsic Policies Affecting Admissibility, 10 Rutgers L.Rev. 574, 590 (1956).

The second sentence of the rule directs attention to the limitations of the rule. Exclusion is called for only when the evidence of subsequent remedial measures is offered as proof of negligence or culpable conduct. In effect it rejects the suggested inference that fault is admitted. Other purposes are, however, allowable, including ownership or control, existence of duty, and feasibility of precautionary measures, if controverted, and impeachment. 2 Wigmore § 283; Annot., 64 A.L.R.2d 1296. Two recent federal cases are illustrative. Boeing Airplane Co. v. Brown, 291 F.2d 310 (9th Cir.1961), an action against an airplane manufacturer for using an allegedly defectively designed alternator shaft which caused a plane crash, upheld the admission of evidence of subsequent design modification for the purpose of showing that design changes and safeguards were feasible. And Powers v. J.B. Michael & Co., 329 F.2d 674 (6th Cir.1964), an action against a road contractor for negligent failure to put out warning signs, sustained the admission of evidence that defendant subsequently put out signs to show that the portion of the road in question was under defendant's control. The requirement that the other purpose be controverted calls for automatic exclusion unless a genuine issue be present and allows the opposing party to lay the groundwork for exclusion by making an admission. Otherwise the factors of undue prejudice, confusion of issues, misleading the jury, and waste of time remain for consideration under Rule 403.

For comparable rules, see Uniform Rule 51; California Evidence Code § 1151; Kansas Code of Civil Procedure § 60–451; New Jersey Evidence Rule 51.

Rule 408. Compromise and Offers to Compromise

Evidence of (1) furnishing or offering or promising to furnish, or (2) accepting or offering or promising to accept, a valuable consideration in compromising or attempting to compromise a claim which was disputed as to either validity or amount, is not admissible to prove liability for or invalidity of the claim or its amount. Evidence of conduct or statements made in compromise negotiations is likewise not admissible. This rule does not require the exclusion of any evidence otherwise discoverable merely because it is presented in the course of compromise negotiations. This rule also does not require exclusion when the evidence is offered for another purpose, such as proving bias or prejudice of a witness, negativing a contention of undue delay, or proving an effort to obstruct a criminal investigation or prosecution.

Section references, McCormick 4th ed.

§ 267

Note by Federal Judicial Center

The rule enacted by the Congress is the rule prescribed by the Supreme Court, amended by the insertion of the third sentence. Other amendments, proposed by the House bill, were not enacted, for reasons stated in the Report of the Senate Committee on the Judiciary and in the Conference Report, set forth below.

Advisory Committee's Note

56 F.R.D. 183, 226

As a matter of general agreement, evidence of an offer to compromise a claim is not receivable in evidence as an admission of, as the case may be, the validity or invalidity of the claim. As with evidence of subsequent remedial measures, dealt with in Rule 407, exclusion may be based on two grounds. (1) The evidence is irrelevant, since the offer may be motivated by a desire for peace rather than from any concession of weakness of position. The validity of this position will vary as the amount of the offer varies in relation to the size of the claim and may also be influenced by other circumstances. (2) A more consistently impressive ground is promotion of the public policy favoring the compromise and settlement of disputes. McCormick §§ 76, 251. While the rule is ordinarily phrased in terms of offers of compromise, it is apparent that a similar attitude must be taken with respect to completed compromises when offered against a party thereto. This latter situation will not, of course, ordinarily occur except when a party to the present litigation has compromised with a third person.

The same policy underlies the provision of Rule 68 of the Federal Rules of Civil Procedure that evidence of an unaccepted offer of judgment is not admissible except in a proceeding to determine costs.

The practical value of the common law rule has been greatly diminished by its inapplicability to admissions of fact, even though made in the course of compromise negotiations, unless hypothetical, stated to be "without prejudice," or so connected with the offer as to be inseparable from it. McCormick § 251, pp. 540–541. An inevitable effect is to inhibit freedom of communication with respect to compromise, even among lawyers. Another effect is the generation of controversy over whether a given statement falls within or without the protected area. These considerations account for the expansion of the rule herewith to include evidence of conduct or statements made in compromise negotiations, as well as the offer or completed compromise itself. For similar provisions see California Evidence Code §§ 1152, 1154.

The policy considerations which underlie the rule do not come into play when the effort is to induce a creditor to settle an admittedly due amount for a lesser sum. McCormick § 251, p. 540. Hence the rule requires that the claim be disputed as to either validity or amount.

The final sentence of the rule serves to point out some limitations upon its applicability. Since the rule excludes only when the purpose is proving the validity or invalidity of the claim or its amount, an offer for another purpose is not within the rule. The illustrative situations mentioned in the rule are supported by the authorities. As to proving bias or prejudice of a witness, see Annot., 161 A.L.R. 395, contra, Fenberg v. Rosenthal, 348 Ill.App. 510, 109 N.E.2d 402 (1952), and negativing a contention of lack of due diligence in presenting a claim, 4 Wigmore § 1061. An effort to "buy off" the prosecution or a prosecuting witness in a criminal case is not within the policy of the rule of exclusion. McCormick § 251, p. 542.

For other rules of similar import, see Uniform Rules 52 and 53; California Evidence Code §§ 1152, 1154; Kansas Code of Civil Procedure §§ 60–452, 60–453; New Jersey Evidence Rules 52 and 53.

Report of House Committee on the Judiciary

House Comm. on Judiciary, Fed.Rules of Evidence, H.R.Rep. No. 650, 93d Cong., 1st Sess., p. 8 (1973); 1974 U.S.Code Cong. & Ad. News 7075, 7081

Under existing federal law evidence of conduct and statements made in compromise negotiations is admissible in subsequent litigation between the parties. The second sentence of Rule 408 as submitted by the Supreme Court proposed to reverse that doctrine in the interest of further promoting non-judicial settlement of disputes. Some agencies of government expressed the view that the Court formulation was likely to impede rather than assist efforts to achieve settlement of disputes. For one thing, it is not always easy to tell when compromise negotiations begin, and informal dealings end. Also, parties dealing with government agencies would be reluctant to furnish factual information at preliminary meetings; they would wait until "compromise negotiations" began and thus hopefully effect an immunity for themselves with respect to the evidence supplied. In light of these considerations, the Committee recast the Rule so that admissions of liability or opinions given during compromise negotiations continue inadmissible, but evidence of unqualified factual assertions is admissible. The latter aspect of the Rule is drafted, however, so as to preserve other possible objections to the introduction of such evidence. The Committee intends no modification of current law whereby a party may protect himself from future use of his statements by couching them in hypothetical conditional form.

Report of Senate Committee on the Judiciary

Senate Comm. on Judiciary, Fed. Rules of Evidence, S.Rep. No. 1277, 93d Cong., 2d Sess., p. 10 (1974); 1974 U.S.Code Cong. & Ad. News 7051, 7056

This rule as reported makes evidence of settlement or attempted settlement of a disputed claim inadmissible when offered as an admission of liability or the amount of liability. The purpose of this rule is to encourage settlements which would be discouraged if such evidence were admissible.

Under present law, in most jurisdictions, statements of fact made during settlement negotiations, however, are excepted from this ban and are admissible. The only escape from admissibility of statements of fact made in a settlement negotiation is if the declarant or his representative expressly states that the statement is hypothetical in nature or is made without prejudice. Rule 408 as submitted by the Court reversed the traditional rule. It would have brought statements of fact within the ban and made them, as well as an offer of settlement, inadmissible.

The House amended the rule and would continue to make evidence of facts disclosed during compromise negotiations admissible. It thus reverted to the traditional rule. The House committee report states that the committee intends to preserve current law under which a party may protect himself by couching his statements in hypothetical form.[1] The real impact of this amendment, however, is to deprive the rule of much of its salutary effect. The exception for factual admissions was believed by the Advisory Committee to

1. See Report No. 93–650, dated November 15, 1973.

hamper free communication between parties and thus to constitute an unjustifiable restraint upon efforts to negotiate settlements—the encouragement of which is the purpose of the rule. Further, by protecting hypothetically phrased statements, it constituted a preference for the sophisticated, and a trap for the unwary.

Three States which had adopted rules of evidence patterned after the proposed rules prescribed by the Supreme Court opted for versions of rule 408 identical with the Supreme Court draft with respect to the inadmissibility of conduct or statements made in compromise negotiations.[2]

For these reasons, the committee has deleted the House amendment and restored the rule to the version submitted by the Supreme Court with one additional amendment. This amendment adds a sentence to insure that evidence, such as documents, is not rendered inadmissible merely because it is presented in the course of compromise negotiations if the evidence is otherwise discoverable. A party should not be able to immunize from admissibility documents otherwise discoverable merely by offering them in a compromise negotiation.

Conference Report

H.R., Fed. Rules of Evidence, Conf. Rep. No. 1597, 93d Cong., 2d Sess., p. 6 (1974); 1974 U.S.Code Cong. & Ad. News 7098, 7099

The House bill provides that evidence of admissions of liability or opinions given during compromise negotiations is not admissible, but that evidence of facts disclosed during compromise negotiations is not inadmissible by virtue of having been first disclosed in the compromise negotiations. The Senate amendment provides that evidence of conduct or statements made in compromise negotiations is not admissible. The Senate amendment also provides that the rule does not require the exclusion of any evidence otherwise discoverable merely because it is presented in the course of compromise negotiations.

The House bill was drafted to meet the objection of executive agencies that under the rule as proposed by the Supreme Court, a party could present a fact during compromise negotiations and thereby prevent an opposing party from offering evidence of that fact at trial even though such evidence was obtained from independent sources. The Senate amendment expressly precludes this result.

The Conference adopts the Senate amendment.

Rule 409. Payment of Medical and Similar Expenses

Evidence of furnishing or offering or promising to pay medical, hospital, or similar expenses occasioned by an injury is not admissible to prove liability for the injury.

Section references, McCormick 4th ed.

§ 267

2. Nev.Rev.Stats. § 48.105; N.Mex.Stats.Anno. (1973 Supp.) § 20-4-408; West's Wis. Stats.Anno. (1973 Supp.) § 904.08.

Note by Federal Judicial Center

The rule enacted by the Congress is the rule prescribed by the Supreme Court without change.

Advisory Committee's Note

56 F.R.D. 183, 228

The considerations underlying this rule parallel those underlying Rules 407 and 408, which deal respectively with subsequent remedial measures and offers of compromise. As stated in Annot., 20 A.L.R.2d 291, 293:

> "[G]enerally, evidence of payment of medical, hospital, or similar expenses of an injured party by the opposing party, is not admissible, the reason often given being that such payment or offer is usually made from humane impulses and not from an admission of liability, and that to hold otherwise would tend to discourage assistance to the injured person."

Contrary to Rule 408, dealing with offers of compromise, the present rule does not extend to conduct or statements not a part of the act of furnishing or offering or promising to pay. This difference in treatment arises from fundamental differences in nature. Communication is essential if compromises are to be effected, and consequently broad protection of statements is needed. This is not so in cases of payments or offers or promises to pay medical expenses, where factual statements may be expected to be incidental in nature.

For rules on the same subject, but phrased in terms of "humanitarian motives," see Uniform Rule 52; California Evidence Code § 1152; Kansas Code of Civil Procedure § 60–452; New Jersey Evidence Rule 52.

Rule 410. Inadmissibility of Pleas, Plea Discussions, and Related Statements

Except as otherwise provided in this rule, evidence of the following is not, in any civil or criminal proceeding, admissible against the defendant who made the plea or was a participant in the plea discussions:

(1) a plea of guilty which was later withdrawn;

(2) a plea of nolo contendere;

(3) any statement made in the course of any proceedings under Rule 11 of the Federal Rules of Criminal Procedure or comparable state procedure regarding either of the foregoing pleas; or

(4) any statement made in the course of plea discussions with an attorney for the prosecuting authority which do not result in a plea of guilty or which result in a plea of guilty later withdrawn.

However, such a statement is admissible (i) in any proceeding wherein another statement made in the course of the same plea or plea discussions has been introduced and the statement ought in fairness be considered contemporaneously with it, or (ii) in a criminal proceeding for perjury or false statement if the statement was made by the defendant under oath, on the record and in the presence of counsel.

(As amended by P.L. 94–149, § 1(9), Dec. 12, 1975, 89 Stat. 805; Apr. 30, 1979, eff. Dec. 1, 1980).

Section references, McCormick 4th ed.

§ 42, § 159, § 257, § 266

Rule 410 as originally enacted

Editorial Note

When first enacted together with the other Federal Rules of Evidence, Rule 410 read as follows:

> Except as otherwise provided by Act of Congress, evidence of a plea of guilty, later withdrawn, or a plea of nolo contendere, or of an offer to plead guilty or nolo contendere to the crime charged or any other crime, or of statements made in connection with any of the foregoing pleas or offers, is not admissible in any civil or criminal action, case, or proceeding against the person who made the plea or offer. This rule shall not apply to the introduction of voluntary and reliable statements made in court on the record in connection with any of the foregoing pleas or offers where offered for impeachment purposes or in a subsequent prosecution of the declarant for perjury or false statement.
>
> This rule shall not take effect until August 1, 1975, and shall be superseded by any amendment to the Federal Rules of Criminal Procedure which is inconsistent with this rule, and which takes effect after the date of the enactment of the Act establishing these Federal Rules of Evidence.

As prescribed by the Supreme Court, the rule had consisted only of the first sentence, without the clause "Except as otherwise provided by Act of Congress". That clause and the remaining language were added by congressional amendment. The theory of the Supreme Court's rule is explained in the Advisory Committee's Note set forth immediately below, and the reasons for the amendments are stated in the congressional reports which follow it. In addition to these latter reports, see Chairman Hungate's explanation. 120 Cong.Rec. 40890 (1974); 1975 U.S.Code Cong. & Ad.News 7108, 7109.

Advisory Committee's Note

56 F.R.D. 183, 228

Withdrawn pleas of guilty were held inadmissible in federal prosecutions in Kercheval v. United States, 274 U.S. 220, 47 S.Ct. 582, 71 L.Ed. 1009 (1927). The Court pointed out that to admit the withdrawn plea would effectively set at naught the allowance of withdrawal and place the accused in a dilemma utterly inconsistent with the decision to award him a trial. The New York Court of Appeals, in People v. Spitaleri, 9 N.Y.2d 168, 212 N.Y.S.2d 53, 173 N.E.2d 35 (1961), reexamined and overturned its earlier decisions which had allowed admission. In addition to the reasons set forth in Kercheval, which was quoted at length, the court pointed out that the effect of admitting the plea was to compel defendant to take the stand by way of explanation and to open the way for the prosecution to call the lawyer who had represented him at the time of entering the plea. State court decisions for and against admissibility are collected in Annot., 86 A.L.R.2d 326.

Pleas of *nolo contendere* are recognized by Rule 11 of the Rules of Criminal Procedure, although the law of numerous States is to the contrary. The present rule gives effect to the principal traditional characteristic of the *nolo* plea, i.e. avoiding the admission of guilt which is inherent in pleas of guilty. This position is consistent with the construction of Section 5 of the Clayton Act, 15 U.S.C. § 16(a), recognizing the inconclusive and compromise nature of judgments based on *nolo* pleas. General Electric Co. v. City of San Antonio, 334 F.2d 480 (5th Cir.1964); Commonwealth Edison Co. v. Allis-Chalmers Mfg. Co., 323 F.2d 412 (7th Cir.1963), cert. denied 376 U.S. 939, 84 S.Ct. 794, 11 L.Ed. 2d 659; Armco Steel Corp. v. North Dakota, 376 F.2d 206 (8th Cir.1967); City of Burbank v. General Electric Co., 329 F.2d 825 (9th Cir.1964). See also state court decisions in Annot., 18 A.L.R.2d 1287, 1314.

Exclusion of offers to plead guilty or *nolo* has as its purpose the promotion of disposition of criminal cases by compromise. As pointed out in McCormick § 251, p. 543.

> "Effective criminal law administration in many localities would hardly be possible if a large proportion of the charges were not disposed of by such compromises."

See also People v. Hamilton, 60 Cal.2d 105, 32 Cal.Rptr. 4, 383 P.2d 412 (1963), discussing legislation designed to achieve this result. As with compromise offers generally, Rule 408, free communication is needed, and security against having an offer of compromise or related statement admitted in evidence effectively encourages it.[1]

Limiting the exclusionary rule to use against the accused is consistent with the purpose of the rule, since the possibility of use for or against other persons will not impair the effectiveness of withdrawing pleas or the freedom of discussion which the rule is designed to foster. See A.B.A. Standards Relating to Pleas of Guilty § 2.2 (1968). See also the narrower provisions of New Jersey Evidence Rule 52(2) and the unlimited exclusion provided in California Evidence Code § 1153.

Report of House Committee on the Judiciary

House Comm. on Judiciary, Fed. Rules of Evidence, H.R.Rep. No. 650, 93d Cong., 1st Sess., p. 8 (1973); 1974 U.S.Code Cong. & Ad. News 7075, 7082

The Committee added the phrase "Except as otherwise provided by Act of Congress" to Rule 410 as submitted by the Court in order to preserve particular congressional policy judgments as to the effect of a plea of guilty or of nolo contendere. See 15 U.S.C. 16(a). The Committee intends that its amendment refers to both present statutes and statutes subsequently enacted.

Report of Senate Committee on the Judiciary

Senate Comm. on Judiciary, Fed. Rules of Evidence, S. Rep. No. 1277, 93d Cong., 2d Sess., p. 10 (1974); 1974 U.S.Code Cong. & Ad. News 7051, 7057

As adopted by the House, rule 410 would make inadmissible pleas of guilty or nolo contendere subsequently withdrawn as well as offers to make such

1. The rule as enacted, it should be noted, allows use of the statements for impeachment or in a subsequent prosecution for perjury or false statement.

pleas. Such a rule is clearly justified as a means of encouraging pleading. However, the House rule would then go on to render inadmissible for any purpose statements made in connection with these pleas or offers as well.

The committee finds this aspect of the House rule unjustified. Of course, in certain circumstances such statements should be excluded. If, for example, a plea is vitiated because of coercion, statements made in connection with the plea may also have been coerced and should be inadmissible on that basis. In other cases, however, voluntary statements of an accused made in court on the record, in connection with a plea, and determined by a court to be reliable should be admissible even though the plea is subsequently withdrawn. This is particularly true in those cases where, if the House rule were in effect, a defendant would be able to contradict his previous statements and thereby lie with impunity.[2] To prevent such an injustice, the rule has been modified to permit the use of such statements for the limited purposes of impeachment and in subsequent perjury or false statement prosecutions.

Conference Report

H.R., Fed. Rules of Evidence, Conf. Rep. No. 1597, 93d Cong., 2d Sess., p. 6 (1974); 1974 U.S.Code Cong. & Ad. News 7098, 7100

The House bill provides that evidence of a guilty or nolo contendere plea, of an offer of either plea, or of statements made in connection with such pleas or offers of such pleas, is inadmissible in any civil or criminal action, case or proceeding against the person making such plea or offer. The Senate amendment makes the rule inapplicable to a voluntary and reliable statement made in court on the record where the statement is offered in a subsequent prosecution of the declarant for perjury or false statement.

The issues raised by Rule 410 are also raised by proposed Rule 11(e)(6) of the Federal Rules of Criminal Procedure presently pending before Congress. This proposed rule, which deals with the admissibility of pleas of guilty or nolo contendere, offers to make such pleas, and statements made in connection with such pleas, was promulgated by the Supreme Court on April 22, 1974, and in the absence of congressional action will become effective on August 1, 1975. The conferees intend to make no change in the presently-existing case law until that date, leaving the courts free to develop rules in this area on a case-by-case basis.

The Conferees further determined that the issues presented by the use of guilty and nolo contendere pleas, offers of such pleas, and statements made in connection with such pleas or offers, can be explored in greater detail during Congressional consideration of Rule 11(e)(6) of the Federal Rules of Criminal Procedure. The Conferees believe, therefore, that it is best to defer its effective date until August 1, 1975. The Conferees intend that Rule 410 would be superseded by any subsequent Federal Rule of Criminal Procedure or Act of Congress with which it is inconsistent, if the Federal Rule of Criminal Procedure or Act of Congress takes effect or becomes law after the date of the enactment of the act establishing the rules of evidence.

The conference adopts the Senate amendment with an amendment that expresses the above intentions.

2. See Harris v. New York, 401 U.S. 222 (1971).

Rule 410 as amended in 1975

Editorial Note

In 1975 the Congress amended Rule 11(e)(6) of the Federal Rules of Criminal Procedure, P.L. 94–64, July 31, 1975, 89 Stat. 371, and then amended Evidence Rule 410 to conform to it. Amended Rule 410 read:

> Except as otherwise provided in this rule, evidence of a plea of guilty, later withdrawn, or a plea of nolo contendere, or of an offer to plead guilty or nolo contendere to the crime charged or any other crime, or of statements made in connection with, and relevant to, any of the foregoing pleas or offers, is not admissible in any civil or criminal proceeding against the person who made the plea or offer. However, evidence of a statement made in connection with, and relevant to, a plea of guilty, later withdrawn, a plea of nolo contendere, or an offer to plead guilty or nolo contendere to the crime charged or any other crime, is admissible in a criminal proceeding for perjury or false statement if the statement was made by the defendant under oath, on the record, and in the presence of counsel. P.L. 94–149, Dec. 12, 1975, 89 Stat. 805.

Report of House Committee on the Judiciary

House Comm. on Judiciary, Fed. Rules of Criminal Procedure, H.R. Rep. No. 247, 94th Cong., 1st Sess. (1975); 1975 U.S.Code Cong. & Ad.News 674, 679

The Committee added an exception to subdivision (e)(6). That subdivision provides:[1]

> Evidence of a plea of guilty, later withdrawn, or a plea of nolo contendere, or of an offer to plead guilty or nolo contendere to the crime charged or any other crime, or of statements made in connection with any of the foregoing pleas or offers, is not admissible in any civil or criminal proceeding against the person who made the plea or offer.

The Committee's exception permits the use of such evidence in a perjury or false statement prosecution where the plea, offer, or related statement was made by the defendant on the record, under oath and in the presence of counsel. The Committee recognizes that even this limited exception may discourage defendants from being completely candid and open during plea negotiations and may even result in discouraging the reaching of plea agreements. However, the Committee believes that, on balance, it is more important to protect the integrity of the judicial process from willful deceit and untruthfulness. [The Committee does not intend its language to be construed as mandating or encouraging the swearing-in of the defendant during proceedings in connection with the disclosure and acceptance or rejection of a plea agreement.] The Committee recast the language of Rule 11(c), which deals with the advice given to a defendant before the court can accept his plea of guilty or nolo contendere. The Committee acted in part because it believed that the warnings given to the defendant ought to include those that Boykin v. Alabama, 395 U.S. 238 (1969), said were constitutionally required. In addition, and as a result of its change in subdivision (e)(6), the Committee thought it only fair that the

1. As prescribed by the Supreme Court and transmitted to the Congress.

defendant be warned that his plea of guilty (later withdrawn) or nolo contendere, or his offer of either plea, or his statements made in connection with such pleas or offers, could later be used against him in a perjury trial if made under oath, on the record, and in the presence of counsel.

Conference Report

H.R., Fed. Rules of Criminal Procedure, Conf. Rep. No. 414, 94th Cong., 1st Sess., (1975); 1976 U.S.Code Cong. & Ad.News 713, 714

Rule 11(e)(6) deals with the use of statements made in connection with plea agreements. The House version permits a limited use of pleas of guilty, later withdrawn, or nolo contendere, offers of such pleas, and statements made in connection with such pleas or offers. Such evidence can be used in a perjury or false statement prosecution if the plea, offer, or related statement was made under oath, on the record, and in the presence of counsel. The Senate version permits evidence of voluntary and reliable statements made in court on the record to be used for the purpose of impeaching the credibility of the declarant or in a perjury or false statement prosecution.

The Conference adopts the House version with changes. The Conference agrees that neither a plea nor the offer of a plea ought to be admissible for any purpose. The Conference-adopted provision, therefore, like the Senate provision, permits only the use of statements made in connection with a plea of guilty, later withdrawn, or a plea of nolo contendere, or in connection with an offer of a guilty or nolo contendere plea.

Rule 410 as revised in 1980

Editorial Note

The Supreme Court adopted and on April 30, 1979, transmitted to the Congress a revision of Rule 11(e)(6) of the Federal Rules of Criminal Procedure, which was to operate also as a revision of Evidence Rule 410. The Congress suspended the effective date of the revision to December 1, 1980, absent congressional action otherwise. P.L. 96–42, July 31, 1979, 93 Stat. 326. Congress having taken no action, the rule as revised became effective on December 1, 1980, and is the present Rule 410, printed at the beginning of these comments.

Advisory Committee's Note

77 F.R.D. 507, 533

The major objective of the amendment to rule 11(e)(6) transmitted by the Supreme Court on April 30, 1979 is to describe more precisely, consistent with the original purpose of the provision, what evidence relating to pleas or plea discussions is inadmissible. The present language is susceptible to interpretation which would make it applicable to a wide variety of statements made under various circumstances other than within the context of those plea discussions authorized by rule 11(e) and intended to be protected by subdivision (e)(6) of the rule. See United States v. Herman, 544 F.2d 791 (5th Cir.1977), discussed herein.

Fed.R.Ev. 410, as originally adopted by Pub.L. 93–595, provided in part that "evidence of a plea of guilty, later withdrawn, or a plea of nolo contendere, or of an offer to plead guilty or nolo contendere to the crime charged or any other crime, or of statements made in connection with any of the foregoing pleas or offers, is not admissible in any civil or criminal action, case, or proceeding against the person who made the plea or offer." (This rule was adopted with the proviso that it "shall be superseded by any amendment to the Federal Rules of Criminal Procedure which is inconsistent with this rule.") As the Advisory Committee Note explained: "Exclusion of offers to plead guilty or nolo has as its purpose the promotion of disposition of criminal cases by compromise." The amendment of Fed.R.Crim.P. 11, transmitted to Congress by the Supreme Court in April 1974, contained a subdivision (e)(6) essentially identical to the rule 410 language quoted above, as a part of a substantial revision of rule 11. The most significant feature of this revision was the express recognition given to the fact that the "attorney for the government and the attorney for the defendant or the defendant when acting pro se may engage in discussions with a view toward reaching" a plea agreement. Subdivision (e)(6) was intended to encourage such discussions. As noted in H.R.Rep. No. 94–247, 94th Cong., 1st Sess. 7 (1975), the purpose of subdivision (e)(6) is to not "discourage defendants from being completely candid and open during plea negotiations." Similarly, H.R.Rep. No. 94–414, 94th Cong., 1st Sess. 10 (1975), states that "Rule 11(e)(6) deals with the use of statements made in connection with plea agreements." (Rule 11(e)(6) was thereafter enacted, with the addition of the proviso allowing use of statements in a prosecution for perjury, and with the qualification that the inadmissible statements must also be "relevant to" the inadmissible pleas or offers. Pub.L. 94–64; Fed.R.Ev. 410 was then amended to conform. Pub.L. 94–149.)

While this history shows that the purpose of Fed.R.Ev. 410 and Fed.R.Crim. P. 11(e)(6) is to permit the unrestrained candor which produces effective plea discussions between the "attorney for the government and the attorney for the defendant or the defendant when acting pro se," given visibility and sanction in rule 11(e), a literal reading of the language of these two rules could reasonably lead to the conclusion that a broader rule of inadmissibility obtains. That is, because "statements" are generally inadmissible if "made in connection with, and relevant to" an "offer to plead guilty," it might be thought that an otherwise voluntary admission to law enforcement officials is rendered inadmissible merely because it was made in the hope of obtaining leniency by a plea. Some decisions interpreting rule 11(e)(6) point in this direction. See United States v. Herman, 544 F.2d 791 (5th Cir.1977) (defendant in custody of two postal inspectors during continuance of removal hearing instigated conversation with them and at some point said he would plead guilty to armed robbery if the murder charge was dropped; one inspector stated they were not "in position" to make any deals in this regard; held, defendant's statement inadmissible under rule 11(e)(6) because the defendant "made the statements during the course of a conversation in which he sought concessions from the government in return for a guilty plea"); United States v. Brooks, 536 F.2d 1137 (6th Cir.1976) (defendant telephoned postal inspector and offered to plead guilty if he got 2-year maximum; statement inadmissible).

The amendment makes inadmissible statements made "in the course of any proceedings under this rule regarding" either a plea of guilty later withdrawn or a plea of nolo contendere, and also statements "made in the course of plea discussions with an attorney for the government which do not result in a plea of guilty or which result in a plea of guilty later withdrawn." It is not limited to statements by the defendant himself, and thus would cover statements by defense counsel regarding defendant's incriminating admissions to him. It thus fully protects the plea discussion process authorized by rule 11 without attempting to deal with confrontations between suspects and law enforcement agents, which involve problems of quite different dimensions. See, e.g., ALI Model Code of Pre-Arraignment Procedure, art. 140 and § 150.2(8) (Proposed Official Draft, 1975) (latter section requires exclusion if "a law enforcement officer induces any person to make a statement by promising leniency"). This change, it must be emphasized, does not compel the conclusion that statements made to law enforcement agents, especially when the agents purport to have authority to bargain, are inevitably admissible. Rather, the point is that such cases are not covered by the per se rule of 11(e)(6) and thus must be resolved by that body of law dealing with police interrogations.

If there has been a plea of guilty later withdrawn or a plea of nolo contendere, subdivision (e)(6)(C) makes inadmissible statements made "in the course of any proceedings under this rule" regarding such pleas. This includes, for example, admissions by the defendant when he makes his plea in court pursuant to rule 11 and also admissions made to provide the factual basis pursuant to subdivision (f). However, subdivision (e)(6)(C) is not limited to statements made in court. If the court were to defer its decision on a plea agreement pending examination of the presentence report, as authorized by subdivision (e)(2), statements made to the probation officer in connection with the preparation of that report would come within this provision.

This amendment is fully consistent with all recent and major law reform efforts on this subject. ALI Model Code of Pre-Arraignment Procedure § 350.7 (Proposed Official Draft, 1975), and ABA Standards Relating to Pleas of Guilty § 3.4 (Approved Draft, 1968) both provide:

> Unless the defendant subsequently enters a plea of guilty or nolo contendere which is not withdrawn, the fact that the defendant or his counsel and the prosecuting attorney engaged in plea discussions or made a plea agreement should not be received in evidence against or in favor of the defendant in any criminal or civil action or administrative proceedings.

The Commentary to the latter states:

> The above standard is limited to discussions and agreements with the prosecuting attorney. Sometimes defendants will indicate to the police their willingness to bargain, and in such instances these statements are sometimes admitted in court against the defendant. State v. Christian, 245 S.W.2d 895 (Mo.1952). If the police initiate this kind of discussion, this may have some bearing on the admissibility of the defendant's statement. However, the policy considerations relevant to this issue are better dealt with in the context of standards governing in-custody interrogation by the police.

Similarly, Unif.R.Crim.P. 441(d) (Approved Draft, 1974), provides that except under limited circumstances "no discussion between the parties or statement by the defendant or his lawyer under this Rule," i.e., the rule providing "the parties may meet to discuss the possibility of pretrial diversion . . . or of a plea agreement," are admissible. The amendment is likewise consistent with the typical state provision on this subject; see, e.g., Ill.S.Ct. Rule 402(f).

The language of the amendment identifies with more precision than the present language the necessary relationship between the statements and the plea or discussion. See the dispute between the majority and concurring opinions in United States v. Herman, 544 F.2d 791 (5th Cir.1977), concerning the meanings and effect of the phrases "connection to" and "relevant to" in the present rule. Moreover, by relating the statements to "plea discussions" rather than "an offer to plead," the amendment ensures "that even an attempt to open plea bargaining [is] covered under the same rule of inadmissibility." United States v. Brooks, 536 F.2d 1137 (6th Cir.1976).

The last sentence of Rule 11(e)(6) is amended to provide a second exception to the general rule of nonadmissibility of the described statements. Under the amendment, such a statement is also admissible "in any proceeding wherein another statement made in the course of the same plea or plea discussions has been introduced and the statement ought in fairness be considered contemporaneously with it." This change is necessary so that, when evidence of statements made in the course of or as a consequence of a certain plea or plea discussions are introduced under circumstances not prohibited by this rule (e.g., not "against" the person who made the plea), other statements relating to the same plea or plea discussions may also be admitted when relevant to the matter at issue. For example, if a defendant upon a motion to dismiss a prosecution on some ground were able to admit certain statements made in aborted plea discussions in his favor, then other relevant statements made in the same plea discussions should be admissible against the defendant in the interest of determining the truth of the matter at issue. The language of the amendment follows closely that in Fed.R.Evid. 106, as the considerations involved are very similar.

The phrase "in any civil or criminal proceeding" has been moved from its present position, following the word "against" for purposes of clarity. An ambiguity presently exists because the word "against" may be read as referring either to the kind of proceeding in which the evidence is offered or the purpose for which it is offered. The change makes it clear that the latter construction is correct. No change is intended with respect to provisions making evidence rules inapplicable in certain situations. See, e.g., Fed.R.Evid. 104(a) and 1101(d).

Unlike ABA Standards Relating to Pleas of Guilty § 3.4 (Approved Draft, 1968), and ALI Model Code of Pre-Arraignment Procedure § 350.7 (Proposed Official Draft, 1975), rule 11(e)(6) does not also provide that the described evidence is inadmissible "in favor of" the defendant. This is not intended to suggest, however, that such evidence will inevitably be admissible in the defendant's favor. Specifically, no disapproval is intended of such decisions as United States v. Verdoorn, 528 F.2d 103 (8th Cir.1976), holding that the trial judge properly refused to permit the defendants to put into evidence at their trial the fact the prosecution had attempted to plea bargain with them, as "meaningful dialogue between the parties would, as a practical matter, be impossible if either party had to assume the risk that plea offers would be admissible in evidence."

Rule 411. Liability Insurance

Evidence that a person was or was not insured against liability is not admissible upon the issue whether the person acted negligently or otherwise wrongfully. This rule does not require the exclusion of evidence of insurance against liability when offered for another purpose, such as proof of agency, ownership, or control, or bias or prejudice of a witness.

(As amended Mar. 2, 1987, eff. Oct. 1, 1987.)

Section references, McCormick 4th ed.

§ 201

Note by Federal Judicial Center

The rule enacted by the Congress is the rule prescribed by the Supreme Court without change.

Advisory Committee's Note

56 F.R.D. 183, 230

The courts have with substantial unanimity rejected evidence of liability insurance for the purpose of proving fault, and absence of liability insurance as proof of lack of fault. At best the inference of fault from the fact of insurance coverage is a tenuous one, as is its converse. More important, no doubt, has been the feeling that knowledge of the presence or absence of liability insurance would induce juries to decide cases on improper grounds. McCormick § 168; Annot., 4 A.L.R.2d 761. The rule is drafted in broad terms so as to include contributory negligence or other fault of a plaintiff as well as fault of a defendant.

The second sentence points out the limits of the rule, using well established illustrations. Id.

For similar rules see Uniform Rule 54; California Evidence Code § 1155; Kansas Code of Civil Procedure § 60–454; New Jersey Evidence Rule 54.

1987 Amendment. The amendment is technical. No substantive change is intended.

Rule 412. Rape Cases; Relevance of Victim's Past Behavior

(a) Notwithstanding any other provision of law, in a criminal case in which a person is accused of rape or of assault with intent to commit rape, reputation or opinion evidence of the past sexual behavior of an alleged victim of such rape or assault is not admissible.

(b) Notwithstanding any other provision of law, in a criminal case in which a person is accused of rape or of assault with intent to commit rape, evidence of a victim's past sexual behavior other than reputation or opinion evidence is also not admissible, unless such evidence other than reputation or opinion evidence is—

(1) admitted in accordance with subdivisions (c)(1) and (c)(2) and is constitutionally required to be admitted; or

(2) admitted in accordance with subdivision (c) and is evidence of—

(A) past sexual behavior with persons other than the accused, offered by the accused upon the issue of whether the accused was or was not, with respect to the alleged victim, the source of semen or injury; or

(B) past sexual behavior with the accused and is offered by the accused upon the issue of whether the alleged victim consented to the sexual behavior with respect to which rape or assault is alleged.

(c)(1) If the person accused of committing rape or assault with intent to commit rape intends to offer under subdivision (b) evidence of specific instances of the alleged victim's past sexual behavior, the accused shall make a written motion to offer such evidence not later than fifteen days before the date on which the trial in which such evidence is to be offered is scheduled to begin, except that the court may allow the motion to be made at a later date, including during trial, if the court determines either that the evidence is newly discovered and could not have been obtained earlier through the exercise of due diligence or that the issue to which such evidence relates has newly arisen in the case. Any motion made under this paragraph shall be served on all other parties and on the alleged victim.

(2) The motion described in paragraph (1) shall be accompanied by a written offer of proof. If the court determines that the offer of proof contains evidence described in subdivision (b), the court shall order a hearing in chambers to determine if such evidence is admissible. At such hearing the parties may call witnesses, including the alleged victim, and offer relevant evidence. Notwithstanding subdivision (b) of rule 104, if the relevancy of the evidence which the accused seeks to offer in the trial depends upon the fulfillment of a condition of fact, the court, at the hearing in chambers or at a subsequent hearing in chambers scheduled for such purpose, shall accept evidence on the issue of whether such condition of fact is fulfilled and shall determine such issue.

(3) If the court determines on the basis of the hearing described in paragraph (2) that the evidence which the accused seeks to offer is relevant and that the probative value of such evidence outweighs the danger of unfair prejudice, such evidence shall be admissible in the trial to the extent an order made by the court specifies evidence which may be offered and areas with respect to which the alleged victim may be examined or cross-examined.

(d) For purposes of this rule, the term "past sexual behavior" means sexual behavior other than the sexual behavior with respect to which rape or assault with intent to commit rape is alleged.

(Added P.L. 95–540, § 2(a), Oct. 28, 1978, 92 Stat. 2046; amended Nov. 18, 1988; Pub.L. 100–690, Title VII, § 7046(a), 102 Stat. 4400.)

Section references, McCormick 4th ed.

§ 43, § 44, § 193

House of Representatives

120 Cong.Rec. 34912 (1978)

Mr. Mann. . . .

Mr. Speaker, for many years in this country, evidentiary rules have permitted the introduction of evidence about a rape victim's prior sexual conduct. Defense lawyers were permitted great latitude in bringing out intimate details about a rape victim's life. Such evidence quite often serves no real purpose and only results in embarrassment to the rape victim and unwarranted public intrusion into her private life.

The evidentiary rules that permit such inquiry have in recent years come under question; and the States have taken the lead to change and modernize their evidentiary rules about evidence of a rape victim's prior sexual behavior. The bill before us similarly seeks to modernize the Federal evidentiary rules.

The present Federal Rules of Evidence reflect the traditional approach. If a defendant in a rape case raises the defense of consent, that defendant may then offer evidence about the victim's prior sexual behavior. Such evidence may be in the form of opinion evidence, evidence of reputation, or evidence of specific instances of behavior. Rule 404(a)(2) of the Federal Rules of Evidence permits the introduction of evidence of a "pertinent character trait." The advisory committee note to that rule cites, as an example of what the rule covers, the character of a rape victim when the issue is consent. Rule 405 of the Federal Rules of Evidence permits the use of opinion or reputation evidence or the use of evidence of specific behavior to show a character trait.

Thus, Federal evidentiary rules permit a wide ranging inquiry into the private conduct of a rape victim, even though that conduct may have at best a tenuous connection to the offense for which the defendant is being tried.

H.R. 4727 amends the Federal Rules of Evidence to add a new rule, applicable only in criminal cases, to spell out when, and under what conditions, evidence of a rape victim's prior sexual behavior can be admitted. The new rule provides that reputation or opinion evidence about a rape victim's prior sexual behavior is not admissible. The new rule also provides that a court cannot admit evidence of specific instances of a rape victim's prior sexual conduct except in three circumstances.

The first circumstance is where the Constitution requires that the evidence be admitted. This exception is intended to cover those infrequent instances where, because of an unusual chain of circumstances, the general rule of inadmissibility, if followed, would result in denying the defendant a constitutional right.

The second circumstance in which the defendant can offer evidence of specific instances of a rape victim's prior sexual behavior is where the defendant raises the issue of consent and the evidence is of sexual behavior with the defendant. To admit such evidence, however, the court must find that the evidence is relevant and that its probative value outweighs the danger of unfair prejudice.

The third circumstance in which a court can admit evidence of specific instances of a rape victim's prior sexual behavior is where the evidence is of behavior with someone other than the defendant and is offered by the defendant on the issue of whether or not he was the source of semen or injury. Again, such evidence will be admitted only if the court finds that the evidence is relevant and that its probative value outweighs the danger of unfair prejudice.

The new rule further provides that before evidence is admitted under any of these exceptions, there must be an in camera hearing—that is, a proceeding that takes place in the judge's chambers out of the presence of the jury and the general public. At this hearing, the defendant will present the evidence he intends to offer and be able to argue why it should be admitted. The prosecution, of course, will be able to argue against that evidence being admitted.

The purpose of the in camera hearing is twofold. It gives the defendant an opportunity to demonstrate to the court why certain evidence is admissible and ought to be presented to the jury. At the same time, it protects the privacy of the rape victim in those instances when the court finds that evidence is inadmissible. Of course, if the court finds the evidence to be admissible, the evidence will be presented to the jury in open court.

The effect of this legislation, therefore, is to preclude the routine use of evidence of specific instances of a rape victim's prior sexual behavior. Such evidence will be admitted only in clearly and narrowly defined circumstances and only after an in camera hearing. In determining the admissibility of such evidence, the court will consider all of the facts and circumstances surrounding the evidence, such as the amount of time that lapsed between the alleged prior act and the rape charged in the prosecution. The greater the lapse of time, of course, the less likely it is that such evidence will be admitted.

Mr. Speaker, the principal purpose of this legislation is to protect rape victims from the degrading and embarrassing disclosure of intimate details about their private lives. It does so by narrowly circumscribing when such evidence may be admitted. It does not do so, however, by sacrificing any constitutional right possessed by the defendant. The bill before us fairly balances the interests involved—the rape victim's interest in protecting her private life from unwarranted public exposure; the defendant's interest in being able adequately to present a defense by offering relevant and probative evidence; and society's interest in a fair trial, one where unduly prejudicial evidence is not permitted to becloud the issues before the jury.

(Proceedings of the Senate leading to passage of the bill are reported in 124 Cong.Rec. 36255 (1978).)

ARTICLE V. PRIVILEGES

Rule 501. General Rule

Except as otherwise required by the Constitution of the United States or provided by Act of Congress or in rules prescribed by the Supreme Court pursuant to statutory authority, the privilege of a witness, person, government, State, or political subdivision thereof shall be governed by the principles of the common law as they may be interpreted by the courts of the United States in the light of reason and experience. However, in civil actions and proceedings, with respect to an element of a claim or defense as to which State law supplies the rule of decision, the privilege of a witness, person, government, State, or political subdivision thereof shall be determined in accordance with State law.

Section references, McCormick 4th ed.

§ 9, § 53, § 66, § 75, § 76, § 78

Note by Federal Judicial Center

The rules enacted by the Congress substituted the single Rule 501 in place of the 13 rules dealing with privilege prescribed by the Supreme Court as Article V. . . . The reasons given in support of the congressional action are stated in the Report of the House Committee on the Judiciary, the Report of the Senate Committee on the Judiciary, and Conference Report, set forth below.

Report of House Committee on the Judiciary

House Comm. of Judiciary, Fed. Rules of Evidence, H.R.Rep. No. 650, 93d Cong., 1st Sess., p. 8 (1973); 1974 U.S.Code Cong. & Ad.News 7075, 7082

Article V as submitted to Congress contained thirteen Rules. Nine of those Rules defined specific non-constitutional privileges which the federal courts must recognize (i.e. required reports, lawyer-client, psychotherapist-patient, husband-wife, communications to clergymen, political vote, trade secrets, secrets of state and other official information, and identity of informer). Another Rule provided that only those privileges set forth in Article V or in some other Act of Congress could be recognized by the federal courts. The three remaining Rules addressed collateral problems as to waiver of privilege by voluntary disclosure, privileged matter disclosed under compulsion or without opportunity to claim privilege, comment upon or inference from a claim of privilege, and jury instruction with regard thereto.

The Committee amended Article V to eliminate all of the Court's specific Rules on privileges. Instead, the Committee, through a single Rule, 501, left the law of privileges in its present state and further provided that privileges shall continue to be developed by the courts of the United States under a uniform standard applicable both in civil and criminal cases. That standard, derived from Rule 26 of the Federal Rules of Criminal Procedure, mandates the application of the principles of the common law as interpreted by the courts of the United States in the light of reason and experience. The words "person, government, State, or political subdivision thereof" were added by the Committee to the lone term "witnesses" used in Rule 26 to make clear that, as under present law, not only witnesses may have privileges. The Committee also included in its amendment a proviso modeled after Rule 302 and similar to language added by the Committee to Rule 601 relating to the competency of witnesses. The proviso is designed to require the application of State privilege law in civil actions and proceedings governed by Erie R. Co. v. Tompkins, 304 U.S. 64 (1938), a result in accord with current federal court decisions. See Republic Gear Co. v. Borg-Warner Corp., 381 F.2d 551, 555–556 n. 2 (2nd Cir. 1967). The Committee deemed the proviso to be necessary in the light of the Advisory Committee's view (see its note to Court Rule 501) that this result is not mandated under *Erie*.

The rationale underlying the proviso is that federal law should not supersede that of the States in substantive areas such as privilege absent a compelling reason. The Committee believes that in civil cases in the federal courts where an element of a claim or defense is not grounded upon a federal question, there is no federal interest strong enough to justify departure from State policy. In addition, the Committee considered that the Court's proposed Article V would have promoted forum shopping in some civil actions, depending upon differences in the privilege law applied as among the State and federal courts. The Committee's proviso, on the other hand, under which the federal courts are bound to apply the State's privilege law in actions founded upon a State-created right or defense, removes the incentive to "shop".

Report of Senate Committee on the Judiciary

Senate Comm. on Judiciary, Fed. Rules of Evidence, S.Rep. No. 1277, 93d Cong., 2d Sess., p. 11 (1974); 1974 U.S.Code Cong. & Ad.News 7051, 7058

Article V as submitted to Congress contained 13 rules. Nine of those rules defined specific nonconstitutional privileges which the Federal courts must recognize (i.e., required reports, lawyer-client, psychotherapist-patient, husband-wife, communications to clergymen, political vote, trade secrets, secrets of state and other official information, and identity of informer). Many of these rules contained controversial modifications or restrictions upon common law privileges. As noted supra, the House amended article V to eliminate all of the Court's specific rules on privileges. Through a single rule, 501, the House provided that privileges shall be governed by the principles of the common law as interpreted by the courts of the United States in the light of reason and experience (a standard derived from rule 26 of the Federal Rules of Criminal Procedure) except in the case of an element of a civil claim or defense as to which State law supplies the rule of decision in which event state privilege law was to govern.

The committee agrees with the main thrust of the House amendment: that a federally developed common law based on modern reason and experience shall apply except where the State nature of the issues renders deference to State privilege law the wiser course, as in the usual diversity case. The committee understands that thrust of the House amendment to require that State privilege law be applied in "diversity" cases (actions on questions of State law between citizens of different States arising under 28 U.S.C. § 1332). The language of the House amendment, however, goes beyond this in some respects, and falls short of it in others: State privilege law applies even in nondiversity, Federal question civil cases, where an issue governed by State substantive law is the object of the evidence (such issues do sometimes arise in such cases); and, in all instances where State privilege law is to be applied, e.g., on proof of a State issue in a diversity case, a close reading reveals that State privilege law is not to be applied unless the matter to be proved is an element of that state claim or defense, as distinguished from a step along the way in the proof of it.

The committee is concerned that the language used in the House amendment could be difficult to apply. It provides that "in civil actions . . . with respect to an element of a claim or defense as to which State law supplies the rule of decision," State law on privilege applies. The question of what is an element of a claim or defense is likely to engender considerable litigation. If the matter in question constitutes an element of a claim, State law supplies the privilege rule; whereas if it is a mere item of proof with respect to a claim, then, even though State law might supply the rule of decision, Federal law on the privilege would apply. Further, disputes will arise as to how the rule should be applied in an antitrust action or in a tax case where the Federal statute is silent as to a particular aspect of the substantive law in question, but Federal cases had incorporated State law by reference to State law.[1] Is a claim (or defense) based on such a reference a claim or defense as to which federal or State law supplies the rule of decision?

Another problem not entirely avoidable is the complexity or difficulty the rule introduces into the trial of a Federal case containing a combination of Federal and State claims and defenses, e.g. an action involving Federal antitrust and State unfair competition claims. Two different bodies of privilege law would need to be consulted. It may even develop that the same witness-testimony might be relevant on both counts and privileged as to one but not the other.[2]

The formulation adopted by the House is pregnant with litigious mischief. The committee has, therefore, adopted what we believe will be a clearer and more practical guideline for determining when courts should respect State rules of privilege. Basically, it provides that in criminal and Federal question civil cases, federally evolved rules on privilege should apply since it is Federal policy which is being enforced.[3] Conversely, in diversity cases where the litigation in question turns on a substantive question of State law, and is brought in the Federal courts because the parties reside in different States, the committee believes it is clear that State rules of privilege should apply unless the proof is directed at a claim or defense for which Federal law supplies the rule of decision (a situation which would not commonly arise.)[4] It is intended that the

1. For a discussion of reference to State substantive law, see note on Federal Incorporation by Reference of State Law, Hart & Wechsler, The Federal Courts and the Federal System, pp. 491–94 (2d ed. 1973).

2. The problems with the House formulation are discussed in Rothstein, The Proposed Amendments to the Federal Rules of Evidence, 62 Georgetown University Law Journal 125 (1973) at notes 25, 26 and 70–74 and accompanying text.

3. It is also intended that the Federal law of privileges should be applied with respect to pendant State law claims when they arise in a Federal question case.

4. While such a situation might require use of two bodies of privilege law, federal and state, in the same case, nevertheless the occasions on which this would be required are considerably reduced as compared with the House version, and confined to situations where the Federal and State interests are such as to justify application of neither privilege law to the case as a whole. If the rule proposed here results in two conflicting

State rules of privilege should apply equally in original diversity actions and diversity actions removed under 28 U.S.C. § 1441(b).

Two other comments on the privilege rule should be made. The committee has received a considerable volume of correspondence from psychiatric organizations and psychiatrists concerning the deletion of rule 504 of the rule submitted by the Supreme Court. It should be clearly understood that, in approving this general rule as to privileges, the action of Congress should not be understood as disapproving any recognition of a psychiatrist-patient, or husband-wife, or any other of the enumerated privileges contained in the Supreme Court rules. Rather, our action should be understood as reflecting the view that the recognition of a privilege based on a confidential relationship and other privileges should be determined on a case-by-case basis.

Further, we would understand that the prohibition against spouses testifying against each other is considered a rule of privilege and covered by this rule and not by rule 601 of the competency of witnesses.

Conference Report

H.R., Fed. Rules of Evidence, Conf.Rep. No. 1597, 93d Cong., 2d Sess., p. 7 (1974); 1974 U.S.Code Cong. & Ad.News 7098, 7100

Rule 501 deals with the privilege of a witness not to testify. Both the House and Senate bills provide that federal privilege law applies in criminal cases. In civil actions and proceedings, the House bill provides that state privilege law applies "to an element of a claim or defense as to which State law supplies the rule of decision." The Senate bill provides that "in civil actions and proceedings arising under 28 U.S.C. § 1332 or 28 U.S.C. § 1335, or between citizens of different States and removed under 28 U.S.C. § 1441(b) the privilege of a witness, person, government, State or political subdivision thereof is determined in accordance with State law, unless with respect to the particular claim or defense, Federal law supplies the rule of decision."

The wording of the House and Senate bills differs in the treatment of civil actions and proceedings. The rule in the House bill applies to evidence that relates to "an element of a claim or defense." If an item of proof tends to support or defeat a claim or defense, or an element of a claim or defense, and if state law supplies the rule of decision for that claim or defense, then state privilege law applies to that item of proof.

Under the provision in the House bill, therefore, state privilege law will usually apply in diversity cases. There may be diversity cases, however, where a claim or defense is based upon federal law. In such instances, federal privilege law will apply to evidence relevant to the federal claim or defense. See Sola Electric Co. v. Jefferson Electric Co., 317 U.S. 173 (1942).

In nondiversity jurisdiction civil cases, federal privilege law will generally apply. In those situations where a federal court adopts or incorporates state

bodies of privilege law applying to the same piece of evidence in the same case, it is contemplated that the rule favoring reception of the evidence should be applied. This policy is based on the present rule 43(a) of the Federal Rules of Civil Procedure which provides: In any case, the statute or rule which favors the reception of the evidence governs and the evidence shall be presented according to the most convenient method prescribed in any of the statutes or rules to which reference is herein made.

law to fill interstices or gaps in federal statutory phrases, the court generally will apply federal privilege law. As Justice Jackson has said:

> A federal court sitting in a non-diversity case such as this does not sit as a local tribunal. In some cases it may see fit for special reasons to give the law of a particular state highly persuasive or even controlling effect, but in the last analysis its decision turns upon the law of the United States, not that of any state.

D'Oench, Duhme & Co. v. Federal Deposit Insurance Corp., 315 U.S. 447, 471 (1942) (Jackson, J., concurring). When a federal court chooses to absorb state law, it is applying the state law as a matter of federal common law. Thus, state law does not supply the rule of decision (even though the federal court may apply a rule derived from state decisions), and state privilege law would not apply. See C.A. Wright, Federal Courts 251–252 (2d ed. 1970); Holmberg v. Armbrecht, 327 U.S. 392 (1946); DeSylva v. Ballentine, 351 U.S. 570, 581 (1956); 9 Wright & Miller, Federal Rules and Procedure § 2408.

In civil actions and proceedings, where the rule of decision as to a claim or defense or as to an element of a claim or defense is supplied by state law, the House provision requires that state privilege law apply.

The Conference adopts the House provision.

ARTICLE VI. WITNESSES

Rule 601. General Rule of Competency

Every person is competent to be a witness except as otherwise provided in these rules. However, in civil actions and proceedings, with respect to an element of a claim or defense as to which State law supplies the rule of decision, the competency of a witness shall be determined in accordance with State law.

Section references, McCormick 4th ed.

§ 9, § 44, § 53, § 62, § 63, § 65, § 66, § 68, § 70, § 71, § 253

Note by Federal Judicial Center

The first sentence of the rule enacted by the Congress is the entire rule prescribed by the Supreme Court, without change. The second sentence was added by congressional action.

Advisory Committee's Note

56 F.R.D. 183, 262

This general ground-clearing eliminates all grounds of incompetency not specifically recognized in the succeeding rules of this Article. Included among the grounds thus abolished are religious belief, conviction of crime, and connection with the litigation as a party or interested person or spouse of a party or interested person. With the exception of the so-called Dead Man's Acts, American jurisdictions generally have ceased to recognize these grounds.

The Dead Man's Acts are surviving traces of the common law disqualification of parties and interested persons. They exist in variety too great to convey conviction of their wisdom and effectiveness. These rules contain no provision of this kind. . . .

No mental or moral qualifications for testifying as a witness are specified. Standards of mental capacity have proved elusive in actual application. A leading commentator observes that few witnesses are disqualified on that ground. Weihofen, Testimonial Competence and Credibility, 34 Geo.Wash.L. Rev. 53 (1965). Discretion is regularly exercised in favor of allowing the testimony. A witness wholly without capacity is difficult to imagine. The question is one particularly suited to the jury as one of weight and credibility, subject to judicial authority to review the sufficiency of the evidence. 2 Wigmore §§ 501, 509. Standards of moral qualification in practice consist essentially of evaluating a person's truthfulness in terms of his own answers about it. Their principal utility is in affording an opportunity on voir dire examination to impress upon the witness his moral duty. This result may, however, be accomplished more directly, and without haggling in terms of legal standards, by the manner of administering the oath or affirmation under Rule 603.

Admissibility of religious belief as a ground of impeachment is treated in Rule 610. Conviction of crime as a ground of impeachment is the subject of Rule 609. Marital relationship is the basis for privilege under Rule 505. Interest in the outcome of litigation and mental capacity are, of course, highly relevant to credibility and require no special treatment to render them admissible along with other matters bearing upon the perception, memory, and narration of witnesses.

Report of House Committee on the Judiciary

House Comm. on Judiciary, Fed. Rules of Evidence, H.R.Rep. No. 650, 93d Cong., 1st Sess., p. 9 (1973); 1974 U.S.Code Cong. & Ad.News 7075, 7083

Rule 601 as submitted to the Congress provided that "Every person is competent to be a witness except as otherwise provided in these rules." One effect of the Rule as proposed would have been to abolish age, mental capacity, and other grounds recognized in some State jurisdictions as making a person incompetent as a witness. The greatest controversy centered around the Rule's rendering inapplicable in the federal courts the so-called Dead Man's Statutes which exist in some States. Acknowledging that there is substantial disagreement as to the merit of Dead Man's Statutes, the Committee nevertheless believed that where such statutes have been enacted they represent State policy which should not be overturned in the absence of a compelling federal interest. The Committee therefore amended the Rule to make competency in civil actions determinable in accordance with State law with respect to elements of claims or defenses as to which State law supplies the rule of decision. Cf. Courtland v. Walston & Co., Inc., 340 F.Supp. 1076, 1087–1092 (S.D.N.Y.1972).

Report of Senate Committee on the Judiciary

Senate Comm. on Judiciary, Fed. Rules of Evidence, S.Rep. No. 1277, 2d Sess., p. 13 (1974); 1974 U.S.Code Cong. & Ad.News 7051, 7059

The amendment to rule 601 parallels the treatment accorded rule 501 discussed immediately above.

Conference Report

H.R., Fed. Rules of Evidence, Conf.Rep. No. 1597, 93d Cong., 2d Sess., p. 8 (1974); 1975 U.S.Code Cong. & Ad.News 7098, 7101

Rule 601 deals with competency of witnesses. Both the House and Senate bills provide that federal competency law applies in criminal cases. In civil actions and proceedings, the House bill provides that state competency law applies "to an element of a claim or defense as to which State law supplies the rule of decision." The Senate bill provides that "in civil actions and proceedings arising under 28 U.S.C. § 1332 or 28 U.S.C. § 1335, or between citizens of different States and removed under 28 U.S.C. § 1441(b) the competency of a witness, person, government, State or political subdivision thereof is determined in accordance with State law, unless with respect to the particular claim or defense, Federal law supplies the rule of decision."

The wording of the House and Senate bills differs in the treatment of civil actions and proceedings. The rule in the House bill applies to evidence that relates to "an element of a claim or defense." If an item of proof tends to support or defeat a claim or defense, or an element of a claim or defense, and if state law supplies the rule of decision for that claim or defense, then state competency law applies to that item of proof.

For reasons similar to those underlying its action on Rule 501, the Conference adopts the House provision.

Rule 602. Lack of Personal Knowledge

A witness may not testify to a matter unless evidence is introduced sufficient to support a finding that the witness has personal knowledge of the matter. Evidence to prove personal knowledge may, but need not, consist of the witness' own testimony. This rule is subject to the provisions of rule 703, relating to opinion testimony by expert witnesses.

(As amended Mar. 2, 1987, eff. Oct. 1, 1987; Apr. 25, 1988, eff. Nov. 1, 1988.)

Section references, McCormick 4th ed.

§ 10, § 11, § 43, § 44, § 71

Note by Federal Judicial Center

The rule enacted by the Congress is the rule prescribed by the Supreme Court without change.

Advisory Committee's Note

56 F.R.D. 183, 263

". . . [T]he rule requiring that a witness who testifies to a fact which can be perceived by the senses must have had an opportunity to observe, and must have actually observed the fact" is a "most pervasive manifestation" of the common law insistence upon "the most reliable sources of information." McCormick § 10, p. 19. These foundation requirements may, of course, be furnished by the testimony of the witness himself; hence personal knowledge is not an absolute but may consist of what the witness thinks he knows from personal perception. 2 Wigmore § 650. It will be observed that the rule is in fact a specialized application of the provisions of Rule 104(b) on conditional relevancy.

This rule does not govern the situation of a witness who testifies to a hearsay statement as such, if he has personal knowledge of the making of the statement. Rules 801 and 805 would be applicable. This rule would, however, prevent him from testifying to the subject matter of the hearsay statement, as he has no personal knowledge of it.

The reference to Rule 703 is designed to avoid any question of conflict between the present rule and the provisions of that rule allowing an expert to express opinions based on facts of which he does not have personal knowledge.

1987 Amendment. The amendments are technical. No substantive change is intended.

1988 Amendment. The amendment is technical. No substantive change is intended.

Rule 603. Oath or Affirmation

Before testifying, every witness shall be required to declare that the witness will testify truthfully, by oath or affirmation administered in a form calculated to awaken the witness' conscience and impress the witness' mind with the duty to do so.

(As amended Mar. 2, 1987, eff. Oct. 1, 1987.)

Section references, McCormick 4th ed.

§ 44, § 46, § 63, § 71, § 245

Note by Federal Judicial Center

The rule enacted by the Congress is the rule prescribed by the Supreme Court without change.

Advisory Committee's Note

56 F.R.D. 183, 263

The rule is designed to afford the flexibility required in dealing with religious adults, atheists, conscientious objectors, mental defectives, and children. Affirmation is simply a solemn undertaking to tell the truth; no special verbal formula is required. As is true generally, affirmation is recognized by federal law. "Oath" includes affirmation, 1 U.S.C. § 1; judges and clerks may administer oaths and affirmations, 28 U.S.C. §§ 459, 953; and affirmations are acceptable in lieu of oaths under Rule 43(d) of the Federal Rules of Civil Procedure. Perjury by a witness is a crime, 18 U.S.C. § 1621.

1987 Amendment. The amendments are technical. No substantive change is intended.

Rule 604. Interpreters

An interpreter is subject to the provisions of these rules relating to qualification as an expert and the administration of an oath or affirmation to make a true translation.

(As amended Mar. 2, 1987, eff. Oct. 1, 1987.)

Section references, McCormick 4th ed.

None

Note by Federal Judicial Center

The rule enacted by the Congress is the rule prescribed by the Supreme Court without change.

Advisory Committee's Note

56 F.R.D. 183, 264

The rule implements Rule 43(f) of the Federal Rules of Civil Procedure and Rule 28(b) of the Federal Rules of Criminal Procedure, both of which contain provisions for the appointment and compensation of interpreters.

1987 Amendment. The amendment is technical. No substantive change is intended.

Rule 605. Competency of Judge as Witness

The judge presiding at the trial may not testify in that trial as a witness. No objection need be made in order to preserve the point.

Section references, McCormick 4th ed.

§ 62, § 68, § 70, § 71

Note by Federal Judicial Center

The rule enacted by the Congress is the rule prescribed by the Supreme Court without change.

Advisory Committee's Note

56 F.R.D. 183, 264

In view of the mandate of 28 U.S.C. § 455 that a judge disqualify himself in "any case in which he . . . is or has been a material witness," the likelihood that the presiding judge in a federal court might be called to testify in the trial over which he is presiding is slight. Nevertheless the possibility is not totally eliminated.

The solution here presented is a broad rule of incompetency, rather than such alternatives as incompetency only as to material matters, leaving the matter to the discretion of the judge, or recognizing no incompetency. The choice is the result of inability to evolve satisfactory answers to questions which arise when the judge abandons the bench for the witness stand. Who rules on objections? Who compels him to answer? Can he rule impartially on the weight and admissibility of his own testimony? Can he be impeached or cross-examined effectively? Can he, in a jury trial, avoid conferring his seal of approval on one side in the eyes of the jury? Can he, in a bench trial, avoid an involvement destructive of impartiality? The rule of general incompetency has substantial support. See Report of the Special Committee on the Propriety of Judges Appearing as Witnesses, 36 A.B.A.J. 630 (1950); cases collected in Annot. 157 A.L.R. 311; McCormick § 68, p. 147; Uniform Rule 42; California Evidence Code § 703; Kansas Code of Civil Procedure § 60–442; New Jersey Evidence Rule 42. Cf. 6 Wigmore § 1909, which advocates leaving the matter to the discretion of the judge, and statutes to that effect collected in Annot., 157 A.L.R. 311.

The rule provides an "automatic" objection. To require an actual objection would confront the opponent with a choice between not objecting, with the result of allowing the testimony, and objecting, with the probable result of excluding the testimony but at the price of continuing the trial before a judge likely to feel that his integrity had been attacked by the objector.

Rule 606. Competency of Juror as Witness

(a) At the trial. A member of the jury may not testify as a witness before that jury in the trial of the case in which the juror is sitting. If the juror is called so to testify, the opposing party shall be afforded an opportunity to object out of the presence of the jury.

(b) Inquiry into validity of verdict or indictment. Upon an inquiry into the validity of a verdict or indictment, a juror may not testify as to any matter or statement occurring during the course of the jury's deliberations or to the effect of anything upon that or any other juror's mind or emotions as influencing the juror to assent to or dissent from the verdict or indictment or concerning the juror's mental processes in connection therewith, except that a juror may testify on the question whether extraneous prejudicial information was improperly brought to the jury's attention or whether any outside influence was improperly brought to bear upon any juror. Nor may a juror's affidavit or evidence of any statement by the juror concerning a matter about which the juror would be precluded from testifying be received for these purposes.

(As amended P.L. 94–149, § 1(10), Dec. 12, 1975, 89 Stat. 805; Mar. 2, 1987, eff. Oct. 1, 1987.)

Section references, McCormick 4th ed.

Generally § 71

(a). § 62, § 68, § 70

(b). § 68

Note by Federal Judicial Center

The rule enacted by the Congress is the rule prescribed by the Supreme Court, amended only by the addition of the concluding phrase "for these purposes." The bill originally passed by the House did not contain in the first sentence the prohibition as to matters or statements during the deliberations or the clause beginning "except."

Advisory Committee's Note

56 F.R.D. 183, 265

Subdivision (a). The considerations which bear upon the permissibility of testimony by a juror in the trial in which he is sitting as juror bear an obvious similarity to those evoked when the judge is called as a witness. See Advisory

Committee's Note to Rule 605. The judge is not, however in this instance so involved as to call for departure from usual principles requiring objection to be made; hence the only provision on objection is that opportunity be afforded for its making out of the presence of the jury. Compare Rule 605.

Subdivision (b). Whether testimony, affidavits, or statements of jurors should be received for the purpose of invalidating or supporting a verdict or indictment, and if so, under what circumstances, has given rise to substantial differences of opinion. The familiar rubric that a juror may not impeach his own verdict, dating from Lord Mansfield's time, is a gross oversimplification. The values sought to be promoted by excluding the evidence include freedom of deliberation, stability and finality of verdicts, and protection of jurors against annoyance and embarrassment. McDonald v. Pless, 238 U.S. 264, 35 S.Ct. 785, 59 L.Ed. 1300 (1915). On the other hand, simply putting verdicts beyond effective reach can only promote irregularity and injustice. The rule offers an accommodation between these competing considerations.

The mental operations and emotional reactions of jurors in arriving at a given result would, if allowed as a subject of inquiry, place every verdict at the mercy of jurors and invite tampering and harassment. See Grenz v. Werre, 129 N.W.2d 681 (N.D.1964). The authorities are in virtually complete accord in excluding the evidence. Fryer, Note on Disqualification of Witnesses, Selected Writings on Evidence and Trial 345, 347 (Fryer ed. 1957); Maguire, Weinstein, et al., Cases on Evidence 887 (5th ed. 1965); 8 Wigmore § 2349 (McNaughton Rev.1961). As to matters other than mental operations and emotional reactions of jurors, substantial authority refuses to allow a juror to disclose irregularities which occur in the jury room, but allows his testimony as to irregularities occurring outside and allows outsiders to testify as to occurrences both inside and out. 8 Wigmore § 2354 (McNaughton Rev.1961). However, the door of the jury room is not necessarily a satisfactory dividing point, and the Supreme Court has refused to accept it for every situation. Mattox v. United States, 146 U.S. 140, 13 S.Ct. 50, 36 L.Ed. 917 (1892).

Under the federal decisions the central focus has been upon insulation of the manner in which the jury reached its verdict, and this protection extends to each of the components of deliberation, including arguments, statements, discussions, mental and emotional reactions, votes, and any other feature of the process. Thus testimony or affidavits of jurors have been held incompetent to show a compromise verdict, Hyde v. United States, 225 U.S. 347, 382 (1912); a quotient verdict, McDonald v. Pless, 238 U.S. 264 (1915); speculation as to insurance coverage, Holden v. Porter, 405 F.2d 878 (10th Cir. 1969), Farmers Coop. Elev. Ass'n v. Strand, 382 F.2d 224, 230 (8th Cir. 1967), cert. denied 389 U.S. 1014; misinterpretation of instructions, Farmers Coop. Elev. Ass'n v. Strand, supra; mistake in returning verdict, United States v. Chereton, 309 F.2d 197 (6th Cir. 1962); interpretation of guilty plea by one defendant as implicating others, United States v. Crosby, 294 F.2d 928, 949 (2d Cir. 1961). The policy does not, however, foreclose testimony by jurors as to prejudicial extraneous information or influences injected into or brought to bear upon the deliberative process. Thus a juror is recognized as competent to testify to statements by the bailiff or the introduction of a prejudicial newspaper account into the jury room, Mattox v. United States, 146 U.S. 140 (1892). See also Parker v. Gladden, 385 U.S. 363 (1966).

This rule does not purport to specify the substantive grounds for setting aside verdicts for irregularity; it deals only with the competency of jurors to testify concerning those grounds.

See also Rule 6(e) of the Federal Rules of Criminal Procedure and 18 U.S.C. § 3500, governing the secrecy of grand jury proceedings. The present rule does not relate to secrecy and disclosure but to the competency of certain witnesses and evidence.

Report of House Judiciary Committee

House Comm. on Judiciary, Fed. Rules of Evidence, H.R.Rep. No. 650, 93d Cong., 1st Sess., p. 9 (1973); 1974 U.S.Code Cong. & Ad.News 7075, 7083

As proposed by the Court, Rule 606(b) limited testimony by a juror in the course of an inquiry into the validity of a verdict or indictment. He could testify as to the influence of extraneous prejudicial information brought to the jury's attention (e.g. a radio newscast or a newspaper account) or an outside influence which improperly had been brought to bear upon a juror (e.g. a threat to the safety of a member of his family), but he could not testify as to other irregularities which occurred in the jury room. Under this formulation a quotient verdict could not be attacked through the testimony of a juror, nor could a juror testify to the drunken condition of a fellow juror which so disabled him that he could not participate in the jury's deliberations.

The 1969 and 1971 Advisory Committee drafts would have permitted a member of the jury to testify concerning these kinds of irregularities in the jury room. The Advisory Committee note in the 1971 draft stated that ". . . the door of the jury room is not a satisfactory dividing point, and the Supreme Court has refused to accept it." The Advisory Committee further commented that—

> The trend has been to draw the dividing line between testimony as to mental processes, on the one hand, and as to the existence of conditions or occurrences of events calculated improperly to influence the verdict, on the other hand, without regard to whether the happening is within or without the jury room. . . . The jurors are the persons who know what really happened. Allowing them to testify as to matters other than their own reactions involves no particular hazard to the values sought to be protected. The rule is based upon this conclusion. It makes no attempt to specify the substantive grounds for setting aside verdicts for irregularity.

Objective jury misconduct may be testified to in California, Florida, Iowa, Kansas, Nebraska, New Jersey, North Dakota, Ohio, Oregon, Tennessee, Texas, and Washington.

Persuaded that the better practice is that provided for in the earlier drafts, the Committee amended subdivision (b) to read in the text of those drafts.

Report of Senate Judiciary Committee

Senate Comm. on Judiciary, Fed. Rules of Evidence, S.Rep. No. 1277, 93d Cong., 2d Sess., p. 13 (1974); 1974 U.S.Code Cong. & Ad.News 7051, 7060

As adopted by the House, this rule would permit the impeachment of verdicts by inquiry into, not the mental processes of the jurors, but what happened in terms of conduct in the jury room. This extension of the ability to impeach a verdict is felt to be unwarranted and ill-advised.

The rule passed by the House embodies a suggestion by the Advisory Committee of the Judicial Conference that is considerably broader than the final version adopted by the Supreme Court, which embodied long-accepted Federal law. Although forbidding the impeachment of verdicts by inquiry into the jurors' mental processes, it deletes from the Supreme Court version the proscription against testimony "as to any matter or statement occurring during the course of the jury's deliberations." This deletion would have the effect of opening verdicts up to challenge on the basis of what happened during the jury's internal deliberations, for example, where a juror alleged that the jury refused to follow the trial judge's instructions or that some of the jurors did not take part in deliberations.

Permitting an individual to attack a jury verdict based upon the jury's internal deliberations has long been recognized as unwise by the Supreme Court. In McDonald v. Pless, the Court stated:

> . . .
>
> [L]et it once be established that verdicts solemnly made and publicly returned into court can be attacked and set aside on the testimony of those who took part in their publication and all verdicts could be, and many would be, followed by an inquiry in the hope of discovering something which might invalidate the finding. Jurors would be harassed and beset by the defeated party in an effort to secure from them evidence of facts which might establish misconduct sufficient to set aside a verdict. If evidence thus secured could be thus used, the result would be to make what was intended to be a private deliberation, the constant subject of public investigation—to the destruction of all frankness and freedom of discussion and conference.[2]
>
> . . .

As it stands then, the rule would permit the harassment of former jurors by losing parties as well as the possible exploitation of disgruntled or otherwise badly-motivated ex-jurors.

Public policy requires a finality to litigation. And common fairness requires that absolute privacy be preserved for jurors to engage in the full and free debate necessary to the attainment of just verdicts. Jurors will not be able to function effectively if their deliberations are to be scrutinized in post-trial litigation. In the interest of protecting the jury system and the citizens who make it work, rule 606 should not permit any inquiry into the internal deliberations of the jurors.

Conference Report

H.R., Fed.Rules of Evidence, Conf.Rep. No. 1597, 93d Cong., 2d Sess., p. 8 (1974); 1974 U.S.Code Cong. & Ad.News 7098, 7102

Rule 606(b) deals with juror testimony in an inquiry into the validity of a verdict or indictment. The House bill provides that a juror cannot testify about his mental processes or about the effect of anything upon his or another juror's mind as influencing him to assent to or dissent from a verdict or indictment.

2. 238 U.S. 264, at 267 (1914).

Thus, the House bill allows a juror to testify about objective matters occurring during the jury's deliberation, such as the misconduct of another juror or the reaching of a quotient verdict. The Senate bill does not permit juror testimony about any matter or statement occurring during the course of the jury's deliberations. The Senate bill does provide, however, that a juror may testify on the question whether extraneous prejudicial information was improperly brought to the jury's attention and on the question whether any outside influence was improperly brought to bear on any juror.

The Conference adopts the Senate amendment. The Conferees believe that jurors should be encouraged to be conscientious in promptly reporting to the court misconduct that occurs during jury deliberations.

1987 Amendment. The amendments are technical. No substantive change is intended.

Rule 607. Who May Impeach

The credibility of a witness may be attacked by any party, including the party calling the witness.

(As amended Mar. 2, 1987, eff. Oct. 1, 1987.)

Section references, McCormick 4th ed.

§ 23, § 38, § 39

Note by Federal Judicial Center

The rule enacted by the Congress is the rule prescribed by the Supreme Court without change.

Advisory Committee's Note

56 F.R.D. 183, 266

The traditional rule against impeaching one's own witness is abandoned as based on false premises. A party does not hold out his witnesses as worthy of belief, since he rarely has a free choice in selecting them. Denial of the right leaves the party at the mercy of the witness and the adversary. If the impeachment is by a prior statement, it is free from hearsay dangers and is excluded from the category of hearsay under Rule 801(d)(1). Ladd, Impeachment of One's Own Witness—New Developments, 4 U.Chi.L.Rev. 69 (1936); McCormick § 38; 3 Wigmore §§ 896–918. The substantial inroads into the old rule made over the years by decisions, rules, and statutes are evidence of doubts as to its basic soundness and workability. Cases are collected in 3 Wigmore § 905. Revised Rule 32(a)(1) of the Federal Rules of Civil Procedure allows any party to impeach a witness by means of his deposition, and Rule 43(b) has allowed the calling and impeachment of an adverse party or person identified with him. Illustrative statutes allowing a party to impeach his own witness under varying circumstances are Ill.Rev.Stats.1967, c. 110, § 60; Mass.Laws Annot. 1959, c. 233 § 23; 20 N.M.Stats. Annot. 1953, § 20–2–4; N.Y. CPLR § 4514 (McKinney 1963); 12 Vt.Stats. Annot. 1959, §§ 1641a, 1642. Complete judicial rejection of the old rule is found in United States v. Freeman, 302 F.2d 347 (2d Cir.1962). The same result is reached in Uniform Rule 20; California

Evidence Code § 785; Kansas Code of Civil Procedure § 60–420. See also New Jersey Evidence Rule 20.

1987 Amendment. The amendment is technical. No substantive change is intended.

Rule 608. Evidence of Character and Conduct of Witness

(a) Opinion and reputation evidence of character. The credibility of a witness may be attacked or supported by evidence in the form of opinion or reputation, but subject to these limitations: (1) the evidence may refer only to character for truthfulness or untruthfulness, and (2) evidence of truthful character is admissible only after the character of the witness for truthfulness has been attacked by opinion or reputation evidence or otherwise.

(b) Specific instances of conduct. Specific instances of the conduct of a witness, for the purpose of attacking or supporting the witness' credibility, other than conviction of crime as provided in rule 609, may not be proved by extrinsic evidence. They may, however, in the discretion of the court, if probative of truthfulness or untruthfulness, be inquired into on cross-examination of the witness (1) concerning the witness' character for truthfulness or untruthfulness, or (2) concerning the character for truthfulness or untruthfulness of another witness as to which character the witness being cross-examined has testified.

The giving of testimony, whether by an accused or by any other witness, does not operate as a waiver of the accused's or the witness' privilege against self-incrimination when examined with respect to matters which relate only to credibility.

(As amended Mar. 2, 1987, eff. Oct. 1, 1987; Apr. 25, 1988, eff. Nov. 1, 1988.)

Section references, McCormick 4th ed.

Generally § 25

(a). § *43*, § 44, § 47

(b). § 41, § 45, § 47

Note by Federal Judicial Center

The rule enacted by the Congress is the rule prescribed by the Supreme Court, changed only by amending the second sentence of subdivision (b). The sentence as prescribed by the Court read: "They may, however, if probative of truthfulness or untruthfulness and not remote in time, be inquired into on cross-examination of the witness himself or on cross-examination of a witness who testifies to his character for truthfulness or untruthfulness." The effect of the amendments was to delete the phrase "and not remote in time," to add the phrase "in the discretion of the court," and otherwise only to clarify the meaning of the sentence. The reasons for the amendments are stated in the

Report of the House Committee on the Judiciary, set forth below. See also Note to Rule 405(a) by Federal Judicial Center, supra.

Advisory Committee's Note

56 F.R.D. 183, 268

Subdivision (a). In Rule 404(a) the general position is taken that character evidence is not admissible for the purpose of proving that the person acted in conformity therewith, subject, however, to several exceptions, one of which is character evidence of a witness as bearing upon his credibility. The present rule develops that exception.

In accordance with the bulk of judicial authority, the inquiry is strictly limited to character for veracity, rather than allowing evidence as to character generally. The result is to sharpen relevancy, to reduce surprise, waste of time, and confusion, and to make the lot of the witness somewhat less unattractive. McCormick § 44.

The use of opinion and reputation evidence as means of proving the character of witnesses is consistent with Rule 405(a). While the modern practice has purported to exclude opinion, witnesses who testify to reputation seem in fact often to be giving their opinions, disguised somewhat misleadingly as reputation. See McCormick § 44. And even under the modern practice, a common relaxation has allowed inquiry as to whether the witnesses would believe the principal witness under oath. United States v. Walker, 313 F.2d 236 (6th Cir.1963), and cases cited therein; McCormick § 44, pp. 94–95, n. 3.

Character evidence in support of credibility is admissible under the rule only after the witness' character has first been attacked, as has been the case at common law. Maguire, Weinstein, et al., Cases on Evidence 295 (5th ed. 1965); McCormick § 49, p. 105; 4 Wigmore § 1104. The enormous needless consumption of time which a contrary practice would entail justifies the limitation. Opinion or reputation that the witness is untruthful specifically qualifies as an attack under the rule, and evidence of misconduct, including conviction of crime, and of corruption also fall within this category. Evidence of bias or interest does not. McCormick § 49; 4 Wigmore §§ 1106, 1107. Whether evidence in the form of contradiction is an attack upon the character of the witness must depend upon the circumstances. McCormick § 49. Cf. 4 Wigmore §§ 1108, 1109.

As to the use of specific instances on direct by an opinion witness, see the Advisory Committee's Note to Rule 405, supra.

Subdivision (b). In conformity with Rule 405, which forecloses use of evidence of specific incidents as proof in chief of character unless character is an issue in the case, the present rule generally bars evidence of specific instances of conduct of a witness for the purpose of attacking or supporting his credibility. There are, however, two exceptions: (1) specific instances are provable when they have been the subject of criminal conviction, and (2) specific instances may be inquired into on cross-examination of the principal witness or of a witness giving an opinion of his character for truthfulness.

(1) Conviction of crime as a technique of impeachment is treated in detail in Rule 609, and here is merely recognized as an exception to the general rule excluding evidence of specific incidents for impeachment purposes.

(2) Particular instances of conduct, though not the subject of criminal conviction, may be inquired into on cross-examination of the principal witness himself or of a witness who testifies concerning his character for truthfulness. Effective cross-examination demands that some allowance be made for going into matters of this kind, but the possibilities of abuse are substantial. Consequently safeguards are erected in the form of specific requirements that the instances inquired into be probative of truthfulness or its opposite . . . . Also, the overriding protection of Rule 403 requires that probative value not be outweighed by danger of unfair prejudice, confusion of issues or misleading the jury, and that of Rule 611 bars harassment and undue embarrassment.

The final sentence constitutes a rejection of the doctrine of such cases as People v. Sorge, 301 N.Y. 198, 93 N.E.2d 637 (1950), that any past criminal act relevant to credibility may be inquired into on cross-examination, in apparent disregard of the privilege against self-incrimination. While it is clear that an ordinary witness cannot make a partial disclosure of incriminating matter and then invoke the privilege on cross-examination, no tenable contention can be made that merely by testifying he waives his right to foreclose inquiry on cross-examination into criminal activities for the purpose of attacking his credibility. So to hold would reduce the privilege to a nullity. While it is true that an accused, unlike an ordinary witness, has an option whether to testify, if the option can be exercised only at the price of opening up inquiry as to any and all criminal acts committed during his lifetime, the right to testify could scarcely be said to possess much vitality. In Griffin v. California, 380 U.S. 609, 85 S.Ct. 1229, 14 L.Ed.2d 106 (1965), the Court held that allowing comment on the election of an accused not to testify exacted a constitutionally impermissible price, and so here. While no specific provision in terms confers constitutional status on the right of an accused to take the stand in his own defense, the existence of the right is so completely recognized that a denial of it or substantial infringement upon it would surely be of due process dimensions. See Ferguson v. Georgia, 365 U.S. 570, 81 S.Ct. 756, 5 L.Ed.2d 783 (1961); McCormick § 131; 8 Wigmore § 2276 (McNaughton Rev.1961). In any event, wholly aside from constitutional considerations, the provision represents a sound policy.

Report of House Committee on the Judiciary

House Comm. on Judiciary, Fed.Rules of Evidence, H.R.Rep. No. 650, 93d Cong., 1st Sess., p. 10 (1973); 1974 U.S.Code Cong. & Ad.News 7075, 7084

The second sentence of Rule 608(b) as submitted by the Court permitted specific instances of misconduct of a witness to be inquired into on cross-examination for the purpose of attacking his credibility, if probative of truthfulness or untruthfulness, "and not remote in time." Such cross-examination could be of the witness himself or of another witness who testifies as to "his" character for truthfulness or untruthfulness.

The Committee amended the Rule to emphasize the discretionary power of the court in permitting such testimony and deleted the reference to remoteness in time as being unnecessary and confusing (remoteness from time of trial or remoteness from the incident involved?). As recast, the Committee amendment also makes clear the antecedent of "his" in the original Court proposal.

1987 Amendment. The amendments are technical. No substantive change is intended.

1988 Amendment. The amendment is technical. No substantive change is intended.

Rule 609. Impeachment by Evidence of Conviction of Crime

(a) General rule. For the purpose of attacking the credibility of a witness,

civil cases

(1) evidence that a witness other than an accused has been convicted of a crime shall be admitted, subject to Rule 403, if the crime was punishable by death or imprisonment in excess of one year under the law under which the witness was convicted, and evidence that an accused has been convicted of such a crime shall be admitted if the court determines that the probative value of admitting this evidence outweighs its prejudicial effect to the accused; and

(2) evidence that any witness has been convicted of a crime shall be admitted if it involved dishonesty or false statement, regardless of the punishment.

(b) Time limit. Evidence of a conviction under this rule is not admissible if a period of more than ten years has elapsed since the date of the conviction or of the release of the witness from the confinement imposed for that conviction, whichever is the later date, unless the court determines, in the interests of justice, that the probative value of the conviction supported by specific facts and circumstances substantially outweighs its prejudicial effect. However, evidence of a conviction more than 10 years old as calculated herein, is not admissible unless the proponent gives to the adverse party sufficient advance written notice of intent to use such evidence to provide the adverse party with a fair opportunity to contest the use of such evidence.

(c) Effect of pardon, annulment, or certificate of rehabilitation. Evidence of a conviction is not admissible under this rule if (1) the conviction has been the subject of a pardon, annulment, certificate of rehabilitation, or other equivalent procedure based on a finding of the rehabilitation of the person convicted, and that person has not been convicted of a subsequent crime which was punishable by death or imprisonment in excess of one year, or (2) the conviction has been the subject of a pardon, annulment, or other equivalent procedure based on a finding of innocence.

(d) Juvenile adjudications. Evidence of juvenile adjudications is generally not admissible under this rule. The court may, however, in a criminal case allow evidence of a juvenile adjudication of a witness other than the accused if conviction of the offense would be admissible to attack the credibility of an adult and the court is satisfied that admission in evidence is necessary for a fair determination of the issue of guilt or innocence.

(e) Pendency of appeal. The pendency of an appeal therefrom does not render evidence of a conviction inadmissible. Evidence of the pendency of an appeal is admissible.

(As amended Mar. 2, 1987, eff. Oct. 1, 1987; Jan. 26, 1990, eff. Dec. 1, 1990.)

Section references, McCormick 4th ed.

Generally § 42

(a). § 42

(b). § 42

(c). § 42

(d). § 42

(e). § 42

Note by Federal Judicial Center

Subdivision (a) of the rule prescribed by the Supreme Court was revised successively in the House, in the Senate, and in the Conference. The nature of the rule prescribed by the Court, the various amendments, and the reasons therefor are stated in the Report of the House Committee on the Judiciary, the Report of the Senate Committee on the Judiciary, and the Conference Report, set forth below.

Subdivision (b) of the rule prescribed by the Supreme Court was also revised successively in the House, in the Senate, and in the Conference. The nature of the rule prescribed by the Court, those amendments and the reasons therefor are likewise stated in the Report of the House Committee on the Judiciary, the Report of the Senate Committee on the Judiciary, and the Conference Report, set forth below.

Subdivision (c) enacted by the Congress is the subdivision prescribed by the Supreme Court, with amendments and reasons therefor stated in the Report of the House Committee on the Judiciary, set forth below.

Subdivision (d) enacted by the Congress is the subdivision prescribed by the Supreme Court, amended in the second sentence by substituting "court" in place of "judge" and by adding the phrase "in a criminal case."

Subdivision (e) enacted by the Congress is the subdivision prescribed by the Supreme Court without change.

Advisory Committee's Note

56 F.R.D. 183, 270

As a means of impeachment, evidence of conviction of crime is significant only because it stands as proof of the commission of the underlying criminal act. There is little dissent from the general proposition that at least some crimes are relevant to credibility but much disagreement among the cases and commentators about which crimes are usable for this purpose. See McCormick § 43; 2 Wright, Federal Practice and Procedure: Criminal § 416 (1969). The weight of traditional authority has been to allow use of felonies generally, without regard to the nature of the particular offense, and of *crimen falsi* without regard to the grade of the offense. This is the view accepted by Congress in the 1970 amendment of § 14–305 of the District of Columbia Code, P.L. 91–358, 84 Stat. 473. Uniform Rule 21 and Model Code Rule 106 permit only crimes involving "dishonesty or false statement." Others have thought that the trial judge should have discretion to exclude convictions if the probative value of the evidence of the crime is substantially outweighed by the danger of unfair prejudice. Luck v. United States, 121 U.S.App.D.C. 151, 348 F.2d 763 (1965); McGowan, Impeachment of Criminal Defendants by Prior Convictions, 1970 Law & Soc. Order 1. . . .

The proposed rule incorporates certain basic safeguards, in terms applicable to all witnesses but of particular significance to an accused who elects to testify. These protections include the imposition of definite time limitations, giving effect to demonstrated rehabilitation, and generally excluding juvenile adjudications.

Subdivision (a). For purposes of impeachment, crimes are divided into two categories by the rule: (1) those of what is generally regarded as felony grade, without particular regard to the nature of the offense, and (2) those involving dishonesty or false statement, without regard to the grade of the offense. Provable convictions are not limited to violations of federal law. By reason of our constitutional structure, the federal catalog of crimes is far from being a complete one, and resort must be had to the laws of the states for the specification of many crimes. For example, simple theft as compared with theft from interstate commerce. Other instances of borrowing are the Assimilative Crimes Act, making the state law of crimes applicable to the special territorial and maritime jurisdiction of the United States, 18 U.S.C. § 13, and the provision of the Judicial Code disqualifying persons as jurors on the grounds of state as well as federal convictions, 28 U.S.C. § 1865. For evaluation of the crime in terms of seriousness, reference is made to the congressional measurement of felony (subject to imprisonment in excess of one year) rather than adopting state definitions which vary considerably. See 28 U.S.C. § 1865, supra, disqualifying jurors for conviction in state or federal court of crime punishable by imprisonment for more than year.

Report of the House Committee on the Judiciary

House Comm. on Judiciary, Fed.Rules of Evidence, H.R.Rep. No. 650, 93d Cong., 1st Sess., p. 11 (1973); 1974 U.S.Code Cong. & Ad.News 7075, 7084

Rule 609(a) as submitted by the Court was modeled after Section 133(a) of Public Law 91–358, 14 D.C.Code 305(b)(1), enacted in 1970. The Rule provided that:

> For the purpose of attacking the credibility of a witness, evidence that he has been convicted of a crime is admissible but only if the crime (1) was punishable by death or imprisonment in excess of one year under the law under which he was convicted or (2) involved dishonesty or false statement regardless of the punishment.

As reported to the Committee by the Subcommittee, Rule 609(a) was amended to read as follows:

> For the purpose of attacking the credibility of a witness, evidence that he has been convicted of a crime is admissible only if the crime (1) was

punishable by death or imprisonment in excess of one year, unless the court determines that the danger of unfair prejudice outweighs the probative value of the evidence of the conviction, or (2) involved dishonesty or false statement.

In full committee, the provision was amended to permit attack upon the credibility of a witness by prior conviction only if the prior crime involved dishonesty or false statement. While recognizing that the prevailing doctrine in the federal courts and in most States allows a witness to be impeached by evidence of prior felony convictions without restriction as to type, the Committee was of the view that, because of the danger of unfair prejudice in such practice and the deterrent effect upon an accused who might wish to testify, and even upon a witness who was not the accused, cross-examination by evidence of prior conviction should be limited to those kinds of convictions bearing directly on credibility, i.e., crimes involving dishonesty or false statement.

Report of the Senate Committee on the Judiciary

Senate Comm. on Judiciary, Fed.Rules of Evidence, S.Rep. No. 1277, 93d Cong., 2d Sess., p. 14 (1974); 1974 U.S.Code Cong. & Ad.News 7051, 7060

As proposed by the Supreme Court, the rule would allow the use of prior convictions to impeach if the crime was a felony or a misdemeanor if the misdemeanor involved dishonesty or false statement. As modified by the House, the rule would admit prior convictions for impeachment purposes only if the offense, whether felony or misdemeanor, involved dishonesty or false statement.

The committee has adopted a modified version of the House-passed rule. In your committee's view, the danger of unfair prejudice is far greater when the accused, as opposed to other witnesses, testifies, because the jury may be prejudiced not merely on the question of credibility but also on the ultimate question of guilt or innocence. Therefore, with respect to defendants, the committee agreed with the House limitation that only offenses involving false statement or dishonesty may be used. By that phrase, the committee means crimes such as perjury or subornation of perjury, false statement, criminal fraud, embezzlement or false pretense, or any other offense, in the nature of crimen falsi the commission of which involves some element of untruthfulness, deceit or falsification bearing on the accused's propensity to testify truthfully.

With respect to other witnesses, in addition to any prior conviction involving false statement or dishonesty, any other felony may be used to impeach if, and only if, the court finds that the probative value of such evidence outweighs its prejudicial effect against the party offering that witness.

Notwithstanding this provision, proof of any prior offense otherwise admissible under rule 404 could still be offered for the purposes sanctioned by that rule. Furthermore, the committee intends that notwithstanding this rule, a defendant's misrepresentation regarding the existence or nature of prior convictions may be met by rebuttal evidence, including the record of such prior convictions. Similarly, such records may be offered to rebut representations made by the defendant regarding his attitude toward or willingness to commit a general category of offense, although denials or other representations by the defendant regarding the specific conduct which forms the basis of the charge against him shall not make prior convictions admissible to rebut such statement.

In regard to either type of representation, of course, prior convictions may be offered in rebuttal only if the defendant's statement is made in response to defense counsel's questions or is made gratuitously in the course of cross-examination. Prior convictions may not be offered as rebuttal evidence if the prosecution has sought to circumvent the purpose of this rule by asking questions which elicit such representations from the defendant.

One other clarifying amendment has been added to this subsection, that is, to provide that the admissibility of evidence of a prior conviction is permitted only upon cross-examination of a witness. It is not admissible if a person does not testify. It is to be understood, however, that a court record of a prior conviction is admissible to prove that conviction if the witness has forgotten or denies its existence.

Conference Report

H.R., Fed.Rules of Evidence, Conf.Rep. No. 1597, 93d Cong., 2d Sess., p. 9 (1974); 1974 U.S.Code Cong. & Ad.News 7098, 7102

The House bill provides that the credibility of a witness can be attacked by proof of prior conviction of a crime only if the crime involves dishonesty or false statement. The Senate amendment provides that a witness' credibility may be attacked if the crime (1) was punishable by death or imprisonment in excess of one year under the law under which he was convicted or (2) involves dishonesty or false statement, regardless of the punishment.

The Conference adopts the Senate amendment with an amendment. The Conference amendment provides that the credibility of a witness, whether a defendant or someone else, may be attacked by proof of a prior conviction but only if the crime: (1) was punishable by death or imprisonment in excess of one year under the law under which he was convicted and the court determines that the probative value of the conviction outweighs its prejudicial effect to the defendant; or (2) involved dishonesty or false statement regardless of the punishment.

By the phrase "dishonesty and false statement" the Conference means crimes such as perjury or subornation of perjury, false statement, criminal fraud, embezzlement, or false pretense, or any other offense in the nature of crimen falsi, the commission of which involves some element of deceit, untruthfulness, or falsification bearing on the accused's propensity to testify truthfully.

The admission of prior convictions involving dishonesty and false statement is not within the discretion of the Court. Such convictions are peculiarly probative of credibility and, under this rule, are always to be admitted. Thus, judicial discretion granted with respect to the admissibility of other prior convictions is not applicable to those involving dishonesty or false statement.

With regard to the discretionary standard established by paragraph (1) of rule 609(a), the Conference determined that the prejudicial effect to be weighed against the probative value of the conviction is specifically the prejudicial effect *to the defendant.* The danger of prejudice to a witness other than the defendant (such as injury to the witness' reputation in his community) was considered and rejected by the Conference as an element to be weighed in determining admissibility. It was the judgment of the Conference that the danger of prejudice to a nondefendant witness is outweighed by the need for the trier of fact to have as much relevant evidence on the issue of credibility as possible. Such evidence should only be excluded where it presents a danger of improperly influencing the outcome of the trial by persuading the trier of fact to convict the defendant on the basis of his prior criminal record.

Advisory Committee's Note

56 F.R.D. 183, 271

Subdivision (b). Few statutes recognize a time limit on impeachment by evidence of conviction. However, practical considerations of fairness and relevancy demand that some boundary be recognized. See Ladd, Credibility Tests—Current Trends, 89 U.Pa.L.Rev. 166, 176–177 (1940). This portion of the rule is derived from the proposal advanced in Recommendation Proposing an Evidence Code, § 788(5), p. 142, Cal.Law Rev.Comm'n (1965), though not adopted. See California Evidence Code § 788.

Report of the House Committee on the Judiciary

House Comm. on Judiciary, Fed.Rules of Evidence, H.R.Rep. No. 650, 93d Cong., 1st Sess, p. 11 (1973); 1974 U.S.Code Cong. & Ad.News 7075, 7085

Rule 609(b) as submitted by the Court was modeled after Section 133(a) of Public Law 91–358, 14 D.C.Code 305(b)(2)(B), enacted in 1970. The Rule provided:

> Evidence of a conviction under this rule is not admissible if a period of more than ten years has elapsed since the date of the release of the witness from confinement imposed for his most recent conviction, or the expiration of the period of his parole, probation, or sentence granted or imposed with respect to his most recent conviction, whichever is the later date.

Under this formulation, a witness' entire past record of criminal convictions could be used for impeachment (provided the conviction met the standard of subdivision (a)), if the witness had been most recently released from confinement, or the period of his parole or probation had expired, within ten years of the conviction.

The Committee amended the Rule to read in the text of the 1971 Advisory Committee version to provide that upon the expiration of ten years from the date of a conviction of a witness, or of his release from confinement for that offense, that conviction may no longer be used for impeachment. The Committee was of the view that after ten years following a person's release from confinement (or from the date of his conviction) the probative value of the conviction with respect to that person's credibility diminished to a point where it should no longer be admissible.

Report of the Senate Committee on the Judiciary

Senate Comm. on Judiciary, Fed.Rules of Evidence, S.Rep. No. 1277, 93d Cong., 2d Sess., p. 15 (1974); 1974 U.S.Code Cong. & Ad.News 7051, 7061

Although convictions over ten years old generally do not have much probative value, there may be exceptional circumstances under which the conviction substantially bears on the credibility of the witness. Rather than exclude all convictions over 10 years old, the committee adopted an amendment in the form of a final clause to the section granting the court discretion to admit convictions over 10 years old, but only upon a determination by the court that the probative value of the convictions supported by specific facts and circumstances, substantially outweighs its prejudicial effect.

It is intended that convictions over 10 years old will be admitted very rarely and only in exceptional circumstances. The rules provide that the decision be supported by specific facts and circumstances thus requiring the court to make specific findings on the record as to the particular facts and circumstances it has considered in determining that the probative value of the conviction substantially outweighs its prejudicial impact. It is expected that, in fairness, the court will give the party against whom the conviction is introduced a full and adequate opportunity to contest its admission.

Conference Report

H.R., Fed.Rules of Evidence, Conf.Rep. No. 1597, 93d Cong., 2d Sess., p. 10 (1974); 1974 U.S.Code Cong. & Ad.News 7098, 7103

The House bill provides in subsection (b) that evidence of conviction of a crime may not be used for impeachment purposes under subsection (a) if more than ten years have elapsed since the date of the conviction or the date the witness was released from confinement imposed for the conviction, whichever is later. The Senate amendment permits the use of convictions older than ten years, if the court determines, in the interests of justice, that the probative value of the conviction, supported by specific facts and circumstances, substantially outweighs its prejudicial effect.

The Conference adopts the Senate amendment with an amendment requiring notice by a party that he intends to request that the court allow him to use a conviction older than ten years. The Conferees anticipate that a written notice, in order to give the adversary a fair opportunity to contest the use of the evidence, will ordinarily include such information as the date of the conviction, the jurisdiction, and the offense or statute involved. In order to eliminate the possibility that the flexibility of this provision may impair the ability of a party-opponent to prepare for trial, the Conferees intend that the notice provision operate to avoid surprise.

Advisory Committee's Note

56 F.R.D. 183, 271

Subdivision (c). A pardon or its equivalent granted solely for the purpose of restoring civil rights lost by virtue of a conviction has no relevance to an inquiry into character. If, however, the pardon or other proceeding is hinged upon a showing of rehabilitation the situation is otherwise. The result under the rule is to render the conviction inadmissible. The alternative of allowing in evidence both the conviction and the rehabilitation has not been adopted for reasons of policy, economy of time, and difficulties of evaluation.

A similar provision is contained in California Evidence Code § 788. Cf. A.L.I. Model Penal Code, Proposed Official Draft § 306.6(3)(e) (1962), and discussion in A.L.I. Proceedings 310 (1961).

Pardons based on innocence have the effect, of course, of nullifying the conviction *ab initio.*

Report of House Committee on the Judiciary

House Comm. on Judiciary, Fed.Rules of Evidence, H.R.Rep. No. 650, 93d Cong., 1st Sess., p. 12 (1973); 1974 U.S.Code Cong. & Ad.News 7075, 7085

Rule 609(c) as submitted by the Court provided in part that evidence of a witness' prior conviction is not admissible to attack his credibility if the conviction was the subject of a pardon, annulment, or other equivalent procedure, based on a showing of rehabilitation, and the witness has not been convicted of a subsequent crime. The Committee amended the Rule to provide that the "subsequent crime" must have been "punishable by death or imprisonment in excess of one year", on the ground that a subsequent conviction of an offense not a felony is insufficient to rebut the finding that the witness has been rehabilitated. The Committee also intends that the words "based on a finding of the rehabilitation of the person convicted" apply not only to "certificate of rehabilitation, or other equivalent procedure", but also to "pardon" and "annulment."

Advisory Committee's Note

56 F.R.D. 183, 271

Subdivision (d). The prevailing view has been that a juvenile adjudication is not usable for impeachment. Thomas v. United States, 74 App.D.C. 167, 121 F.2d 905 (1941); Cotton v. United States, 355 F.2d 480 (10th Cir.1966). This conclusion was based upon a variety of circumstances. By virtue of its informality, frequently diminished quantum of required proof, and other departures from accepted standards for criminal trials under the theory of *parens patriae,* the juvenile adjudication was considered to lack the precision and general probative value of the criminal conviction. While In re Gault, 387 U.S. 1, 87 S.Ct. 1428, 18 L.Ed.2d 527 (1967), no doubt eliminates these characteristics insofar as objectionable, other obstacles remain. Practical problems of administration are raised by the common provisions in juvenile legislation that records be kept confidential and that they be destroyed after a short time. While *Gault* was skeptical as to the realities of confidentiality of juvenile records, it also saw no constitutional obstacles to improvement. 387 U.S. at 25, 87 S.Ct. 1428. See also Note, Rights and Rehabilitation in the Juvenile Courts, 67 Colum.L.Rev. 281, 289 (1967). In addition, policy considerations much akin to those which dictate exclusion of adult convictions after rehabilitation has been established strongly suggest a rule of excluding juvenile adjudications. Admittedly, however, the rehabilitative process may in a given case be a demonstrated failure, or the strategic importance of a given witness may be so great as to require the overriding of general policy in the interests of particular justice. See Giles v. Maryland, 386 U.S. 66, 87 S.Ct. 793, 17 L.Ed.2d 737 (1967). Wigmore was outspoken in his condemnation of the disallowance of juvenile adjudications to impeach, especially when the witness is the complainant in a case of molesting a minor. 1 Wigmore § 196; 3 id. §§ 924a, 980. The rule recognizes discretion in the judge to effect an accommodation among these various factors by departing from the general principle of exclusion. In deference to the general pattern and policy of juvenile statutes, however, no discretion is accorded when the witness is the accused in a criminal case.

Subdivision (e). The presumption of correctness which ought to attend judicial proceedings supports the position that pendency of an appeal does not preclude use of a conviction for impeachment. United States v. Empire Packing Co., 174 F.2d 16 (7th Cir.1949), cert. denied 337 U.S. 959, 69 S.Ct. 1534, 93 L.Ed. 1758; Bloch v. United States, 226 F.2d 185 (9th Cir.1955), cert. denied 350 U.S. 948, 76 S.Ct. 323, 100 L.Ed. 826 and 353 U.S. 959, 77 S.Ct. 868, 1 L.Ed. 2d 910; and see Newman v. United States, 331 F.2d 968 (8th Cir.1964). Contra, Campbell v. United States, 85 U.S.App.D.C. 133, 176 F.2d 45 (1949). The pendency of an appeal is, however, a qualifying circumstance properly considerable.

1987 Amendment. The amendments are technical. No substantive change is intended.

1990 Amendment. The amendment to Rule 609(a) makes two changes in the rule. The first change removes from the rule the limitation that the conviction may only be elicited during cross-examination, a limitation that virtually every circuit has found to be inapplicable. It is common for witnesses to reveal on direct examination their convictions to "remove the sting" of the impeachment. See e.g., United States v. Bad Cob, 560 F.2d 877 (8th Cir.1977). The amendment does not contemplate that a court will necessarily permit proof of prior convictions through testimony, which might be time-consuming and more prejudicial than proof through a written record. Rules 403 and 611(a) provide sufficient authority for the court to protect against unfair or disruptive methods of proof.

The second change effected by the amendment resolves an ambiguity as to the relationship of Rules 609 and 403 with respect to impeachment of witnesses other than the criminal defendant. See, Green v. Bock Laundry Machine Co., 109 S.Ct. ___, ___ U.S. ___ (1989). The amendment does not disturb the special balancing test for the criminal defendant who chooses to testify. Thus, the rule recognizes that, in virtually every case in which prior convictions are used to impeach the testifying defendant, the defendant faces a unique risk of prejudice—i.e., the danger that convictions that would be excluded under Fed.R. Evid. 404 will be misused by a jury as propensity evidence despite their introduction solely for impeachment purposes. Although the rule does not forbid all use of convictions to impeach a defendant, it requires that the government show that the probative value of convictions as impeachment evidence outweighs their prejudicial effect.

Prior to the amendment, the rule appeared to give the defendant the benefit of the special balancing test when defense witnesses other than the defendant were called to testify. In practice, however, the concern about unfairness to the defendant is most acute when the defendant's own convictions are offered as evidence. Almost all of the decided cases concern this type of impeachment, and the amendment does not deprive the defendant of any meaningful protection, since Rule 403 now clearly protects against unfair impeachment of any defense witness other than the defendant. There are cases in which a defendant might be prejudiced when a defense witness is impeached. Such cases may arise, for example, when the witness bears a special relationship to the defendant such that the defendant is likely to suffer some spill-over effect from impeachment of the witness.

The amendment also protects other litigants from unfair impeachment of their witnesses. The danger of prejudice from the use of prior convictions is not confined to criminal defendants. Although the danger that prior convictions will be misused as character evidence is particularly acute when the defendant is impeached, the danger exists in other situations as well. The amendment reflects the view that it is desirable to protect all litigants from the unfair use of prior convictions, and that the ordinary balancing test of Rule 403, which provides that evidence shall not be excluded unless its prejudicial effect substantially outweighs its probative value, is appropriate for assessing the admissibility of prior convictions for impeachment of any witness other than a criminal defendant.

The amendment reflects a judgment that decisions interpreting Rule 609(a) as requiring a trial court to admit convictions in civil cases that have little, if anything, to do with credibility reach undesirable results. See, e.g., Diggs v. Lyons, 741 F.2d 577 (3d Cir.1984), cert. denied, 105 S.Ct. 2157 (1985). The amendment provides the same protection against unfair prejudice arising from prior convictions used for impeachment purposes as the rules provide for other evidence. The amendment finds support in decided cases. See, e.g., Petty v. Ideco, 761 F.2d 1146 (5th Cir.1985); Czaka v. Hickman, 703 F.2d 317 (8th Cir. 1983).

Fewer decided cases address the question whether Rule 609(a) provides any protection against unduly prejudicial prior convictions used to impeach government witnesses. Some courts have read Rule 609(a) as giving the government no protection for its witnesses. See, e.g., United States v. Thorne, 547 F.2d 56 (8th Cir.1976); United States v. Nevitt, 563 F.2d 406 (9th Cir.1977), cert. denied, 444 U.S. 847 (1979). This approach also is rejected by the amendment. There are cases in which impeachment of government witnesses with prior convictions that have little, if anything, to do with credibility may result in unfair prejudice to the government's interest in a fair trial and unnecessary embarrassment to a witness. Fed.R.Evid. 412 already recognizes this and excluded certain evidence of past sexual behavior in the context of prosecutions for sexual assaults.

The amendment applies the general balancing test of Rule 403 to protect all litigants against unfair impeachment of witnesses. The balancing test protects civil litigants, the government in criminal cases, and the defendant in a criminal case who calls other witnesses. The amendment addresses prior convictions offered under Rule 609, not for other purposes, and does not run afoul, therefore, of Davis v. Alaska, 415 U.S. 308 (1974). Davis involved the use of a prior juvenile adjudication not to prove a past law violation, but to prove bias. The defendant in a criminal case has the right to demonstrate the bias of a witness and to be assured a fair trial, but not to unduly prejudice a trier of fact. See generally Rule 412. In any case in which the trial court believes that confrontation rights require admission of impeachment evidence, obviously the Constitution would take precedence over the rule.

The probability that prior convictions of an ordinary government witness will be unduly prejudicial is low in most criminal cases. Since the behavior of the witness is not the issue in dispute in most cases, there is little chance that the trier of fact will misuse the convictions offered as impeachment evidence as propensity evidence. Thus, trial courts will be skeptical when the government objects to impeachment of its witnesses with prior convictions. Only when the government is able to point to a real danger of prejudice that is sufficient to outweigh substantially the probative value of the conviction for impeachment purposes will the conviction be excluded.

The amendment continues to divide subdivision (a) into subsections (1) and (2) thus facilitating retrieval under current computerized research programs which distinguish the two provisions. The Committee recommended no substantive change in subdivision (a)(2), even though some cases raise a concern about the proper interpretation of the words "dishonesty or false statement." These words were used but not explained in the original Advisory Committee Note accompanying Rule 609. Congress extensively debated the rule, and the Report of the House and Senate Conference Committee states that "[b]y the phrase 'dishonesty and false statement,' the Conference means crimes such as perjury, subornation of perjury, false statement, criminal fraud, embezzlement, or false pretense, or any other offense in the nature of *crimen falsi*, commission of which involves some element of deceit, untruthfulness, or falsification bearing on the accused's propensity to testify truthfully." The Advisory Committee concluded that the Conference Report provides sufficient guidance to trial courts and that no amendment is necessary, notwithstanding some decisions that take an unduly broad view of "dishonesty," admitting convictions such as for bank robbery or bank larceny. Subsection (a)(2) continues to apply to any witness, including a criminal defendant.

Finally, the Committee determined that it was unnecessary to add to the rule language stating that, when a prior conviction is offered under Rule 609, the trial court is to consider the probative value of the prior conviction *for impeachment*, not for other purposes. The Committee concluded that the title of the rule, its first sentence, and its placement among the impeachment rules clearly establish that evidence offered under Rule 609 is offered only for purposes of impeachment.

Rule 610. Religious Beliefs or Opinions

Evidence of the beliefs or opinions of a witness on matters of religion is not admissible for the purpose of showing that by reason of their nature the witness' credibility is impaired or enhanced.

(As amended Mar. 2, 1987, eff. Oct. 1, 1987.)

Section references, McCormick 4th ed.

§ 46

Note by Federal Judicial Center

The rule enacted by the Congress is the rule prescribed by the Supreme Court without change.

Advisory Committee's Note

56 F.R.D. 183, 272

While the rule forecloses inquiry into the religious beliefs or opinions of a witness for the purpose of showing that his character for truthfulness is affected by their nature, an inquiry for the purpose of showing interest or bias because of them is not within the prohibition. Thus disclosure of affiliation with a church which is a party to the litigation would be allowable under the rule. Cf. Tucker v. Reil, 51 Ariz. 357, 77 P.2d 203 (1938). To the same effect, though less specifically worded, is California Evidence Code § 789. See 3 Wigmore § 936.

1987 Amendment. The amendment is technical. No substantive change is intended.

Rule 611. Mode and Order of Interrogation and Presentation

(a) Control by court. The court shall exercise reasonable control over the mode and order of interrogating witnesses and presenting evidence so as to (1) make the interrogation and presentation effective for the ascertainment of the truth, (2) avoid needless consumption of time, and (3) protect witnesses from harassment or undue embarrassment.

(b) Scope of cross-examination. Cross-examination should be limited to the subject matter of the direct examination and matters affecting the credibility of the witness. The court may, in the exercise of discretion, permit inquiry into additional matters as if on direct examination.

(c) Leading questions. Leading questions should not be used on the direct examination of a witness except as may be necessary to develop the witness' testimony. Ordinarily leading questions should be permitted on cross-examination. When a party calls a hostile witness, an adverse party, or a witness identified with an adverse party, interrogation may be by leading questions.

(As amended Mar. 2, 1987, eff. Oct. 1, 1987.)

Section references, McCormick 4th ed.

Generally § 4, § 5, § 16, § 25, § 36, § 56, § 57, § 60

(a). § 4, § 5, § 6, § 7, § 16, § 29, § 32, § 40, § 41, § 42, § 44, § 51, § 52, § 55, § 56, § 58

(b). § 20, § 21, § 22, § 23, § 24, § 25, § 26, § 27, § 29, § 33, § 40, § 134

(c). § 6, § 20, § 25, § 26

Note by Federal Judicial Center

Subdivision (a) of the rule enacted by the Congress is the subdivision prescribed by the Supreme Court, amended only by substituting "court" in place of "judge."

Subdivision (b) of the rule enacted by the Congress is substantially different from the subdivision prescribed by the Supreme Court. The nature of the changes and the reasons therefor are stated in the Report of the House Committee on the Judiciary, set forth below.

The first two sentences of subdivision (c) of the rule enacted by the Congress are the same as prescribed by the Supreme Court. The third sentence has been amended in the manner and for the reasons stated in the Report of the House Committee on the Judiciary, set forth below.

Advisory Committee's Note

56 F.R.D. 183, 273

Subdivision (a). Spelling out detailed rules to govern the mode and order of interrogating witnesses and presenting evidence is neither desirable nor feasible. The ultimate responsibility for the effective working of the adversary system rests with the judge. The rule sets forth the objectives which he should seek to attain.

Item (1) restates in broad terms the power and obligation of the judge as developed under common law principles. It covers such concerns as whether testimony shall be in the form of a free narrative or responses to specific questions, McCormick § 5, the order of calling witnesses and presenting evidence, 6 Wigmore § 1867, the use of demonstrative evidence, McCormick § 179, and the many other questions arising during the course of a trial which can be solved only by the judge's common sense and fairness in view of the particular circumstances.

Item (2) is addressed to avoidance of needless consumption of time, a matter of daily concern in the disposition of cases. A companion piece is found in the discretion vested in the judge to exclude evidence as a waste of time in Rule 403(b).

Item (3) calls for a judgment under the particular circumstances whether interrogation tactics entail harassment or undue embarrassment. Pertinent circumstances include the importance of the testimony, the nature of the inqury, its relevance to credibility, waste of time, and confusion. McCormick § 42. In Alford v. United States, 282 U.S. 687, 694, 51 S.Ct. 218, 75 L.Ed. 624 (1931), the Court pointed out that, while the trial judge should protect the witness from questions which "go beyond the bounds of proper cross-examination merely to harass, annoy or humiliate," this protection by no means forecloses efforts to discredit the witness. Reference to the transcript of the prosecutor's cross-examination in Berger v. United States, 295 U.S. 78, 55 S.Ct. 629, 79 L.Ed. 1314 (1935), serves to lay at rest any doubts as to the need for judicial control in this area.

The inquiry into specific instances of conduct of a witness allowed under Rule 608(b) is, of course, subject to this rule.

Subdivision (b) *. The tradition in the federal courts and in numerous state courts has been to limit the scope of cross-examination to matters testified to on direct, plus matters bearing upon the credibility of the witness. Various reasons have been advanced to justify the rule of limited cross-examination. (1)

* The Advisory Committee's Note to subdivision (b) is from the 1969 Preliminary Draft. 46 F.R.D. 161, 304.—Federal Judicial Center.

A party vouches for his own witness but only to the extent of matters elicited on direct. Resurrection Gold Mining Co. v. Fortune Gold Mining Co., 129 Fed. 668, 675 (8th Cir.1904), quoted in Maguire, Weinstein, et al., Cases on Evidence 277, n. 38 (5th ed. 1965). But the concept of vouching is discredited, and Rule 6–07[607] rejects it. (2) A party cannot ask his own witness leading questions. This is a problem properly solved in terms of what is necessary for a proper development of the testimony rather than by a mechanistic formula similar to the vouching concept. See discussion under subdivision (c). (3) A practice of limited cross-examination promotes orderly presentation of the case. Finch v. Weiner, 109 Conn. 616, 145 Atl. 31 (1929). In the opinion of the Advisory Committee this latter reason has merit. It is apparent, however, that the rule of limited cross-examination thus viewed becomes an aspect of the judge's general control over the mode and order of interrogating witnesses and presenting evidence, to be administered as such. The matter is not one in which involvement at the appellate level is likely to prove fruitful. See, for example, Moyer v. Aetna Life Ins. Co., 126 F.2d 141 (3rd Cir.1942); Butler v. New York Central R. Co., 253 F.2d 281 (7th Cir.1958); United States v. Johnson, 285 F.2d 35 (9th Cir.1960); Union Automobile Indemnity Ass'n v. Capitol Indemnity Ins. Co., 310 F.2d 318 (7th Cir.1962). In view of these considerations, the rule is phrased in terms of a suggestion rather than a mandate to the trial judge.

The qualification "as if on direct examination," applicable when inquiry into additional matters is allowed is designed to terminate at that point the asking of leading questions as a matter of right and to bring into operation subdivision (c) of the rule.

The rule does not purport to determine the extent to which an accused who elects to testify thereby waives his privilege against self-incrimination. The question is a constitutional one, rather than a mere matter of administering the trial. Under United States v. Simmons, 390 U.S. 377 (1968), no general waiver occurs when the accused testifies on such preliminary matters as the validity of a search and seizure or the admissibility of a confession. Rule 1–04(d) [104(d)], supra. When he testifies on the merits, however, can he foreclose inquiry into an aspect or element of the crime by avoiding it on direct? The affirmative answer given in Tucker v. United States, 5 F.2d 818 (8th Cir.1925), is inconsistent with the description of the waiver as extending to "all other relevant facts" in Johnson v. United States, 318 U.S. 189, 195 (1943). See also Brown v. United States, 356 U.S. 148 (1958). The situation of an accused who desires to testify on some but not all counts of a multiple-count indictment is one to be approached, in the first instance at least, as a problem of severance under Rule 14 of the Federal Rules of Criminal Procedure. Cross v. United States, 335 F.2d 987 (D.C.Cir.1964). Cf. United States v. Baker, 262 F.Supp. 657, 686 (D.D.C.1966). In all events, the extent of the waiver of the privilege against self-incrimination ought not to be determined as a by-product of a rule on scope of cross-examination.

Report of House Committee on the Judiciary

House Comm. on Judiciary, Fed.Rules of Evidence, H.R.Rep. No. 650, 93d Cong., 1st Sess., p. 12 (1973); 1974 U.S.Code Cong. & Ad.News 7075, 7085

As submitted by the Court, Rule 611(b) provided:

> A witness may be cross-examined on any matter relevant to any issue in the case, including credibility. In the interests of justice, the judge may limit cross-examination with respect to matters not testified to on direct examination.

The Committee amended this provision to return to the rule which prevails in the federal courts and thirty-nine State jurisdictions. As amended, the Rule is in the text of the 1969 Advisory Committee draft. It limits cross-examination to credibility and to matters testified to on direct examination, unless the judge permits more, in which event the cross-examiner must proceed as if on direct examination. This traditional rule facilitates orderly presentation by each party at trial. Further, in light of existing discovery procedures, there appears to be no need to abandon the traditional rule.

Report of Senate Committee on the Judiciary

Senate Comm. on Judiciary, Fed.Rules of Evidence, S.Rep. No. 1277, 93d Cong., 2d Sess., p. 25 (1974); 1974 U.S.Code Cong. & Ad.News 7051, 7071

Rule 611(b) as submitted by the Supreme Court permitted a broad scope of cross-examination: "cross-examination on any matter relevant to any issue in the case" unless the judge, in the interests of justice, limited the scope of cross-examination.

The House narrowed the Rule to the more traditional practice of limiting cross-examination to the subject matter of direct examination (and credibility), but with discretion in the judge to permit inquiry into additional matters in situations where that would aid in the development of the evidence or otherwise facilitate the conduct of the trial.

The committee agrees with the House amendment. Although there are good arguments in support of broad cross-examination from perspectives of developing all relevant evidence, we believe the factors of insuring an orderly and predictable development of the evidence weigh in favor of the narrower rule, especially when discretion is given to the trial judge to permit inquiry into additional matters. The committee expressly approves this discretion and believes it will permit sufficient flexibility allowing a broader scope of cross-examination whenever appropriate.

The House amendment providing broader discretionary cross-examination permitted inquiry into additional matters only as if on direct examination. As a general rule, we concur with this limitation, however, we would understand that this limitation would not preclude the utilization of leading questions if the conditions of subsection (c) of this rule were met, bearing in mind the judge's discretion in any case to limit the scope of cross-examination.[1]

1. See McCormick on Evidence, §§ 24–26 (especially 24) (2d ed. 1972).

Further, the committee has received correspondence from Federal judges commenting on the applicability of this rule to section 1407 of title 28. It is the committee's judgment that this rule as reported by the House is flexible enough to provide sufficiently broad cross-examination in appropriate situations in multidistrict litigation.

Advisory Committee's Note

56 F.R.D. 183, 275

Subdivision (c). The rule continues the traditional view that the suggestive powers of the leading question are as a general proposition undesirable. Within this tradition, however, numerous exceptions have achieved recognition: The witness who is hostile, unwilling, or biased; the child witness or the adult with communication problems; the witness whose recollection is exhausted; and undisputed preliminary matters. 3 Wigmore §§ 774–778. An almost total unwillingness to reverse for infractions has been manifested by appellate courts. See cases cited in 3 Wigmore § 770. The matter clearly falls within the area of control by the judge over the mode and order of interrogation and presentation and accordingly is phrased in words of suggestion rather than command.

The rule also conforms to tradition in making the use of leading questions on cross-examination a matter of right. The purpose of the qualification "ordinarily" is to furnish a basis for denying the use of leading questions when the cross-examination is cross-examination in form only and not in fact, as for example the "cross-examination" of a party by his own counsel after being called by the opponent (savoring more of re-direct) or of an insured defendant who proves to be friendly to the plaintiff.

The final sentence deals with categories of witnesses automatically regarded and treated as hostile. Rule 43(b) of the Federal Rules of Civil Procedure has included only "an adverse party or an officer, director, or managing agent of a public or private corporation or of a partnership or association which is an adverse party." This limitation virtually to persons whose statements would stand as admissions is believed to be an unduly narrow concept of those who may safely be regarded as hostile without further demonstration. See, for example, Maryland Casualty Co. v. Kador, 225 F.2d 120 (5th Cir.1955), and Degelos v. Fidelity and Casualty Co., 313 F.2d 809 (5th Cir.1963), holding despite the language of Rule 43(b) that an insured fell within it, though not a party in an action under the Louisiana direct action statute. The phrase of the rule, "witness identified with" an adverse party, is designed to enlarge the category of persons thus callable.

Report of House Committee on the Judiciary

House Comm. on Judiciary, Fed.Rules of Evidence, H.R.Rep. No. 650, 93d Cong., 1st Sess., p. 12 (1973); 1974 U.S.Code Cong. & Ad.News 7075, 7086

The third sentence of Rule 611(c) as submitted by the Court provided that:

> In civil cases, a party is entitled to call an adverse party or witness identified with him and interrogate by leading questions.

The Committee amended this Rule to permit leading questions to be used with respect to any hostile witness, not only an adverse party or person identified with such adverse party. The Committee also substituted the word "When" for the phrase "In civil cases" to reflect the possibility that in criminal cases a defendant may be entitled to call witnesses identified with the government, in which event the Committee believed the defendant should be permitted to inquire with leading questions.

Report of Senate Committee on the Judiciary

Senate Comm. on Judiciary, Fed.Rules of Evidence, S.Rep. No. 1277, 93d Cong., 2d Sess., p. 25 (1974); 1974 U.S.Code Cong. & Ad.News 7051, 7072

As submitted by the Supreme Court, the rule provided: "In civil cases, a party is entitled to call an adverse party or witness identified with him and interrogate by leading questions."

The final sentence of subsection (c) was amended by the House for the purpose of clarifying the fact that a "hostile witness"—that is a witness who is hostile in fact—could be subject to interrogation by leading questions. The rule as submitted by the Supreme Court declared certain witnesses hostile as a matter of law and thus subject to interrogation by leading questions without any showing of hostility in fact. These were adverse parties or witnesses identified with adverse parties. However, the wording of the first sentence of subsection (c) while generally prohibiting the use of leading questions on direct examination, also provides "except as may be necessary to develop his testimony." Further, the first paragraph of the Advisory Committee note explaining the subsection makes clear that they intended that leading questions could be asked of a hostile witness or a witness who was unwilling or biased and even though that witness was not associated with an adverse party. Thus, we question whether the House amendment was necessary.

However, concluding that it was not intended to affect the meaning of the first sentence of the subsection and was intended solely to clarify the fact that leading questions are permissible in the interrogation of a witness, who is hostile in fact, the committee accepts that House amendment.

The final sentence of this subsection was also amended by the House to cover criminal as well as civil cases. The committee accepts this amendment, but notes that it may be difficult in criminal cases to determine when a witness is "identified with an adverse party," and thus the rule should be applied with caution.

1987 Amendment. The amendment is technical. No substantive change is intended.

Rule 612. Writing Used to Refresh Memory

Except as otherwise provided in criminal proceedings by section 3500 of title 18, United States Code, if a witness uses a writing to refresh memory for the purpose of testifying, either—

(1) while testifying, or

(2) before testifying, if the court in its discretion determines it is necessary in the interests of justice,

an adverse party is entitled to have the writing produced at the hearing, to inspect it, to cross-examine the witness thereon, and to introduce in evidence those portions which relate to the testimony of the witness. If it is claimed that the writing contains matters not related to the subject matter of the testimony the court shall examine the writing in camera, excise any portions not so related, and order delivery of the remainder to the party entitled thereto. Any portion withheld over objections shall be preserved and made available to the appellate court in the event of an appeal. If a writing is not produced or delivered pursuant to order under this rule, the court shall make any order justice requires, except that in criminal cases when the prosecution elects not to comply, the order shall be one striking the testimony or, if the court in its discretion determines that the interests of justice so require, declaring a mistrial.

(As amended Mar. 2, 1987, eff. Oct. 1, 1987.)

Section references, McCormick 4th ed.

§ 9, § 93, § 97

Note by Federal Judicial Center

The rule enacted by the Congress is the rule prescribed by the Supreme Court, amended by substituting "court" in place of "judge," with appropriate pronominal change, and in the first sentence, by substituting "the writing" in place of "it" before "produced," and by substituting the phrase "(1) while testifying, or (2) before testifying if the court in its discretion determines it is necessary in the interests of justice" in place of "before or while testifying." The reasons for the latter amendment are stated in the Report of the House Committee on the Judiciary, set forth below.

Advisory Committee's Note

56 F.R.D. 183, 277

The treatment of writings used to refresh recollection while on the stand is in accord with settled doctrine. McCormick § 9, p. 15. The bulk of the case law has, however, denied the existence of any right to access by the opponent when the writing is used prior to taking the stand, though the judge may have discretion in the matter. Goldman v. United States, 316 U.S. 129, 62 S.Ct. 993, 86 L.Ed. 1322 (1942); Needelman v. United States, 261 F.2d 802 (5th Cir.1958), cert. dismissed 362 U.S. 600, 80 S.Ct. 960, 4 L.Ed.2d 980, rehearing denied 363 U.S. 858, 80 S.Ct. 1606, 4 L.Ed.2d 1739, Annot., 82 A.L.R.2d 473, 562 and 7 A.L.R.3d 181, 247. An increasing group of cases has repudiated the distinction, People v. Scott, 29 Ill.2d 97, 193 N.E.2d 814 (1963); State v. Mucci, 25 N.J. 423, 136 A.2d 761 (1957); State v. Hunt, 25 N.J. 514, 138 A.2d 1 (1958); State v. Deslovers, 40 R.I. 89, 100 A. 64 (1917), and this position is believed to be correct. As Wigmore put it, "the risk of imposition and the need of safeguard is just as great" in both situations. 3 Wigmore § 762, p. 111. To the same effect is McCormick § 9, p. 17.

The purpose of the phrase "for the purpose of testifying" is to safeguard against using the rule as a pretext for wholesale exploration of an opposing party's files and to insure that access is limited only to those writings which may fairly be said in fact to have an impact upon the testimony of the witness.

The purpose of the rule is the same as that of the *Jencks* statute, 18 U.S.C. § 3500: to promote the search of credibility and memory. The same sensitivity to disclosure of government files may be involved; hence the rule is expressly made subject to the statute, subdivision (a) of which provides: "In any criminal prosecution brought by the United States, no statement or report in the possession of the United States which was made by a Government witness or prospective Government witness (other than the defendant) shall be the subject of subpena, discovery, or inspection until said witness has testified on direct examination in the trial of the case." Items falling within the purview of the statute are producible only as provided by its terms, Palermo v. United States, 360 U.S. 343, 351 (1959), and disclosure under the rule is limited similarly by the statutory conditions. With this limitation in mind, some differences of application may be noted. The *Jencks* statute applies only to statements of witnesses; the rule is not so limited. The statute applies only to criminal cases; the rule applies to all cases. The statute applies only to government witnesses; the rule applies to all witnesses. The statute contains no requirement that the statement be consulted for purposes of refreshment before or while testifying; the rule so requires. Since many writings would qualify under either statute or rule, a substantial overlap exists, but the identity of procedures makes this of no importance.

The consequences of nonproduction by the government in a criminal case are those of the *Jencks* statute, striking the testimony or in exceptional cases a mistrial. 18 U.S.C. § 3500(d). In other cases these alternatives are unduly limited, and such possibilities as contempt, dismissal, finding issues against the offender, and the like are available. See Rule 16(g) of the Federal Rules of Criminal Procedure and Rule 37(b) of the Federal Rules of Civil Procedure for appropriate sanctions.

Report of House Committee on the Judiciary

House Comm. on Judiciary, Fed.Rules of Evidence, H.R.Rep. No. 650, 93d Cong., 1st Sess., p. 13 (1973); 1974 U.S.Code Cong. & Ad.News 7075, 7086

As submitted to Congress, Rule 612 provided that except as set forth in 18 U.S.C. § 3500, if a witness uses a writing to refresh his memory for the purpose of testifying, "either before or while testifying," an adverse party is entitled to have the writing produced at the hearing, to inspect it, to cross-examine the witness on it, and to introduce in evidence those portions relating to the witness' testimony. The Committee amended the Rule so as still to require the production of writings used by a witness while testifying, but to render the production of writings used by a witness to refresh his memory before testifying discretionary with the court in the interests of justice, as is the case under existing federal law. See Goldman v. United States, 316 U.S. 129 (1942). The Committee considered that permitting an adverse party to require the production of writings used before testifying could result in fishing expeditions among a multitude of papers which a witness may have used in preparing for trial.

The Committee intends that nothing in the Rule be construed as barring the assertion of a privilege with respect to writings used by a witness to refresh his memory.

1987 Amendment. The amendment is technical. No substantive change is intended.

Rule 613. Prior Statements of Witnesses

(a) Examining witness concerning prior statement. In examining a witness concerning a prior statement made by the witness, whether written or not, the statement need not be shown nor its contents disclosed to the witness at that time, but on request the same shall be shown or disclosed to opposing counsel.

(b) Extrinsic evidence of prior inconsistent statement of witness. Extrinsic evidence of a prior inconsistent statement by a witness is not admissible unless the witness is afforded an opportunity to explain or deny the same and the opposite party is afforded an opportunity to interrogate the witness thereon, or the interests of justice otherwise require. This provision does not apply to admissions of a party-opponent as defined in rule 801(d)(2).

(As amended Mar. 2, 1987, eff. Oct. 1, 1987; Apr. 25, 1988, eff. Nov. 1, 1988.)

Section references, McCormick 4th ed.

Generally § 34, § 37, § 39

(a). § 28, § 37, § 39

(b). § 37

Note by Federal Judicial Center

The rule enacted by the Congress is the rule prescribed by the Supreme Court, amended only by substituting "nor" in the place of "or" in subdivision (a).

Advisory Committee's Note

56 F.R.D. 183, 278

Subdivision (a). The Queen's Case, 2 Br. & B. 284, 129 Eng.Rep. 976 (1820), laid down the requirement that a cross-examiner, prior to questioning the witness about his own prior statement in writing, must first show it to the witness. Abolished by statute in the country of its origin, the requirement nevertheless gained currency in the United States. The rule abolishes this useless impediment, to cross-examination. Ladd, Some Observations on Credibility: Impeachment of Witnesses, 52 Cornell L.Q. 239, 246–247 (1967); McCormick § 28; 4 Wigmore §§ 1259–1260. Both oral and written statements are included.

The provision for disclosure to counsel is designed to protect against unwarranted insinuations that a statement has been made when the fact is to the contrary.

The rule does not defeat the application of Rule 1002 relating to production of the original when the contents of a writing are sought to be proved. Nor does it defeat the application of Rule 26(b)(3) of the Rules of Civil Procedure, as revised, entitling a person on request to a copy of his own statement, though the operation of the latter may be suspended temporarily.

Subdivision (b). The familiar foundation requirement that an impeaching statement first be shown to the witness before it can be proved by extrinsic evidence is preserved but with some modifications. See Ladd, Some Observations on Credibility: Impeachment of Witnesses, 52 Cornell L.Q. 239, 247 (1967). The traditional insistence that the attention of the witness be directed to the statement on cross-examination is relaxed in favor of simply providing the witness an opportunity to explain and the opposite party an opportunity to examine on the statement, with no specification of any particular time or sequence. Under this procedure, several collusive witnesses can be examined before disclosure of a joint prior inconsistent statement. See Comment to California Evidence Code § 770. Also, dangers of oversight are reduced. See McCormick § 37, p. 68.

In order to allow for such eventualities as the witness becoming unavailable by the time the statement is discovered, a measure of discretion is conferred upon the judge. Similar provisions are found in California Evidence Code § 770 and New Jersey Evidence Rule 22(b).

Under principles of *expression unius* the rule does not apply to impeachment by evidence of prior inconsistent conduct. The use of inconsistent statements to impeach a hearsay declaration is treated in Rule 806.

1987 Amendment. The amendments are technical. No substantive change is intended.

1988 Amendment. The amendment is technical. No substantive change is intended.

Rule 614. Calling and Interrogation of Witnesses by Court

(a) Calling by court. The court may, on its own motion or at the suggestion of a party, call witnesses, and all parties are entitled to cross-examine witnesses thus called.

(b) Interrogation by court. The court may interrogate witnesses, whether called by itself or by a party.

(c) Objections. Objections to the calling of witnesses by the court or to interrogation by it may be made at the time or at the next available opportunity when the jury is not present.

Section references, McCormick 4th ed.

§ 8

Note by Federal Judicial Center

The rule enacted by the Congress is the rule prescribed by the Supreme Court, amended only by substituting "court" in place of "judge," with conforming pronominal changes.

Advisory Committee's Note

56 F.R.D. 183, 279

Subdivision (a). While exercised more frequently in criminal than in civil cases, the authority of the judge to call witnesses is well established. McCormick § 8, p. 14; Maguire, Weinstein, et al., Cases on Evidence 303–304

(5th ed. 1965); 9 Wigmore § 2484. One reason for the practice, the old rule against impeaching one's own witness, no longer exists by virtue of Rule 607, supra. Other reasons remain, however, to justify the continuation of the practice of calling court's witnesses. The right to cross-examine, with all it implies, is assured. The tendency of juries to associate a witness with the party calling him, regardless of technical aspects of vouching, is avoided. And the judge is not imprisoned within the case as made by the parties.

Subdivision (b). The authority of the judge to question witnesses is also well established. McCormick § 8, pp. 12–13; Maguire, Weinstein, et al., Cases on Evidence 737–739 (5th ed. 1965); 3 Wigmore § 784. The authority is, of course, abused when the judge abandons his proper role and assumes that of advocate, but the manner in which interrogation should be conducted and the proper extent of its exercise are not susceptible of formulation in a rule. The omission in no sense precludes courts of review from continuing to reverse for abuse.

Subdivision (c). The provision relating to objections is designed to relieve counsel of the embarrassment attendant upon objecting to questions by the judge in the presence of the jury, while at the same time assuring that objections are made in apt time to afford the opportunity to take possible corrective measures. Compare the "automatic" objection feature of Rule 605 when the judge is called as a witness.

Rule 615. Exclusion of Witnesses

At the request of a party the court shall order witnesses excluded so that they cannot hear the testimony of other witnesses and it may make the order of its own motion. This rule does not authorize exclusion of (1) a party who is a natural person, or (2) an officer or employee of a party which is not a natural person designated as its representative by its attorney, or (3) a person whose presence is shown by a party to be essential to the presentation of the party's cause.

(As amended Mar. 2, 1987, eff. Oct. 1, 1987; Apr. 25, 1988, eff. Nov. 1, 1988; Nov. 18, 1988, Pub.L. 100–690, Title VII, § 7075(a), 102 Stat. 4405.)

Section references, McCormick 4th ed.

§ 50

Note by Federal Judicial Center

The rule enacted by the Congress is the rule prescribed by the Supreme Court, amended only by substituting "court," in place of "judge," with conforming pronominal changes.

Advisory Committee's Note

56 F.R.D. 183, 280

The efficacy of excluding or sequestering witnesses has long been recognized as a means of discouraging and exposing fabrication, inaccuracy, and collusion. 6 Wigmore §§ 1837–1838. The authority of the judge is admitted, the only question being whether the matter is committed to his discretion or one of right. The rule takes the latter position. No time is specified for making the request.

Several categories of persons are excepted. (1) Exclusion of persons who are parties would raise serious problems of confrontation and due process. Under accepted practice they are not subject to exclusion. 6 Wigmore § 1841. (2) As the equivalent of the right of a natural-person party to be present, a party which is not a natural person is entitled to have a representative present. Most of the cases have involved allowing a police officer who has been in charge of an investigation to remain in court despite the fact that he will be a witness. United States v. Infanzon, 235 F.2d 318 (2d Cir.1956); Portomene v. United States, 221 F.2d 582 (5th Cir.1955); Powell v. United States, 208 F.2d 618 (6th Cir.1953); Jones v. United States, 252 F.Supp. 781 (W.D.Okl.1966). Designation of the representative by the attorney rather than by the client may at first glance appear to be an inversion of the attorney-client relationship, but it may be assumed that the attorney will follow the wishes of the client, and the solution is simple and workable. See California Evidence Code § 777. (3) The category contemplates such persons as an agent who handled the transaction being litigated or an expert needed to advise counsel in the management of the litigation. See 6 Wigmore § 1841, n. 4.

Report of Senate Committee on the Judiciary

Senate Comm. on Judiciary, Fed.Rules of Evidence, S.Rep. No. 1277, 93d Cong., 2d Sess., p. 26 (1974); 1974 U.S.Code Cong. & Ad.News 7051, 7072

Many district courts permit government counsel to have an investigative agent at counsel table throughout the trial although the agent is or may be a witness. The practice is permitted as an exception to the rule of exclusion and compares with the situation defense counsel finds himself in—he always has the client with him to consult during the trial. The investigative agent's presence may be extremely important to government counsel, especially when the case is complex or involves some specialized subject matter. The agent, too, having lived with the case for a long time, may be able to assist in meeting trial surprises where the best-prepared counsel would otherwise have difficulty. Yet, it would not seem the Government could often meet the burden under rule 615 of showing that the agent's presence is essential. Furthermore, it could be dangerous to use the agent as a witness as early in the case as possible, so that he might then help counsel as a nonwitness, since the agent's testimony could be needed in rebuttal. Using another, nonwitness agent from the same investigative agency would not generally meet government counsel's needs.

This problem is solved if it is clear that investigative agents are within the group specified under the second exception made in the rule, for "an officer or employee of a party which is not a natural person designated as its representative by its attorney." It is our understanding that this was the intention of the House committee. It is certainly this committee's construction of the rule.

1987 Amendment. The amendment is technical. No substantive change is intended.

1988 Amendment. The amendment is technical. No substantive change is intended.

ARTICLE VII. OPINIONS AND EXPERT TESTIMONY

Rule 701. Opinion Testimony by Lay Witnesses

If the witness is not testifying as an expert, the witness' testimony in the form of opinions or inferences is limited to those opinions or inferences which are (a) rationally based on the perception of the witness and (b) helpful to a clear understanding of the witness' testimony or the determination of a fact in issue.

(As amended Mar. 2, 1987, eff. Oct. 1, 1987.)

Section references, McCormick 4th ed.

§ 11, § 12, § 14, § 35, § 43, § 313

Note by Federal Judicial Center

The rule enacted by the Congress is the rule prescribed by the Supreme Court without change.

Advisory Committee's Note

56 F.R.D. 183, 281

The rule retains the traditional objective of putting the trier of fact in possession of an accurate reproduction of the event.

Limitation (a) is the familiar requirement of first-hand knowledge or observation.

Limitation (b) is phrased in terms of requiring testimony to be helpful in resolving issues. Witnesses often find difficulty in expressing themselves in language which is not that of an opinion or conclusion. While the courts have made concessions in certain recurring situations, necessity as a standard for permitting opinions and conclusions has proved too elusive and too unadaptable to particular situations for purposes of satisfactory judicial administration. McCormick § 11. Moreover, the practical impossibility of determining by rule what is a "fact," demonstrated by a century of litigation of the question of what is a fact for purposes of pleading under the Field Code, extends into evidence also. 7 Wigmore § 1919. The rule assumes that the natural characteristics of the adversary system will generally lead to an acceptable result, since the detailed account carries more conviction than the broad assertion, and a lawyer can be expected to display his witness to the best advantage. If he fails to do so, cross-examination and argument will point up the weakness. See Ladd, Expert Testimony, 5 Vand.L.Rev. 414, 415–417 (1952). If, despite these considerations, attempts are made to introduce meaningless assertions which amount to little more than choosing up sides, exclusion for lack of helpfulness is called for by the rule.

The language of the rule is substantially that of Uniform Rule 56(1). Similar provisions are California Evidence Code § 800; Kansas Code of Civil Procedure § 60–456(a); New Jersey Evidence Rule 56(1).

1987 Amendment. The amendments are technical. No substantive change is intended.

Rule 702. Testimony by Experts

If scientific, technical, or other specialized knowledge will assist the trier of fact to understand the evidence or to determine a fact in issue, a witness qualified as an expert by knowledge, skill, experience, training, or education, may testify thereto in the form of an opinion or otherwise.

Section references, McCormick 4th ed.

§ 12, § 13, § 14, § 202, § 203

Note by Federal Judicial Center

The rule enacted by the Congress is the rule prescribed by the Supreme Court without change.

Advisory Committee's Note

56 F.R.D. 183, 282

An intelligent evaluation of facts is often difficult or impossible without the application of some scientific, technical, or other specialized knowledge. The most common source of this knowledge is the expert witness, although there are other techniques for supplying it.

Most of the literature assumes that experts testify only in the form of opinions. The assumption is logically unfounded. The rule accordingly recognizes that an expert on the stand may give a dissertation or exposition of scientific or other principles relevant to the case, leaving the trier of fact to apply them to the facts. Since much of the criticism of expert testimony has centered upon the hypothetical question, it seems wise to recognize that opinions are not indispensable and to encourage the use of expert testimony in nonopinion form when counsel believes the trier can itself draw the requisite inference. The use of opinions is not abolished by the rule, however. It will continue to be permissible for the expert to take the further step of suggesting the inference which should be drawn from applying the specialized knowledge to the facts. See Rules 703 to 705.

Whether the situation is a proper one for the use of expert testimony is to be determined on the basis of assisting the trier. "There is no more certain test for determining when experts may be used than the common sense inquiry whether the untrained layman would be qualified to determine intelligently and to the best possible degree the particular issue without enlightenment from those having a specialized understanding of the subject involved in the dispute." Ladd, Expert Testimony, 5 Vand.L.Rev. 414, 418 (1952). When opinions are excluded, it is because they are unhelpful and therefore superfluous and a waste of time. 7 Wigmore § 1918.

The rule is broadly phrased. The fields of knowledge which may be drawn upon are not limited merely to the "scientific" and "technical" but extend to all "specialized" knowledge. Similarly, the expert is viewed, not in a narrow sense, but as a person qualified by "knowledge, skill, experience, training, or education." Thus within the scope of the rule are not only experts in the strictest sense of the word, e.g. physicians, physicists, and architects, but also the large group sometimes called "skilled" witnesses, such as bankers or landowners testifying to land values.

Rule 703. Bases of Opinion Testimony by Experts

The facts or data in the particular case upon which an expert bases an opinion or inference may be those perceived by or made known to the expert at or before the hearing. If of a type reasonably relied upon by experts in the particular field in forming opinions or inferences upon the subject, the facts or data need not be admissible in evidence.

(As amended Mar. 2, 1987, eff. Oct. 1, 1987.)

Section references, McCormick 4th ed.

§ 10, § 13, § 14, § 15, § 203, § 208, § 324.3

Note by Federal Judicial Center

The rule enacted by the Congress is the rule prescribed by the Supreme Court without change.

Advisory Committee's Note

56 F.R.D. 183, 283

Facts or data upon which expert opinions are based may, under the rule, be derived from three possible sources. The first is the firsthand observation of the witness, with opinions based thereon traditionally allowed. A treating physician affords an example. Rheingold, The Basis of Medical Testimony, 15 Vand.L.Rev. 473, 489 (1962). Whether he must first relate his observations is treated in Rule 705. The second source, presentation at the trial, also reflects existing practice. The technique may be the familiar hypothetical question or having the expert attend the trial and hear the testimony establishing the facts. Problems of determining what testimony the expert relied upon, when the latter technique is employed and the testimony is in conflict, may be resolved by resort to Rule 705. The third source contemplated by the rule consists of presentation of data to the expert outside of court and other than by his own perception. In this respect the rule is designed to broaden the basis for expert opinions beyond that current in many jurisdictions and to bring the judicial practice into line with the practice of the experts themselves when not in court. Thus a physician in his own practice bases his diagnosis on information from numerous sources and of considerable variety, including statements by patients and relatives, reports and opinions from nurses, technicians and other doctors, hospital records, and X rays. Most of them are admissible in evidence, but only with the expenditure of substantial time in producing and examining various authenticating witnesses. The physician makes life-and-death decisions in reliance upon them. His validation, expertly performed and subject to cross-examination, ought to suffice for judicial purposes. Rheingold, supra, at 531; McCormick § 15. A similar provision is California Evidence Code § 801(b).

The rule also offers a more satisfactory basis for ruling upon the admissibility of public opinion poll evidence. Attention is directed to the validity of the techniques employed rather than to relatively fruitless inquiries whether hearsay is involved. See Judge Feinberg's careful analysis in Zippo Mfg. Co. v. Rogers Imports, Inc., 216 F.Supp. 670 (S.D.N.Y.1963). See also Blum et al., The Art of Opinion Research: A Lawyer's Appraisal of an Emerging Service, 24 U.Chi.L.Rev. 1 (1956); Bonynge, Trademark Surveys and Techniques and Their Use in Litigation, 48 A.B.A.J. 329 (1962); Zeisel, The Uniqueness of Survey Evidence, 45 Cornell L.Q. 322 (1960); Annot., 76 A.L.R.2d 919.

If it be feared that enlargement of permissible data may tend to break down the rules of exclusion unduly, notice should be taken that the rule requires that the facts or data "be of a type reasonably relied upon by experts in the particular field." The language would not warrant admitting in evidence the opinion of an "accidentologist" as to the point of impact in an automobile collision based on statements of bystanders, since this requirement is not satisfied. See Comment, Cal.Law Rev.Comm'n, Recommendation Proposing an Evidence Code 148–150 (1965).

1987 Amendment. The amendment is technical. No substantive change is intended.

Rule 704. Opinion on Ultimate Issue

(a) Except as provided in subdivision (b), testimony in the form of an opinion or inference otherwise admissible is not objectionable because it embraces an ultimate issue to be decided by the trier of fact.

(b) No expert witness testifying with respect to the mental state or condition of a defendant in a criminal case may state an opinion or inference as to whether the defendant did or did not have the mental state or condition constituting an element of the crime charged or of a defense thereto. Such ultimate issues are matters for the trier of fact alone.

(As amended Pub.L. 98–473, Title II, § 406, Oct. 12, 1984, 98 Stat. 2067.)

Section references, McCormick 4th ed.

§ 12, § 14, § 206, § 313

Editorial Note

Subdivision (a) is the entire rule prescribed by the Supreme Court and enacted without change by the Congress when it enacted the Rules of Evidence in 1974, except for the addition of the matter preceding the comma, which was added by the Congress in 1984.

Subdivision (b) was added by the Congress in 1984 as a part of the Insanity Defense Reform Act of 1984. P.L. 98–473, Title II, ch. IV, § 406.

Advisory Committee's Note

56 F.R.D. 183, 284

Subdivision (a).

The basic approach to opinions, lay and expert, in these rules is to admit them when helpful to the trier of fact. In order to render this approach fully effective and to allay any doubt on the subject, the so-called "ultimate issue" rule is specifically abolished by the instant rule.

The older cases often contained strictures against allowing witnesses to express opinions upon ultimate issues, as a particular aspect of the rule against opinions. The rule was unduly restrictive, difficult of application, and generally served only to deprive the trier of fact of useful information. 7 Wigmore §§ 1920, 1921; McCormick § 12. The basis usually assigned for the rule, to prevent the witness from "usurping the province of the jury," is aptly characterized as "empty rhetoric." 7 Wigmore § 1920, p. 17. Efforts to meet the felt needs of particular situations led to odd verbal circumlocutions which were said not to violate the rule. Thus a witness could express his estimate of the criminal responsibility of an accused in terms of sanity or insanity, but not in terms of ability to tell right from wrong or other more modern standard. And in cases of medical causation, witnesses were sometimes required to couch their opinions in cautious phrases of "might or could," rather than "did," though the result was to deprive many opinions of the positiveness to which they were entitled, accompanied by the hazard of a ruling of insufficiency to support a verdict. In other instances the rule was simply disregarded, and, as concessions to need, opinions were allowed upon such matters as intoxication, speed, handwriting, and value, although more precise coincidence with an ultimate issue would scarcely be possible.

Many modern decisions illustrate the trend to abandon the rule completely. People v. Wilson, 25 Cal.2d 341, 153 P.2d 720 (1944), whether abortion necessary to save life of patient; Clifford-Jacobs Forging Co. v. Industrial Comm., 19 Ill.2d 236, 166 N.E.2d 582 (1960), medical causation; Dowling v. L.H. Shattuck, Inc., 91 N.H. 234, 17 A.2d 529 (1941), proper method of shoring ditch; Schweiger v. Solbeck, 191 Or. 454, 230 P.2d 195 (1951), cause of landslide. In each instance the opinion was allowed.

The abolition of the ultimate issue rule does not lower the bars so as to admit all opinions. Under Rules 701 and 702, opinions must be helpful to the trier of fact, and Rule 403 provides for exclusion of evidence which wastes time. These provisions afford ample assurances against the admission of opinions which would merely tell the jury what result to reach, somewhat in the manner of the oath-helpers of an earlier day. They also stand ready to exclude opinions phrased in terms of inadequately explored legal criteria. Thus the question,

"Did T have capacity to make a will?" would be excluded, while the question, "Did T have sufficient mental capacity to know the nature and extent of his property and the natural objects of his bounty and to formulate a rational scheme of distribution?" would be allowed. McCormick § 12.

For similar provisions see Uniform Rule 56(4); California Evidence Code § 805; Kansas Code of Civil Procedure § 60–456(d); New Jersey Evidence Rule 56(3).

Report of House Committee on the Judiciary

H.R. Report 98–1030, 98th Cong., 2d Sess., p. 230; 1984 U.S.Code Cong. & Ad.News 232 (Legislative History)

Subdivision (b).

The purpose of this amendment is to eliminate the confusing spectacle of competing expert witnesses testifying to directly contradictory conclusions as to the ultimate legal issue to be found by the trier of fact. Under this proposal, expert psychiatric testimony would be limited to presenting and explaining their diagnosis, such as whether the defendant had a severe mental disease or defect and what the characteristics of such a disease or defect, if any, may have been. * * *

Rule 705. Disclosure of Facts or Data Underlying Expert Opinion

The expert may testify in terms of opinion or inference and give reasons therefor without prior disclosure of the underlying facts or data, unless the court requires otherwise. The expert may in any event be required to disclose the underlying facts or data on cross-examination.

(As amended Mar. 2, 1987, eff. Oct. 1, 1987.)

Section references, McCormick 4th ed.

§ 13, § 14, § 15, § 16, § 31, § 324.3

Note by Federal Judicial Center

The rule enacted by the Congress is the rule prescribed by the Supreme Court, amended only by substituting "court" in place of "judge."

Advisory Committee's Note

56 F.R.D. 183, 285

The hypothetical question has been the target of a great deal of criticism as encouraging partisan bias, affording an opportunity for summing up in the middle of the case, and as complex and time consuming. Ladd, Expert Testimony, 5 Vand.L.Rev. 414, 426–427 (1952). While the rule allows counsel to make disclosure of the underlying facts or data as a preliminary to the giving of an expert opinion, if he chooses, the instances in which he is required to do so are reduced. This is true whether the expert bases his opinion on data furnished him at secondhand or observed by him at firsthand.

The elimination of the requirement of preliminary disclosure at the trial of underlying facts or data has a long background of support. In 1937 the Commissioners on Uniform State Laws incorporated a provision to this effect in their Model Expert Testimony Act, which furnished the basis for Uniform Rules 57 and 58. Rule 4515, N.Y.CPLR (McKinney 1963), provides:

> "Unless the court orders otherwise, questions calling for the opinion of an expert witness need not be hypothetical in form, and the witness may state his opinion and reasons without first specifying the data upon which it is based. Upon cross-examination, he may be required to specify the data . . . ."

See also California Evidence Code § 802; Kansas Code of Civil Procedure §§ 60–456, 60–457; New Jersey Evidence Rules 57, 58.

If the objection is made that leaving it to the cross-examiner to bring out the supporting data is essentially unfair, the answer is that he is under no compulsion to bring out any facts or data except those unfavorable to the opinion. The answer assumes that the cross-examiner has the advance knowledge which is essential for effective cross-examination. This advance knowledge has been afforded, though imperfectly, by the traditional foundation requirement. Rule 26(b)(4) of the Rules of Civil Procedure, as revised, provides for substantial discovery in this area, obviating in large measure the obstacles which have been raised in some instances to discovery of findings, underlying data, and even the identity of the experts. Friedenthal, Discovery and Use of an Adverse Party's Expert Information, 14 Stan.L.Rev. 455 (1962).

These safeguards are reinforced by the discretionary power of the judge to require preliminary disclosure in any event.

1987 Amendment. The amendment is technical. No substantive change is intended.

Rule 706. Court Appointed Experts

(a) Appointment. The court may on its own motion or on the motion of any party enter an order to show cause why expert witnesses should not be appointed, and may request the parties to submit nominations. The court may appoint any expert witnesses agreed upon by the parties, and may appoint expert witnesses of its own selection. An expert witness shall not be appointed by the court unless the witness consents to act. A witness so appointed shall be informed of the witness' duties by the court in writing, a copy of which shall be filed with the clerk, or at a conference in which the parties shall have opportunity to participate. A witness so appointed shall advise the parties of the witness' findings, if any; the witness' deposition may be taken by any party; and the witness may be called to testify by the court or any party. The witness shall be subject to cross-examination by each party, including a party calling the witness.

(b) Compensation. Expert witnesses so appointed are entitled to reasonable compensation in whatever sum the court may allow. The compensation thus fixed is payable from funds which may be provided by law in criminal cases and civil actions and proceedings involving just compensation under the fifth amendment. In other civil actions and proceedings the compensation shall be paid by the parties in such proportion and at such time as the court directs, and thereafter charged in like manner as other costs.

(c) Disclosure of appointment. In the exercise of its discretion, the court may authorize disclosure to the jury of the fact that the court appointed the expert witness.

(d) Parties' experts of own selection. Nothing in this rule limits the parties in calling expert witnesses of their own selection.

(As amended Mar. 2, 1987, eff. Oct. 1, 1987.)

Section references, McCormick 4th ed.

§ 8, § 17

Note by Federal Judicial Center

The rule enacted by the Congress is the rule prescribed by the Supreme Court, amended by substituting "court" in place of "judge," with conforming pronominal changes, and, in subdivision (b), by substituting the phrase "and civil actions and proceedings" in place of "and cases" before "involving" in the second sentence.

Advisory Committee's Note

56 F.R.D. 183, 286

The practice of shopping for experts, the venality of some experts, and the reluctance of many reputable experts to involve themselves in litigation, have been matters of deep concern. Though the contention is made that court appointed experts acquire an aura of infallibility to which they are not entitled, Levy, Impartial Medical Testimony—Revisited, 34 Temple L.Q. 416 (1961), the trend is increasingly to provide for their use. While experience indicates that actual appointment is a relatively infrequent occurrence, the assumption may be made that the availability of the procedure in itself decreases the need for resorting to it. The ever-present possibility that the judge *may* appoint an expert in a given case must inevitably exert a sobering effect on the expert witness of a party and upon the person utilizing his services.

The inherent power of a trial judge to appoint an expert of his own choosing is virtually unquestioned. Scott v. Spanjer Bros., Inc., 298 F.2d 928 (2d Cir.1962); Danville Tobacco Assn. v. Bryant-Buckner Associates, Inc., 333 F.2d 202 (4th Cir.1964); Sink, The Unused Power of a Federal Judge to Call His Own Expert Witnesses, 29 S.Cal.L.Rev. 195 (1956); 2 Wigmore § 563, 9 id. § 2484; Annot., 95 A.L.R.2d 383. Hence the problem becomes largely one of detail.

The New York plan is well known and is described in Report by Special Committee of the Association of the Bar of the City of New York: Impartial Medical Testimony (1956). On recommendation of the Section of Judicial Administration, local adoption of an impartial medical plan was endorsed by the American Bar Association. 82 A.B.A.Rep. 184–185 (1957). Descriptions and analyses of plans in effect in various parts of the country are found in Van Dusen, A United States District Judge's View of the Impartial Medical Expert

System, 32 F.R.D. 498 (1963); Wick and Kightlinger, Impartial Medical Testimony Under the Federal Civil Rules: A Tale of Three Doctors, 34 Ins. Counsel J. 115 (1967); and numerous articles collected in Klein, Judicial Administration and the Legal Profession 393 (1963). Statutes and rules include California Evidence Code §§ 730–733; Illinois Supreme Court Rule 215(d), Ill.Rev.Stat. 1969, c. 110A, § 215(d); Burns Indiana Stats.1956, § 9–1702; Wisconsin Stats. Annot.1958, § 957.27.

In the federal practice, a comprehensive scheme for court appointed experts was initiated with the adoption of Rule 28 of the Federal Rules of Criminal Procedure in 1946. The Judicial Conference of the United States in 1953 considered court appointed experts in civil cases, but only with respect to whether they should be compensated from public funds, a proposal which was rejected. Report of the Judicial Conference of the United States 23 (1953). The present rule expands the practice to include civil cases.

Subdivision (a) is based on Rule 28 of the Federal Rules of Criminal Procedure, with a few changes, mainly in the interest of clarity. Language has been added to provide specifically for the appointment either on motion of a party or on the judge's own motion. A provision subjecting the court appointed expert to deposition procedures has been incorporated. The rule has been revised to make definite the right of any party, including the party calling him, to cross-examine.

Subdivision (b) combines the present provision for compensation in criminal cases with what seems to be a fair and feasible handling of civil cases, originally found in the Model Act and carried from there into Uniform Rule 60. See also California Evidence Code §§ 730–731. The special provision for Fifth Amendment compensation cases is designed to guard against reducing constitutionally guaranteed just compensation by requiring the recipient to pay costs. See Rule 71A(*l*) of the Rules of Civil Procedure.

Subdivision (c) seems to be essential if the use of court appointed experts is to be fully effective. Uniform Rule 61 so provides.

Subdivision (d) is in essence the last sentence of Rule 28(a) of the Federal Rules of Criminal Procedure.

1987 Amendment. The amendments are technical. No substantive change is intended.

ARTICLE VIII. HEARSAY

Advisory Committee's Note

INTRODUCTORY NOTE: THE HEARSAY PROBLEM

The factors to be considered in evaluating the testimony of a witness are perception, memory, and narration. Morgan, Hearsay Dangers and the Application of the Hearsay Concept, 62 Harv.L.Rev. 177 (1948), Selected Writings on Evidence and Trial 764, 765 (Fryer ed. 1957); Shientag, Cross-Examination—A Judge's Viewpoint, 3 Record 12 (1948); Strahorn, A Reconsideration of the Hearsay Rule and Admissions, 85 U.Pa.L.Rev. 484, 485 (1937), Selected Writings, supra, 756, 757; Weinstein, Probative Force of Hearsay, 46 Iowa L.Rev. 331 (1961). Sometimes a fourth is added, sincerity, but in fact it seems merely to be an aspect of the three already mentioned.

In order to encourage the witness to do his best with respect to each of these factors, and to expose any inaccuracies which may enter in, the Anglo-American tradition has evolved three conditions under which witnesses will ideally be required to testify: (1) under oath, (2) in the personal presence of the trier of fact, (3) subject to cross-examination.

(1) Standard procedure calls for the swearing of witnesses. While the practice is perhaps less effective than in an earlier time, no disposition to relax the requirement is apparent, other than to allow affirmation by persons with scruples against taking oaths.

(2) The demeanor of the witness traditionally has been believed to furnish trier and opponent with valuable clues. Universal Camera Corp. v. N.L.R.B., 340 U.S. 474, 495–496, 71 S.Ct. 456, 95 L.Ed. 456 (1951); Sahm, Demeanor Evidence: Elusive and Intangible Imponderables, 47 A.B.A.J. 580 (1961), quoting numerous authorities. The witness himself will probably be impressed with the solemnity of the occasion and the possibility of public disgrace. Willingness to falsify may reasonably become more difficult in the presence of the person against whom directed. Rules 26 and 43(a) of the Federal Rules of Criminal and Civil Procedure, respectively, include the general requirement that testimony be taken orally in open court. The Sixth Amendment right of confrontation is a manifestation of these beliefs and attitudes.

(3) Emphasis on the basis of the hearsay rule today tends to center upon the condition of cross-examination. All may not agree with Wigmore that cross-examination is "beyond doubt the greatest legal engine ever invented for the discovery of truth," but all will agree with his statement that it has become a "vital feature" of the Anglo-American system. 5 Wigmore, § 1367, p. 29. The belief, or perhaps hope, that cross-examination, is effective in exposing imperfections of perception, memory, and narration is fundamental. Morgan, Foreword to Model Code of Evidence 37 (1942).

The logic of the preceding discussion might suggest that no testimony be received unless in full compliance with the three ideal conditions. No one advocates this position. Common sense tells that much evidence which is not given under the three conditions may be inherently superior to much that is. Moreover, when the choice is between evidence which is less than best and no evidence at all, only clear folly would dictate an across-the-board policy of doing without. The problem thus resolves itself into effecting a sensible accommodation between these considerations and the desirability of giving testimony under the ideal conditions.

The solution evolved by the common law has been a general rule excluding hearsay but subject to numerous exceptions under circumstances supposed to furnish guarantees of trustworthiness. Criticisms of this scheme are that it is bulky and complex, fails to screen good from bad hearsay realistically, and inhibits the growth of the law of evidence.

Since no one advocates excluding all hearsay, three possible solutions may be considered: (1) abolish the rule against hearsay and admit all hearsay; (2) admit hearsay possessing sufficient probative force, but with procedural safeguards; (3) revise the present system of class exceptions.

(1) Abolition of the hearsay rule would be the simplest solution. The effect would not be automatically to abolish the giving of testimony under ideal conditions. If the declarant were available, compliance with the ideal conditions would be optional with either party. Thus the proponent could call the declarant as a witness as a form of presentation more impressive than his hearsay statement. Or the opponent could call the declarant to be cross-

examined upon his statement. This is the tenor of Uniform Rule 63(1), admitting the hearsay declaration of a person "who is present at the hearing and available for cross-examination." Compare the treatment of declarations of available declarants in Rule 801(d)(1) of the instant rules. If the declarant were unavailable, a rule of free admissibility would make no distinctions in terms of degrees of noncompliance with the ideal conditions and would exact no quid pro quo in the form of assurances of trustworthiness. Rule 503 of the Model Code did exactly that, providing for the admissibility of any hearsay declaration by an unavailable declarant, finding support in the Massachusetts act of 1898, enacted at the instance of Thayer, Mass.Gen.L.1932, c. 233 § 65, and in the English act of 1938, St.1938, c. 28, Evidence. Both are limited to civil cases. The draftsmen of the Uniform Rules chose a less advanced and more conventional position. Comment, Uniform Rule 63. The present Advisory Committee has been unconvinced of the wisdom of abandoning the traditional requirement of some particular assurance of credibility as a condition precedent to admitting the hearsay declaration of an unavailable declarant.

In criminal cases, the Sixth Amendment requirement of confrontation would no doubt move into a large part of the area presently occupied by the hearsay rule in the event of the abolition of the latter. The resultant split between civil and criminal evidence is regarded as an undesirable development.

(2) Abandonment of the system of class exceptions in favor of individual treatment in the setting of the particular case, accompanied by procedural safeguards, has been impressively advocated. Weinstein, The Probative Force of Hearsay, 46 Iowa L.Rev. 331 (1961). Admissibility would be determined by weighing the probative force of the evidence against the possibility of prejudice, waste of time, and the availability of more satisfactory evidence. The bases of the traditional hearsay exceptions would be helpful in assessing probative force. Ladd, The Relationship of the Principles of Exclusionary Rules of Evidence to the Problem of Proof, 18 Minn.L.Rev. 506 (1934). Procedural safeguards would consist of notice of intention to use hearsay, free comment by the judge on the weight of the evidence, and a greater measure of authority in both trial and appellate judges to deal with evidence on the basis of weight. The Advisory Committee has rejected this approach to hearsay as involving too great a measure of judicial discretion, minimizing the predictability of rulings, enhancing the difficulties of preparation for trial, adding a further element to the already over-complicated congeries of pretrial procedures, and requiring substantially different rules for civil and criminal cases. The only way in which the probative force of hearsay differs from the probative force of other testimony is in the absence of oath, demeanor, and cross-examination as aids in determining credibility. For a judge to exclude evidence because he does not believe it has been described as "altogether atypical, extraordinary. . . ." Chadbourn, Bentham and the Hearsay Rule—A Benthamic View of Rule 63(4)(c) of the Uniform Rules of Evidence, 75 Harv.L.Rev. 932, 947 (1962).

(3) The approach to hearsay in these rules is that of the common law, i.e., a general rule excluding hearsay, with exceptions under which evidence is not required to be excluded even though hearsay. The traditional hearsay exceptions are drawn upon for the exceptions, collected under two rules, one dealing with situations where availability of the declarant is regarded as immaterial and the other with those where unavailability is made a condition to the admission of the hearsay statement. Each of the two rules concludes with a

provision for hearsay statements not within one of the specified exceptions "but having comparable [equivalent] circumstantial guarantees of trustworthiness." Rules 803(24) and 804(b)(6)[5]. This plan is submitted as calculated to encourage growth and development in this area of the law, while conserving the values and experience of the past as a guide to the future.

CONFRONTATION AND DUE PROCESS

Until very recently, decisions invoking the confrontation clause of the Sixth Amendment were surprisingly few, a fact probably explainable by the former inapplicability of the clause to the states and by the hearsay rule's occupancy of much the same ground. The pattern which emerges from the earlier cases invoking the clause is substantially that of the hearsay rule, applied to criminal cases: an accused is entitled to have the witnesses against him testify under oath, in the presence of himself and trier, subject to cross-examination; yet considerations of public policy and necessity require the recognition of such exceptions as dying declarations and former testimony of unavailable witnesses. Mattox v. United States, 156 U.S. 237, 15 S.Ct. 337, 39 L.Ed. 409 (1895); Motes v. United States, 178 U.S. 458, 20 S.Ct. 993, 44 L.Ed. 1150 (1900); Delaney v. United States, 263 U.S. 586, 44 S.Ct. 206, 68 L.Ed. 462 (1924). Beginning with Snyder v. Massachusetts, 291 U.S. 97, 54 S.Ct. 330, 78 L.Ed. 674 (1934), the Court began to speak of confrontation as an aspect of procedural due process, thus extending its applicability to state cases and to federal cases other than criminal. The language of *Snyder* was that of an elastic concept of hearsay. The deportation case of Bridges v. Wixon, 326 U.S. 135, 65 S.Ct. 1443, 89 L.Ed. 2103 (1945), may be read broadly as imposing a strictly construed right of confrontation in all kinds of cases or narrowly as the product of a failure of the Immigration and Naturalization Service to follow its own rules. In re Oliver, 333 U.S. 257, 68 S.Ct. 499, 92 L.Ed. 682 (1948), ruled that cross-examination was essential to due process in a state contempt proceeding, but in United States v. Nugent, 346 U.S. 1, 73 S.Ct. 991, 97 L.Ed. 1417 (1953), the court held that it was not an essential aspect of a "hearing" for a conscientious objector under the Selective Service Act. Stein v. New York, 346 U.S. 156, 196, 73 S.Ct. 1077, 97 L.Ed. 1522 (1953), disclaimed any purpose to read the hearsay rule into the Fourteenth Amendment, but in Greene v. McElroy, 360 U.S. 474, 79 S.Ct. 1400, 3 L.Ed.2d 1377 (1959), revocation of security clearance without confrontation and cross-examination was held unauthorized, and a similar result was reached in Willner v. Committee on Character, 373 U.S. 96, 83 S.Ct. 1175, 10 L.Ed.2d 224 (1963). Ascertaining the constitutional dimensions of the confrontation-hearsay aggregate against the background of these cases is a matter of some difficulty, yet the general pattern is at least not inconsistent with that of the hearsay rule.

In 1965 the confrontation clause was held applicable to the states. Pointer v. Texas, 380 U.S. 400, 85 S.Ct. 1065, 13 L.Ed.2d 923 (1965). Prosecution use of former testimony given at a preliminary hearing where petitioner was not represented by counsel was a violation of the clause. The same result would have followed under conventional hearsay doctrine read in the light of a constitutional right to counsel, and nothing in the opinion suggests any difference in essential outline between the hearsay rule and the right of confrontation. In the companion case of Douglas v. Alabama, 380 U.S. 415, 85 S.Ct. 1074, 13 L.Ed.2d 934 (1965), however, the result reached by applying the confrontation clause is one reached less readily via the hearsay rule. A confession implicating petitioner was put before the jury by reading it to the witness in portions and asking if he made that statement. The witness refused to answer on grounds of self-incrimination. The result, said the Court, was to deny cross-examination, and hence confrontation. True, it could broadly be said that the confession was a hearsay statement which for all practical purposes was put in evidence. Yet a more easily accepted explanation of the opinion is that its real thrust was in the direction of curbing undesirable prosecutorial behavior, rather than merely applying rules of exclusion, and that the confrontation clause was the means selected to achieve this end. Comparable facts and a like result appeared in Brookhart v. Janis, 384 U.S. 1, 86 S.Ct. 1245, 16 L.Ed.2d 314 (1966).

The pattern suggested in *Douglas* was developed further and more distinctly in a pair of cases at the end of the 1966 term. United States v. Wade, 388 U.S. 218, 87 S.Ct. 1926, 18 L.Ed.2d 1149 (1967), and Gilbert v. California, 388 U.S. 263, 87 S.Ct. 1951, 18 L.Ed.2d 1178 (1967), hinged upon practices followed in identifying accused persons before trial. This pretrial identification was said to be so decisive an aspect of the case that accused was entitled to have counsel present; a pretrial identification made in the absence of counsel was not itself receivable in evidence and, in addition, might fatally infect a courtroom identification. The presence of counsel at the earlier identification was described as a necessary prerequisite for "a meaningful confrontation at trial." United States v. Wade, supra, 388 U.S. at p. 236, 87 S.Ct. at p. 1937. *Wade* involved no evidence of the fact of a prior identification and hence was not susceptible of being decided on hearsay grounds. In *Gilbert,* witnesses did testify to an earlier identification, readily classifiable as hearsay under a fairly strict view of what constitutes hearsay. The Court, however, carefully avoided basing the decision on the hearsay ground, choosing confrontation instead. 388 U.S. 263, 272, n. 3, 87 S.Ct. 1951. See also Parker v. Gladden, 385 U.S. 363, 87 S.Ct. 468, 17 L.Ed.2d 420 (1966), holding that the right of confrontation was violated when the baliff made prejudicial statements to jurors, and Note, 75 Yale L.J. 1434 (1966).

Under the earlier cases, the confrontation clause may have been little more than a constitutional embodiment of the hearsay rule, even including traditional exceptions but with some room for expanding them along similar lines. But under the recent cases the impact of the clause clearly extends beyond the confines of the hearsay rule. These considerations have led the Advisory Committee to conclude that a hearsay rule can function usefully as an adjunct to the confrontation right in constitutional areas and independently in nonconstitutional areas. In recognition of the separateness of the confrontation clause and the hearsay rule, and to avoid inviting collisions between them or between the hearsay rule and other exclusionary principles, the exceptions set forth in Rules 803 and 804 are stated in terms of exemption from the general exclusionary mandate of the hearsay rule, rather than in positive terms of admissibility. See Uniform Rule 63(1) to (31) and California Evidence Code §§ 1200–1340.

Rule 801. Definitions

The following definitions apply under this article:

(a) Statement. A "statement" is (1) an oral or written assertion or (2) nonverbal conduct of a person, if it is intended by the person as an assertion.

(b) Declarant. A "declarant" is a person who makes a statement.

(c) Hearsay. "Hearsay" is a statement, other than one made by the declarant while testifying at the trial or hearing, offered in evidence to prove the truth of the matter asserted.

(d) Statements which are not hearsay. A statement is not hearsay if—

(1) Prior statement by witness. The declarant testifies at the trial or hearing and is subject to cross-examination concerning the statement, and the statement is (A) inconsistent with the declarant's testimony, and was given under oath subject to the penalty of perjury at a trial, hearing, or other proceeding, or in a deposition, or (B) consistent with the declarant's testimony and is offered to rebut an express or implied charge against the declarant of recent fabrication or improper influence or motive, or (C) one of identification of a person made after perceiving the person; or

(2) Admission by party-opponent. The statement is offered against a party and is (A) the party's own statement, in either an individual or a representative capacity or (B) a statement of which the party has manifested an adoption or belief in its truth, or (C) a statement by a person authorized by the party to make a statement concerning the subject, or (D) a statement by the party's agent or servant concerning a matter within the scope of the agency or employment, made during the existence of the relationship, or (E) a statement by a coconspirator of a party during the course and in furtherance of the conspiracy.

(As amended Pub.L. 94–113, § 1, Oct. 16, 1975, 89 Stat. 576; Mar. 2, 1987, eff. Oct. 1, 1987.)

Section references, McCormick 4th ed.

General. § 246

(a). § 250

(c). § 245

(d)(1). § 34, § 36, § 37, § 36, § 251, § 324.1, § 326

(A). § 50, § 324.3

(B). § 47, § 324.3

(C). § 251

(d)(2). § 35, § 144, § 160, § 254, § 255, § 256

(A). § 251, § 263, § 264, § 265

(B). § 251, § 259, § 261, § 262

(C). § 251, § 259

(D). § 255, § 259

(E). § 53, § 259

Note by Federal Judicial Center

The rule enacted by the Congress is the rule prescribed by the Supreme Court, with [an] amendment[s] to subdivision (d)(1). The amendment[s] inserted in item (A), after "testimony," [adds] the phrase "and was given under oath subject to the penalty of perjury at a trial, hearing, or other proceeding, or in a deposition." The reasons for [the] amendment[s] are stated in the Report of the House Committee on the Judiciary, the Report of the Senate Committee on the Judiciary, and the Conference Report, set forth below.

Advisory Committee's Note

56 F.R.D. 183, 293

Subdivision (a). The definition of "statement" assumes importance because the term is used in the definition of hearsay in subdivision (c). The effect of the definition of "statement" is to exclude from the operation of the hearsay rule all evidence of conduct, verbal or nonverbal, not intended as an assertion. The key to the definition is that nothing is an assertion unless intended to be one.

It can scarcely be doubted that an assertion made in words is intended by the declarant to be an assertion. Hence verbal assertions readily fall into the category of "statement." Whether nonverbal conduct should be regarded as a statement for purposes of defining hearsay requires further consideration. Some nonverbal conduct, such as the act of pointing to identify a suspect in a lineup, is clearly the equivalent of words, assertive in nature, and to be regarded as a statement. Other nonverbal conduct, however, may be offered as evidence that the person acted as he did because of his belief in the existence of the condition sought to be proved, from which belief the existence of the condition may be inferred. This sequence is, arguably, in effect an assertion of the existence of the condition and hence properly includable within the hearsay concept. See Morgan, Hearsay Dangers and the Application of the Hearsay Concept, 62 Harv.L.Rev. 177, 214, 217 (1948), and the elaboration in Finman, Implied Assertions as Hearsay: Some Criticisms of the Uniform Rules of Evidence, 14 Stan.L.Rev. 682 (1962). Admittedly evidence of this character is untested with respect to the perception, memory, and narration (or their equivalents) of the actor, but the Advisory Committee is of the view that these dangers are minimal in the absence of an intent to assert and do not justify the loss of the evidence on hearsay grounds. No class of evidence is free of the possibility of fabrication, but the likelihood is less with nonverbal than with assertive verbal conduct. The situations giving rise to the nonverbal conduct are such as virtually to eliminate questions of sincerity. Motivation, the nature of the conduct, and the presence or absence of reliance will bear heavily upon the weight to be given the evidence. Falknor, The "Hear-Say" Rule as a "See-Do" Rule: Evidence of Conduct, 33 Rocky Mt.L.Rev. 133 (1961). Similar considerations govern nonassertive verbal conduct and verbal conduct which is assertive but offered as a basis for inferring something other than the matter asserted, also excluded from the definition of hearsay by the language of subdivision (c).

When evidence of conduct is offered on the theory that it is not a statement, and hence not hearsay, a preliminary determination will be required to determine whether an assertion is intended. The rule is so worded as to place the burden upon the party claiming that the intention existed; ambiguous and doubtful cases will be resolved against him and in favor of admissibility. The determination involves no greater difficulty than many other preliminary questions of fact. Maguire, The Hearsay System: Around and Through the Thicket, 14 Vand.L.Rev. 741, 765–767 (1961).

For similar approaches, see Uniform Rule 62(1); California Evidence Code §§ 225, 1200; Kansas Code of Civil Procedure § 60–459(a); New Jersey Evidence Rule 62(1).

Subdivision (c). The definition follows along familiar lines in including only statements offered to prove the truth of the matter asserted. McCormick § 225; 5 Wigmore § 1361, 6 id. § 1766. If the significance of an offered statement lies solely in the fact that it was made, no issue is raised as to the truth of anything asserted, and the statement is not hearsay. Emich Motors Corp. v. General Motors Corp., 181 F.2d 70 (7th Cir.1950), rev'd on other grounds 340 U.S. 558, 71 S.Ct. 408, 95 L.Ed. 534, letters of complaint from customers offered as a reason for cancellation of dealer's franchise, to rebut contention that franchise was revoked for refusal to finance sales through affiliated finance company. The effect is to exclude from hearsay the entire category of "verbal acts" and "verbal parts of an act," in which the statement itself affects the legal rights of the parties or is a circumstance bearing on conduct affecting their rights.

The definition of hearsay must, of course, be read with reference to the definition of statement set forth in subdivision (a).

Testimony given by a witness in the course of court proceedings is excluded since there is compliance with all the ideal conditions for testifying.

Subdivision (d). Several types of statements which would otherwise literally fall within the definition are expressly excluded from it:

(1) *Prior statement by witness.* Considerable controversy has attended the question whether a prior out-of-court statement by a person now available for cross-examination concerning it, under oath and in the presence of the trier of fact, should be classed as hearsay. If the witness admits on the stand that he made the statement and that it was true, he adopts the statement and there is no hearsay problem. The hearsay problem arises when the witness on the stand denies having made the statement or admits having made it but denies its truth. The argument in favor of treating these latter statements as hearsay is based upon the ground that the conditions of oath, cross-examination, and demeanor observation did not prevail at the time the statement was made and cannot adequately be supplied by the later examination. The logic of the situation is troublesome. So far as concerns the oath, its mere presence has never been regarded as sufficient to remove a statement from the hearsay category, and it receives much less emphasis than cross-examination as a truth-compelling device. While strong expressions are found to the effect that no conviction can be had or important right taken away on the basis of statements not made under fear of prosecution for perjury, Bridges v. Wixon, 326 U.S. 135, 65 S.Ct. 1443, 89 L.Ed. 2103 (1945), the fact is that, of the many common law exceptions to the hearsay rule, only that for reported testimony has required the statement to have been made under oath. [It should be noted, however, that rule 801(d)(1)(A), as enacted by the Congress, requires that a prior inconsistent statement have been made under oath.] Nor is it satisfactorily explained why cross-examination cannot be conducted subsequently with success. The

decisions contending most vigorously for its inadequacy in fact demonstrate quite thorough exploration of the weaknesses and doubts attending the earlier statement. State v. Saporen, 205 Minn. 358, 285 N.W. 898 (1939); Ruhala v. Roby, 379 Mich. 102, 150 N.W.2d 146 (1967); People v. Johnson, 68 Cal.2d 646, 68 Cal.Rptr. 599, 441 P.2d 111 (1968). In respect to demeanor, as Judge Learned Hand observed in Di Carlo v. United States, 6 F.2d 364 (2d Cir.1925), when the jury decides that the truth is not what the witness says now, but what he said before, they are still deciding from what they see and hear in court. The bulk of the case law nevertheless has been against allowing prior statements of witnesses to be used generally as substantive evidence. Most of the writers and Uniform Rule 63(1) have taken the opposite position.

The position taken by the Advisory Committee in formulating this part of the rule is founded upon an unwillingness to countenance the general use of prior prepared statements as substantive evidence, but with a recognition that particular circumstances call for a contrary result. The judgment is one more of experience than of logic. The rule requires in each instance, as a general safeguard, that the declarant actually testify as a witness, and it then enumerates three situations in which the statement is excepted from the category of hearsay. Compare Uniform Rule 63(1) which allows any out-of-court statement of a declarant who is present at the trial and available for cross-examination.

(A) Prior inconsistent statements traditionally have been admissible to impeach but not as substantive evidence. Under the rule they are substantive evidence. As has been said by the California Law Revision Commission with respect to a similar provision:

"Section 1235 admits inconsistent statements of witnesses because the dangers against which the hearsay rule is designed to protect are largely nonexistent. The declarant is in court and may be examined and cross-examined in regard to his statements and their subject matter. In many cases, the inconsistent statement is more likely to be true than the testimony of the witness at the trial because it was made nearer in time to the matter to which it relates and is less likely to be influenced by the controversy that gave rise to the litigation. The trier of fact has the declarant before it and can observe his demeanor and the nature of his testimony as he denies or tries to explain away the inconsistency. Hence, it is in as good a position to determine the truth or falsity of the prior statement as it is to determine the truth or falsity of the inconsistent testimony given in court. Moreover, Section 1235 will provide a party with desirable protection against the 'turncoat' witness who changes his story on the stand and deprives the party calling him of evidence essential to his case." Comment, California Evidence Code § 1235. See also McCormick § 39. The Advisory Committee finds these views more convincing than those expressed in People v. Johnson, 68 Cal.2d 646, 68 Cal.Rptr. 599, 441 P.2d 111 (1968). The constitutionality of the Advisory Committee's view was upheld in California v. Green, 399 U.S. 149, 90 S.Ct. 1930, 26 L.Ed.2d 489 (1970). Moreover, the requirement that the statement be inconsistent with the testimony given assures a thorough exploration of both versions while the witness is on the stand and bars any general and indiscriminate use of previously prepared statements. [It should be noted that the rule as enacted by the Congress also requires that the prior inconsistent statement have been made under oath.]

Report of House Committee on the Judiciary

House Comm. on Judiciary, Fed.Rules of Evidence, H.R.Rep. No. 650, 93d Cong., 1st Sess., p. 13 (1973); 1975 U.S. Code Cong. & Ad.News 7075, 7086

Present federal law, except in the Second Circuit, permits the use of prior inconsistent statements of a witness for impeachment only. Rule 801(d)(1) as proposed by the Court would have permitted all such statements to be admissible as substantive evidence, an approach followed by a small but growing number of State jurisdictions and recently held constitutional in California v. Green, 399 U.S. 149 (1970). Although there was some support expressed for the Court Rule, based largely on the need to counteract the effect of witness intimidation in criminal cases, the Committee decided to adopt a compromise version of the Rule similar to the position of the Second Circuit. The Rule as amended draws a distinction between types of prior inconsistent statements (other than statements of identification of a person made after perceiving him which are currently admissible, see United States v. Anderson, 406 F.2d 719, 720 (4th Cir.), cert. denied, 395 U.S. 967 (1969)) and allows only those made while the declarant was subject to cross-examination at a trail [trial] or hearing or in a deposition, to be admissible for their truth. Compare United States v. DeSisto, 329 F.2d 929 (2nd Cir.), cert. denied, 377 U.S. 979 (1964); United States v. Cunningham, 446 F.2d 194 (2nd Cir.1971) (restricting the admissibility of prior inconsistent statements as substantive evidence to those made under oath in a formal proceeding, but not requiring that there have been an opportunity for cross-examination). The rationale for the Committee's decision is that (1) unlike in most other situations involving unsworn or oral statements, there can be no dispute as to whether the prior statement was made; and (2) the context of a formal proceeding, an oath, and the opportunity for cross-examination provide firm additional assurances of the reliability of the prior statement.

Report of Senate Committee on the Judiciary

Senate Comm. on Judiciary, Fed.Rules of Evidence, S.Rep. No. 1277, 93d Cong., 2d Sess., p. 15 (1974); 1974 U.S. Code Cong. & Ad.News 7051, 7062

Rule 801 defines what is and what is not hearsay for the purpose of admitting a prior statement as substantive evidence. A prior statement of a witness at a trial or hearing which is inconsistent with his testimony is, of course, always admissible for the purpose of impeaching the witness' credibility.

As submitted by the Supreme Court, subdivision (d)(1)(A) made admissible as substantive evidence the prior statement of a witness inconsistent with this present testimony.

The House severely limited the admissibility of prior inconsistent statements by adding a requirement that the prior statement must have been subject to cross-examination, thus precluding even the use of grand jury statements. The requirement that the prior statement must have been subject to cross-examination appears unnecessary since this rule comes into play only when the witness testifies in the present trial. At that time, he is on the stand and can explain an earlier position and be cross-examined as to both.

The requirement that the statement be under oath also appears unnecessary. Notwithstanding the absence of an oath contemporaneous with the statement, the witness, when on the stand, qualifying or denying the prior statement, is under oath. In any event, of all the many recognized exceptions to the hearsay rule, only one (former testimony) requires that the out-of-court statement have been made under oath. With respect to the lack of evidence of the demeanor of the witness at the time of the prior statement, it would be difficult to improve upon Judge Learned Hand's observation that when the jury decides that the truth is not what the witness says now but what he said before, they are still deciding from what they see and hear in court.[1]

The rule as submitted by the Court has positive advantages. The prior statement was made nearer in time to the events, when memory was fresher and intervening influences had not been brought into play. A realistic method is provided for dealing with the turncoat witness who changes his story on the stand.[2]

New Jersey, California, and Utah have adopted a rule similar to this one; and Nevada, New Mexico, and Wisconsin have adopted the identical Federal rule.

For all of these reasons, we think the House amendment should be rejected and the rule as submitted by the Supreme Court reinstated.[3]

Conference Report

H.R., Fed.Rules of Evidence, Conf.Rep. No. 1597, 93d Cong., 2d Sess., p. 10 (1974); 1974 U.S. Code Cong. & Ad.News 7098, 7104

The House bill provides that a statement is not hearsay if the declarant testifies and is subject to cross-examination concerning the statement and if the statement is inconsistent with his testimony and was given under oath subject to cross-examination and subject to the penalty of perjury at a trial or hearing or in a deposition. The Senate amendment drops the requirement that the prior statement be given under oath subject to cross-examination and subject to the penalty of perjury at a trial or hearing or in a deposition.

The Conference adopts the Senate amendment with an amendment, so that the rule now requires that the prior inconsistent statement be given under oath subject to the penalty of perjury at a trial, hearing, or other proceeding, or in a deposition. The rule as adopted covers statements before a grand jury. Prior inconsistent statements may, of course, be used for impeaching the credibility of a witness. When the prior inconsistent statement is one made by a defendant in a criminal case, it is covered by Rule 801(d)(2).

1. Di Carlo v. United States, 6 F.2d 364 (2d Cir.1925).

2. See Comment, California Evidence Code § 1235; McCormick, Evidence, § 38 (2nd ed. 1972).

3. It would appear that some of the opposition to this Rule is based on a concern that a person could be convicted solely upon evidence admissible under this Rule. The Rule, however, is not addressed to the question of the sufficiency of evidence to send a case to the jury, but merely as to its admissibility. Factual circumstances could well arise where, if this were the sole evidence, dismissal would be appropriate.

Advisory Committee's Note

56 F.R.D. 183, 296

(B) Prior consistent statements traditionally have been admissible to rebut charges of recent fabrication or improper influence or motive but not as substantive evidence. Under the rule they are substantive evidence. The prior statement is consistent with the testimony given on the stand and, if the opposite party wishes to open the door for its admission in evidence, no sound reason is apparent why it should not be received generally.

Editorial Note

Subdivision (d)(1)(C) was included in the rule as prescribed by the Supreme Court but was deleted by the Congress in enacting the rules, as indicated in the Conference Report above. However, the subdivision was restored by Act effective Oct. 31, 1975. Therefore the Advisory Committee's Note to the subdivision is now reprinted below.

Advisory Committee's Note

56 F.R.D. 183, 296

(C) The admission of evidence of identification finds substantial support, although it falls beyond a doubt in the category of prior out-of-court statements. Illustrative are People v. Gould, 54 Cal.2d 621, 7 Cal.Rptr. 273, 354 P.2d 865 (1960); Judy v. State, 218 Md. 168, 146 A.2d 29 (1958); State v. Simmons, 63 Wash.2d 17, 385 P.2d 389 (1963); California Evidence Code § 1238; New Jersey Evidence Rule 63(1)(c); N.Y.Code of Criminal Procedure § 393–b. Further cases are found in 4 Wigmore § 1130. The basis is the generally unsatisfactory and inconclusive nature of courtroom identifications as compared with those made at an earlier time under less suggestive conditions. The Supreme Court considered the admissibility of evidence of prior identification in Gilbert v. California, 388 U.S. 263, 87 S.Ct. 1951, 18 L.Ed.2d 1178 (1967). Exclusion of lineup identification was held to be required because the accused did not then have the assistance of counsel. Significantly, the Court carefully refrained from placing its decision on the ground that testimony as to the making of a prior out-of-court identification ("That's the man") violated either the hearsay rule or the right of confrontation because not made under oath, subject to immediate cross-examination, in the presence of the trier. Instead the Court observed:

> "There is a split among the States concerning the admissibility of prior extra-judicial identifications, as independent evidence of identity, both by the witness and third parties present at the prior identification. See 71 A.L.R.2d 449. It has been held that the prior identification is hearsay, and, when admitted through the testimony of the identifier, is merely a prior consistent statement. The recent trend, however, is to admit the prior identification under the exception that admits as substantive evidence a prior communication by a witness who is available for cross-examination at the trial. See 5 A.L.R.2d Later Case Service 1225–1228. . . ." 388 U.S. at 272, n. 3, 87 S.Ct. at 1956.[1]

1. See also 121 Cong.Rec. 19752 and 31866 (1975) for action reinstating item (C).

(2) *Admissions.* Admissions by a party-opponent are excluded from the category of hearsay on the theory that their admissibility in evidence is the result of the adversary system rather than satisfaction of the conditions of the hearsay rule. Strahorn, A Reconsideration of the Hearsay Rule and Admissions, 85 U.Pa.L.Rev. 484, 564 (1937); Morgan, Basic Problems of Evidence 265 (1962); 4 Wigmore § 1048. No guarantee of trustworthiness is required in the case of an admission. The freedom which admissions have enjoyed from technical demands of searching for an assurance of trustworthiness in some against-interest circumstance, and from the restrictive influences of the opinion rule and the rule requiring firsthand knowledge, when taken with the apparently prevalent satisfaction with the results, calls for generous treatment of this avenue to admissibility.

The rule specifies five categories of statements for which the responsibility of a party is considered sufficient to justify reception in evidence against him:

(A) A party's own statement is the classic example of an admission. If he has a representative capacity and the statement is offered against him in that capacity, no inquiry whether he was acting in the representative capacity in making the statement is required; the statement need only be relevant to representative affairs. To the same effect is California Evidence Code § 1220. Compare Uniform Rule 63(7), requiring a statement to be made in a representative capacity to be admissible against a party in a representative capacity.

(B) Under established principles an admission may be made by adopting or acquiescing in the statement of another. While knowledge of contents would ordinarily be essential, this is not inevitably so: "X is a reliable person and knows what he is talking about." See McCormick § 246, p. 527, n. 15. Adoption or acquiescence may be manifested in any appropriate manner. When silence is relied upon, the theory is that the person would, under the circumstances, protest the statement made in his presence, if untrue. The decision in each case calls for an evaluation in terms of probable human behavior. In civil cases, the results have generally been satisfactory. In criminal cases, however, troublesome questions have been raised by decisions holding that failure to deny is an admission: the inference is a fairly weak one, to begin with; silence may be motivated by advice of counsel or realization that "anything you say may be used against you"; unusual opportunity is afforded to manufacture evidence; and encroachment upon the privilege against self-incrimination seems inescapably to be involved. However, recent decisions of the Supreme Court relating to custodial interrogation and the right to counsel appear to resolve these difficulties. Hence the rule contains no special provisions concerning failure to deny in criminal cases.

(C) No authority is required for the general proposition that a statement authorized by a party to be made should have the status of an admission by the party. However, the question arises whether only statements to third persons should be so regarded, to the exclusion of statements by the agent to the principal. The rule is phrased broadly so as to encompass both. While it may be argued that the agent authorized to make statements to his principal does not speak for him, Morgan, Basic Problems of Evidence 273 (1962), communication to an outsider has not generally been thought to be an essential characteristic of an admission. Thus a party's books or records are usable against him, without regard to any intent to disclose to third persons. 5 Wigmore § 1557. See also McCormick § 78, pp. 159–161. In accord is New Jersey Evidence Rule

63(8)(a). Cf. Uniform Rule 63(8)(a) and California Evidence Code § 1222 which limit status as an admission in this regard to statements authorized by the party to be made "for" him, which is perhaps an ambiguous limitation to statements to third persons. Falknor, Vicarious Admissions and the Uniform Rules, 14 Vand.L.Rev. 855, 860–861 (1961).

(D) The tradition has been to test the admissibility of statements by agents, as admissions, by applying the usual test of agency. Was the admission made by the agent acting in the scope of his employment? Since few principals employ agents for the purpose of making damaging statements, the usual result was exclusion of the statement. Dissatisfaction with this loss of valuable and helpful evidence has been increasing. A substantial trend favors admitting statements related to a matter within the scope of the agency or employment. Grayson v. Williams, 256 F.2d 61 (10th Cir.1958); Koninklijke Luchtvaart Maatschappij N.V. KLM Royal Dutch Airlines v. Tuller, 110 U.S.App.D.C. 282, 292 F.2d 775, 784 (1961); Martin v. Savage Truck Lines, Inc., 121 F.Supp. 417 (D.D.C.1954) , and numerous state court decisions collected in 4 Wigmore, 1964 Supp., pp. 66–73, with comments by the editor that the statements should have been excluded as not within scope of agency. For the traditional view see Northern Oil Co. v. Socony Mobile [sic] Oil Co., 347 F.2d 81, 85 (2d Cir.1965) and cases cited therein. Similar provisions are found in Uniform Rule 63(9)(a), Kansas Code of Civil Procedure § 60–460(i)(1), and New Jersey Evidence Rule 63(9)(a).

(E) The limitation upon the admissibility of statements of co-conspirators to those made "during the course and in furtherance of the conspiracy" is in the accepted pattern. While the broadened view of agency taken in item (iv) might suggest wider admissibility of statements of co-conspirators, the agency theory of conspiracy is at best a fiction and ought not to serve as a basis for admissibility beyond that already established. See Levie, Hearsay and Conspiracy, 52 Mich.L.Rev. 1159 (1954); Comment, 25 U.Chi.L.Rev. 530 (1958). The rule is consistent with the position of the Supreme Court in denying admissibility to statements made after the objectives of the conspiracy have either failed or been achieved. Krulewitch v. United States, 336 U.S. 440, 69 S.Ct. 716, 93 L.Ed. 790 (1949); Wong Sun v. United States, 371 U.S. 471, 490, 83 S.Ct. 407, 9 L.Ed.2d 441 (1963). For similarly limited provisions see California Evidence Code § 1223 and New Jersey Rule 63(9)(b). Cf. Uniform Rule 63(9)(b).

Report of Senate Committee on the Judiciary

Senate Comm. on Judiciary, Fed.Rules of Evidence, S.Rep. No. 1277, 93d Cong., 2d Sess., p. 26 (1974); 1974 U.S. Code Cong. & Ad.News 7051, 7073

The House approved the long-accepted rule that "a statement by a coconspirator of a party during the course and in furtherance of the conspiracy" is not hearsay as it was submitted by the Supreme Court. While the rule refers to a coconspirator, it is this committee's understanding that the rule is meant to carry forward the universally accepted doctrine that a joint venturer is considered as a coconspirator for the purposes of this rule even though no conspiracy has been charged. United States v. Rinaldi, 393 F.2d 97, 99 (2d Cir.), cert. denied 393 U.S. 913 (1968); United States v. Spencer, 415 F.2d 1301, 1304 (7th Cir.1969).

1987 Amendment. The amendments are technical. No substantive change is intended.

Rule 802. Hearsay Rule

Hearsay is not admissible except as provided by these rules or by other rules prescribed by the Supreme Court pursuant to statutory authority or by Act of Congress.

Section references, McCormick 4th ed.

§ 246, § 299

Note by Federal Judicial Center

The rule enacted by the Congress is the rule prescribed by the Supreme Court, amended by substituting "prescribed" in place of "adopted" and by inserting the phrase "pursuant to statutory authority."

Advisory Committee's Note

56 F.R.D. 183, 299

The provision excepting from the operation of the rule hearsay which is made admissible by other rules adopted by the Supreme Court or by Act of Congress continues the admissibility thereunder of hearsay which would not qualify under these Evidence Rules. The following examples illustrate the working of the exception:

FEDERAL RULES OF CIVIL PROCEDURE

Rule 4(g): proof of service by affidavit.

Rule 32: admissibility of depositions.

Rule 43(e): affidavits when motion based on facts not appearing of record.

Rule 56: affidavits in summary judgment proceedings.

Rule 65(b): showing by affidavit for temporary restraining order.

FEDERAL RULES OF CRIMINAL PROCEDURE

Rule 4(a): affidavits to show grounds for issuing warrants.

Rule 12(b)(4): affidavits to determine issues of fact in connection with motions.

ACTS OF CONGRESS

10 U.S.C. § 7730: affidavits of unavailable witnesses in actions for damages caused by vessel in naval service, or towage or salvage of same, when taking of testimony or bringing of action delayed or stayed on security grounds.

29 U.S.C. § 161(4): affidavit as proof of service in NLRB proceedings.

38 U.S.C. § 5206: affidavit as proof of posting notice of sale of unclaimed property by Veterans Administration.

Rule 803. Hearsay Exceptions; Availability of Declarant Immaterial

The following are not excluded by the hearsay rule, even though the declarant is available as a witness:

(1) Present sense impression. A statement describing or explaining an event or condition made while the declarant was perceiving the event or condition, or immediately thereafter.

(2) Excited utterance. A statement relating to a startling event or condition made while the declarant was under the stress of excitement caused by the event or condition.

(3) Then existing mental, emotional, or physical condition. A statement of the declarant's then existing state of mind, emotion, sensation, or physical condition (such as intent, plan, motive, design, mental feeling, pain, and bodily health), but not including a statement of memory or belief to prove the fact remembered or believed unless it relates to the execution, revocation, identification, or terms of declarant's will.

(4) Statements for purposes of medical diagnosis or treatment. Statements made for purposes of medical diagnosis or treatment and describing medical history, or past or present symptoms, pain, or sensations, or the inception or general character of the cause or external source thereof insofar as reasonably pertinent to diagnosis or treatment.

(5) Recorded recollection. A memorandum or record concerning a matter about which a witness once had knowledge but now has insufficient recollection to enable the witness to testify fully and accurately, shown to have been made or adopted by the witness when the matter was fresh in the witness' memory and to reflect that knowledge correctly. If admitted, the memorandum or record may be read into evidence but may not itself be received as an exhibit unless offered by an adverse party.

(6) Records of regularly conducted activity. A memorandum, report, record, or data compilation, in any form, of acts, events, conditions, opinions, or diagnoses, made at or near the time by, or from information transmitted by, a person with knowledge, if kept in the course of a regularly conducted business activity, and if it was the regular practice of that business activity to make the memorandum, report, record, or data compilation, all as shown by the testimony of the custodian or other qualified witness, unless the source of information or the method or circumstances of preparation indicate lack of trustworthiness. The term "business" as used in this paragraph includes business, institution, association, profession, occupation, and calling of every kind, whether or not conducted for profit.

(7) Absence of entry in records kept in accordance with the provisions of paragraph (6). Evidence that a matter is not included in the memoranda, reports, records, or data compilations, in any form, kept in accordance with the provisions of paragraph (6), to prove the nonoccurrence or nonexistence of the matter, if the matter was of a kind of which a memorandum, report, record, or data compilation was regularly made and preserved, unless the sources of information or other circumstances indicate lack of trustworthiness.

(8) Public records and reports. Records, reports, statements, or data compilations, in any form, of public offices or agencies, setting forth (A) the activities of the office or agency, or (B) matters observed pursuant to duty imposed by law as to which matters there was a duty to report, excluding, however, in criminal cases matters observed by police officers and other law enforcement personnel, or (C) in civil actions and proceedings and against the Government in criminal cases, factual findings resulting from an investigation made pursuant to authority granted by law, unless the sources of information or other circumstances indicate lack of trustworthiness.

(9) Records of vital statistics. Records or data compilations, in any form, of births, fetal deaths, deaths, or marriages, if the report thereof was made to a public office pursuant to requirements of law.

(10) Absence of public record or entry. To prove the absence of a record, report, statement, or data compilation, in any form, or the nonoccurrence or nonexistence of a matter of which a record, report, statement, or data compilation, in any form, was regularly made and preserved by a public office or agency, evidence in the form of a certification in accordance with rule 902, or testimony, that diligent search failed to disclose the record, report, statement, or data compilation, or entry.

(11) Records of religious organizations. Statements of births, marriages, divorces, deaths, legitimacy, ancestry, relationship by blood or marriage, or other similar facts of personal or family history, contained in a regularly kept record of a religious organization.

(12) Marriage, baptismal, and similar certificates. Statements of fact contained in a certificate that the maker performed a marriage or other ceremony or administered a sacrament, made by a clergyman, public official, or other person authorized by the rules or practices of a religious organization or by law to perform the act certified, and purporting to have been issued at the time of the act or within a reasonable time thereafter.

(13) Family records. Statements of fact concerning personal or family history contained in family Bibles, genealogies, charts, engravings on rings, inscriptions on family portraits, engravings on urns, crypts, or tombstones, or the like.

(14) Records of documents affecting an interest in property. The record of a document purporting to establish or affect an interest in property, as proof of the content of the original recorded document and its execution and delivery by each person by whom it purports to have been executed, if the record is a record of a public office and an applicable statute authorizes the recording of documents of that kind in that office.

(15) Statements in documents affecting an interest in property. A statement contained in a document purporting to establish or affect an interest in property if the matter stated was relevant to the purpose of the document, unless dealings with the property since the document was made have been inconsistent with the truth of the statement or the purport of the document.

(16) Statements in ancient documents. Statements in a document in existence twenty years or more the authenticity of which is established.

(17) Market reports, commercial publications. Market quotations, tabulations, lists, directories, or other published compilations, generally used and relied upon by the public or by persons in particular occupations.

(18) Learned treatises. To the extent called to the attention of an expert witness upon cross-examination or relied upon by the expert witness in direct examination, statements contained in published treatises, periodicals, or pamphlets on a subject of history, medicine, or other science or art, established as a reliable authority by the testimony or admission of the witness or by other expert testimony or by judicial notice. If admitted, the statements may be read into evidence but may not be received as exhibits.

(19) Reputation concerning personal or family history. Reputation among members of a person's family by blood, adoption, or marriage, or among a person's associates, or in the community, concerning a person's birth, adoption, marriage, divorce, death, legitimacy, relationship by blood, adoption, or marriage, ancestry, or other similar fact of his personal or family history.

(20) Reputation concerning boundaries or general history. Reputation in a community, arising before the controversy, as to boundaries of or customs affecting lands in the community, and reputation as to events of general history important to the community or State or nation in which located.

(21) Reputation as to character. Reputation of a person's character among associates or in the community.

(22) Judgment of previous conviction. Evidence of a final judgment, entered after a trial or upon a plea of guilty (but not upon a plea of nolo contendere), adjudging a person guilty of a crime punishable by death or imprisonment in excess of one year, to prove any fact essential to sustain the judgment, but not including, when offered by the Government in a criminal prosecution for purposes other than impeachment, judgments against persons other than the accused. The pendency of an appeal may be shown but does not affect admissibility.

(23) Judgment as to personal, family, or general history, or boundaries. Judgments as proof of matters of personal, family or general history, or boundaries, essential to the judgment, if the same would be provable by evidence of reputation.

(24) Other exceptions. A statement not specifically covered by any of the foregoing exceptions but having equivalent circumstantial guarantees of trustworthiness, if the court determines that (A) the statement is offered as evidence of a material fact; (B) the statement is more probative on the point for which it is offered than any other evidence which the proponent can procure through reasonable efforts; and (C) the general purposes of these rules and the interests of justice will best be served by admission of the statement into evidence. However, a statement may not be admitted under this exception unless the proponent of it makes known to the adverse party sufficiently in advance of the trial or hearing to provide the adverse party with a fair opportunity to prepare to meet it, the proponent's intention to offer the statement and the particulars of it, including the name and address of the declarant.

(As amended P.L. 94–149, § 1(11), Dec. 12, 1975, 89 Stat. 805; Mar. 2, 1987, eff. Oct. 1, 1987.)

Section references, McCormick 4th ed.

Generally *§ 253,* § 326

(1). § 271

(2). § 272

(3). § 273, § 274, § 275, § 276

(4). § 277, § 278, § 324.3

(5). § 144, § 279, § 281, § 282, § 283

(6). § 250, § 286, § 287, § 288, § 289, § 290, § 291, § 292, § 293, § 294, § 296, § 324.1

(7). § 287

(8). § 288, § 295

(A). § 296

(B). § 296, § 297

(C). § 296, § 297

(9). § 297

(10). § 300

(11). § 288, § 299

(12). § 299

(13). § 322

(14). § 323

(15). § 323

(16). § 323

(17). § 321

(18). § 321

(19). § 322

(20). § 324

(21). § 191

(22). § 42, § 252, § 257, § 298

(23). § 322

(24). § 208, § 324, § 324.3, § 353

Note by Federal Judicial Center

The rule enacted by the Congress retains the 24 exceptions set forth in the rule prescribed by the Supreme Court. Three of the exceptions, numbered (6), (8), and (24) have been amended in respects that may fairly be described as substantial. Others, numbered (5), (7), (14), and (16), have been amended in lesser ways. The remaining 17 are unchanged. The amendments are, in numerical order, as follows.

Exception (5) as prescribed by the Supreme Court was amended by inserting after "made" the phrase "or adopted by the witness."

Exception (6) as prescribed by the Supreme Court was amended by substituting the phrase, "if kept in the course of a regularly conducted business activity, and if it was the regular practice of that business activity to make the memorandum, report, record, or data compilation, all," in place of "all in the course of a regularly conducted activity"; by substituting "source" in place of "sources"; by substituting the phrase, "the method or circumstances of preparation," in place of "other circumstances"; and by adding the second sentence.

Exception (7) as prescribed by the Supreme Court was amended by substituting the phrase, "kept in accordance with the provisions of paragraph (6)," in place of "of a regularly conducted activity." The exception prescribed by the Supreme Court included a comma after "memoranda," while the congressional enactment does not.

Exception (8) as prescribed by the Supreme Court was amended by inserting in item (B) after "law" the phrase, "as to which matters there was a duty to report, excluding, however, in criminal cases matters observed by police officers and other law enforcement personnel," and by substituting in item (C) the phrase "civil actions and proceedings," in place of "civil cases."

Exception (14) as prescribed by the Supreme Court was amended by substituting "authorizes" in place of "authorized."

Exception (16) as prescribed by the Supreme Court was amended by substituting the phrase, "the authenticity of which," in place of "whose authenticity."

Exception (24) as prescribed by the Supreme Court was amended by substituting "equivalent" in place of "comparable," and adding all that appears after "trustworthiness" in the exception as enacted by the Congress.

Advisory Committee's Note

56 F.R.D. 183, 303

The exceptions are phrased in terms of nonapplication of the hearsay rule, rather than in positive terms of admissibility, in order to repel any implication that other possible grounds for exclusion are eliminated from consideration.

The present rule proceeds upon the theory that under appropriate circumstances a hearsay statement may possess circumstantial guarantees of trustworthiness sufficient to justify nonproduction of the declarant in person at the trial even though he may be available. The theory finds vast support in the many exceptions to the hearsay rule developed by the common law in which unavailability of the declarant is not a relevant factor. The present rule is a synthesis of them, with revision where modern developments and conditions are believed to make that course appropriate.

In a hearsay situation, the declarant is, of course, a witness, and neither this rule nor Rule 804 dispenses with the requirement of firsthand knowledge. It may appear from his statement or be inferable from circumstances. See Rule 602.

Exceptions (1) and (2). In considerable measure these two [exceptions] overlap, though based on somewhat different theories. The most significant practical difference will lie in the time lapse allowable between event and statement.

The underlying theory of Exception (1) is that substantial contemporaneity of event and statement negative the likelihood of deliberate or conscious misrepresentation. Moreover, if the witness is the declarant, he may be examined on the statement. If the witness is not the declarant, he may be examined as to the circumstances as an aid in evaluating the statement. Morgan, Basic Problems of Evidence 340–341 (1962).

The theory of Exception (2) is simply that circumstances may produce a condition of excitement which temporarily stills the capacity of reflection and produces utterances free of conscious fabrication. 6 Wigmore § 1747, p. 135. Spontaneity is the key factor in each instance, though arrived at by somewhat different routes. Both are needed in order to avoid needless niggling.

While the theory of Exception (2) has been criticized on the ground that excitement impairs accuracy of observation as well as eliminating conscious fabrication, Hutchins and Slesinger, Some Observations on the Law of Evidence: Spontaneous Exclamations, 28 Colum.L.Rev. 432 (1928), it finds support in cases without number. See cases in 6 Wigmore § 1750; Annot., 53 A.L.R.2d 1245 (statements as to cause of or responsibility for motor vehicle accident); Annot., 4 A.L.R.3d 149 (accusatory statements by homicide victims). Since unexciting events are less likely to evoke comment, decisions involving Exception (1) are far less numerous. Illustrative are Tampa Elec. Co. v. Getrost, 151 Fla. 558, 10 So.2d 83 (1942); Houston Oxygen Co. v. Davis, 139 Tex. 1, 161 S.W.2d 474 (1942); and cases cited in McCormick § 273, p. 585, n. 4.

With respect to the *time element,* Exception (1) recognizes that in many, if not most, instances precise contemporaneity is not possible, and hence a slight lapse is allowable. Under Exception (2) the standard of measurement is the duration of the state of excitement. "How long can excitement prevail? Obviously there are no pat answers and the character of the transaction or event will largely determine the significance of the time factor." Slough, Spontaneous Statements and State of Mind, 46 Iowa L.Rev. 224, 243 (1961); McCormick § 272, p. 580.

Participation by the declarant is not required: a non-participant may be moved to describe what he perceives, and one may be startled by an event in which he is not an actor. Slough, supra; McCormick, supra; 6 Wigmore § 1755; Annot., 78 A.L.R.2d 300.

Whether *proof of the startling event* may be made by the statement itself is largely an academic question, since in most cases there is present at least circumstantial evidence that something of a startling nature must have occurred. For cases in which the evidence consists of the condition of the declarant (injuries, state of shock), see Insurance Co. v. Mosely, 75 U.S. (8 Wall.) 397, 19 L.Ed. 437 (1869); Wheeler v. United States, 93 U.S.App.D.C. 159, 211 F.2d 19 (1953), cert. denied 347 U.S. 1019, 74 S.Ct. 876, 98 L.Ed. 1140; Wetherbee v. Safety Casualty Co., 219 F.2d 274 (5th Cir.1955); Lampe v. United States, 97 U.S.App.D.C. 160, 229 F.2d 43 (1956). Nevertheless, on occasion the only evidence may be the content of the statement itself, and rulings that it may be sufficient are described as "increasing," Slough, supra at 246, and as the "prevailing practice," McCormick § 272, p. 579. Illustrative are Armour & Co. v. Industrial Commission, 78 Colo. 569, 243 P. 546 (1926); Young v. Stewart, 191 N.C. 297, 131 S.E. 735 (1926). Moreover, under Rule 104(a) the judge is not limited by the hearsay rule in passing upon preliminary questions of fact.

Proof of declarant's perception by his statement presents similar considerations when declarant is identified. People v. Poland, 22 Ill.2d 175, 174 N.E.2d 804 (1961). However, when declarant is an unidentified bystander, the cases indicate hesitancy in upholding the statement alone as sufficient, Garrett v. Howden, 73 N.M. 307, 387 P.2d 874 (1963); Beck v. Dye, 200 Wash. 1, 92 P.2d 1113 (1939), a result which would under appropriate circumstances be consistent with the rule.

Permissible *subject matter* of the statement is limited under Exception (1) to description or explanation of the event or condition, the assumption being that spontaneity, in the absence of a startling event, may extend no farther. In Exception (2), however, the statement need only "relate" to the startling event or condition, thus affording a broader scope of subject matter coverage. 6 Wigmore §§ 1750, 1754. See Sanitary Grocery Co. v. Snead, 67 App.D.C. 129, 90 F.2d 374 (1937), slip-and-fall case sustaining admissibility of clerk's statement, "That has been on the floor for a couple of hours," and Murphy Auto Parts Co., Inc. v. Ball, 101 U.S.App.D.C. 416, 249 F.2d 508 (1957), upholding admission, on issue of driver's agency, of his statement that he had to call on a customer and was in a hurry to get home. Quick, Hearsay, Excitement, Necessity and the Uniform Rules: A Reappraisal of Rule 63(4), 6 Wayne L.Rev. 204, 206–209 (1960).

Similar provisions are found in Uniform Rule 63(4)(a) and (b); California Evidence Code § 1240 (as to Exception (2) only); Kansas Code of Civil Procedure § 60–460(d)(1) and (2); New Jersey Evidence Rule 63(4).

Exception (3) is essentially a specialized application of Exception (1), presented separately to enhance its usefulness and accessibility. See McCormick §§ 265, 268.

The exclusion of "statements of memory or belief to prove the fact remembered or believed" is necessary to avoid the virtual destruction of the hearsay rule which would otherwise result from allowing state of mind, provable by a hearsay statement, to serve as the basis for an inference of the happening of the event which produced the state of mind. Shepard v. United States, 290 U.S. 96, 54 S.Ct. 22, 78 L.Ed. 196 (1933); Maguire, The Hillmon Case—Thirty-three Years After, 38 Harv.L.Rev. 709, 719–731 (1925); Hinton, States of Mind and the Hearsay Rule, 1 U.Chi.L.Rev. 394, 421–423 (1934). The rule of Mutual Life Ins. Co. v. Hillmon, 145 U.S. 285, 12 S.Ct. 909, 36 L.Ed. 706 (1892), allowing evidence of intention as tending to prove the doing of the act intended, is, of course, left undisturbed.

The carving out, from the exclusion mentioned in the preceding paragraph, of declarations relating to the execution, revocation, identification, or terms of declarant's will represents an *ad hoc* judgment which finds ample reinforcement in the decisions, resting on practical grounds of necessity and expediency rather than logic. McCormick § 271, pp. 577–578; Annot., 34 A.L.R.2d 588, 62 A.L.R.2d 855. A similar recognition of the need for and practical value of this kind of evidence is found in California Evidence Code § 1260.

Report of House Committee on the Judiciary

House Comm. on Judiciary, Fed.Rules of Evidence, H.R.Rep. No. 650, 93d Cong., 1st Sess., p. 13 (1973); 1974 U.S.Code Cong. & Ad.News 7075, 7087

Rule 803(3) was approved in the form submitted by the Court to Congress. However, the Committee intends that the Rule be construed to limit the doctrine of Mutual Life Insurance Co. v. Hillmon, 145 U.S. 285, 295–300 (1892), so as to render statements of intent by a declarant admissible only to prove his future conduct, not the future conduct of another person.

Advisory Committee's Note

56 F.R.D. 183, 306

Exception (4). Even those few jurisdictions which have shied away from generally admitting statements of present condition have allowed them if made to a physician for purposes of diagnosis and treatment in view of the patient's strong motivation to be truthful. McCormick § 266, p. 563. The same guarantee of trustworthiness extends to statements of past conditions and medical history, made for purposes of diagnosis or treatment. It also extends to statements as to causation, reasonably pertinent to the same purposes, in accord with the current trend, Shell Oil Co. v. Industrial Commission, 2 Ill.2d 590, 119 N.E.2d 224 (1954); McCormick § 266, p. 564; New Jersey Evidence Rule 63(12)(c). Statements as to fault would not ordinarily qualify under this latter language. Thus a patient's statement that he was struck by an automobile would qualify but not his statement that the car was driven through a red light. Under the exception the statement need not have been made to a physician. Statements to hospital attendants, ambulance drivers, or even members of the family might be included.

Conventional doctrine has excluded from the hearsay exception, as not within its guarantee of truthfulness, statements to a physician consulted only for the purpose of enabling him to testify. While these statements were not admissible as substantive evidence, the expert was allowed to state the basis of his opinion, including statements of this kind. The distinction thus called for was one most unlikely to be made by juries. The rule accordingly rejects the limitation. This position is consistent with the provision of Rule 703 that the facts on which expert testimony is based need not be admissible in evidence if of a kind ordinarily relied upon by experts in the field.

Report of House Committee on the Judiciary

House Comm. on Judiciary, Fed.Rules of Evidence, H.R.Rep. No. 650, 93d Cong., 1st Sess., p. 14 (1973); 1974 U.S.Code Cong. & Ad.News 7075, 7087

After giving particular attention to the question of physical examination made solely to enable a physician to testify, the Committee approved Rule 803(4) as submitted to Congress, with the understanding that it is not intended in any way to adversely affect present privilege rules or those subsequently adopted.

Report of Senate Committee on the Judiciary

Senate Comm. on Judiciary, Fed.Rules of Evidence, S.Rep. No. 1277, 93d Cong., 2d Sess., p. 27 (1974); 1974 U.S.Code Cong. & Ad.News 7051, 7073

The House approved this rule as it was submitted by the Supreme Court "with the understanding that it is not intended in any way to adversely affect present privilege rules." We also approve this rule, and we would point out with respect to the question of its relation to privileges, it must be read in conjunction with rule 35 of the Federal Rules of Civil Procedure which provides that whenever the physical or mental condition of a party (plaintiff or defendant) is in controversy, the court may require him to submit to an examination by a physician. It is these examinations which will normally be admitted under this exception.

Advisory Committee's Note

56 F.R.D. 183, 306

Exception (5). A hearsay exception for recorded recollection is generally recognized and has been described as having "long been favored by the federal and practically all the state courts that have had occasion to decide the question." United States v. Kelly, 349 F.2d 720, 770 (2d Cir.1965), citing numerous cases and sustaining the exception against a claimed denial of the right of confrontation. Many additional cases are cited in Annot., 82 A.L.R.2d 473, 520. The guarantee of trustworthiness is found in the reliability inherent in a record made while events were still fresh in mind and accurately reflecting them. Owens v. State, 67 Md. 307, 316, 10 A. 210, 212 (1887).

The principal controversy attending the exception has centered, not upon the propriety of the exception itself, but upon the question whether a preliminary requirement of impaired memory on the part of the witness should be imposed. The authorities are divided. If regard be had only to the accuracy of the evidence, admittedly impairment of the memory of the witness adds nothing to it and should not be required. McCormick § 277, p. 593; 3 Wigmore § 738, p. 76; Jordan v. People, 151 Colo. 133, 376 P.2d 699 (1962), cert. denied

373 U.S. 944, 83 S.Ct. 1553, 10 L.Ed.2d 699; Hall v. State, 223 Md. 158, 162 A.2d 751 (1960); State v. Bindhammer, 44 N.J. 372, 209 A.2d 124 (1965). Nevertheless, the absence of the requirement, it is believed, would encourage the use of statements carefully prepared for purposes of litigation under the supervision of attorneys, investigators, or claim adjusters. Hence the example includes a requirement that the witness not have "sufficient recollection to enable him to testify fully and accurately." To the same effect are California Evidence Code § 1237 and New Jersey Rule 63(1)(b), and this has been the position of the federal courts. Vicksburg & Meridian R.R. v. O'Brien, 119 U.S. 99, 7 S.Ct. 118, 30 L.Ed. 299 (1886); Ahern v. Webb, 268 F.2d 45 (10th Cir.1959); and see N.L. R.B. v. Hudson Pulp and Paper Corp., 273 F.2d 660, 665 (5th Cir.1960); N.L.R.B. v. Federal Dairy Co., 297 F.2d 487 (1st Cir.1962). But cf. United States v. Adams, 385 F.2d 548 (2d Cir.1967).

No attempt is made in the exception to spell out the method of establishing the initial knowledge or the contemporaneity and accuracy of the record, leaving them to be dealt with as the circumstances of the particular case might indicate. Multiple person involvement in the process of observing and recording, as in Rathbun v. Brancatella, 93 N.J.L. 222, 107 A. 279 (1919), is entirely consistent with the exception.

Locating the exception at this place in the scheme of the rules is a matter of choice. There were two other possibilities. The first was to regard the statement as one of the group of prior statements of a testifying witness which are excluded entirely from the category of hearsay by Rule 801(d)(1). That category, however, requires that declarant be "subject to cross-examination," as to which the impaired memory aspect of the exception raises doubts. The other possibility was to include the exception among those covered by Rule 804. Since unavailability is required by that rule and lack of memory is listed as a species of unavailability by the definition of the term in Rule 804(a)(3), that treatment at first impression would seem appropriate. The fact is, however, that the unavailability requirement of the exception is of a limited and peculiar nature. Accordingly, the exception is located at this point rather than in the context of a rule where unavailability is conceived of more broadly.

Report of House Committee on the Judiciary

House Comm. on Judiciary, Fed.Rules of Evidence, H.R.Rep. No. 650, 93d Cong., 1st Sess., p. 14 (1973); 1974 U.S.Code Cong. & Ad.News 7075, 7087

Rule 803(5) as submitted by the Court permitted the reading into evidence of a memorandum or record concerning a matter about which a witness once had knowledge but now has insufficient recollection to enable him to testify accurately and fully, "shown to have been made when the matter was fresh in his memory and to reflect that knowledge correctly." The Committee amended this Rule to add the words "or adopted by the witness" after the phrase "shown to have been made", a treatment consistent with the definition of "statement" in the Jencks Act, 18 U.S.C. 3500. Moreover, it is the Committee's understanding that a memorandum or report, although barred under this Rule, would nonetheless be admissible if it came within another hearsay exception. This last stated principle is deemed applicable to all the hearsay rules.

Report of Senate Committee on the Judiciary

Senate Comm. on Judiciary, Fed.Rules of Evidence, S.Rep. No. 1277, 93d Cong., 2d Sess., p. 27 (1974); 1974 U.S.Code Cong. & Ad.News 7051, 7073

Rule 803(5) as submitted by the Court permitted the reading into evidence of a memorandum or record concerning a matter about which a witness once had knowledge but now has insufficient recollection to enable him to testify accurately and fully, "shown to have been made when the matter was fresh in his memory and to reflect that knowledge correctly." The House amended the rule to add the words "or adopted by the witness" after the phrase "shown to have been made," language parallel to the Jencks Act.[1]

The committee accepts the House amendment with the understanding and belief that it was not intended to narrow the scope of applicability of the rule. In fact, we understand it to clarify the rule's applicability to a memorandum adopted by the witness as well as one made by him. While the rule as submitted by the Court was silent on the question of who made the memorandum, we view the House amendment as a helpful clarification, noting, however, that the Advisory Committee's note to this rule suggests that the important thing is the accuracy of the memorandum rather than who made it.

The committee does not view the House amendment as precluding admissibility in situations in which multiple participants were involved.

When the verifying witness has not prepared the report, but merely examined it and found it accurate, he has adopted the report, and it is therefore admissible. The rule should also be interpreted to cover other situations involving multiple participants, e.g., employer dictating to secretary, secretary making memorandum at direction of employer, or information being passed along a chain of persons, as in Curtis v. Bradley.[2]

The committee also accepts the understanding of the House that a memorandum or report, although barred under this rule, would nonetheless be admissible if it came within another hearsay exception. We consider this principle to be applicable to all the hearsay rules.

Advisory Committee's Note

56 F.R.D. 183, 307

Exception (6) represents an area which has received much attention from those seeking to improve the law of evidence. The Commonwealth Fund Act was the result of a study completed in 1927 by a distinguished committee under the chairmanship of Professor Morgan. Morgan et al., The Law of Evidence: Some Proposals for its Reform 63 (1927). With changes too minor to mention, it was adopted by Congress in 1936 as the rule for federal courts. 28 U.S.C. § 1732. A number of states took similar action. The Commissioners on Uniform State Laws in 1936 promulgated the Uniform Business Records as Evidence Act, 9A U.L.A. 506, which has acquired a substantial following in the states. Model Code Rule 514 and Uniform Rule 63(13) also deal with the

1. 18 U.S.C. § 3500.

2. 65 Conn. 99, 31 Atl. 591 (1894). See also, Rathbun v. Brancatella, 93 N.J.L. 222, 107 Atl. 279 (1919); see also McCormick on Evidence, § 303 (2d ed. 1972).

subject. Difference of varying degrees of importance exist among these various treatments.

These reform efforts were largely within the context of business and commercial records, as the kind usually encountered, and concentrated considerable attention upon relaxing the requirement of producing as witnesses, or accounting for the nonproduction of, all participants in the process of gathering, transmitting, and recording information which the common law had evolved as a burdensome and crippling aspect of using records of this type. In their areas of primary emphasis on witnesses to be called and the general admissibility of ordinary business and commercial records, the Commonwealth Fund Act and the Uniform Act appear to have worked well. The exception seeks to preserve their advantages.

On the subject of what witnesses must be called, the Commonwealth Fund Act eliminated the common law requirement of calling or accounting for all participants by failing to mention it. United States v. Mortimer, 118 F.2d 266 (2d Cir.1941); La Porte v. United States, 300 F.2d 878 (9th Cir.1962); McCormick § 290, p. 608. Model Code Rule 514 and Uniform Rule 63(13) did likewise. The Uniform Act, however, abolished the common law requirement in express terms, providing that the requisite foundation testimony might be furnished by "the custodian or other qualified witness." Uniform Business Records as Evidence Act, § 2; 9A U.L.A. 506. The exception follows the Uniform Act in this respect.

The element of unusual reliability of business records is said variously to be supplied by systematic checking, by regularity and continuity which produce habits of precision, by actual experience of business in relying upon them, or by a duty to make an accurate record as part of a continuing job or occupation. McCormick §§ 281, 286, 287; Laughlin, Business Entries and the Like, 46 Iowa L.Rev. 276 (1961). The model statutes and rules have sought to capture these factors and to extend their impact by employing the phrase "regular course of business," in conjunction with a definition of "business" far broader than its ordinarily accepted meaning. The result is a tendency unduly to emphasize a requirement of routineness and repetitiveness and an insistence that other types of records be squeezed into the fact patterns which give rise to traditional business records. . . .

Amplification of the kinds of activities producing admissible records has given rise to problems which conventional business records by their nature avoid. They are problems of the source of the recorded information, of entries in opinion form, of motivation, and of involvement as participant in the matters recorded.

Sources of information presented no substantial problem with ordinary business records. All participants, including the observer or participant furnishing the information to be recorded, were acting routinely, under a duty of accuracy, with employer reliance on the result, or in short "in the regular course of business." If, however, the supplier of the information does not act in the regular course, an essential link is broken; the assurance of accuracy does not extend to the information itself, and the fact that it may be recorded with scrupulous accuracy is of no avail. An illustration is the police report incorporating information obtained from a bystander: the officer qualifies as acting in the regular course but the informant does not. The leading case, Johnson v. Lutz, 253 N.Y. 124, 170 N.E. 517 (1930), held that a report thus prepared was inadmissible. Most of the authorities have agreed with the decision. Gencarella v. Fyfe, 171 F.2d 419 (1st Cir.1948); Gordon v. Robinson, 210 F.2d 192 (3d Cir. 1954); Standard Oil Co. of California v. Moore, 251 F.2d 188, 214 (9th Cir.1957), cert. denied 356 U.S. 975, 78 S.Ct. 1139, 2 L.Ed.2d 1148; Yates v. Bair Transport, Inc., 249 F.Supp. 681 (S.D.N.Y.1965); Annot., 69 A.L.R.2d 1148. Cf. Hawkins v. Gorea Motor Express, Inc., 360 F.2d 933 (2d Cir.1966). Contra, 5 Wigmore § 1530a, n. 1, pp. 391–392. The point is not dealt with specifically in the Commonwealth Fund Act, the Uniform Act, or Uniform Rule 63(13). However, Model Code Rule 514 contains the requirement "that it was the regular course of that business for one with personal knowledge . . . to make such a memorandum or record or to transmit information thereof to be included in such a memorandum or record . . .." The rule follows this lead in requiring an informant with knowledge acting in the course of the regularly conducted activity.

Entries in the form of opinions were not encountered in traditional business records in view of the purely factual nature of the items recorded, but they are now commonly encountered with respect to medical diagnoses, prognoses, and test results, as well as occasionally in other areas. The Commonwealth Fund Act provided only for records of an "act, transaction, occurrence, or event," while the Uniform Act, Model Code Rule 514, and Uniform Rule 63(13) merely added the ambiguous term "condition." The limited phrasing of the Commonwealth Fund Act, 28 U.S.C. § 1732, may account for the reluctance of some federal decisions to admit diagnostic entries. New York Life Ins. Co. v. Taylor, 79 U.S.App.D.C. 66, 147 F.2d 297 (1945); Lyles v. United States, 103 U.S.App.D.C. 22, 254 F.2d 725 (1957), cert. denied 356 U.S. 961, 78 S.Ct. 997, 2 L.Ed.2d 1067; England v. United States, 174 F.2d 466 (5th Cir.1949); Skogen v. Dow Chemical Co., 375 F.2d 692 (8th Cir.1967). Other federal decisions, however, experienced no difficulty in freely admitting diagnostic entries. Reed v. Order of United Commercial Travelers, 123 F.2d 252 (2d Cir.1941); Buckminster's Estate v. Commissioner of Internal Revenue, 147 F.2d 331 (2d Cir.1944); Medina v. Erickson, 226 F.2d 475 (9th Cir.1955); Thomas v. Hogan, 308 F.2d 355 (4th Cir.1962); Glawe v. Rulon, 284 F.2d 495 (8th Cir.1960). In the state courts, the trend favors admissibility. Borucki v. MacKenzie Bros. Co., 125 Conn. 92, 3 A.2d 224 (1938); Allen v. St. Louis Public Service Co., 365 Mo. 677, 285 S.W.2d 663, 55 A.L.R.2d 1022 (1956); People v. Kohlmeyer, 284 N.Y. 366, 31 N.E.2d 490 (1940); Weis v. Weis, 147 Ohio St. 416, 72 N.E.2d 245 (1947). In order to make clear its adherence to the latter position, the rule specifically includes both diagnoses and opinions, in addition to acts, events, and conditions, as proper subjects of admissible entries.

Problems of the motivation of the informant have been a source of difficulty and disagreement. In Palmer v. Hoffman, 318 U.S. 109, 63 S.Ct. 477, 87 L.Ed. 645 (1943), exclusion of an accident report made by the since deceased engineer, offered by defendant railroad trustees in a grade crossing collision case, was upheld. The report was not "in the regular course of business," not a record of the systematic conduct of the business as a business, said the Court. The report was prepared for use in litigating, not railroading. While the opinion mentions the motivation of the engineer only obliquely, the emphasis on records of routine operations is significant only by virtue of impact on motivation to be accurate. Absence of routineness raises lack of motivation to be accurate. The opinion of the Court of Appeals had gone beyond mere lack of motive to be accurate: the engineer's statement was "dripping with motivations to misrepresent." Hoffman v. Palmer, 129 F.2d 976, 991 (2d Cir.1942). The direct introduction of motivation is a disturbing factor, since absence of motive to misrepresent has not traditionally been a requirement of the rule; that records might be self-serving has not been a ground for exclusion. Laughlin, Business Records and the Like, 46 Iowa L.Rev. 276, 285 (1961). As Judge Clark said in his dissent, "I submit that there is hardly a grocer's account book which could not be excluded on that basis." 129 F.2d at 1002. A physician's evaluation report of a personal injury litigant would appear to be in the routine of his business. If the report is offered by the party at whose instance it was made, however, it has been held inadmissible, Yates v. Bair Transport, Inc., 249 F.Supp. 681 (S.D.N.Y.1965), otherwise if offered by the opposite party, Korte v. New York, N.H. & H.R. Co., 191 F.2d 86 (2d Cir.1951), cert. denied 342 U.S. 868, 72 S.Ct. 108, 96 L.Ed. 652.

The decisions hinge on motivation and which party is entitled to be concerned about it. Professor McCormick believed that the doctor's report or the accident report were sufficiently routine to justify admissibility. McCormick § 287, p. 604. Yet hesitation must be experienced in admitting everything which is observed and recorded in the course of a regularly conducted activity. Efforts to set a limit are illustrated by Hartzog v. United States, 217 F.2d 706 (4th Cir.1954), error to admit worksheets made by since deceased deputy collector in preparation for the instant income tax evasion prosecution, and United States v. Ware, 247 F.2d 698 (7th Cir.1957), error to admit narcotics agents' records of purchases. See also Exception (8), infra, as to the public record aspects of records of this nature. Some decisions have been satisfied as to motivation of an accident report if made pursuant to statutory duty, United States v. New York Foreign Trade Zone Operators, 304 F.2d 792 (2d Cir.1962); Taylor v. Baltimore & O.R. Co., 344 F.2d 281 (2d Cir.1965), since the report was oriented in a direction other than the litigation which ensued. Cf. Matthews v. United States, 217 F.2d 409 (5th Cir.1954). The formulation of specific terms which would assure satisfactory results in all cases is not possible. Consequently the rule proceeds from the base that records made in the course of a regularly conducted activity will be taken as admissible but subject to authority to exclude if "the sources of information or other circumstances indicate lack of trustworthiness."

Occasional decisions have reached for enhanced accuracy by requiring involvement as a participant in matters reported. Clainos v. United States, 82 U.S.App.D.C. 278, 163 F.2d 593 (1947), error to admit police records of convictions; Standard Oil Co. of California v. Moore, 251 F.2d 188 (9th Cir.1957), cert. denied 356 U.S. 975, 78 S.Ct. 1139, 2 L.Ed.2d 1148, error to admit employees' records of observed business practices of others. The rule includes no requirement of this nature. Wholly acceptable records may involve matters merely observed, e.g. the weather.

The form which the "record" may assume under the rule is described broadly as a "memorandum, report, record, or data compilation, in any form." The expression "data compilation" is used as broadly descriptive of any means of storing information other than the conventional words and figures in written or documentary form. It includes, but is by no means limited to, electronic computer storage. The term is borrowed from revised Rule 34(a) of the Rules of Civil Procedure.

Report of House Committee on the Judiciary

House Comm. on Judiciary, Fed.Rules of Evidence, H.R.Rep. No. 650, 93d Cong., 1st Sess., p. 14 (1973); 1974 U.S.Code Cong. & Ad.News 7075, 7087

Rule 803(6) as submitted by the Court permitted a record made "in the course of a regularly conducted activity" to be admissible in certain circumstances. The Committee believed there were insufficient guarantees of reliability in records made in the course of activities falling outside the scope of "business" activities as that term is broadly defined in 28 U.S.C. 1732. Moreover, the Committee concluded that the additional requirement of Section 1732 that it must have been the regular practice of a business to make the record is a necessary further assurance of its trustworthiness. The Committee accordingly amended the Rule to incorporate these limitations.

Report of Senate Committee on the Judiciary

Senate Comm. on Judiciary, Fed.Rules of Evidence, S.Rep. No. 1277, 93d Cong., 2d Sess., p. 16 (1974); 1974 U.S.Code Cong. & Ad.News 7051, 7063

Rule 803(6) as submitted by the Supreme Court permitted a record made in the course of a regularly conducted activity to be admissible in certain circumstances. This rule constituted a broadening of the traditional business records hearsay exception which has been long advocated by scholars and judges active in the law of evidence.

The House felt there were insufficient guarantees of reliability of records not within a broadly defined business records exception. We disagree. Even under the House definition of "business" including profession, occupation, and "calling of every kind," the records of many regularly conducted activities will, or may be, excluded from evidence. Under the principle of ejusdem generis, the intent of "calling of every kind" would seem to be related to work-related endeavors—e.g., butcher, baker, artist, etc.

Thus, it appears that the records of many institutions or groups might not be admissible under the House amendments. For example, schools, churches, and hospitals will not normally be considered businesses within the definition. Yet, these are groups which keep financial and other records on a regular basis in a manner similar to business enterprises. We believe these records are of equivalent trustworthiness and should be admitted into evidence.

Three states, which have recently codified their evidence rules, have adopted the Supreme Court version of rule 803(6), providing for admission of memoranda of a "regularly conducted activity." None adopted the words "business activity" used in the House amendment.[3]

Therefore, the committee deleted the word "business" as it appears before the word "activity". The last sentence then is unnecessary and was also deleted.

It is the understanding of the committee that the use of the phrase "person with knowledge" is not intended to imply that the party seeking to introduce

3. See Nev.Rev.Stats. § 15.135; N.Mex.Stats. (1973 Supp.) § 20–4–803(6); West's Wis. Stats.Anno. (1973 Supp.) § 908.03(6).

the memorandum, report, record, or data compilation must be able to produce, or even identify, the specific individual upon whose first-hand knowledge the memorandum, report, record or data compilation was based. A sufficient foundation for the introduction of such evidence will be laid if the party seeking to introduce the evidence is able to show that it was the regular practice of the activity to base such memorandums, reports, records, or data compilations upon a transmission from a person with knowledge, e.g., in the case of the content of a shipment of goods, upon a report from the company's receiving agent or in the case of a computer printout, upon a report from the company's computer programmer or one who has knowledge of the particular record system. In short, the scope of the phrase "person with knowledge" is meant to be coterminous with the custodian of the evidence or other qualified witness. The committee believes this represents the desired rule in light of the complex nature of modern business organizations.

Conference Report

H.R., Fed.Rules of Evidence, Conf.Rep. No. 1597, 93d Cong., 2d Sess., p. 11 (1974); 1974 U.S.Code Cong. & Ad.News 7098, 7104

The House bill provides in subsection (6) that records of a regularly conducted "business" activity qualify for admission into evidence as an exception to the hearsay rule. "Business" is defined as including "business, profession, occupation and calling of every kind." The Senate amendment drops the requirement that the records be those of a "business" activity and eliminates the definition of "business." The Senate amendment provides that records are admissible if they are records of a regularly conducted "activity."

The Conference adopts the House provision that the records must be those of a regularly conducted "business" activity. The Conferees changed the definition of "business" contained in the House provision in order to make it clear that the records of institutions and associations like schools, churches and hospitals are admissible under this provision. The records of public schools and hospitals are also covered by Rule 803(8), which deals with public records and reports.

Advisory Committee's Note

56 F.R.D. 183, 311

Exception (7). Failure of a record to mention a matter which would ordinarily be mentioned is satisfactory evidence of its nonexistence. Uniform Rule 63(14), Comment. While probably not hearsay as defined in Rule 801, supra, decisions may be found which class the evidence not only as hearsay but also as not within any exception. In order to set the question at rest in favor of admissibility, it is specifically treated here. McCormick § 289, p. 609; Morgan, Basic Problems of Evidence 314 (1962); 5 Wigmore § 1531; Uniform Rule 63(14); California Evidence Code § 1272; Kansas Code of Civil Procedure § 60–460(n); New Jersey Evidence Rule 63(14).

Report of House Committee on the Judiciary

House Comm. on Judiciary, Fed.Rules of Evidence, H.R.Rep. No. 650, 93d Cong., 1st Sess., p. 14 (1973); 1974 U.S.Code Cong. & Ad.News 7075, 7088

Rule 803(7) as submitted by the Court concerned the *absence* of entry in the records of a "regularly conducted activity." The Committee amended this Rule to conform with its action with respect to Rule 803(6).

Advisory Committee's Note

56 F.R.D. 183, 311

Exception (8). Public records are a recognized hearsay exception at common law and have been the subject of statutes without number. McCormick § 291. See, for example, 28 U.S.C. § 1733, the relative narrowness of which is illustrated by its nonapplicability to non-federal public agencies, thus necessitating resort to the less appropriate business record exception to the hearsay rule. Kay v. United States, 255 F.2d 476 (4th Cir.1958). The rule makes no distinction between federal and nonfederal offices and agencies.

Justification for the exception is the assumption that a public official will perform his duty properly and the unlikelihood that he will remember details independently of the record. Wong Wing Foo v. McGrath, 196 F.2d 120 (9th Cir.1952), and see Chesapeake & Delaware Canal Co. v. United States, 250 U.S. 123, 39 S.Ct. 407, 63 L.Ed. 889 (1919). As to items (A) and (B), further support is found in the reliability factors underlying records of regularly conducted activities generally. See Exception (6), supra.

(A) Cases illustrating the admissibility of records of the office's or agency's own activities are numerous. Chesapeake & Delaware Canal Co. v. United States, 250 U.S. 123, 39 S.Ct. 407, 63 L.Ed. 889 (1919), Treasury records of miscellaneous receipts and disbursements; Howard v. Perrin, 200 U.S. 71, 26 S.Ct. 195, 50 L.Ed. 374 (1906), General Land Office records; Ballew v. United States, 160 U.S. 187, 16 S.Ct. 263, 40 L.Ed. 388 (1895), Pension Office records.

(B) Cases sustaining admissibility of records of matters observed are also numerous. United States v. Van Hook, 284 F.2d 489 (7th Cir.1960), remanded for resentencing 365 U.S. 609, 81 S.Ct. 823, 5 L.Ed.2d 821, letter from induction officer to District Attorney, pursuant to army regulations, stating fact and circumstances of refusal to be inducted; T'Kach v. United States, 242 F.2d 937 (5th Cir.1957), affidavit of White House personnel officer that search of records showed no employment of accused, charged with fraudulently representing himself as an envoy of the President; Minnehaha County v. Kelley, 150 F.2d 356 (8th Cir.1945); Weather Bureau records of rainfall; United States v. Meyer, 113 F.2d 387 (7th Cir.1940), cert. denied 311 U.S. 706, 61 S.Ct. 174, 85 L.Ed. 459, map prepared by government engineer from information furnished by men working under his supervision.

(C) The more controversial area of public records is that of the so-called "evaluative" report. The disagreement among the decisions has been due in part, no doubt, to the variety of situations encountered, as well as to differences in principle. Sustaining admissibility are such cases as United States v. Dumas, 149 U.S. 278, 13 S.Ct. 872, 37 L.Ed. 734 (1893), statement of account certified by Postmaster General in action against postmaster; McCarty v.

United States, 185 F.2d 520 (5th Cir.1950), reh. denied 187 F.2d 234, Certificate of Settlement of General Accounting Office showing indebtedness and letter from Army official stating Government had performed, in action on contract to purchase and remove waste food from Army camp; Moran v. Pittsburgh-Des Moines Steel Co., 183 F.2d 467 (3d Cir.1950), report of Bureau of Mines as to cause of gas tank explosion; Petition of W___, 164 F.Supp. 659 (E.D.Pa.1958), report by Immigration and Naturalization Service investigator that petitioner was known in community as wife of man to whom she was not married. To the opposite effect and denying admissibility are Franklin v. Skelly Oil Co., 141 F.2d 568 (10th Cir.1944), State Fire Marshal's report of cause of gas explosion; Lomax Transp. Co. v. United States, 183 F.2d 331 (9th Cir.1950), Certificate of Settlement from General Accounting Office in action for naval supplies lost in warehouse fire; Yung Jin Teung v. Dulles, 229 F.2d 244 (2d Cir.1956), "Status Reports" offered to justify delay in processing passport applications. . . . Various kinds of evaluative reports are admissible under federal statutes: 7 U.S.C. § 78, findings of Secretary of Agriculture prima facie evidence of true grade of grain; 7 U.S.C. § 210(f), findings of Secretary of Agriculture prima facie evidence in action for damages against stockyard owner; 7 U.S.C. § 292, order by Secretary of Agriculture prima facie evidence in judicial enforcement proceedings against producers association monopoly; 7 U.S.C. § 1622(h), Department of Agriculture inspection certificates of products shipped in interstate commerce prima facie evidence; 8 U.S.C. § 1440(c), separation of alien from military service on conditions other than honorable provable by certificate from department in proceedings to revoke citizenship; 18 U.S.C. § 4245, certificate of Director of Prisons that convicted person has been examined and found probably incompetent at time of trial prima facie evidence in court hearing on competency; 42 U.S.C. § 269(b), bill of health by appropriate official prima facie evidence of vessel's sanitary history and condition and compliance with regulations; 46 U.S.C. § 679, certificate of consul presumptive evidence of refusal of master to transport destitute seamen to United States. While these statutory exceptions to the hearsay rule are left undisturbed, Rule 802, the willingness of Congress to recognize a substantial measure of admissibility for evaluative reports is a helpful guide.

Factors which may be of assistance in passing upon the admissibility of evaluative reports include: (1) the timeliness of the investigation, McCormick, Can the Courts Make Wider Use of Reports of Official Investigations? 42 Iowa L.Rev. 363 (1957); (2) the special skill or experience of the official, *id.,* (3) whether a hearing was held and the level at which conducted, Franklin v. Skelly Oil Co., 141 F.2d 568 (10th Cir.1944); (4) possible motivation problems suggested by Palmer v. Hoffman, 318 U.S. 109, 63 S.Ct. 477, 87 L.Ed. 645 (1943). Others no doubt could be added.

The formulation of an approach which would give appropriate weight to all possible factors in every situation is an obvious impossibility. Hence the rule, as in Exception (6), assumes admissibility in the first instance but with ample provision for escape if sufficient negative factors are present. In one respect, however, the rule with respect to evaluative reports under item (C) is very specific: they are admissible only in civil cases and against the government in criminal cases in view of the almost certain collision with confrontation rights which would result from their use against the accused in a criminal case.

Report of House Committee on the Judiciary

House Comm. on Judiciary, Fed.Rules of Evidence, H.R.Rep. No. 650, 93d Cong., 1st Sess., p. 14 (1973); 1974 U.S.Code Cong. & Ad.News 7075, 7088

The Committee approved Rule 803(8) without substantive change from the form in which it was submitted by the Court. The Committee intends that the phrase "factual findings" be strictly construed and that evaluations or opinions contained in public reports shall not be admissible under this Rule.

House of Representatives

Feb. 6, 1974, 120 Cong.Rec. 2387 (1974)

Amendment offered by Ms. Holtzman

Ms. HOLTZMAN. Mr. Chairman, I offer an amendment.

The Clerk read as follows:

> Amendment offered by Ms. Holtzman: On page 94, line 11, after the word "law" and before the comma, insert the following: "as to which matters there was a duty to report".

Ms. HOLTZMAN. Mr. Chairman, I will try to be very brief, because it is late in the day.

My amendment is offered to clarify and narrow a provision on the hearsay rule (Rule 803(8)(B)). This rule now provides that if any Government employee in the course of his duty observes something—in fact, anything—and makes a report of that observation, that report can be entered into evidence at a trial whether criminal or civil, without the opportunity to cross-examine the author of the report.

While I respect Government employees, I think we would all concede that they are fallible, exactly like every other human. We do not provide such broad exceptions to the hearsay rule for ordinary mortals.

My amendment makes it crystal clear that random observations by a Government employee cannot be introduced as an exception to the hearsay rule and be insulated from cross-examination. My amendment would allow reports of "matters observed" by a public official only if he had a duty to report about such matters. One operating under such a duty is far more likely to observe and report accurately.

I urge adoption of this amendment in order to narrow and restrict the broad exception to the hearsay rule in the bill.

Mr. HUNGATE. Mr. Chairman, I rise in opposition to the amendment.

This is a matter that was considered in the subcommittee, and we decided to stay with the language as presented to the House here, which states as follows:

> Records, reports, statements, or data compilations, in any form, of public offices or agencies, setting forth (A) the activities of the office or agency, or (B) matters observed pursuant to duty imposed by law. . . .

Mr. Chairman, this is where the point of disagreement occurred. We stayed with that version of the bill, and I would recommend that version to the Committee of the Whole House.

Mr. DANIELSON. Mr. Chairman, I rise in support of the amendment offered by the gentlewoman from New York (Ms. Holtzman).

I think if we leave this language in the proposed bill, we are opening the door to a host of problems, the like of which we have probably never seen in a trial court.

I think the proper approach, in order to eliminate this, is simply to adopt the gentlewoman's amendment, and eliminate this provision, simply because there is absolutely no restriction on the sort of material which could come in under the language as proposed.

I urge the adoption of the gentlewoman's amendment.

Mr. DENNIS. Mr. Chairman, I rise in support of the gentlewoman's amendment.

So that the committee will know what we are talking about here, this permits the introduction in evidence as an exception to the hearsay rule of public records and reports, statements, or data compilations in any form of matters observed pursuant to duty imposed by law. The gentlewoman would add "as to which matters there was a duty to report."

Again it is a matter of judgment, but the difference would be this: Supposing you had a divorce case and you tried to put in a report of a social worker, rather than putting the social worker on the stand; under the committee's language anything she said in the report which would be observed by her pursuant to her general duties would be admissible. Under the amendment, only those things as to which she had some duty to make a report would be admissible.

If the law required her to observe and report certain things about a condition in the home, that could come in, but if she put in a lot of other stuff there, she could not put that in without calling her as a witness and giving the opposition a chance to cross-examine her.

On the whole I think the amendment improves the bill, and I support it.

The CHAIRMAN. The question is on the amendment offered by the gentlewoman from New York (Ms. Holtzman).

The amendment was agreed to.

Amendment offered by Mr. Dennis

Mr. DENNIS. Mr. Chairman, I offer an amendment.

The Clerk read as follows:

> Amendment offered by Mr. Dennis: On page 94, line 11 of the bill, after the word "law", insert the words "excluding, however, in criminal cases matters observed by police officers and other law enforcement personnel".

Mr. DENNIS. Mr. Chairman, this goes to the same subject matter as the last amendment. It deals with official statements and reports.

What I am saying here is that in a criminal case, only, we should not be able to put in the police report to prove your case without calling the policeman. I think in a criminal case you ought to have to call the policeman on the beat and give the defendant the chance to cross examine him, rather than just reading the report into evidence, that is the purpose of this amendment.

Ms. HOLTZMAN. Mr. Chairman, I rise in support of the amendment.

I will be very brief again.

I commend my colleague for raising this point. Again his purpose is to restrict the possible abuse of hearsay evidence.

I think the gentleman's amendment is very valuable and reaffirms the right of cross-examination to the accused. It also permits those engaged in civil trials the right of cross-examination. Cross-examination guarantees due process of law and a fair trial.

(Ms. HOLTZMAN asked and was given permission to revise and extend her remarks.)

Mr. SMITH of New York. Mr. Chairman, I rise in opposition to the amendment.

Mr. Chairman, in reading this amendment it seems to me that the effect of the gentleman's amendment is to treat police officers and other law enforcement officers as second-class citizens, because we have already agreed that we are going to allow in as exceptions to the hearsay rule matters observed pursuant to duty imposed by law. The gentleman from Indiana would exclude from that as follows: "Excluding however, in criminal cases, matters observed by police officers and other law enforcement personnel." This would be so even though they were matters observed pursuant to a duty imposed by law.

I just think we are treading in an area the impact of which will be very unfortunate and the effect of which is to make police officers and law enforcement officers second-class citizens and persons less trustworthy than social workers or garbage collectors.

. . .

Mr. DENNIS. Mr. Chairman, I would like to say on that point that of course that is not my idea. I think the point is that we are dealing here with criminal cases, and in a criminal case the defendant should be confronted with the accuser to give him the chance to cross-examine. This is not any reflection on the police officer, but in a criminal case that is the type of report with which, in fact, one is going to be concerned.

. . .

Mr. JOHNSON of Colorado. Mr. Chairman, as an ex-prosecutor I cannot imagine that the gentleman would be advocating that a policeman's report could come in to help convict a man, and not have the policeman himself subject to cross-examination.

Is that what the gentleman is advocating?

Mr. SMITH of New York. That is what I am advocating in that the policeman's report, if he is not available, should be admissible when it is made pursuant to a duty imposed on that law enforcement officer by law. This is the amendment we have just adopted, and for other public officers these police reports ought to be admissible, whatever their probative value might be.

Mr. JOHNSON of Colorado. Mr. Chairman, if the gentleman will yield further, as I said, I was a prosecutor in a State court, and there were so many cases where good cross-examination indicated a lack of investigative ability on the part of the man who made the report that I became more and more convinced that good cross-examination was one of the principal elements in any criminal trial. If the officer who made the investigation is not available for cross-examination, then you cannot have a fair trial.

I cannot believe the gentleman would be saying that we should be able to convict people where the police officer's statement is not subject to cross-examination.

Mr. SMITH of New York. All I am saying to the gentleman from Colorado is that—and I will concede that the gentleman has probably had greater experience in this field than I have had—all I am saying is that it seems to me that it should be allowed for the jury to consider such a report, together with all of the other aspects of the case, if this report was made by a police officer pursuant to a duty imposed upon that police officer by law.

I will have to admit to the gentleman from Colorado that it is not the best evidence.

Mr. JOHNSON of Colorado. If the gentleman will yield still further, I will have to say that in my opinion the Supreme Court would have to ultimately declare that kind of a rule unconstitutional if we did pass it, and that the present amendment is one that would have to be passed if we are going to preserve the rights and traditions of individuals that have been in existence since 1066—I think that is when it started.

Mr. BRASCO. Mr. Chairman, I move to strike the requisite number of words.

(Mr. BRASCO asked and was given permission to revise and extend his remarks.)

Mr. BRASCO. Mr. Chairman, I would like to ask the author of the amendment, the gentleman from Indiana (Mr. Dennis) a question. I am deeply disturbed and troubled about these rules that have been brought out today.

It seems to me that many critical areas have been overlooked.

One of the basic tenets of our law is that one should be confronted by one's accuser and be able to cross-examine the accuser.

There are many, many exceptions to the hearsay rule here.

As I understand it the gentleman from New York (Mr. Smith) is advocating, in opposition to the amendment offered by the gentleman from Indiana (Mr. Dennis) that if a police officer made a report that he saw Mr. X with a gun on such and such an occasion, and then thereafter that police officer is unavailable that that statement could be used in a criminal trial against Mr. X without the defense attorney having the opportunity to cross-examine the officer with respect to his position with relation to Mr. X, the time of the day, whether he was under a light, or whether there was no light, how much time did he have in which to see the gun, and all other observations relevant to the case.

Mr. DENNIS. Mr. Chairman, I would say in answer to the question raised by the gentleman from New York (Mr. Brasco) that if the statements of the police officer in his report would, in the language of this bill, be "matters observed pursuant to a duty imposed by law, and as to which he was under a duty to make a report," and I rather think they might be, that then what the gentleman says is true, and would be true.

I am trying to remove that possibility, by saying that the rule will not apply in the case the gentleman is talking about.

Mr. BRASCO. I support the gentleman. I am just standing up talking, because I cannot believe that we would for one moment entertain any other rule. I would hope we would do it with all cases of hearsay.

. . .

Mr. HUNT. I had no intention of getting into this argument, but when the gentleman brings in the word "investigator," then I have to get in.

Mr. BRASCO. I did not say it.

Mr. HUNT. I know the gentleman from New York did not, but it was discussed. The only time I can recall in my 34 years of law enforcement that a report of an investigator was admissible in court was to test the credibility of an officer. We would never permit a report to come in unchallenged. We would never even think about bringing in a report in lieu of the officer being there to have that officer cross-examined; but reports were admitted as evidentiary fact for the purpose of testing the officer's credibility and perhaps to refresh his memory. That has always been the rule of law in the State of New Jersey, and I hope it will always remain that way—and even the Federal canons.

Mr. BRASCO. I do not think that the gentleman's amendment interferes with that at all. I think what he is talking about is that the prosecution could use this to prove its case in chief with the possibility of no other evidence being presented.

Mr. HUNT. He is talking about bringing the report in in lieu of an officer, and that certainly is not the case.

Mr. DENNIS. Mr. Chairman, will the gentleman yield?

Mr. BRASCO. I yield to the gentleman from Indiana.

Mr. DENNIS. I thank the gentleman for yielding. I certainly agree this amendment has nothing to do with what my friend, the gentleman from New Jersey, is talking about. This applies only to a hearsay exception, where it would be attempted to bring this report in instead of the officer to prove one's case in chief, which one could do if we do not pass this amendment; but we could still use the report to contradict him and cross-examine him.

Mr. HUNT. Certainly, but the gentleman is speaking of the best evidence available then in lieu of the direct evidence.

Mr. DENNIS. I say we should bring in the man who saw it and put him on the stand.

Mr. HUNT. Certainly, the gentleman is right.

The CHAIRMAN. The question is on the amendment offered by the gentleman from Indiana (Mr. Dennis).

The amendment was agreed to.

Report of Senate Committee on the Judiciary

Senate Comm. on Judiciary, Fed.Rules of Evidence, S.Rep. No. 1277, 93d Cong., 2d Sess., p. 17 (1974); 1974 U.S.Code Cong. & Ad.News 7051, 7064

The House approved rule 803(8), as submitted by the Supreme Court, with one substantive change. It excluded from the hearsay exception reports containing matters observed by police officers and other law enforcement personnel in criminal cases. Ostensibly, the reason for this exclusion is that observations by police officers at the scene of the crime or the apprehension of the defendant are not as reliable as observations by public officials in other cases because of the adversarial nature of the confrontation between the police and the defendant in criminal cases.

The committee accepts the House's decision to exclude such recorded observations where the police officer is available to testify in court about his observation. However, where he is unavailable as unavailability is defined in rule 804(a)(4) and (a)(5), the report should be admitted as the best available evidence. Accordingly, the committee has amended rule 803(8) to refer to the provision of rule 804(b)(5), which allows the admission of such reports, records or other statements where the police officer or other law enforcement officer is unavailable because of death, then existing physical or mental illness or infirmity, or not being successfully subject to legal process. [This version of rule 804(b)(5) was not included in the rules as enacted.]

The House Judiciary Committee report contained a statement of intent that "the phrase 'factual findings' in subdivision (c) be strictly construed and that evaluations or opinions contained in public reports shall not be admissible under this rule." The committee takes strong exception to this limiting understanding of the application of the rule. We do not think it reflects an understanding of the intended operation of the rule as explained in the Advisory Committee notes to this subsection. The Advisory Committee notes on subsection (c) of this subdivision point out that various kinds of evaluative reports are now admissible under Federal statutes. 7 U.S.C. § 78, findings of Secretary of Agriculture prima facie evidence of true grade of grain; 42 U.S.C. § 269(b), bill of health by appropriate official prima facie evidence of vessel's sanitary history and condition and compliance with regulations. These statutory exceptions to the hearsay rule are preserved. Rule 802. The willingness of Congress to recognize these and other such evaluative reports provides a helpful guide in determining the kind of reports which are intended to be admissible under this rule. We think the restrictive interpretation of the House overlooks the fact that while the Advisory Committee assumes admissibility in the first instance of evaluative reports, they are not admissible if, as the rule states, "the sources of information or other circumstances indicate lack of trustworthiness."

The Advisory Committee explains the factors to be considered:

* * *

Factors which may be assistance in passing upon the admissibility of evaluative reports include: (1) the timeliness of the investigation, McCormick, Can the Courts Make Wider Use of Reports of Official Investigations? 42 Iowa L.Rev. 363 (1957); (2) the special skill or experience of the official, id.; (3) whether a hearing was held and the level at which conducted, Franklin v. Skelly Oil Co., 141 F.2d 568 (19th Cir.1944): (4) possible motivation problems suggested by Palmer v. Hoffman, 318 U.S. 109, 63 S.Ct. 477, 87 L.Ed. 645 (1943). Others no doubt could be added.[4]

* * *

The committee concludes that the language of the rule together with the explanation provided by the Advisory Committee furnish sufficient guidance on the admissibility of evaluative reports.

Conference Report

H.R., Fed.Rules of Evidence, Conf.Rep. No. 1597, 93d Cong., 2d Sess., p. 11 (1974); 1974 U.S.Code Cong. & Ad.News 7098, 7104

The Senate amendment adds language, not contained in the House bill, that refers to another rule that was added by the Senate in another amendment (Rule 804(b)(5)—Criminal law enforcement records and reports).

In view of its action on Rule 804(b)(5) (Criminal law enforcement records and reports), the Conference does not adopt the Senate amendment and restores the bill to the House version.

Advisory Committee's Note

56 F.R.D. 183, 313

Exception (9). Records of vital statistics are commonly the subject of particular statutes making them admissible in evidence, Uniform Vital Statistics Act, 9C U.L.A. 350 (1957). The rule is in principle narrower than Uniform Rule 63(16) which includes reports required of persons performing functions authorized by statute, yet in practical effect the two are substantially the same. Comment Uniform Rule 63(16). The exception as drafted is in the pattern of California Evidence Code § 1281.

Exception (10). The principle of proving nonoccurrence of an event by evidence of the absence of a record which would regularly be made of its occurrence, developed in Exception (7) with respect to regularly conducted [business] activities, is here extended to public records of the kind mentioned in Exceptions (8) and (9). 5 Wigmore § 1633(6), p. 519. Some harmless duplication no doubt exists with Exception (7). For instances of federal statutes recognizing this method of proof, see 8 U.S.C. § 1284(b), proof of absence of alien crewman's name from outgoing manifest prima facie evidence of failure to detain or deport, and 42 U.S.C. § 405(c)(3), (4)(B), (4)(C), absence of HEW record prima facie evidence of no wages or self-employment income.

The rule includes situations in which absence of a record may itself be the ultimate focal point of inquiry, e.g. People v. Love, 310 Ill. 558, 142 N.E. 204 (1923), certificate of Secretary of State admitted to show failure to file documents required by Securities Law, as well as cases where the absence of a record is offered as proof of the non-occurrence of an event ordinarily recorded.

The refusal of the common law to allow proof by certificate of the lack of a record or entry has no apparent jusitification, 5 Wigmore § 1678(7), p. 752. The rule takes the opposite position, as do Uniform Rule 63(17); California

4. Advisory Committee's notes, to rule 803(8)(c).

Evidence Code § 1284; Kansas Code of Civil Procedure § 60–460(*c*); New Jersey Evidence Rule 63(17). Congress has recognized certification as evidence of the lack of a record. 8 U.S.C. § 1360(d), certificate of Attorney General or other designated officer that no record of Immigration and Naturalization Service of specified nature or entry therein is found, admissible in alien cases.

Exception (11). Records of activities of religious organizations are currently recognized as admissible at least to the extent of the business records exception to the hearsay rule, 5 Wigmore § 1523, p. 371, and Exception (6) would be applicable. However, both the business record doctrine and Exception (6) require that the person furnishing the information be one in the business or activity. The result is such decisions as Daily v. Grand Lodge, 311 Ill. 184, 142 N.E. 478 (1924), holding a church record admissible to prove fact, date, and place of baptism, but not age of child except that he had at least been born at the time. In view of the unlikelihood that false information would be furnished on occasions of this kind, the rule contains no requirement that the informant be in the course of the activity. See California Evidence Code § 1315 and Comment.

Exception (12). The principle of proof by certification is recognized as to public officials in Exceptions (8) and (10), and with respect to authentication in Rule 902. The present exception is a duplication to the extent that it deals with a certificate by a public official, as in the case of a judge who performs a marriage ceremony. The area covered by the rule is, however, substantially larger and extends the certification procedure to clergymen and the like who perform marriages and other ceremonies or administer sacraments. Thus certificates of such matters as baptism or confirmation, as well as marriage, are included. In principle they are as acceptable evidence as certificates of public officers. See 5 Wigmore § 1645, as to marriage certificates. When the person executing the certificate is not a public official, the self-authenticating character of documents purporting to emanate from public officials, see Rule 902, is lacking and proof is required that the person was authorized and did make the certificate. The time element, however, may safely be taken as supplied by the certificate, once authority and authenticity are established, particularly in view of the presumption that a document was executed on the date it bears.

For similar rules, some limited to certificates of marriage, with variations in foundation requirements, see Uniform Rule 63(18); California Evidence Code § 1316; Kansas Code of Civil Procedure § 60–460(p); New Jersey Evidence Rule 63(18).

Exception (13). Records of family history kept in family Bibles have by long tradition been received in evidence. 5 Wigmore §§ 1495, 1496, citing numerous statutes and decisions. See also Regulations, Social Security Administration, 20 C.F.R. § 404.703(c), recognizing family Bible entries as proof of age in the absence of public or church records. Opinions in the area also include inscriptions on tombstones, publicly displayed pedigrees, and engravings on rings. Wigmore, supra. The rule is substantially identical in coverage with California Evidence Code § 1312.

Report of House Committee on the Judiciary

House Comm. on Judiciary, Fed.Rules of Evidence, H.R.Rep. No. 650, 93d Cong., 1st Sess., p. 15 (1973); 1974 U.S.Code Cong. & Ad.News 7075, 7088

The Committee approved this Rule in the form submitted by the Court, intending that the phrase "Statements of fact concerning personal or family history" be read to include the specific types of such statements enumerated in Rule 803(11).

Advisory Committee's Note

56 F.R.D. 183, 315

Exception (14). The recording of title documents is a purely statutory development. Under any theory of the admissibility of public records, the records would be receivable as evidence of the contents of the recorded document, else the recording process would be reduced to a nullity. When, however, the record is offered for the further purpose of proving execution and delivery, a problem of lack of first-hand knowledge by the recorder, not present as to contents, is presented. This problem is solved, seemingly in all jurisdictions, by qualifying for recording only those documents shown by a specified procedure, either acknowledgement or a form of probate, to have been executed and delivered. 5 Wigmore §§ 1647–1651. Thus what may appear in the rule, at first glance, as endowing the record with an effect independently of local law and inviting difficulties of an *Erie* nature under Cities Service Oil Co. v. Dunlap, 308 U.S. 208, 60 S.Ct. 201, 84 L.Ed. 196 (1939), is not present, since the local law in fact governs under the example [exception].

Exception (15). Dispositive documents often contain recitals of fact. Thus a deed purporting to have been executed by an attorney in fact may recite the existence of the power of attorney, or a deed may recite that the grantors are all the heirs of the last record owner. Under the rule, these recitals are exempted from the hearsay rule. The circumstances under which dispositive documents are executed and the requirement that the recital be germane to the purpose of the document are believed to be adequate guarantees of trustworthiness, particularly in view of the nonapplicability of the rule if dealings with the property have been inconsistent with the document. The age of the document is of no significance, though in practical application the document will most often be an ancient one. See Uniform Rule 63(29), Comment.

Similar provisions are contained in Uniform Rule 63(29); California Evidence Code § 1330; Kansas Code of Civil Procedure § 60–460(aa); New Jersey Evidence Rule 63(29).

Exception (16). Authenticating a document as ancient, essentially in the pattern of the common law, as provided in Rule 901(b)(8), leaves open as a separate question the admissibility of assertive statements contained therein as against a hearsay objection. 7 Wigmore § 2145a. Wigmore further states that the ancient document technique of authentication is universally conceded to apply to all sorts of documents, including letters, records, contracts, maps, and certificates, in addition to title documents, citing numerous decisions. Id. § 2145. Since most of these items are significant evidentially only insofar as they are assertive, their admission in evidence must be as a hearsay exception.

But see 5 id. § 1573, p. 429, referring to recitals in ancient deeds as a "limited" hearsay exception. The former position is believed to be the correct one in reason and authority. As pointed out in McCormick § 298, danger of mistake is minimized by authentication requirements, and age affords assurance that the writing antedates the present controversy. See Dallas County v. Commercial Union Assurance Co., 286 F.2d 388 (5th Cir.1961), upholding admissibility of 58-year-old newspaper story. Cf. Morgan, Basic Problems of Evidence 364 (1962), but see id. 254.

For a similar provision, but with the added requirement that "the statement has since generally been acted upon as true by persons having an interest in the matter," see California Evidence Code § 1331.

Exception (17). Ample authority at common law supported the admission in evidence of items falling in this category. While Wigmore's text is narrowly oriented to lists, etc., prepared for the use of a trade or profession, 6 Wigmore § 1702, authorities are cited which include other kinds of publications, for example, newspaper market reports, telephone directories, and city directories. Id. §§ 1702–1706. The basis of trustworthiness is general reliance by the public or by a particular segment of it, and the motivation of the compiler to foster reliance by being accurate.

For similar provisions, see Uniform Rule 63(30); California Evidence Code § 1340; Kansas Code of Civil Procedure § 60–460(bb); New Jersey Evidence Rule 63(30). Uniform Commercial Code § 2–724 provides for admissibility in evidence of "reports in official publications or trade journals or in newspapers or periodicals of general circulation published as the reports of such [established commodity] market."

Exception (18). The writers have generally favored the admissibility of learned treatises, McCormick § 296, p. 621; Morgan, Basic Problems of Evidence 366 (1962); 6 Wigmore § 1692, with the support of occasional decisions and rules, City of Dothan v. Hardy, 237 Ala. 603, 188 So. 264 (1939); Lewandowski v. Preferred Risk Mut. Ins. Co., 33 Wis.2d 69, 146 N.W.2d 505 (1966), 66 Mich.L.Rev. 183 (1967); Uniform Rule 63(31); Kansas Code of Civil Procedure § 60–460(cc), but the great weight of authority has been that learned treatises are not admissible as substantive evidence though usable in the cross-examination of experts. The foundation of the minority view is that the hearsay objection must be regarded as unimpressive when directed against treatises since a high standard of accuracy is engendered by various factors: the treatise is written primarily and impartially for professionals, subject to scrutiny and exposure for inaccuracy, with the reputation of the writer at stake. 6 Wigmore § 1692. Sound as this position may be with respect to trustworthiness, there is, nevertheless, an additional difficulty in the likelihood that the treatise will be misunderstood and misapplied without expert assistance and supervision. This difficulty is recognized in the cases demonstrating unwillingness to sustain findings relative to disability on the basis of judicially noticed medical texts. Ross v. Gardner, 365 F.2d 554 (6th Cir.1966); Sayers v. Gardner, 380 F.2d 940 (6th Cir.1967); Colwell v. Gardner, 386 F.2d 56 (6th Cir.1967); Glendenning v. Ribicoff, 213 F.Supp. 301 (W.D.Mo.1962); Cook v. Celebrezze, 217 F.Supp. 366 (W.D.Mo.1963); Sosna v. Celebrezze, 234 F.Supp. 289 (E.D.Pa.1964); and see McDaniel v. Celebrezze, 331 F.2d 426 (4th Cir.1964). The rule avoids the danger of misunderstanding and misapplication by limiting the use of treatises as substantive evidence to situations in which an expert is on the stand and available to explain and assist in the application of the treatise if desired. The limitation upon receiving the publication itself physically in evidence, contained in the last sentence, is designed to further this policy.

The relevance of the use of treatises on cross-examination is evident. This use of treatises has been the subject of varied views. The most restrictive position is that the witness must have stated expressly on direct his reliance upon the treatise. A slightly more liberal approach still insists upon reliance but allows it to be developed on cross-examination. Further relaxation dispenses with reliance but requires recognition as an authority by the witness, developable on cross-examination. The greatest liberality is found in decisions allowing use of the treatise on cross-examination when its status as an authority is established by any means. Annot., 60 A.L.R.2d 77. The exception is hinged upon this last position, which is that of the Supreme Court, Reilly v. Pinkus, 338 U.S. 269, 70 S.Ct. 110, 94 L.Ed. 63 (1949), and of recent well considered state court decisions, City of St. Petersburg v. Ferguson, 193 So.2d 648 (Fla.App.1967), cert. denied Fla., 201 So.2d 556; Darling v. Charleston Memorial Community Hospital, 33 Ill.2d 326, 211 N.E.2d 253 (1965); Dabroe v. Rhodes Co., 64 Wash.2d 431, 392 P.2d 317 (1964).

In Reilly v. Pinkus, supra, the Court pointed out that testing of professional knowledge was incomplete without exploration of the witness' knowledge of and attitude toward established treatises in the field. The process works equally well in reverse and furnishes the basis of the rule.

The rule does not require that the witness rely upon or recognize the treatise as authoritative, thus avoiding the possibility that the expert may at the outset block cross-examination by refusing to concede reliance or authoritativeness. Dabroe v. Rhodes Co., supra. Moreover, the rule avoids the unreality of admitting evidence for the purpose of impeachment only, with an instruction to the jury not to consider it otherwise. The parallel to the treatment of prior inconsistent statements will be apparent. See Rules 613(b) and 801(d)(1).

Exceptions (19), (20), and (21). Trustworthiness in reputation evidence is found "when the topic is such that the facts are likely to have been inquired about and that persons having personal knowledge have disclosed facts which have thus been discussed in the community; and thus the community's conclusion, if any has been formed, is likely to be a trustworthy one." 5 Wigmore § 1580, p. 444, and see also § 1583. On this common foundation, reputation as to land boundaries, customs, general history, character, and marriage have come to be regarded as admissible. The breadth of the underlying principle suggests the formulation of an equally broad exception, but tradition has in fact been much narrower and more particularized, and this is the pattern of these exceptions in the rule.

Exception (19) is concerned with matters of personal and family history. Marriage is universally conceded to be a proper subject of proof by evidence of reputation in the community. 5 Wigmore § 1602. As to such items as legitimacy, relationship, adoption, birth, and death, the decisions are divided. Id. § 1605. All seem to be susceptible to being the subject of well founded repute. The "world" in which the reputation may exist may be family, associates, or community. This world has proved capable of expanding with changing times from the single uncomplicated neighborhood, in which all activities take place, to the multiple and unrelated worlds of work, religious affiliation, and social activity, in each of which a reputation may be generated.

People v. Reeves, 360 Ill. 55, 195 N.E. 443 (1935); State v. Axilrod, 248 Minn. 204, 79 N.W.2d 677 (1956); Mass.Stat.1947, c. 410, M.G.L.A. c. 233 § 21A; 5 Wigmore § 1616. The family has often served as the point of beginning for allowing community reputation. 5 Wigmore § 1488. For comparable provisions see Uniform Rule 63(26), (27)(c); California Evidence Code §§ 1313, 1314; Kansas Code of Civil Procedure § 60–460(x), (y)(3); New Jersey Evidence Rule 63(26), (27)(c).

The first portion of Exception (20) is based upon the general admissibility of evidence of reputation as to land boundaries and land customs, expanded in this country to include private as well as public boundaries. McCormick § 299, p. 625. The reputation is required to antedate the controversy, though not to be ancient. The second portion is likewise supported by authority, id., and is designed to facilitate proof of events when judicial notice is not available. The historical character of the subject matter dispenses with any need that the reputation antedate the controversy with respect to which it is offered. For similar provisions see Uniform Rule 63(27)(a), (b); California Evidence Code §§ 1320–1322; Kansas Code of Civil Procedure § 60–460(y), (1), (2); New Jersey Evidence Rule 63(27)(a), (b).

Exception (21) recognizes the traditional acceptance of reputation evidence as a means of proving human character. McCormick §§ 44, 158. The exception deals only with the hearsay aspect of this kind of evidence. Limitations upon admissibility based on other grounds will be found in Rules 404, relevancy of character evidence generally, and 608, character of witness. The exception is in effect a reiteration, in the context of hearsay, of Rule 405(a). Similar provisions are contained in Uniform Rule 63(28); California Evidence Code § 1324; Kansas Code of Civil Procedure § 60–460(z); New Jersey Evidence Rule 63(28).

Exception (22). When the status of a former judgment is under consideration in subsequent litigation, three possibilities must be noted: (1) the former judgment is conclusive under the doctrine of res judicata, either as a bar or a collateral estoppel; or (2) it is admissible in evidence for what it is worth; or (3) it may be of no effect at all. The first situation does not involve any problem of evidence except in the way that principles of substantive law generally bear upon the relevancy and materiality of evidence. The rule does not deal with the substantive effect of the judgment as a bar or collateral estoppel. When, however, the doctrine of res judicata does not apply to make the judgment either a bar or a collateral estoppel, a choice is presented between the second and third alternatives. The rule adopts the second for judgments of criminal conviction of felony grade. This is the direction of the decisions, Annot., 18 A.L.R.2d 1287, 1299, which manifest an increasing reluctance to reject *in toto* the validity of the law's factfinding processes outside the confines of res judicata and collateral estoppel. While this may leave a jury with the evidence of conviction but without means to evaluate it, as suggested by Judge Hinton, Note 27 Ill.L.Rev. 195 (1932), it seems safe to assume that the jury will give it substantial effect unless defendant offers a satisfactory explanation, a possibility not foreclosed by the provision. But see North River Ins. Co. v. Militello, 104 Colo. 28, 88 P.2d 567 (1939), in which the jury found for plaintiff on a fire policy despite the introduction of his conviction for arson. For supporting federal decisions see Clark, J., in New York & Cuba Mail S.S. Co. v. Continental Cas.

Co., 117 F.2d 404, 411 (2d Cir.1941); Connecticut Fire Ins. Co. v. Farrara, 277 F.2d 388 (8th Cir.1960).

Practical considerations require exclusion of convictions of minor offenses, not because the administration of justice in its lower echelons must be inferior, but because motivation to defend at this level is often minimal or nonexistent. Cope v. Goble, 39 Cal.App.2d 448, 103 P.2d 598 (1940); Jones v. Talbot, 87 Idaho 498, 394 P.2d 316 (1964); Warren v. Marsh, 215 Minn. 615, 11 N.W.2d 528 (1943); Annot., 18 A.L.R.2d 1287, 1295–1297; 16 Brooklyn L.Rev. 286 (1950); 50 Colum.L.Rev. 529 (1950); 35 Cornell L.Q. 872 (1950). Hence the rule includes only convictions of felony grade, measured by federal standards.

Judgments of conviction based upon pleas of *nolo contendere* are not included. This position is consistent with the treatment of *nolo* pleas in Rule 410 and the authorities cited in the Advisory Committee's Note in support thereof.

While these rules do not in general purport to resolve constitutional issues, they have in general been drafted with a view to avoiding collision with constitutional principles. Consequently the exception does not include evidence of the conviction of a third person, offered against the accused in a criminal prosecution to prove any fact essential to sustain the judgment of conviction. A contrary position would seem clearly to violate the right of confrontation. Kirby v. United States, 174 U.S. 47, 19 S.Ct. 574, 43 L.Ed. 890 (1899), error to convict of possessing stolen postage stamps with the only evidence of theft being the record of conviction of the thieves. The situation is to be distinguished from cases in which conviction of another person is an element of the crime, e.g. 15 U.S.C. § 902(d), interstate shipment of firearms to a known convicted felon, and, as specifically provided, from impeachment.

For comparable provisions see Uniform Rule 63(20); California Evidence Code § 1300; Kansas Code of Civil Procedure § 60–460(r); New Jersey Evidence Rule 63(20).

Exception (23). A hearsay exception in this area was originally justified on the ground that verdicts were evidence of reputation. As trial by jury graduated from the category of neighborhood inquests, this theory lost its validity. It was never valid as to chancery decrees. Nevertheless the rule persisted, though the judges and writers shifted ground and began saying that the judgment or decree was as good evidence as reputation. See City of London v. Clerke, Carth. 181, 90 Eng.Rep. 710 (K.B. 1691); Neill v. Duke of Devonshire, 8 App.Cas. 135 (1882). The shift appears to be correct, since the process of inquiry, sifting, and scrutiny which is relied upon to render reputation reliable is present in perhaps greater measure in the process of litigation. While this might suggest a broader area of application, the affinity to reputation is strong, and paragraph (23) goes no further, not even including character.

The leading case in the United States, Patterson v. Gaines, 47 U.S. (6 How.) 550, 599, 12 L.Ed. 553 (1847), follows in the pattern of the English decisions, mentioning as illustrative matters thus provable: manorial rights, public rights of way, immemorial custom, disputed boundary, and pedigree. More recent recognition of the principle is found in Grant Bros. Construction Co. v. United States, 232 U.S. 647, 34 S.Ct. 452, 58 L.Ed. 776 (1914), in action for penalties under Alien Contract Labor Law, decision of board of inquiry of Immigration Service admissible to prove alienage of laborers, as a matter of pedigree; United States v. Mid-Continent Petroleum Corp., 67 F.2d 37 (10th Cir.1933), records of commission enrolling Indians admissible on pedigree; Jung Yen Loy v. Cahill, 81 F.2d 809 (9th Cir.1936), board decisions as to citizenship of plaintiff's father admissible in proceeding for declaration of citizenship. Contra, In re Estate of Cunha, 49 Haw. 273, 414 P.2d 925 (1966).

Exception (24). The preceding 23 exceptions of Rule 803 and the first five [four] exceptions of Rule 804(b), infra, are designed to take full advantage of the accumulated wisdom and experience of the past in dealing with hearsay. It would, however, be presumptuous to assume that all possible desirable exceptions to the hearsay rule have been catalogued and to pass the hearsay rule to oncoming generations as a closed system. Exception (24) and its companion provision in Rule 804(b)(6)[5] are accordingly included. They do not contemplate an unfettered exercise of judicial discretion, but they do provide for treating new and presently unanticipated situations which demonstrate a trustworthiness within the spirit of the specifically stated exceptions. Within this framework, room is left for growth and development of the law of evidence in the hearsay area, consistently with the broad purposes expressed in Rule 102. See Dallas County v. Commercial Union Assur. Co., 286 F.2d 388 (5th Cir. 1961).

Report of House Committee on the Judiciary

House Comm. on Judiciary, Fed.Rules of Evidence, H.R.Rep. No. 650, 93d Cong., 1st Sess., p. 5 (1973); 1974 U.S.Code Cong. & Ad.News 7075, 7079

The proposed Rules of Evidence submitted to Congress contained identical provisions in Rules 803 and 804 (which set forth the various hearsay exceptions), to the effect that the federal courts could admit any hearsay statement not specifically covered by any of the stated exceptions, if the hearsay statement was found to have "comparable circumstantial guarantees of trustworthiness."

The Committee deleted these provisions (proposed Rules 803(24) and 804(b)(6)) as injecting too much uncertainty into the law of evidence and impairing the ability of practitioners to prepare for trial. It was noted that Rule 102 directs the courts to construe the Rules of Evidence so as to promote "growth and development." The Committee believed that if additional hearsay exceptions are to be created, they should be by amendments to the Rules, not on a case-by-case basis.

Report of Senate Committee on the Judiciary

Senate Comm. on Judiciary, Fed.Rules of Evidence, S.Rep. No. 1277, 93d Cong., 2d Sess., p. 18 (1974); 1974 U.S.Code Cong. & Ad.News 7051, 7065

The proposed Rules of Evidence submitted to Congress contained identical provisions in rules 803 and 804 (which set forth the various hearsay exceptions), admitting any hearsay statement not specifically covered by any of the stated exceptions, if the hearsay statement was found to have "comparable circumstantial guarantees of trustworthiness." The House deleted these provisions (proposed rules 803(24) and 804(b)(6)) as injecting "too much uncertainty" into the law of evidence and impairing the ability of practitioners to prepare for trial. The House felt that rule 102, which directs the courts to construe the

Rules of Evidence so as to promote growth and development, would permit sufficient flexibility to admit hearsay evidence in appropriate cases under various factual situations that might arise.

We disagree with the total rejection of a residual hearsay exception. While we view rule 102 as being intended to provide for a broader construction and interpretation of these rules, we feel that, without a separate residual provision, the specifically enumerated exceptions could become tortured beyond any reasonable circumstances which they were intended to include (even if broadly construed). Moreover, these exceptions, while they reflect the most typical and well recognized exceptions to the hearsay rule, may not encompass every situation in which the reliability and appropriateness of a particular piece of hearsay evidence make clear that it should be heard and considered by the trier of fact.

The committee believes that there are certain exceptional circumstances where evidence which is found by a court to have guarantees of trustworthiness equivalent to or exceeding the guarantees reflected by the presently listed exceptions, and to have a high degree of probativeness and necessity could properly be admissible.

The case of Dallas County v. Commercial Union Assoc. Co., Ltd., 286 F.2d 388 (5th Cir.1961) illustrates the point. The issue in that case was whether the tower of the county courthouse collapsed because it was struck by lightning (covered by insurance) or because of structural weakness and deterioration of the structure (not covered). Investigation of the structure revealed the presence of charcoal and charred timbers. In order to show that lightning may not have been the cause of the charring, the insurer offered a copy of a local newspaper published over 50 years earlier containing an unsigned article describing a fire in the courthouse while it was under construction. The Court found that the newspaper did not qualify for admission as a business record or an ancient document and did not fit within any other recognized hearsay exception. The court concluded, however, that the article was trustworthy because it was inconceivable that a newspaper reporter in a small town would report a fire in the courthouse if none had occurred. See also United States v. Barbati, 284 F.Supp. 409 (E.D.N.Y.1968).

Because exceptional cases like the *Dallas County* case may arise in the future, the committee has decided to reinstate a residual exception for rules 803 and 804(b).

The committee, however, also agrees with those supporters of the House version who felt that an overly broad residual hearsay exception could emasculate the hearsay rule and the recognized exceptions or vitiate the rationale behind codification of the rules.

Therefore, the committee has adopted a residual exception for rules 803 and 804(b) of much narrower scope and applicability than the Supreme Court version. In order to qualify for admission, a hearsay statement not falling within one of the recognized exceptions would have to satisfy at least four conditions. First, it must have "equivalent circumstantial guarantees of trustworthiness." Second, it must be offered as evidence of a material fact. Third, the court must determine that the statement "is more probative on the point for which it is offered than any other evidence which the proponent can procure through reasonable efforts." This requirement is intended to insure that only statements which have high probative value and necessity may qualify for admission under the residual exceptions. Fourth, the court must determine that "the general purposes of these rules and the interests of justice will best be served by admission of the statement into evidence."

It is intended that the residual hearsay exceptions will be used very rarely, and only in exceptional circumstances. The committee does not intend to establish a broad license for trial judges to admit hearsay statements that do not fall within one of the other exceptions contained in rules 803 and 804(b). The residual exceptions are not meant to authorize major judicial revisions of the hearsay rule, including its present exceptions. Such major revisions are best accomplished by legislative action. It is intended that in any case in which evidence is sought to be admitted under these subsections, the trial judge will exercise no less care, reflection and caution than the courts did under the common law in establishing the now-recognized exceptions to the hearsay rule.

In order to establish a well-defined jurisprudence, the special facts and circumstances which, in the court's judgment, indicates that the statement has a sufficiently high degree of trustworthiness and necessity to justify its admission should be stated on the record. It is expected that the court will give the opposing party a full and adequate opportunity to contest the admission of any statement sought to be introduced under these subsections.

Conference Report [1]

H.R., Fed.Rules of Evidence, Conf.Rep. No. 1597, 93d Cong., 2d Sess., p. 11 (1974); 1974 U.S.Code Cong. & Ad.News 7098, 7105

The Senate amendment adds a new subsection, (24), which makes admissible a hearsay statement not specifically covered by any of the previous twenty-three subsections, if the statement has equivalent circumstantial guarantees of trustworthiness and if the court determines that (A) the statement is offered as evidence of a material fact; (B) the statement is more probative on the point for which it is offered than any other evidence the proponent can procure through reasonable efforts; and (C) the general purposes of these rules and the interests of justice will best be served by admission of the statement into evidence.

The House bill eliminated a similar, but broader, provision because of the conviction that such a provision injected too much uncertainty into the law of evidence regarding hearsay and impaired the ability of a litigant to prepare adequately for trial.

The Conference adopts the Senate amendment with an amendment that provides that a party intending to request the court to use a statement under this provision must notify any adverse party of this intention as well as of the particulars of the statement, including the name and address of the declarant. This notice must be given sufficiently in advance of the trial or hearing to provide any adverse party with a fair opportunity to prepare to contest the use of the statement.

1987 Amendment. The amendments are technical. No substantive change is intended.

1. The Conference Report contains a like provision with regard to Rule 804(b)(5).—Ed.

Rule 804. Hearsay Exceptions; Declarant Unavailable

(a) Definition of unavailability. "Unavailability as a witness" includes situations in which the declarant—

(1) is exempted by ruling of the court on the ground of privilege from testifying concerning the subject matter of the declarant's statement; or

(2) persists in refusing to testify concerning the subject matter of the declarant's statement despite an order of the court to do so; or

(3) testifies to a lack of memory of the subject matter of the declarant's statement; or

(4) is unable to be present or to testify at the hearing because of death or then existing physical or mental illness or infirmity; or

(5) is absent from the hearing and the proponent of statement has been unable to procure the declarant's attendance (or in the case of a hearsay exception under subdivision (b)(2), (3), or (4), the declarant's attendance or testimony) by process or other reasonable means.

A declarant is not unavailable as a witness if exemption, refusal, claim of lack of memory, inability, or absence is due to the procurement or wrongdoing of the proponent of a statement for the purpose of preventing the witness from attending or testifying.

(b) Hearsay exceptions. The following are not excluded by the hearsay rule if the declarant is unavailable as a witness:

(1) Former testimony. Testimony given as a witness at another hearing of the same or a different proceeding, or in a deposition taken in compliance with law in the course of the same or another proceeding, if the party against whom the testimony is now offered, or, in a civil action or proceeding, a predecessor in interest, had an opportunity and similar motive to develop the testimony by direct, cross, or redirect examination.

(2) Statement under belief of impending death. In a prosecution for homicide or in a civil action or proceeding, a statement made by a declarant while believing that the declarant's death was imminent, concerning the cause or circumstances of what the declarant believed to be impending death.

(3) Statement against interest. A statement which was at the time of its making so far contrary to the declarant's pecuniary or proprietary interest, or so far tended to subject the declarant to civil or criminal liability, or to render invalid a claim by the declarant against another, that a reasonable person in the declarant's position would not have made the statement unless believing it to be true. A statement tending to expose the declarant to criminal liability and offered to exculpate the accused is not admissible unless corroborating circumstances clearly indicate the trustworthiness of the statement.

(4) Statement of personal or family history. (A) A statement concerning the declarant's own birth, adoption, marriage, divorce, legitimacy, relationship by blood, adoption, or marriage, ancestry, or other similar fact of personal or family history, even though declarant had no means of acquiring personal knowledge of the matter stated; or (B) a statement concerning the foregoing matters, and death also, of another person, if the declarant was related to the other by blood, adoption, or marriage or was so intimately associated with the other's family as to be likely to have accurate information concerning the matter declared.

(5) Other exceptions. A statement not specifically covered by any of the foregoing exceptions but having equivalent circumstantial guarantees of trustworthiness, if the court determines that (A) the statement is offered as evidence of a material fact; (B) the statement is more probative on the point for which it is offered than any other evidence which the proponent can procure through reasonable efforts; and (C) the general purposes of these rules and the interests of justice will best be served by admission of the statement into evidence. However, a statement may not be admitted under this exception unless the proponent of it makes known to the adverse party sufficiently in advance of the trial or hearing to provide the adverse party with a fair opportunity to prepare to meet it, the proponent's intention to offer the statement and the particulars of it, including the name and address of the declarant.

(As amended P.L. 94–149, § 1(12), (13), Dec. 12, 1975, 89 Stat. 806; Mar. 2, 1987, eff. Oct. 1, 1987; Nov. 18, 1988, P.L. 100–690, Title VII, § 7075(b), 102 Stat. 4405.)

Section references, McCormick 4th ed.

Generally, § 253, § 326

(a). § 253

(b). § 320

(1). § 301, § 302, § 303, § 304, § 308

(2). § 310, § 311, § 312, § 313, § 315

(3). § 254, § 316, § 317, § 318, § 319, § 271

(4). § 322

(5). § 324, § 324.3, § 353

Note by Federal Judicial Center

The rule prescribed by the Supreme Court was amended by the Congress in a number of respects as follows:

Subdivision (a). Paragraphs (1) and (2) were amended by substituting "court" in place of "judge," and paragraph (5) was amended by inserting "(or in the case of a hearsay exception under subdivision (b)(2), (3), or (4), his attendance or testimony)".

Subdivision (b). Exception (1) was amended by inserting "the same or" after "course of," and by substituting the phrase "if the party against whom the testimony is now offered, or, in a civil action or proceeding, a predecessor in interest, had an opportunity and similar motive to develop the testimony by direct, cross, or redirect examination" in place of "at the instance of or against a party with an opportunity to develop the testimony by direct, cross, or redirect examination, with motive and interest similar to those of the party against whom now offered."

Exception (2) as prescribed by the Supreme Court, dealing with statements of recent perception, was deleted by the Congress.

. . . Exception (2) as enacted by the Congress is Exception (3) prescribed by the Supreme Court, amended by inserting at the beginning, "In a prosecution for homicide or in a civil action or proceeding".

Exception (3) as enacted by the Congress is Exception (4) prescribed by the Supreme Court, amended in the first sentence by deleting, after "another," the phrase "or to make him an object of hatred, ridicule, or disgrace," and amended in the second sentence by substituting, after "unless," the phrase, "corroborating circumstances clearly indicate the trustworthiness of the statement," in place of "corroborated."

Exception (4) as enacted by the Congress is Exception (5) prescribed by the Supreme Court without change.

Exception (5) as enacted by the Congress is Exception (6) prescribed by the Supreme Court, amended by substituting "equivalent" in place of "comparable" and by adding all after "trustworthiness."

Advisory Committee's Note

56 F.R.D. 183, 322

As to firsthand knowledge on the part of hearsay declarants, see the introductory portion of the Advisory Committee's Note to Rule 803.

Subdivision (a). The definition of unavailability implements the division of hearsay exceptions into two categories by Rules 803 and 804(b).

At common law the unavailability requirement was evolved in connection with particular hearsay exceptions rather than along general lines. For example, see the separate explications of unavailability in relation to former testimony, declarations against interest, and statements of pedigree, separately developed in McCormick §§ 234, 257, and 297. However, no reason is apparent for making distinctions as to what satisfies unavailability for the different exceptions. The treatment in the rule is therefore uniform although differences in the range of process for witnesses between civil and criminal cases will lead to a less exacting requirement under item (5). See Rule 45(e) of the Federal Rules of Civil Procedure and Rule 17(e) of the Federal Rules of Criminal Procedure.

Five instances of unavailability are specified:

(1) Substantial authority supports the position that exercise of a claim of privilege by the declarant satisfies the requirement of unavailability (usually in connection with former testimony). Wyatt v. State, 35 Ala.App. 147, 46 So.2d

837 (1950); State v. Stewart, 85 Kan. 404, 116 P. 489 (1911); Annot., 45 A.L.R.2d 1354; Uniform Rule 62(7)(a); California Evidence Code § 240(a)(1); Kansas Code of Civil Procedure § 60–459(g)(1). A ruling by the judge is required, which clearly implies that an actual claim of privilege must be made.

(2) A witness is rendered unavailable if he simply refuses to testify concerning the subject matter of his statement despite judicial pressures to do so, a position supported by similar considerations of practicality. Johnson v. People, 152 Colo. 586, 384 P.2d 454 (1963); People v. Pickett, 339 Mich. 294, 63 N.W.2d 681, 45 A.L.R.2d 1341 (1954). Contra, Pleau v. State, 255 Wis. 362, 38 N.W.2d 496 (1949).

(3) The position that a claimed lack of memory by the witness of the subject matter of his statement constitutes unavailability likewise finds support in the cases, though not without dissent. McCormick § 234, p. 494. If the claim is successful, the practical effect is to put the testimony beyond reach, as in the other instances. In this instance, however, it will be noted that the lack of memory must be established by the testimony of the witness himself, which clearly contemplates his production and subjection to cross-examination.

Report of House Committee on the Judiciary

House Comm. on Judiciary, Fed.Rules of Evidence, H.R.Rep. No. 650, 93d Cong., 1st Sess., p. 15 (1973); 1974 U.S.Code Cong. & Ad.News 7075, 7088

Rule 804(a)(3) was approved in the form submitted by the Court. However, the Committee intends no change in existing federal law under which the court may choose to disbelieve the declarant's testimony as to his lack of memory. See United States v. Insana, 423 F.2d 1165, 1169–1170 (2nd Cir.), cert. denied, 400 U.S. 841 (1970).

Advisory Committee's Note

56 F.R.D. 183, 322

(4) Death and infirmity find general recognition as grounds. McCormick §§ 234, 257, 297; Uniform Rule 62(7)(c); California Evidence Code § 240(a)(3); Kansas Code of Civil Procedure § 60–459(g)(3); New Jersey Evidence Rule 62(6)(c). See also the provisions on use of depositions in Rule 32(a)(3) of the Federal Rules of Civil Procedure and Rule 15(e) of the Federal Rules of Criminal Procedure.

(5) Absence from the hearing coupled with inability to compel attendance by process or other reasonable means also satisfies the requirement. McCormick § 234; Uniform Rule 62(7)(d) and (e); California Evidence Code § 240(a)(4) and (5); Kansas Code of Civil Procedure § 60–459(g)(4) and (5); New Jersey Rule 62(6)(b) and (d). See the discussion of procuring attendance of witnesses who are nonresidents or in custody in Barber v. Page, 390 U.S. 719, 88 S.Ct. 1318, 20 L.Ed.2d 255 (1968).

If the conditions otherwise constituting unavailability result from the procurement or wrongdoing of the proponent of the statement, the requirement is not satisfied. . . .

Report of House Committee on the Judiciary

House Comm. on Judiciary, Fed.Rules of Evidence, H.R.Rep. No. 650, 93d Cong., 1st Sess., p. 15 (1973); 1974 U.S.Code Cong. & Ad.News 7075, 7088

Rule 804(a)(5) as submitted to the Congress provided, as one type of situation in which a declarant would be deemed "unavailable", that he be "absent from the hearing and the proponent of his statement has been unable to procure his attendance by process or other reasonable means." The Committee amended the Rule to insert after the word "attendance" the parenthetical expression "(or, in the case of a hearsay exception under subdivision (b)(2), (3), or (4), his attendance or testimony)". The amendment is designed primarily to require that an attempt be made to depose a witness (as well as to seek his attendance) as a precondition to the witness being deemed unavailable. The Committee, however, recognized the propriety of an exception to this additional requirement when it is the declarant's former testimony that is sought to be admitted under subdivision (b)(1).

Report of Senate Committee on the Judiciary

Senate Comm. on Judiciary, Fed.Rules of Evidence, S.Rep. No. 1277, 93d Cong., 2d Sess., p. 20 (1974); 1974 U.S.Code Cong. & Ad.News 7051, 7066

Subdivision (a) of rule 804 as submitted by the Supreme Court defined the conditions under which a witness was considered to be unavailable. It was amended in the House.

The purpose of the amendment, according to the report of the House Committee on the Judiciary, is "primarily to require that an attempt be made to depose a witness (as well as to seek his attendance) as a precondition to the witness being unavailable." [1]

Under the House amendment, before a witness is declared unavailable, a party must try to depose a witness (declarant) with respect to dying declarations, declarations against interest, and declarations of pedigree. None of these situations would seem to warrant this needless, impractical and highly restrictive complication. A good case can be made for eliminating the unavailability requirement entirely for declarations against interest cases.[2]

In dying declaration cases, the declarant will usually, though not necessarily, be deceased at the time of trial. Pedigree statements which are admittedly and necessarily based largely on word of mouth are not greatly fortified by a deposition requirement.

Depositions are expensive and time-consuming. In any event, deposition procedures are available to those who wish to resort to them. Moreover, the deposition procedures of the Civil Rules and Criminal Rules are only imperfectly adapted to implementing the amendment. No purpose is served unless the deposition, if taken, may be used in evidence. Under Civil Rule (a)(3) and Criminal Rule 15(e), a deposition, though taken, may not be admissible, and under Criminal Rule 15(a) substantial obstacles exist in the way of even taking a deposition.

1. H.Rept. 93–650, at p. 15.
2. Uniform rule 63(10); Kan.Stat.Anno. 60–460(j); 2A N.J.Stats.Anno. 84–63(10).

For these reasons, the committee deleted the House amendment.

The committee understands that the rule as to unavailability, as explained by the Advisory Committee "contains no requirement that an attempt be made to take the deposition of a declarant." In reflecting the committee's judgment, the statement is accurate insofar as it goes. Where, however, the proponent of the statement, with knowledge of the existence of the statement, fails to confront the declarant with the statement at the taking of the deposition, then the proponent should not, in fairness, be permitted to treat the declarant as "unavailable" simply because the declarant was not amenable to process compelling his attendance at trial. The committee does not consider it necessary to amend the rule to this effect because such a situation abuses, not conforms to, the rule. Fairness would preclude a person from introducing a hearsay statement on a particular issue if the person taking the deposition was aware of the issue at the time of the deposition but failed to depose the unavailable witness on that issue.

Conference Report

H.R., Fed.Rules of Evidence, Conf.Rep. No. 1597, 93d Cong., 2d Sess., p. 12 (1974); 1974 U.S.Code Cong. & Ad. News 7098, 7105

Subsection (a) defines the term "unavailability as a witness". The House bill provides in subsection (a)(5) that the party who desires to use the statement must be unable to procure the declarant's attendance by process or other reasonable means. In the case of dying declarations, statements against interest and statements of personal or family history, the House bill requires that the proponent must also be unable to procure the declarant's *testimony* (such as by deposition or interrogatories) by process or other reasonable means. The Senate amendment eliminates this latter provision.

The Conference adopts the provision contained in the House bill.

Advisory Committee's Note

56 F.R.D. 183, 323

Subdivision (b). Rule 803, supra, is based upon the assumption that a hearsay statement falling within one of its exceptions possesses qualities which justify the conclusion that whether the declarant is available or unavailable is not a relevant factor in determining admissibility. The instant rule proceeds upon a different theory: hearsay which admittedly is not equal in quality to testimony of the declarant on the stand may nevertheless be admitted if the declarant is unavailable and if his statement meets a specified standard. The rule expresses preferences: testimony given on the stand in person is preferred over hearsay, and hearsay, if of the specified quality, is preferred over complete loss of the evidence of the declarant. The exceptions evolved at common law with respect to declarations of unavailable declarants furnish the basis for the exceptions enumerated in the proposal. The term "unavailable" is defined in subdivision (a).

Exception [1]. Former testimony does not rely upon some set of circumstances to substitute for oath and cross-examination, since both oath and opportunity to cross-examine were present in fact. The only missing one of the ideal conditions for the giving of testimony is the presence of trier and opponent ("demeanor evidence"). This is lacking with all hearsay exceptions.

Hence it may be argued that former testimony is the strongest hearsay and should be included under Rule 803, supra. However, opportunity to observe demeanor is what in a large measure confers depth and meaning upon oath and cross-examination. Thus in cases under Rule 803 demeanor lacks the significance which it possesses with respect to testimony. In any event, the tradition, founded in experience, uniformly favors production of the witness if he is available. The exception indicates continuation of the policy. This preference for the presence of the witness is apparent also in rules and statutes on the use of depositions, which deal with substantially the same problem.

Under the exception, the testimony may be offered (1) against the party *against* whom it was previously offered or (2) against the party *by* whom it was previously offered. In each instance the question resolves itself into whether fairness allows imposing, upon the party against whom now offered, the handling of the witness on the earlier occasion. (1) If the party against whom now offered is the one against whom the testimony was offered previously, no unfairness is apparent in requiring him to accept his own prior conduct of cross-examination or decision not to cross-examine. Only demeanor has been lost, and that is inherent in the situation. (2) If the party against whom now offered is the one *by* whom the testimony was offered previously, a satisfactory answer becomes somewhat more difficult. One possibility is to proceed somewhat along the line of an adoptive admission, i.e. by offering the testimony proponent in effect adopts it. However, this theory savors of discarded concepts of witnesses' belonging to a party, of litigants' ability to pick and choose witnesses, and of vouching for one's own witnesses. Cf. McCormick § 246, pp. 526–527; 4 Wigmore § 1075. A more direct and acceptable approach is simply to recognize direct and redirect examination of one's own witness as the equivalent of cross-examining an opponent's witness. Falknor, Former Testimony and the Uniform Rules: A Comment, 38 N.Y.U.L.Rev. 651, n. 1 (1963); McCormick § 231, p. 483. See also 5 Wigmore § 1389. Allowable techniques for dealing with hostile, double-crossing, forgetful, and mentally deficient witnesses leave no substance to a claim that one could not adequately develop his own witness at the former hearing. An even less appealing argument is presented when failure to develop fully was the result of a deliberate choice.

The common law did not limit the admissibility of former testimony to that given in an earlier trial of the same case, although it did require identity of issues as a means of insuring that the former handling of the witness was the equivalent of what would now be done if the opportunity were presented. Modern decisions reduce the requirement to "substantial" identity. McCormick § 233. Since identity of issues is significant only in that it bears on motive and interest in developing fully the testimony of the witness, expressing the matter in the latter terms is preferable. Id. Testimony given at a preliminary hearing was held in California v. Green, 399 U.S. 149, 90 S.Ct. 1930, 26 L.Ed.2d 489 (1970), to satisfy confrontation requirements in this respect.

As a further assurance of fairness in thrusting upon a party the prior handling of the witness, the common law also insisted upon identity of parties, deviating only to the extent of allowing substitution of successors in a narrowly construed privity. Mutuality as an aspect of identity is now generally discredited, and the requirement of identity of the offering party disappears except as it might affect motive to develop the testimony. Falknor, supra, at 652;

McCormick § 232, pp. 487–488. The question remains whether strict identity, or privity, should continue as a requirement with respect to the party against whom offered. . . .

Report of House Committee on the Judiciary

House Comm. on Judiciary, Fed.Rules of Evidence, H.R.Rep. No. 650, 93d Cong., 1st Sess., p. 15 (1973); 1974 U.S.Code Cong. & Ad.News 7075, 7088

Rule 804(b)(1) as submitted by the Court allowed prior testimony of an unavailable witness to be admissible if the party against whom it is offered or a person "with motive and interest similar" to his had an opportunity to examine the witness. The Committee considered that it is generally unfair to impose upon the party against whom the hearsay evidence is being offered responsibility for the manner in which the witness was previously handled by another party. The sole exception to this, in the Committee's view, is when a party's predecessor in interest in a civil action or proceeding had an opportunity and similar motive to examine the witness. The Committee amended the Rule to reflect these policy determinations.

Advisory Committee's Note

56 F.R.D. 183, 326

Exception [2]. The exception is the familiar dying declaration of the common law, expanded somewhat beyond its traditionally narrow limits. While the original religious justification for the exception may have lost its conviction for some persons over the years, it can scarcely be doubted that powerful psychological pressures are present. See 5 Wigmore § 1443 and the classic statement of Chief Baron Eyre in Rex v. Woodcock, 1 Leach 500, 502, 168 Eng.Rep. 352, 353 (K.B.1789).

The common law required that the statement be that of the victim, offered in a prosecution for criminal homicide. Thus declarations by victims in prosecutions for other crimes, e.g. a declaration by a rape victim who dies in childbirth, and all declarations in civil cases were outside the scope of the exception. An occasional statute has removed these restrictions, as in Colo.R.S. § 52–1–20, or has expanded the area of offenses to include abortions, 5 Wigmore § 1432, p. 224, n. 4. Kansas by decision extended the exception to civil cases. Thurston v. Fritz, 91 Kan. 468, 138 P. 625 (1914). While the common law exception no doubt originated as a result of the exceptional need for the evidence in homicide cases, the theory of admissibility applies equally in civil cases . . .. The same considerations suggest abandonment of the limitation to circumstances attending the event in question, yet when the statement deals with matters other than the supposed death, its influence is believed to be sufficiently attenuated to justify the limitation. Unavailability is not limited to death. See subdivision (a) of this rule. Any problem as to declarations phrased in terms of opinion is laid at rest by Rule 701, and continuation of a requirement of first-hand knowledge is assured by Rule 602.

Comparable provisions are found in Uniform Rule 63(5); California Evidence Code § 1242; Kansas Code of Civil Procedure § 60–460(e); New Jersey Evidence Rule 63(5).

Report of House Committee on the Judiciary

House Comm. on Judiciary, Fed.Rules of Evidence, H.R.Rep. No. 650, 93d Cong., 1st Sess., p. 15 (1973); 1974 U.S.Code Cong. & Ad.News 7075, 7089

Rule 804(b)(3) as submitted by the Court (now Rule 804(b)(2) in the bill) proposed to expand the traditional scope of the dying declaration exception (i.e. a statement of the victim in a homicide case as to the cause or circumstances of his believed imminent death) to allow such statements in all criminal and civil cases. The Committee did not consider dying declarations as among the most reliable forms of hearsay. Consequently, it amended the provision to limit their admissibility in criminal cases to homicide prosecutions, where exceptional need for the evidence is present. This is existing law. At the same time, the Committee approved the expansion to civil actions and proceedings where the stakes do not involve possible imprisonment, although noting that this could lead to forum shopping in some instances.

Advisory Committee's Note

46 F.R.D. 183, 327

Exception [3]. The circumstantial guaranty of reliability for declarations against interest is the assumption that persons do not make statements which are damaging to themselves unless satisfied for good reason that they are true. Hileman v. Northwest Engineering Co., 346 F.2d 668 (6th Cir.1965). If the statement is that of a party, offered by his opponent, it comes in as an admission, Rule 803(d)(2), and there is no occasion to inquire whether it is against interest, this not being a condition precedent to admissibility of admissions by opponents.

The common law required that the interest declared against be pecuniary or proprietary but within this limitation demonstrated striking ingenuity in discovering an against-interest aspect. Higham v. Ridgway, 10 East 109, 103 Eng.Rep. 717 (K.B.1808); Reg. v. Overseers of Birmingham, 1 B. & S. 763, 121 Eng.Rep. 897 (Q.B.1861); McCormick, § 256, p. 551, nn. 2 and 3.

The exception discards the common law limitation and expands to the full logical limit. One result is to remove doubt as to the admissibility of declarations tending to establish a tort liability against the declarant or to extinguish one which might be asserted by him, in accordance with the trend of the decisions in this country. McCormick, § 254, pp. 548–549. . . . And finally, exposure to criminal liability satisfies the against-interest requirement. The refusal of the common law to concede the adequacy of a penal interest was no doubt indefensible in logic, see the dissent of Mr. Justice Holmes in Donnelly v. United States, 228 U.S. 243, 33 S.Ct. 449, 57 L.Ed. 820 (1913), but one senses in the decisions a distrust of evidence of confessions by third persons offered to exculpate the accused arising from suspicions of fabrication either of the fact of the making of the confession or in its contents, enhanced in either instance by the required unavailability of the declarant. Nevertheless, an increasing amount of decisional law recognizes exposure to punishment for crime as a sufficient stake. People v. Spriggs, 60 Cal.2d 868, 36 Cal.Rptr. 841, 389 P.2d 377 (1964); Sutter v. Easterly, 354 Mo. 282, 189 S.W.2d 284 (1945); Band's Refuse Removal, Inc. v. Fairlawn Borough, 62 N.J.Super. 522, 163 A.2d 465

(1960); Newberry v. Commonwealth, 191 Va. 445, 61 S.E.2d 318 (1950); Annot., 162 A.L.R. 446. The requirement of corroboration is included in the rule in order to effect an accommodation between these competing considerations. When the statement is offered by the accused by way of exculpation, the resulting situation is not adapted to control by rulings as to the weight of the evidence, and hence the provision is cast in terms of a requirement preliminary to admissibility. Cf. Rule 406(a). The requirement of corroboration should be construed in such a manner as to effectuate its purpose of circumventing fabrication.

Ordinarily the third-party confession is thought of in terms of exculpating the accused, but this is by no means always or necessarily the case: it may include statements implicating him, and under the general theory of declarations against interest they would be admissible as related statements. Douglas v. Alabama, 380 U.S. 415, 85 S.Ct. 1074, 13 L.Ed.2d 934 (1965), and Bruton v. United States, 389 U.S. 818, 88 S.Ct. 126, 19 L.Ed.2d 70 (1968), both involved confessions by codefendants which implicated the accused. While the confession was not actually offered in evidence in *Douglas,* the procedure followed effectively put it before the jury, which the Court ruled to be error. Whether the confession might have been admissible as a declaration against penal interest was not considered or discussed. *Bruton* assumed the inadmissibility, as against the accused, of the implicating confession of his codefendant, and centered upon the question of the effectiveness of a limiting instruction. These decisions, however, by no means require that all statements implicating another person be excluded from the category of declarations against interest. Whether a statement is in fact against interest must be determined from the circumstances of each case. Thus a statement admitting guilt and implicating another person, made while in custody, may well be motivated by a desire to curry favor with the authorities and hence fail to qualify as against interest. See the dissenting opinion of Mr. Justice White in *Bruton.* On the other hand, the same words spoken under different circumstances, e.g., to an acquaintance, would have no difficulty in qualifying. The rule does not purport to deal with questions of the right of confrontation.

The balancing of self-serving against disserving aspects of a declaration is discussed in McCormick § 256.

For comparable provisions, see Uniform Rule 63(10); California Evidence Code § 1230; Kansas Code of Civil Procedure § 60–460(j); New Jersey Evidence Rule 63(10).

Report of House Committee on the Judiciary

House Comm. on Judiciary, Fed.Rules of Evidence, H.R.Rep. No. 650, 93d Cong., 1st Sess., p. 16 (1973); 1974 U.S.Code Cong. & Ad.News 7075, 7089

Rule 804(b)(4) as submitted by the Court (now Rule 804(b)(3) in the bill) provided as follows:

> *Statement against interest.*—A statement which was at the time of its making so far contrary to the declarant's pecuniary or proprietary interest or so far tended to subject him to civil or criminal liability or to render invalid a claim by him against another or to make him an object of hatred, ridicule, or disgrace, that a reasonable man in his position would not have

made the statement unless he believed it to be true. A statement tending to exculpate the accused is not admissible unless corroborated.

The Committee determined to retain the traditional hearsay exception for statements against pecuniary or proprietary interest. However, it deemed the Court's additional references to statements tending to subject a declarant to civil liability or to render invalid a claim by him against another to be redundant as included within the scope of the reference to statements against pecuniary or proprietary interest. See Gichner v. Antonio Triano Tile and Marble Co., 410 F.2d 238 (D.C.Cir.1968). Those additional references were accordingly deleted.

The Court's Rule also proposed to expand the hearsay limitation from its present federal limitation to include statements subjecting the declarant to criminal liability and statements tending to make him an object of hatred, ridicule, or disgrace. The Committee eliminated the latter category from the subdivision as lacking sufficient guarantees of reliability. See United States v. Dovico, 380 F.2d 325, 327 nn. 2, 4 (2nd Cir.), cert. denied, 389 U.S. 944 (1967). As for statements against penal interest, the Committee shared the view of the Court that some such statements do possess adequate assurances of reliability and should be admissible. It believed, however, as did the Court, that statements of this type tending to exculpate the accused are more suspect and so should have their admissibility conditioned upon some further provision insuring trustworthiness. The proposal in the Court Rule to add a requirement of simple corroboration was, however, deemed ineffective to accomplish this purpose since the accused's own testimony might suffice while not necessarily increasing the reliability of the hearsay statement. The Committee settled upon the language "unless corroborating circumstances clearly indicate the trustworthiness of the statement" as affording a proper standard and degree of discretion. It was contemplated that the result in such cases as Donnelly v. United States, 228 U.S. 243 (1912), where the circumstances plainly indicated reliability, would be changed. The Committee also added to the Rule the final sentence from the 1971 Advisory Committee draft, designed to codify the doctrine of Bruton v. United States, 391 U.S. 123 (1968). The Committee does not intend to affect the existing exception to the *Bruton* principle where the codefendant takes the stand and is subject to cross-examination, but believed there was no need to make specific provision for this situation in the Rule, since in that event the declarant would not be "unavailable".

Report of Senate Committee on the Judiciary

Senate Comm. on Judiciary, Fed.Rules of Evidence, S.Rep. No. 1277, 93d Cong., 2d Sess., p. 21 (1974); 1974 U.S.Code Cong. & Ad.News 7051, 7067

The rule defines those statements which are considered to be against interest and thus of sufficient trustworthiness to be admissible even though hearsay. With regard to the type of interest declared against, the version submitted by the Supreme Court included inter alia, statements tending to subject a declarant to civil liability or to invalidate a claim by him against another. The House struck these provisions as redundant. In view of the conflicting case law construing pecuniary or proprietary interests narrowly so as to exclude, e.g., tort cases, this deletion could be misconstrued.

Three States which have recently codified their rules of evidence have followed the Supreme Court's version of this rule, i.e., that a statement is against interest if it tends to subject a declarant to civil liability.[3]

The committee believes that the reference to statements tending to subject a person to civil liability constitutes a desirable clarification of the scope of the rule. Therefore, we have reinstated the Supreme Court language on this matter.

The Court rule also proposed to expand the hearsay limitation from its present federal limitation to include statements subjecting the declarant to statements tending to make him an object of hatred, ridicule, or disgrace. The House eliminated the latter category from the subdivision as lacking sufficient guarantees of reliability. Although there is considerable support for the admissibility of such statements (all three of the State rules referred to supra, would admit such statements), we accept the deletion by the House.

The House amended this exception to add a sentence making inadmissible a statement or confession offered against the accused in a criminal case, made by a codefendant or other person implicating both himself and the accused. The sentence was added to codify the constitutional principle announced in Bruton v. United States, 391 U.S. 123 (1968). *Bruton* held that the admission of the extrajudicial hearsay statement of one codefendant inculpating a second codefendant violated the confrontation clause of the sixth amendment.

The committee decided to delete this provision because the basic approach of the rules is to avoid codifying, or attempting to codify, constitutional evidentiary principles, such as the fifth amendment's right against self-incrimination and, here, the sixth amendment's right of confrontation. Codification of a constitutional principle is unnecessary and, where the principle is under development, often unwise. Furthermore, the House provision does not appear to recognize the exceptions to the *Bruton* rule, e.g. where the codefendant takes the stand and is subject to cross examination; where the accused confessed, see United States v. Mancusi, 404 F.2d 296 (2d Cir.1968), cert. denied 397 U.S. 942 (1907); where the accused was placed at the scene of the crime, see United States v. Zelker, 452 F.2d 1009 (2d Cir.1971). For these reasons, the committee decided to delete this provision.

Conference Report

H.R., Fed.Rules of Evidence, Conf.Rep. No. 1597, 93d Cong., 2d Sess., p. 12 (1974); 1974 U.S.Code Cong. & Ad.News 7098, 7105

The Senate amendment to subsection (b)(3) provides that a statement is against interest and not excluded by the hearsay rule when the declarant is unavailable as a witness, if the statement tends to subject a person to civil or criminal liability or renders invalid a claim by him against another. The House bill did not refer specifically to civil liability and to rendering invalid a claim against another. The Senate amendment also deletes from the House bill the provision that subsection (b)(3) does not apply to a statement or confession, made by a codefendant or another, which implicates the accused and the person who made the statement, when that statement or confession is offered against the accused in a criminal case.

3. Nev.Rev.Stats. § 51.345; N.Mex.Stats. (1973 Supp.) § 20–4–804(4); West's Wis. Stats.Anno. (1973 Supp.) § 908.045(4).

The Conference adopts the Senate amendment. The Conferees intend to include within the purview of this rule, statements subjecting a person to civil liability and statements rendering claims invalid. The Conferees agree to delete the provision regarding statements by a codefendant, thereby reflecting the general approach in the Rules of Evidence to avoid attempting to codify constitutional evidentiary principles.

Advisory Committee's Note

56 Fed.R.Evid. 183, 328

Exception [4]. The general common law requirement that a declaration in this area must have been made *ante litem motam* has been dropped, as bearing more appropriately on weight than admissibility. See 5 Wigmore § 1483. Item (i) specifically disclaims any need of firsthand knowledge respecting declarant's own personal history. In some instances it is self-evident (marriage) and in others impossible and traditionally not required (date of birth). Item (ii) deals with declarations concerning the history of another person. As at common law, declarant is qualified if related by blood or marriage. 5 Wigmore, § 1489. In addition, and contrary to the common law, declarant qualifies by virtue of intimate association with the family. Id., § 1487. The requirement sometimes encountered that when the subject of the statement is the relationship between two other persons the declarant must qualify as to both is omitted. Relationship is reciprocal. Id., § 1491.

For comparable provisions, see Uniform Rule 63(23), (24), (25); California Evidence Code §§ 1310, 1311; Kansas Code of Civil Procedure § 60–460(u), (v), (w); New Jersey Evidence Rules 63(23), 63(24), 63(25).

Exception [5]. In language and purpose, this exception is identical with Rule 803(24). See the Advisory Committee's Note to that provision.

Reports of House and Senate Committees on the Judiciary

[This exception and its companion exception in rule 803(24) are discussed together in the congressional committee reports. The reports are set forth under rule 803(24), supra.]

Conference Report [1]

The Senate amendment adds a new subsection, (b)(6), [2] which makes admissible a hearsay statement not specifically covered by any of the five [four] previous subsections, if the statement has equivalent circumstantial guarantees of trustworthiness and if the court determines that (A) the statement is offered as evidence of a material fact; (B) the statement is more probative on the point for which it is offered than any other evidence the proponent can procure through reasonable efforts; and (C) the general purposes of these rules and the interests of justice will best be served by admission of the statement into evidence.

The House bill eliminated a similar, but broader, provision because of the conviction that such a provision injected too much uncertainty into the law of

1. The Conference Report contains a like provision with respect to Rule 803(24).—Ed.
2. Numbered (b)(5) as finally enacted.—Ed.

evidence regarding hearsay and impaired the ability of a litigant to prepare adequately for trial.

The Conference adopts the Senate amendment with an amendment that renumbers this subsection and provides that a party intending to request the court to use a statement under this provision must notify any adverse party of this intention as well as of the particulars of the statement, including the name and address of the declarant. This notice must be given sufficiently in advance of the trial or hearing to provide any adverse party with a fair opportunity to prepare to contest the use of the statement.

1987 Amendment. The amendments are technical. No substantive change is intended.

Rule 805. Hearsay Within Hearsay

Hearsay included within hearsay is not excluded under the hearsay rule if each part of the combined statements conforms with an exception to the hearsay rule provided in these rules.

Section references, McCormick 4th ed.

§ 255, § 324.1

Note by Federal Judicial Center

The rule enacted by the Congress is the rule prescribed by the Supreme Court without change.

Advisory Committee's Note

56 F.R.D. 183, 329

On principle it scarcely seems open to doubt that the hearsay rule should not call for exclusion of a hearsay statement which includes a further hearsay statement when both conform to the requirements of a hearsay exception. Thus a hospital record might contain an entry of the patient's age based on information furnished by his wife. The hospital record would qualify as a regular entry except that the person who furnished the information was not acting in the routine of the business. However, her statement independently qualifies as a statement of pedigree (if she is unavailable) or as a statement made for purposes of diagnosis or treatment, and hence each link in the chain falls under sufficient assurances. Or, further to illustrate, a dying declaration may incorporate a declaration against interest by another declarant. See McCormick § 290, p. 611.

Rule 806. Attacking and Supporting Credibility of Declarant

When a hearsay statement, or a statement defined in Rule 801(d)(2), (C), (D), or (E), has been admitted in evidence, the credibility of the declarant may be attacked, and if attacked may be supported, by any evidence which would be admissible for those purposes if declarant had testified as a witness. Evidence of a statement or conduct by the declarant at any time, inconsistent with the declarant's hearsay statement, is not subject to any requirement that the declarant may have been afforded an opportunity to deny or explain. If the party against whom a hearsay statement has been admitted calls the declarant as a witness, the party is entitled to examine the declarant on the statement as if under cross-examination.

(As amended Mar. 2, 1987, eff. Oct. 1, 1987.)

Section references, McCormick 4th ed.

§ 37, § 324.2

Note by Federal Judicial Center

The rule enacted by the Congress is the rule prescribed by the Supreme Court, amended by inserting the phrase "or a statement defined in Rule 801(d)(2), (C), (D), or (E)."

Advisory Committee's Note

56 F.R.D. 183, 329

The declarant of a hearsay statement which is admitted in evidence is in effect a witness. His credibility should in fairness be subject to impeachment and support as though he had in fact testified. See Rules 608 and 609. There are however, some special aspects of the impeaching of a hearsay declarant which require consideration. These special aspects center upon impeachment by inconsistent statement, arise from factual differences which exist between the use of hearsay and an actual witness and also between various kinds of hearsay, and involve the question of applying to declarants the general rule disallowing evidence of an inconsistent statement to impeach a witness unless he is afforded an opportunity to deny or explain. See Rule 613(b).

The principal difference between using hearsay and an actual witness is that the inconsistent statement will in the case of the witness almost inevitably of necessity in the nature of things be a *prior* statement, which it is entirely possible and feasible to call to his attention, while in the case of hearsay the inconsistent statement may well be a *subsequent* one, which practically precludes calling it to the attention of the declarant. The result of insisting upon observation of this impossible requirement in the hearsay situation is to deny the opponent, already barred from cross-examination, any benefit of this important technique of impeachment. The writers favor allowing the subsequent statement. McCormick, § 37, p. 69; 3 Wigmore § 1033. The cases, however, are divided. Cases allowing the impeachment include People v. Collup, 27 Cal.2d 829, 167 P.2d 714 (1946); People v. Rosoto, 58 Cal.2d 304, 23 Cal.Rptr. 779, 373 P.2d 867 (1962); Carver v. United States, 164 U.S. 694, 17 S.Ct. 228, 41 L.Ed. 602 (1897). Contra, Mattox v. United States, 156 U.S. 237, 15 S.Ct. 337, 39 L.Ed. 409 (1895); People v. Hines, 284 N.Y. 93, 29 N.E.2d 483 (1940). The force of *Mattox,* where the hearsay was the former testimony of a deceased witness and the denial of use of a subsequent inconsistent statement was upheld, is much diminished by *Carver,* where the hearsay was a dying declaration and denial of use of a subsequent inconsistent statement resulted in reversal. The difference in the particular brand of hearsay seems unimportant when the inconsistent statement is a *subsequent* one. True, the opponent is not totally deprived of cross-examination when the hearsay is former testimony or a deposition but he is deprived of cross-examining on the statement or along lines suggested by it. Mr. Justice Shiras, with two justices joining him, dissented vigorously in *Mattox.*

When the impeaching statement was made *prior* to the hearsay statement, differences in the kinds of hearsay appear which arguably may justify differences in treatment. If the hearsay consisted of a simple statement by the witness, e.g. a dying declaration or a declaration against interest, the feasibility of affording him an opportunity to deny or explain encounters the same practical impossibility as where the statement is a subsequent one, just discussed, although here the impossibility arises from the total absence of anything resembling a hearing at which the matter could be put to him. The courts by a large majority have ruled in favor of allowing the statement to be used under these circumstances. McCormick § 37, p. 69; 3 Wigmore § 1033. If, however, the hearsay consists of former testimony or a deposition, the possibility of calling the prior statement to the attention of the witness or deponent is not ruled out, since the opportunity to cross-examine was available. It might thus be concluded that with former testimony or depositions the conventional foundation should be insisted upon. Most of the cases involve depositions, and Wigmore describes them as divided. 3 Wigmore § 1031. Deposition procedures at best are cumbersome and expensive, and to require the laying of the foundation may impose an undue burden. Under the federal practice, there is no way of knowing with certainty at the time of taking a deposition whether it is merely for discovery or will ultimately end up in evidence. With respect to both former testimony and depositions the possibility exists that knowledge of the statement might not be acquired until after the time of the cross-examination. Moreover, the expanded admissibility of former testimony and depositions under Rule 804(b)(1) calls for a correspondingly expanded approach to impeachment. The rule dispenses with the requirement in all hearsay situations, which is readily administered and best calculated to lead to fair results.

Notice should be taken that Rule 26(f) of the Federal Rules of Civil Procedure, as originally submitted by the Advisory Committee, ended with the following:

> ". . . and, without having first called them to the deponent's attention, may show statements contradictory thereto made at any time by the deponent."

This language did not appear in the rule as promulgated in December, 1937. See 4 Moore's Federal Practice ¶¶ 26.01[9], 26.35 (2d ed. 1967). In 1951, Nebraska adopted a provision strongly resembling the one stricken from the federal rule:

> "Any party may impeach any adverse deponent by self-contradiction without having laid foundation for such impeachment at the time such deposition was taken." R.S.Neb. § 25–1267.07.

For similar provisions, see Uniform Rule 65; California Evidence Code § 1202; Kansas Code of Civil Procedure § 60–462; New Jersey Evidence Rule 65.

The provision for cross-examination of a declarant upon his hearsay statement is a corollary of general principles of cross-examination. A similar provision is found in California Evidence Code § 1203.

Report of Senate Committee on the Judiciary

Senate Comm. on Judiciary, Fed.Rules of Evidence, S.Rep. No. 1277, 93d Cong., 2d Sess., p. 22 (1974); 1974 U.S.Code Cong. & Ad.News 7051, 7068

Rule 906 [806], as passed by the House and as proposed by the Supreme Court provides that whenever a hearsay statement is admitted, the credibility of the declarant of the statement may be attacked, and if attacked may be supported, by any evidence which would be admissible for those purposes if the declarant had testified as a witness. Rule 801 defines what is a hearsay statement. While statements by a person authorized by a party-opponent to make a statement concerning the subject, by the party-opponent's agent or by a coconspirator of a party—see rule 801(d)(2)(c), (d) and (e)—are traditionally defined as exceptions to the hearsay rule, rule 801 defines such admission by a party-opponent as statements which are not hearsay. Consequently, rule 806 by referring exclusively to the admission of hearsay statements, does not appear to allow the credibility of the declarant to be attacked when the declarant is a coconspirator, agent or authorized spokesman. The committee is of the view that such statements should open the declarant to attacks on his credibility. Indeed, the reason such statements are excluded from the operation of rule 806 is likely attributable to the drafting technique used to codify the hearsay rule, viz. some statements, instead of being referred to as exceptions to the hearsay rule, are defined as statements which are not hearsay. The phrase "or a statement defined in rule 801(d)(2)(c), (d) and (e)" is added to the rule in order to subject the declarant of such statements, like the declarant of hearsay statements, to attacks on his credibility.[1]

Conference Report

H.R., Fed.Rules of Evidence, Conf.Rep. No. 1597, 93d Cong., 2d Sess., p. 13 (1974); 1974 U.S.Code Cong. & Ad.News 7098, 7106

The Senate amendment permits an attack upon the credibility of the declarant of a statement if the statement is one by a person authorized by a party-opponent to make a statement concerning the subject, only by an agent of a party-opponent, or one by a coconspirator of the party-opponent, as these statements are defined in Rules 801(d)(2)(C), (D) and (E). The House bill has no such provision.

The Conference adopts the Senate amendment. The Senate amendment conforms the rule to present practice.

1987 Amendment. The amendments are technical. No substantive change is intended.

1. The committee considered it unnecessary to include statements contained in rule 801(d)(2)(A) and (B)—the statement by the party-opponent himself or the statement of which he has manifested his adoption—because the credibility of the party-opponent is always subject to an attack on his credibility.

ARTICLE IX. AUTHENTICATION AND IDENTIFICATION

Rule 901. Requirement of Authentication or Identification

(a) General provision. The requirement of authentication or identification as a condition precedent to admissibility is satisfied by evidence sufficient to support a finding that the matter in question is what its proponent claims.

(b) Illustrations. By way of illustration only, and not by way of limitation, the following are examples of authentication or identification conforming with the requirements of this rule:

(1) Testimony of witness with knowledge. Testimony that a matter is what it is claimed to be.

(2) Nonexpert opinion on handwriting. Nonexpert opinion as to the genuineness of handwriting, based upon familiarity not acquired for purposes of the litigation.

(3) Comparison by trier or expert witness. Comparison by the trier of fact or by expert witnesses with specimens which have been authenticated.

(4) Distinctive characteristics and the like. Appearance, contents, substance, internal patterns, or other distinctive characteristics, taken in conjunction with circumstances.

(5) Voice identification. Identification of a voice, whether heard firsthand or through mechanical or electronic transmission or recording, by opinion based upon hearing the voice at any time under circumstances connecting it with the alleged speaker.

(6) Telephone conversations. Telephone conversations, by evidence that a call was made to the number assigned at the time by the telephone company to a particular person or business, if (A) in the case of a person, circumstances, including self-identification, show the person answering to be the one called, or (B) in the case of a business, the call was made to a place of business and the conversation related to business reasonably transacted over the telephone.

(7) Public records or reports. Evidence that a writing authorized by law to be recorded or filed and in fact recorded or filed in a public office, or a purported public record, report, statement, or data compilation, in any form, is from the public office where items of this nature are kept.

(8) Ancient documents or data compilation. Evidence that a document or data compilation, in any form, (A) is in such condition as to create no suspicion concerning its authenticity, (B) was in a place where it, if authentic, would likely be, and (C) has been in existence 20 years or more at the time it is offered.

(9) Process or system. Evidence describing a process or system used to produce a result and showing that the process or system produces an accurate result.

(10) Methods provided by statute or rule. Any method of authentication or identification provided by Act of Congress or by other rules prescribed by the Supreme Court pursuant to statutory authority.

Section references, McCormick 4th ed.

Generally § 207, § 218

(a). § 222, § 224, § 227

(b)(1). § 214, § 219

(2). § 221

(3). § 221

(4). § 222, § 225

(5). § 226

(6). § 226

(7). § 224

(8). § 223, § 323

(9). § 214, § 293

Note by Federal Judicial Center

The rule enacted by the Congress is the rule prescribed by the Supreme Court, amended in subdivison (b)(10) by substituting "prescribed" in place of "adopted," and by adding "pursuant to statutory authority."

Advisory Committee's Note

56 F.R.D. 183, 332

Subdivison (a). Authentication and identification represent a special aspect of relevancy. Michael and Adler, Real Proof, 5 Vand.L.Rev. 344, 362 (1952); McCormick §§ 179, 185; Morgan, Basic Problems of Evidence 378 (1962). Thus a telephone conversation may be irrelevant because on an unrelated topic or because the speaker is not identified. The latter aspect is the one here involved. Wigmore describes the need for authentication as "an inherent logical necessity." 7 Wigmore § 2129, p. 564.

This requirement of showing authenticity or identity falls in the category of relevancy dependent upon fulfillment of a condition of fact and is governed by the procedure set forth in Rule 104(b).

The common law approach to authentication of documents has been criticized as an "attitude of agnosticism," McCormick, Cases on Evidence 388, n. 4 (3rd ed. 1956), as one which "departs sharply from men's customs in ordinary affairs," and as presenting only a slight obstacle to the introduction of forgeries in comparison to the time and expense devoted to proving genuine writings which correctly show their origin on their face, McCormick § 185, pp. 395, 396. Today, such available procedures as requests to admit and pretrial conference afford the means of eliminating much of the need for authentication or identification. Also, significant inroads upon the traditional insistence on authentication and identification have been made by accepting as at least prima facie genuine items of the kind treated in Rule 902, infra. However, the need for suitable methods of proof still remains, since criminal cases pose their own obstacles to the use of preliminary procedures, unforeseen contingencies may arise, and cases of genuine controversy will still occur.

Subdivision (b). The treatment of authentication and identification draws largely upon the experience embodied in the common law and in statutes to furnish illustrative applications of the general principle set forth in subdivision (a). The examples are not intended as an exclusive enumeration of allowable methods but are meant to guide and suggest, leaving room for growth and development in this area of the law.

The examples relate for the most part to documents, with some attention given to voice communications and computer print-outs. As Wigmore noted, no special rules have been developed for authenticating chattels. Wigmore, Code of Evidence § 2086 (3rd ed. 1942).

It should be observed that compliance with requirements of authentication or identification by no means assures admission of an item into evidence, as other bars, hearsay for example, may remain.

Example (1) contemplates a broad spectrum ranging from testimony of a witness who was present at the signing of a document to testimony establishing narcotics as taken from an accused and accounting for custody through the period until trial, including laboratory analysis. See California Evidence Code § 1413, eyewitness to signing.

Example (2) states conventional doctrine as to lay identification of handwriting, which recognizes that a sufficient familiarity with the handwriting of another person may be acquired by seeing him write, by exchanging correspondence, or by other means, to afford a basis for identifying it on subsequent occasions. McCormick § 189. See also California Evidence Code § 1416. Testimony based upon familiarity acquired for purposes of the litigation is reserved to the expert under the example which follows.

Example (3). The history of common law restrictions upon the technique of proving or disproving the genuineness of a disputed specimen of handwriting through comparison with a genuine specimen, by either the testimony of expert witnesses or direct viewing by the triers themselves, is detailed in 7 Wigmore §§ 1991–1994. In breaking away, the English Common Law Procedure Act of 1854, 17 and 18 Vict., c. 125, § 27, cautiously allowed expert or trier to use exemplars "proved to the satisfaction of the judge to be genuine" for purposes of comparison. The language found its way into numerous statutes in this country, e.g., California Evidence Code §§ 1417, 1418. While explainable as a measure of prudence in the process of breaking with precedent in the handwriting situation, the reservation to the judge of the question of the genuiness of exemplars and the imposition of an unusually high standard of persuasion are at variance with the general treatment of relevancy which depends upon fulfillment of a condition of fact. Rule 104(b). No similar attitude is found in other comparison situations, e.g., ballistics comparison by jury, as in Evans v. Commonwealth, 230 Ky. 411, 19 S.W.2d 1091 (1929), or by experts, Annot., 26 A.L.R.2d 892, and no reason appears for its continued existence in handwriting cases. Consequently Example (3) sets no higher standard for handwriting specimens and treats all comparison situations alike, to be governed by Rule 104(b). This approach is consistent with 28 U.S.C. § 1731: "The admitted or proved handwriting of any person shall be admissible, for purposes of comparison, to determine genuineness of other handwriting attributed to such person."

Precedent supports the acceptance of visual comparison as sufficiently satisfying preliminary authentication requirements for admission in evidence. Brandon v. Collins, 267 F.2d 731 (2d Cir.1959); Wausau Sulphate Fibre Co. v. Commissioner of Internal Revenue, 61 F.2d 879 (7th Cir.1932); Desimone v. United States, 227 F.2d 864 (9th Cir.1955).

Example (4). The characteristics of the offered item itself, considered in the light of circumstances, afford authentication techniques in great variety. Thus a document or telephone conversation may be shown to have emanated from a particular person by virtue of its disclosing knowledge of facts known peculiarly to him; Globe Automatic Sprinkler Co. v. Braniff, 89 Okl. 105, 214 P. 127 (1923); California Evidence Code § 1421; similarly, a letter may be authenticated by content and circumstances indicating it was in reply to a duly authenticated one. McCormick § 192; California Evidence Code § 1420. Language patterns may indicate authenticity or its opposite. Magnuson v. State, 187 Wis. 122, 203 N.W. 749 (1925); Arens and Meadow, Psycholinguistics and the Confession Dilemma, 56 Colum.L.Rev. 19 (1956).

Example (5). Since aural voice identification is not a subject of expert testimony, the requisite familiarity may be acquired either before or after the particular speaking which is the subject of the identification, in this respect resembling visual identification of a person rather than identification of handwriting. Cf. Example (2), supra, People v. Nichols, 378 Ill. 487, 38 N.E.2d 766 (1942); McGuire v. State, 200 Md. 601, 92 A.2d 582 (1952); State v. McGee, 336 Mo. 1082, 83 S.W.2d 98 (1935).

Example (6). The cases are in agreement that a mere assertion of his identity by a person talking on the telephone is not sufficient evidence of the authenticity of the conversation and that additional evidence of his identity is required. The additional evidence need not fall in any set pattern. Thus the content of his statements or the reply technique, under Example (4), supra, or voice identification under Example (5), may furnish the necessary foundation. Outgoing calls made by the witness involve additional factors bearing upon authenticity. The calling of a number assigned by the telephone company reasonably supports the assumption that the listing is correct and that the number is the one reached. If the number is that of a place of business, the mass of authority allows an ensuing conversation if it relates to business reasonably transacted over the telephone, on the theory that the maintenance of the telephone connection is an invitation to do business without further identification. Matton v. Hoover Co., 350 Mo. 506, 166 S.W.2d 557 (1942); City of Pawhuska v. Crutchfield, 147 Okl. 4, 293 P. 1095 (1930); Zurich General Acc. & Liability Ins. Co. v. Baum, 159 Va. 404, 165 S.E. 518 (1932). Otherwise, some additional circumstance of identification of the speaker is required. The authorities divide on the question whether the self-identifying statement of the person answering suffices. Example (6) answers in the affirmative on the assumption that usual conduct respecting telephone calls furnish adequate assurances of regularity, bearing in mind that the entire matter is open to exploration before the trier of fact. In general, see McCormick § 193; 7 Wigmore § 2155; Annot., 71 A.L.R. 5, 105 id. 326.

Example (7). Public records are regularly authenticated by proof of custody, without more. McCormick § 191; 7 Wigmore §§ 2158, 2159. The example extends the principle to include data stored in computers and similar methods, of which increasing use in the public records area may be expected. See California Evidence Code §§ 1532, 1600.

Example (8). The familiar ancient document rule of the common law is extended to include data stored electronically or by other similar means. Since the importance of appearance diminishes in this situation, the importance of custody or place where found increases correspondingly. This expansion is necessary in view of the widespread use of methods of storing data in forms other than conventional written records.

Any time period selected is bound to be arbitrary. The common law period of 30 years is here reduced to 20 years, with some shift of emphasis from the probable unavailability of witnesses to the unlikeliness of a still viable fraud after the lapse of time. The shorter period is specified in the English Evidence Act of 1938, 1 & 2 Geo. 6, c. 28, and in Oregon R.S.1963, § 41.360(34). See also the numerous statutes prescribing periods of less than 30 years in the case of recorded documents. 7 Wigmore § 2143.

The application of Example (8) is not subject to any limitation to title documents or to any requirement that possession, in the case of a title document, has been consistent with the document. See McCormick § 190.

Example (9) is designed for situations in which the accuracy of a result is dependent upon a process or system which produces it. X rays afford a familiar instance. Among more recent developments is the computer, as to which see Transport Indemnity Co. v. Seib, 178 Neb. 253, 132 N.W.2d 871 (1965); State v. Veres, 7 Ariz.App. 117, 436 P.2d 629 (1968); Merrick v. United States Rubber Co., 7 Ariz.App. 433, 440 P.2d 314 (1968); Freed, Computer Print-Outs as Evidence, 16 Am.Jur.Proof of Facts 273; Symposium, Law and Computers in the Mid-Sixties, ALI–ABA (1966); 37 Albany L.Rev. 61 (1967). Example (9) does not, of course, foreclose taking judicial notice of the accuracy of the process or system.

Example (10). The example makes clear that methods of authentication provided by Act of Congress and by the Rules of Civil and Criminal Procedure or by Bankruptcy Rules are not intended to be superseded. Illustrative are the provisions for authentication of official records in Civil Procedure Rule 44 and Criminal Procedure Rule 27, for authentication of records of proceedings by court reporters in 28 U.S.C. § 753(b) and Civil Procedure Rule 80(c), and for authentication of depositions in Civil Procedure Rule 30(f).

Rule 902. Self-Authentication

Extrinsic evidence of authenticity as a condition precedent to admissibility is not required with respect to the following:

(1) Domestic public documents under seal. A document bearing a seal purporting to be that of the United States, or of any State, district, Commonwealth, territory, or insular possession thereof, or the Panama Canal Zone, or the Trust Territory of the Pacific Islands, or of a political subdivision, department, officer, or agency thereof, and a signature purporting to be an attestation or execution.

(2) Domestic public documents not under seal. A document purporting to bear the signature in the official capacity of an officer or employee of any entity included in paragraph (1) hereof, having no seal, if a public officer having a seal and having official duties in the district or political subdivision of the officer or employee certifies under seal that the signer has the official capacity and that the signature is genuine.

(3) Foreign public documents. A document purporting to be executed or attested in an official capacity by a person authorized by the laws of a foreign country to make the execution or attestation, and accompanied by a final certification as to the genuineness of the signature and official position (A) of the executing or attesting person, or (B) of any foreign official whose certificate of genuineness of signature and official position relates to the execution or attestation or is in a chain of certificates of genuineness of signature and official position relating to the execution or attestation. A final certification may be made by a secretary of embassy or legation, consul general, consul, vice consul, or consular agent of the United States, or a diplomatic or consular official of the foreign country assigned or accredited to the United States. If reasonable opportunity has been given to all parties to investigate the authenticity and accuracy of official documents, the court may, for good cause shown, order that they be treated as presumptively authentic without final certification or permit them to be evidenced by an attested summary with or without final certification.

(4) Certified copies of public records. A copy of an official record or report or entry therein, or of a document authorized by law to be recorded or filed and actually recorded or filed in a public office, including data compilations in any form, certified as correct by the custodian or other person authorized to make the certification, by certificate complying with paragraph (1), (2), or (3) of this rule or complying with any Act of Congress or rule prescribed by the Supreme Court pursuant to statutory authority.

(5) Official publications. Books, pamphlets, or other publications purporting to be issued by public authority.

(6) Newspapers and periodicals. Printed materials purporting to be newspapers or periodicals.

(7) Trade inscriptions and the like. Inscriptions, signs, tags, or labels purporting to have been affixed in the course of business and indicating ownership, control, or origin.

(8) Acknowledged documents. Documents accompanied by a certificate of acknowledgment executed in the manner provided by law by a notary public or other officer authorized by law to take acknowledgments.

(9) Commercial paper and related documents. Commercial paper, signatures thereon, and documents relating thereto to the extent provided by general commercial law.

(10) Presumptions under Acts of Congress. Any signature, document, or other matter declared by Act of Congress to be presumptively or prima facie genuine or authentic.

(As amended Mar. 2, 1987, eff. Oct. 1, 1987; Apr. 25, 1988, eff. Nov. 1, 1988.)

Section references, McCormick 4th ed.

Generally § 218

(1). § 228

(2). § 228

(3). § 228

(4). § 228, § 300

(5). § 228

(6). § 228

(7). § 218, § 228

(8). § 228

Note by Federal Judicial Center

The rule enacted by the Congress is the rule prescribed by the Supreme Court, amended as follows:

Paragraph (4) was amended by substituting "prescribed" in place of "adopted," and by adding "pursuant to statutory authority."

Paragraph (8) was amended by substituting "in the manner provided by law by" in place of "under the hand and seal of."

Advisory Committee's Note

56 F.R.D. 183, 337

Case law and statutes have, over the years, developed a substantial body of instances in which authenticity is taken as sufficiently established for purposes of admissibility without extrinsic evidence to that effect, sometimes for reasons of policy but perhaps more often because practical considerations reduce the possibility of unauthenticity to a very small dimension. The present rule collects and incorporates these situations, in some instances expanding them to occupy a larger area which their underlying considerations justify. In no instance is the opposite party foreclosed from disputing authenticity.

Paragraph (1). The acceptance of documents bearing a public seal and signature, most often encountered in practice in the form of acknowledgments or certificates authenticating copies of public records, is actually of broad application. Whether theoretically based in whole or in part upon judicial notice, the practical underlying considerations are that forgery is a crime and detection is fairly easy and certain. 7 Wigmore § 2161, p. 638; California Evidence Code § 1452. More than 50 provisions for judicial notice of official seals are contained in the United States Code.

Paragraph (2). While statutes are found which raise a presumption of genuineness of purported official signatures in the absence of an official seal, 7 Wigmore § 2167; California Evidence Code § 1453, the greater ease of effecting a forgery under these circumstances is apparent. Hence this paragraph of the rule calls for authentication by an officer who has a seal. Notarial acts by members of the armed forces and other special situations are covered in paragraph (10).

Paragraph (3) provides a method for extending the presumption of authenticity to foreign official documents by a procedure of certification. It is derived from Rule 44(a)(2) of the Rules of Civil Procedure but is broader in applying to public documents rather than being limited to public records.

Paragraph (4). The common law and innumerable statutes have recognized the procedure of authenticating copies of public records by certificate. The certificate qualifies as a public document, receivable as authentic when in conformity with paragraph (1), (2), or (3). Rule 44(a) of the Rules of Civil Procedure and Rule 27 of the Rules of Criminal Procedure have provided authentication procedures of this nature for both domestic and foreign public records. It will be observed that the certification procedure here provided extends only to public records, reports, and recorded documents, all including data compilations, and does not apply to public documents generally. Hence documents provable when presented in original form under paragraphs (1), (2), or (3) may not be provable by certified copy under paragraph (4).

Paragraph (5). Dispensing with preliminary proof of the genuineness of purportedly official publications, most commonly encountered in connection with statutes, court reports, rules, and regulations, has been greatly enlarged by statutes and decisions. 5 Wigmore § 1684. Paragraph (5), it will be noted, does not confer admissibility upon all official publications; it merely provides a means whereby their authenticity may be taken as established for purposes of admissibility. Rule 44(a) of the Rules of Civil Procedure has been to the same effect.

Paragraph (6). The likelihood of forgery of newspapers or periodicals is slight indeed. Hence no danger is apparent in receiving them. Establishing the authenticity of the publication may, of course, leave still open questions of authority and responsibility for items therein contained. See 7 Wigmore § 2150. Cf. 39 U.S.C. § 4005(b), public advertisement prima facie evidence of agency of person named, in postal fraud order proceeding; Canadian Uniform Evidence Act, Draft of 1936, printed copy of newspaper prima facie evidence that notices or advertisements were authorized.

Paragraph (7). Several factors justify dispensing with preliminary proof of genuineness of commercial and mercantile labels and the like. The risk of forgery is minimal. Trademark infringement involves serious penalties. Great efforts are devoted to inducing the public to buy in reliance on brand names, and substantial protection is given them. Hence the fairness of this treatment finds recognition in the cases. Curtiss Candy Co. v. Johnson, 163 Miss. 426, 141 So. 762 (1932), Baby Ruth candy bar; Doyle v. Continental Baking Co., 262 Mass. 516, 160 N.E. 325 (1928), loaf of bread; Weiner v. Mager & Throne, Inc., 167 Misc. 338, 3 N.Y.S.2d 918 (1938), same. And see W.Va.Code 1966, § 47–3–5, trade-mark on bottle prima facie evidence of ownership. Contra, Keegan v. Green Giant Co., 150 Me. 283, 110 A.2d 599 (1954); Murphy v. Campbell Soup Co., 62 F.2d 564 (1st Cir.1933). Cattle brands have received similar acceptance in the western states. Rev.Code Mont.1947, § 46–606; State v. Wolfley, 75 Kan. 406, 89 P. 1046 (1907); Annot., 11 L.R.A.(N.S.) 87. Inscriptions on trains and vehicles are held to be prima facie evidence of ownership or control. Pittsburgh, Ft. W. & C. Ry. v. Callaghan, 157 Ill. 406, 41 N.E. 909 (1895); 9 Wigmore § 2510a. See also the provision of 19 U.S.C. § 1615(2) that marks, labels, brands, or stamps indicating foreign origin are prima facie evidence of foreign origin of merchandise.

Paragraph (8). In virtually every state, acknowledged title documents are receivable in evidence without further proof. Statutes are collected in 5 Wigmore § 1676. If this authentication suffices for documents of the importance of those affecting titles, logic scarcely permits denying this method when other kinds of documents are involved. Instances of broadly inclusive statutes are California Evidence Code § 1451 and N.Y.CPLR 4538, McKinney's Consol. Laws 1963.

Report of House Committee on the Judiciary

House Comm. on Judiciary, Fed.Rules of Evidence, H.R.Rep. No. 650, 93d Cong., 1st Sess., p. 17 (1973); 1974 U.S.Code Cong. & Ad.News 7075, 7090

Rule 902(8) as submitted by the Court referred to certificates of acknowledgment "under the hand and seal of" a notary public or other officer authorized by law to take acknowledgments. The Committee amended the Rule to eliminate the requirement, believed to be inconsistent with the law in some States, that a notary public must affix a seal to a document acknowledged before him. As amended the Rule merely requires that the document be executed in the manner prescribed by State law.

Advisory Committee's Note

56 F.R.D. 183, 339

Paragraph (9). Issues of the authenticity of commercial paper in federal courts will usually arise in diversity cases, will involve an element of a cause of action or defense, and with respect to presumptions and burden of proof will be controlled by Erie Railroad Co. v. Tompkins, 304 U.S. 64, 58 S.Ct. 817, 82 L.Ed 1188 (1938). Rule 302, supra. There may, however, be questions of authenticity involving lesser segments of a case or the case may be one governed by federal common law. Clearfield Trust Co. v. United States, 318 U.S. 363, 63 S.Ct. 573, 87 L.Ed. 838 (1943). Cf. United States v. Yazell, 382 U.S. 341, 86 S.Ct.

500, 15 L.Ed.2d 404 (1966). In these situations, resort to the useful authentication provisions of the Uniform Commercial Code is provided for. While the phrasing is in terms of "general commercial law," in order to avoid the potential complications inherent in borrowing local statutes, today one would have difficulty in determining the general commercial law without referring to the Code. See Williams v. Walker-Thomas Furniture Co., 121 U.S.App.D.C. 315, 350 F.2d 445 (1965). Pertinent Code provisions are sections 1-202, 3-307, and 3-510, dealing with third-party documents, signatures on negotiable instruments, protests, and statements of dishonor.

Report of House Committee on the Judiciary

House Comm. on Judiciary, Fed.Rules of Evidence, H.R.Rep. No. 650, 93d Cong., 1st Sess., p. 17 (1973); 1974 U.S.Code Cong. & Ad.News 7075, 7090

The Committee approved Rule 902(9) as submitted by the Court. With respect to the meaning of the phrase "general commercial law", the Committee intends that the Uniform Commercial Code, which has been adopted in virtually every State, will be followed generally, but that federal commercial law will apply where federal commercial paper is involved. See Clearfield Trust Co. v. United States, 318 U.S. 363 (1943). Further, in those instances in which the issues are governed by Erie R. Co. v. Tompkins, 304 U.S. 64 (1938), State law will apply irrespective of whether it is the Uniform Commercial Code.

Advisory Committee's Note

56 F.R.D. 183, 340

Paragraph (10). The paragraph continues in effect dispensations with preliminary proof of genuineness provided in various Acts of Congress. See, for example, 10 U.S.C. § 936, signature, without seal, together with title, prima facie evidence of authenticity of acts of certain military personnel who are given notarial powers; 15 U.S.C. § 77f(a), signature on SEC registration presumed genuine; 26 U.S.C. § 6064, signature to tax return prima facie genuine.

1987 Amendment. The amendments are technical. No substantive change is intended.

1988 Amendment. Two sentences were inadvertently eliminated from the 1987 amendment. The amendment is technical. No substantive change is intended.

Rule 903. Subscribing Witness' Testimony Unnecessary

The testimony of a subscribing witness is not necessary to authenticate a writing unless required by the laws of the jurisdiction whose laws govern the validity of the writing.

Section references, McCormick 4th ed.

§ 218, § 220

Note by Federal Judicial Center

The rule enacted by the Congress is the rule prescribed by the Supreme Court without change.

Advisory Committee's Note

56 F.R.D. 183, 340

The common law required that attesting witnesses be produced or accounted for. Today the requirement has generally been abolished except with respect to documents which must be attested to be valid, e.g. wills in some states. McCormick § 188. Uniform Rule 71; California Evidence Code § 1411; Kansas Code of Civil Procedure § 60–468; New Jersey Evidence Rule 71; New York CPLR Rule 4537.

ARTICLE X. CONTENTS OF WRITINGS, RECORDINGS, AND PHOTOGRAPHS

Rule

Rule 1001. Definitions

For purposes of this article the following definitions are applicable:

(1) **Writings and recordings.** "Writings" and "recordings" consist of letters, words, or numbers, or their equivalent, set down by handwriting, typewriting, printing, photostating, photographing, magnetic impulse, mechanical or electronic recording, or other form of data compilation.

(2) **Photographs.** "Photographs" include still photographs, X-ray films, video tapes, and motion pictures.

(3) **Original.** An "original" of a writing or recording is the writing or recording itself or any counterpart intended to have the same effect by a person executing or issuing it. An "original" of a photograph includes the negative or any print therefrom. If data are stored in a computer or similar device, any printout or other output readable by sight, shown to reflect the data accurately, is an "original".

(4) **Duplicate.** A "duplicate" is a counterpart produced by the same impression as the original, or from the same matrix, or by means of photography, including enlargements and miniatures, or by mechanical or electronic re-recording, or by chemical reproduction, or by other equivalent technique which accurately reproduces the original.

Section references, McCormick 4th ed.

Generally § 236

(1). § 232

(2). § 232

(3). § 230, § 236

(4). § 236

Note by Federal Judicial Center

The rule enacted by the Congress is the rule prescribed by the Supreme Court, amended in paragraph (2) by inserting "video tapes."

Advisory Committee's Note

56 F.R.D. 183, 341

In an earlier day, when discovery and other related procedures were strictly limited, the misleading named "best evidence rule" afforded substantial guarantees against inaccuracies and fraud by its insistence upon production of original documents. The great enlargement of the scope of discovery and related procedures in recent times has measurably reduced the need for the rule. Nevertheless important areas of usefulness persist: discovery of documents outside the jurisdiction may require substantial outlay of time and money; the unanticipated document may not practically be discoverable; criminal cases have built-in limitations on discovery. Cleary and Strong, The Best Evidence Rule: An Evaluation in Context, 51 Iowa L.Rev. 825 (1966).

Paragraph (1). Traditionally the rule requiring the original centered upon accumulations of data and expressions affecting legal relations set forth in words and figures. This meant that the rule was one essentially related to writings. Present day techniques have expanded methods of storing data, yet the essential form which the information ultimately assumes for usable purposes is words and figures. Hence the considerations underlying the rule dictate its expansion to include computers, photographic systems, and other modern developments.

Paragraph (2).

Report of House Committee on the Judiciary

House Comm. on Judiciary, Fed.Rules of Evidence, H.R.Rep. No. 650, 93d Cong., 1st Sess., p. 17 (1973); 1974 U.S.Code Cong. & Ad.News 7075, 7090

The Committee amended this Rule expressly to include "video tapes" in the definition of "photographs."

Advisory Committee's Note

56 F.R.D. 183, 341

Paragraph (3). In most instances, what is an original will be self-evident and further refinement will be unnecessary. However, in some instances particularized definition is required. A carbon copy of a contract executed in duplicate becomes an original, as does a sales ticket carbon copy given to a customer. While strictly speaking the original of a photograph might be thought to be only the negative, practicality and common usage require that any print from the negative be regarded as an original. Similarly, practicality and usage confer the status of original upon any computer printout. Transport Indemnity Co. v. Seib, 178 Neb. 253, 132 N.W.2d 871 (1965).

Paragraph (4). The definition describes "copies" produced by methods possessing an accuracy which virtually eliminates the possibility of error. Copies thus produced are given the status of originals in large measure by Rule 1003, infra. Copies subsequently produced manually, whether handwritten or typed, are not within the definition. It should be noted that what is an original for some purposes may be a duplicate for others. Thus a bank's microfilm record of checks cleared is the original as a record. However, a print offered as a copy of a check whose contents are in controversy is a duplicate. This result is substantially consistent with 28 U.S.C. § 1732(b). Compare 26 U.S.C. § 7513(c), giving full status as originals to photographic reproductions of tax returns and other documents, made by authority of the Secretary of the Treasury, and 44 U.S.C. § 399(a), giving original status to photographic copies in the National Archives.

Rule 1002. Requirement of Original

To prove the content of a writing, recording, or photograph, the original writing, recording, or photograph is required, except as otherwise provided in these rules or by Act of Congress.

Note by Federal Judicial Center

The rule enacted by the Congress is the rule prescribed by the Supreme Court without change.

Section references, McCormick 4th ed.

§ 230

Advisory Committee's Note

56 F.R.D. 183, 342

The rule is the familiar one requiring production of the original of a document to prove its contents, expanded to include writings, recordings, and photographs, as defined in Rule 1001(1) and (2), supra.

Application of the rule requires a resolution of the question whether contents are sought to be proved. Thus an event may be proved by nondocumentary evidence, even though a written record of it was made. If, however, the event is sought to be proved by the written record, the rule applies. For example, payment may be proved without producing the written receipt which was given. Earnings may be proved without producing books of account in which they are entered. McCormick § 198; 4 Wigmore § 1245. Nor does the rule apply to testimony that books or records have been examined and found not to contain any reference to a designated matter.

The assumption should not be made that the rule will come into operation on every occasion when use is made of a photograph in evidence. On the contrary, the rule will seldom apply to ordinary photographs. In most instances a party *wishes* to introduce the item and the question raised is the propriety of receiving it in evidence. Cases in which an offer is made of the testimony of a witness as to what he saw in a photograph or motion picture, without producing the same, are most unusual. The usual course is for a witness on the stand to identify the photograph or motion picture as a correct representation of events which he saw or of a scene with which he is familiar. In fact he adopts the picture as his testimony, or, in common parlance, uses the picture to illustrate his testimony. Under these circumstances, no effort is made to prove the contents of the picture, and the rule is inapplicable. Paradis, The Celluloid Witness, 37 U.Colo.L.Rev. 235, 249–251 (1965).

On occasion, however, situations arise in which contents are sought to be proved. Copyright, defamation, and invasion of privacy by photograph or motion picture falls in this category. Similarly as to situations in which the picture is offered as having independent probative value, e.g. automatic photograph of bank robber. See People v. Doggett, 83 Cal.App.2d 405, 188 P.2d 792 (1948), photograph of defendants engaged in indecent act; Mouser and Philbin, Photographic Evidence—Is There a Recognized Basis for Admissibility? 8 Hastings L.J. 310 (1957). The most commonly encountered of this latter group is of course, the X-ray, with substantial authority calling for production of the original. Daniels v. Iowa City, 191 Iowa 811, 183 N.W. 415 (1921); Cellamare v. Third Ave. Transit Corp., 273 App.Div. 260, 77 N.Y.S.2d 91 (1948); Patrick & Tilman v. Matkin, 154 Okl. 232, 7 P.2d 414 (1932); Mendoza v. Rivera, 78 P.R.R. 569 (1955).

It should be noted, however, that Rule 703, supra, allows an expert to give an opinion based on matters not in evidence, and the present rule must be read as being limited accordingly in its application. Hospital records which may be admitted as business records under Rule 803(6) commonly contain reports interpreting X rays by the staff radiologist, who qualifies as an expert, and these reports need not be excluded from the records by the instant rule.

The references to Acts of Congress is made in view of such statutory provisions as 26 U.S.C. § 7513, photographic reproductions of tax returns and documents, made by authority of the Secretary of the Treasury, treated as originals, and 44 U.S.C. § 399(a), photographic copies in National Archives treated as originals.

Rule 1003. Admissibility of Duplicates

A duplicate is admissible to the same extent as an original unless (1) a genuine question is raised as to the authenticity of the original or (2) in the circumstances it would be unfair to admit the duplicate in lieu of the original.

Section references, McCormick 4th ed.

§ 231, § 236, § 243, § 354

Note by Federal Judicial Center

The rule enacted by the Congress is the rule prescribed by the Supreme Court without change.

Advisory Committee's Note

56 F.R.D. 183, 343

When the only concern is with getting the words or other contents before the court with accuracy and precision, then a counterpart serves equally as well as the original, if the counterpart is the product of a method which insures accuracy and genuineness. By definition in Rule 1001(4), supra, a "duplicate" possesses this character.

Therefore, if no genuine issue exists as to authenticity and no other reason exists for requiring the original, a duplicate is admissible under the rule. This position finds support in the decisions, Myrick v. United States, 332 F.2d 279 (5th Cir.1964), no error in admitting photostatic copies of checks instead of original microfilm in absence of suggestion to trial judge that photostats were incorrect; Johns v. United States, 323 F.2d 421 (5th Cir.1963), not error to admit concededly accurate tape recording made from original wire recording; Sauget v. Johnston, 315 F.2d 816 (9th Cir.1963), not error to admit copy of agreement when opponent had original and did not on appeal claim any discrepancy. Other reasons for requiring the original may be present when only a part of the original is reproduced and the remainder is needed for cross-examination or may disclose matters qualifying the part offered or otherwise useful to the opposing party. United States v. Alexander, 326 F.2d 736 (4th Cir. 1964). And see Toho Bussan Kaisha, Ltd. v. American President Lines, Ltd., 265 F.2d 418, 76 A.L.R.2d 1344 (2d Cir.1959).

Report of House Committee on the Judiciary

House Comm. on Judiciary, Fed.Rules of Evidence, 93d Cong., 1st Sess., p. 17 (1973); 1974 U.S.Code Cong. & Ad.News 7075, 7090

The Committee approved this Rule in the form submitted by the Court, with the expectation that the courts would be liberal in deciding that a "genuine question is raised as to the authenticity of the original."

Rule 1004. Admissibility of Other Evidence of Contents

The original is not required, and other evidence of the contents of a writing, recording, or photograph is admissible if—

(1) Originals lost or destroyed. All originals are lost or have been destroyed, unless the proponent lost or destroyed them in bad faith; or

(2) Original not obtainable. No original can be obtained by any available judicial process or procedure; or

(3) Original in possession of opponent. At a time when an original was under the control of the party against whom offered, that party was put on notice, by the pleadings or otherwise, that the contents would be a subject of proof at the hearing, and that party does not produce the original at the hearing; or

(4) Collateral matters. The writing, recording, or photograph is not closely related to a controlling issue.

(As amended Mar. 2, 1987, eff. Oct. 1, 1987.)

Section references, McCormick 4th ed.

Generally § 236, § 241

(1). § 237

(2). § 238

(3). § 239

(4). § 234

Note by Federal Judicial Center

The rule enacted by the Congress is the rule prescribed by the Supreme Court without change.

Advisory Committee's Note

56 F.R.D. 183, 344

Basically the rule requiring the production of the original as proof of contents has developed as a rule of preference: if failure to produce the original is satisfactorily explained, secondary evidence is admissible. The instant rule specifies the circumstances under which production of the original is excused.

The rule recognizes no "degrees" of secondary evidence. While strict logic might call for extending the principle of preference beyond simply preferring the original, the formulation of a hierarchy of preferences and a procedure for making it effective is believed to involve unwarranted complexities. Most, if not all, that would be accomplished by an extended scheme of preferences will, in any event, be achieved through the normal motivation of a party to present the most convincing evidence possible and the arguments and procedures available to his opponent if he does not. Compare McCormick § 207.

Paragraph (1). Loss or destruction of the original, unless due to bad faith of the proponent, is a satisfactory explanation of nonproduction. McCormick § 201.

Report of House Committee on the Judiciary

House Comm. on Judiciary, Fed.Rules of Evidence, H.R.Rep. No. 650, 93d Cong., 1st Sess., p. 17 (1973); 1974 U.S.Code Cong. & Ad.News 7075, 7090

The Committee approved Rule 1004(1) in the form submitted to Congress. However, the Committee intends that loss or destruction of an original by another person at the instigation of the proponent should be considered as tantamount to loss or destruction in bad faith by the proponent himself.

Advisory Committee's Note

56 F.R.D. 183, 344

Paragraph (2). When the original is in the possession of a third person, inability to procure it from him by resort to process or other judicial procedure is a sufficient explanation of nonproduction. Judicial procedure includes subpoena duces tecum as an incident to the taking of a deposition in another jurisdiction. No further showing is required. See McCormick § 202.

Paragraph (3). A party who has an original in his control has no need for the protection of the rule if put on notice that proof of contents will be made. He can ward off secondary evidence by offering the original. The notice procedure here provided is not to be confused with orders to produce or other discovery procedures, as the purpose of the procedure under this rule is to afford the opposite party an opportunity to produce the original, not to compel him to do so. McCormick § 203.

Paragraph (4). While difficult to define with precision, situations arise in which no good purpose is served by production of the original. Examples are the newspaper in an action for the price of publishing defendant's advertisement, Foster-Holcomb Investment Co. v. Little Rock Publishing Co., 151 Ark. 449, 236 S.W. 597 (1922), and the streetcar transfer of plaintiff claiming status as a passenger, Chicago City Ry. Co. v. Carroll, 206 Ill. 318, 68 N.E. 1087 (1903). Numerous cases are collected in McCormick § 200, p. 412, n. 1.

1987 Amendment. The amendments are technical. No substantive change is intended.

Rule 1005. Public Records

The contents of an official record, or of a document authorized to be recorded or filed and actually recorded or filed, including data compilations in any form, if otherwise admissible, may be proved by copy, certified as correct in accordance with rule 902 or testified to be correct by a witness who has compared it with the original. If a copy which complies with the foregoing cannot be obtained by the exercise of reasonable diligence, then other evidence of the contents may be given.

Section references, McCormick 4th ed.

§ 240, § 300

Note by Federal Judicial Center

The rule enacted by the Congress is the rule prescribed by the Supreme Court without change.

Advisory Committee's Note

56 F.R.D. 183, 345

Public records call for somewhat different treatment. Removing them from their usual place of keeping would be attended by serious inconvenience to the public and to the custodian. As a consequence judicial decisions and statutes commonly hold that no explanation need be given for failure to produce the original of a public record. McCormick § 204; 4 Wigmore §§ 1215–1228. This blanket dispensation from producing or accounting for the original would open the door to the introduction of every kind of secondary evidence of contents of public records were it not for the preference given certified or compared copies. Recognition of degrees of secondary evidence in this situation is an appropriate *quid pro quo* for not applying the requirement of producing the original.

The provisions of 28 U.S.C. § 1733(b) apply only to departments or agencies of the United States. The rule, however, applies to public records generally and is comparable in scope in this respect to Rule 44(a) of the Rules of Civil Procedure.

Rule 1006. Summaries

The contents of voluminous writings, recordings, or photographs which cannot conveniently be examined in court may be presented in the form of a chart, summary, or calculation. The originals, or duplicates, shall be made available for examination or copying, or both, by other parties at reasonable time and place. The court may order that they be produced in court.

Section references, McCormick 4th ed.

§ 233

Note by Federal Judicial Center

The rule enacted by the Congress is the rule prescribed by the Supreme Court without change.

Advisory Committee's Note

56 F.R.D. 183, 346

The admission of summaries of voluminous books, records, or documents offers the only practicable means of making their contents available to judge and jury. The rule recognizes this practice, with appropriate safeguards. 4 Wigmore § 1230.

Rule 1007. Testimony or Written Admission of Party

Contents of writings, recordings, or photographs may be proved by the testimony or deposition of the party against whom offered or by that party's written admission, without accounting for the nonproduction of the original.

(As amended Mar. 2, 1987, eff. Oct. 1, 1987.)

Section references, McCormick 4th ed.

§ 242

Note by Federal Judicial Center

The rule enacted by the Congress is the rule prescribed by the Supreme Court without change.

Advisory Committee's Note

56 F.R.D. 183, 356

While the parent case, Slatterie v. Pooley, 6 M. & W. 664, 151 Eng.Rep. 579 (Exch.1840), allows proof of contents by evidence of an oral admission by the party against whom offered, without accounting for nonproduction of the original, the risk of inaccuracy is substantial and the decision is at odds with the purpose of the rule giving preference to the original. See 4 Wigmore § 1255. The instant rule follows Professor McCormick's suggestion of limiting this use of admissions to those made in the course of giving testimony or in writing. McCormick § 208, p. 424. The limitation, of course, does not call for excluding evidence of an oral admission when nonproduction of the original has been accounted for and secondary evidence generally has become admissible. Rule 1004, supra.

A similar provision is contained in New Jersey Evidence Rule 70(1)(h).

1987 Amendment. The amendment is technical. No substantive change is intended.

Rule 1008. Functions of Court and Jury

When the admissibility of other evidence of contents of writings, recordings, or photographs under these rules depends upon the fulfillment of a condition of fact, the question whether the condition has been fulfilled is ordinarily for the court to determine in accordance with the provisions of rule 104. However, when an issue is raised (a) whether the asserted writing ever existed, or (b) whether another writing, recording, or photograph produced at the trial is the original, or (c) whether other evidence of contents correctly reflects the contents, the issue is for the trier of fact to determine as in the case of other issues of fact.

Section references, McCormick 4th ed.

§ 53, § 54

Note by Federal Judicial Center

The rule enacted by the Congress is the rule prescribed by the Supreme Court, amended by substituting "court" in place of "judge," and by adding at the end of the first sentence the phrase "in accordance with the provisions of rule 104."

Advisory Committee's Note

56 F.R.D. 183, 347

Most preliminary questions of fact in connection with applying the rule preferring the original as evidence of contents are for the judge, under the general principles announced in Rule 104, supra. Thus, the question whether the loss of the originals has been established, or of the fulfillment of other conditions specified in Rule 1004, supra, is for the judge. However, questions may arise which go beyond the mere administration of the rule preferring the original and into the merits of the controversy. For example, plaintiff offers secondary evidence of the contents of an alleged contract, after first introducing evidence of loss of the original, and defendant counters with evidence that no such contract was ever executed. If the judge decides that the contract was never executed and excludes the secondary evidence, the case is at an end without ever going to the jury on a central issue. Levin, Authentication and Content of Writings, 10 Rutgers L.Rev. 632, 644 (1956). The latter portion of the instant rule is designed to insure treatment of these situations as raising jury questions. The decision is not one for uncontrolled discretion of the jury but is subject to the control exercised generally by the judge over jury determinations. See Rule 104(b), supra.

For similar provisions, see Uniform Rule 70(2); Kansas Code of Civil Procedure § 60–467(b); New Jersey Evidence Rule 70(2), (3).

ARTICLE XI. MISCELLANEOUS RULES

Rule 1101. Applicability of Rules

(a) Courts and magistrates. These rules apply to the United States district courts, the District Court of Guam, the District Court of the Virgin Islands, the District Court for the Northern Mariana Islands, the United States courts of appeals, the United States Claims Court, and to United States bankruptcy judges and United States magistrates, in the actions, cases, and proceedings and to the extent hereinafter set forth. The terms "judge" and "court" in these rules include United States bankruptcy judges and United States magistrates.

(b) Proceedings generally. These rules apply generally to civil actions and proceedings, including admiralty and maritime cases, to criminal cases and proceedings, to contempt proceedings except those in which the court may act summarily, and to proceedings and cases under title 11, United States Code.

(c) Rule of privilege. The rule with respect to privileges applies at all stages of all actions, cases, and proceedings.

(d) Rules inapplicable. The rules (other than with respect to privileges) do not apply in the following situations:

(1) Preliminary questions of fact. The determination of questions of fact preliminary to admissibility of evidence when the issue is to be determined by the court under rule 104.

(2) Grand jury. Proceedings before grand juries.

(3) Miscellaneous proceedings. Proceedings for extradition or rendition; preliminary examinations in criminal cases; sentencing, or granting or revoking probation; issuance of warrants for arrest, criminal summonses, and search warrants; and proceedings with respect to release on bail or otherwise.

(e) Rules applicable in part. In the following proceedings these rules apply to the extent that matters of evidence are not provided for in the statutes which govern procedure therein or in other rules prescribed by the Supreme Court pursuant to statutory authority: the trial of minor and petty offenses by United States magistrates; review of agency actions when the facts are subject to trial de novo under section 706(2)(F) of title 5, United States Code; review of orders of the Secretary of Agriculture under section 2 of the Act entitled "An Act to authorize association of producers of agricultural products" approved February 18, 1922 (7 U.S.C. 292), and under sections 6 and 7(c) of the Perishable Agricultural Commodities Act, 1930 (7 U.S.C. 499f, 499g(c)); naturalization and revocation of naturalization under sections 310–318 of the Immigration and Nationality Act (8 U.S.C. 1421–1429); prize proceedings in admiralty under sections 7651–7681 of title 10, United States Code; review of orders of the Secretary of the Interior under section 2 of the Act entitled "An Act authorizing associations of producers of aquatic products" approved June 25, 1934 (15 U.S.C. 522); review of orders of petroleum control boards under section 5 of the Act entitled "An Act to regulate interstate and foreign commerce in petroleum and its products by prohibiting the shipment in such commerce of petroleum and its products produced in violation of State law, and for other purposes", approved February 22, 1935 (15 U.S.C. 715d); actions for fines, penalties, or forfeitures under part V of title IV of the Tariff Act of 1930 (19 U.S.C. 1581–1624), or under the Anti-Smuggling Act (19 U.S.C. 1701–1711); criminal libel for condemnation, exclusion of imports, or other proceedings under the Federal Food, Drug, and Cosmetic Act (21 U.S.C. 301–392); disputes between seamen under sections 4079, 4080, and 4081 of the Revised Statutes (22 U.S.C. 256–258); habeas corpus under sections 2241–2254 of title 28, United States Code; motions to vacate, set aside or correct sentence under section 2255 of title 28, United States Code; actions for penalties for refusal to transport destitute seamen under section 4578 of the Revised Statutes (46 U.S.C. 679); actions against the United States under the Act entitled "An Act authorizing suits against the United States in admiralty for damage caused by and salvage service rendered to public vessels belonging to the United States, and for other purposes", approved March 3, 1925 (46 U.S.C. 781–790), as implemented by section 7730 of title 10, United States Code.

(As amended P.L. 94–149, § 1(14), Dec. 12, 1975, 89 Stat. 806; P.L. 95–598, Title II, § 251, Nov. 6, 1978, 92 Stat. 2673; P.L. 97–164, Title I, § 142, Apr. 2, 1982, 96 Stat. 45; Mar. 2, 1987, eff. Oct. 1, 1987; Apr. 25, 1988, eff. Nov. 1, 1988; Nov. 18, 1988, Pub.L. 100–690, Title VII, § 7075(c), 102 Stat. 4405.)

Section references, McCormick 4th ed.

None

Note by Federal Judicial Center

The rule enacted by the Congress is the rule prescribed by the Supreme Court, amended as follows:

Subdivision (a) was amended in the first sentence by inserting "the Court of Claims" and by inserting "actions, cases, and." It was amended in the second sentence by substituting "terms" in place of "word," by inserting the phrase "and 'court'," and by adding "commissioners of the Court of Claims."

Subdivision (b) was amended by substituting "civil actions and proceedings" in place of "civil actions," and by substituting "criminal cases and proceedings" in place of "criminal proceedings."

Subdivision (c) was amended by substituting "rule" in place of "rules" and by changing the verb to the singular.

Subdivision (d) was amended by deleting "those" after "other than" and by substituting "Rule 104" in place of "Rule 104(a)."

Subdivision (e) was amended by substituting "prescribed" in place of "adopted" and by adding "pursuant to statutory authority." The form of the statutory citations was also changed.

Advisory Committee's Note

56 F.R.D. 183, 348

Subdivision (a). [This portion of the Advisory Committee's Note discussed the courts for which the various enabling acts granted the Supreme Court power to prescribe rules. Congressional enactment of the rules has rendered the discussion moot. The enabling acts did not include the Court of Claims which the Congress added to Rule 1101(a)].

Report of House Committee on the Judiciary

House Comm. on Judiciary, Fed.Rules of Evidence, H.R.Rep. No. 650, 93d Cong., 1st Sess., p. 17 (1973); 1974 U.S.Code Cong. & Ad.News 7075, 7090

Subdivision (a) as submitted to the Congress, in stating the courts and judges to which the Rules of Evidence apply, omitted the Court of Claims and commissioners of that Court. At the request of the Court of Claims, the

Committee amended the Rule to include the Court and its commissioners within the purview of the Rules.

Advisory Committee's Note

56 F.R.D. 183, 351

Subdivision (b) is a combination of the language of the enabling acts, supra, with respect to the kinds of proceedings in which the making of rules is authorized. It is subject to the qualifications expressed in the subdivisions which follow.

Subdivision (c), singling out the rules of privilege for special treatment, is made necessary by the limited applicability of the remaining rules.

Subdivision (d). The rule is not intended as an expression as to when due process or other constitutional provisions may require an evidentiary hearing. Paragraph (1) restates, for convenience, the provisions of the second sentence of Rule 104(a), supra. See Advisory Committee's Note to that rule.

(2) While some states have statutory requirements that indictments be based on "legal evidence," and there is some case law to the effect that the rules of evidence apply to grand jury proceedings, 1 Wigmore § 4(5), the Supreme Court has not accepted this view. In Costello v. United States, 350 U.S. 359, 76 S.Ct. 406, 100 L.Ed. 397 (1965), the Court refused to allow an indictment to be attacked, for either constitutional or policy reasons, on the ground that only hearsay evidence was presented.

> "It would run counter to the whole history of the grand jury institution, in which laymen conduct their inquiries unfettered by technical rules. Neither justice nor the concept of a fair trial requires such a change." Id. at 364.

The rule as drafted does not deal with the evidence required to support an indictment.

(3) The rule exempts preliminary examinations in criminal cases. Authority as to the applicability of the rules of evidence to preliminary examinations has been meagre and conflicting. Goldstein, The State and the Accused: Balance of Advantage in Criminal Procedure, 69 Yale L.J. 1149, 1168, n. 53 (1960); Comment, Preliminary Hearings on Indictable Offenses in Philadelphia, 106 U. of Pa.L.Rev. 589, 592–593 (1958). Hearsay testimony is, however, customarily received in such examinations. Thus in a Dyer Act case, for example, an affidavit may properly be used in a preliminary examination to prove ownership of the stolen vehicle, thus saving the victim of the crime the hardship of having to travel twice to a distant district for the sole purpose of testifying as to ownership. It is believed that the extent of the applicability of the Rules of Evidence to preliminary examinations should be appropriately dealt with by the Federal Rules of Criminal Procedure which regulate those proceedings.

Extradition and rendition proceedings are governed in detail by statute. 18 U.S.C. §§ 3181–3195. They are essentially administrative in character. Traditionally the rules of evidence have not applied. 1 Wigmore § 4(6). Extradition proceedings are accepted from the operation of the Rules of Criminal Procedure. Rule 54(b)(5) of Federal Rules of Criminal Procedure.

The rules of evidence have not been regarded as applicable to sentencing or probation proceedings, where great reliance is placed upon the presentence investigation and report. Rule 32(c) of the Federal Rules of Criminal Procedure requires a presentence investigation and report in every case unless the court otherwise directs. In Williams v. New York, 337 U.S. 241, 69 S.Ct. 1079, 93 L.Ed. 1337 (1949), in which the judge overruled a jury recommendation of life imprisonment and imposed a death sentence, the Court said that due process does not require confrontation or cross-examination in sentencing or passing on probation, and that the judge has broad discretion as to the sources and types of information relied upon. Compare the recommendation that the substance of all derogatory information be disclosed to the defendant, in A.B.A. Project on Minimum Standards for Criminal Justice, Sentencing Alternatives and Procedures § 4.4, Tentative Draft (1967, Sobeloff, Chm.). Williams was adhered to in Specht v. Patterson, 386 U.S. 605, 87 S.Ct. 1209, 18 L.Ed.2d 326 (1967), but not extended to a proceeding under the Colorado Sex Offenders Act, which was said to be a new charge leading in effect to punishment, more like the recidivist statutes where opportunity must be given to be heard on the habitual criminal issue.

Warrants for arrest, criminal summonses, and search warrants are issued upon complaint or affidavit showing probable cause. Rules 4(a) and 41(c) of the Federal Rules of Criminal Procedure. The nature of the proceedings makes application of the formal rules of evidence inappropriate and impracticable.

Criminal contempts are punishable summarily if the judge certifies that he saw or heard the contempt and that it was committed in the presence of the court. Rule 42(a) of the Federal Rules of Criminal Procedure. The circumstances which preclude application of the rules of evidence in this situation are not present, however, in other cases of criminal contempt.

Proceedings with respect to release on bail or otherwise do not call for application of the rules of evidence. The governing statute specifically provides:

> "Information stated in, or offered in connection with, any order entered pursuant to this section need not conform to the rules pertaining to the admissibility of evidence in a court of law." 18 U.S.C.A. § 3146(f).

This provision is consistent with the type of inquiry contemplated in A.B.A. Project on Minimum Standards for Criminal Justice, Standards Relating to Pretrial Release, § 4.5(b), (c), p. 16 (1968). The references to the weight of the evidence against the accused, in Rule 46(a)(1), (c) of the Federal Rules of Criminal Procedure and in 18 U.S.C.A. § 3146(b), as a factor to be considered, clearly do not have in view evidence introduced at a hearing under the rules of evidence.

The rule does not exempt habeas corpus proceedings. The Supreme Court held in Walker v. Johnston, 312 U.S. 275, 61 S.Ct. 574, 85 L.Ed. 830 (1941), that the practice of disposing of matters of fact on affidavit, which prevailed in some circuits, did not "satisfy the command of the statute that the judge shall proceed 'to determine the facts of the case, by hearing the testimony and arguments.'" This view accords with the emphasis in Townsend v. Sain, 372 U.S. 293, 83 S.Ct. 745, 9 L.Ed.2d 770 (1963), upon trial-type proceedings, id. 311, 83 S.Ct. 745, with demeanor evidence as a significant factor, id. 322, 83 S.Ct. 745, in applications by state prisoners aggrieved by unconstitutional detentions.

Hence subdivision (e) applies the rules to habeas corpus proceedings to the extent not inconsistent with the statute.

Subdivision (e). In a substantial number of special proceedings, *ad hoc* evaluation has resulted in the promulgation of particularized evidentiary provisions, by Act of Congress or by rule adopted by the Supreme Court. Well adapted to the particular proceedings, though not apt candidates for inclusion in a set of general rules, they are left undisturbed. Otherwise, however, the rules of evidence are applicable to the proceedings enumerated in the subdivision.

Report of House Committee on the Judiciary

House Comm. on Judiciary, Fed.Rules of Evidence, H.R.Rep. No. 650, 93d Cong., 1st Sess., p. 17 (1973); 1974 U.S.Code Cong. & Ad.News 7075, 7090

Subdivision (b)[E] was amended merely to substitute positive law citations for those which were not.

1987 Amendment. Subdivision (a) is amended to delete the reference to the District Court for the District of the Canal Zone, which no longer exists, and to add the District Court for the Northern Mariana Islands. The United States bankruptcy judges are added to conform the subdivision with Rule 1101(b) and Bankruptcy Rule 9017.

1988 Amendment. The amendment is technical. No substantive change is intended.

Rule 1102. Amendments

Amendments to the Federal Rules of Evidence may be made as provided in section 2072 of title 28 of the United States Code.

(As amended Apr. 30, 1991, eff. Dec. 1, 1991.)

Note by Federal Judicial Center

This rule was not included among those prescribed by the Supreme Court. The rule prescribed by the Court as 1102 now appears as 1103.

Advisory Committee's Note

1991 Amendment. The amendment is technical. No substantive change is intended.

Rule 1103. Title

These rules may be known and cited as the Federal Rules of Evidence.

Note by Federal Judicial Center

The rule enacted by the Congress is the rule prescribed by the Supreme Court as Rule 1102 without change.

Sec. 2. (a) Title 28 of the United States Code is amended—

(1) by inserting immediately after section 2075 the following new section:

"§ 2076. Rules of evidence

"The Supreme Court of the United States shall have the power to prescribe amendments to the Federal Rules of Evidence. Such amendments shall not take effect until they have been reported to Congress by the Chief Justice at or after the beginning of a regular session of Congress but not later than the first day of May, and until the expiration of one hundred and eighty days after they have been so reported; but if either House of Congress within that time shall by resolution disapprove any amendment so reported it shall not take effect. The effective date of any amendment so reported may be deferred by either House of Congress to a later date or until approved by Act of Congress. Any rule whether proposed or in force may be amended by Act of Congress. Any provision of law in force at the expiration of such time and in conflict with any such amendment not disapproved shall be of no further force or effect after such amendment has taken effect. Any such amendment creating, abolishing, or modifying a privilege shall have no force or effect unless it shall be approved by act of Congress"; and

(2) by adding at the end of the table of sections of chapter 131 the following new item:

"2076. Rules of evidence."

(b) Section 1732 of title 28 of the United States Code is amended by striking out subsection (a), and by striking out "(b)".

(c) Section 1733 of title 28 of the United States Code is amended by adding at the end thereof the following new subsection:

"(c) This section does not apply to cases, actions, and proceedings to which the Federal Rules of Evidence apply."

Approved Jan. 2, 1975.

INDEX
TO
FEDERAL RULES OF EVIDENCE

INDEX TO FEDERAL RULES OF EVIDENCE

INDEX TO FEDERAL RULES OF EVIDENCE

INDEX TO FEDERAL RULES OF EVIDENCE

INDEX TO FEDERAL RULES OF EVIDENCE

INDEX TO FEDERAL RULES OF EVIDENCE

Appendix I

EMERGING PROBLEMS UNDER THE FEDERAL RULES OF EVIDENCE *

Second Edition

A Product of the Trial Evidence Committee Section of Litigation American Bar Association

David A. Schlueter
Editor-in-Chief

Stephen A. Saltzburg
Reporter

Gregory P. Joseph
Reporter

John E.S. Scott
Chair, Trial Evidence Committee

APPENDIX I

ANALYSIS

TABLE OF CONTENTS

APPENDIX I

ACKNOWLEDGEMENTS

Special thanks are in order for a number of individuals who over the last several years toiled to update the first edition of this report which was published in 1983. Working with the contributions of approximately 20 practitioners, judges, and professors, the initial edition was prepared by a group of attorneys in the Fried, Frank, Harris, Shriver & Jacobson firm in New York working under the leadership of Gregory P. Joseph.

Drafts of the commentary for this second edition were prepared by approximately 30 lawyers, judges, and law professors who generously donated their time to the project:

Professor Michael J. Ahlen, Grand Forks, North Dakota

T. Maxfield Bahner, Esq., Chattanooga, Tennessee

Gena E. Cadieux, Esq., Washington, D.C.

David T. Case, Esq., Washington, D.C.

John J. Cruze, Esq., Cincinnati, Ohio

Anthony DiResta, Esq., Atlanta, Georgia

Michael W. Donaldson, Esq., Columbus, Ohio

A. Michael Ferrill, Esq., San Antonio, Texas

Hon. Ralph Adam Fine, Milwaukee, Wisconsin

Professor Teree E. Foster, Norman, Oklahoma

Hon. John E. Jennings, Little Rock, Arkansas

Bruce E.H. Johnson, Esq., Seattle, Washington

Robert Hanaford, Esq., Chicago, Illinois

Daniel A. Harvey, Esq., Moline, Illinois

Jed Horwitt, Esq., New Haven, Connecticut

Professor Michael Hutter, Albany, New York

Mark R. Kravitz, Esq., New Haven, Connecticut

Robert Magill, Esq., Ann Arbor, Michigan

Clarence E. Martin, III, Esq., Martinsburg, West Virginia

David Nagle, Esq., Chattanooga, Tennessee

Phillip D. Noble, Esq., Seattle, Washington

Professor Mary E. Phelan, Lansing, Michigan

Michael J. Progar, Chicago, Illinois

Professor Myrna Raeder, Los Angeles, California

Mary L. Richards, Esq., Milwaukee, Wisconsin

Gary Rosen, Esq., Philadelphia, Pennsylvania

Daniel J. Ryan, Esq., Kansas City, Missouri

Janet L. Schafer, Houston, Texas

John R. Stegner, Esq., Lewiston, Idaho

Linda Hitt Thatcher, Esq., Washington, D.C.

William R. Wilson, Jr., Esq., Little Rock, Arkansas

Charles P. Wisdom, Louisville, Kentucky

The Report was coordinated and edited by Professor Dave Schlueter of Saint Mary's University School of Law in San Antonio, Texas. He was assisted by Ms. Janet Schafer and Ms. Theresa Waldrop who provided indispensable editorial assistance on the project. The manuscript was typed by Ms. Maria Klatt. Professor Stephen A. Saltzburg and Gregory P. Joseph served as Reporters for the project and provided invaluable insight and suggestions on the commentary.

Finally, the publication and distribution of this work by the West Publishing Company, at no cost to the American Bar Association, is gratefully acknowledged.

APPENDIX I

INTRODUCTION

This text was prepared by a special committee of lawyers from the Trial Evidence Committee of the Section of Litigation of the American Bar Association. Although the First Edition began as a response to an inquiry by the Australian Law Reform Commission, which was studying the codification of Australian Rules of Evidence, the Section determined that any report that involved a systematic and careful review of the Federal Rules of Evidence would be of as much interest to American lawyers and judges as to the Australian Commission. As it developed, the first edition was well received by the federal judiciary and was relied upon in several appellate court decisions. See, e.g., United States v. Scop, 846 F.2d 135 (2d Cir.1988); Barrel of Fun, Inc. v. State Farm Fire & Cas. Co., 739 F.2d 1028 (5th Cir.1984); White v. Southern Rwy Co., No. 89–6307, 1991 U.S.App. Lexis 3335 (6th Cir. 1991); Nachtscheim v. Beech Aircraft Corp., 847 F.2d 1261 (7th Cir. 1988); Paddock v. Dave Christenson, Inc., 745 F.2d 1254 (9th Cir.1984).

Because the Rules have been amended infrequently since they took effect in 1975, there has been substantial opportunity to analyze how they are working. The special committee endeavored to examine the experience under the Rules in order to better understand its strengths by focusing upon the weaknesses that have become apparent. The committee hopes that its work product will be helpful whenever future amendments to the Rules are considered, will provide useful information for states still in the process of codifying evidence rules or amending their state codes, and will be of interest to lawyers in other lands who seek to learn about the American evidence experiment.

To examine the Rules fully, the committee determined that it would consider every one of the eleven Articles that comprise the Rules and that it would individually examine each rule. Thus, the report examines the overall structure of the Rules as a group, the structure and workings of all articles, and the specifics of individual rules.

The goal of the study was to see whether the Rules have been working in federal courts as the drafters intended. When the Rules were adopted, it was thought that they would promote uniformity in the law of evidence, that they would provide clearer guidance to lawyers preparing to litigate or to settle a case, that they would make the task of discovering the law of evidence less costly, and that the litigation process in federal courts would improve as a result of having a readily accessible code of evidence. In evaluating the Rules, the committee sought to determine whether the advantages claimed for the Rules have been evident, whether some Rules have done more harm than good, whether there have been unexpected benefits from having all or some of the Rules, and finally, whether problems unforeseen by the drafters of the Rules have been encountered.

EMERGING PROBLEMS

As the title itself suggests, a report like this is always negative to some extent. Problem areas inevitably command attention, while areas without problems are taken for granted. Although both strengths and weaknesses are recorded in this Report, weaknesses are its focus and may get more attention than they deserve. There is less to say about Rules that are working well and causing few, if any, problems than there is to say about Rules that are causing trouble. Although some effort has been made to identify problem areas that may not yet be apparent, generally the assumption is that Rules now working well are likely to continue to work well.

Problems come in different forms, and there are at least eight kinds that must be faced in any analysis of the Federal Rules of Evidence. These may be identified as follows:

1. Problems of omission—e.g., Article V on privileges which contains no specific rules.

2. Problems of internal contradiction—e.g., when an inconsistent statement offered under Rule 607 to impeach a witness called by that party is deemed inadmissible under Rule 801(d)(1).

3. Problems of vagueness as to the drafters' intent—e.g., whether one person's statement of an intention to do something in the future is admissible under Rule 803(3) to show what someone else did; or whether a subsequent remedial measure is admissible in a products liability case under Rule 407.

4. Problems of inconsistent case law interpretation—e.g., the foundation necessary in criminal cases to warrant admission of evidence of a defendant's prior crimes.

5. Problems of policy—e.g., whether Rule 803(8)(C) goes too far in admitting factual findings.

6. Problems of drafting quality—e.g., the wording regarding the use of specific instances of conduct to test a character witness under Rules 405 and 608.

7. Problems of procedure—e.g., when should in limine motions on evidence questions be considered.

8. Problems of constitutional law—e.g., whether admission under Rule 803(6) of certain scientific reports in criminal cases that might be excluded under Rule 803(8) would violate the confrontation clause of the Sixth Amendment.

The Special committee was asked to consider these problems and any others that it might observe as it examined Articles and individual rules. It became obvious that what some observers regard as problems others regard as strengths. Because this was intended to be a general study, no effort has been made to resolve the controversies that have developed in connection with some rules or to renew debate on policy questions that were resolved during the course of adopting the Rules (e.g., whether a presumption should shift the burden of persuasion). The committee deemed it sufficient to identify the areas in which there is respectable opinion suggesting that practical problems exist and to indicate the nature of the problems from the perspective of those who have identified them. It also has attempted to discover whether problems that have been identified have had an appreciable negative impact on practice under the Rules or whether they have been more a subject of academic concern.

Because the focus of this Report is on identifying potential problems, not in resolving controversies, the citations are principally to cases that illustrate the points considered. No effort has been made to indicate the views of all the various commentators who have taken positions on controversial issues.

Aside from the advantages claimed for federal courts as a result of the adoption of the Rules, many saw the Rules as likely to encourage rethinking and improvement of the law of evidence in many states. Thirty-four of the states have adopted the Rules, with some modifications, of course. Thus, it appears that the foresight was accurate. The committee thought that, in connection with some rules, it would be worthwhile to note how states have departed from the federal model. Their actions may be of interest to lawyers in states still considering codification or amendments to existing codes, to lawyers in other nations and to anyone who contemplates changing the Rules any time in the future.

The Trial Evidence Committee has separately published a four volume Treatise examining state adoption and adaptation of the Rules. That treatise, G. Joseph & S. Saltzburg, *Evidence in America: The Federal Rules in the States* (1987; Supp.1990), is cited in this text as *Evidence in America* and referenced where appropriate to reflect the states' experience.

During the final stages of the committee's work on the First Edition, it drew upon the deliberations of another committee, one appointed by the Federal Judicial Center to study the Rules, that met in Williamsburg in May 1981. That committee undertook to examine the Rules in some detail. Many of the problems identified in this Report were also identified by the Williamsburg committee.

In working on this Second Edition the committee, composed of 30 or so practitioners, judges, and law professors, carried forward the focus and purpose of the original committee and its work. In some instances problems addressed in the First Edition have been resolved. For example, Rule 609(a) has been amended to address some of the issues concerning the applicability of Rule 403 to impeachment by conviction. In still other areas, the problems remain. It is important to note that the committee did not believe that a massive rewriting of the Rules was required. The Rules seem to be working well and although an amendment here and there might solve selected problems, judicial interpretation and resolution might be just as appropriate.

It should be noted that most problem, or potential problem areas are identified, but there has been some selectivity in the material included in the Report. Some judgments have been made that certain alleged problems are not serious enough to warrant mention. Usually, however, the committee has erred on the side of inclusion rather than exclusion.

APPENDIX I

ARTICLE I. GENERAL PROVISIONS

Introduction

Article I contains general provisions of the Rules. Some people have described the six rules found in this Article as "housekeeping rules," and the rules do fit that description. Like the rules in Article XI, to which they are closely related, the rules in Article I do not set forth evidentiary principles of admission and exclusion. Rather, they describe how a judge should go about making decisions on evidentiary issues. The Articles other than Articles I and XI contain the rules that dictate what evidence should, or may be, admitted or excluded.

Rule 101 defines the scope of the Rules and provides that they generally govern proceedings in all courts of the United States and before all United States magistrates, subject to Rule 1101. Rule 102 sets forth the general purposes of the Rules. Rule 103 provides procedures for raising and disposing of evidence questions. Rule 104 allocates functions between judge and jury. Rule 105 sets forth the doctrine of limited admissibility. Finally, Rule 106 is a rule of completeness covering writings and recordings. While none of the Article I rules requires that evidence be admitted or excluded, all are important to the determination of whether, and how, evidence will be received.

RULE 101

I. TEXT OF RULE

RULE 101. Scope

These rules govern proceedings in the courts of the United States and before United States bankruptcy judges and United States magistrates, to the extent and with the exceptions stated in Rule 1101.

II. DISCUSSION

In tandem with Rule 1101, Rule 101 effectively provides that the Rules will apply, *inter alia,* in all United States district courts and in all courts of appeals. The Rules apply in both civil and criminal proceedings, irrespective of whether an Article III judge, a federal magistrate, or a bankruptcy judge is presiding.[1] Rule 1101 specifies the circumstances in which the Rules do not apply.

There is little controversy over the scope and application of Rule 101, which eliminated the uneven application of state rules of evidence in federal cases. The rule is intended to ensure that one body of rules will be used by all federal courts, as illustrated by *United States v. Flores.*[2] In *Flores,* the High Court of Spain ordered extradition of a fugitive to the United States for trial on the condition that the fugitive, Flores, would be prosecuted only for a particular crime committed after a certain date. The trial court barred the government from introducing relevant evidence of Flores' criminal conduct committed prior to the date specified in the extradition order on the ground that the order barred it. The Second Circuit reversed, relying on Rule 101. It reasoned that, although the trial court was correct in recognizing the limitations imposed by the extradition order under the international law doctrine of speciality, that doctrine had never been construed to permit foreign intrusion into the evidentiary rules of the requisitioning state. Consequently, because Flores was to be tried only for the crime specified in the extradition order, the customary rules of evidence—including the rule permitting use of prior criminal acts—were applicable.[3]

Rule 101 has presented no difficulty for the courts, either on the federal level or in the state courts.[4]

1. The Rule was amended in 1988 specifically to include bankruptcy judges.

2. 538 F.2d 939 (2d Cir.1976), *cert. denied,* 429 U.S. 1066 (1977).

3. *Id.* at 944–945.

4. Almost all states that have adopted codes of evidence patterned after the Rules have included identical or substantially similar versions of Rule 101. *See* 1 *Evidence in America* §§ 1.2–1.4. Throughout this work notations will be made of those Rules.

RULE 102

I. TEXT OF RULE

RULE 102. Purpose and Construction

These rules shall be construed to secure fairness in administration, elimination of unjustifiable expense and delay, and promotion of growth and development of the law of evidence to the end that the truth may be ascertained and proceedings justly determined.

II. DISCUSSION

Rule 102, much like its counterparts in Federal Rule of Civil Procedure 1 and Federal Rule of Criminal Procedure 2, describes the goals that the evidence Rules seek to achieve. The breadth of its language, however, is potentially problematic. The apparent flexibility which the Rule affords is not entirely consistent with the concept of a uniform set of evidentiary rules governing in all federal cases. To the extent that the Rule is construed to permit the judge to ignore other, more specifically applicable rules in order to achieve the goals stated in Rule 102, the uniformity which the Rules were promulgated to achieve is at least theoretically at risk.

There are signs that some courts may apply Rule 102 to achieve results they perceive to be preferable to those dictated by other rules. In *United States v. American Cyanamid Co.,*[1] for example, the government sought an order of criminal contempt for the defendant's alleged willful violation of a longstanding antitrust consent decree and judgment. On a motion to strike a large number of documents which the defendant offered into evidence, including letters written by the defendant's competitors to the Justice Department in response to a Justice Department inquiry, the trial court admitted the documents under Rule 803(24). The government argued that Rule 803(24) applied only in exceptional cases, but the district court disagreed, interpreting Rule 803(24) in light of the broad mandate of Rule 102.[2]

The inclination to rely periodically on Rule 102 in order to avoid the results dictated by other rules is illustrated in *United States v. Batts.*[3] Batts, a passenger in a truck owned by a third party, was returning to the United States from a trip to Canada. Customs officials searched the truck and found 15 bricks of hashish. Batts was arrested and was found to be wearing a "coke spoon" around his neck. He was subsequently tried for importation and possession of hashish.

1. 427 F.Supp. 859 (S.D.N.Y.1977).

2. *Id.* at 865–866.

3. 558 F.2d 513 (9th Cir.), *opinion withdrawn,* 573 F.2d 599 (1978), *cert. denied,* 439 U.S. 859 (1978).

Batts took the stand in his own defense. The government elicited from him a denial that he knew what a coke spoon was used for, a claim that the spoon was a necklace given him by his girlfriend, and a further denial of general knowledge about cocaine use. Then the government sought to introduce rebuttal evidence that, seven months prior to trial, Batts had sold a large amount of cocaine to an undercover agent. The cocaine had been illegally seized and therefore was ruled inadmissible in the previous proceedings, which did not result in a conviction. The trial court admitted the evidence, Rule 608(b) notwithstanding, and Batts was convicted.[4]

A divided panel of the United States Court of Appeals for the Ninth Circuit affirmed the conviction, originally relying in large part on Rule 102. It reasoned that the evidentiary issue raised a conflict between the prohibition of extrinsic evidence of a crime in Rule 608(b) and the general purpose of the rules as stated in Rule 102.[5] Ultimately, it concluded that a mechanical application of Rule 608(b) was contrary to the intent of the rules as enunciated in Rule 102 and upheld introduction of the other-crime evidence.[6] Subsequently, however, the Ninth Circuit withdrew its original opinion and held that the evidence was admissible not under Rule 102 but under Rule 404(b), upon which the court had originally relied only for "further support." [7] The second opinion did not address whether the specific constraints imposed by another rule may be overridden by Rule 102.

It may be that the potential clash between the general language of Rule 102 and the specific language of other rules is of more theoretical than practical concern. *Batts* appears to be an unusual case, and the *Batts* court ultimately withdrew the opinion that surfaced the problem. *American Cyanamid* suggests, moreover, that by paying close attention to the introductory language of Rule 102—which emphasizes that the rule is a guide to construction—and by bearing in mind that rules like 403, 611(a), 803(24) and 804(b)(5) leave room for the sound exercise of judgment and discretion, the courts will find that they can interpret other, specific rules to promote the goals articulated in Rule 102. If Rule 102 were routinely construed to permit the clear language of other rules to be ignored, the potential for uneven treatment of litigants could be significant and concern about this rule would be warranted.[8]

4. 558 F.2d at 516.

5. 558 F.2d at 517.

6. *Id.*

7. *Compare* 573 F.2d at 603 *with* 558 F.2d at 518.

8. For the states' experience under this Rule, *see* 1 *Evidence in America* §§ 2.2–2.4.

RULE 103

I. TEXT OF RULE

RULE 103. Rulings on Evidence

(a) Effect of erroneous ruling. Error may not be predicated upon a ruling which admits or excludes evidence unless a substantial right of the party is affected, and

(1) Objection. In case the ruling is one admitting evidence, a timely objection or motion to strike appears of record, stating the specific ground of objection, if the specific ground was not apparent from the context; or

(2) Offer of proof. In case the ruling is one excluding evidence, the substance of the evidence was made known to the court by offer or was apparent from the context within which questions were asked.

(b) Record of offer and ruling. The court may add any other or further statement which shows the character of the evidence, the form in which it was offered, the objection made, and the ruling thereon. It may direct the making of an offer in question and answer form.

(c) Hearing of jury. In jury cases, proceedings shall be conducted, to the extent practicable, so as to prevent inadmissible evidence from being suggested to the jury by any means, such as making statements or offers of proof or asking questions in the hearing of the jury.

(d) Plain error. Nothing in this rule precludes taking notice of plain errors affecting substantial rights although they were not brought to the attention of the court.

II. DISCUSSION

This rule is clear and causes few problems, probably because for the most part it codifies pre-existing law.

Perhaps more than any other rule, Rule 103 requires some knowledge and understanding of the common law principles that governed litigation in federal courts prior to the adoption of the rules. Rule 103 imposes certain obligations on litigants but neglects to define them. For example, the rule requires a "timely" objection to preserve a complaint about evidence admitted on behalf of an opponent, and it insists upon an "offer of proof" by a proponent of evidence who wishes to complain about its exclusion. Yet, the rule defines neither term. Despite its bare bones nature, however, trial lawyers understand what the rule requires because it carries forward a traditional approach to making a record on evidence questions. Reported cases do reveal instances in which some litigants have lost opportunities to object to or support the admission or exclusion of evidence because of the failure of counsel to take appropriate action,[1] but the problem in such cases lies with counsel, not with the rule.

One of the interesting developments in modern litigation is the increased use of motions in limine. Although that term nowhere appears in the evidence Rules, they are frequently used to obtain evidentiary rulings before trial or before a certain point in a trial.[2] It is important to note that nothing in Rule 103 requires the court to make in limine rulings or inhibits it from doing so. Federal district judges frequently have ruled on evidence questions in advance of trial, but in most situations they have the discretion to delay a ruling in order to see how issues look as a trial progresses. It seems clear that certain questions—e.g., those involving the government's use of prior convictions to impeach a criminal defendant, those involving the government's use of conspiracy statements, and those surrounding claims of privilege—are most likely to be raised in limine. Particular problems with the rules that govern these questions are covered in the discussion of those rules.

Aside from establishing what counsel must do to make a record, Rule 103 sets forth a traditional limitation on a party's ability to benefit from demonstrating an error in the trial court: the harmless error rule. Harmless errors will not require reversal. The rule also recognizes a traditional exception from the general proposition that the failure to make a proper record prevents a later complaint: the plain error doctrine. Plain errors may be recognized, and judgments may be reversed because of them, even though no proper objection or offer of proof was made at trial.

One perceived difficulty with Rule 103 arises out of the use of the same term—"substantial right"—in defining both harmless and plain error. A harmless error is one that does not affect a substantial right. Thus, it would seem that a harmful error is one that does affect a substantial right. Yet, a plain error also is one that affects a substantial right. As a result, it is sometimes argued that any error which is not "harmless" must be "plain." The use of identical language to define both terms is unfortunate, but it does not seem to have created many actual problems in administering the rules. It seems clear that only the rare error will rise to the level of plain error. A party who does not give the trial judge a chance to correct a mistake will not receive the same consideration as a party who does.

1. *See, e.g.,* United States v. Long, 574 F.2d 761 (3d Cir.), *cert. denied,* 439 U.S. 985 (1978); United States v. Brady, 595 F.2d 359 (6th Cir.), *cert. denied,* 444 U.S. 862 (1979).

2. Since August 1, 1983, pretrial rulings on evidence issues have been expressly authorized in civil cases by Fed.R.Civ.P. 16(c)(3) and 16(d). Motions in limine are further addressed in the Discussion of Rule 609, *infra.*

Chapman v. California,[3] requires that a judgment in a criminal case be reversed where constitutional error occurs, unless that error is harmless beyond a reasonable doubt. In assessing the impact of non-constitutional error, however, lower courts have vacillated in the standards that they employ.[4] Some users of the Rules have suggested that it might be preferable to have a harmless error standard specified in the rule. This, it is suggested, might promote greater consistency in appellate rulings. It should be noted, however, that almost every standard utilized by federal courts involves some appellate judgment about the importance of a trial error. Different appellate courts are concerned about different sorts of errors. A uniform standard could not make the law less clear than it now is, but it probably is unduly optimistic to believe that because a standard is stated it will be significantly easier to distinguish harmful from harmless error.

One practical problem that trial lawyers note with some frequency involves not Rule 103 but the way certain judges inhibit its use. Some courts refuse to permit lawyers much leeway in stating a specific objection or much time to make an adequate offer of proof. No change in the Rule, however, is likely to ameliorate this problem. It existed before the Rules were adopted and it survives. Counsel must respect the rules imposed by the judges before whom they appear, but judges are obliged to provide an adequate opportunity for counsel to protect the interests of their clients. Rule 103, if anything, makes this point even clearer than it was previously.

Rule 103 has operated equally well in the states, few of which have modified it in any substantive respect.[5]

3. 386 U.S. 18 (1967).

4. A brief summary of their approaches can be found in 1 Saltzburg & Martin, *Federal Rules of Evidence Manual* 16–17 (5th ed. 1990).

5. 1 *Evidence in America* §§ 3.2–3.4.

RULE 104

I. TEXT OF RULE

RULE 104. Preliminary Questions

(a) Questions of admissibility generally. Preliminary questions concerning the qualifications of a person to be a witness, the existence of a privilege, or the admissibility of evidence shall be determined by the court, subject to the provisions of subdivision (b). In making its determination it is not bound by the rules of evidence except those with respect to privileges.

(b) Relevancy conditioned on fact. When the relevancy of evidence depends upon the fulfillment of a condition of fact, the court shall admit it upon, or subject to, the introduction of evidence sufficient to support a finding of the fulfillment of the condition.

(c) Hearing of jury. Hearings on the admissibility of confessions shall in all cases be conducted out of the hearing of the jury. Hearings on other preliminary matters shall be so conducted when the interests of justice require or, when an accused is a witness and so requests.

(d) Testimony by accused. The accused does not, by testifying upon a preliminary matter, become subject to cross-examination as to other issues in the case.

(e) Weight and credibility. This rule does not limit the right of a party to introduce before the jury evidence relevant to weight or credibility.

II. DISCUSSION

Rule 104 governs every decision that a trial judge is called upon to make on evidence questions. It is the Rule that dictates which issues are for the court to resolve and which are to be left for the jury. Generally, it follows the separation of functions that was well established in common law cases.

The theme of the rule is easily stated: the trial judge is expected to apply the rules of evidence to the evidence offered at trial, but he or she is not to usurp the factfinding function of the jury. Thus, the trial judge decides judicial notice issues under Article II, presumption issues under Article III, privilege questions under Article V, expert witness questions under Article VII, hearsay questions under Article VIII, most best evidence questions under Article X [1] and most issues that arise under Article IV. Moreover, the judge decides what evidence is relevant according to the definition found in Rule 401. This is the import of subdivision (a) of Rule 104.

1. *But see* Rule 1008.

Subdivision (b) reflects what remains for the jury: once the judge decides that evidence, if credited, is relevant and is not excluded under some other rule, it is for the jury to decide whether to credit that evidence. And, if one piece of evidence is helpful only if another piece is also believed, the judge leaves to the jury the decision whether to believe them both, after initially determining that the jury properly could do so and that neither piece is excluded by some other rule of evidence.

Subdivision (e) explicitly adds that once evidence is admitted, a party who had opposed its admission can offer evidence suggesting that the jury should give it little weight. A judge may find that evidence is admissible but the jury, if it wishes, may choose to give the evidence no weight.

The major difficulty in applying Rule 104 has arisen in cases in which the judge's ruling involves an issue that is similar, perhaps identical, to an issue that the jury is asked to decide. The archetypical case is that of conspirator statements offered against a conspirator who did not make statements. The judge must determine that a statement was made during and in furtherance of conspiracy before admitting the statement under Rule 801. Such a finding obviously requires that the judge find that there was a conspiracy. Yet, this may be the very question the jury is asked to decide. The functions of judge and jury are different, but the difference can be confusing, as the discussion of Rule 801 indicates.

The confusion existed at common law, and the cases decided under the Rules may have produced more agreement on how judges handle fact finding associated with evidence issues than existed prior to the Rules' adoption. The conspiracy questions, and several others, are complicated. It is doubtful, however, that any change in a basic rule like 104, which tracks a common law distinction, will make the questions any easier to handle.

The role of judges in making preliminary factual findings under Rule 104(b) was addressed and reaffirmed by the Supreme Court in *Huddleston v. United States.*[2] At trial on charges of possession and sale of 500 stolen videotapes, the prosecution introduced evidence under Rule 404(b) that the defendant had been connected with other stolen televisions and appliances. The Court rejected the defendant's argument that before admitting this evidence the trial judge was required by Rule 104(a) to determine by a preponderance of the evidence that the alleged extrinsic acts occurred and that the defendant committed the acts.[3] Rule 104(b), said the Court, is the operative rule. The trial

2. 485 U.S. 681 (1988).

3. A split had developed in the Circuits over the standard of admissibility of extrinsic offense evidence. The First, Fourth, Fifth and Eleventh Circuits had ruled that such evidence was admissible if there was sufficient evidence to permit the jury to determine that the defendant committed the extrinsic offense. *See, e.g.,* United States v. Beechum,

court is only required to examine the evidence and determine whether the jury could reasonably find that the alleged extrinsic acts occurred by a preponderance of the evidence.

In response, the American Bar Association at the request of its Criminal Justice Section adopted a resolution encouraging an amendment to Rule 404(b) which would have required the judge under Rule 104(a) to determine finally the admissibility of extrinsic offense evidence. The resolution was presented to the Advisory Committee in 1989 but to date has not been added to Rule 404(b).[4]

There are few problems associated with subdivisions (c) and (d), although they do fail to state whether a criminal accused, protected by these subdivisions, may be impeached with the testimony given on a preliminary matter if he or she subsequently testifies at trial. Cases like *Harris v. New York,*[5] and *United States v. Havens,*[6] suggest that the Supreme Court might be inclined to give an affirmative answer. A clear answer in the Rule itself would be desirable. Two states, Alaska and Iowa, did add language to address this issue in their versions of Rule 104(d). In both states, the impeachment is permitted.[7]

582 F.2d 898 (5th Cir.1978) (en banc), *cert. denied,* 440 U.S. 920 (1979). The Sixth and Second Circuits had applied the preponderance of the evidence test and the Seventh, Eighth, Ninth and District of Columbia Circuits had applied a clear and convincing evidence standard. 485 U.S. at 685, n. 2.

4. The Draft Advisory Committee's Note to a proposed amendment to Rule 404(b) which would require notice of an intent to introduce extrinsic act evidence indicates that the Committee was not inclined at this point to overrule *Huddleston* through an amendment to Rule 404(b). *See* Rule 404(b) *infra.*

5. 401 U.S. 222 (1971).

6. 446 U.S. 620 (1980).

7. *See* 1 *Evidence in America* §§ 4.2–4.4.

RULE 105

I. TEXT OF RULE

RULE 105. Limited Admissibility

When evidence which is admissible as to one party or for one purpose but not admissible as to another party or for another purpose is admitted, the court, upon request, shall restrict the evidence to its proper scope and instruct the jury accordingly.

II. DISCUSSION

The straightforward principle embodied in Rule 105—that the trial court must give a limiting instruction if limited-purpose or limited-person evidence is admitted and a specific and timely request for the instruction is made—generates little litigation. Occasional appellate opinions, however, consider one or more of three recurring Rule 105 issues: timing of the request, specificity of the request, and content of the instruction.

The timing and specificity issues are well illustrated by *United States v. Thirion.*[1] In *Thirion,* a multiple-defendant fraud prosecution, the trial court refused one defendant's request for "an instruction limiting the jury's 'consideration of all of [the testimony of a particular witness] except his testimony concerning contacts with [the requesting defendant] and that they may not be considered against [the requesting defendant], with the exception of those that directly deal with him.' "[2] The request was made after the prosecution and two co-defendants had examined the witness, but before the requestor's examination began. Affirming the trial court's refusal, the appellate panel found the request to be neither timely nor specific, but made two noteworthy observations:

> [The] request may have been specific enough had it immediately followed the offending testimony. Likewise, the request would have been timely had it been made with greater specificity identifying the subject of the testimony to be limited.[3]

Litigators accordingly would do well to recall the phrase "too little, too late" whenever limited admissibility evidence is offered.

Litigation concerning the content of limiting instructions covers a broad spectrum of issues. The scenario examined in *Hale v. Firestone Tire & Rubber Co.,*[4] a product liability case, is illustrative. The *Hale* decision involved the following limiting instruction, which was given in connection with admitted evidence of prior product accidents:

1. 813 F.2d 146 (8th Cir.1987).
2. 813 F.2d at 155.
3. *Id.*
4. 820 F.2d 928 (8th Cir.1987).

> [T]he stipulation and the reports that were just read to you here are for the purpose of notice of the allegations of claims of defect in the [product] related to the issues in this case.[5]

The product supplier complained on appeal that the instruction failed to admonish the jury not to consider the evidence as proof of defect or causation. The Eighth Circuit rejected this challenge, finding no abuse of the trial court's discretion, even though it would have preferred that the instruction identify the evidence's prohibited uses.

The appellant in *Hale* undoubtedly anticipated a more receptive audience in light of the Eighth Circuit's earlier decision in *Sprynczynatyk v. General Motors Corp.*[6] In *Sprynczynatyk,* General Motors successfully challenged a limiting instruction concerning admitted videotapes of the plaintiff under hypnosis. The appellate court accepted GM's argument that the instruction must expressly prohibit consideration of the videotapes as proof of the matters recounted in them, and went so far as to draft an acceptable instruction for use in the ordered retrial. In its analysis, the court noted GM's request, in the jury's presence, for specific "prohibited use" language and emphasized the danger that the jury would interpret the court's refusal as an endorsement of the use GM had legitimately sought to bar.

Read together, *Sprynczynatyk* and *Hale* suggest that trial lawyers may have to "stick their necks out" before the jury, and risk the negative inference of endorsement noted in *Sprynczynatyk,* if they hope to bind trial judges to particular content of limiting instructions.

The preceding issues as a group have received far less judicial attention and scholarly debate than the more vexing problem of confessions in joint criminal trials. This problem, repeatedly examined by the United States Supreme Court, arises when the prosecution, in a multiple-defendant criminal trial, seeks to admit one defendant's pretrial confession into evidence against the confessor, but the confessor refuses to testify. Where the confession in some manner implicates another defendant, a clash of constitutional values—the privilege against self-incrimination and the right of confrontation—results.

The confession-in-joint-trials problem relates less to the substance of Rule 105 than to the underlying notion that limiting instructions will be understood and diligently obeyed by juries. The validity of this "obedience presumption" is frequently questioned, occasionally by particularly noteworthy critics.[7] Nonetheless, the presumption remains

5. 820 F.2d at 935.

6. 771 F.2d 1112 (8th Cir.1985), *cert. denied,* 475 U.S. 1046 (1986).

7. *See, e.g.,* Delli Paoli v. United States, 352 U.S. 232, 245 (1957) (Frankfurter, J, dissenting); Nash v. United States, 54 F.2d 1006, 1007 (2d Cir.) (L. Hand, J.) (The limiting instruction is a "recommendation to the jury of a mental gymnastic which is beyond, not only their powers, but anybody's else"), *cert. denied,* 285 U.S. 556 (1932).

essentially unassailable in civil litigation, and has survived vigorous challenge in many criminal cases.[8]

The obedience presumption is constitutionally curtailed, however, in the implicating co-defendant confession scenario. In *Bruton v. United States,*[9] the Supreme Court found a Confrontation Clause violation in the admission, in a multi-defendant criminal trial, of the specifically inculpating confession of a non-testifying co-defendant, despite the trial court's specific and repeated instruction restricting use of the confession to the confessor. Underlying the court's decision were its perceptions of the risk of juror disobedience under the circumstances and the "powerfully incriminating" nature and "suspect" reliability of the evidence.[10]

Rule 105's most confounding "emerging problem" has involved application of *Bruton* in light of "the infinite variability of inculpatory statements (whether made by defendants or co-defendants), and of their likely effect on juries." *Parker v. Randolph,* 442 U.S. 62, 84 (1979) (Stevens, J., dissenting). The cases are legion. Of them, *Richardson v. Marsh* [11] and *Cruz v. New York* [12] decided the same day, are particularly important and insightful.

Cruz v. New York involved "interlocking" confessions. The two defendants had confessed separately to the charged joint crime, and the two confessions corroborated one another. At the defendants' joint trial, both confessions were admitted into evidence, and the jury was given corresponding limited-person instructions. On appeal from the convictions that followed, the Supreme Court sustained a *Bruton*-based challenge to admission of the confessions. En route to its conclusion, the Court noted that while the existence of an interlocking confession generally enhances the reliability of the co-defendant's corresponding confession, it in no way reduces the risk of juror disobedience or the degree of devastation visited upon the complaining defendant. Notably, the *Cruz* opinion specifically repudiated the Court's eight-year-old plurality opinion in *Parker v. Randolph* [13] which had considered *Bruton* inapplicable to interlocking confessions because the complaining defendant's own confession would leave little for the co-defendant's confession to "devastate."

8. *See e.g.,* Greer v. Miller, 483 U.S. 756, 766 n. 8, (1987) (instruction to disregard prosecutor's question to accused, suggesting guilt be inferred from post-arrest silence); Harris v. New York, 401 U.S. 222, 223 (1971) (instruction limiting use of statements inadmissible under *Miranda* to issue of defendant's credibility); United States v. Tussa, 816 F.2d 58, 68 (2d Cir.1987) (instruction limiting use of prior drug crimes to issue of intent in drug prosecution).

9. 391 U.S. 123 (1968).

10. 391 U.S. at 135–36.

11. 481 U.S. 200 (1987).

12. 481 U.S. 186 (1987).

13. 442 U.S. 62 (1979).

Richardson v. Marsh concerned the "redacted" confession, a species alluded to but not at issue in *Bruton.* The *Richardson* confession, which inculpated defendant Marsh in its unabridged form, was edited for admission to omit any indication that anyone other than the confessor and a third person, not a party to the litigation, was involved in the crime. Upon admitting the redacted confession, the trial court admonished the jury not to use it against Marsh. Rejecting Marsh's *Bruton*-based Confrontation Clause challenge, the Supreme Court found the limiting instruction constitutionally sufficient, even though the confession did tend to incriminate Marsh "when linked with evidence introduced later at trial." [14] The decision rested on the Court's view that "inferentially inculpatory" co-defendant confessions, requiring "linkage" to the complaining defendant, are less "powerfully incriminating" than the "expressly inculpating" confession at issue in *Bruton* and, further, that "[w]here the necessity of such linkage is involved, it is a less valid generalization that the jury will not likely obey the instruction to disregard the evidence." [15]

Chief Justice Rehnquist and Justices White, Powell and O'Connor dissented in *Cruz,* while Justices Stevens, Brennan, and Marshall dissented in *Richardson.*

Countless permutations undoubtedly remain unresolved by the Supreme Court. One example, expressly left unaddressed in *Richardson,*[16] is the confession redacted not by elimination, but by substitution of some neutral symbol or pronoun. Such redactions have received extensive treatment in the lower courts.[17] Ultimate Supreme Court

14. 481 U.S. at 208.

15. *Id.*

16. 481 U.S. at 211.

17. *See* United States v. Danzey, 594 F.2d 905, 917–19 (2d Cir.) (finding *Bruton* violation in admission of co-defendant's written statement, which was read to jury with the work "blank" substituted for the name of an identified accomplice; also disapproving allowance of testimony of agent, to whom co-defendant made oral statements, that co-defendant had named his accomplices, though names given were not disclosed), *cert denied,* 441 U.S. 951 (1979); United States v. Holleman, 575 F.2d 139, 142–43 (7th Cir. 1978) (upholding admission, in three-defendant prosecution, of one defendant's confession that implicated two accomplices "unnamed and not identified by race, age, size or any other means except by sex"); Hodges v. Rose, 570 F.2d 643 (6th Cir.) (finding *Bruton* violation in admission of co-defendant's statement, which implicated an accomplice, where statement after redaction referred to the accomplice as "blank"), *cert. denied,* 436 U.S. 909 (1978); United States v. DiGilio, 538 F.2d 972, 981–83 (3d Cir.1976) (finding *Bruton* violation in use of word "blank" in place of co-defendants' identification of accomplice, despite trial court's instruction that "blank" was used to aid jury "in adhering to" court's person-limiting instruction), *cert. denied,* 429 U.S. 1038 (1977); United States ex rel. Joseph v. LaVallee, 290 F.Supp. 90, 94–95 (N.D.N.Y.1968) (finding *Bruton* violation in admission of testimony of police officers, to whom co-defendant had confessed, concerning co-defendant's statements, where "he," "the other person," and "someone else" were substituted for identification of accomplice), *rev'd,* 415 F.2d 150, 153 (2d Cir.1969) (any *Bruton* violation was harmless error), *cert. denied,* 397 U.S. 951 (1970); *cf.* Harrington v. California, 395 U.S. 250, 253 (1969) (assuming that references to "the

intervention seems likely. Precedent indicates that the Court's view of this and other co-defendant confession issues will be guided by its perceptions of the risk of juror disobedience, the degree of devastation caused by the evidence, and its reliability. In light of the Court's flexibility on these points,[18] the co-defendant confession problem may continue to emerge for a long time to come.[19]

white guy" in co-defendants' confessions "made it as clear as pointing and shouting that the person referred to was the white man in the dock with the three Negroes").

18. *Compare* Delli Paoli v. United States, 352 U.S. 232, 239 (1957), with *Bruton,* 391 U.S. at 126, (overruling *Delli Paoli*), and Parker v. Randolph, 442 U.S. 62, 73 (1979) (plurality opinion), with *Cruz,* 481 U.S. at 191–92 (rejecting *Parker* plurality view).

19. For the states' experience under this Rule, *see* 1 *Evidence in America* §§ 5.2–5.4.

RULE 106

I. TEXT OF RULE

RULE 106. Remainder of or Related Writings or Recorded Statements

When a writing or recorded statement or part thereof is introduced by a party, an adverse party may require the introduction at that time of any other part or any other writing or recorded statement which ought in fairness to be considered contemporaneously with it.

II. DISCUSSION

The "rule of completeness" expressed in Rule 106 addresses the obvious dangers associated with receiving out-of-context excerpts of writings or recordings. Courts frequently reiterate the two key reasons for the rule: taking matters out of context may create a misleading impression, and delaying "repair work" until a later point in the trial may render it ineffective.[1] Consistent with this rationale, Rule 106 does not require introduction of additional excerpts that are neither relevant to the admitted portion nor necessary to qualify, explain, or clarify it.[2]

United States v. Dorrell[3] illustrates this point. Security guards apprehended Dorrell at a United States military installation and obtained from him a written statement admitting various acts of vandalism. The statement also set forth Dorrell's political and religious motivations for the acts. The trial court redacted Dorrell's statement, eliminating all references to his motivations, in response to a prosecution motion in limine, and admitted the redacted version into evidence. Noting that redaction of a confession comports with Rule 106 so long as it "neither 'distorts the meaning of the statement or excludes information substantially exculpatory of the declarant,' . . . nor excludes 'portions of a statement that are . . . neither explanatory of [or] relevant to the admitted passages,'" the appellate court affirmed:

> In this case, removing Dorrell's explanation of the political and religious motivations for his actions did not change the meaning of the portions of his confession submitted to the jury. The redaction did not alter the fact that he admitted committing the acts with which he was charged. Further, because the defense of necessity was unavailable, Dorrell's motivation did not excuse the crimes he

1. *E.g.,* United States v. Pendas–Martinez, 845 F.2d 938, 943 (11th Cir.1988).

2. *E.g., id.* at 944; United States v. Green, 694 F.Supp. 107, 110 (E.D.Pa.1988), *aff'd,* 875 F.2d 312 (3d Cir.1989).

3. 758 F.2d 427 (9th Cir.1985).

committed. The omitted portions of his confession were therefore not exculpatory.[4]

An interesting variation on the "confession completeness" theme is presented in *United States v. Castro.*[5] In the course of a drug raid, a police officer asked Castro where the drugs were kept. Castro responded by pointing to a bag and stating that it contained drugs. When asked how he knew this, Castro replied that the bag belonged to another person, Acosta, who had put it there. At their joint trial, Castro and Acosta urged differing treatments of Castro's statement. Acosta insisted upon deletion of the references to him, on the authority of the Confrontation Clause and *Bruton v. United States.*[6] Castro countered that Rule 106 barred redaction of the statement, as deletion of the portion concerning Acosta would cause his statement to suggest that he owned the bag. At the trial court's suggestion, the officer omitted specific reference to Acosta in his testimony, but acknowledged Castro "in substance" had denied owning the bag. On appeal from the convictions, the Second Circuit affirmed. Although the opinion rests, at least in part, on the "harmless error" rule, the court did note its inability to find an abuse of discretion in the trial court's accommodation of Acosta's confrontation right and Castro's entitlement to completeness.[7]

Of the few problems to emerge under Rule 106, the by far most intriguing involves its use to admit otherwise incompetent evidence. Such use generally has been rejected summarily by the courts, on the theory that Rule 106 concerns only the order—not the content—of proof.[8] The three states to address this issue expressly in their versions of Rule 106—Iowa, Ohio and Oregon—codified this position.[9] The contrary view, that otherwise incompetent evidence becomes admissible, under Rule 106, when necessary to put admitted evidence in proper context, has gained credibility from an important recent decision.

United States v. Sutton[10] specifically and squarely rejects the notion that Rule 106's procedural function has no substantive counter-

4. 758 F.2d at 435.

5. 813 F.2d 571 (2d Cir.), *cert. denied,* 484 U.S. 844 (1987).

6. 391 U.S. 123 (1968) (discussed in connection with Rule 105, *supra*).

7. Although the *Castro* court appropriately notes Rule 106's inapplicability to oral statements and refers to the court's broader discretion under Rule 611, its discussion suggests equivalent propriety under Rule 106. *See* 813 F.2d at 576.

8. *See, e.g.,* United States Football League v. National Football League, 842 F.2d 1335, 1375–76 (2d Cir.1988); United States v. Woolbright, 831 F.2d 1390, 1395 (8th Cir.1987); United States v. Terry, 702 F.2d 299, 314 (2d Cir.), *cert. denied sub nom.* Williams v. United States, 461 U.S. 931 (1983); United States v. Costner, 684 F.2d 370, 373 (6th Cir. 1982); United States v. Burreson, 643 F.2d 1344, 1349 (9th Cir.), *cert. denied,* 454 U.S. 847 (1981).

9. *See* 1 *Evidence in America* §§ 6.2–6.4.

10. 801 F.2d 1346 (D.C.Cir.1986).

part. Occasional admission of otherwise inadmissible evidence will be essential, according to *Sutton,* to the Rule's distortion-avoidance function. Rule 106 accordingly can independently support the admission of otherwise inadmissible evidence, provided the usual requirements for its use are satisfied. This view clearly expands Rule 106's offensive utility considerably beyond its more generally accepted use to reorder proof.

A second decision, *United States v. LeFevour,*[11] also reflects an expansive view of Rule 106. While the *LeFevour* opinion unremarkably rejects an attempt to invoke Rule 106 on the ground that omission of the proffered context evidence created no danger of a misleading impression, it does contain some important dicta:

> If otherwise inadmissible evidence is necessary to correct a misleading impression, then either it is admissible for this limited purpose by force of Rule 106 . . . or, if it is inadmissible (maybe because of privilege), the misleading evidence must be excluded too. . . . Rule 106 was not intended to override every privilege and other exclusionary rule of evidence in the legal armamentarium, so there must be cases where if an excerpt is misleading the only cure is to exclude it rather than to put in other excerpts.[12]

In contrast to the *Sutton* approach, *LeFevour* may support a defensive use of Rule 106, barring the admission of distorting evidence whenever the needed clarification is itself inadmissible.

While *Sutton* and *LeFevour* may signal the emergence of Rule 106 as both an important offensive and defensive weapon in the litigator's arsenal, it remains to be seen whether its full potential will be realized.

The Supreme Court addressed the applicability of Rule 106 in *Beech Aircraft v. Rainey.*[13] In that case the plaintiff was called to testify as an adverse witness for the defendant aircraft company. During direct examination counsel questioned the plaintiff about a statement he had made in a letter concerning the cause of a crash which killed the plaintiff's wife. But the trial court would not permit the plaintiff's counsel to refer to other statements in the same letter which would have given a different impression to the jury. That limitation, said the Court, was improper. Noting that Rule 106 is a partial codification of the "rule of completeness," the Court declined to address its scope and meaning. Instead, it concluded that the trial court had erred because the offered evidence (other statements in the letter) were independently relevant.[14]

11. 798 F.2d 977 (7th Cir.1986).

12. 798 F.2d at 981.

13. 109 S.Ct. 439 (1988).

14. For the states' experience under this Rule, *see* 1 *Evidence in America* §§ 6.2–6.4.

APPENDIX I

ARTICLE II. JUDICIAL NOTICE

Introduction

Article II consists of a single rule which deals with judicial notice of adjudicative facts. It is the only evidence rule concerning judicial notice. Adjudicative facts constitute only a portion of those facts and matters of which a court may take notice. There are, for example, nonadjudicative, or legislative, facts which may be the object of judicial notice pursuant to the common law. These are not governed by Rule 201. Similarly, judicial notice of the law of a sister state or a foreign country, also unregulated by the rule, may be taken at common law or in accordance with the applicable rule of civil or criminal procedure.

Rule 201 substantially codifies the common law requirements for taking judicial notice and, probably for that reason, has presented few, if any, problems for the courts. In most respects, the rule applies uniformly to civil and criminal cases. Subdivision (g), however, provides that a jury in a criminal case need not accept as conclusive those facts judicially noticed while a jury in a civil case is instructed that it has no such discretion.

RULE 201

I. TEXT OF RULE

RULE 201. Judicial Notice of Adjudicative Facts

(a) Scope of rule. This rule governs only judicial notice of adjudicative facts.

(b) Kinds of facts. A judicially noticed fact must be one not subject to reasonable dispute in that it is either (1) generally known within the territorial jurisdiction of the trial court or (2) capable of accurate and ready determination by resort to sources whose accuracy cannot reasonably be questioned.

(c) When discretionary. A court may take judicial notice, whether requested or not.

(d) When mandatory. A court shall take judicial notice if requested by a party and supplied with the necessary information.

(e) Opportunity to be heard. A party is entitled upon timely request to an opportunity to be heard as to the propriety of taking judicial notice and the tenor of the matter noticed. In the absence of prior notification, the request may be made after judicial notice has been taken.

(f) Time of taking notice. Judicial notice may be taken at any stage of the proceeding.

(g) Instructing jury. In a civil action or proceeding, the court shall instruct the jury to accept as conclusive any fact judicially noticed. In a criminal case, the court shall instruct the jury that it may, but is not required to, accept as conclusive any fact judicially noticed.

II. DISCUSSION

Rule 201 has generated few problems for the courts in routine civil cases,[1] primarily because it is a codification of pre-existing common law requirements for taking judicial notice. In certain instances, courts have taken judicial notice of facts necessary to establish a plaintiff's cause of action.[2]

1. *See, e.g.,* Lovvorn v. City of Chattanooga, 846 F.2d 1539, 1562 (6th Cir.) (drug problem in work force) (Guy, J., dissenting), *vacated* 861 F.2d 1388 (6th Cir.1988); Grant v. Meyer, 828 F.2d 1446, 1453 (D.C.Cir.1987) (recognizing that it is more often difficult to get people to work without compensation than it is to get them to work for pay) *aff'd,* 486 U.S. 414 (1988); Martin v. Solem, 801 F.2d 324, 334 (8th Cir.1986) (state of farm economy) (Bright, J., dissenting).

2. *See, e.g.,* Durham v. Independence Bank of Chicago, 629 F.Supp. 983, 991 & n. 9 (N.D.Ill.1986) (judicial notice in civil RICO case that corporation was an "enterprise" within meaning of Act where complaint did not allege "enterprise" status).

As a result of the jury's right in a criminal case not to accept as conclusive any fact judicially noticed, courts are generally reluctant to judicially notice facts in criminal cases that they would typically judicially notice in civil cases.[3] Courts often refuse to judicially notice facts necessary to establish an essential element of the government's case in criminal matters.[4] Criminal defendants who request judicial notice under Rule 201, however, have fared no better than the prosecution.[5]

Courts will, even in criminal cases, take judicial notice of facts which are easily confirmed,[6] of indisputable facts,[7] or of facts within the common knowledge of the jury.[8] Geography and distances are frequently judicially noticed in criminal cases, even when they constitute an element of the government's case in chief.[9]

3. *Compare* United States v. Judge, 846 F.2d 274, 276–77 (5th Cir.1988) (in criminal case, declining to take judicial notice of DEA regulations establishing standardized inventory search procedures), *aff'd,* 864 F.2d 1144 (5th Cir.1989) with Policeman's Benevolent Ass'n. of New Jersey v. Township of Washington, 850 F.2d 133 (3d Cir.1988) (in civil case, judicial notice of local regulations governing police force), *cert. denied,* 490 U.S. 1004 (1989).

4. *See, e.g.,* United States v. Mentz, 840 F.2d 315, 322 (6th Cir.1988) (declining to take judicial notice, in criminal action for bank robbery, that deposits of financial institution robbed were insured by FDIC). *But see* United States v. McCargo, 783 F.2d 507, 509 (5th Cir.1986) (findings of fact by United States Magistrate in proceeding for criminal contempt); United States v. Anderson, 782 F.2d 908, 917 (11th Cir.1986) (existence of state arson statute in criminal RICO proceeding).

5. *See, e.g.,* United States v. Mosely, 810 F.2d 93, 99 (6th Cir.1987) (judges' use of sentencing recommendations), *cert. denied,* 484 U.S. 841 (1988); United States v. Risk, 672 F.Supp. 346, 359 (S.D.Ind.1987) (facts underlying government's alleged selective, discriminatory prosecution of defendant), *aff'd,* 843 F.2d 1059 (7th Cir.1988).

6. *E.g.,* United States v. Comstock, 805 F.2d 1194, 1201 n. 7 (5th Cir.1986) (state judge who issued search warrant was a lawyer), *cert. denied,* 481 U.S. 1022 (1987); United States v. Kabat, 797 F.2d 580, 593 & n. 4 (8th Cir.1986) (great disparity of sentences imposed on nuclear protesters) (Bright, J., dissenting), *cert. denied,* 481 U.S. 1030 (1987).

7. *E.g.,* Blake v. United States, 841 F.2d 203, 206 n. 3 (7th Cir.1988) (kilogram of cocaine weighs approximately 2.2 pounds); United States v. Deckard, 816 F.2d 426, 428 (8th Cir.1987) (interstate character of telephone lines of Southwestern Bell).

8. *E.g.,* United States v. Rodriguez, 803 F.2d 318, 321 (7th Cir.1986) (authority of United States over Puerto Rico), *cert. denied,* 480 U.S. 908 (1987); *see also* United States v. Sweiss, 800 F.2d 684, 690 (7th Cir.1986) (result at trial of using informant to secretly tape-record conversations), *aff'd,* 814 F.2d 1208 (7th Cir.1987). *But cf.* United States v. Grassi, 783 F.2d 1572, 1577 n. 3 (11th Cir.1986) (command to "show respect" is mobster language), *cert. denied,* 479 U.S. 985, (1986).

9. *See, e.g.,* United States v. Perez, 776 F.2d 797, 801–02 (9th Cir.1985) (travel between Guam and Rota necessarily involved travel through international waters); United States v. Judd, 687 F.Supp. 1052, 1054 (N.D.Miss.1988) (distances and approximate time of travel between towns), *aff'd,* 889 F.2d 1410 (5th Cir.1989); United States v. Robertson, 638 F.Supp. 1202, 1203 (E.D.Va.1986) (property on which offenses occurred was federal property).

In making such determinations, a court may judicially notice facts from another, related criminal proceeding.[10] But it is prohibited from relying upon its own personal experience to support the taking of judicial notice in a criminal proceeding if it denies the parties the opportunity to test the basis for the court's opinion.[11] In any event, care should be taken by the court to identify the fact it is noticing and its justification for doing so.[12]

Appellate courts are entitled, but are not required, to take judicial notice of facts even when such facts are not part of the record on appeal.[13] However, use of judicial notice on appeal could be viewed as violating due process and confrontation rights despite Rule 201(f)'s clear statement that "[j]udicial notice may be taken at any stage of the proceeding." [14] Two problems analogous to the one relating to judicial notice on appeal involve situations where the trial court takes judicial notice of facts in a criminal proceeding in which the jury is not allowed to be present, as in hearings on the defendant's motion to suppress,[15] and evidentiary rulings which are not within the province of the jury.[16]

The trend is to apply the "plain error" rule to facts judicially noticed in criminal proceedings. In one case, for example, the court of appeals recognized that the district court had erred in judicially noticing a fact because the fact was subject to reasonable dispute,[17] but

10. *See* United States v. Author Serv., Inc., 804 F.2d 1520, 1523 (9th Cir.1986) (denying defendant's request for evidentiary hearing on ground that allegations of IRS' bad faith had been raised and held insubstantial in related tax case), *modified,* 811 F.2d 1264 (9th Cir.1987); *cf.* United States v. Estep, 760 F.2d 1060, 1063 (10th Cir.1985) (in hearing on request for return of property voluntarily given for use as evidence in criminal trial, judicial notice of all evidence admitted in criminal trial phase not reversible error).

11. *See* United States v. Lewis, 833 F.2d 1380, 1385–86 (9th Cir.1987) (condition following surgery under general anesthetic), *cert. denied,* 486 U.S. 1056 (1988).

12. United States v. Mentz, 840 F.2d 315, 322 (6th Cir.1988); Colonial Leasing Co. of New England v. Logistics Control Group Int'l., 762 F.2d 454, 459 (5th Cir.1985).

13. *Compare* United States v. O'Dell, 805 F.2d 637, 643 (6th Cir.1986) (declining to enlarge record by taking judicial notice of extra-record facts for first time on appeal), *cert. denied,* 484 U.S. 859 (1987), with United States v. LaChance, 788 F.2d 856, 862 (2d Cir.) (judicial notice on appeal of plan for random selection of grand jurors), *cert. denied,* 479 U.S. 883 (1986).

14. *See, e.g.,* Garner v. Louisiana, 368 U.S. 157, 173 (1961).

15. *See* United States v. Johnson, 726 F.2d 1018, 1021–22 (4th Cir.1984) (distances involved in crimes, concluding that automobile was connected with crimes, thereby justifying search of automobile); United States v. Rembert, 694 F.Supp. 163, 175 (W.D. N.C.1988) (departure time of commercial bus in determining whether departure was delayed and, thus, whether passengers were "seized," in motion to suppress physical evidence found during search).

16. *See* United States v. Hing Shair Chan, 680 F.Supp. 521, 524 (E.D.N.Y.1988) (facts making it "likely" that foreign hotel records were as authentic and accurate as they appeared to be).

17. *See* Rule 201(b).

concluded that the district court had committed no plain error by its erroneous admission of the evidence.[18]

Another emerging problem is the use of judicial notice in cases involving alleged constitutional infirmities in the method of jury selection in criminal proceedings. Prior to *Batson v. Kentucky,*[19] the area of most concern in criminal proceedings was the use of judicial notice of adjudicative facts necessary to establish an essential element of the government's case after trial or on appeal. In *Batson,* the Supreme Court of the United States held that a defendant could make a *prima facie* showing of discrimination against the defendant's cognizable racial group in the use of peremptory challenges to the venire based on evidence concerning the defendant's own trial without showing repeated instances of such discriminatory conduct over a number of cases. In order to make a *prima facie* showing of discriminatory peremptory challenges under the Equal Protection clause, a defendant must show: (1) that he is a member of a cognizable racial group and that the prosecutor has exercised peremptory challenges to remove from the venire members of the defendant's group, and (2) that these facts and other relevant circumstances raise an inference that the prosecutor used that practice to exclude the veniremen from the petit jury on account of their membership in that group.

The first prong of the *Batson* test is ideally suited for the exercise of judicial notice. Courts have routinely determined the cognizability of a group through the use of judicial notice.[20] Use of judicial notice, however, to establish the inference that the prosecutor exercised peremptory challenges to exclude from the jury panel members of a certain cognizable group[21] tends to blur the distinction between adjudicative facts and legislative facts. Only the former are addressed by Rule 201.[22]

18. *See* United States v. Lebron–Gonzalez, 816 F.2d 823, 827 (1st Cir.1987) (admission of questionable birth certificate where essential element of crime was proof of citizenship of victim), *cert. denied,* 484 U.S. 843, (1988). *See also* United States v. Hernandez, 780 F.2d 113, 121 (D.C.Cir.1986) (not plain error for district court to judicially notice matters outside record).

19. 476 U.S. 79 (1986).

20. *See, e.g.,* Roman v. Abrams, 822 F.2d 214, 227–28 (2d Cir.1987) (Caucasians), *cert. denied,* 489 U.S. 1052 (1989); United States v. Biaggi, 673 F.Supp. 96, 101 (E.D.N.Y.1987) (Italian–Americans), *aff'd,* 853 F.2d 89 (2d Cir.1988), *cert. denied,* 489 U.S. 1052 (1989).

21. *See, e.g.,* United States v. Hughes, 864 F.2d 78, 79–80 (8th Cir.1988) (frequency of charges of systematic exclusion of black jurors in criminal cases in particular federal judicial district), *aff'd,* 880 F.2d 101 (8th Cir.1989).

22. Adjudicative facts are defined as the facts of the particular case. Legislative facts are those which have relevance to legal reasoning and the law-making process, whether in the formulation of a legal principle or ruling by a court or the enactment of a statute by a legislative body. 1 Joseph and Saltzburg, Evidence in America § 7.3 (1987). Legislative facts are predictions about the effects of legal rules and are by their very nature disputable. *See* Woolhandler, *Rethinking the Judicial Reception of Legislative Facts,* 41 Vand.L. rev. 111, 123 (1988).

This result may depend, in part, upon the courts' presumption of discrimination as a causative factor in the use of peremptory challenges. One commentator presents the argument that if legislative facts merely reinforce pre-existing presumptions, as they did in *Brown v. Board of Education,*[23] where the Court referred to the social science appendix detailing the deleterious effects of segregation on black children, then the reception of legislative facts is likely to by sympathetic and unremarkable.[24]

The evaluation of the statistical evidence of racial bias in *McCleskey v. Kemp*[25] demonstrates the fate of legislative facts that seek to undermine pre-existing legal and personal presumptions that discrimination is not an important causative factor in the disproportionate racial effects of the death penalty.[26] Thus, depending upon the courts' views on the cause of alleged racially discriminatory use of peremptory challenges, the emerging problem of using judicial notice in such cases may eventually be resolved by the United States Supreme Court.

Judicial notice of the jury selection process is appropriate, however, when the systematic exclusion of a protected class is not an issue[27] and judicial notice of a court's own records or the records of other courts appears to be expanding in civil[28] and criminal proceedings.[29]

23. 347 U.S. 483, 494 N. 11 (1954).

24. Woolhandler, *Rethinking the Judicial Reception of Legislative Facts,* 41 Vand.L. Rev. 111, 120–21 (1988).

25. 481 U.S. 279 (1987).

26. Woolhandler, 41 Vand.L.Rev. at 121.

27. *See, e.g.,* United States v. Cecil, 836 F.2d 1431, 1449 & n. 8 (4th Cir.) (en banc) (finding by courts that voter registration lists represent fair cross-section of community), *cert. denied,* 487 U.S. 1205 (1988); United States v. LaChance, 788 F.2d 856, 862 (2d Cir. 1986) (plan for random selection of grand jurors), *cert. denied,* 479 U.S. 883 (1986); *see generally* Barber v. Ponte, 772 F.2d 982, 984–86 (1st Cir.1985) (en banc) (reviewing history of right to venire comprised of fair cross-section of community), *cert. denied,* 475 U.S. 1050 (1986).

28. *See, e.g.,* United Food and Commercial Workers Int'l, Union v. IBP, Inc., 857 F.2d 422, 432 & n. 13 (8th Cir.1988) (recent prosecution under state mass picketing statute); Oneida Motor Freight, Inc. v. United Jersey Bank, 848 F.2d 414, 416 n. 3 (3d Cir.1988) (record of prior bankruptcy proceeding in making ruling on dispositive, pre-trial motion) *cert. denied,* 488 U.S. 967 (1988); Reynolds v. Ellingsworth, 843 F.2d 712, 714 n. 1 (3d Cir. 1988) (all relevant parts of state court record, whether or not they appeared in joint appendix prepared by parties to appeal), *cert. denied,* 488 U.S. 960 (1988); Weil v. Markowitz, 829 F.2d 166, 173 n. 15 (D.C.Cir.1987) (related proceeding in another court to establish fact that individual owned substantial interest in realty).

29. *See, e.g.,* Person v. Miller, 854 F.2d 656, 660 (4th Cir.1988) (court's own order in action for criminal contempt), *cert. denied,* 484 U.S. 830 (1989); United States v. Rey, 811 F.2d 1453, 1457 n. 5 (11th Cir.1987) (records, including transcript of prior trial, of former Fifth Circuit Court of Appeals), *cert. denied,* 484 U.S. 830 (1987); *cf.* Lettsome v. Waggoner, 672 F.Supp. 858, 864 (D. Virgin Islands 1987) (not error to take judicial notice of criminal conviction and facts contained therein although criminal defendant had been pardoned and the criminal records "expunged").

Despite potential problems encountered through use of judicial notice in certain criminal proceedings, nothing indicates that any modification to Rule 201 is necessary or would be useful in light of the constitutional concerns involved. State modifications have generally expanded this Rule into judicial notice of law.[30]

30. *See* 1 *Evidence in America* §§ 7.2–7.4.

ARTICLE III. PRESUMPTIONS IN CIVIL ACTIONS AND PROCEEDINGS

Introduction

Article III covers what at common law were known as rebuttal presumptions, presumptions which invite and often require rebuttal evidence and which are not conclusive in the face of the rebuttal evidence. The Article is limited to civil cases. Not covered by the Article are jury instructions on permissible inferences, judicial comment on the weight of evidence or the credibility of witnesses, and so-called "conclusive presumptions" of the type considered by the Supreme Court in a number of cases—e.g., *Vlandix v. Kline,* 412 U.S. 441 (1973); *Weinberger v. Salfi,* 422 U.S. 749 (1975); *Elkins v. Moreno,* 435 U.S. 647 (1978).

The Article contains two rules. Rule 301 provides the basic framework for treatment of rebuttable presumptions where federal law defines the rights, duties and defenses of the parties. Rule 302, like Rules 501 and 601, defers to state law where that law defines the rights, duties and defenses of the parties.

Although the Supreme Court approved a proposed Rule 303 in November 1972 and sent it to Congress, Congress declined to adopt a rule for criminal cases. For the reader's convenience, proposed (but unenacted) Rule 303 is included in the Discussion that accompanies Rule 301.

RULE 301

I. TEXT OF RULE

RULE 301. Presumptions in General in Civil Actions and Proceedings

In all civil actions and proceedings not otherwise provided for by Act of Congress, or by these rules, a presumption imposes on the party against whom it is directed the burden of going forward with evidence to rebut or meet the presumption, but does not shift the burden of proof in the sense of the risk of nonpersuasion, which remains throughout the trial upon the party on whom it was originally cast.

II. DISCUSSION

Prior to the adoption of the Federal Rules of Evidence, there were a number of approaches to rebuttable presumptions evident in reported decisions, especially in state court decisions. Two approaches among the many that could be found were most significant and both were associated with great names in the history of the law of evidence. The most familiar was the Thayer or "bursting bubble" rule, identified with James Bradley Thayer. The other, often referred to as the shifting-the-burden-of-persuasion rule, was associated with Professors Morgan and McCormick.

Both rules had much in common. They both gave the benefit of a presumed fact to a party who triggered the operation of a presumption by proving a basic fact. For example, a party who proved that a letter was mailed got the benefit of a presumption that the letter was received. That is, this party would get the benefit as long as an opponent did not offer evidence to contradict the presumed fact (that the latter was in fact received). In this fashion, both rules imposed the same burden on the party opposing the presumed fact to come forward with some evidence. Absent rebuttal evidence, the presumption governed.

The principal difference between the rules was in the treatment of a presumption following the introduction of rebuttal evidence. Under the Thayer view, the presumption disappeared, having served its purpose by requiring the opponent to produce evidence. With the presumption gone, the case proceeded on the basis of the evidence actually produced.

Under the Morgan–McCormick approach, the presumption shifted the burden to the party opposing it to disprove the presumed fact. So, if one party—the plaintiff, for example—proved that a letter was mailed, another party—the defendant, for example—would have to offer evidence that it was not received and also bear the burden of persuading the jury that it was not received. Under the Thayer view, if the plaintiff generally bore the burden of persuasion on the issue, he would continue to bear it once the defendant produced rebuttal evidence.

When the Supreme Court approved the Rules in 1972, it opted for the Morgan–McCormick view. Congress went through different drafts until it settled in Rule 301 on what is essentially the Thayer view. Rule 301 explicitly states that the burden of persuasion does not shift because of the operation of a presumption, unless a specific statute or another rule provides for a shift in the persuasion burden.

It is not surprising that some lawyers preferred the language that appeared in the Supreme Court's draft, while others applauded Congress' more traditional approach. It is not the purpose of this study to re-open the debate on the draft but, rather, to see how the language Congress has chosen has worked in practice.

Because rule tracks the traditional Thayer approach rather closely, it is not surprising that there have been few problems in the judicial handling of presumption problems in civil cases. Rule 301 is not a rule that has given the judiciary much trouble.

There are questions, however, that are unanswered by the rule. For example, how much rebuttal evidence is required to make the presumption disappear? Should the trial judge tell the jury about a permissible inference after rebuttal evidence is offered? And, if the presumption disappears, when might a directed verdict or summary judgment for one party be proper in light of the evidence actually presented by both sides?

Judges appear to be answering such questions by relying on authorities that were developed in connection with the Thayer rule at common law. Sufficient rebuttal evidence to warrant a jury in accepting a fact as true will generally be required.[1] Judges in federal court, who have the power to comment on evidence, will use their discretion in deciding whether to speak about a permissible inference, and if so, determining what to say.[2] And judges will rule on directed verdict and summary judgment requests by examining whether a reasonable jury could reach only one result just as they would were no presumption involved in a case.[3]

The greatest difficulty presented by the Rule has little to do with its specific language. Judges have experience with it and seem to use it well. The difficulty arises in deciding when another statute or rule requires that the burden of persuasion be shifted. For example, it took

1. *See, e.g.,* Patti v. Schweiker, 669 F.2d 582 (9th Cir.1982) (insufficient rebuttal evidence to make the presumptions disappear).

2. *See generally* 1 Saltzburg & Martin, Federal Rules of Evidence Manual 100 (5th ed. 1990). Some states have provided jury instructions in their presumption rules. *See, e.g.,* Nev.Rev.Stat. §§ 47.200, 47.210, and 47.220.

3. *See, e.g.,* Legille v. Dann, 544 F.2d 1 (D.C.Cir.1976).

the Supreme Court several decisions before it finally clarified in *Texas Dep't of Community Affairs v. Burdine*[4] what burden an employer is required to bear in employment discrimination cases after the plaintiff presents sufficient evidence to give rise to an inference of unlawful discrimination in disparate treatment cases. In *Burdine* the burden of persuasion remained on the plaintiff once the employer offered a nondiscriminatory reason for an action.

On the other hand, in *Smiddy v. Varney,*[5] the Ninth Circuit said that, where the plaintiff in a civil rights case offers to rebut the presumption that a prosecutor used independent judgment in filing a complaint following an arrest by police officers, the burden is on defendant police officers to prove that, if the arrest was unlawful, an independent, intervening cause insulates the prosecutor from tort liability. And the burden of persuasion on the question of patent invalidity was held to be on the party opposing the presumption of validity in *Solder Removable Co. v. United States Int'l Trade Comm'n.*[6]

In *James v. River Parishes Co., Inc.,*[7] the court held that traditional admiralty law placing the burden of persuasion on the question of negligence on a party whose boat caused damage while adrift remained in effect. A majority of the court reasoned that Rule 301 was not intended to change the result in admiralty cases where judge-made law had a force similar to statutes in other areas. One judge dissented and would have relied on Rule 301 to hold that only a burden of producing evidence should be placed on the party whose boat was adrift.

These cases indicate that it may be difficult to ascertain legislative intent or, in the admiralty case, to decide exactly when Rule 301 should defer to other law. But the difficulties in these cases are not likely to go away. Any rule that defers to statutes or other law requires that the other law be interpreted. These problems may be inevitable in any approach, except adoption of a single rule for all rebuttable presumptions in all cases. Such an approach may be unattractive because it does not allow different situations to be handled differently.

Rule 301 offers a clearer approach for courts than is presently available in criminal cases. The rule approved by the Supreme Court

4. 450 U.S. 248 (1981). *See also* Patterson v. McLean Credit Union, 109 S.Ct. 2363 (1989).

5. 665 F.2d 261 (9th Cir.1981), *cert. denied,* 459 U.S. 829 (1982).

6. 582 F.2d 628 (Ct.Cust. & Pat.App.1978). *See also* City of Boston v. S.S. Texaco Texas, 773 F.2d 1396 (1st Cir.1985).

7. 686 F.2d 1129 (5th Cir.1982). A divided Tenth Circuit reached an analogous result under the National Labor Relations Act in Beth Israel Hosp. & Ger. Ctr. v. NLRB, 688 F.2d 697 (10th Cir.1982) (holding, over the dissent of two judges, that Rule 301 does not apply to "informal and nonadversarial" representation proceedings notwithstanding a statutory provision stating that the Rules shall apply in all unfair labor practice proceedings so far as practicable).

to govern criminal cases, was not enacted by the Congress.[8] Presumptions in criminal cases pose special problems because they may be inconsistent with the government's responsibility to prove certain elements of an offense beyond a reasonable doubt.[9]

8. *See* Appendix B, Rule 303. Presumptions in Criminal Cases. Several states, however, have adopted provisions akin to proposed Fed.R.Evid. 303. *See* 1 *Evidence in America* §§ 10.2–10.4.

9. For a discussion of such problems, *see* Francis v. Franklin, 471 U.S. 307 (1985); Ulster County Court v. Allen, 442 U.S. 140 (1979); Sandstrom v. Montana, 442 U.S. 510 (1979). For a discussion of the states' experience under this Rule, *see* 1 *Evidence in America* §§ 8.2–8.4.

RULE 302

I. TEXT OF RULE

RULE 302. Applicability of State Law in Civil Actions and Proceedings

In civil actions and proceedings, the effect of a presumption respecting a fact which is an element of a claim or defense as to which State law supplies the rule of decision is determined in accordance with State law.

II. DISCUSSION

This Rule poses a theoretical problem that has not proved to be much of an actual problem. The Rule directs federal courts to use state presumptions when state law supplies the rule of decision in a case and the presumption relates to a fact that is an element of a claim or defense. Although this should cause little problem in a typical diversity case where state law controls virtually all substantive issues, in a pendent (now, supplemental) jurisdiction case or any case in which state and federal issues are joined, one presumption may be relevant to both state and federal issues and its treatment could be different under state law from the treatment provided in Rule 301. Should this happen, a court would have to decide whether to tell a jury to treat a fact differently on the federal and state claims or whether one approach, either state or federal, should predominate.

Thus far, there are no reported cases in which the theoretical problem has given federal courts much trouble. A similar theoretical problem arises under Rules 501 and 601, and under those rules the problems also have been few.

There is some disagreement among commentators as to whether Rule 302's deference to state presumption law should be liberally or conservatively construed. There is no reason to believe that the scholarly disagreement reflects problems that federal courts are actually experiencing. No problems appear in reported cases.

As the court observed in *Melville v. American Home Assurance Co.,*[1] Rule 302 provides little guidance as to which state's law should apply. Presumably, it will be the state law that governs the claim or defense to which the presumption relates.

A number of states have opted to follow the Supreme Court's proposed approach and to shift the burden of persuasion in connection with civil presumptions. Thirteen states do this.[2] Some states follow the approach used by California Evid.Code § 600, *et seq.,* and divided presumptions into two categories, some of which follow the Thayer

1. 443 F.Supp. 1064 (E.D.Pa.1977), *rev'd on other grounds,* 584 F.2d 1306 (3d Cir.1978).

2. *See* 1 *Evidence in America* §§ 8.2–8.4.

approach, and others of which follow the Morgan–McCormick approach.[3] Because the states have not chosen to be consistent, the theoretical problem identified above may at some point become a real one. This is not yet the case.

3. *Id.*

APPENDIX I

ARTICLE IV. RELEVANCY AND ITS LIMITS

Introduction

Article IV treats the subject of relevancy and the limitations imposed on the admissibility of plainly relevant evidence by various policy considerations inherited from the common law, embodied in statute or articulated definitively in the Rules themselves.

Rule 401 sets forth a broad definition of "relevant evidence" which subsumes the common law concept of materiality. Rule 402 states the general rule that relevant evidence is admissible and irrelevant evidence inadmissible. Rule 403 articulates the fundamental balancing test under which relevant evidence may properly be excluded if its probative value is substantially outweighed by any of several considerations, including prejudice, confusion or delay.

Rules 404 and 405 deal, respectively, with the admissibility of character evidence for substantive purposes and the proper methods of proving it. They should be read in conjunction with Rule 608 which prescribes the parameters of using character evidence for attacking or rehabilitating credibility. Rule 406 covers the related question of the admissibility of evidence of habit or routine practice.

Rules 407 through 412 deal with a series of thorny common law issues. Rule 407 addresses the admissibility of evidence of subsequent remedial measures. Rule 408 concerns proof of compromise and offers to compromise. Rule 409 precludes evidence that a party paid, or offered to pay, any other party's medical expenses. Rule 410 deals with the general inadmissibility of guilty or nolo contendere pleas and related statements. Rule 411 covers evidence of liability insurance. Finally, Rule 412, enacted by Congress in 1978, addresses the admissibility in sexual assault cases of evidence of the past sexual behavior of the victim.

RULE 401

I. TEXT OF RULE

RULE 401. Definition of "Relevant Evidence"

"Relevant evidence" means evidence having any tendency to make the existence of any fact that is of consequence to the determination of the action more probable or less probable than it would be without the evidence.

II. DISCUSSION

Rule 401 defines the kind of evidence that Rule 402 makes admissible, subject to specific exceptions provided in Article IV and other federal and state laws. Although this definition has generally been well understood and implemented by the courts, minor problems in the application of Rule 401 have occurred in the areas of undisputed evidence and scientific evidence.

Rule 401 does not require that the proffered evidence be relevant to a fact which is in dispute. This departure from the practice prior to adoption of the Federal Rules is intended to give the trial court greater freedom to admit background evidence and evidence of surrounding circumstances which may aid the trier of fact in understanding the context of events.[1] On occasion, however, courts have continued to approve the exclusion of evidence on the ground that the issue to which it is relevant is not disputed.[2] The better practice is to hold that such evidence is relevant and is therefore admissible unless a particular exclusionary rule (such as Rule 403 which authorizes the exclusion of cumulative evidence) is applicable.[3]

There is also some confusion in the courts with respect to the method for determining the relevance of scientific evidence. Prior to adoption of the Rules, the admissibility of scientific evidence depended primarily on satisfaction of the *Frye* test.[4] Under that test, the court determines whether the scientific principle has gained general acceptance in the particular field of study before the evidence may be

1. *See* Fed.R.Evid. 401, Advisory Committee Note.

2. United States v. Wasman, 700 F.2d 663, 665 (11th Cir.1983) (in prosecution for making false statement in passport application, defendant had no right to introduce evidence that statement in drivers license application was true when government did not challenge that application), *aff'd,* 468 U.S. 559 (1984).

3. *See* Government of Virgin Islands v. Grant, 775 F.2d 508, 513 (3d Cir.1985) (jurisprudence of background evidence is essentially undeveloped, is not mentioned in the evidence rules, and has received no attention in treatises; but there is a wide practice of admitting background evidence, although admission is discretionary); *see also* Conway v. Chemical Leaman Tank Lines, Inc., 525 F.2d 927, 930 (5th Cir.1976) (evidence of surviving spouse's remarriage was admissible as background evidence in wrongful death action).

4. The test is derived from the court's opinion in Frye v. United States, 293 F. 1013 (D.C.Cir.1923).

admitted. Since the Rules were adopted, some courts have continued to follow *Frye*,[5] while other courts have rejected *Frye* or adopted a modified version of the *Frye* test.[6] In any event, the relevance of scientific evidence should also be analyzed under the definition in Rule 401.[7]

As explained by the Advisory Committee, the definition of relevance in Rule 401 is intended to embrace relationships between proffered evidence and the proposition to be proved that find support in experience or science and logic. The goal of the Federal Rules of Evidence, to promote the admission of evidence unless there is a specific reason for exclusion, has been well-served by the breadth of this definition.[8] The problems arising under this Rule result more from lack of attention to the language of the Rule than from any weakness in the Rule itself.[9]

5. United States v. Shorter, 809 F.2d 54, 59–60 (D.C.Cir.), *cert. denied*, 484 U.S. 817 (1987); United States v. Metzger, 778 F.2d 1195, 1203 (6th Cir.1985), *cert. denied*, 477 U.S. 906 (1986); Barrel of Fun, Inc. v. State Farm Fire and Casualty Co., 739 F.2d 1028, 1031 n. 9 (5th Cir.1984).

6. United States v. Ferri, 778 F.2d 985, 988 (3d Cir.1985) (rejecting *Frye* and adopting two part test: (1) determine reliability and (2) balance reliability against potential for misleading the jury), *cert. denied*, 476 U.S. 1172 (1986); United States v. Gould, 741 F.2d 45, 48–49 & n. 2 (4th Cir.1984) (modifying *Frye* test and holding expert testimony on compulsive gambling disorder is relevant if scientific hypothesis has substantial acceptance in relevant discipline).

7. Scientific evidence must also satisfy the requirements of Fed.R.Evid. 702. *See generally* the Discussion of Rule 702, *infra*, on this issue. Justices White and Brennan would have granted certiorari in Mustafa v. United States, 479 U.S. 953 (1986), to resolve the question of whether *Frye* retains validity following adoption of the Federal Rules of Evidence.

8. *E.g.*, Bettius v. Sanderson, P.C. v. National Union Fire Ins. Co., 839 F.2d 1009, 1014 (4th Cir.1988) (proof of compensation paid to principals was relevant to net profit of professional corporation although it would not be relevant to net profit of commercial corporation). *See* Riordan v. Kempiners, 831 F.2d 690, 697–98 (7th Cir.1987) (plaintiff's ability to prove case must not be crippled by evidentiary rulings that keep out probative evidence because of crabbed notions of relevance); Young v. Illinois Cent. Gulf R.R., 618 F.2d 332, 337 (5th Cir.1980) (trial court's exclusion of evidence on grounds of irrelevance gutted plaintiff's case).

9. For the states' experience under this Rule, *see* 1 *Evidence in America* §§ 11.2–11.4.

RULE 402

I. TEXT OF RULE

RULE 402. Relevant Evidence Admissible; Irrelevant Evidence Inadmissible

All relevant evidence is admissible, except as otherwise provided by the Constitution of the United States, by Act of Congress, by these rules, or by other rules prescribed by the Supreme Court pursuant to statutory authority. Evidence which is not relevant is not admissible.

II. DISCUSSION

Under Rule 402, relevance, as defined in Rule 401, is the threshold criterion of admissibility and the foundation of our system of evidence. Rule 402 enumerates the sources of exceptions to the general principle that relevant evidence is admissible and expressly provides that irrelevant evidence is inadmissible.

The determination of relevance is essentially an exercise in legal reasoning and analysis, accomplished by applying the definition in Rule 401 to the proffered evidence and the substantive issues in the case.[1] Rules 401 and 402 combine to diminish the discretion previously afforded the trial court in the admission or exclusion of evidence. Nevertheless, the majority of the federal Circuit Courts of Appeal have held that relevance rulings are discretionary.[2] Appellate courts tend to scrutinize the trial court's reasoning more carefully, and are more apt to reverse a finding of irrelevance which is not satisfactorily explained by the trial court, when evidence is excluded.[3]

It has been suggested that there is a continuing problem with unfairness in relevance rulings.[4] As Professor Wright noted, the potential for unfairness is inherent in the American system of justice.[5] It is

1. *See* Fed.R.Evid. 401, Advisory Committee Note.

2. *See, e.g.,* Marshall v. El Paso Natural Gas Co., 874 F.2d 1373, 1380 (10th Cir.1989); Benford v. Richards Medical Co., 792 F.2d 1537, 1540 (11th Cir.1986); Smith v. Firestone Tire & Rubber Co., 755 F.2d 129, 134 (8th Cir.1985); McLaurin v. Fischer, 768 F.2d 98, 104 (6th Cir.1985); Charles v. Daley, 749 F.2d 452, 463 (7th Cir.1984), *appeal dismissed,* 476 U.S. 54 (1986).

3. "Discretion does not sanction the exclusion of competent evidence without a sound, practical reason." Borden, Inc. v. Florida East Coast Ry., 772 F.2d 750, 754 (11th Cir. 1985) (reversing exclusion of prior accident evidence); Anderson v. Malloy, 700 F.2d 1208, 1212 (8th Cir.1983) (reversing exclusion of evidence of similar security measures at other hotels); Ramos v. Liberty Mut. Ins. Co., 615 F.2d 334, 340 (5th Cir.1980) (reversing exclusion of evidence of similar accident and design changes in products liability case), *cert. denied,* 449 U.S. 1112 (1981).

4. 22 C. Wright & K. Graham, *Federal Practice and Procedure* § 5180 (1978 and Supp. 1989) (citing cases in which relevance rulings appear to be skewed in favor of one party).

5. *Id.* § 5180 at 165. *See also* 1 *Evidence in America* §§ 12.2–12.4.

doubtful that any reform of the Rules relating to relevance will alleviate this problem. Indeed, the liberal definition of relevance in Rule 401 should assist courts in realizing greater evenhandedness in the admission of evidence. Less emphasis on discretion in relevance rulings and greater focus by counsel and courts on the analysis required by the Rules will do more to abate inequity than any change in the Rules.

RULE 403

I. TEXT OF RULE

RULE 403. Exclusion of Relevant Evidence on Grounds of Prejudice, Confusion, or Waste of Time

Although relevant, evidence may be excluded if its probative value is substantially outweighed by the danger of unfair prejudice, confusion of the issues, or misleading the jury, or by considerations of undue delay, waste of time, or needless presentation of cumulative evidence.

II. DISCUSSION

Rule 403 authorizes the trial court to exclude relevant evidence that it finds, in essence, will do more harm than good to the truth-finding process or the efficiency of the judicial process. Two issues that have arisen under this Rule concern the trial court's assessment of the probative value of evidence for purposes of conducting the balancing test required by Rule 403, and the use of techniques for minimizing the "danger[s]" and "considerations" enumerated in the Rule.

No specific guidelines are given in Rule 403 to aid the court in assessing the probative value of evidence. The Advisory Committee's Note indicates only that the court may also take into account the need for the proffered evidence. The court's judgment of probative value is particularly critical because this value becomes part of the balancing equation under Rule 403. The court must therefore be careful to avoid assessing the credibility of that evidence. Probative value must be judged from the standpoint of the value of the evidence if it is believed, and not by the degree to which the court finds it to be believable.[1]

Rule 403 outlines three "danger[s]" and three "considerations" against which the court must balance the probative value of the evidence. Courts have employed a variety of techniques to minimize the negative side of the balancing equation in order to promote the admissibility of evidence. Unfair prejudice and the potential for confusion and misleading the jury can be diminished through use of curative or limiting instructions.[2] This method of controlling the adverse effect

1. *See, e.g.,* Ballou v. Henri Studios, Inc., 656 F.2d 1147, 1154 (5th Cir.1981) (trial court erroneously excluded results of blood alcohol test because test results "lacked credibility" and court believed witness' testimony that decedent was not intoxicated); United States v. Thompson, 615 F.2d 329, 333 (5th Cir.1980) (Rule 403 did not authorize expungement of witness' testimony because trial court found it unworthy of belief); Bowden v. McKenna, 600 F.2d 282, 284–85 (1st Cir.) (trial court improperly excluded evidence that decedent committed robbery because court believed alibi), *cert. denied,* 444 U.S. 899 (1979).

2. *See, e.g.,* United States v. Markowski, 772 F.2d 358, 366 (7th Cir.1985) (trial court carefully considered proffered testimony outside hearing of jury and instructed witness to relate only what he was told and not how he felt to avoid inflaming the jury to prejudice), *cert. denied,* 475 U.S. 1018 (1986); Forro Precision, Inc. v. International Business Mach. Corp., 673 F.2d 1045, 1057 (9th Cir.1982) (limiting instruction that evidence be used only

of evidence is expressly approved by the Advisory Committee. Considerations of undue delay, waste of time and repetitious evidence may be lessened through use of the court's inherent power to control the mode and presentation of evidence.[3] These efforts to use the inherent powers of the court to enhance the admissibility of evidence are commendable. Courts should be encouraged to utilize innovative techniques of minimizing prejudice when appropriate.

State modifications of this Rule have been modest and their experience relatively unproblematic.[4]

to show state of mind), *cert. denied,* 471 U.S. 1130 (1985); United States v. Guerrero, 667 F.2d 862, 867 (10th Cir.1981) (trial court viewed, in camera, videotape of defendant committing crime, and admitted only visual portion to minimize prejudice to defendant), *cert. denied,* 456 U.S. 964 (1982).

3. Walker v. Action Indus., Inc., 802 F.2d 703, 712 (4th Cir.1986) (court properly required plaintiff to present oral summaries of lengthy depositions rather than reading depositions verbatim to jury), *cert. denied,* 479 U.S. 1065 (1987); Hill v. Bache Halsey Stuart Shields Inc., 790 F.2d 817, 826 (10th Cir.1986) (to avoid confusion and delay, the court retained power to require a less elaborate presentation of evidence, through either written summaries of securities transactions or through expert testimony recapitulating transactions); McLaurin v. Fischer, 768 F.2d 98, 104 (6th Cir.1985) (exclusion of witnesses was not error when plaintiff called 10 witnesses and court did not impose absolute prohibition on further witnesses, but required plaintiff to demonstrate cause). *See generally* the Discussion of Rule 611.

4. 1 *Evidence in America* §§ 13.2–13.4.

RULE 404

I. TEXT OF RULE

RULE 404. Character Evidence Not Admissible to Prove Conduct; Exceptions; Other Claims

(a) Character evidence generally. Evidence of a person's character or a trait of his character is not admissible for the purpose of proving action in conformity therewith on a particular occasion, except:

(1) Character of accused. Evidence of a pertinent trait of character offered by an accused, or by the prosecution to rebut the same;

(2) Character of victim. Evidence of a pertinent trait of character of the victim of the crime offered by an accused, or by the prosecution to rebut the same, or evidence of a character trait of peacefulness of the victim offered by the prosecution in a homicide case to rebut evidence that the victim was the first aggressor;

(3) Character of witness. Evidence of the character of a witness, as provided in Rules 607, 608, and 609.

(b) Other crimes, wrongs, or acts. Evidence of other crimes, wrongs, or acts is not admissible to prove the character of a person in order to show action in conformity therewith. It may, however, be admissible for other purposes, such as proof of motive, opportunity, intent, preparation, plan, knowledge, identity, or absence of mistake or accident.

II. DISCUSSION

Rule 404, like the common law, recognizes some basic rules concerning the admissibility of character evidence and establishes that evidence of specific acts offered for a purpose other than to prove a character trait is not affected by these rules. Subsection (b) of the rule has caused the most controversy amongst the courts because of various problems in admitting "other acts" evidence. For example, courts have struggled with the standard of proof the government must bear before there can be a determination that the other act occurred. Additionally, there has been conflict over whether the court or the jury will make that determination. Finally, the "other acts" evidence must be balanced under Rule 403 to determine whether it is too prejudicial.[1]

Prior to the Supreme Court decision in *Huddleston v. United States,*[2] some courts followed the practice of requiring clear and con-

1. *See* United States v. Fortenberry, 860 F.2d 628 (5th Cir.1988).

2. 108 S.Ct. 1496 (1988).

vincing evidence of the other act or crime.[3] The Fifth Circuit led others to treat the question as one of conditional relevance under Rule 104(b).[4] Other courts required only a preponderance of the evidence of the other act.[5] In *Huddleston,* the Supreme Court affirmatively ruled that the court decides "whether the jury could reasonably find the conditional fact . . . by a preponderance of the evidence."[6]

In recognition of the potentially prejudicial effect of this holding, the Court further explained that the defendant was still protected because of three requirements.[7] First, the evidence may be admitted for one of the nine proper purposes.[8] Second, the evidence must be relevant under Rule 401 and 402. Third, there must still be a balancing under Rule 403 to exclude evidence the prejudicial dangers of which substantially outweigh its probative value.

This decision settles the controversy between the circuits and should lead to a greater certainty with respect to the standard of proof. However, the wording and interpretation of Rule 404(b) is still criticized.[9] While the standard of proof may not be changed, suggestions have been made to include a notice provision to Rule 404(b).[10] It is thought that such a provision would prevent the defendant from being surprised. Florida has provided a ten-day notice requirement[11] and Texas simply provides that "reasonable" notice must be given in criminal cases.[12] Other states require notice as a matter of decisional

3. *See, e.g.,* United States v. O'Brien, 618 F.2d 1234 (7th Cir.1980); United States v. Frederickson, 601 F.2d 1358 (8th Cir.1979).

4. United States v. Beechum, 582 F.2d 898 (5th Cir.1978), *cert. denied,* 440 U.S. 920 (1979).

5. *E.g.,* United States v. Schleicher, 862 F.2d 1320 (8th Cir.1988), *cert. denied,* 109 S.Ct. 1326 (1989).

6. 108 U.S. at 1501.

7. *Id.* at 1502.

8. Fed.R.Evid. 404(b) provides that evidence may be offered to prove motive, opportunity, intent, preparation, plan, knowledge, identity, absence of mistake or accident.

9. The ABA proposed changes in Rule 404(b) to require clear and convincing evidence of the other act and a determination to be made by the court, not the jury. This recommendation has not been adopted by the Advisory Committee. American Bar Association Resolution, Adopted by the House of Delegates February 6–7, 1989, Report No. 109B.

10. The Advisory Committee to the Federal Rules of Evidence recently submitted a proposed amendment providing: "that upon request by the accused, the prosecution in a criminal case shall provide reasonable notice in advance of trial, or during trial if the court excuses pretrial notice on good cause shown, of the general nature of any such evidence it intends to introduce at trial." For an excellent discussion of the proposed notice provision, *see* Saltzburg, *Other Act Evidence: A Change in Discovery Practice,* 5 Criminal Justice 34 (1991).

11. Fla.Stat.Ann. § 90.404.

12. Tex.R.Crim.Evid. 404.

law construing their versions of Rule 404(b).[13] The Advisory Committee did not specify a proposed time limit, recognizing that this would rest on the circumstances of the particular case.

Another issue that has arisen under Rule 404(b) is whether the government can offer evidence on an issue before it is clear that the issue actually is disputed. For example, there is no doubt that where intent is in dispute, other crime or act evidence may be admissible to prove that intent.[14] Where intent is plainly disputed, the government can offer evidence in its case in chief.[15] There are a number of cases suggesting, however, that if it is doubtful that the defendant will contest intent, it is preferable for the other crime or act evidence to be reserved for rebuttal and offered if intent becomes an issue.[16] If the defendant attempts to conceal whether intent is disputed, courts may not be sympathetic and may allow the government to offer proof early in its case.[17] As a general rule, though, evidence of matters not disputed, especially prejudicial evidence, ought not to be readily accepted.

The greatest problem with Rule 404(b) is the tendency some courts have to permit prosecutors to rely on a "laundry list" of reasons for offering other act evidence.[18] In every case trial judges must balance the possible misuse of other act evidence as propensity evidence against its probative value. It is common for appellate courts to recommend that trial judges carefully set forth reasons justifying their decision to admit evidence.[19] It can be helpful if trial judges compel the party offering other act evidence to articulate with precision the use it seeks to make of the evidence and the inferences it seeks to have the trier of fact draw. In some cases, the trial judge may decide to exclude the other act evidence during the government's case in chief and to determine whether it should be admitted only after it is clear what issues, if any, are disputed in the defendant's case.

Although character evidence is generally inadmissible in civil cases under subdivision (a),[20] and although the Advisory Committee's Note suggests that the distinction between civil and criminal cases is adver-

13. *See* 1 *Evidence in America* § 14.3 at 7 & n. 37.

14. *See, e.g.,* United States v. Johnson, 634 F.2d 735, 737–738 (4th Cir.1980), *cert. denied,* 451 U.S. 907 (1981); United States v. Grimes, 620 F.2d 587, 587–588 (6th Cir. 1980).

15. *See, e.g.,* United States v. Alessi, 638 F.2d 466 (2d Cir.1980); United States v. Deloach, 654 F.2d 763, 769 (D.C.Cir.1980).

16. *See, e.g.,* United States v. Figueroa, 618 F.2d 934 (2d Cir.1980).

17. United States v. Webb, 625 F.2d 709, 710–711 (5th Cir.1980).

18. *See, e.g.,* United States v. Harvey, 845 F.2d 760 (8th Cir.1988).

19. *See, e.g.,* United States v. Robinson, 700 F.2d 205 (5th Cir.1983), *cert. denied,* 469 U.S. 1008 (1984).

20. Advisory Committee Note to Rule 404.

tent,[21] subdivision (b) does not distinguish between civil and criminal cases. Nor did the common law.

Use of other crime or act evidence is particularly important when discrimination is claimed. Intent is an issue and, where the defendant is an individual, Rule 404(b) is frequently invoked to admit other crime or extensive act evidence.[22] Where the defendant is a governmental entity or a corporation, the evidence may be admitted under Rules 404, 405 and 406.[23]

There is every reason to believe that the *Huddleston* analysis applies equally to civil cases. Just as co-conspirator statements are equally admissible in civil and criminal pricefixing trials, other act evidence is as welcome in civil as in criminal cases. In some civil cases, other act evidence may tend to be less prejudicial than in a criminal context, e.g., when an entity's acts are offered. The prejudice may be less because the entity may be comprised of several individuals and a trier of fact may understand that a bad act by one entity employee does not necessarily suggest that the entire entity is bad. But, in other civil cases, evidence of uncharged acts can be as prejudicial as in a criminal context. In civil as in criminal cases, trial judges perform their best when they articulate reasons for their rulings. And their rulings are most informed when the party offering other act evidence justifies the offer with a clear statement of purpose.

21. *See, e.g.,* Nakasian v. Incontrade, Inc., 78 F.R.D. 229 (S.D.N.Y.1978); Blake v. Cich, 79 F.R.D. 398 (D.Minn.1979); Hackbart v. Cincinnati Bengals, Inc., 601 F.2d 516 (10th Cir. 1979).

22. Miller v. Poretsky, 595 F.2d 780, 785, 790 (D.C.Cir.1978).

23. Comw. of Pennsylvania v. Parter, 659 F.2d 306, 320 (3d Cir.1981).

RULE 405

I. TEXT OF RULE

RULE 405. Methods of Proving Character

(a) Reputation or opinion. In all cases in which evidence of character or a trait of character of a person is admissible, proof may be made by testimony as to reputation or by testimony in the form of an opinion. On cross-examination, inquiry is allowable into relevant specific instances of conduct.

(b) Specific instances of conduct. In cases in which character or a trait of character of a person is an essential element of a charge, claim, or defense, proof may also be made of specific instances of that person's conduct.

II. DISCUSSION

This Rule has presented no significant problems in application. The signal innovation embodied in Rule 405 is the provision for proof "by testimony in the form of an opinion." Although persuaded in significant part by the value of testimony by witnesses personally familiar with the defendant, the drafters expressly welcomed the evidence of "the opinion of the psychiatrist based on examination and testing," and implicitly of analogous experts using equivalent means.[1] Some decisions, however, do evince a reluctance to make such use of psychiatric evidence or even to treat proffers of expert character evidence under the Rule.[2] Such evidence tends to ignore inquiries into the facts of the case.

The question when character is in issue, and whether to admit expert testimony on the subject, may be difficult in certain cases. However, it is not clear that any amendment to the Rule would resolve the question. The facts and circumstances of each case tend to be dispositive, and meticulousness in analyzing the facts is essential.

The law has clearly and correctly developed that specific act evidence does not qualify for admission to prove an "essential element of a charge, claim or defense" simply because it makes the existence of a charge, claim or defense more or less probable. Otherwise, all specific act evidence would be admissible because relevant evidence by

1. Advisory Committee Note to Rule 405. *See, e.g.,* United States v. Hill, 655 F.2d 512 (3rd Cir.1981) (reversing trial court exclusion of expert character testimony by clinical psychologist).

2. *See, e.g.,* United States v. West, 670 F.2d 675, 682 (7th Cir.1982), in which the court upheld exclusion of a psychiatrist's testimony that the defendant's limited intelligence made it unlikely that he understood that he was accepting a bribe. *See also* United States v. Webb, 625 F.2d 709, 711 (5th Cir.1980) (upholding exclusion of psychiatrist's testimony, offered to show, in support of alibi, defendant's peaceableness and likelihood of being elsewhere, because the trait is "within 'the ken of lay jurors'" and "a proper subject for lay testimony," under Rules 404(a)(1), 405(a), and 702).

definition (Rule 401) tends to make something which is disputed more or less likely. Specific act evidence is admissible when the charge, claim or defense has a character or propensity aspect that cannot be avoided. For example, if entrapment requires a defendant to prove the absence of predisposition, the government must be permitted to offer specific acts to demonstrate predisposition.[3]

Alaska adopted Rule 405 but elaborated on the reputation evidence by permitting reputation of a person in the community with which the person is habitually associated. This would allow testimony of reputation where the person works, goes to school, or lives.[4] This appears to reflect a growing trend in state court decisions.[5]

3. The entrapment cases are set out in 1 Saltzburg & Martin, *Federal Rules of Evidence Manual* 312–14 (5th ed. 1990).

4. Alaska R.Evid. 405.

5. 1 *Evidence in America* §§ 15.2–15.3. *Compare* United States v. Mandel, 591 F.2d 1347, *vacated,* 602 F.2d 653 (4th Cir.1979) (en banc), *cert. denied,* 445 U.S. 959 (1980) (argument raised that reputation could be from work community but court did not address this point).

RULE 406

I. TEXT OF RULE

RULE 406. Habit; Routine Practice

Evidence of the habit of a person or the routine practice of an organization, whether corroborated or not and regardless of the presence of eyewitnesses, is relevant to prove that the conduct of the person or organization on a particular occasion was in conformity with the habit or routine practice.

II. DISCUSSION

Rule 406 permits introduction of habit evidence used to show that conduct on a particular occasion was in conformity therewith. Because Rule 404 generally forbids the use of character evidence for this purpose, the courts must distinguish between habit and character. As at common law, drawing this distinction under the Rules can be difficult.

One element distinguishing habit from character evidence is the more routine repetitive nature of a "habit." For example, in *Reyes v. Missouri Pacific R.R.,*[1] the plaintiff's intoxication convictions were held inadmissible as character evidence for the purpose of showing intoxication on the occasion of the accident. As evidence of habit, they would have been admissible for that purpose, but the court held they did not constitute habit evidence because the behavior did not rise to the sufficient level of consistency. Yet, in *Keltner v. Ford Motor Co.,*[2] the court allowed testimony of plaintiff's habit of drinking a six-pack of beer four nights a week in light of the fact that plaintiff smelled of alcohol after the accident.

Whether juries can properly infer individual conduct from organizational habit or routine was addressed in *United States v. Angelilli,*[3] a RICO, extortion and mail fraud prosecution of four marshals arising from fraudulent auctions of judgment debtors' property. The government introduced testimony depicting "a regular custom and practice of New York City marshals" in taking illicit "top money" in such sales, conduct which was characterized as pervasive and not limited to the defendants or the transactions charged in the indictment.[4] The Second Circuit held the evidence admissible under Rule 404(b) to show a continuous plan and, as a reflection of conduct pursuant to the conspir-

1. 589 F.2d 791 (5th Cir.1979). *See also* Wilson v. Volkswagen of America, Inc., 561 F.2d 494, 509–512 (4th Cir.1977), *cert. denied,* 434 U.S. 1020 (1978) (court noted that determination of existence of habit should be carefully scrutinized).

2. 748 F.2d 1265 (8th Cir.1984).

3. 660 F.2d 23 (2d Cir.1981), *cert. denied,* 455 U.S. 910 (1982).

4. *Id.* at 26–28, 37.

acy alleged, unaffected by the Rule because "the conduct did not present *other* acts." [5]

The trial court had, however, given an interim instruction permitting an inference from the custom and practice evidence that the defendants individually had engaged in the custom and practice. Although harmless, this was held error under Rule 404 and, because it "require[d] an inference that the individual defendants committed certain acts based on evidence that other acts were performed by other persons," could not be saved by Rule 404. Similarly, because it "require[d] an inference that the individual defendants committed certain acts based on evidence that other acts were performed by other persons," it could not be saved by Rule 406. The court noted that the evidence dealt with the practice of marshals as a class, not the habits of individuals. Although there had been testimony of the defendants' specific receipt of "top money," there had been none of their habit of doing so.

Most of the decided cases have resisted efforts to blur the distinction between habit and character.[6] Habit requires a uniformity and regularity of specific acts that is different in kind from general character evidence. As one court of appeals said, habit and pattern evidence is not lightly established and the key criteria are "adequacy of sampling and uniformity of ratio of reactions to situations." [7]

Florida's version of Rule 406 refers only to "the routine practice of an organization," deleting any reference to evidence of any "habit of a person." [8] According to the Sponsor's Note, the section is expressly inapplicable to "the habit of an individual." [9] Like most other states,[10] Wisconsin adopted the uniform version of Rule 406 but modified it to include an exception for Wisconsin's "rape shield" act.[11] Three states, Montana, Tennessee and Oregon, have defined "habit" in their codes (Montana and Tennessee also define "routine practice"), but these definitions have not affected decisionmaking under the Rule.[12]

5. *Id.* at 39.

6. This is not always the case. Some decisions—*e.g.,* Perrin v. Anderson, 784 F.2d 1040 (10th Cir.1986) (holding that five violent acts by a deceased against police officers was admitting, based on representation that other acts could also be proved)—appear to come perilously close to admitting character evidence that hardly appears to be a uniform response to a particularized stimulus.

7. Loughan v. Firestone Tire & Rubber Co., 749 F.2d 1519 (11th Cir.1985).

8. Fla.Stat.Ann. § 90.406.

9. West's Fla.Stat.Ann.Evid.Code at 38 (1979 Spec.Pamphlet).

10. 1 *Evidence in America* § 16.2.

11. Wis.Stat.Ann. § 904.06.

12. 1 *Evidence in America* §§ 16.2–16.4.

RULE 407

I. TEXT OF RULE

RULE 407. Subsequent Remedial Measures

When, after an event, measures are taken which, if taken previously, would have made the event less likely to occur, evidence of the subsequent measures is not admissible to prove negligence or culpable conduct in connection with the event. This rule does not require the exclusion of evidence of subsequent measures when offered for another purpose, such as proving ownership, control, or feasibility of precautionary measures, if controverted, or impeachment.

II. DISCUSSION

Rule 407 restates the common law "subsequent repairs" doctrine, but it has been interpreted with a twist. The principal question emerging in the cases concerns whether subsequent remedial measures are admissible in products liability actions because neither "negligence [n]or culpable conduct" are at issue. The courts are split in resolving this question.

One line of products liability cases bars admission of the subsequent repairs evidence for the traditional reason: to avoid discouraging defendants from taking remedial measures beneficial to the public at large.[1] These courts reject the argument that products cases, unlike traditional tort cases, focus solely on the characteristics of the product rather than the behavior of the defendant. Other courts reason that exclusion of remedial measures in products liability cases serves no deterrent function because mass market manufacturers cannot afford to be exposed to the financial risk that attends marketing defective products, and subsequent repairs will therefore be made irrespective of their admissibility at individual trials.[2]

Among the thirty-four states that have adopted Rule 407, six have expressly dealt with the strict liability issue.[3] The second sentence of Hawaii R.Evid. 407, for example, expressly permits use of subsequent repairs to prove a "dangerous defect in products liability cases." And Tex.R.Evid. 407 expressly states that the Rule does not "preclude

1. *See, e.g.,* Cann v. Ford Motor Co., 658 F.2d 54 (2d Cir.1981); Oberst v. International Harvester Co., 640 F.2d 863 (7th Cir.1980); Werner v. Upjohn Co., 628 F.2d 848 (4th Cir. 1980), *cert. denied,* 449 U.S. 1080 (1981).

2. *See, e.g.,* Farnar v. Paccar, Inc., 562 F.2d 518 (8th Cir.1977).

3. Alaska, Hawaii, Iowa, Nebraska, Tennessee and Texas. *See* 1 *Evidence in America* § 17.2. A state rule at variance with Rule 407 may be so closely tied to substantive law that it must be applied in a diversity action. *Compare* Moe v. Avions Marcel Dassault-Brequet Aviation, 727 F.2d 917 (10th Cir.1984), *cert. denied,* 469 U.S. 853 (1984), *with* Flaminio v. Honda Motor Co., Ltd., 733 F.2d 463 (7th Cir.1984). See also 1 *Evidence in America* § 17.5.

admissibility in products liability cases based on strict liability." Colorado and Wyoming, in addition, note in committee comments that "culpable conduct" does not encompass strict liability defects.[4]

It is easy to fashion an argument in favor of modifying the rule to state plainly how it affects products liability actions. However, that argument may be too quick. Recent cases indicate that not all products liability cases involve similar theories of liability. Whether or not the exclusionary provision of Rule 407 should be applied in a particular products liability case—or in other types of strict liability cases [5]—may depend on precisely how liability is gauged under the applicable law. Additional cases may clarify the state of the law.[6]

Several decisions have considered whether Rule 407 applies not only to the "evidence of the subsequent measures" taken by the defendant, but also to reports or other evidence relating to the investigation of the particular events that led to the changes in policy or design.[7] These cases have articulated a so-called "critical self-analysis" privilege. This privilege rests on the strong public policies "to assure fairness to persons who have been required by law to engage in self-evaluation . . . and to make the self-evaluation process more effective by creating an effective incentive structure for candid and unconstrained self-evaluation." [8] One of the purposes of the doctrine is to encourage the necessary "self-analysis and self-evaluation . . . for the purpose of protecting the public by instituting practices assuring safer operations." [9] The early cases regarding "critical self-analysis" concerned whether such documents were discoverable not whether they were admissible. Other decisions, relying upon Rule 407 and noting that the Rule is not applicable to pretrial discovery, have rejected

4. 7B Colo.Rev.Stat. (1981 Cum.Supp. at 271); Wyo.Ct.R.Ann. at 315 (1982).

5. *See, e.g.,* Hall v. American S.S. Co., 688 F.2d 1062 (6th Cir.1982) (although operation of unseaworthy vessel is a species of strict liability, it is "culpable conduct" within the meaning of the Rule because such conduct would impose liability upon the defendant); R.W. Murray Co. v. Shatterproof Glass Corp., 758 F.2d 266 (8th Cir.1985) (breach of warranty action does not involve culpable conduct).

6. *See, e.g.,* Gauthier v. AMF, Inc., 788 F.2d 634 (9th Cir.1986); Herndon v. Seven Bar Flying Service, Inc., 716 F.2d 1322 (10th Cir.1983), *cert. denied,* 466 U.S. 958 (1984); DeLurza v. Winthrop Laboratories, 697 F.2d 222 (8th Cir.1983).

7. One case has held that, in a civil rights action brought by the estate of a man who died after being subjected to a police choke hold, evidence about a subsequent police disciplinary proceeding was properly excluded under Rule 407. Maddox v. City of Los Angeles, 792 F.2d 1408 (9th Cir.1986), *But see* Rocky Mountain Helicopters, Inc. v. Bell Helicopters Textron, 805 F.2d 907 (10th Cir.1986) (post-event tests, which are investigative rather than directly remedial in nature, are not excluded by Rule 407); Westmoreland v. CBS, Inc., 601 F.Supp. 66 (S.D.N.Y.1984) (Rule 407 does not bar admission of internal investigative reports—indeed, these are among the most accurate sources of information for injured claimants). *See* Banks v. Lockheed–Georgia Co., 53 F.R.D. 283 (N.D.Ga.1971).

8. O'Connor v. Chrysler Corp., 86 F.R.D. 211, 218 (D.Mass.1980).

9. Granger v. National R.R. Passenger Corp., 116 F.R.D. 507, 509 (E.D.Pa.1987).

application of the privilege—at least at the discovery stage.[10] Somewhat inconsistently, other courts have held such reports admissible despite the application of Rule 407 because their confidentiality had been lost upon disclosure by the defendants.[11]

10. *See* Capellupo v. FMC Corp., 46 F.E.P. Cases 1193, 1194–98 (D.Minn.1988).

11. *See* Bergman v. Kemp, 97 F.R.D. 413 (W.D.Mich.1983).

RULE 408

I. TEXT OF RULE

RULE 408. Compromise and Offers to Compromise

Evidence of (1) furnishing or offering or promising to furnish, or (2) accepting or offering or promising to accept, a valuable consideration in compromising or attempting to compromise a claim which was disputed as to either validity or amount, is not admissible to prove liability for or invalidity of the claim or its amount. Evidence of conduct or statements made in compromise negotiations is likewise not admissible. This rule does not require the exclusion of any evidence otherwise discoverable merely because it is presented in the course of compromise negotiations. The rule also does not require exclusion where the evidence is offered for another purpose, such as proving bias or prejudice of a witness, negativing a contention of undue delay, or proving an effort to obstruct a criminal investigation or prosecution.

II. DISCUSSION

Rule 408 excludes evidence, if offered for proscribed purposes, of promising, furnishing, or accepting of consideration in compromising "a claim which was disputed as to either validity or amount." The decisional law defining when a "claim" is "disputed," [1] and distinguishing business communications from compromise negotiations,[2] is essential to the application of the Rule. However, these problems antedated promulgation of the Rule and are attributable not to the language of the Rule but the difficulties inherent in applying the underlying policy.

Paralleling other sections of Article IV, Rule 408 enumerates exceptions to its exclusionary mandate on a "such as" basis. This structure leaves open the question of whether otherwise excluded

1. *See, e.g.,* United States v. Meadows, 598 F.2d 984, 989 (5th Cir.1979) (CETA employee's admission to superiors that he had improperly negotiated mistakenly-issued checks soon after the discrepancy was discovered in an informal investigation did not constitute an offer to compromise as "there was no claim to compromise"); Burns v. Des Perez, 534 F.2d 103, 112 & n. 9 (8th Cir.1976), *cert. denied,* 429 U.S. 861 (1976) (upholding exclusion of all evidence relating to settlement negotiations in zoning dispute and rejecting as purposeless the "fine semantical distinction" between "compromise" and "settlement" and noting on the basis of the legislative history that, under the rule, "evidence relating to settlement negotiations is treated the same as compromise negotiations"); Playboy Enterprises, Inc. v. Chuckleberry Pub., Inc., 486 F.Supp. 414, 423 n. 10 (S.D.N.Y.1980) (terms of settlement accepted by present plaintiff in similar trademark litigation inadmissible, reflecting policy of encouraging settlement, *inter alia*).

2. *See, e.g.,* Fozdar v. City of Manchester, 24 Fed.R.Evid.Serv. 168 (D.N.H.1987) (demand letter by plaintiff and response by defendant are not excluded, where neither letter represented an effort to compromise); Big O Tire Dealers v. Goodyear Tire & Rubber Co., 561 F.2d 1365 (10th Cir.1977) (discussions prior to first threat of litigation admissible as business communications), *cert. dismissed,* 434 U.S. 1052 (1978).

statements made in a settlement context may be admitted for impeachment purposes if the settlement negotiations prove fruitless or at least do not resolve the claims against all defendants. To admit them is, of course, inconsistent with the announced policy of encouraging settlements. At the same time, such evidence may be quite valuable to the truth-finding process. The few decisions note but do not purport to resolve the tension between these two concerns.[3] Alaska and Tennessee explicitly forbid such impeachment in their versions of Rule 408.[4]

In adopting its version of Rule 408, Florida deleted the last two sentences of the Rule. Fla.Stat.Ann. § 90.408. The accompanying Sponsor's Note clearly indicates that the deletion was designed to preserve the integrity, and inadmissibility, of settlement discussions. Fla.Stat.Ann.Evid.Code at 39–40 (1979 Spec.Pamphlet).

3. *Compare* Estate of Spinosa v. International Harvester Co., 621 F.2d 1154 (1st Cir. 1980) (excluding proffer of settlement between plaintiff and another defendant), *with* John McShain, Inc. v. Cessna Aircraft Co., 563 F.2d 632 (3d Cir.1977) (admitting same). *See also* Reichenbach v. Smith, 528 F.2d 1072, 1075–1076 (5th Cir.1976) (affirming trial court's admission of evidence for impeachment purposes with a caveat that "this affirmance is not to be considered an approval for the future of the trial court's approach").

4. *See* 1 *Evidence in America* § 18.2.

RULE 409

I. TEXT OF RULE

RULE 409. Payment of Medical and Similar Expenses

Evidence of furnishing or offering or promising to pay medical, hospital, or similar expenses occasioned by an injury is not admissible to prove liability for the injury.

II. DISCUSSION

The underlying theory of Rule 409 is that public policy demands that good Samaritan instincts should not be construed as an admission of liability.[1] This in turn should encourage others to voluntarily lend support to injured parties without fear of admitting fault.

Although few reported decisions interpret Rule 409, one area that poses a potential problem concerns the admissibility of statements made in connection with offers to pay medical expenses. An example of this might be, "I'm sorry you are hurt, let me pay your medical expenses." Should the statement of remorse be admitted? While not technically within the purview of Rule 409, some commentators believe that such statements have little probative value and thus should be inadmissible so as to avoid misuse by the jury.[2] Other commentators believe that statements of remorse are always implicit in offers of payment and thus, the offerer should not be penalized for expressing his or her reasons for paying.[3] Of the thirty-four states adopting this Rule, Montana seems to be the only state to eliminate this confusion. Its rule provides that only evidence of the act of paying itself is excluded not evidence of promises or offers.[4] Thus any accompanying statements would not be excluded by this Rule.

The second area addressed in litigation is the admissibility of payments of expenses for purposes other than proving liability. In *Savoie v. Otto Candies, Inc.*,[5] the court held that such evidence may be admissible to show that the offerer is the plaintiff's employer. However, in *Eisenhart v. Patchett*,[6] the district court held that payment of medical expenses sent from West Virginia to Pennsylvania could not be used to establish minimum contacts for the purpose of establishing diversity jurisdiction. The Rule would not seem to require the latter result.

1. *See, e.g.*, Ferguson v. Graddy, 263 Ark. 413, 565 S.W.2d 600 (1978); Merva v. Super Fresh Food Markets, Inc., 1989 WL 32757 (E.D.Pa.1989).

2. 1 Saltzburg & Martin, *Federal Rules of Evidence Manual* 368 (5th ed. 1990).

3. Wendorf & Schlueter, *Texas Rules of Evidence Manual* 100 (2d ed. 1988).

4. Mont.R.Evid. 409. *See generally* 1 *Evidence in America* § 19.2; 3 & 4 *id.* (Louisiana, Rhode Island and Tennessee Rules).

5. 692 F.2d 363, 370 n. 7 (5th Cir.1982).

6. 1988 WL 91125 (E.D.Pa.1988).

RULE 410

I. TEXT OF RULE

RULE 410. Inadmissibility of Plea Discussions, and Related Statements

Except as otherwise provided in this rule, evidence of the following is not, in any civil or criminal proceedings, admissible against the defendant who made the plea or was a participant in the plea discussions:

(1) a plea of guilty which was later withdrawn;

(2) a plea of nolo contendere;

(3) any statement made in the course of any proceedings under Rule 11 of the Federal Rules of Criminal Procedure or comparable state procedure regarding either of the foregoing pleas; or

(4) any statement made in the course of plea discussions with an attorney for the prosecuting authority which do not result in a plea of guilty or which result in a plea of guilty later withdrawn.

However, such a statement is admissible (i) in any proceeding wherein another statement made in the course of the same plea or plea discussions has been introduced and the statement ought in fairness to be considered contemporaneously with it, or (ii) in a criminal proceeding for perjury or false statement if the statement was made by the defendant under oath, on the record and in the presence of counsel.

II. DISCUSSION

Rule 410, which embodies a public policy of encouraging plea bargaining in criminal cases,[1] is the only rule to have been rewritten twice since 1975. It tracks the language of Rule 11(e)(6) of the Federal Rules of Criminal Procedure, differing only to the extent that subparagraph (4) of Rule 410 refers to discussions with an attorney "for the prosecuting authority," while subparagraph (D) of Fed.R.Crim.P. 11(e)(6) speaks of an attorney "for the government." Indeed, as originally promulgated, Rule 410 was by its terms to be superseded by an amendment to the Federal Rules of Criminal Procedure.[2] It has been

1. *See* Myers v. Secretary of Health & Human Services, 893 F.2d 840, 843 (6th Cir. 1990) (while Rule 410 protects a nolo contendere plea in criminal and civil cases, the rule does not apply to administrative proceedings).

2. Such an amendment appeared in the 1975 version of Rule 11(e)(6), which, as it then stood, eliminated a provision in the original Rule 410 that admitted plea bargaining statements for impeachment. Rule 11(e)(6) also restricted admissibility to sworn statements, where the original would have admitted those deemed "voluntary and reliable." This constituted the 1975 or first amendment to the rule. Rule 410 was again amended

analogized, in its protection of plea bargaining discussions, to Rule 408 which addresses admissibility of compromise negotiations.[3]

The policy of encouraging plea negotiations is implemented in Rule 410 by protecting negotiations with "the attorney for the prosecuting authority." Conversely, the protection was not extended to other contacts that a defendant may have with the law enforcement system because of the risk of "substantial adverse effect on important law enforcement interests," notably that in obtaining confessions.[4] Consequently, who qualifies as an "attorney for the prosecuting authority," is a question of controlling significance.

United States v. Grant,[5] presented the question whether law enforcement personnel, other than government attorneys, who engaged in plea bargain negotiations were the subject of the evidentiary proscriptions of Rule 410. The court held the rule applicable to statements which the defendant made to an FBI agent authorized to negotiate, but inapplicable to post-bargain statements to an agent who was not so authorized.

Stressing consideration of the "totality of the circumstances" of each case, the Fifth Circuit (before the second amendment of the rule) formulated a two-tier analysis in *United States v. Robertson.*[6] The first inquiry was into "the accused's perceptions of the discussion, in context"; the second, into its reasonableness "given the totality of the objective circumstances." Because the *Robertson* defendants evinced no perception of participating in plea negotiations, neither made nor contemplated pleas, and sought no concessions but the release of one wife and one lady friend, and because the officers had not misled the defendants in any way, Rule 410 was held inapposite.

In *United States v. Swidan,*[7] the trial court relied upon a string of cases interpreting *United States v. Robertson* and suppressed the defendant's statements to a DEA agent who promised that he would relay an offer to the prosecution but stated that he lacked the authority to plea bargain. But in *United States v. Guerrero*[8] the defendant was hooked on both of the prongs of the *Robertson* test. The court concluded that even if the defendant believed that his statements to FBI agents were

in conjunction with Rule of Criminal Procedure 11(e)(6), effective December 1, 1980, adding the present subparagraphs (1) through (4) to ensure that the rule did not cover discussions between suspects and law enforcement agents.

3. *See, e.g.,* United States v. Grant, 622 F.2d 312 (8th Cir.1980); United States v. Robertson, 582 F.2d 1356, 1365 (5th Cir.1978).

4. United States v. Robertson, 582 F.2d at 1368.

5. 622 F.2d 308 (8th Cir.1980).

6. 582 F.2d 1356, 1366 (5th Cir.1978).

7. 689 F.Supp. 726 (E.D.Mich.1988).

8. 847 F.2d 1363 (9th Cir.1988).

part of plea discussions, that belief would have been objectively unreasonable.[9]

The rule covers discussions leading to a plea that is itself later withdrawn, and it has not been extended to statements made pursuant to a consummated plea bargain which the defendant later decides to breach.[10] In *United States v. Stirling,*[11] the defendant had negotiated formally through his attorney an exchange of his testimony for a limitation of prosecution to a single indictment count, to which he would plead guilty. Pursuant to his agreement, the defendant testified before the grand jury. Reacting to the contents of the indictment, however, he withdrew his plea, stood trial, was convicted, and on appeal invoked Rule 11(e)(6) to contest admission of the grand jury testimony. Upholding admission, the court pointed out that the statement had not been made in the course of plea discussion but in fulfillment of the finalized bargain, that exclusion would not be consistent with either the structure or the policy of the rule, and that, in the instance of grand jury testimony, extension of the rule might invite deceptive and manipulative abuses.[12]

It should be noted that the Rule does not address the issue of whether the government's attempts to negotiate a plea bargain should be admissible as evidence for the defendant. In *United States v. Verdoorn* [13] the Eighth Circuit analogized this situation to Rule 408, and held that government proposals concerning pleas are excludable as offers of compromise. However, in *United States v. Biaggi,*[14] the court held that evidence of immunity negotiations by the government was admissible against the government. It reasoned that most defendants would welcome immunity from prosecution and, if a defendant rejects the offer because he claims that he has no knowledge of wrongdoing, then the jury could find this probative of defendant's lack of guilty knowledge. Alaska is the only state to provide explicitly that statements made in connection with guilty pleas or nolo contendere pleas are not admissible against the defendant or government.[15] Minnesota and North Carolina bar use of the statements "for or against" the defendant, while the Florida and Nevada provisions render the statements flatly inadmissible regardless of whom they are offered by or against.[16]

9. *See also* U.S. v. Aponte–Suarez, 905 F.2d 483 (1st Cir.1990).

10. United States v. Stirling, 571 F.2d 708 (2d Cir.1978), *cert. denied,* 439 U.S. 824 (1979). *See also* United States v. Perez–Franco, 873 F.2d 455, 460–61 (1st Cir.1989) (recognizing that defendant may breach plea bargain, court held that statements regarding charges to which defendant did not plead guilty are admissible).

11. *Id.*

12. *Accord* United States v. Davis, 617 F.2d 677 (D.C.Cir.1979).

13. 528 F.2d 103 (8th Cir.1976).

14. 1990 WL 92821 (2d Cir.1990).

15. *See* Alaska R.Evid. 410.

16. *See generally* 1 *Evidence in America* §§ 20.2–20.4.

RULE 411

I. TEXT OF RULE

RULE 411. Liability Insurance

Evidence that a person was or was not insured against liability is not admissible upon the issue whether the person acted negligently or otherwise wrongfully. This rule does not require the exclusion of evidence of insurance against liability when offered for another purpose, such as proof of agency, ownership, or control, or bias or prejudice of a witness.

II. DISCUSSION

Central to Rule 411, which is consistent with the common law, is the feeling that knowledge of the presence or absence of liability insurance would induce juries to decide cases on improper grounds.[1] Justice Holmes' observation that most tort cases are decided on the theory of the nearest rich man would seem to lie somewhere in the background of the drafters' thinking. As at common law, the principal problem associated with the Rule involves ensuring that parties do not smuggle insurance evidence into the case on theories or pretexts that undercut the policy forbidding such evidence.

The formula of two Third Circuit decisions,[2] requiring the court to find the presence of a validating purpose and then to weigh relative prejudice to proponent and opponent seems well adapted to effectuating the drafters' intent. The absence of an articulable approved purpose is held to signal an offer made for a proscribed purpose.[3] However, the mere presence of such a purpose does not suffice for admission.[4] Moreover, direct evidence on the subject of insurance does not necessarily open the topic to cross-examination on the same basis as any other.[5]

Rule 411 problems more typically call for a balancing. A crucial issue in *Posttape Associates v. Eastman Kodak Co.*,[6] was whether the plaintiff knew of an alleged custom of the trade limiting the liability of sellers such as the defendant. The fact that the plaintiff had insured itself against the loss at issue was of obvious relevance, and the uniqueness of the coverage enhanced its probative value. Moreover, the fact that the case involved the purely commercial character of the parties and their litigation made it improbable, in the eyes of the

1. *See* the Advisory Committee Note to Rule 411.

2. Hunziker v. Scheidemantle, 543 F.2d 489 (3d Cir.1976), and Posttape Associates v. Eastman Kodak Co., 537 F.2d 751 (3d Cir.1976).

3. Cleveland v. Peter Kiewit Sons' Co., 624 F.2d 749 (6th Cir.1980); Hunziker v. Scheidemantle, 543 F.2d 489 (3d Cir.1976).

4. Varlack v. SWC Caribbean, Inc., 550 F.2d 171 (3d Cir.1977).

5. Hannah v. Haskins, 612 F.2d 373 (8th Cir.1980).

6. 537 F.2d 751 (3d Cir.1976).

appellate court that any responsive prejudicial chord would be struck in the minds of the jury. The Third Circuit held that exclusion constituted reversible error.

And in *Morrissey v. Welsh Co.*,[7] the Eighth Circuit affirmed the trial court's admission of references to liability insurance to show the reason safety inspections were made. It is important to note that this holding was limited to a statement that such admission was within the trial court's discretion. Thus, the trial court also had discretion to refuse the evidence. The mere articulation of some proper purpose does not guarantee that evidence of insurance will be admitted.[8]

The Michigan, Ohio, Texas and West Virginia Rules provide that the evidence of liability insurance may be offered to prove things other than liability but only if the issue is controverted.[9] If the issue is not controverted, the probative value of the evidence is likely to be low and the prejudicial effect—i.e., the misuse of the evidence to prove a "deep pocket"—is likely to be high. While only the New Hampshire version of Rule 411 expressly incorporates a Rule 403 type of balance, the remaining state courts—like the federal courts—require the judge to weigh probative value against prejudicial effect.[10]

7. 821 F.2d 1294 (8th Cir.1987).

8. *See* Palmer v. Krueger, 897 F.2d 1529, 1538 (10th Cir.1990) (evidence of liability insurance was admissible to prove family discord although court recognizes this admission as discretionary).

9. Mich.R.Evid. 411, Ohio R.Evid. 411, Tex.R.Civ. and Crim.Evid. 411, W.Va.R.Evid. 411.

10. *See* 1 *Evidence in America* §§ 21.2–21.3.

RULE 412

I. TEXT OF RULE

RULE 412. Sex Offense Cases; Relevance of Victim's Past Behavior

(a) Notwithstanding any other provision of law, in a criminal case in which a person is accused of an offense under chapter 109A of title 18, United States Code, reputation or opinion evidence of the past sexual behavior of an alleged victim of such offense is not admissible.

(b) Notwithstanding any other provision of law, in a criminal case in which a person is accused of an offense under chapter 109A of title 18, United States Code, evidence of a victim's past sexual behavior other than reputation or opinion evidence is also not admissible, unless such evidence other than reputation or opinion evidence is—

(1) admitted in accordance with subdivision (c)(1) and (c)(2) and is constitutionally required to be admitted; or

(2) admitted in accordance with subdivision (c) and is evidence of—

(A) past sexual behavior with persons other than the accused, offered by the accused upon the issue of whether the accused was or was not, with respect to the alleged victim, the source of semen or injury; or

(B) past sexual behavior with the accused and is offered by the accused upon the issue of whether the alleged victim consented to the sexual behavior with respect to which such offense is alleged.

(c)(1) If the person accused of committing an offense under chapter 109A of title 18, United States Code intends to offer under subdivision (b) evidence of specific instances of the alleged victim's past sexual behavior, the accused shall make a written motion to offer such evidence not later than fifteen days before the date on which the trial in which such evidence is to be offered is scheduled to begin, except that the court may allow the motion to be made at a later date, including during trial, if the court determines either that the evidence is newly discovered and could not have been obtained earlier through the exercise of due diligence or that the issue to which such evidence relates has newly arisen in the case. Any motion made under this paragraph shall be served on all other parties and on the alleged victim.

(2) The motion described in paragraph (1) shall be accompanied by a written offer of proof. If the court determines that the offer of proof contains evidence described in subdivi-

sion (b), the court shall order a hearing in chambers to determine if such evidence is admissible. At such hearing the parties may call witnesses, including the alleged victim, and offer relevant evidence. Notwithstanding subdivision (b) of rule 104, if the relevancy of the evidence which the accused seeks to offer in the trial depends upon the fulfillment of a condition of fact, the court, at the hearing in chambers or at a subsequent hearing in chambers scheduled for such purpose, shall accept evidence on the issue of whether such condition of fact is fulfilled and shall determine such issue.

(3) If the court determines on the basis of the hearing described in paragraph (2) that the evidence which the accused seeks to offer is relevant and that the probative value of such evidence outweighs the danger of unfair prejudice, such evidence shall be admissible in the trial to the extent an order made by the court specifies evidence which may be offered and areas with respect to which the alleged victim may be examined or cross-examined.

(d) For purposes of this rule, the term "past sexual behavior" means sexual behavior other than the sexual behavior with respect to which an offense under chapter 109A of title 18, United States Code is alleged.

II. DISCUSSION

Rule 412 is the Privacy Protection for Rape Victims Act of 1978, one of more than 20 roughly contemporaneous "rape shield" enactments. Re-written in Section 7046(a) of the Anti-Drug Abuse Act of 1988, the rule eliminates the words "rape or of assault with intent to commit rape" for "offense." No other substantive changes have been made. Although federal jurisdiction is infrequently invoked over this crime, the Rule was designed in part to "serve as a model to suggest to the remaining states that reform of existing rape laws is important to the equity of our criminal justice system." [1] A uniform version of Rule 412 was adopted in 1986 but has not been adopted by any state. However, 48 states have enacted rape shield statutes, five of them closely following the federal counterpart.[2]

While Rule 412 is well intentioned, it seems almost certain to trigger constitutional attacks, the first being based on the Sixth Amendment. Among the problems is the possibility of interpreting subdivision (a) to preclude testimony that the accused mistook the victim's reaction because of the victim's reputation for sexual promiscuity. Exclusion of such evidence might make it impossible for the accused to negate intent.

1. 124 Cong.Rec. H 34913 (daily ed. Oct. 10, 1978) (remarks of Rep. Holtzman).

2. Hawaii, Idaho, Iowa, Mississippi and Oregon follow the more restrictive provisions of the Federal Rule. *See* 1 *Evidence in America* § 22.2.

Subdivision (a) in effect requires the defendant wishing to prove any fact permissible under subdivision (b) to seek out and present individual witnesses. Where such individuals cannot be located or brought to court in time, the subdivision, literally read, prevents the defendant from presenting any evidence. Evidence in other forms is admissible, however, under subdivision (b)(1) if "constitutionally required to be admitted." [3] In *United States v. Bartlett,*[4] the defendant relied on section (b)(1) and the Sixth Amendment right of confrontation as imposing a constitutional right to impeach the victim for prior false allegations. The court concluded that this evidence was properly excluded because of its "minimal probative value and highly prejudicial effect."

There are two instances under subdivision (b)(2) which allow evidence of past sexual behavior. These include showings of whether the accused was or was not the source of semen or injury and whether the victim consented to the behavior. "Injury" usually refers to the condition of the victim's vaginal area where the condition might be relevant as to defendant's case and the defendant offers evidence to show someone else caused that condition. In *United States v. Azure,*[5] evidence of an alleged prior sexual activity with a 13–year–old boy was excluded as irrelevant to the source of a laceration on the 10–year–old victim's vaginal wall where physicians testified that such injury would have been painful and the victim did not express prior discomfort.

Additionally, in *United States v. Shaw,*[6] in an extensive discussion of Rule 412, evidence offered by a foster father of his daughter's sexual relations with other boys was properly excluded where the defendant failed to establish that an "injury" occurred. It ruled that the rupturing of a hymen does not constitute an injury under section (b)(2)(A). Moreover, the court in *Shaw* held that emotional injuries are not within Rule 412 exception when unaccompanied by certain physical consequences.

Another Sixth Amendment challenge might arise from the notice provision of section (c) where the motion and offer are not timely filed thus rising to an argument of ineffective assistance of counsel. The Court in *United States v. Eagle Thunder,*[7] ruled that a failure to file written notice of intent under section (c)(1) was alone sufficient to deny

3. The Rule thus establishes a presumption of exclusion subject to a judicial finding that evidence offered for a specific purpose must be admitted, in accordance with Giles v. Maryland, 386 U.S. 66 (1967).

4. 856 F.2d 1071 (8th Cir.1988).

5. 845 F.2d 1503 (8th Cir.1988).

6. 824 F.2d 601 (8th Cir.1987), *cert. denied,* 484 U.S. 1068 (1988).

7. 893 F.2d 950 (8th Cir.1990).

the offer of proof.[8] The requirements of section (c)(2) may also allow the introduction of defense evidence to turn on the proponent's articulation of its purpose, removing the burden of objection from the government. Moreover, subdivision (c)(3), unlike Rule 403, does not premise exclusion on a finding that probative value is substantially outweighed, and thus implicitly favors exclusion where the decision is close.[9]

Most importantly, subdivision (c)(2) may take from the jury issues it has traditionally decided and, but for this Rule, would continue to decide under Rule 104(b). It confides to the judge the finding of a condition of fact on which the relevancy of proffered evidence depends. The decision is clearly one that will often require determinations of witness credibility or other truth finding. The provision thus risks infringing on the defendant's right to trial by jury. Consequently, some commentators believe the rule should require the trial judge to determine whether the defendant has presented sufficient evidence for a reasonable jury to find the proposition asserted by the defendant to be true.[10] Because of the real constitutional concerns raised by the Rule, its operation continues to necessitate a watchful eye.

8. *See also* United States v. Provost, 875 F.2d 172 (8th Cir.) (defendant barred from offering statement by victim because he failed to give 15 days notice), *cert. denied,* 110 S.Ct. 170 (1989).

9. *See* United States v. Blue Horse, 856 F.2d 1037 (8th Cir.1988) (medical record showing date of victim's last sexual contact excluded as prejudicial).

10. 1 Saltzburg & Martin, *Federal Rules of Evidence Manual* 396 (5th ed. 1990).

APPENDIX I

ARTICLE V. PRIVILEGES

Introduction

Article V of the Rules deals with privileges. It is, in its brevity, perhaps more significant for what it does not attempt to do than for what it does. To begin with, it does not address constitutional privileges. Moreover, in enacting this single-rule Article, Congress specifically rejected the Advisory Committee's attempt to enumerate the recognized constitutional privileges and to define their scope. See Appendix B. Congress further rejected the Committee's attempt to create a uniform federal law of privilege, mandating instead that in cases where state law governs substantively state privilege law also governs.

In rejecting the committee's recommendations, Congress was motivated by a concern that the proposed rules intruded upon legitimate state interests in having state substantive law applied. More broadly, Congress was motivated by a concern that the proposed rules would have tended to "freeze" standards in an area of law which, Congress felt, was best left to grow and develop on a case by case basis and in the light of changing circumstances.

The following discussion focuses on both the manner in which Article V resolves federal-state choice of law questions in the privilege areas and on the present state of the federal common law of privilege, including analyses of each of the various specific privileges.

RULE 501

I. TEXT OF RULE

RULE 501. General Rule

Except as otherwise required by the Constitution of the United States or provided by Act of Congress or in rules prescribed by the Supreme Court pursuant to statutory authority, the privilege of a witness, person, government, State, or political subdivision thereof shall be governed by the principles of the common law as they may be interpreted by the courts of the United States in the light of reason and experience. However, in civil actions and proceedings with respect to an element of a claim or defense as to which State law supplies the rule of decision, the privilege of a witness, person, government, state, or political subdivision thereof shall be determined in accordance with State law.

II. DISCUSSION

Congress enacted Article V, consisting of Rule 501 only, after it scrapped the Advisory Committee's thirteen proposed rules for a uniform, specific law of privilege in the federal courts. In place of Proposed Rules 501–513,[1] Congress passed the present Rule 501 which (1) requires the application of state law of privilege on substantive questions as to which state law supplies the rule of decision and (2) seems to have endorsed the common law approach that federal courts followed in criminal proceedings pursuant to Fed.R.Crim.P. 26 prior to the adoption of the Federal Rules of Evidence. In a separate statute, designed to further protect the substantive considerations Congress considered inherent in the law of privilege, Congress set out the requirement that any attempt to change that law by way of a rule devised by the Supreme Court would be invalid absent affirmative approval by Congress.[2]

State Law Privileges

Rule 501 regarding the application of state privileges under the *Erie* doctrine [3] has not caused major problems for practitioners or the courts and has been the subject of favorable commentary generally.[4] Rule 501's language may raise certain *Erie* ambiguities. However,

1. These rejected rules have served as significant guidelines for federal courts and are set forth in Appendix B to this Report. This Discussion of particular privileges largely follows the order of the Supreme Court's rejected rules.

2. 28 U.S.C. § 2076 (1975). Proposed Rule 501, as approved by the Supreme Court, would have bound federal courts to recognize only the privileges set forth in Proposed Rules 502–513 and other privileges enacted by Congress or required by the Constitution. *See* Appendix B.

3. Erie R.R. v. Tompkins, 304 U.S. 64 (1938).

4. *See, e.g.,* 2 Louisell & Mueller, *Federal Evidence* §§ 200, 204 (Supp.1982).

these are for the most part clarified by the legislative history, and no serious problems have emerged in practice.

Thus, the phrase "with respect to an element of a claim or defense" may, on its face, appear to be unclear and of potentially problematic breadth. The Congressional Conference Report, however, clarifies that: "If an item of proof tends to support or defeat a claim or defense, or an element of a claim or defense, and if state law supplies the rule of decision for that claim or defense, then state privilege law applies to that item of proof." [5] That clarification superseded the comment in the earlier Senate Judiciary Committee Report that "the Federal law of privileges should be applied with respect to pendant [*sic*] State law claims when they arise in a Federal question case." [6] The legislative history might be considered as effectively inserting the words "proof of a fact relevant to" before the words "an element of a claim or defense," resolving doubts which might otherwise linger.

Rule 501's language also gives rise to the question whether state law of privilege applies if a suit is brought under federal law but federal law adopts or incorporates state substantive law. The Conference Report answers with a resounding "No." [7] Some commentators, however, have expressed uncertainty on the point, at least "where Congress has directed application of state substantive law *in toto.*" [8] No problems have, however, arisen in the case law on this score.[9] Similarly, a theoretical problem, regarding the application of inconsistent state and federal law of privilege in a case containing both federal and state claims, does not appear to have caused any significant difficulties in practice.[10]

Although the conflict problem thus far remains more theoretical than practical, it could become more troubling in the future, especially as a result of the Supreme Court's decision on corporate attorney-client privilege in *Upjohn Co. v. United States.*[11] As discussed *infra,* that case rejects the "control group" limitation on the corporate attorney-client

5. H.R.Rep. No. 93–1597, 93d Cong., 2d Sess., reprinted in West's 1990 *Federal Rules of Evidence for United States Courts and Magistrates* at 60.

6. Sen.Rep. No. 93–1277, 93d Cong., 2d Sess., reprinted in West's 1990 *Federal Rules of Evidence for United States Courts and Magistrates* at 60. *See* 1 Saltzburg & Martin, *Federal Rules of Evidence Manual* 230 (5th ed. 1990).

7. *See* H.R.Rep. No. 93–1597, 93d Cong., 2d Sess., reprinted in West's 1990 *Federal Rules of Evidence for United States Courts and Magistrates* at 60.

8. *See* 2 Louisell & Mueller, *Federal Evidence* § 201 at 415–16 (Supp.1982) ("It is not certain what the result should be in cases where Congress has directed application of state substantive law *in toto,* as it did, for example, in the Federal Tort Claims Act").

9. *See* Wm. T. Thompson Co. v. Gen. Nutrition Corp., 671 F.2d 100, 104 (3d Cir.1982).

10. *See, e.g.,* Los Angeles Memorial Coliseum Commission v. NFL, 89 F.R.D. 489 (C.D. Cal.1981) (state and federal law of privilege easily coincided).

11. 449 U.S. 383 (1981).

privilege—a limitation which is still retained by a number of states.[12] In litigation involving corporate matters, it is not uncommon to have state law claims raised in conjunction with federal claims. Where a state rule denies a corporation the broad protection that *Upjohn* may provide and evidence, protected under *Upjohn,* is sought or offered on a state claim, a federal court may find that deciding how to reconcile the conflicting privilege rules is problematic.

When state law governs, courts have had to decide which state's law to apply.[13] There is some uncertainty as to whether a federal court should use the evidence law that a court in the state in which the federal court is located would use or whether the federal court should use its own conflict rules to make that determination. There are arguments in favor of each approach. In many cases both produce the same result, and no choice need be made. The issue certainly is of academic interest. To date, it has not been the subject of much judicial concern in reported cases.

The following discussion addresses some of the more commonly encountered privileges generally falling within the topic of Rule 501. As noted throughout the discussion, many of the states which have adopted the federal rules of evidence have also included specific privilege rules and many of those are patterned in some way after the privilege rules proposed by the Supreme Court.[14]

Attorney–Client Privilege

The attorney-client privilege is one of the oldest of the privileges for confidential communications.[15] As a general rule, a client may assert the privilege to protect confidential communications made to the client's attorney to enable the attorney to render legal advice or services to the client.[16] Proposed Rule 503(b) would merely have restated, rather than modified, the common law privilege.[17]

Nevertheless, the privilege is not absolute—and not without some gray areas.[18] And despite various well accepted restrictions, recent

12. At least ten states retain a version of the control group test in their versions of Proposed Fed.R.Evid. 503. *See* 1 *Evidence in America* §§ 24.2–24.3.

13. *See, e.g.,* Mitsui & Co., v. Puerto Rico Water Resources Auth., 79 F.R.D. 72 (D.P.R. 1978).

14. *See* Appendix B and 1 *Evidence in America* §§ 23.1–34.4.

15. *See generally,* Upjohn Co. v. United States, 449 U.S. 383, 389 (1981); 8 J. Wigmore, *Evidence* § 2291 (McNaughton rev. 1961); McCormick, *Evidence* § 87 at 175 (Cleary ed. 1984).

16. *See* 1 Saltzburg & Martin, *Federal Rules of Evidence Manual* 411 (5th ed. 1990).

17. *See* Appendix B.

18. Although it is beyond the scope of this Discussion, counsel should be alert that the testimonial privilege under Rule 501 may conflict with ethical responsibilities under applicable state codes of professional responsibility or the model rules of professional

caselaw suggests that questions of scope and waiver continue to perplex the courts.

The common law attorney-client privilege is subject to a number of exceptions. The communication must, for example, relate to an attorney's status as a legal advisor; communications regarding non-legal activities of an attorney are not privileged.[19] Courts have specifically held that communications relating or responding to requests for business, scientific or economic advice are not privileged.[20] But the fact that a nonlawyer could perform the service in question will not automatically preclude the privilege.[21]

Several restrictions are also recognized, as for example (a) where the communication is made in contemplation or furtherance of a crime or fraud,[22] (b) where the communications were made to or by former clients while they were represented jointly but who later litigate against each other,[23] (c) where the communications concern legal services rendered by the attorney who is defending a suit by the client over those services,[24] and (d) where the attorney is called to testify in a case contesting the will of a deceased client.[25] Proposed Rule 503(b) and (d) would substantially have codified the foregoing but not significantly altered them.[26]

In addition to these situational exceptions, federal courts have also generally held that the privilege does not include information that relates to (a) the existence of the attorney-client relationship,[27] (b) the

conduct. Similar ethical issues may also arise between other professional oaths and Rule 501, including for example, the priest-penitent and doctor-patient relationships.

19. Cannaday v. United States, 384 F.2d 849 (8th Cir.1966); United States v. Bartone, 400 F.2d 459 (6th Cir.1968).

20. For example, an attorney who receives information to do a client's tax returns has no privilege vis-a-vis the IRS. *See* United States v. Willis, 565 F.Supp. 1186 (S.D.Iowa, 1983).

21. United States v. Summe, 208 F.Supp. 925, 928 (E.D.Ky.1962).

22. *See, e.g.,* In re Impounded Case (Law Firm), 879 F.2d 1211 (3d Cir.1989); United States v. Rosenstein, 474 F.2d 705, 715 (2d Cir.1973); United States v. Shewfelt, 455 F.2d 836 (9th Cir.), *cert. denied,* 406 U.S. 944 (1972).

23. *See, e.g.,* Popovitch v. Kasperlik, 70 F.Supp. 376, 381 (W.D.Pa.1947); United States v. Schwimmer, 892 F.2d 237 (2d Cir.1989); In re Crazy Eddie Securities Litigation, 131 F.R.D. 374, 378 (E.D.N.Y.1990) ("joint defense" exception protects communications in a criminal case between counsel and their laymen codefendants who have "common interests"). *But see* In re Grand Jury Subpoenas 89–3 & 89–4, 902 F.2d 244 (4th Cir.1990) (disclosure of documents generated in common interest required movant's consent).

24. *See, e.g.,* In re Nat. Mtg. Equity Corp. Mtg. Pool Certificates Sec. Litig., 120 F.R.D. 687 (C.D.Cal.1988).

25. Glover v. Patten, 165 U.S. 394 (1987); Sorrels v. Alexander, 142 F.2d 769 (D.C.Cir. 1944).

26. *See* Appendix B.

27. National Union Fire Ins. Co. of Pittsburgh v. Aetna Casualty & Surety Co., 384 F.2d 316 (D.C.Cir.1967).

client's address,[28] or (c) the attorney's fee.[29] More recently, in cases where the privilege is claimed to protect the client's identity, the courts have applied a "last link" doctrine that will protect nonprivileged information when disclosure would reveal otherwise privileged information.[30]

Because it is a prerequisite of the privilege that the communication be intended to be confidential, disclosure to a third party will ordinarily waive the privilege [31]—except perhaps in certain cases where the disclosure is inadvertent [32] or where public policy dictates otherwise.[33] And some courts have held that the privilege must be asserted document by document.[34] But neither Proposed Rule 503(b), which restated the common law confidentiality criterion, nor Proposed Rule 511, which concerned "voluntary" waiver, addresses the waiver questions raised by inadvertent disclosure or public policy considerations.[35]

Proposed Rule 503(a)(1) was also just as vague when it came to identifying to whom the privilege extends. Although it recognized that the privilege extends beyond an individual to corporations,[36] it did not identify which corporate employees' communications with counsel would fall within the privilege.[37] But that once vigorously litigated

28. Litton Industries v. Lehman Bros. Kuhn Loeb, 130 F.R.D. 25, 26 (S.D.N.Y.1990) (client's address was not related to the legal advice requested).

29. In re Shargel, 742 F.2d 61 (2d Cir.1984).

30. In re Grand Jury Proceedings, 869 F.2d 1267 (11th Cir.1990); *See e.g.,* In re Witness–Attorney Before Grand Jury No. 83–1, 613 F.Supp. 394 (S.D.Fla.1984); In re Grand Jury Proceedings 88–9 (MIA), 899 F.2d 1039 (11th Cir.1990). And some courts will not allow disclosure where it would reveal the client's motive for seeking legal advice. *See e.g.,* In re Grand Jury Proceeding (Cherney), 898 F.2d 565 (7th Cir.1990); Baird v. Koerner, 279 F.2d 623, 633 (9th Cir.1960); Tillotson v. Boughner, 350 F.2d 663 (7th Cir. 1965); *But cf* United States v. Ponder, 475 F.2d 37 (5th Cir.1973); Dole v. Molinas, 889 F.2d 885 (9th Cir.1989).

31. "However, where the third parties are the agents or subordinates of the attorney or his client [or] are necessary for communication . . ., their presence does not defeat the existence of the privilege." Saltzburg, *supra* note b, at 411 (citations omitted).

32. *See e.g.,* Transamerica Computer Co. v. IBM, 573 F.2d 646, 651–652 (9th Cir.1978), and SCM Corp. v. Xerox Corp., 70 F.R.D. 508, 519 (D.Conn.1976) (both holding no waiver). *But see, e.g.,* United States v. Mendelsohn, 896 F.2d 1183 (9th Cir.1990) (defendant's disclosure to an undercover detective about misstated legal advice waived privilege).

33. *Compare* the conflicting approaches in Diversified Industries, Inc. v. Meredith, 572 F.2d 596 (8th Cir.1978) (limited waiver), Permian Corp. v. United States, 665 F.2d 1214 (D.C.Cir.1981) (full waiver) and Teachers Ins. & Ann Ass'n v. Shamrock Broadcasting Co., 521 F.Supp. 638 (S.D.N.Y.1981) (conditional waiver).

34. *See, e.g.,* United States v. Rockwell Int'l, 897 F.2d 1255, 1265 (3d Cir.1990); Holified v. United States, 909 F.2d 201, 203–204 (7th Cir.1990) (failure to allege specific facts document by document did not raise privilege claim to documents requested in three production requests).

35. *See* Appendix B.

36. *See* Appendix B.

37. *Id.*

issue was resolved, for federal law purposes,[38] in *Upjohn Co. v. United States,* 449 U.S. 383 (1981), in which the Supreme Court rejected the control-group test and held that communications by corporate personnel would be privileged if they were made to corporate attorneys (a) in connection with their duties and (b) in order to provide the attorneys with information they require to advise the corporation. The Court indicated that a case-by-case approach was appropriate to determine the extent of a corporation's privilege and who may invoke it. However, neither the Court nor Proposed Rule 503 address the question of what happens when the corporate entity is dissolved and the effect of certain employees' waiver of the privilege.

Therefore, although certain standards regarding the scope of the attorney-client privilege are well accepted, because Proposed Rule 503 would only have restated established law, where uncertainties exist it is unlikely that codification would have removed them. Proposed Rule 503 would have provided no help to the Supreme Court in deciding *Upjohn* given its case-by-case approach in this area. Especially in the area of waiver, further clarification and uniformity would be desirable.

Proposed Rule 503 would have clarified exactly what communication falls within the privilege. About the only proposition undisputed in the caselaw is that communications from the client to the attorney for the purpose of obtaining legal services qualify for protection. As for communications from the attorney to the client and communications among attorneys representing different clients, the law is not so clear. Proposed Rule 503 would have provided some guidance. And guidance of some sort would be most helpful.

A number of evidence codes adopted by the following jurisdictions contain codified attorney-client privileges, many of which are based on Proposed Rule 503 or the 1974 version of Uniform Rule of Evidence 502. *See generally* 1 *Evidence in America* §§ 24.2–24.4. In August 1986, Uniform Rule 502(a)(2) was amended in light of *Upjohn,* and a number of states have similarly broad provisions. *Id.*

Clergy–Penitent Privilege

For over a century, the federal courts have recognized the existence of a clergy-penitent privilege which extends to the "confidences of the confessional." [39] The privilege is rooted in the imperative need for confidence and trust in clergy-penitent relationships:

> The priest-penitent privilege recognizes the human need to disclose to a spiritual counselor, in total and absolute confidence, what are

38. Of course, where application of state privilege law is mandated by Rule 501, a contrary rule may apply in federal court. *E.g.,* Consolidation Coal Co. v. Bucyrus–Erie Co., 432 N.E.2d 250 (Ill.1982).

39. Totten v. United States, 92 U.S. 105 (1876). *See generally* 1 Saltzburg & Martin, *Federal Rules of Evidence Manual* 414 (5th ed. 1990).

believed to be flawed acts or thoughts and to receive priestly consolation and guidance in return.

Trammel v. United States, 445 U.S. 40, 51 (1980). Although the privilege is not restricted to situations where the religion itself mandates no disclosure, such as a Catholic's confession to a priest, not all communications with a member of the clergy are privileged. In particular, the privilege applies only to confidential confessions or communications of a penitent seeking spiritual rehabilitation.[40] Accordingly, litigation revolves around the issues of (a) whether an individual is seeking spiritual relief and (b) whether the individual to whom the statement is made qualifies as a "clergyman."

Turning first to whether the communication itself qualifies for protection under the privilege, protected conversations must involve spiritual relationships and they must be made in confidence to a clergy member in his or her spiritual capacity.[41] Accordingly, conversations which relate to business relationships are not made in a clergy-penitent setting and do not qualify for the privilege.[42] Moreover, reasonable efforts must be made to insure that a communication is confidential. Thus, when a prisoner confesses to a crime in the presence of prison chaplain and officer, the confession is not privileged.[43]

Recently the Third Circuit addressed the existence of a "clergy-communicant" privilege in an appeal from an order denying motion to compel grand jury testimony of a Lutheran Pastor. In *In re Grand Jury Investigation,*[44] the Court held that a clergy-communicant privilege does exist but vacated the order for a determination of whether the people present at the counseling session were "third parties" so as to determine if the privilege was properly invoked.[45] In a thorough analysis of the history of this privilege, the court stated that the clergy-communicant privilege satisfies the four requirements set forth by Dean Wigmore for recognizing privileges.[46]

40. United States v. Wells, 446 F.2d 2 (2d Cir.1971). At least one federal court, following a state statute, has held that the privilege may only be waived by the clergyman, thus "safeguarding [a] clergyman's status as a secure repository for the confessant's confidences." Eckmann v. Board of Educ. Hawthorn School Dist., 106 F.R.D. 70, 73 (E.D.Mo.1985), *citing* Seidman v. Fishburne–Hudgins Educ. Found. Inc., 724 F.2d 413, 415 (4th Cir.1984).

41. United States v. Gordon, 493 F.Supp. 822 (N.D.N.Y.1980), *aff'd,* U.S. v. Gordon, 655 F.2d 478 (2d Cir.1981).

42. United States v. Gordon, 493 F.Supp. at 823. *See also* United States v. Dube, 820 F.2d 886 (7th Cir.1987) (if one seeks out the clergy only for income tax avoidance, then that person is not a penitent seeking spiritual relief from his sins, but is only a citizen seeking relief from his obligation to pay taxes).

43. United States v. Webb, 615 F.2d 828 (9th Cir.1980).

44. 918 F.2d 374 (3d Cir.1990).

45. *Id.* at 377.

46. *Id.* at 384.

While noting nothing in the privilege which limits group discussions to family members, the court did state that the focus should be on whether a third party's presence was essential to the counseling session.[47]

The privilege is not limited to communications with clergy members per se. Individuals who function as spiritual advisors or who otherwise perform activities that generally conform with a significant portion of activities normally performed by the clergy may invoke the privilege as well.[48] Proposed Rule 506 provided some guidance concerning to whom the privilege applies [49] and may serve as a guideline for the federal courts to follow. In general, however, application of this privilege has not proved problematic for the courts.

Family Privileges

Marital privileges. Two privileges protect the marital relationship. The adverse testimony privilege (sometimes called "spousal immunity") protects one spouse from being compelled to testify against the other spouse on any subject while they are married. The confidential communications privilege (sometimes called the "marital communications" privilege) shields communications made in confidence during marriage and may be asserted even after the marriage has terminated. Federal courts recognize both privileges.[50]

The adverse testimony privilege was originally based on the incompetency of one spouse to testify for or against the other spouse. The United States Supreme Court abolished this absolute disqualification in federal courts and permitted a defendant's spouse to testify on the defendant's behalf.[51] However, the Court left intact the rule that either spouse could prevent the other from giving adverse testimony.

The stated purpose of the adverse testimony privilege is to preserve marital harmony by avoiding the potentially irreparable rifts that may result from requiring one spouse to testify against the other. Critics point out, however, that if a spouse is willing to testify *voluntarily* against the other spouse, the justification for the privilege no longer

47. 918 F.2d at 386.

48. *See* Eckman v. Board of Education, 106 F.R.D. at 73 (position as a spiritual advisor is enough to invoke the priest-penitent privilege under Missouri and federal law); *see also* In re Verplank, 329 F.Supp. 433 (C.D.Cal.1971) (draft counselors perform activities that generally conform with a significant portion of activities normally performed by clergy and are thus brought within the privilege).

49. *See* Appendix B.

50. Only a slight majority of states recognize the adverse testimony privilege. However, virtually all states recognize the confidential communications privilege. McCormick on Evidence § 78 at 189–203 (3d ed. 1984); Note, *Developments in the Law—Privileged Communications,* 98 Harv.L.Rev. 1450 (1985).

51. *See* Funk v. United States, 290 U.S. 371 (1933).

exists since the marriage has probably already been damaged beyond repair.

This consideration persuaded the Supreme Court in *Trammel v. United States*[52] to rule unanimously that the adverse testimony privilege belongs to the witness spouse, not the defendant spouse. Thus, the defendant in a federal criminal trial may not prevent the spouse's testimony—only the witness spouse may assert or waive the right. The Court reasoned that "when one spouse is willing to testify against the other in a criminal proceeding . . . their relationship is almost certainly in disrepair; there is probably little in the way of marital harmony for the privilege to preserve."[53] This is contrary to Proposed Rule 505(a)–(b), which allows either the accused or the spouse to claim the privilege. *See* Appendix B.

In federal courts, and in most state courts, the adverse testimony privilege applies only in criminal cases.[54] Some commentators argue that the rationale behind the privilege applies equally in civil cases,[55] but federal courts have declined to extend the privilege to civil cases, at least where they did not perceive any serious threat to the marital relationship.[56]

Generally, the adverse testimony is given. However, the privilege has been held not to apply where the marriage was entered into fraudulently[57] or where marital differences were irreconcilable.[58] Some courts are reluctant to inquire into the viability of a marriage, instead opting for bright-line rules, while other courts believe such an inquiry is necessary to give effect to the underlying rationale for the privilege.[59]

If the witness spouse participated in a joint criminal venture with the defendant spouse, the adverse testimony privilege might not be available to the witness spouse who refuses to testify. The circuits disagree over the "joint participants" exception to the privilege. The

52. 445 U.S. 40 (1980).

53. 445 U.S. at 52.

54. Proposed Rule 505(a) limits the privilege to criminal cases. *See* Appendix B. *See also* 1 *Evidence in America* §§ 26.2–26.4.

55. 2 Louisell and Mueller, *Federal Evidence* § 218 (Supp.1990).

56. *See* Ryan v. C.I.R., 568 F.2d 531 (7th Cir.1977), *cert. denied,* 439 U.S. 820 (1978); *see also* In re Martenson, 779 F.2d 461 (8th Cir.1985) (declining to decide whether privilege is limited to criminal cases). *See generally* Medine, *The Adverse Testimony Privilege: Time to Dispose of a "Sentimental Relic,"* 67 Or.L.Rev. 519, 521–22 n. 8 (1988).

57. *Compare* United States v. Apodaca, 522 F.2d 568 (10th Cir.1975) (privilege inapplicable to marriage occurring three days before trial) with Emo v. United States, 777 F.2d 508 (9th Cir.1985) (privilege applicable despite marriage between date of subpoena and grand jury testimony).

58. *See* In re Witness Before Grand Jury, 791 F.2d 234 (2d Cir.1986).

59. *See* discussion of this issue *infra* under the marital communication privilege.

Seventh and Tenth Circuits have endorsed the exception,[60] the Second and Third Circuits have rejected it,[61] and the Fifth Circuit has refused to rule on it.[62] Proposed Rule 505(c) notably contains no exception for joint criminal activity.

Despite *Trammel,* only fifteen states follow the federal approach of vesting the privilege only in the witness spouse. Twenty states have abolished the privilege altogether, most doing so prior to *Trammel.* The remaining states retain spousal immunity in one form or another.[63] Moreover, some states explicitly extend the privilege to civil as well as criminal cases.[64] Under Federal Rule 501, these broader versions of the privilege would apply to civil claims or defenses based on state law in diversity cases.

The confidential communications privilege excludes from evidence confidential communications made by one spouse to the other during marriage. The underlying rationale for this privilege is somewhat different than that for the adverse testimony privilege.

> The testimonial privilege looks forward with reference to the particular marriage at hand: the privilege is meant to protect against the impact of the testimony on the marriage. The marital communications privilege in a sense, is broader and more abstract: it exists to insure that spouses . . . feel free to communicate their deepest feelings to each other without fear of eventual exposure in a court of law.[65]

The confidential communications privilege differs from the adverse testimony privilege in other fundamental respects. Whereas the adverse testimony privilege applies only if the parties are still married at the time of the trial, the confidential communications privilege applies as long as the parties were married at the time of the communication, even if the marriage has subsequently ended. Further, while spousal immunity may only be invoked by the witness spouse, either spouse may invoke the marital communication privilege. Additionally, the marital communication privilege is generally available to civil and

60. United States v. Keck, 773 F.2d 759 (7th Cir.1985); United States v. Clark, 712 F.2d 299 (7th Cir.1983); United States v. Trammel, 538 F.2d 1166 (10th Cir.1978), *aff'd on other grounds,* 445 U.S. 40 (1980).

61. In re Grand Jury Subpoena United States, 755 F.2d 1022 (2d Cir.1985), *vacated as moot,* 475 U.S. 133 (1986); United States v. Ammar, 714 F.2d 238 (3d Cir.), *cert. denied,* 464 U.S. 936 (1983); Appeal of Malfitano, 633 F.2d 276 (3d Cir.1980).

62. United States v. Archer, 733 F.2d 354 (5th Cir.), *cert. denied,* 469 U.S. 861 (1984).

63. The non-party spouse or the party spouse controls the privilege in ten states; the party spouse alone controls in one state; four states treat the non-party spouse as incompetent to testify. Uniform Rule 504 was amended in 1986 to codify the *Trammel* holding which restricts the privilege to the spouse of the accused.

64. *See, e.g.,* Cal.Evid.Code § 970; Del.R.Evid. 504; Fla.Stat.Ann. § 90.504. *See generally* 1 *Evidence in America* § 26.2.

65. United States v. Byrd, 750 F.2d 585, 590 (7th Cir.1984).

criminal litigants alike.[66] Finally, the adverse testimony privilege will protect the witness spouse from testifying even as to *acts* committed by the defendant spouse; by contrast, the confidential communications privilege will usually not prevent such testimony, since it applies only to private marital *communications* intended to be confidential.[67]

Confidential communications, made before a separation or divorce occurs, remain protected by the privilege even after termination of the marriage. However, several circuits have held that a marital separation destroys the communications privilege. Thus, any communications that occur after the separation are not protected by the privilege. The importance of the search for truth in a criminal trial supposedly outweighs the interest in protecting a separated couple's confidentiality.

The circuit courts differ on how to apply this exception. The Seventh Circuit has adopted a categorical rule: proof of a permanent separated status at the time of the communication renders the communication privilege automatically inapplicable.[68] The Second Circuit has indicated that the duration of physical estrangement is the guiding factor in determining "permanent separation," but allows either party to show special circumstances that render more or less likely the possibility of reconciliation at the time of the communication.[69] The Ninth Circuit follows a similar approach. If husband and wife are separated at the time of the communication, the court should undertake a more detailed inquiry into the irreconcilability of the marriage, considering all relevant circumstances such as the duration of the separation and the stability of the marriage at the time of the communication.[70] The Eighth Circuit has also adopted the permanent separation standard without elaboration.[71] Notably, all of these decisions involved criminal defendants. Whether this exception would apply to civil proceedings is still an open question.

66. *See* the 1986 version of Uniform Rule 504 (applicable in civil cases except when spouses are adverse parties). Some states limit the marital communication privilege to criminal proceedings. *See generally* 1 *Evidence in America* §§ 26.2–26.3.

67. Proposed Rule 505 did not recognize the confidential communication privilege. *See* Appendix B. This omission was criticized during the Congressional hearings on the Supreme Court's draft. Several states have adopted versions of Proposed Rule 505 which add a marital communication privilege.

68. United States v. Fulk, 816 F.2d 1202 (7th Cir.1987); United States v. Byrd, 750 F.2d 585 (7th Cir.1984). Declining to become involved in such a difficult factual inquiry, the *Byrd* court rejected the argument that where communications are made in a "deteriorated marriage," the privilege cannot apply.

69. In re Witness Before Grand Jury, 791 F.2d 234 (2d Cir.1986).

70. United States v. Roberson, 859 F.2d 1376 (9th Cir.1988) (distinguishing prior cases involving estranged couples).

71. United States v. Frank, 869 F.2d 1177 (8th Cir.) (citing above cases from Ninth, Seventh, and Second Circuits), *cert. denied,* 110 S.Ct. 121 (1989).

Federal courts widely agree that the "joint participants" exception applies to the confidential communications privilege. Eight circuits have ruled that communications between spouses pertaining to ongoing or future criminal activity are not protected against disclosure by the marital communication privilege.[72] The Sixth Circuit narrowly construes this exception, limiting it to only those conversations that pertain to "patently illegal activity." [73] The Fourth Circuit extends the exception to "statements made in the course of successfully formulating and commencing joint participation in criminal activity." [74] Two circuits disagree as to statements made after the crime is committed. The Tenth Circuit holds that the exception applies when the spouse participates in the "fruits" of the crime or covers up evidence thereof.[75] Reaching a somewhat different result, the Second Circuit allows the privilege even if the spouse is an accessory after the fact.[76]

The refusal to codify privileges under the Federal Rules was widely-criticized. However, federal courts, utilizing "reason and experience," have demonstrated both the predictability inherent in a common law system and the flexibility of the common law to respond to changes in social values and attitudes. Proposed Rule 505 would have abolished the marital confidential communications privilege and restricted the adverse testimony privilege to the criminal defendant. Yet the Supreme Court in *Trammel* reaffirmed the vitality of the confidential communications privilege and placed the decision to invoke spousal immunity exclusively in the hands of the testifying spouse. The circuit courts have further defined the contours of these privileges so as to present no substantial problems in their application.

Parent–Child Privilege. Because Federal Rule 501 provides for the creation of new privileges, some have urged the adoption of a parent-child privilege to further protect family privacy. Such a privilege was not recognized at common law and apparently was not seriously considered by the drafters of the Federal Rules. Proponents of the parent-child privilege support their arguments by policies similar to those

72. *See, e.g.,* United States v. Parker, 834 F.2d 408 (4th Cir.1987), *cert. denied,* 485 U.S. 938 (1988); United States v. Estes, 793 F.2d 465 (2d Cir.1986); United States v. Picciandra, 788 F.2d 39 (1st Cir.), *cert. denied,* 479 U.S. 936 (1983); United States v. Keck, 773 F.2d 759 (7th Cir.1985); United States v. Sims, 755 F.2d 1239 (6th Cir.), *cert. denied,* 473 U.S. 907 (1985); United States v. Harrelson, 754 F.2d 1153 (5th Cir.), *cert. denied,* 474 U.S. 908 (1985); United States v. Neal, 743 F.2d 1441 (10th Cir.1984), *cert. denied,* 470 U.S. 1086 (1985); United States v. Ammar, 714 F.2d 238 (3d Cir.), *cert. denied,* 464 U.S. 936 (1983). The marital privilege also does not protect those conversations made in furtherance of a conspiracy. *See* United States v. Malekzadeh, 855 F.2d 1492 (11th Cir.1988), *cert. denied,* 489 U.S. 1024 (1989).

73. *United States v. Sims,* 755 F.2d at 1243.

74. *United States v. Parker,* 834 F.2d at 413 n. 9 (declining to follow *Estes,* 793 F.2d at 466, to extent it holds contrary).

75. *United States v. Neal,* 743 F.2d at 1446.

76. *United States v. Estes,* 793 F.2d at 466 (declining to follow *Neal*).

underlying the marital privileges, including the promotion of family harmony and unity.[77]

Only three states have a statutory parent-child privilege. In Idaho and Minnesota, parents cannot be forced to reveal certain communications from their minor children in civil or criminal cases.[78] In Massachusetts minor children who live at home are disqualified from testifying against their parents in criminal proceedings.[79] Most state courts which have considered the issue have declined to recognize a parent-child privilege,[80] while only a few, mostly in New York, have adopted it.[81]

Federal courts likewise have overwhelmingly refused to create a parent-child privilege. Each of the circuit courts which have considered the claimed parent-child or "family" privilege have rejected it.[82] Only two federal courts have recognized or applied the privilege.[83] Widespread acceptance of the parent-child privilege seems unlikely at this time. However, with the flexibility of Rule 501, federal courts may embrace a limited form of the privilege, especially if it proves workable in state jurisdictions.

Other Family Privileges. The marital privileges apply only to valid marriages. Courts have refused to recognize either privilege for common-law, or "live-in," arrangements.[84] Other types of "family" privileges that go beyond the marital and parental relationships also have

77. *See generally,* Note, *Parent–Child Loyalty and Testimonial Privilege,* 100 Harv.L. Rev. 910 (1987) (strong and supportive parent-child bonds are centrally important to society and should be protected by testimonial privilege). *But see* Schlueter, *The Parent Child Privilege: A Response to Calls for Adoption,* 19 St. Mary's L.J. 35 (1987) (opposes codification of parent-child privilege).

78. *See* Idaho Code § 9–203(7) (Supp.1986); Minn.Stat.Ann. § 595.02(i) (West 1986). Neither statute permits a child to refuse to testify against a parent.

79. *See* Mass.Ann.Laws. ch. 233, § 20 (Law.Co-op.Supp.1987).

80. *See, e.g.,* State v. Willoughby, 532 A.2d 1020 (Me.1987); Hope v. State, 449 So.2d 1319 (Fla.Dist.Ct.App.1984).

81. *See* People v. Fitzgerald, 422 N.Y.2d 309 (Westchester County Ct.1979). All New York cases involve the protection of confidential communications *from* the child *to* the parent.

82. *See, e.g.,* In re Grand Jury Proceedings of John Doe, 842 F.2d 244 (10th Cir.), *cert. denied,* 488 U.S. 894 (1988); United States v. Davies, 768 F.2d 893 (7th Cir.), *cert. denied,* 474 U.S. 1008 (1985); Port v. Heard, 764 F.2d 423 (5th Cir.1985); United States v. Ismail, 756 F.2d 1253 (6th Cir.1985); In re Grand Jury Subpoena of Santarelli, 740 F.2d 816 (11th Cir.1984).

83. In re Agosto, 553 F.Supp. 1298 (D.Nev.1983); In re Grand Jury Proceedings, 11 Fed.R.Evid.Serv. 579 (1982).

84. *See, e.g.,* United States v. Lustig, 555 F.2d 737 (9th Cir.) (neither marital privilege applied for couple living together but not legally married, where common-law marriages not valid in Alaska), *cert. denied,* 434 U.S. 926 (1977); United States v. White, 545 F.2d 1129 (8th Cir.1976) (no privilege for defendant and alleged common-law wife, where state did not recognize common-law marriages); State v. Watkins, 126 Ariz. 293, 614 P.2d 835 (1980) (no privilege where couple living together in "de facto" marriage).

little prospect of judicial or legislative recognition.[85] Beyond the most intimate forms of family relationships, the courts and legislatures apparently believe there is no compelling interest to justify limiting the truth-finding process.

Physician–Patient and Psychotherapist–Patient Privileges

There is no general recognition of a physician-patient privilege under federal common law.[86] Neither is there any federal statutory law recognizing such a privilege.[87] Nevertheless, a majority of the states have enacted statutory privileges for physician-patient relationships.[88] Thus, under the mandates of Rule 501, the state privileges often *must* be applied by federal courts exercising diversity jurisdiction.[89] And they *may* be applied in federal law or criminal cases if, "in light of reason and experience," the courts decide to make them part of the federal common law.[90]

85. *See, e.g.,* In re Matthews, 714 F.2d 223 (2d Cir.1983) (no family privilege to avoid incriminating in-laws).

86. Wei v. Bodner, 127 F.R.D. 91 (D.N.J.1989); In re Grand Jury Proceedings, 876 F.2d 562 (9th Cir.), *cert. denied sub. nom,* Doe v. United States, 867 U.S. ——, 110 S.Ct. 265 (1989) ("When Congress chose not to enact the physician-patient privilege, it may not have been aware that that privilege did not have common law foundations.") (*citing* S.Rep. No. 93–1277, 93rd Cong., 2d Sess. (1974), *reprinted in* 1974 U.S.Code Cong. & Admin.News, 7051, 7059); United States v. Corona, 849 F.2d 562 (11th Cir.1988), *cert. denied,* 489 U.S. 1084 (1989); Slaken v. Porter, 737 F.2d 368, 377 (4th Cir.1984), *cert. denied,* 470 U.S. 1035 (1985); In re Doe, 711 F.2d 1187 (2d Cir.1983) (the physician-patient privilege was unknown at federal common law).

The privilege was not recognized at common law because "the considerations which relate to physicians and their patients do not require that an exception should be made to the general liability of all persons to give testimony upon all facts that are the subject of legitimate inquiry in the administration of justice." Recent Decisions, *The Psychotherapist–Patient Privilege in Federal Courts,* 59 Notre Dame L.Rev. 791, 795 (1984) (*citing* United States v. Kansas City Lutheran Home & Hosp. Ass'n., 297 F.Supp. 239, 244 (W.D. Mo.1969)).

But see In re Zuniga, 714 F.2d 632 (6th Cir.1983), *cert. denied,* 464 U.S. 983 (1983), (recognizing a psychotherapist-patient privilege under federal common law).

87. However, such a privilege has been asserted under the fifth amendment right against self-incrimination and the first amendment right of privacy. United States v. Layton, 90 F.R.D. 520, 523 (D.C.Cal.1981) (although the court did not recognize a psychotherapist-patient privilege under federal common law, it noted that the defendant's rights to privacy vis-a-vis his psychiatric records outweighed the government's need for the information).

Proposed Rule 504 would have created a psychotherapist-patient privilege, but not a general physician-patient privilege. *See* Appendix B.

88. Note, *The Ohio Physician–Patient Privilege: Modified, Revised, and Defined,* 49 Ohio St.L.J. 1147, 1148 (1989). *See generally* Rule 504 Advisory Committee Note, 56 F.R.D. 183, 242 (1973).

89. Erie R.R. v. Tompkins, 304 U.S. 64 (1938) (state privilege should apply); Fed.R. Evid. 501.

90. *See* S.Rep. No. 1277, 93rd Cong. 2d Sess. n. 17, *reprinted in* 1974 U.S.Code Cong. & Admin.News 7051, 7059. As Congress noted: "It should be clearly understood that, in

Generally, the privilege belongs to the patient and extends only to confidential communications from the patient to the physician made in the course of a visit seeking diagnosis or treatment.[91] Under the majority rule, the privilege is waived whenever the patient makes an issue of the patient's medical condition and the privileged communication is relevant.[92] Two minority views, however, hold that there is no automatic waiver upon the filing of a lawsuit. Under one view, there is no waiver until the patient testifies or proffers the physician's testimony at trial. Under a second minority view, the filing of a lawsuit creates a limited waiver of the privilege for discovery purposes, but prohibits any use of the privileged matter until the plaintiff testifies at trial.[93]

approving the general rule [Rule 501] as to privileges, the action of Congress should not be understood as disapproving any recognition of . . . the enumerated privileges contained in the Supreme Court [proposed] rules"; Note, *The Case For a Federal Psychotherapist–Patient Privilege That Protects Patient Identity,* 1985 Duke L.J. 1217, 1220: "The rationale for eliminating the several enumerated privileges in favor of a broad general rule is consistent with an expansive rather than a restrictive view of the role of the federal courts in recognizing evidentiary privileges." *But cf.* In re Grand Jury Proceedings, 867 F.2d 562 (9th Cir.) ("[W]e note that the Hippocratic tradition of physician non-disclosure of patient secrets is ancient; we decline to reach the merits of the efficiency of the . . . privilege by this holding. If it is to be recognized in federal criminal proceedings, it is up to Congress to define it—not the court"), *cert. denied sub. nom.* Doe v. United States, — U.S. ——, 110 S.Ct. 265 (1989); Herbert v. Lando, 441 U.S. 153 (1979) ("Evidentiary privileges in litigation are not favored"); United States v. Nixon, 418 U.S. 683, 711 (1974) ("Whatever their origins, these exceptions to the demand for everyman's evidence are not lightly created nor expansively construed").

91. Sipes v. United States, 111 F.R.D. 59, 61 (S.D.Cal.1986) ("[I]t is only 'confidential communications' from the patient to the physician that are privileged prior to the initiation of the lawsuit. The Physician's measurement and observation, unaided by protected communications are never cloaked with the privilege").

The *Sipes* court also noted that it is improper to name treating physicians as expert witnesses where the physicians are in fact "percipient fact witnesses," and their information and opinions "should be freely accessible to both parties to . . . the litigation." *Id.* (*citing* Rule 26 of the Fed.R.Civ.Proc.).

92. Doe v. Eli Lilly & Co., 99 F.R.D. 126 (D.D.C.1983) (applying federal evidentiary rubric, the court held that the filing a malpractice suit which puts the plaintiff's medical condition at issue constitutes a waiver of the physician-patient privilege viv-a-vis the plaintiff's treating physicians); Thomsen v. Mayo Foundation, No. 4–84–1239 (D.Minn. 1986) (WL 9159). In this unreported decision, the district court held not only that the filing of a lawsuit that places the plaintiff's medical condition at issue constitutes waiver of the plaintiff's physician-patient privilege, but that it also allows for ex parte interviews of plaintiffs' treating physicians by defense counsel under Fed.R.Evid. 501. *See also* Fed. R.Civ.P. 35.

93. Noggle v. Marshall, 706 F.2d 1408 (6th Cir.), *cert. denied,* 464 U.S. 1010 (1983). *See also* Urseth v. City of Dayton, Ohio, 653 F.Supp. 1057, 1063 (S.D.Ohio 1986) (there is no implied waiver by virtue of plaintiff having filed a lawsuit, applying privilege law).

There is also some disagreement whether the production of records will constitute waiver. For example, in Schuler v. United States, 113 F.R.D. 518, 521 (W.D.Mich.1986), the court held that the plaintiff had waived his physician-patient privilege when he produced his medical records on several occasions without asserting his privilege in writing as required under Michigan law.

The Advisory Committee's proposed rules did not recognize a physician-patient privilege and would, indeed, have precluded its assertion even in diversity actions based on state law in jurisdictions recognizing the privilege. But as noted, under Rule 501, the federal courts *must* apply the privilege in cases brought under state law and may choose to apply it even in cases brought under federal law or in criminal cases if "in light of reason and experience" the courts decide to make it a part of federal common law.[94]

Proposed Rule 504 would have recognized a "special case" of that privilege, namely a psychotherapist-patient privilege.[95] Without it, when a federal court is faced with a claim of that privilege, the court must fend for itself on a case-by-case basis under the generalized standards of Rule 501. And approaches by the federal courts to the question of a psychotherapist-patient privilege have varied, rendering conflicting results.[96]

Though the federal courts as a whole have not definitively recognized the privilege, many appear to be increasingly sympathetic to the

94. For detailed discussion of the proposed rules and Rule 501, see generally the Senate Judiciary Committee Report, at West's 1990 *Federal Rules of Evidence for United States Courts and Magistrates.*

95. Under Proposed Rule 504, the privilege would have extended to communications made by a person who "consults or is examined by or interviewed by" a psychotherapist, provided that the communication was not intended to be disclosed to persons other than "those present to further the interest of the patient" or persons necessary to transmit the communications to others participating in the diagnosis and treatment. The language used apparently would extend the privilege to statements made in "group therapy" sessions. The rule specifically would have provided that members of a patient's family could be included as persons participating in the diagnosis and treatment.

Exceptions were recognized for proceedings for hospitalization, for communications made in the course of a court-ordered examination, and for cases where the patient asserts his own mental condition as part of a claim or defense (or, after the patient's death, if any party bases a claim or defense on that condition).

96. The federal district and circuit courts are divided as to the existence of a psychotherapist-patient privilege under federal common law. The Sixth and Seventh Circuits apparently recognize such a privilege. In re Pebsworth, 705 F.2d 261, 263 (7th Cir.1983); In re Zuniga, 714 F.2d 632 (6th Cir.), *cert. denied,* 464 U.S. 983 (1983). However, the Fifth, Ninth, and Eleventh Circuits appear to refuse to recognize the privilege. U.S. v. Meagher, 531 F.2d 752 (5th Cir.), *cert. denied,* 429 U.S. 853 (1976); In re Grand Jury Proceedings, 867 F.2d 562 (9th Cir.), *cert. denied sub. nom.,* Doe v. United States, —— U.S. ——, 110 S.Ct. 265 (1989); United States v. Corona, 849 F.2d 562 (11th Cir.1988). And some districts and some circuits, such as the Second and Fourth Circuits, reach conflicting conclusions as to its existence. *Compare* Lora v. Board of Education, 74 F.R.D. 565 (E.D.N.Y.1972) (where it was found to be a matter of social policy to protect psychotherapist-patient confidences) with United States v. Witt, 542 F.Supp. 696 (S.D. N.Y.) *aff'd,* 697 F.2d 301 (2d Cir.1982) (where the court refused to recognize the privilege. *Compare also* Flora v. Hamilton, 81 F.R.D. 576 (M.D.N.C.1978) (though the action was brought under federal law, because the state recognized the psychotherapist-patient privilege, the court recognized a strong policy of comity between the state and federal jurisdictions, and thus allowed the privilege) with United States v. Brown, 479 F.Supp. 1247 (D.Md.1979) (where the court found no general psychotherapist-patient privilege exists to bar the production of documents under the federal rules of evidence).

assertion of such a privilege—though not perhaps going so far as to absorb Proposed Rule 504 into the federal common law.[97] Generally, courts that have refused to recognize the psychotherapist-patient privilege either equate it with the physician-patient privilege, ignoring judicial pronouncements that "confidentiality is a *sine qua non* for successful psychiatric treatment.[98] Or, they adhere to the Supreme Court's disfavor of evidentiary privileges in litigation because they are "in derogation of the search for the truth." [99]

Courts recognizing the privilege tend to follow the spirit of the Proposed Rules and Congressional acknowledgement that the breadth of Rule 501 is more consistent with an expansive—as opposed to a restrictive—view of the role of federal courts in recognizing evidentiary privileges.[100]

97. *See* Cunningham v. Southlake Center for Mental Health, Inc., 125 F.R.D. 474 (N.D. Ind.1989) (holding that neither state nor federal psychotherapist-patient privilege extends to a supervisor with master's degree in social work who was neither a medical doctor nor a licensed certified psychologist).

See generally Note, *The Case For a Psychotherapist–Patient Privilege That Protects Patient Identity,* 1985 Duke L.J. 1217; Comment, *The Psychotherapist–Patient Privilege Under Federal Rule 501,* 23 Washburn L.J. 706 (1984); Saltzburg, *Privileges and Professionals: Lawyers and Psychiatrists,* 66 Va.L.Rev. 597 (1980); Slovenko, *Psychiatry and A Second Look at the Medical Privilege,* 6 Wayne L.Rev. 175 (1960); and 1 Saltzburg & Martin, *Federal Rules of Evidence Manual* 423 (5th ed. 1990).

Like the physician-patient privilege, the psychotherapist-patient privilege raises questions concerning the waiver of the privilege. *For example,* in Sabree v. United Bhd. of Carpenters and Joiners of Am., 126 F.R.D. 422, 426 (D.Mass.1989), the court held that where a plaintiff did not place his mental condition directly at issue by making a claim of psychic injury or psychiatric disorder, but rather made an ordinary claim of emotional distress, the state psychotherapist-patient privilege was not waived. And in Simpson v. Braider, 104 F.R.D. 512 (D.D.C.1985), the court held that the privilege under the District of Columbia's law applies to communications from a psychiatrist or psychologist to parents of a penitent who was a minor at the time of treatment. The court also held that disclosures of therapist's names and dates and general purposes of treatment did not justify finding a waiver of the privilege.

98. Report No. 45, Group for the Advancement of Psychiatry 92 (1960) *quoted* in Advisory Committee's Notes to Proposed Rules, *supra.*

99. United States v. Nixon, *supra* note 5, 418 U.S. at 711.

Indeed, as one commentator has noted: "Privileges are not all equally important; they vary with the interests they protect and the policies they promote." Saltzburg, *supra* at 622.

100. United States v. Gillock, 445 U.S. 360, 368 (1980). Where the Supreme Court noted that Rule 501 "provide[s] the courts with greater flexibility in developing rules of privilege on a case-by-case basis."

Courts recognizing the privilege also tend to find support in social policy which encourages the mentally disabled to seek help. Cunningham v. Southlake Center for Mental Health Inc., 125 F.R.D. 474 (N.D.Ind.1989); Jennings v. D.H.L. Airlines, 101 F.R.D. 549, 550–551 (N.D.Ill.1984) ("Unlike the patient with physical complaints who will consult a physician regardless of whether confidentiality is guaranteed, a neurotic or psychotic individual may seek help only if he is assured that his confidences will not be divulged, even in a courtroom").

The relationship between the attorney-client privilege and the psychotherapist-patient privilege has also caused concern—especially in cases in which the patient is a criminal defendant raising an insanity or other diminished capacity defense. Courts disagree whether a defendant-patient who offers psychiatric testimony waives the privilege for communications made to all psychiatrists who examined the defendant, or only to those communications made to psychiatrists actually called by the defendant to testify. Defendants have argued, with limited success, that communications made to psychiatrists consulted before trial fall within both the attorney-client and psychotherapist-patient privileges, and that if the defendant waives the medical privilege by producing a defense expert, this does not also waive the attorney-client privilege.[101] The proposed rules offer no guidance here.

Unfortunately, the lack of any federal codified scheme regarding either the physician-patient or the psychotherapist-patient [102] privilege has created confusion, a split among the federal circuits, and arguably disparate treatment for federal litigants. Thus, until Congress acts, or the Supreme Court grants certiorari, federal courts and federal litigants are confined to the courts' "reason and experience."

Political Vote Privilege

Many states, either on a common-law or statutory basis, recognize an individual's privilege to refuse to testify as to his lawful vote in a public election conducted by secret ballot.[103] Indeed, it has been sug-

Some courts use a balancing test, weighing the need for the information against the importance of the confidential relationship and the likelihood that recognizing the privilege will in fact protect confidentiality. Ryan v. C.I.R., 568 F.2d 531, 543 (7th Cir. 1977), *cert. denied,* 439 U.S. 820 (1978).

101. *See* United States v. Layton, 90 F.R.D. 520 (D.C.Cal.1981), where the court held that the attorney-client privilege would shield disclosure of a tape recording of a conversation between the defendant and a psychiatrist because the tapes were made at least in part for purposes of obtaining legal advice.

However, other courts hold that once the psychotherapist privilege is waived, this precludes assertion of the attorney-client privilege. Edney v. Smith, 425 F.Supp. 1038 (S.D.N.Y.1976) (defendant waived privilege when he offered his own testimony), *aff'd mem.,* 556 F.2d 556, *cert. denied,* 431 U.S. 958 (1977).

And at least one court has held that the use of statements made by a defendant to psychiatrist during a psychiatric consultation in preparation for trial, is not precluded by the attorney-client privilege where the defendant talked to the psychiatrist without any expectation of privacy. United States v. Alvarez, 519 F.2d 1036 (3d Cir.1975).

102. However, almost every state, the District of Columbia, Puerto Rico and the United States Military has recognized some form of a psychotherapist- or psychologist-patient privilege. *See generally* Annot., 44 A.L.R.3d 24 (1972). Since each jurisdiction's privilege statute differs in scope and applicability, each statute should be analyzed to determine whether the privilege attaches to a given situation.

103. Among the jurisdictions with Federal Rules-based codes, Alaska, Arkansas, Delaware, Hawaii, Idaho, Maine, Nebraska, Nevada, New Mexico, North Dakota, Oklahoma, South Dakota, Texas, Wisconsin and the military have codified this privilege. *See* 1 *Evidence in America* § 28.2.

gested that the "secret of the ballot" may have constitutional overtones.[104] Perhaps because the important role this privilege plays in our elective system is widely recognized,[105] and because cases are rare in which the content of a citizen's vote would satisfy the relevance standard of Rule 401, or otherwise be discoverable under Federal Rule of Civil Procedure 26(b), there appear to be no reported federal cases addressing this privilege. Accordingly, this privilege has not proved significant in the litigation process,[106] and the uncodified status of this privilege has not presented problems for the federal courts. Nor do there appear to be any reported decisions of the state courts applying this privilege.[107] Arguably, the only situation in which the tenor of an individual's vote would be relevant would be a case of voter fraud, which clearly falls outside the protection of this privilege.[108]

Governmental Privileges

"Governmental privileges" encompass a variety of privileges which may be asserted by the government or a governmental agency. The federal courts ordinarily recognize the following governmental privileges: (a) a state secrets privilege; (b) a deliberative process privilege covering predecisional governmental communications connected with the development of policy; (c) an investigatory files privilege concerning information gathered in the course of an investigation; (d) an informant's privilege; and (e) an executive privilege covering communications between the President of the United States and his advisors.[109] While these governmental privileges differ substantively and procedurally, they all reflect a sensitivity to the separation of powers inherent

104. *See, e.g.,* United States v. Executive Committee of Democratic Party, 254 F.Supp. 543, 546 (N.D.Ala.1966) ("the secrecy of the ballot is one of the fundamental civil liberties upon which a democracy must rely most heavily in order for it to survive").

105. *See, e.g.,* Nutting, *Freedom of Silence; Constitutional Protection Against Government Intrusions in Political Affairs,* 47 Mich.L.Rev. 181, 195 (1948) ("social interest in honest elections is of the greatest importance").

106. *See* Louisell & Mueller, *Federal Evidence* § 220 (1985).

107. *Cf.* Kaufman v. La Crosse City Board of Canvassers, 98 N.W.2d 422, 424 (Wis. 1959) (a voter may waive his right of secrecy and reveal how he voted).

108. *See, e.g.,* Moffat v. Township of Princeton, 361 A.2d 74, 78 (N.J.Sup.1976) (it is possible in the case of illegal voting to compel disclosure of how an individual voted). This case involved an election contest in which a malfunctioning voting machine resulted in the rejection of legal votes. In dicta, the court noted that since the legality of the votes was not in question, voters would have possessed the privilege against disclosing the tenor of their votes. *Id.* at 78.

109. Some statutes also make specific provision for the confidentiality of certain kinds of information, usually in the context of protecting the confidentiality of reports made to the government. *See, e.g.,* Labor Management Relations Act, 29 U.S.C. § 181(a); Federal Aviation Act, 49 U.S.C. § 1441(e). Rule 501 of the Federal Rules of Evidence is not intended to affect the operation or effect of these statutorily-created privileges, for the Rule's federal common law standard is qualified with a savings clause stating "[e]xcept as otherwise . . . provided by Act of Congress". Fed.R.Evid. 501.

in the federal system and a concern that the judicial branch not unnecessarily impede the essential working of the other branches of the government.

Despite Congressional rejection of Proposed Rule 509, the common law concerning government privileges has been significantly affected by the Freedom of Information Act ("FOIA"), 5 U.S.C. § 552. In particular, to effectuate a policy of broad disclosure, FOIA requires government agencies to afford individuals access to documents unless a document is specifically exempted by the exceptions in the Act.[110] Because some of the FOIA exemptions correspond with the common law governmental privileges, litigation under FOIA has occasioned decisions concerning the disclosure of government documents that provide guidance on the scope of various governmental privileges.[111]

Although precedents interpreting FOIA exemptions are useful to an analysis of governmental privileges, the Supreme Court has admonished that the discovery rules can only be applied under FOIA "by way of rough analogy." [112] For example, documents which might be protected from FOIA disclosure as pre-decisional documents under Exemption 5, may be ordered disclosed in litigation because of a compelling need on the part of a litigant.[113] Conversely, it is possible that information disclosed under FOIA may, in some instances, be precluded from trial because the public interest may justify *access* to agency records, but will limit the *use* of that information in litigation.

The State Secrets Privilege

The state secrets privilege has a long tradition of acceptance by the courts and was given its modern formulation in *United States v. Reynolds,* 345 U.S. 1 (1953). The Court explained this privilege as follows:

> [T]he privilege belongs to the Government and must be asserted by it; it can neither be claimed nor waived by a private party. It is not to be lightly invoked. There must be a formal claim of privilege, lodged by the head of the department which has control over the matter, after actual personal consideration by that officer. The court must itself determine whether the circumstances are appropriate for the claim of privilege, and yet do so without forcing a disclosure of the very thing the privilege is designed to protect.[114]

The FOIA counterpart of the state secrets privilege is Exemption 1, which excludes from disclosure those documents:

110. Jordan v. United States Dept. of Justice, 591 F.2d 753, 755–56 (D.C.Cir.1978).

111. McClelland v. Andrus, 606 F.2d 1278, 1287 n. 54 (D.C.Cir.1979).

112. Environmental Protection Agency v. Mink, 410 U.S. 73, 8 (1973).

113. N.L.R.B. v. Sears, Roebuck & Co., 421 U.S. 132, 148–49 (1975).

114. United States v. Reynolds, 345 U.S. at 7–8.

(A) specifically authorized under criteria established by an Executive order to be kept secret in the interest of national defense or foreign policy and

(B) are in fact properly classified pursuant to such an Executive order. . . ."

5 U.S.C. § 552(b)(1). The justification for this privilege is the protection of national security concerns, including defense secrets, intelligence capabilities and diplomatic relations.[115]

When properly invoked, the state secrets privilege is absolute and cannot be compromised by any showing of need by the party seeking the information.[116] Because this privilege is absolute when correctly invoked, the courts often scrutinize whether the privilege has been properly invoked by examining documents *in camera.*[117] On the other hand, neither FOIA nor the common law require *in camera* review, so with respect to certain claims involving military security, even *in camera* review of the information involved may be inappropriate.[118] It would seem the courts have not experienced difficulty looking at the particular facts and circumstances before them and determining whether *in camera* examinations should be conducted to assess whether the privilege has been properly invoked. Moreover, where it is possible to "separate out" classified materials from less sensitive but relevant information, the courts can and will do so.[119]

115. Ellsberg v. Mitchell, 709 F.2d 51, 57 (D.C.Cir.1983), *cert. denied,* 465 U.S. 1038 (1984).

116. Northrop Corp. v. McDonnell Douglas Corp., 751 F.2d 395, 399 (D.C.Cir.1984); Ellsberg v. Mitchell, 709 F.2d at 57. The Supreme Court described the absolute nature of this privilege as follows:

> Where there is a strong showing of necessity [for the allegedly privileged information], the claim of privilege should not be lightly accepted, *but even the most compelling necessity cannot overcome the claim of privilege if the court is ultimately satisfied that military secrets are at stake.* [Emphasis added.]

117. United States v. Reynolds, 345 U.S. at 11 (emphasis added). It is well accepted that *in camera* review is available to assess whether the common law privilege for state secrets is properly invoked. *See* Northrop Corp. v. McDonnell Douglas, 751 F.2d at 401; Ellsberg v. Mitchell, 709 F.2d at 61; U.S. v. Kampiles, 609 F.2d 1233, 1248 (7th Cir.1979), *cert. denied,* 446 U.S. 954 (1980). Similarly, FOIA provides the option of *in camera* review to assess whether the documents in dispute have been properly classified. Alfred A. Knopf, Inc. v. Colby, 509 F.2d 1362, 1367 (4th Cir.), *cert. denied,* 421 U.S. 908 (1975).

118. Northrop Corp. v. McDonnell Douglas, 751 F.2d at 401. As the Supreme Court stated:

> It may be possible to satisfy the court from all the circumstances of the case, that there is a reasonable danger which in the interest of national security, should not be divulged. When this is the case, the occasion for the privilege is appropriate, and *the court should not jeopardize the security which the privilege is meant to protect by insisting upon an examination of the evidence even by the judge alone in his chambers.*

United States v. Reynolds, 345 U.S. at 9 (emphasis added).

119. Ellsberg v. Mitchell, 709 F.2d at 57.

To assist the courts in using classified information, Congress passed the Classified Information Procedures Act ("CIPA") in 1980. 18 U.S.C. App. §§ 1–16 (1982). CIPA applies to criminal trials and addresses the use of "graymail," a tactic where the defense alleges the need to discover or use classified information in order to pressure the prosecution into dropping the case.[120] CIPA therefore addresses situations where the defendant seeks to discover classified information or reasonably expects to disclose classified information during the course of the defense.[121] In particular, CIPA creates a pretrial procedure for ruling upon the admission of classified information and authorizes several procedures which will safeguard the classified information from public disclosure, yet make such information available for use at trial.[122] Such procedures include the substitution of summaries of classified information or statements admitting the facts that the classified information would tend to prove.[123]

Deliberative Process Privilege

The deliberative process privilege protects the "consultative functions" of government by maintaining the confidentiality of the opinions and recommendations expressed by government personnel in the formulation of government policies or decisions.[124] The deliberative process privilege is often addressed in the context of FOIA Exemption 5, which exempts from disclosure:

> inter-agency or intra-agency memorandum or letters which would not be available by law to a party other than an agency in litigation with an agency.

120. United States v. Sarkissian, 841 F.2d 959, 965 (9th Cir.1988); S.Rep. No. 823, 96th Cong., 2d Sess. 4, *reprinted in* 1980 U.S.Code Cong. & Admin.News 4294, 4297.

121. CIPA was used extensively in the widely followed trial of Colonel Oliver North. *See* United States v. North, 708 F.Supp. 389 (D.D.C.1988) and United States v. North, 708 F.Supp. 399 (D.D.C.1988), *aff'd in relevant part,* 910 F.2d 843 (D.C.Cir.1990).

122. United States v. Zettl, 835 F.2d 1059, 1062–63 (4th Cir.1987).

123. *See* 18 U.S.C.App. § 6(c). Pursuant to CIPA and a government request, one trial court permitted a procedure denominated "the silent witness rule." United States v. Zettl, 835 F.2d at 1063. Under this rule, the witness will not discuss classified information in open court. Rather, the witness, along with the judge, the counsel and the jury, will have copies of the classified document so that classified information can be referenced by its location within the document. *Id.* The result of this method is to permit the use of classified information by the defendant while preventing the information from being made public.

124. Although the courts commonly refer to this privilege as the "deliberative process" privilege, it has also been referred to as the "official information" privilege, the "executive" privilege, and the "governmental" privilege. Gomez v. City of Nashua, 126 F.R.D. 432, 434 (D.N.H.1989); Zinker v. Doty, 637 F.Supp. 138, 140 (D.Conn.1986). Moreover, federal courts have applied this privilege to the deliberative functions of state agencies. *See* Moorhead v. Lane, 125 F.R.D. 680, 685 (C.D.Ill.1989) (the court refers to this privilege as an "executive predecisional deliberative process privilege").

5 U.S.C. § 552(b)(5) (1988). This privilege serves to preserve the quality of agency decisions by encouraging open discussions in connection with policy-making and to protect the integrity of the decision-making process by confirming that officials will be judged by what they decide, not what they considered before making a decision.[125]

This privilege is limited to materials that are both predecisional and connected with the deliberative process.[126] Because the privilege applies only to materials that are predecisional, when opinions and recommendations become the actual and effective policy of an agency, they—and any other post-decisional communications—are no longer privileged.[127]

In addressing the requirement of a connection with the "deliberative process," the courts have held that to be protected by the privilege, information must "reflect the give-and-take of the consultative process." [128] Accordingly, factual matters, as opposed to opinions, are not protected if they can be separated from the opinions and recommendations.[129]

Unlike the state secrets privilege, the deliberative process privilege is not absolute, even when properly invoked.[130] Thus, when material is covered by the deliberative process privilege, the court must assess whether to order disclosure by balancing the litigant's need for the report against the agency's need to protect its deliberative process.[131] This balancing process is generally conducted in an *in camera* inspection of the documents, with the court assessing such factors as:

(1) the relevance of the evidence sought to be protected;

(2) the availability of other evidence;

(3) the seriousness of the litigation and the issues involved;

(4) the role of the government in the litigation; and

125. NLRB v. Sears, Roebuck & Co., 421 U.S. 132 (1975); Jordan v. United States Dept. of Justice, 591 F.2d 753, (D.C.Cir.1978); Carl Zeiss Stiftung v. V.E.B. Carl Zeiss, Jena, 40 F.R.D. 318 (D.D.C.), *aff'd*, 384 F.2d 979 (D.C.Cir.), *cert. denied*, 389 U.S. 952 (1966); Kaiser Aluminum & Chemical Corp. v. United States, 157 F.Supp. 939 (Ct.Cl. 1958).

126. Formaldehyde Inst. v. Dept. of Health and Human Serv., 889 F.2d 1118, 1121 (D.C.Cir.1989); Wolfe v. Dept. of Health and Human Serv., 839 F.2d 768, 774 (D.C.Cir. 1988) (en banc).

127. Wolfe v. Dept. of Health and Human Serv., 839 F.2d at 774. *See also* 5 U.S.C. § 552(a)(2)(A)–(B); NLRB v. Sears Roebuck and Co., 421 U.S. 132 (1975).

128. Coastal States Gas Corp. v. Department of Energy, 617 F.2d 854 (D.C.Cir.1980).

129. McClelland v. Andrus, 606 F.2d 1278, 1287–1289 (D.C.Cir.1979); EPA v. Mink, 410 U.S. 73, 91 (1973). Furthermore, the courts do not "mechanically apply the fact/opinion test," but make their determination by considering the policies underlying the privilege. Wolfe v. Dept. of Health and Human Services, 839 F.2d at 774–76.

130. McClelland v. Andrus, 606 F.2d 1278 (D.C.Cir.1979); Gomez v. City of Nashua, N.H., 126 F.R.D. 432 (D.N.H.1989).

131. *Id.*

(5) the possibility of future timidity by government employees who will be forced to recognize that their secrets are voilable.[132]

Indeed, a recent bankruptcy decision uses just such an analysis in requiring disclosure of information over a claim of protection under the "bank examination privilege," a privilege claim which the court analyzed in terms of the deliberative process privilege.[133]

The Investigatory Files Privilege

The investigatory files privilege covers materials gathered and used in connection with law enforcement.[134] This privilege has often been construed in the context of FOIA Exemption 7, which exempts from mandatory disclosure:

> records or information compiled for law enforcement purposes, but only to the extent that the production of such law enforcement records or information (A) could reasonably be expected to interfere with enforcement proceedings, (B) would deprive a person of a right to a fair trial or an impartial adjudication, (C) could reasonably be expected to constitute an unwarranted invasion of personal privacy, (D) could reasonably be expected to disclose the identity of a confidential source . . . information furnished only by the confidential source, (E) would disclose techniques and procedures for law enforcement investigations . . ., or (F) could reasonably be expected to endanger the life or physical safety of any individual.

5 U.S.C. § 552(b)(7) (1988). The policy behind the privilege is the need to protect the law enforcement process, because disclosure could undercut prosecution efforts by disclosing investigative techniques, forewarning suspects, deterring witnesses from coming forward and prematurely revealing the facts of the government's case.

The burden of persuasion is upon the government[135] and the proper party to assert the privilege is the relevant agency or the individual department head.[136] The investigatory files privilege is not

132. Zinker v. Doty, 637 F.Supp. 138, 141 (D.Conn.1986).

133. In re SunRise Securities Litigation, 109 B.R. 658 (E.D.Pa.1990).

134. This privilege is generally called the "law enforcement investigatory files" privilege. Friedman v. Bache Halsey Stuart Shields, Inc., 738 F.2d 1336, 1341 (D.C.Cir. 1984). For a general discussion of this privilege, see Association for Reduction of Violence v. Hall, 734 F.2d 63 (1st Cir.1984); Black v. Sheraton Corp. of America, 564 F.2d 531 (D.C.Cir.1977).

135. *See, e.g.,* Smith v. FTC, 403 F.Supp. 1000 (D.Del.1975).

136. Friedman v. Bache Halsey Stuart Shields, Inc., 738 F.2d 1336, (D.C.Cir.1984); McClelland v. Andrus, 606 F.2d 1278, 1290 n. 59 (D.C.Cir.1979); Black v. Sheraton Corp. of America, 564 F.2d 531 (D.C.Cir.1977). Proposed Rule 509 would have altered this requirement and allowed any government lawyer to assert this privilege. It is not certain that all courts will insist that the agency head made the claim. Where it is clear that authority rests with a subordinate, courts may "in light of reason and experience" permit this person to make the privilege claim. Of course, in balancing competing

absolute and the government's need for confidentiality is measured against the private litigant's need for the allegedly privileged information.[137] The customary method of judicial evaluation of the validity of the assertion is an *in camera* inspection of the materials subject to the claim.[138] Among the factors which may militate against disclosure are a police officer's safety or privacy, the impact on the effectiveness of a law enforcement program, citizen candor and compliance with state privacy law.[139] Other factors which must be considered in determining whether disclosure is proper include the relevance of the information, the importance of the information to the case, and the public interest.[140] Moreover, a strong factor in favor of disclosure is the unavailability of information from other sources.[141]

It has been recognized in the FOIA context that, due to the vast amounts of written material that may be involved in such an inspection, it should be the task of the government to undertake the burdensome task of preparing these materials in such a form that the court may effectively focus on them.[142]

Informer–Identity Privilege

The informer-identity privilege generally refers to the government's privilege to withhold from disclosure the identity of persons who furnish information regarding violations or possible violations of the law to law enforcement officers. The purpose of this privilege is to further the public interest in effective law enforcement by encouraging citizens—through assurances of anonymity—to come forward with information and knowledge regarding the commission of crimes.[143]

The scope of the privilege is limited by its underlying purpose. Thus, only the informant's identity is privileged; communications to or by the informer which will not tend to reveal that identity are not.

interests, a court may take into account the responsibilities of the government officer asserting a privilege claim.

137. King v. Conde, 121 F.R.D. 180, 190–95 (E.D.N.Y.1988).

138. Kerr v. United States District Court, 426 U.S. 394, 405 (1976) ("[I]n camera review is a highly appropriate and useful means of dealing with claims of government privilege").

139. King v. Conde, *supra,* 121 F.R.D. at 190–94.

140. *Id.* at 194–95.

141. In re Franklin Nat. Bank Sec. Litig., 478 F.Supp. 577 (E.D.N.Y.1979). (Lists five factors to be balances.)

142. Frankenhauser v. Rizzo, 59 F.R.D. 339 (E.D.Pa.1973). In Vaughn v. Rosen, 484 F.2d 820 (D.C.Cir.1973), *cert. denied,* 415 U.S. 977 (1974), the Court of Appeals established detained procedures for indexing and itemizing materials incumbent upon the government in asserting the privilege as to a large quantity of documents allegedly exempt under the FOIA. *Accord.* Cuneo v. Schlesinger, 484 F.2d 1086 (D.C.Cir.1973), *cert. denied,* 415 U.S. 977 (1974).

143. Rovario v. United States, 353 U.S. 53 (1957); Dole v. Local 1942, IBEW, AFL–CIO, 870 F.2d 368 (7th Cir.1989).

Furthermore, once the informer's identity has been revealed to those whom the informer fears, the privilege disappears. The government possesses no absolute right to withhold informer's identities, and parties seeking disclosure never have an absolute right to disclosure. The issue is to be resolved by the court by balancing the competing public and private interests involved and:

> Where the disclosure of an informer's identity, or of the contents of his communication, is relevant and helpful to the defense of an accused, or is essential to a fair determination of a cause, the privilege must give way.[144]

Although this privilege commonly arises in the context of criminal actions, it is applicable in civil cases as well.[145] In fact, one court has suggested that the scope of the privilege is greater in a civil case because certain constitutional guarantees apply only to criminal defendants.[146]

In determining whether the facts and circumstances justify application of the privilege, *in camera* proceedings, sometimes including an interview of the informant, are common and proper.[147] Factors to be considered would include the nature of the charged crime, the possible defenses, the possible significance of the informer's testimony and the informer's degree of participation, if any, in the crime.[148]

Proposed Rule 510(c)(2) would have entitled the government to an *in camera* hearing and would have barred opposing counsel and parties from these proceedings. With the rejection of the proposed rules, these issues remain discretionary with the judge. The absence of codification has not created notable problems for the courts in applying this privilege, and in view of the constitutional issues permeating application of this privilege, it is doubtful that clarification other than by case law is feasible.

144. Rovario v. United States, 353 U.S. 53, 60–61 (1957).

145. *See, e.g.,* Hodgson v. Charles Martin Inspectors of Petroleum, Inc., 459 F.2d 303, 305 (5th Cir.1972) (the Fair Labor Standards Act); Westinghouse Electric Corp. v. Burlington, 351 F.2d 762, 769 (D.C.Cir.1965) (civil antitrust action); Bocchicchio v. Curtis Publishing Co., 203 F.Supp. 403, 407 (E.D.Pa.1962) (libel action). *But see* Brennan v. Automatic Toll Systems, Inc., 60 F.R.D. 195 (S.D.N.Y.1973) (rejecting informer's privilege in a civil case).

146. Dole v. Local 1942, IBEW, AFL–CIO, 870 F.2d 368 (7th Cir.1989).

147. Rovario v. United States, 353 U.S. 53, 60–61 (1957). *See also* United States v. Freund, 525 F.2d 873, 877 (5th Cir.), *cert. denied,* 426 U.S. 923 (1976); United States v. Doe, 525 F.2d 878 (5th Cir.), *cert. denied,* 425 U.S. 976 (1976); United States v. Lloyd, 400 F.2d 414 (6th Cir.1968); United States v. Rawlinson, 487 F.2d 5 (9th Cir.1973), *cert. denied,* 415 U.S. 984 (1974).

148. *Id.* at 62. United States v. Reardon, 787 F.2d 512, 517 (10th Cir.1986).

The Executive Privilege

The "executive privilege" that covers communications between the President of the United States and his advisors received a great deal of public attention when it was invoked during the Watergate crisis. In *United States v. Nixon,*[149] the Supreme Court recognized the constitutional underpinnings of the privilege but held that it was not unqualified and must yield "to the demonstrated specific need for evidence in a pending criminal trial." While of significant historical and political import, the executive privilege is of little significance in ordinary litigation. Important cases concerning it have arisen almost solely in the context of the Watergate affair. The fundamental constitutional basis and controversial nature of the executive privilege render it an unlikely subject for codification, and its limited applicability have limited the need for clarification of its parameters.

Trade Secrets

The House and Senate Conference Committee reports on the Federal Rules of Evidence indicate that the proposed trade secrets privilege did not give rise to any particular controversy.[150] Hence, it is generally accepted that the privilege proposed in Rule 508 adequately reflected the "principles of common law" referenced in Rule 501.[151]

The trade secrets "privilege," which protects the confidentiality of technological and other proprietary business secrets, is subject even more than most privileges to a balancing test.[152] It is widely recognized that there is no absolute privilege from disclosure of trade secrets,[153] and that courts should balance the requesting party's need for the information against the owner's need for secrecy.[154] For this reason,

149. 418 U.S. 683 (1974).

150. *See* Wearly v. F.T.C., 462 F.Supp. 589, 595 (D.N.J.1978) (discussing the trade secrets privilege and noting the sharply differing views on the inclusion of newsperson's shield law and the scope of other privileges), *cert. denied,* 449 U.S. 822 (1980).

151. *Id. See also* Friction Div. Products v. E.I. DuPont de Nemours, 658 F.Supp. 998, 1006 (D.Del.1987) (applying trade secrets privilege in a patent infringement case), *aff'd,* 883 F.2d 1027 (Fed.Cir.1989); Microwave Research Corp. v. Sanders Associates Inc., 110 F.R.D. 669, 672 (D.Mass.1986) (applying trade secrets privilege in action for misappropriation of trade secrets). *But see* Natta v. Zletz, 405 F.2d 99, 101 (7th Cir.1968), *cert. denied,* 395 U.S. 909 (1969) (no privilege barring discovery of trade secrets).

152. *See* Federal Open Market Committee v. Merrill, 443 U.S. 340, 362 (1979) (court must weigh claim to privacy against the need for disclosure); Coca–Cola Bottling Co. v. Coca–Cola Co., 107 F.R.D. 288, 293 (D.Del.1985) ("must balance the need for the information against the injury that would ensue if disclosure is ordered").

153. Friction Div. Products, 658 F.Supp. at 1006.

154. Coca–Cola Bottling Co., 107 F.R.D. at 292–93. "In order to resist discovery of a trade secret, a party must first demonstrate by competent evidence that the information sought through discovery is a trade secret and that disclosure of the secret might be harmful." *Id.* at 292. Once these requirements are met, the burden shifts to the

several courts and commentators suggest that the protection of trade secrets does not amount to a privilege at all.[155] Complete protection from disclosure is rare, and discovery usually is ordered once the information is shown to be relevant and necessary.[156] The courts generally endeavor to permit access to the sensitive information while controlling access to, and use of, that information so as to protect the legitimate interests of the resisting party.[157]

The uncodified status of this privilege has not created particular problems for the federal courts.[158] Regardless of whether it is labelled a "privilege," the policy of extending protection to trade secrets is uniformly recognized by the federal courts, and the broad language of proposed Rule 508 recognized the need for the fact-specific balancing reflected in the case law. Indeed this process is expressly provided for in Federal Rule of Civil Procedure 26(c)(7).[159]

In retrospect, it is mildly ironic that one of the stated purposes for adopting Rule 501 in lieu of proposed Rule 508 was the belief that federal law "should not supersede that of the states in substantive areas such as privilege absent a compelling reason." Since the adoption of Rule 501, fifteen states[160] have codified the trade secrets

requesting party to establish that the information sought is necessary and relevant to the action. If this is shown, the court will balance these competing interests. *Id.*

155. *See, e.g.,* Natta v. Zletz, 405 F.2d 99, 101 (7th Cir.1968), *cert. denied,* 395 U.S. 909 (1969); Davis v. General Motors Corp., 64 F.R.D. 420, 422 (N.D.Ill.1974); 4 J. Moore, *Federal Practice* § 26.60[4] (2d ed. 1982). Whether a court uses the label "privilege" appears to be of limited practical significance. In each of these cases the court recognized that the resisting party was entitled to protection against unnecessary disclosure, even though the court was reluctant to use the term "privilege."

156. *See, e.g.,* Federal Open Market Committee v. Merrill, 443 U.S. 340, 362 n. 24 (1979) ("orders forbidding any disclosure of trade secrets or confidential commercial information are rare"); St. Jude Medical, Inc. v. Intermedics, Inc., 107 F.R.D. 398, 400 (D.Minn.1985) (since trade secrets sought to be discovered were calculated to lead to admissible evidence information was discoverable); Pfeiffer v. K–Mart Corp., 106 F.R.D. 235, 236–37 (S.D.Fla.1985) (trade secrets discoverable since they were relevant to case).

157. *See, e.g.,* Centurion Industries, Inc. v. Warren Steurer, 665 F.2d 323, 326 (10th Cir.1981) (if trade secrets are deemed discoverable "the appropriate safeguards should attend their disclosure"); Struthers Scientific & International Corp. v. General Foods Corp., 45 F.R.D. 375, 378 (S.D.Tex.1968).

158. In contrast, the federal courts have applied differing definitions of a "trade secret" in the context of civil claims for misappropriation of trade secrets. *See, e.g.,* Sikes v. McGraw–Edison Co., 671 F.2d 150, 151 (5th Cir.1982) (recognizing that Texas law has "followed a course somewhat different" from other states in the area of trade secret actions), *cert. denied,* 458 U.S. 1108 (1982).

159. This rule provides that the court should issue a protective order to prevent the disclosure of a trade secret or to permit disclosure only in a designated way. *Id.*

160. Alaska, Arkansas, Delaware, Florida, Hawaii, Maine, Nebraska, Nevada, New Hampshire, New Mexico, North Dakota, Oklahoma, South Dakota, Texas, and Wisconsin adopted versions of the trade secrets privilege in their Federal Rules-based codes of evidence. There are no substantive differences in the wordings of the various rules. *See* 1 *Evidence in America* § 29.2.

privilege in substantially the same form submitted by the Advisory Committee. Thus, by allowing the states to supply the rule of privilege, the federal courts ironically often find themselves applying the very rule (in the form of state law) omitted from the Federal Rules of Evidence.

Journalist's Privilege

The proposed privilege Rules failed to include among them one for a reporter or journalist. See Appendix B. The Advisory Committee gave no reason for the omission.[161] This omission was one of the primary focuses of the Congressional review of the proposed evidentiary rules, stemming in part from the "nationwide discussions of the newspaperman's privilege." [162] Following testimony on behalf of groups such as the Reporter's Committee for Freedom of the Press,[163] the privilege rule was revised to eliminate the proposed specific rules on privileges and to leave the law of privilege in its current state to be developed by the federal courts.[164]

Given this backdrop, the courts through their "reason and experience" have provided journalists, under the First Amendment to the United States Constitution, a qualified privilege against disclosure of their newsgathering activities. As succinctly stated in *Loadholtz v. Fields,* 389 F.Supp. 1299 (M.D.Fla.1975):

> The concept of freedom of the press as guaranteed by the First Amendment is the keystone of our constitutional democracy and is broad enough to include virtually all activities for the press to fulfill its First Amendment functions.

Id. at 1300.

161. Advisory Committee's Notes. HR Doc. No. 46, 93d Cong., 1st Sess. 78 (1973).

162. Rules of Evidence, Hearings Before the House Special Subcommittee on Reform of Federal Criminal Laws of the Committee on the Judiciary, 93d Cong., 1st Sess. 5 (Rep. Holtzman).

163. *Id.* at 367.

164. S.Rep. No. 1277, 93d Cong., 2d Sess. 11 (1974); H.Rep. No. 650, 93d Cong., 1st Sess. 8 (1973).

The Third Circuit, in Matter of Grand Jury Impaneled January 21, 1975, 541 F.2d 373, 379 n. 11 (3rd Cir.1976), referred to the following comment by Congressman Hungate, the principal drafter of the Federal Rules of Evidence:

> For example, the Supreme Court's rule of evidence contained no rule of privilege for a newspaperperson. The language of Rule 501 permits the courts to develop a privilege for newspaperpeople on a case-by-case basis. The language cannot be interpreted as a congressional expression in favor of having no such privilege, nor can the conference action be interpreted as denying to newspaperpeople any protection they may have from State newsperson's privilege laws.

120 Cong.Rec.H. 12253–54 (daily ed. Dec. 18, 1974) (explaining the final Conference Report version of the Rules).

The seminal case is *Branzburg v. Hayes,*[165] where the Supreme Court expressly recognized that newsgathering by the media qualifies for First Amendment protection, emphasizing the "without some protection for seeking out the news, freedom of the press would be eviscerated."[166] Specifically, in *Branzburg,* the Court held in a four-one-four decision that a court could require a reporter to testify before a grand jury about a crime that the reporter had witnessed. However, Justice Powell, in casting the deciding fifth vote, stressed in a concurring opinion the limited holding of the Court: "[I]f the newsman is called upon to give information bearing only a remote or tenuous relationship to the subject of the investigation . . . he will have access to the court on a motion to quash and an appropriate protective order may be entered." [167]

Subsequent to the decision in *Branzburg,* the courts have broadly construed the scope of the reporter's first amendment qualified privilege. They have applied it to: (1) civil as well as criminal actions; [168] (2) non-confidential as well as confidential sources; [169] and (3) the mere fact gathering process of the reporter,[170] such that the privilege applies to a reporter's documents or resource materials as well as his or her testimony.[171]

Courts utilize a four-prong test to evaluate the privilege, holding that a reporter is protected from a subpoena unless:

(1) the information sought from the reporter is relevant and goes to the "heart of the case;"

(2) a compelling need exists for the information sought from the reporter;

(3) the party moving for disclosure from the reporter has exhausted other possible sources of information; and

(4) there is no alternative source for the information sought from the reporter.[172]

165. 408 U.S. 665 (1972).

166. *Id.* at 681.

167. *Id.* at 710 (Powell J., concurring).

168. *See, e.g.,* Zerilli v. Smith, 656 F.2d 705, 712 (D.C.Cir.1981); United States v. Cuthbertson, 630 F.2d 139 (3rd Cir.1980), *cert. denied,* 449 U.S. 1126 (1981); In re Consumer's Union of United States, Inc., 495 F.Supp. 582 (S.D.N.Y.1980); Loadholtz v. Fields, 389 F.Supp. 1299 (M.D.Fla.1975).

169. *See, e.g.,* Miller v. Mecklenburg County, 602 F.Supp. 675, 678 (W.D.N.C.1985); Loadholtz v. Fields, 389 F.Supp. 1299 (M.D.Fla.1975).

170. Palandjian v. Pahlavi, 11 Media L.Rep. (BNA) 1028 (D.D.C.1984).

171. *See, e.g.,* United States v. Cuthbertson, 630 F.2d 139, 147 (3rd Cir.1980), *cert. denied,* 449 U.S. 1126 (1981); Damico v. Lemen, 14 Media L.Rep. (BNA) 1031 (Fla.Cir.Ct. 1987); In re Consumer's Union of United States, Inc., 495 F.Supp. 582, 586 (S.D.N.Y.1980).

172. *See, e.g.,* Miller v. Transamerica Press, Inc., 621 F.2d 721, 725 (5th Cir.1980); Miller v. Mecklenburg County, 602 F.Supp. 675, 679 (W.D.N.C.1985); United States v.

The United States Department of Justice also recognizes these factors. The Attorney General has promulgated guidelines which provide that no subpoena shall be issued to a journalist under any circumstances unless:

> [There is] reasonable ground to believe that the information sought is essential to a successful investigation—particularly with reference to directly establishing guilt or innocence; "and" The government [has] unsuccessfully attempted to obtain the information from alternative nonmedia sources.

28 C.F.R. § 50.10(f)(1), (3). The Justice Department guidelines also provide that subpoenas to newsmen "should, except under exigent circumstance, be limited to the verification of published information and to such surrounding circumstances as relate to the accuracy of the published information." 28 C.F.R. § 50.10(f)(4).

Journalists' privileges have received extensive attention in the states, but generally outside their evidence codes.[173]

New Privileges

The federal courts have been reluctant to extend the scope of nonconstitutional privileges beyond the traditional types discussed above. Thus, the federal courts have rejected various purported privileges for bankers,[174] insurance companies,[175] accountants [176] and social workers.[177] Nonetheless, the recognition of both the journalist's privilege and of a parent-child privilege [178] demonstrate that some courts are not unwilling to permit growth in this field of the law. Furthermore, because many state law privileges not recognized under federal law are, under Rule 501, applicable in diversity cases, growth in the state laws of privilege will find their way into federal litigation and possibly into federal law. Thus, the federal law of privilege remains subject to broad change and development—plainly the intended result of Congress' decision to resist codification of the proposed rules.

Lance, 5 Media L.Rep. (DNA) 2306 (N.D.Ga.1979); United States v. Hubbard, 493 F.Supp. 202, 205 (D.D.C.1979), *cert. denied,* 102 S.Ct. 1971.

173. *See generally* 1 *Evidence in America* § 23.5.

174. Harris v. United States, 413 F.2d 316, 319 (9th Cir.1969); Rosenblatt v. Northwest Airlines, Inc., 54 F.R.D. 21, 23 (S.D.N.Y.1971).

175. Gottleib v. Bresler, 24 F.R.D. 371 (D.D.C.1959).

176. United States v. Wainwright, 413 F.2d 796, 802 (10th Cir.1969), *cert. denied,* 396 U.S. 1009 (1970); Himmelfarb v. United States, 175 F.2d 924 (9th Cir.), *cert. denied,* 338 U.S. 860 (1949); United States v. Schmidt, 343 F.Supp. 444 (M.D.Pa.1972).

177. Matter of Wood, 430 F.Supp. 41, 46 (S.D.N.Y.1977).

178. In re Grand Jury Proceedings (Witnesses Mary Agosto, et al.), 553 F.Supp. 1298 (D.Nev. January 4, 1983). *See discussion, supra,* of this privilege.

Summary

The law of privileges has developed smoothly under Rule 501. Congress believed that privileges were so important that the adoption of rules in this area was too important a task to be left to the Supreme Court alone. Ironically, Congress enacted a rule and a statute that resulted in the Supreme Court's having as much, if not more, control over privileges than it would have had if specific rules had been adopted along with the remainder of the Rules.

This is explained by Rule 501's direction to courts to apply the common law in light of reason and experience. In carrying out this directive, courts lost no time in looking to the proposed rules, the very rules that had the imprimatur of the Supreme Court, for guidance as to what the common law was. Consequently, the privilege rules that failed to receive Congressional approbation became nonetheless influential. This fact, coupled with the authority implicit in the grant to the courts—including the Supreme Court—to decide privilege questions in light of reason and experience, has afforded the Supreme Court the ability to mold the law of privileges as it has seen fit.

Had Congress adopted specific rules, it could have exercised some control over the scope of federal privileges. Of course, Congress has the authority to consider rules at any time, and the Supreme Court can resubmit privilege rules if it wishes. However, because of 28 U.S.C. § 2076, it is doubtful that the court will be in a hurry to draft rules. As a result, it appears that, in an effort to control the Supreme Court, Congress actually produced legislation that accomplished in practice what in theory Congress wished to avoid. Whether this is a welcome turn of fortune or something to be regretted may depend either upon one's view of the current state of the law or of which body, the Court or the Congress, is in a better position to formulate rules of privilege.

Whichever view is correct, it appears that the Supreme Court's formulation of basic privileges has provided useful guidance to lower courts. Even though the Court itself departed from its own proposed rule in deciding *Trammel,* and even though the proposed rules in places appear to depart from, rather than to track, the common law—e.g., in eliminating the marital communications privilege—the rules and the Advisory Committee's Notes have furnished ample material with which to begin research.

There is something to be said for codification of the basic privilege concepts. As this Discussion has noted, most of the cases appear to be falling into place. Through the process of adjudication, courts have been working to establish, define, refine and improve the law of privileges. The advantage afforded by some codification is that rules state more clearly than cases generally do the core concepts of various privileges; research into the different circuit and district court opinions becomes less necessary; and such rules might provide help in the areas touched upon in this Discussion that need clarification.

It is doubtful that rules could, or should, attempt to resolve all of the questions concerning privileges. Perhaps the lesson of the journalist's privilege is the importance of leaving a little room for privileges to be nurtured and for case-by-case development, particularly in the case of new privileges. With established privileges, however, identifying core doctrines and stating them clearly could help to avoid repetitive litigation on familiar points and to remove some uncertainty concerning the coverage of the privileges.

Whether or not privilege rules are codified, it appears that the trend is away from "absolute rules." The attorney client privilege and the marital privileges, while admitting of exceptions, are absolute when properly invoked and do not give way even to a strong showing of need by an adverse party. The clergy-penitent privilege also appears to be absolute, but is so rarely invoked that it is not very important in practice. In many jurisdictions the physician-patient privilege is more flexible. The governmental privileges (except perhaps for military secrets), the trade secrets privilege, and the journalist's privilege involve the balancing of competing interests and may be quite case-specific. Even if privilege rules are codified, it is doubtful that rules will make it very much easier for judges to balance one party's need for evidence against another's claimed need for privacy or secrecy.

APPENDIX I

ARTICLE VI. WITNESSES

Introduction

Article VI, which deals generally with the subject of witnesses, contains rules of three different sorts. First, it includes rules concerning witness competency. Rule 601 sets forth a liberal general rule of competency. Rule 602 refines this with a traditional statement of the rule requiring firsthand knowledge, carving out an exception for expert opinion testimony admissible under Rule 703. Rule 603 states the oath or affirmation requirement. Rule 604 specifically extends this requirement to interpreters. Rules 605 and 606 address, respectively, the competency of the judge or any juror to be a witness in any trial before either of them.

Second, Article VI includes impeachment rules. Rule 607 abolishes the common law "voucher" rule, permitting any party, including the party who calls a witness, to impeach that witness. Rule 608 addresses impeachment by evidence of character and conduct. Rule 609 covers impeachment by evidence of a criminal conviction. Rule 610 bars impeachment of a witness on the basis of his religious beliefs. Rule 613 deals with use of prior statements of witnesses.

Third, Article VI includes rules setting forth the trial court's role. Rule 611 places the mode and order of witness interrogation and evidence presentation within the discretion of the trial court. Rule 614 concerns interrogation of witnesses called by the court. Finally, Rule 615 deals with the exclusion of witnesses from the courtroom.

RULE 601

I. TEXT OF RULE

RULE 601. General Rule of Competency

Every person is competent to be a witness except as otherwise provided in these rules. However, in civil actions and proceedings with respect to an element of a claim or defense as to which State law supplies the rule of decision, the competency of a witness shall be determined in accordance with State law.

II. DISCUSSION

Rule 601 establishes a very strong presumption of witness competency. Indeed, although federal courts generally analyze competency questions in terms of their discretion to exclude testimony pursuant to Rule 601, this study has revealed no reported federal case upholding a challenge to a witness's competency based upon such once-accepted grounds as mental incapacity or intoxication.[1] Rather, Rule 601 has encouraged the bench to treat these issues as matters of credibility and to leave them to the jury.[2] The suggestion has been made that the trial judge may exercise some control over the jury by commenting on the evidence and, to the extent permitted, by exerting the power to direct or set aside jury verdicts.[3] The extent to which judges should comment on the credibility of witnesses is a subject about which many lawyers and judges disagree. It is likely, however, that all judges will instruct the jury on its role in assessing the credibility of witnesses. Any general instruction that invites the jury to consider the capacities of witnesses ought to be acceptable and is consistent with the approach of the rule. When a judge should set aside a jury verdict is a question beyond the scope of this evidence study.

Because Rule 601 declares that all witnesses are competent unless other Rules of Evidence state otherwise, it is not all that clear that trial judges have the discretion to even conduct a voir dire of the witness in deciding if a particular witness is competent. That is, if all witnesses are otherwise competent, there is no need to determine if they are indeed competent. It has been suggested, however, that if a particular witness is not precluded from testifying by any other Rule in Article VI, the judge may nonetheless use the Rule 403 balancing test to determine whether the probative value of the witness's testimony is outweighed by

1. *See, e.g.,* United States v. Lightly, 677 F.2d 1027 (4th Cir.1982) (criminally insane witness who was found incompetent to stand trial held competent to testify despite hallucinations); United States v. Van Meerbeke, 548 F.2d 415 (2d Cir.1976), *cert. denied,* 430 U.S. 974 (1977) (narcotic addict held competent to testify despite ingestion of opium while on the witness stand).

2. *See, e.g.,* United States v. Peyro, 786 F.2d 826 (8th Cir.1986).

3. 3 J. Weinstein & M. Berger, Weinstein's Evidence, ¶ 601[05] at p. 601–38 (Supp. 1982).

the prejudicial dangers listed in that rule. To that end, some judicial inquiry of the witness may be appropriate.[4] Another approach is to apply Rule 601 in conjunction with Rule 603. If the witness is not able to comprehend the nature of the required oath, the witness is not competent to testify. Again, determining whether the witness understands the nature of the oath might require some judicial questioning of the witness.

Rule 601 is silent about child witnesses, a topic of increasing attention in the courts and legislatures.[5] Given the broad first sentence in the Rule, one might conclude that all children would be considered competent. But it is apparently common practice for trial judges to conduct some form of inquiry of child witnesses to insure that they understand what is being required of them in the proceeding. Thus, Rule 601 may not be as absolute as it first seems—at least with regard to child witnesses.

Finally, there is the question of whether a hearsay declarant must otherwise be competent under Rule 601. There are several cases which indicate that they may not be required. In *Idaho v. Wright,*[6] a two and one-half year old child abuse victim was not considered competent to testify under Rule 601.[7] The Supreme Court assumed, however, that the child's out-of-court hearsay statement might be admitted under one of the exceptions to the hearsay rule. It ultimately concluded that the statement was not admissible under the state's residual hearsay exception. In *Morgan v. Foretich,*[8] the court concluded that a four-year-old child abuse victim's hearsay statements were admissible under Rules 803(2) and (4), regardless of whether the child was competent to testify.

4. *See* 1 Saltzburg & Martin, *Federal Rules of Evidence Manual* 519 (5th ed. 1990).

5. *Cf.* Tex.R.Civ.Evid. 601 which specifically addresses the competency of insane persons, child witnesses and other witnesses who "after being examined by the court, appear not to possess sufficient intellect to relate transactions with respect to which they are interrogated." *Compare* Ohio R.Evid. 601(A), which excepts children under 10 "who appear incapable of receiving just impressions . . . or of relating them truly. . . ." However, even in Ohio, children's testimony is liberally received. *See generally* 1 *Evidence in America* §§ 35.2–35.4.

6. 110 S.Ct. 3139 (1990).

7. 110 S.Ct. at 3147.

8. 846 F.2d 941 (4th Cir.1988).

RULE 602

I. TEXT OF RULE

RULE 602. Lack of Personal Knowledge

A witness may not testify to a matter unless evidence is introduced sufficient to support a finding that the witness has personal knowledge of the matter. Evidence to prove personal knowledge may, but need not, consist of the witness' own testimony. This rule is subject to the provisions of Rule 703, relating to opinion testimony by expert witnesses.

II. DISCUSSION

Rule 602 has presented no problems in application. Together with Article VIII (the hearsay rule), the personal knowledge requirement operates to exclude speculative testimony. For example, in ordering a new trial for Maryland officials charged with racketeering and mail fraud, the Fourth Circuit cited Rule 602 in finding inadmissible legislators' testimony concerning their own beliefs at the relevant time as to the defendant governor's position on a veto override.[1] Although the proffered testimony was not technically hearsay, it was so substantially based upon inadmissible hearsay—rumors—that it failed the first-hand knowledge requirement of Rule 602.[2]

There appears to be slight confusion in some cases [3] as to whether personal knowledge is something that the trial court decides under Rule 104(a) or whether it is left for the jury under Rule 104(b). Both at common law and under the Rules, the basic decision whether or not to believe a witness who claims to have knowledge is a jury question. If a witness claims to have personal knowledge and a reasonable jury could believe the witness, the witness should not be barred from testifying. In the rare case in which the court finds that, despite a claim of personal knowledge, no reasonable jury could find a basis to believe the witness, the judge will exclude the testimony.

The most difficult problem that has yet arisen in connection with this Rule involves its relationship to various hearsay rules. As noted in the discussion of Rule 801, it is unclear whether a vicarious admission may be offered against a party when the person who made the state-

1. United States v. Mandel, 591 F.2d 1347 (4th Cir.), *aff'd by equally divided court,* 602 F.2d 653 (4th Cir.1979), *cert. denied,* 445 U.S. 961 (1980).

2. *See also* United States v. Lanci, 669 F.2d 391, 394–395 (6th Cir.), *cert. denied,* 457 U.S. 1134 (1982) (citing Rule 602 to exclude co-defendant's testimony from separate trial regarding what he "imagined" would explain certain fingerprints); United States v. Lang, 589 F.2d 92, 97–98 (2d Cir.1978) (citing Rule 602 to exclude witness' otherwise admissible out-of-court declaration as to defendant's intent, where witness dealt only through intermediary).

3. *See, e.g.,* United States v. Lyon, 567 F.2d 777, 783–784 (8th Cir.1977), *cert. denied,* 435 U.S. 918 (1978).

ment might not have had personal knowledge. The Rules have not created the difficulty, which existed at common law also. It is doubtful that the problem could be resolved by any simple rule change because it is debatable whether all vicarious admissions should be treated in the same way. Clarification of the relationship between Rule 801 and Rule 602 is likely to come through judicial decisions, and it is likely to come slowly.

RULE 603

I. TEXT OF RULE

RULE 603. Oath or Affirmation

Before testifying, every witness shall be required to declare that the witness will testify truthfully, by oath or affirmation administered in a form calculated to awaken the witness' conscience and impress the witness' mind with the duty to do so.

II. DISCUSSION

This rule has caused the courts no difficulties.

The oath in many courts is administered under circumstances in which it is difficult to imagine that it impresses anyone, least of all the witness who takes it, with its seriousness. The Rule states that the oath should be administered in a *form* calculated to awaken the witness's conscience. If the oath is to have any significance, it probably ought also to be administered in a *manner* that impresses upon the witness that the court takes the oath seriously. This is not a matter of evidence law but of orderly procedure. It should be apparent, though, that the contents of the oath are significant only if the oath is presented in a way that focuses the witness's attention on the contents. If the procedure suggests that the court and its officers do not take the oath seriously, it is doubtful that anyone else will.

RULE 604

I. TEXT OF RULE

RULE 604. Interpreters

An interpreter is subject to the provisions of these rules relating to qualification as an expert and the administration of an oath or affirmation to make a true translation.

II. DISCUSSION

This rule has presented no problems in application. The more general goal of ensuring fair trial proceedings for non-English-speaking and hearing-impaired parties has created some difficulties for the courts as they exercise their rather wide discretion in this area to determine the method and extent of translation.[1] However, the problems inhere in the attempt to achieve substantial justice in the circumstances are not generated by the Rule.

Whenever an interpreter is used, problems may arise concerning the nature of the translation provided. Because it is important to make a record accurately depicting trial problems, the suggestion has been made it might be useful to provide for audio, and even video, recording of translations as a supplement to stenographic recording.[2]

1. *See, e.g.,* United States v. Reyes–Padron, 538 F.2d 33 (2d Cir.1976), *cert. denied,* 429 U.S. 1046 (1977) (upholding refusal to require written translation of Jencks Act material); United States v. Diaz Berrios, 441 F.2d 1125 (2d Cir.1971) (commenting favorable upon continuous translation at criminal trial).

2. *See* 1 Saltzburg & Martin, *Federal Rules of Evidence Manual* 538 (5th ed. 1990).

RULE 605

I. TEXT OF RULE

RULE 605. Competency of Judge as Witness

The judge presiding at the trial may not testify in that trial as a witness. No objection need be made in order to preserve the point.

II. DISCUSSION

Rule 605 continues to present only minor problems in application. The automatic requirement of disqualifying the presiding judge from testifying has been an adequate prophylactic measure against jeopardizing the rights of parties in both civil and criminal actions.[1] The "gray area" in applying Rule 605 emerges when the presiding judge acts as a witness without physically taking the stand. A number of recent cases have attempted to clarify at what point a presiding judge begins to act as a witness, although not on the stand.

In *Hersch v. United States,*[2] the court permitted the trial judge to bring his experience and knowledge to bear in assessing the evidence submitted at trial by relying on his military background and sailing experience in plotting the courses of two aircraft.

The appellate court recognized that a trial judge or his clerk may not "deliberately set about gathering facts outside the record of a bench trial over which he presides," and may not "interject his personal evidentiary observation." The court stated:

> The trial judge, however, like a juror, is permitted to bring his experience and knowledge to bear in assessing the evidence submitted at trial. The trial judge did not overstep the bounds of propriety in this case.[3]

However, in *United States v. Lewis,*[4] the court held that the trial judge had erred in ruling that defendant's confession was involuntary because it was given in her hospital room shortly after surgery. The judge's ruling was based on his own personal experience with anaesthetic, and his belief that "as you come out of a general anaesthetic you

1. Automatic disqualification of the presiding judge from testifying spares the parties from having to choose between either allowing highly prejudicial testimony or risking the judge's antagonism. The policy of Rule 605 has been extended to exclude use of the presiding judge's law clerks, both as witnesses and as informal sources of evidence. Kennedy v. Great Atlantic & Pacific Tea Co., 551 F.2d 593 (5th Cir.1977); Price Brothers Co. v. Philadelphia Gear Corp., 629 F.2d 444 (6th Cir.1980), *cert. denied,* 454 U.S. 1099 (1981).

2. 719 F.2d 873 (6th Cir.1983).

3. *Id.* at 878.

4. 833 F.2d 1380 (9th Cir.1987), *cert. denied sub nom.* Fultz v. Rose, 486 U.S. 1056 (1988).

are not accountable for what you do." The Ninth Circuit held that the judge was not a competent witness on anesthetics, and was prohibited from relying on personal experience to support the taking of judicial notice. "It is therefore plainly accepted that the judge is not to use from the bench, under the guise of judicial knowledge, that which he knows only as an individual observer outside the court." [5]

The courts have vacillated in assessing what types of personal experience will be allowed before prejudice occurs, and recusal or trial *de novo* is required. The Eleventh Circuit expanded the potential for judges to rely on outside information in *Johnson v. United States,*[6] when it held that a trial judge may do "outside research" to familiarize himself with the complex technical facts of a case. The court, relying in part on *Roe v. Wade,*[7] held that it was common for judges to "occasionally consult sources not in evidence, ranging anywhere from dictionaries to medical treatises." [8] The court emphasized that the trial judge stated that he did not rely on those outside sources in reaching his conclusions.

Sometimes, the presiding judge can, by his or her treatment of the facts, but without doing outside research, come close to testifying on behalf of one of the parties. In the drug prosecution case of *United States v. Sanchez,*[9] the defendant was tried in absentia. The trial judge instructed the jury that they could consider defendant's flight or nonappearance as evidence of guilt. The appellate court did not regard the trial judge's instruction as purported or implied testimony by the judge in violation of Rule 605.[10]

Rule 605 can also prevent the use of a trial court's pretrial ruling as evidence. In *Jones v. Benefit Trust Life Ins. Co.,*[11] the defendant (insurance company) sought to introduce the district court's original order denying plaintiff's motion for summary judgment on the issue of insurance contract interpretation. The court's summary judgment denial however, was nullified when it later decided to grant plaintiff's motion. The appellate court noted that to allow such evidence would seem at odds with Rule 605, and that the defendant had cited no authorities supporting the relevance of the judge's pretrial ruling to an issue of fact before a jury.

5. *Id.* at 1385, *quoting* 9 J. Wigmore, Evidence in Trials at Common Law § 2569, at 723 (J. Chabourn rev. ed. 1981).

6. 780 F.2d 902 (11th Cir.1986).

7. 410 U.S. 113, 129–162 (1973).

8. 780 F.2d at 910.

9. 790 F.2d 245 (2d Cir.1986).

10. *See* United States v. Sanchez, 790 F.2d 245, 252 (2d Cir.), *cert. denied,* 479 U.S. 989 (1986).

11. 800 F.2d 1397 (5th Cir.1986).

Thirty-three states have adopted Federal Rule of Evidence 605, verbatim or with only insignificant linguistic modifications.[12] Rule 605 appears to work well and has prevented the occurrence of the procedural problems it was intended to prevent. However, appellate courts differ as to when the presiding judge begins to act as a witness although not taking the stand. And the cases that seem most troubling arise when a judge employs personal experiences to assess the material facts and draw legal conclusions.

12. Of these, only Florida expressly permits the parties to consent to testimony from the trial judge. *See* 1 *Evidence in America* § 39.2.

RULE 606

I. TEXT OF RULE

RULE 606. Competency of Juror as Witness

(a) At the trial. A member of the jury may not testify as a witness before that jury in the trial of the case in which the juror is sitting as a juror. If the juror is called so to testify, the opposing party shall be afforded an opportunity to object out of the presence of the jury.

(b) Inquiry into validity of verdict or indictment. Upon an inquiry into the validity of a verdict or indictment, a juror may not testify as to any matter or statement occurring during the course of the jury's deliberations or to the effect of anything upon that or any other juror's mind or emotions as influencing the juror to assent to or dissent from the verdict or indictment or concerning the juror's mental processes in connection therewith, except that a juror may testify on the question whether extraneous prejudicial information was improperly brought to the jury's attention or whether any outside influence was improperly brought to bear upon any juror. Nor may a juror's affidavit or evidence of any statement by the juror concerning a matter about which the juror would be precluded from testifying be received for these purposes.

II. DISCUSSION

The absolute prohibition against juror testimony at trial, as contained in Rule 606(a), has presented no problems in application. However, Rule 606(b) uses a case-by-case approach to the use of juror testimony or other evidence derived from jury deliberations to attack the validity of the verdict or indictment. This approach continues to produce inconsistent results, particularly in close cases attempting to define the type of outside influence that will suffice to admit this type of evidence.

The law is clear that alleged irregularities in jury deliberations such as confusion, misunderstanding or disregard of the law, and excessive concern on the part of jurors with time or family pressures, do not constitute proper areas for inquiry under Rule 606(b).[1] Conversely, such behavior as unauthorized viewing or experiments, discussions with third parties, exposure to media publicity and attempted

1. *See, e.g.,* Robles v. Exxon Corp., 862 F.2d 1201 (5th Cir.1989) (misunderstanding of judge's instructions not allowable by Rule 606); United States v. Jelsma, 630 F.2d 778 (10th Cir.1980) (inquiry into factors influencing a juror's decision not allowed); Poches v. J.J. Newberry Co., 549 F.2d 1166 (8th Cir.1977) (juror's excessive concern with time pressures insufficient to impeach verdict).

bribery, are plainly permissible evidentiary subject areas under Rule 606(b).[2]

Questions of juror mental competence have been considered permissible areas of inquiry but present closer cases. Generally, courts have been reluctant to permit inquiry into juror mental competence absent a very strong showing of prejudice. Thus, in *United States v. Dioguardi,*[3] a pre-Rules case, the court found defendant's receipt ten days after the verdict of an unsolicited letter from a juror, which referred to her alleged clairvoyant powers, to be an insufficient basis to order a hearing on the matter of her competency. Yet, in *Sullivan v. Fogg,*[4] the same court found that a juror's statements one month after the verdict that he had heard voices and vibrations at the trial and during jury deliberations, were not only cause for inquiry, but sufficient to mandate an evidentiary hearing on competency with an opportunity for cross-examination by defendant.

The Supreme Court considered the question of juror competence in *Tanner v. United States,*[5] a mail fraud prosecution in which two jurors testified about drug and alcohol use by some jurors. In a 5–4 decision, Justice O'Connor writing for the majority, the Court rejected the contention that substance abuse was an outside influence capable of allowing testimony in under Rule 606(b). The Court reasoned that drug or alcohol use by jurors is "no more an 'outside influence' than . . . poorly prepared food or lack of sleep." In his dissenting opinion, Justice Marshall argued that drug use during deliberations is not the sort of incompetency which would come to light on voir dire. Furthermore, Sixth Amendment guarantees would be rendered meaningless if post-verdict investigations of this type of misconduct were not allowed.

Courts have also viewed allegations of racial bias as impermissible areas of inquiry.[6] However, when a strong likelihood of prejudice appears, or there is cause to believe that a juror lied on voir dire concerning bias or prejudice, fundamental fairness considerations may

2. *E.g.,* Hard v. Burlington N.R.R. Co., 870 F.2d 1454 (9th Cir.1989) (juror who lied on voir dire about prior experience with railroad constituted extraneous influences); Stockton v. Commonwealth of Virginia, 852 F.2d 740 (4th Cir.1988) (statement by restaurant owner to jurors that "they ought to fry the son of a bitch" made during punishment phase was clearly an outside influence), *cert. denied,* 489 U.S. 1071 (1989); United States v. Bruscino, 662 F.2d 450 (7th Cir.1981) (documents which although not in evidence went into jury room were not prejudicial to defendants).

3. 492 F.2d 70 (2d Cir.), *cert. denied,* 419 U.S. 873 (1974).

4. 613 F.2d 465 (2d Cir.1980).

5. 483 U.S. 107 (1987).

6. *See, e.g.,* Shillcutt v. Gagnon, 827 F.2d 155 (7th Cir.1987) (racial slur made during deliberations not an outside influence); Wright v. United States, 559 F.Supp. 1139 (E.D. N.Y.1983), *aff'd,* 732 F.2d 1048 (2d Cir.1984), *cert. denied,* 469 U.S. 1106 (1985); United States v. Duzac, 622 F.2d 911 (5th Cir.), *cert. denied,* 449 U.S. 1012 (1980).

mandate a hearing, with such prejudice being treated as an outside influence for Rule 606(b) purposes.[7]

Where a question is raised as to threats and coercion from within the jury room,[8] the prevailing view under Rule 606(b) has been that evidence concerning such aspects of deliberations is not admissible to attack the verdict. Thus in *United States v. Casamayor,*[9] the court held that strong-arm tactics used by the foreman against another juror were insufficient to impeach the verdict. Such intra-juror behavior is considered part and parcel of the deliberations process, and hence not an outside influence.[10] However, in one case decided immediately prior to the effective date of the Rules, *Virgin Islands v. Gereau,*[11] the line between external threats and internal coercive pressure was not so clearly drawn. The court, citing Rule 606, refused to order a new trial or to permit further proof to impeach the verdict, even though juror affidavits were proffered indicating that rumors of other killings in the Virgin Islands had been circulated and acted to pressure the jury.

In general, courts have taken the strict limitations contained in Rule 606(b) as an invitation to assert a substantial degree of control over post-verdict efforts by counsel to contact the jurors.[12] Some commentators have suggested that serious consideration should be given to permit the trial court "a somewhat broader inquiry." [13]

The inconsistencies that are identified in the decisions might be unavoidable whenever judgments must be made as to whether irregularities warrant an intrusion into the private deliberations of the jury. Line-drawing in this area is always difficult. Rule 606(b) enunciates a fairly restrictive attitude towards impeachment of jury decisions. Federal courts appear to accept this approach of the Rule and are cautious in evaluating impeachment attempts.

7. Tobias v. Smith, 468 F.Supp. 1287 (W.D.N.Y.1979); Smith v. Brewer, 444 F.Supp. 482, 490 (S.D.Iowa), *aff'd,* 577 F.2d 466 (8th Cir.), *cert. denied,* 439 U.S. 967 (1978).

8. External threats, as from persons interested in the outcome of the case, are permissible subjects for inquiry and may impeach the resulting verdict. Krause v. Rhodes, 570 F.2d 563 (6th Cir.1977), *cert. denied,* 435 U.S. 924 (1978).

9. 837 F.2d 1509 (11th Cir.1988), *cert. denied,* 488 U.S. 1017 (1989); *see also* United States v. Norton, 867 F.2d 1354 (11th Cir.1989) (duress used by one juror against another was insufficient to impeach verdict), *cert. denied,* 491 U.S. 907 (1989).

10. *See, e.g.,* United States v. Blackburn, 446 F.2d 1089 (5th Cir.1971), *cert. denied,* 404 U.S. 1017 (1972); United States v. Stoppelman, 406 F.2d 127 (1st Cir.), *cert. denied,* 395 U.S. 981 (1969).

11. 523 F.2d 140 (3d Cir.1975), *cert. denied,* 424 U.S. 917 (1976).

12. United States v. Moten, 582 F.2d 654 (2d Cir.1978).

13. 1 Saltzburg & Martin, *Federal Rules of Evidence Manual* 547–548 (5th ed. 1990).

RULE 607

I. TEXT OF RULE

RULE 607. Who May Impeach

The credibility of a witness may be attacked by any party, including the party calling the witness.

II. DISCUSSION

Rule 607 is a change from the common-law rule that a party calling a witness to testify on its behalf vouches for that witness and could not, therefore, impeach that witness. As explained by the United States Supreme Court in *Chambers v. Mississippi:*

> Although the historical origins of the "voucher" rule are uncertain, it appears to be a remnant of primitive English trial practice in which "oath-takers" or "compurgators" were called to stand behind a particular party's position in any controversy. Their assertions were strictly partisan and, quite unlike witnesses in criminal trials today, their role bore little relation to the impartial ascertainment of the facts.[1]

As a common-law remnant, the "voucher" rule was often applied blindly by courts. Rule 607 accepted the reality of modern-day trial practice and eliminated the rule. The Rule implicitly recognizes that impeachment of a witness' credibility is an important part of the trial's quest for truth, but it is not always clear when a party is actually "impeaching" as opposed to trying to circumvent another rule of evidence.

Prior Inconsistent Statements

An effective way to impeach a witness' credibility under Rule 607 is to introduce prior inconsistent statements. See Rule 613, *infra.* Rule 801(d)(1)(A) permits a witness' prior inconsistent statements to be used as substantive evidence as well as for impeachment as long as the prior statements were "given under oath subject to the penalty of perjury at a trial, hearing, or other proceeding, or in a deposition." [2] A witness' prior inconsistent statement that was not given under oath at a proceeding can nevertheless be received for impeachment purposes

1. 410 U.S. 284, 296 (1973).

2. As originally proposed, Rule 801(d)(1)(A) would have applied to all prior inconsistent statements, irrespective of whether they were made under oath at a proceeding. *See* 2 Saltzburg & Martin, *Federal Rules of Evidence Manual* 141 (5th ed. 1990). Of the thirty-four states that have adopted Rule 801 in whole or in part, ten states (Alaska, Arizona, Colorado, Delaware, Montana, Nevada, New Mexico, Rhode Island, Utah, and Wisconsin) have eliminated the requirement that the prior inconsistent statements must have been made under oath at a proceeding. 2 *Evidence in America* § 56.2. Three states (Arkansas, North Dakota, and Wyoming) have imposed the oath requirement in criminal cases only. *Id.*

under Rule 607, even though it may not be considered by the factfinder as substantive evidence. This creates room for mischief however because few, if any, jurors are able totally to ignore the substantive impact of a prior statement despite Rule 105's assumption to the contrary.[3] Accordingly, courts should be careful that witnesses are not called merely "as a stratagem to get before the jury otherwise inadmissible evidence."[4]

The line between bona fide impeachment and the circumvention of Rule 801(d)(1)(A)'s prohibition against using prior inconsistent statements that were not made under oath at a proceeding as substantive evidence can, at times, be thin, and courts have approached the problem on a case-by-case basis. Generally, courts favor admitting the evidence. Thus, the mere fact that the bulk of a witness' testimony is favorable to the party calling that witness will not necessarily prevent the party from impeaching the non-favorable portions with the witness' prior inconsistent statements.[5] Additionally, a party may elicit prior inconsistent statements by the witness to lessen the sting of the inconsistency prior to the opposing party's cross-examination of that witness.[6] In an attempt to add some structure and preclude circumvention of Rule 801(d)(1)(A), some commentators suggest that a party must first suffer prejudicial surprise by the testimony of a witness called by that party before impeachment with a prior inconsistent statement that is not given under oath at a proceeding should be permitted.[7]

Bias

Although the Federal Rules of Evidence do not by their express terms deal with bias, the Supreme Court in *United States v. Abel*[8] acknowledged that the rules permit the impeachment of a witness' credibility by evidence that demonstrates bias. The Court concluded that admissibility of bias evidence is supported by the relevance rules, the references to bias in the Advisory Committee Notes to Rules 608 and 610, and by Rules 607 and 611(b). Referring to Rules 401 and 402, the Court reasoned: "A successful showing of bias on the part of a witness would have a tendency to make the facts to which he testified

3. Rule 105 provides that "[w]hen evidence which is admissible . . . for one purpose but not admissible . . . for another purpose is admitted, the court, upon request, shall restrict the evidence to its proper scope and instruct the jury accordingly."

4. United States v. Gossett, 877 F.2d 901, 907 (11th Cir.1989) (per curiam), *cert. denied,* 110 S.Ct. 1141 (1990); United States v. Webster, 734 F.2d 1191, 1192 (7th Cir.1984).

5. *See* United States v. DeLillo, 620 F.2d 939, 946–947 (2d Cir.), *cert. denied,* 449 U.S. 835 (1980).

6. *See* United States v. Livingston, 816 F.2d 184, 191 (5th Cir.1987).

7. *See* 1 Saltzburg & Martin, *Federal Rules of Evidence Manual* 569 n. 3 (5th ed. 1990); *cf.* United States v. Peterman, 841 F.2d 1474, 1480 (10th Cir.1988) (government permitted to impeach own witness with prior conviction when witness testifies differently than expected), *cert. denied,* 488 U.S. 1004 (1989).

8. 469 U.S. 45 (1984).

less probable in the eyes of the jury than it would be without such testimony." [9]

Bias exists where certain relationships and circumstances may affect the impartiality of a witness, thus causing the witness, unconsciously or otherwise, to color his or her testimony in favor of or against a party, such as where there are family, business, or personal relationships between the witness and a party, where the witness has an interest in the litigation, or where the witness might fear a party.[10]

An important method of showing the bias of a witness is by reference to something the witness has either said or done. Prior to the effective date of the Rules, a witness' written prior statement indicative of bias could be not received into evidence unless the witness was given an opportunity to explain the statement.[11] This is true under the Rules as well.[12] The opportunity to explain was not, however, necessary for the receipt of evidence concerning conduct by the witness that displayed bias,[13] and, although the Rules are silent on this point, this is apparently the current practice.[14] Nevertheless, some commentators argue that it would be better to require that a witness be given the opportunity to explain both statements and conduct.[15]

A significant problem arises when evidence that ostensibly is offered to prove bias also shows propensity, which, subject to narrowly drawn exceptions, is an impermissible purpose under Rule 404. In *Young v. Rabideau,*[16] for example, a civil rights action brought by a prisoner against two correctional officers, the officers argued that the prisoner's disciplinary record at the institution was admissible to show his bias against authority. The Seventh Circuit Court of Appeals rejected this contention, recognizing that the evidence permitted the

9. *Id.* at 51.

10. *See id.* at 49–54; Clark v. O'Leary, 852 F.2d 999, 1005–1008 (7th Cir.1988) (membership in rival gang); *see also* 27 C. Wright & V. Gold, *Federal Practice and Procedure* §§ 6092 & 6095, at 487 (1990); 3A J. Wigmore, *Evidence* §§ 949–950 (Chadbourn rev. ed. 1970).

11. *See* United States v. Marzano, 537 F.2d 257, 265 (7th Cir.1976), *cert. denied,* 429 U.S. 1038 (1977); United States v. Kahn, 472 F.2d 272, 281–282 (2d Cir.), *cert. denied,* 411 U.S. 982 (1973).

12. *See* Rule 613(b) ("Extrinsic evidence of a prior inconsistent statement by a witness is not admissible unless the witness is afforded an opportunity to explain or deny the same and the opposite party is afforded an opportunity to interrogate the witness thereon, or the interests of justice otherwise require"); United States v. Harvey, 547 F.2d 720, 722 (2d Cir.1976).

13. *See* Comer v. Pennsylvania R.R. Co., 323 F.2d 863 (2d Cir.1963) (per curiam); *see also* 3A Wigmore, *supra,* § 953 & n. 2.

14. *See* 3 J. Weinstein & M. Berger, *supra,* ¶ 607[03], at 53–54. *See also* 27 C. Wright & V. Gold, *supra,* § 6095, at 535–536 (suggesting that Rule 613(b) is persuasive only as to how courts should apply Rules 403 and 611 in this circumstance).

15. *See* 27 C. Wright & V. Gold, *supra,* § 6095, at 536.

16. 821 F.2d 373 (7th Cir.), *cert. denied,* 484 U.S. 915 (1987).

inference "that the prisoner acted in conformity with his prior bad acts," and that this violated Rule 404. The court also noted that the prisoner was a party, and that impeachment with evidence of bias is generally permitted only with respect to witnesses and not parties. Although Rule 105 provides that the jury must upon request be told to limit evidence to its proper purpose, there is, as noted earlier, a very real problem whether juries can observe this distinction.

Reputation and Opinion Evidence; Specific Acts

One of the most effective ways of impeaching a witness is to show that the witness has a reputation for not telling the truth or to show through opinion testimony that the witness does not tell the truth. See Rule 608(a).

Generally, extrinsic evidence of a witness' conduct may not be used to attack or support the witness' credibility. The exceptions rest in Rules 609 and 608(b). Specifically, Rule 608(b) permits counsel in the court's discretion, to inquire into specific acts on "cross-examination." Although Rule 608(b) does not purport to authorize this type of inquiry on direct examination—even though the witness is hostile or adverse—it would seem that such inquiry should be permitted as a matter of common sense.[17] Nevertheless, some commentators argue that the distinction between cross and direct examination is "sensible" because impeachment needs on direct examination are different than those on cross-examination.[18] Significantly, a recent amendment to Rule 609 has eliminated the requirement that impeachment of a witness by criminal-conviction evidence be limited to the cross-examination of that witness.

Conclusion

By abrogating the common law's prohibition against impeaching one's own witness, Rule 607 recognizes that parties must use witnesses that are available even if they are less than ideal. Its general language, in synergism with the other rules affecting impeachment has, however, created few major problems that would require any change in the Rule itself. Perhaps more than any other area of evidence, the law governing impeachment is most susceptible to a common-law, case-by-case development under the overall aegis of Rule 403's balancing and the trial court's discretion to control the conduct of trial under Rule 611.

17. *See* United States v. Cosentino, 844 F.2d 30, 32–35 (2d Cir.) (admission of entire cooperation agreement, including its bolstering aspects, on the government's direct examination permitted when witness' credibility attacked during the defense's opening statement, noting that impeaching portions of the agreement could be admitted to lessen the sting irrespective of whether there was a prior attack), *cert. denied,* 488 U.S. 923 (1988).

18. 1 S. Saltzburg & M. Martin, *supra,* at 143.

RULE 608

I. TEXT OF RULE

RULE 608. Evidence of Character and Conduct of Witness

(a) Opinion and reputation evidence of character. The credibility of a witness may be attacked or supported by evidence in the form of opinion or reputation, but subject to these limitations: (1) the evidence may refer only to character for truthfulness or untruthfulness, and (2) evidence of truthful character is admissible only after the character of the witness for truthfulness has been attacked by opinion or reputation evidence or otherwise.

(b) Specific instances of conduct. Specific instances of the conduct of a witness, for the purpose of attacking or supporting the witness' credibility, other than conviction of crime as provided in Rule 609, may not be proved by extrinsic evidence. They may, however, in the discretion of the court, if probative of truthfulness or untruthfulness, be inquired into on cross-examination of the witness (1) concerning his character for truthfulness or untruthfulness, or (2) concerning the character for truthfulness or untruthfulness of another witness as to which character the witness being cross-examined has testified.

The giving of testimony, whether by an accused or by any other witness, does not operate as a waiver of the accused's or the witness' privilege against self-incrimination when examined with respect to matters which relate only to credibility.

II. DISCUSSION

The use of character witnesses to attack and, where proper, to rehabilitate a witness is much the same under Rule 608 as it was at common law, except that under the rule, opinion, as well as reputation testimony is admissible. This inclusion of opinion testimony has caused no major problems.

Rule 608(a)(2) permits introduction of evidence of a witness' truthfulness where such veracity has been attacked, apparently by any means. Although the Rules' drafters clearly did not intend every instance of a vigorous and successful cross-examination to invite rebuttal evidence of truthfulness, the determination of whether or when the door has been opened remains *ad hoc.* Even so, few real problems of interpretation have arisen.

In *Beard v. Mitchell,*[1] the court permitted the introduction of evidence of good reputation for truth once a witness had been impeached with a prior inconsistent statement. Similarly, where the government brought out its own witness' criminal record on direct and

1. 604 F.2d 485, 503 (7th Cir.1979).

the defense then engaged in vigorous cross-examination, the Second Circuit found the government entitled to rehabilitate its witness with good character evidence—but, the court noted that such rehabilitation could not have been elicited prior to defendant's cross.

Additionally, one court has held that presenting evidence of the "truthfulness" portions of cooperation agreements is not improper vouching. In *United States v. Bowie,*[2] the government's witness testified to the terms of the agreement which required truthful testimony. In noting that Rule 608(a)(2) allows evidence of truthful character only after it has been attacked, the court held that there was harmless error, if any, given the defense's subsequent attack during cross-examination. However, in *United States v. Borello,*[3] the Second Circuit refused to allow premature bolstering of the witness' credibility following an earlier line of cases prohibiting this practice.

In attacking or supporting credibility of a witness, Rule 608(b) excludes much extrinsic evidence concerning specific so-called "bad acts," but permits cross-examination where the acts involved reflect upon veracity.[4] However, unlike the somewhat comparable *crimen falsi* reference in Rule 609(a)(2), discussed below, this Rule reposes wide discretion in that trial judge's hands.[5]

Moreover, Rule 608(b) comes into play only in the context of attempts to use bad act evidence to attack or support credibility. All other uses[6] are governed by other rules, chiefly Rules 403 and 404.

2. 892 F.2d 1494 (10th Cir.1990). *See also* United States v. Martin, 815 F.2d 818 (1st Cir.), *cert. denied,* 484 U.S. 825 (1987). *But see* United States v. Roberts, 618 F.2d 530 (9th Cir.1980) (statement that witness truthfulness was monitored constituted vouching).

3. 766 F.2d 46 (2d Cir.1985). *See also* United States v. Arroyo–Angulo, 580 F.2d 1137 (2d Cir.), *cert. denied,* 439 U.S. 913 (1978). *See generally* Saltzburg, *Bolstering and Attacking the Cooperating Witness,* 6 Criminal Justice 43 (Spring 1991); 1 *Evidence in America* § 41.5 (Anticipatory Rehabilitation of Witnesses).

4. Cross-examination concerning bad acts is also permissible if directed toward establishing bias, or toward rebuttal of a defendant witness' material claims. United States v. Hodnett, 537 F.2d 828 (5th Cir.1976); United States v. Contreras, 602 F.2d 1237, 1241–1242 (5th Cir.), *cert. denied,* 444 U.S. 971 (1979).

5. Thus, the range of cases precluding defense cross-examination of prosecution witnesses includes United States v. Hastings, 577 F.2d 38, 41 (8th Cir.1978) (participation in drug transactions, less than honorable military discharge for failure to wear uniform); United States v. Kizer, 568 F.2d 504, 505–506 (9th Cir.), *cert. denied,* 435 U.S. 976 (1978) (past drug use and hospitalization); United States v. Young, 567 F.2d 799, 803 (9th Cir. 1977), *cert. denied,* 434 U.S. 1079 (1978) (offer to pay money to have former husband killed); United States v. Bynum, 566 F.2d 914, 923 (5th Cir.), *cert. denied,* 439 U.S. 840 (1978) (holding foster children unlawfully); and United States v. Estell, 539 F.2d 697, 700 (10th Cir.), *cert. denied,* 429 U.S. 982 (1976) (stealing meat, passing bad checks). Among the cases consistently allowing bad act cross-examination are those involving an attorney witness concurrently or previously subject to Bar disciplinary procedures. *See* United States v. Blitstein, 626 F.2d 774, 783–784 (10th Cir.1980), *cert. denied,* 449 U.S. 1102 (1981); United States v. Whitehead, 618 F.2d 523, 529 (4th Cir.1980).

6. Perhaps the least controversial common use of such evidence is that directed toward establishing the witness' *bias,* rather than credibility. *See, e.g.,* United States v.

Some substantial areas of dispute have arisen in the context of attempts to use extrinsic evidence of bad acts to impeach witnesses—especially defendants—by contradiction. For example, where a defendant opens the door to the same incident on direct or gratuitously volunteers a material denial on cross, impeachment use of extrinsic evidence to contradict may be allowed.[7] However, where the defendant's statement is invited by cross-examination, or where the defendant may have interpreted the line of questioning as limited to the charged offense (rather than including prior incidents), courts are generally cautious and prohibit resort to extrinsic evidence merely to contradict the witness' denial.[8] Rule 608(b) is also cited in precluding such evidence where the issue denied or misstated is collateral and does not reflect significantly on credibility.[9] By the same token, where the defendant relies for a material element of the defense upon testimony which may be contravened by extrinsic evidence, Rule 608(b) provides no basis for exclusion—and Rule 404(b) affirmatively supports admission—at least for rebuttal purposes.[10] In *Carson v. Polley,*[11] evidence of an old performance evaluation on losing his temper was admitted to rebut a civil rights defendant's denial of possibility of temper loss with prisoner.

Finally, where the defendant is questioned and admits the act in issue, Rule 608(b) may not necessarily operate as a bar to extrinsic evidence. In *Carter v. Hewitt,*[12] the prisoner plaintiff admitted writing a letter which the defense interpreted as suggesting that another inmate bring a fraudulent lawsuit. After the plaintiff testified, the letter itself was admitted into evidence. Although the court discussed Rule 608(b) at some length, the existence of a plan to cause fraudulent instigation of claims goes beyond a mere collateral attempt to impeach

James, 609 F.2d 36, 46 (2d Cir.1979), *cert. denied,* 445 U.S. 905 (1980); United States v. Rios Ruiz, 579 F.2d 670, 673 (1st Cir.1978); United States v. Alvarez–Lopez, 559 F.2d 1155, 1158 (9th Cir.1977); United States v. Brown, 547 F.2d 438, 445–446 (8th Cir.), *cert. denied,* 430 U.S. 937 (1977); United States v. Robinson, 530 F.2d 1076 (D.C.Cir.1976); Johnson v. Brewer, 521 F.2d 556 (8th Cir.1975).

7. *See, e.g.,* United States v. Garcia, 900 F.2d 571 (2d Cir.1990); United States v. Wright, 542 F.2d 975, 980 (7th Cir.1976), *cert. denied,* 429 U.S. 1073 (1977).

8. United States v. Green, 648 F.2d 587 (9th Cir.1981); United States v. Bosley, 615 F.2d 1274, 1277 (9th Cir.1980); United States v. Herman, 589 F.2d 1191, 1196–1197 (3d Cir.1978), *cert. denied,* 441 U.S. 913 (1979).

9. United States v. Herzberg, 558 F.2d 1219 (5th Cir.1977), *cert. denied,* 434 U.S. 930 (1977); United States v. Blackshire, 538 F.2d 569 (4th Cir.), *cert. denied,* 429 U.S. 840 (1976).

10. United States v. Opager, 589 F.2d 799, 801–802 (5th Cir.1979) (evidence of predisposition to sell drugs offered to rebut entrapment defense); United States v. Batts, 573 F.2d 599 (9th Cir.), *cert. denied,* 439 U.S. 859 (1978) (evidence of familiarity with drugs offered to rebut defense of lack of intent).

11. 689 F.2d 562, 574–575 (5th Cir.1982).

12. 617 F.2d 961 (3d Cir.1980).

credibility. Under Rule 404(b), the evidence could have come in to counter plaintiff's substantive claims as well.

Prior to the adoption of the Rules, most federal courts did not permit impeachment through proof of bad acts not the subject of criminal convictions. Rule 608(b) therefore made a major change in the permissible scope of impeachment. The Rule gives vast discretion to the trial judge to decide when an act actually relates to credibility. Only when it relates to credibility may it be the subject of questioning under this Rule. Further, even if this Rule is satisfied, a trial judge who is concerned that questions about prior acts may unfairly prejudice a party may bar the questions under Rule 403.

There is one trend that is slightly disturbing. Some courts have permitted counsel to ask witnesses whether third parties have accepted as true allegations of bad acts rather than whether the witnesses admit the acts. For example, in *United States v. Whitehead,*[13] the court of appeals held that a defendant was properly questioned concerning his suspension from the practice of law as well as about the underlying facts. This flies in the face of the restriction on extrinsic evidence and permits such evidence to be smuggled in the back door. If a witness is asked, "Did you commingle funds in violation of your duty to your client?" and the answer is "No," the examiner should not be permitted to ask, "Weren't you punished or suspended for just that reason?" Such a question is directed to attacking the witness's denial, and the witness's denial is the end of the matter as far as bad act impeachment and Rule 608 are concerned.

Thus far, the Rule has not caused significant problems. In some instances, it is apparent that parties have looked to Rule 608 when they should have been looking at Rule 404(b), but that is not a function of the language of Rule 608.

13. 618 F.2d 523 (4th Cir.1980).

RULE 609

I. TEXT OF RULE

(a) General rule. For the purpose of attacking the credibility of a witness,

(1) evidence that a witness other than an accused has been convicted of a crime shall be admitted, subject to Rule 403, if the crime was punishable by death or imprisonment in excess of one year under the law under which the witness was convicted, and evidence that an accused has been convicted of such a crime shall be admitted if the court determines that the probative value of admitting this evidence outweighs its prejudicial effect to the accused; and

(2) evidence that any witness has been convicted of a crime shall be admitted if it involved dishonesty or false statement, regardless of the punishment.

(b) Time limit. Evidence of a conviction under this rule is not admissible if a period of more than ten years has elapsed since the date of the conviction or of the release of the witness from the confinement imposed for that conviction, whichever is the later date, unless the court determines, in the interests of justice, that the probative value of the conviction supported by specific facts and circumstances substantially outweighs its prejudicial effect. However, evidence of a conviction more than 10 years old as calculated herein, is not admissible unless the proponent gives to the adverse party sufficient advance written notice of intent to use such evidence to provide the adverse party with a fair opportunity to contest the use of such evidence.

(c) Effect of pardon, annulment or certificate of rehabilitation. Evidence of a conviction is not admissible under this rule if (1) the conviction has been the subject of a pardon, annulment, certificate of rehabilitation, or other equivalent procedure based on a finding of the rehabilitation of the person convicted, and that person has not been convicted of a subsequent crime which was punishable by death or imprisonment in excess of one year, or (2) the conviction has been the subject of a pardon, annulment, or other equivalent procedure based on a finding of innocence.

(d) Juvenile adjudications. Evidence of juvenile adjudications is generally not admissible under this rule. The court may, however, in a criminal case allow evidence of a juvenile adjudication of a witness other than the accused if conviction of the offense would be admissible to attack the credibility of an adult and the court is satisfied that admission in evidence is necessary for a fair determination of the issue of guilt or innocence.

(e) Pendency of appeal. The pendency of an appeal therefrom does not render evidence of a conviction inadmissible. Evidence of the pendency of an appeal is admissible.

II. DISCUSSION

No rule of evidence has provoked commentary so passionate or profuse as that which permits impeachment of a testifying witness by introducing that witness' previous convictions. Rule 609, which embodies that impeachment tool, has always provoked controversy, and scholars continue to criticize the rationale and construction of this evidence rule.[1]

The 1990 Amendments

Subsection (a) of the Rule has been amended[2] to accommodate criticism that Rule 609(a) was ambiguous regarding impeachment of witnesses other than the criminal defendant. As amended, Rule 609(a) incorporates two revisions.

First, amended Rule 609(a) deletes the restriction that required elicitation of the conviction during cross-examination of the witness to be impeached. Congress had inserted this proviso as a guarantee that only witnesses who actually testified would be impeached by their previous convictions.[3] Virtually every circuit, however, had determined this restriction to be superfluous, recognizing that it is commonplace in trials for witnesses to reveal their past convictions during direct examination in order to "draw the sting" from introduction of their past malefactions.[4] Revised Rule 609(a) affords flexibility to the

1. *See, e.g.,* Gold, *Sanitizing Prior Conviction Evidence to Reduce Its Prejudicial Effects,* 27 Ariz.L.Rev. 691 (1985); Betro, *The Use of Prior Convictions to Impeach Criminal Defendants—Do the Risks Outweigh the Benefits?,* 4 Antioch L.J. 211 (1986); Foster, *Rule 609(a) in the Civil Context: A Recommendation for Reform,* 57 Fordham L.Rev. 1 (1988); Note, *Balancing Prejudice in Admitting Prior Felony Convictions in Civil Actions: Resolving the 609(a)(1)–403 Conflict,* 63 Notre Dame L.Rev. 333 (1988).

2. The amendment is effective as of December 1, 1990.

3. *See* S.Rep. No. 1277, 93d Cong., 2d Sess. 15, *reprinted in* 1974 U.S.Code Cong. & Ad. News 7051, 7061. Apparently, the committee overlooked Rule 806, which allows a hearsay declarant to be subject to impeachment on the same basis as any other witness regardless of whether the hearsay declarant actually testifies at trial. *See, e.g.,* United States v. Newman, 849 F.2d 156, 163 (5th Cir.1988) (criminal defendant whose hearsay declarations are admitted can be impeached under Rule 806). *See also* Schmertz, *The First Decade Under Article VI of the Federal Rules of Evidence: Some Suggested Amendments to Fill Gaps and Cure Confusion,* 30 Villanova L.Rev. 1367, 1441 (1985).

4. Advisory Committee Note to amended Rule 609. *See* United States v. Handly, 591 F.2d 1125, 1128 n. 1 (5th Cir.1979); United States v. Hasenstab, 575 F.2d 1035 (2d Cir.), *cert. denied,* 439 U.S. 827 (1978); United States v. Bad Cob, 560 F.2d 877 (8th Cir.1977). Moreover, Fed.R.Evid. 607 permits an attorney to impeach his or her own witness; presumably, this impeachment would be accomplished during direct examination.

trial judge in selecting the manner in which this form of impeachment evidence is to be introduced.[5]

Second, Rule 609(a)(1) has been amended to clarify the use of prior convictions to impeach witnesses in civil cases and witnesses other than the accused in criminal cases. As initially enacted, Rule 609(a)(1) obliged the trial judge to balance the probative value of the previous conviction for determining the witness' veracity against its "prejudicial effect to the defendant." Congress extensively debated the ramifications of prior convictions evidence upon the criminal defendant.[6] Yet, despite the vigorous debate and conscientious consideration lavished upon the implications of Rule 609 for criminal defendants, the Rule's application to prosecution witnesses and civil litigants appears to have emerged as a consequence of legislative ennui. Congress simply overlooked the effects of the Rule's language on prosecution witnesses and civil litigants, or at best, cast a weary, apathetic glance in that direction.

Judicial construction of the balancing provision of Rule 609(a)(1) reflected a number of divergent viewpoints. Most courts agreed that "the defendant" referred to the criminal accused; otherwise, Rule 609(a)(1) would permit the civil defendant, but not the plaintiff, to object to the use of his criminal record for impeachment purposes.[7] Similarly, most courts agreed that Congress intended to permit broad impeachment of prosecution witnesses without taking cognizance of any prejudicial effect to the prosecution.[8] However, three distinct judicial views emerged as to the standard by which the trial judge should decide whether to admit felony convictions offered to impeach civil litigants and their witnesses.

Under one view, all felony convictions of all civil witnesses should be automatically admissible, because Rule 609(a)(1) literally allowed discretion only in evaluating convictions that adversely affect the

5. Advisory Committee Note amended Rule 609:

> The amendment does not contemplate that a court will necessarily permit proof of prior convictions through testimony, which might be time-consuming and more prejudicial than proof through a written record.

See Fed.R.Evid. 403, 611(a).

6. The legislative history of Rule 609 is exhaustively catalogued in Tobias, *Impeachment of the Accused by Prior Convictions and the Proposed Federal Rules of Evidence: The Tortured Path of Rule 609, Hearings Before the Special Subcomm. on Reform of Federal Criminal Laws of the Comm. of the Judiciary,* H.R.Rep. No. 2, 93d Cong., 1st Sess. 105–15 (1973). *See also* Diggs v. Lyons, 741 F.2d 577 (3d Cir.1984) (describing the extensive legislative history of Rule 609), *cert. denied,* 471 U.S. 1078 (1985).

7. *See* Campbell v. Greer, 831 F.2d 700 (7th Cir.1987). *But see* Diggs v. Lyons, 741 F.2d 577 (3d Cir.1984) (apparently reads "to the defendant" as encompassing both civil and criminal defendants), *cert. denied,* 471 U.S. 1078 (1985).

8. *See, e.g.,* United States v. Pandozzi, 878 F.2d 1526 (1st Cir.1989); United States v. Bay, 762 F.2d 1314 (9th Cir.1984); United States v. Garza, 754 F.2d 1202 (5th Cir.1985).

criminal defendant.[9] These courts reasoned that Congress intended Rule 609(a) to be the sole provision governing witness impeachment by former convictions. The residual discretion afforded by Rule 403 was deemed inapplicable because Rule 609(a) specifically addresses circumstances under which judicial discretion is permitted. Under this absolutist approach, all felony convictions of all civil witnesses were available for impeachment under Rule 609(a)(1). Moreover, all convictions for crimes of dishonesty and false statement were available under Rule 609(a)(2).

A second approach evaluated the civil witness' felony convictions under the prescribed balancing test of Rule 609(a)(1).[10] This construction treated the Rule's specification of "to the defendant" as the equivalent of "to the witness against whom the conviction is offered" in a civil case. Consequently, felony convictions of civil witnesses were admitted when the conviction was more helpful in assessing veracity than it was prejudicial.

The third view resorted to the residual balancing provision, Rule 403. Some courts in this third group deemed the Rule 609(a) balancing process inapplicable to civil cases, holding that Congress' preoccupation with mitigating prejudice to the criminal defendant and defense witnesses did not reflect an intent to restrict judicial discretion in civil cases.[11] Rules 102 and 611 vest discretion in the trial judge to construe the Federal Rules of Evidence in accordance with principles of justice and fairness, and to control the mode and manner of witness interrogation. Further, Rule 403 allocates minimal residual discretion to the judge to exclude unduly prejudicial evidence. These courts admitted felony convictions offered to impeach civil witnesses unless the evidence was substantially more prejudicial than useful in evaluating credibility.[12]

9. *See, e.g.,* Campbell v. Greer, 831 F.2d 700 (7th Cir.1987); Diggs v. Lyons, 741 F.2d 577 (3d Cir.1984), *cert. denied,* 471 U.S. 1078 (1985); NLRB v. Jacob E. Decker & Sons, 569 F.2d 357 (5th Cir.1978).

10. *See, e.g.,* Petty v. Ideco, 761 F.2d 1146 (5th Cir.1985); Murr v. Stinson, 752 F.2d 233 (6th Cir.1985); Green v. Shearson Lehman/American Express, Inc., 625 F.Supp. 382 (E.D. Pa.1985) (dictum).

11. *See, e.g.,* Donald v. Wilson, 847 F.2d 1191 (6th Cir.1988); Moore v. Volkswagenwerk, A.G., 575 F.Supp. 919 (D.Md.1983); Tussel v. Witco Chem. Corp., 555 F.Supp. 979 (W.D.Pa.1983).

12. Other courts that adopted this third view construed Rule 403 as an overriding provision "that cuts across the rules of evidence," and did not reach the issue of Rule 609(a)(1)'s scope. Shows v. M/V Red Eagle, 695 F.2d 114 (5th Cir.1983). *See also* Jones v. Board of Police Comm'rs, 844 F.2d 500, (8th Cir.1988), *cert. denied,* 490 U.S. 1092 (1989); Diaz v. Cianci, 737 F.2d 138 (1st Cir.1984).

Regardless of the application of Rule 609(a)(1) to civil litigation, Rule 403 affords the trial judge a modicum of discretion to exclude a civil witness' unduly prejudicial felony conviction. But, reliance upon the Rule 403 balancing standard affords only slight protection to civil witnesses against prejudicial effects of their previous transgressions because it is an inclusionary test, and affords the trial court only minimal discretion to

The Supreme Court addressed the appropriate construction of Rule 609(a)(1), and resolved the judicial division in favor of the absolutist position in *Green v. Bock Laundry Machine Co.*[13] Green, a nineteen year-old who worked at a car wash under a prison release program, suffered the loss of his arm when he reached inside a large dryer in an attempt to stop its motion. At the trial of his product liability suit against the machine's manufacturer, Green testified that he had been neither adequately trained in the machine's use, nor adequately instructed as to its hazardous character. On cross-examination, defendant was permitted to impeach Green by eliciting his felony convictions for burglary and conspiracy to commit burglary. The jury returned a verdict for defendant, which was affirmed by the Court of Appeals.

The Supreme Court, after an exhaustive review of the legislative history, concluded that Rule 609(a)(1) is ambiguous in its application to civil cases. But, the Court reasoned, the Rule could not be read literally to favor the civil defendant. Rather, the Rule's command to consider "prejudice to the defendant" must be construed as referring only to the criminal accused. However, the Court determined Congress' reference to "the defendant" to be a deliberate compromise between the House version of Rule 609(a), which would have allowed impeachment only by *crimen falsi* offenses, and the Senate version, which would have abrogated judicial discretion and required admissibility of all felony crimes and *crimen falsi* offenses. Thus, only the criminal accused was protected by the balancing proposition of Rule 609(a)(1). Moreover, the inclusion of a specific balancing provision in Rule 609(a)(1) overrides the residual balancing proposition contained in Rule 403. The Court concluded that, properly construed, Rule 609(a)(1) mandates admissibility of all felony convictions against all other witnesses. Rule 609(a)(1) permitted no intervening judicial discretion to protect a witness, or the party who had presented the witness' testimony, from ensuing unfair prejudice.[14]

The recent amendment to Rule 609(a)(1) mitigates the absolutist position espoused by the Court in *Green.* The criminal defendant's prior non-*crimen falsi* felony convictions are available for impeachment purposes only if the trial judge determines that the probative value of the conviction for evaluating the defendant's credibility outweighs prejudicial harm to him.[15] Non-*crimen falsi* felony convictions of other

exclude. *See* Boyer v. Chicago & N.W. Transp. Co., 603 F.Supp. 132 (D.Minn.1985); Moore v. Volkswagenwerk, A.G., 575 F.Supp. 919 (D.Md.1983).

13. 490 U.S. 504 (1989).

14. 490 U.S. at 527; *see also* Coursey v. Broadhurst, 888 F.2d 338 (5th Cir.1989) (trial judge has no discretion to exclude prior felony cattle theft conviction of personal injury plaintiff).

15. The Advisory Committee observes that witnesses who bear a special relationship to the criminal accused might also be the beneficiaries of the enhanced "probative value exceeds prejudice" balancing standard, at least in situations where the accused "is likely

witnesses are admissible only upon the exercise of discretion under 403 by the trial judge.

Prior conviction evidence is concededly less prejudicial in civil cases than in criminal cases. However, in civil cases, all energies and resources of litigants and jurors should be concentrated on reconstructing the past event that forms the basis for the lawsuit, not upon a litigant's or a witness' character. The law of evidence does not relegate other types of evidence infused with prejudicial potential to the trial judge's discretion. Instead, the law declares such proof inadmissible.[16] The nature and extent of prejudice endemic in prior convictions evidence should persuade trial judges to evaluate carefully the claimed probity of felony convictions in evaluating a witness' veracity, and make careful use of their discretion to allow this avenue of impeachment.

In exercising the discretion afforded by Rule 609(a)(1), trial judges should be cognizant of the factors that bear on admissibility of prior convictions as impeachment evidence. Federal courts adhere to the *Luck–Gordon* approach in determining the probative value/prejudicial effect calculus for previous convictions offered as impeachment evidence.[17] Five factors are considered by the trial judge: (1) the impeachment value of the prior crime; (2) the point in time of the conviction and the witness' subsequent history; (3) the similarity between the past crime and the charged crime; (4) the importance of the defendant's testimony; and (5) the centrality of the credibility issue.[18]

In performing the balancing mandated by Rule 609(a)(1), the trial judge should strive to articulate findings regarding probative value and prejudicial effect on the record, in order to apprise the reviewing court of the factors considered and the weight accorded to each. Of course, the trial judge who, in the heat of trial, omits the explicit findings and implicitly performs the required balancing, does not necessarily abuse his or her discretion.[19]

to suffer some spill-over effect from impeachment of the witness." Advisory Committee Note to amended Rule 609.

16. *See, e.g.,* the exclusionary evidence provisions incorporated in Article IV of the Federal Rules of Evidence.

17. Luck v. United States, 348 F.2d 763 (D.C.Cir.1965); Gordon v. United States, 383 F.2d 936 (D.C.Cir.1967), *cert. denied,* 390 U.S. 1029 (1968). *See also* United States v. Rein, 848 F.2d 777 (7th Cir.1988).

18. Obviously, the *Luck–Gordon* approach was crafted with the accused's former convictions in mind. For prosecution witnesses, as well as civil litigants and witnesses, the first and second factors relate to the probative value assessment. Prejudicial effect inheres in the ever-present potential that the trier of fact will use the conviction as substantive evidence of conduct, or will over-value it as credibility proof.

19. United States v. Alvarez, 833 F.2d 724 (7th Cir.1987), *rev'd on other grounds,* United States v. Durrive, 902 F.2d 1221 (7th Cir.1990); United States v. Walker, 817 F.2d 461 (8th Cir.), *cert. denied,* 484 U.S. 863 (1987).

Additional Suggestions

Several additional troublesome aspects of Rule 609, both of which relate to subsection (a)(2), were not addressed by the Advisory Committee. As initially adopted, Rule 609(a)(2) prescribes a *per se* rule of admissibility, for impeachment purposes, of certain crimes—those that "involved dishonesty or false statement, regardless of the punishment." Legislative history incorporates the proposition that a witness' commission of these types of crimes is particularly telling on the issue of that witness' character for veracity.[20] Similarly, courts unanimously agree that Rule 609(a)(2) mandates admission of all convictions for any "dishonesty or false statement" offenses, even misdemeanors; the acute probative value of these *crimen falsi* offenses is deemed to be so weighty that the balance of prejudice versus probative value is inapplicable.[21] The scope and application of Rule 609(a)(2)'s mandate of impeachment use for "dishonesty and false statement" offenses has spawned several subsidiary issues.[22]

The first issue concerns the scope of Rule 609(a)(2). Courts have not been unanimous in sculpting the parameters of this "dishonesty and false statement" category. Clearly, crimes of violence do not qualify as veracity-related offenses.[23] Conversely, crimes that qualified at common law as *crimen falsi*—such as fraud, embezzlement, swindling—are almost indisputably convincing as indicators of veracity.[24]

20. Conf.Rep. No. 1597, 93d Cong., 2d Sess. 9, *reprinted in* 1974 U.S.Code Cong. & Ad. News 7098, 7013. The drafters contemplated that "dishonesty and false statement" crimes include: "perjury or subornation of perjury, false statement, criminal fraud, embezzlement, or false pretense, or any other offense in the nature of crimen falsi, the commission of which involves some element of deceit, untruthfulness, or falsification bearing on the accused's propensity to testify truthfully."

21. *See, e.g.,* United States v. Kuecker, 740 F.2d 496 (7th Cir.1984); United States v. Wong, 703 F.2d 65 (3d Cir.), *cert. denied,* 464 U.S. 842 (1983); United States v. Kiendra, 663 F.2d 349 (1st Cir.1981), *overruled on other grounds,* Luce v. United States, 469 U.S. 38 (1984); United States v. Toney, 615 F.2d 277 (5th Cir.), *cert. denied,* 449 U.S. 985 (1980).

22. The party seeking to admit the prior conviction as impeachment evidence bears the burden of demonstrating that it is a crime of "dishonesty and false statement" and falls within the *per se* confines of rule 609(a)(1). United States v. Livingston, 816 F.2d 184 (5th Cir.1987); United States v. Givens, 767 F.2d 574, 579 n. 1 (9th Cir.), *cert. denied,* 474 U.S. 953 (1985).

23. *See, e.g.,* United States v. Cameron, 814 F.2d 403, 405 (7th Cir.1987) (possession of switchblade); Czajka v. Hickman, 703 F.2d 317 (8th Cir.1983) (rape); United States v. Mansaw, 714 F.2d 785 (8th Cir.) (prostitution), *cert. denied,* 464 U.S. 986 (1983); Reyes v. Missouri Pac. R.R. Co., 589 F.2d 791, 795 n. 10 (5th Cir.1979) (misdemeanor public intoxication); United States v. Harvey, 588 F.2d 1201 (8th Cir.1978) (misdemeanor assault).

24. *See, e.g.,* Altobello v. Borden Confectionery Products, Inc., 872 F.2d 215 (7th Cir. 1989) (misdemeanor meter tampering); United States v. Rogers, 853 F.2d 249 (4th Cir.) (misdemeanor worthless check convictions), *cert. denied,* 488 U.S. 946 (1988); United States v. Huddleston, 811 F.2d 974 (6th Cir.) (misdemeanor failure to file tax return), *aff'd,* 484 U.S. 894 (1987); United States v. Noble, 754 F.2d 1324 (7th Cir.) (counterfeit-

The difficult question is the treatment of those offenses that reflect less lack of respect for the obligation to conduct oneself with veracity than lack of respect for the possessions of another, such as property crimes, or the person of another, such as narcotics offenses. Courts are in disarray concerning the availability of property-related offenses such as robbery, burglary, larceny, theft and shoplifting,[25] and of narcotics offenses,[26] as impeachment evidence under Rule 609(a)(2).

The Criminal Justice Section of the American Bar Association proposed a revision to Rule 609(a)(2) that would have restricted *per se* admissibility to crimes that included "untruthfulness or falsehood" as a statutory element.[27] However, the Advisory Committee chose not to

ing), *cert. denied,* 474 U.S. 818 (1985); United States v. Coats, 652 F.2d 1002 (D.C.Cir.1981) (uttering).

25. Not admissible under Rule 609(a)(2): United States v. Yeo, 739 F.2d 385 (8th Cir. 1984) (theft); United States v. Hendershot, 614 F.2d 648 (9th Cir.1980) (robbery); McHenry v. Chadwock, 896 F.2d 184 (6th Cir.1990) (shoplifting); United States v. Newman, 849 F.2d 156 (5th Cir.1988) (theft and felony theft). Admissible under Rule 609(a)(2): United States v. Kinslow, 860 F.2d 963 (9th Cir.1988) (armed robbery), *cert. denied,* 110 S.Ct. 96, 107 (1989); United States v. Del Toro Soto, 676 F.2d 13 (1st Cir.1982) (grand larceny).

26. Not admissible under Rule 609(a)(2): United States v. Mehrmanesh, 689 F.2d 822 (9th Cir.1982) (smuggling hashish); United States v. Lewis, 626 F.2d 940 (D.C.Cir.1980) (distribution of heroin); United States v. McLister, 608 F.2d 785 (9th Cir.1979) (possession of one marijuana cigarette). Admissible under Rule 609(a)(2): United States v. Parrish, 736 F.2d 152 (5th Cir.1984) (selling methamphetamine); United States v. Moore, 735 F.2d 289 (8th Cir.1984) (previous narcotics offenses).

The rationale for allowing proof of previous narcotics offenses is expressed in United States v. Ortiz, 553 F.2d 782, 784 (2d Cir.), *cert. denied,* 434 U.S. 897 (1977), where the impeachment offenses were convictions for two heroin sales:

> [T]he District Judge in his discretion was entitled to recognize that a narcotics trafficker lives a life of secrecy and dissembling in the course of that activity, being prepared to say whatever is required by the demands of the moment, whether the truth or a lie. From this he could rationally conclude that such activity in a witness' past is probative on the issue of credibility.

See also United States v. Trejo–Bambrano, 582 F.2d 460 (9th Cir.), *cert. denied,* 439 U.S. 1005 (1978), *citing Ortiz.*

27. The Criminal Justice Section's version of Rule 609(a) provided:

(a) General Rule.

For the purpose of attacking the credibility of a witness, evidence that the witness has been convicted of a crime shall be admitted only if the crime:

(1) was punishable by death or imprisonment in excess of one year under the law under which the witness was convicted, and the court determines that the probative value of admitting this evidence outweighs its prejudicial effect; or

(2) involved untruthfulness or falsification, regardless of the punishment, unless the court determines that the probative value of admitting this evidence is substantially outweighed by the danger of unfair prejudice. This subsection (2) applies only to those crimes whose statutory elements necessarily involve untruthfulness or falsification.

alter the "dishonesty and false statement" categorization in favor of the more narrow "untruthfulness or falsification" formulation.[28]

The legislative history is unambiguous in articulating the intent of the drafters concerning property and narcotics crimes. Although property and narcotics crimes display disregard for the law and are thus perhaps indicative of "dishonesty", the *per se* rule of impeachment is restricted to crimes that require deception as an element of the offense. Admissibility of property and narcotics crimes, as well as crimes of violence, should be assessed under subsection (a)(1), and subject to the balancing tests promulgated therein. The cause of clarity would be served by deleting the "dishonesty" language from subsection (a)(2), and instead redirecting the focus of Rule 609(a)(2) to those crimes that elementally implicate deception or prevarication.

The second issue concerns whether, and if so to what degree, the trial judge should probe into the circumstances surrounding the witness' commission of the prior offense in order to determine whether witness' underlying conduct is indicative of untruthfulness. For example, misdemeanor assault is neither a felony crime nor an offense of "dishonesty or false statement," and thus would not be admissible as impeachment evidence under either subsection (a)(1) or (a)(2) of Rule 609. Should the misdemeanor assault be admissible impeachment evidence if the proponent demonstrated that the witness accomplished the assault by luring the victim into an alley by deceit?[29] Some courts have manifested an inclination to delve into contextual facts and circumstances surrounding the prior crime.[30] Although investigation of the manner in which the prior crime was committed provides a more precise evaluation of the extent to which deception pervaded the witness' conduct, this examination of details takes time and places undue emphasis upon the significance of this form of impeaching information. Fairness, efficiency and convenience are better served by

28. The Advisory Committee deemed the guidance provided by the Conference Report to be sufficient, and declined the opportunity to clarify further the scope of Rule 609(a)(2), "notwithstanding some decisions that take an unduly broad view of 'dishonesty,' admitting convictions such as for bank robbery or bank larceny." Advisory Committee Note to amended Rule 609.

29. 3 J. Weinstein and M. Berger, *Weinstein's Evidence* ¶ 609[04], at 609–85 (1988).

30. *See, e.g.,* the following cases, where the court reasoned that the impeachment convictions offered did not entail "dishonesty or false statement," but stated that the conviction could be admitted under Rule 609(a)(2) if the particular offense was accomplished by fraudulent or deceitful means: United States v. Yeo, 739 F.2d 385, 388 (8th Cir.) (theft crimes); United States v. Grandmont, 680 F.2d 867 (1st Cir.1982) (purse snatchings); United States v. Glenn, 667 F.2d 1269 (9th Cir.1982) (burglary or theft); United States v. Whitman, 665 F.2d 313 (10th Cir.1981) (larceny); United States v. Dorsey, 591 F.2d 922 (D.C.Cir.1978) (shoplifting).

See also United States v. Lipscomb, 702 F.2d 1049 (D.C.Cir.1983) (en banc), where the court held that examination of the facts and circumstances underlying commission of the prior crime is an appropriate consideration in conducting the balancing process required by Rule 609(a)(1).

the simple, mechanical rule that only those convictions for crimes whose statutory elements include deception, untruthfulness or falsehood are admissible under Rule 609(a)(2).[31]

A final issue concerning Rule 609 involves the procedure by which the trial judge determines admissibility of prior convictions to impeach. Generally, a pretrial *motion in limine* is available to aid the attorney presenting the witness whose convictions will be offered to undermine his believability in assessing the risks of using that witness.

The Supreme Court held in *Luce v. United States* [32] that a criminal defendant who seeks to appeal an adverse *motion in limine* ruling concerning admissibility of his own prior convictions must actually testify and be impeached in order to preserve any claim of error in the pretrial ruling. The Court rejected the position, adopted by a number of circuit courts,[33] that an erroneous pretrial ruling burdened the accused's right to testify by inflicting an unnecessary chill upon the decision whether to take the stand. Instead, the Court focused upon the unavailability on review of precise data concerning prejudice and probative value if the accused does not testify.[34] The Court observed that no one factor generally motivates the decision to testify, so that the reviewing court could not assume that defendant's reluctance to take the stand is attributable solely to the pretrial ruling on admissibility of his prior record. Moreover, the Court declined to provide an avenue for automatic reversals, reasoning that if pretrial *motions in limine* were reviewable, a reviewing court "could not logically term 'harmless' an error that presumptively kept the defendant from testifying." [35]

Although *Luce* arose in the context of an appeal by a criminal defendant, the Court's rationale concerning speculative nature of the effect of the conviction as an impeachment device, and the undesirability of fashioning any *per se* rules concerning prejudice and prejudicial error, is readily transferable to the civil context. Thus, it is likely that the same result obtains in civil cases.

31. *See* United States v. Lewis, 626 F.2d 940 (D.C.Cir.1980). This was the position advanced by the Criminal Justice Section of the American Bar Association in its proposed revision and by the New York State Bar Association Commercial and Federal Litigation Section. Judge Weinstein also endorses this position. 3 J. Weinstein and M. Berger, *Weinstein's Evidence* ¶ 609[04], at 609–84 to 609–85 (1988).

32. 469 U.S. 38 (1984).

33. *See, e.g.,* United States v. Cook, 608 F.2d 1175 (9th Cir.1979), *cert. denied,* 444 U.S. 1034 (1980); United States v. Washington, 746 F.2d 104 (2d Cir.1984).

34. The Court was not persuaded that an offer of proof would suffice to demonstrate either the prejudice to the defendant or probative value to the government. The defendant's trial testimony might differ from that stated in the offer of proof or the government might not offer to impeach the defendant if he did testify.

35. 469 U.S. at 42.

Finally, it should be noted that an accused who testifies after an adverse preliminary ruling and reveals his convictions during direct examination in anticipation of the expected impeachment, in all likelihood, has waived any claim of error in the pretrial ruling.[36]

36. Jones v. Collier, 762 F.2d 71 (8th Cir.1985).

RULE 610

I. TEXT OF RULE

RULE 610. Religious Beliefs or Opinions

Evidence of the beliefs or opinions of a witness on matters of religion is not admissible for the purpose of showing that by reason of their nature the witness' credibility is impaired or enhanced.

II. DISCUSSION

Rule 610 is rarely noted in the reported decisions, which is testimony to the fact that it has caused no real problems for the courts. The Rule is broadly worded and proscribes use of a witness' religious beliefs either to attack [1] or support that witness' credibility.[2]

The Rule does not prohibit counsel from inquiring into a witness' affiliations which might demonstrate bias. As the Advisory Committee Note points out, the Rule would not prohibit inquiry into a witness' affiliation with a church which was a party to the litigation. But what if the particular religious organization is not a party? Would bias evidence still be admissible? In *United States v. Abel,*[3] the Supreme Court held that it was proper for the prosecutor to introduce evidence that the defendant and defense witness belonged to a secret prison gang, called the Aryan Brotherhood, which required the members to deny that that organization existed and to commit perjury, murder, and theft on each other's behalf. Noting that bias evidence is relevant, the Court concluded that the witness' affiliation in this organization was evidence of bias which the jury was entitled to hear. The question posed by this case is whether it would also apply even if the court concluded that the particular organization was "religious." Arguably it would because any members who testified would be biased because of their affiliation with each other, even if the association was religious in nature.

1. United States v. Kalaydjian, 784 F.2d 53 (2d Cir.1986) (improper to question witness about his reasons for affirming, but not swearing, on the Koran).

2. *See, e.g.,* Virgin Islands v. Petersen, 553 F.2d 324 (3d Cir.1977) (religious beliefs of defense witness not admissible to enhance credibility).

3. 469 U.S. 45 (1984).

RULE 611

I. TEXT OF RULE

RULE 611. Mode and Order of Interrogation and Presentation

(a) Control by court. The court shall exercise reasonable control over the mode and order of interrogating witnesses and presenting evidence so as to (1) make the interrogation and presentation effective for the ascertainment of the truth, (2) avoid needless consumption of time, and (3) protect witnesses from harassment or undue embarrassment.

(b) Scope of cross-examination. Cross-examination should be limited to the subject matter of the direct examination and matters affecting the credibility of the witness. The court may, in the exercise of discretion, permit inquiry into additional matters as if on direct examination.

(c) Leading questions. Leading questions should not be used on the direct examination of a witness except as may be necessary to develop the witness' testimony. Ordinarily leading questions should be permitted on cross-examination. When a party calls a hostile witness, an adverse party, or a witness identified with an adverse party, interrogation may be by leading questions.

II. DISCUSSION

Rule 611 codifies the common law traditions concerning the scope of cross-examination and the use of leading questions, while broadly authorizing the exercise of the court's discretion, for example, to control the order of proof,[1] to allow a wider scope of questioning on cross in some instances,[2] to permit leading questions to be used with hostile or adverse witnesses or to refuse to allow such questioning on nominal cross-examination.[3]

This Rule, together with Rule 403, was cited by critics of the Rules as conferring upon trial judges too much control and discretion in handling evidence problems. So far, it is difficult to find any evidence that Rule 611 has caused major problems. In the few instances in which judges seem to have substituted their own views concerning how evidence should be presented for the approach provided in specific rules, appellate courts have been quick to insist upon adherence to the rules. In *Lis v. Robert Packer Hospital,*[4] for example, the court of

1. *See, e.g.,* United States v. DeLuna, 763 F.2d 897 (8th Cir.), *cert. denied sub. nom.* Thomas v. United States, 474 U.S. 980 (1985) (testimony in installments from one witness).

2. *See, e.g.,* United States v. Alvarez, 833 F.2d 724, 729 (7th Cir.1987).

3. *See, e.g.,* Schultz v. Rice, 809 F.2d 643, 654 (10th Cir.1986) (rejected by *Edwards v. City of Philadelphia,* 860 F.2d 568 (3rd Cir.1988)).

4. 579 F.2d 819 (3d Cir.), *cert. denied,* 439 U.S. 955 (1978).

appeals reasoned that a trial judge erred in allowing, as a general rule, cross-examination beyond the scope of the direct. Similarly, in *United States v. Ledesma,*[5] the court criticized the trial judge's no side-bar conference rule where Rule 103(c) indicates that evidence questions generally shall be decided outside the hearing of the jury. In *United States v. Reed,*[6] defendant's conviction for embezzlement and theft of mail was reversed when the prosecution impeached the defendant with extrinsic evidence of marijuana possession by the defendant in violation of the prohibition of Fed.R.Evid. 608. And in *Johnson v. Ashby,*[7] the appellate court criticized the trial court's arbitrary time limits on portions of the trial. The trial court's judgment was affirmed due to failure of the party to raise a timely objection.

Rule 611 presents a problem with regard to research. Although courts often use the Rule to make the trial effective for the ascertainment of the truth, they often fail to cite the Rule.[8] Almost all decisions which cite the Rule simply quote the Rule and hold that under the facts of the given case there has not been an abuse of discretion but if there has been an error the error is harmless.[9]

5. 632 F.2d 670 (7th Cir.), *cert. denied,* 449 U.S. 998 (1980).

6. 700 F.2d 638 (11th Cir.1983).

7. 808 F.2d 676 (8th Cir.1987).

8. 1 Saltzburg and Martin, *Federal Rules of Evidence Manual,* 564 (5th ed. 1990).

9. *See e.g.,* United States v. Tindle, 808 F.2d 319, 328 (4th Cir.1986), *cert. denied,* 490 U.S. 1114 (1989).

RULE 612

I. TEXT OF RULE

RULE 612. Writing Used to Refresh Memory

Except as otherwise provided in criminal proceedings by section 3500 of title 18, United States Code, if a witness uses a writing to refresh his memory for the purpose of testifying, either—

(1) while testifying, or

(2) before testifying, if the court in its discretion determines it is necessary in the interests of justice, an adverse party is entitled to have the writing produced at the hearing, to inspect it, to cross-examine the witness thereon, and to introduce in evidence those portions which relate to the testimony of the witness. If it is claimed that the writing contains matters not related to the subject matter of the testimony the courts shall examine the writing in camera, excise any portions not so related, and order delivery of the remainder to the party entitled thereto. Any portion withheld over objections shall be preserved and made available to the appellate court in the event of an appeal. If a writing is not ordered or delivered pursuant to order under this rule, the court shall make any order justice requires, except that in criminal cases when the prosecution elects not to comply, the order shall be one striking the testimony or, if the court in its discretion determines that the interests of justice so require, declaring a mistrial.

II. DISCUSSION

The primary objective of Rule 612, detection of fabricated testimony through inspection of materials used to refresh the memory of a witness, was accomplished at common law through the inspection of materials used to refresh memory while a witness was testifying.[1] The Rule expands the means of protection by allowing inspection of writings used to refresh a witness's memory prior to testifying, "if the court in its discretion determines it is necessary in the interest of justice." [2] It is sometimes very difficult to determine precisely what writings a witness may have used to refresh memory prior to testifying because of the extended period of time over which the witness may refresh memory, the large number of writings reviewed, and the seemingly limitless ways in which memories may be refreshed.[3]

1. C. McCormick, *Evidence* § 9 (Cleary ed. 1984); R. Marcus & E. Sherman, *Complex Litigation* 563 (1985).

2. Saltzburg & Martin, *Federal Rules of Evidence Manual* 705 (5th ed. 1990).

3. *See* M. Graham, *Handbook of Federal Evidence* § 612.2 (2d ed. 1986).

Rule 612 has not been troublesome in sofar as it allows an adverse party the right to inspect writings used by a witness to refresh memory while testifying. Troublesome questions have arisen, however, with regard to writings used to refresh the memory of a witness before testifying, particularly when a writing contains materials which are subject to the attorney-client privilege or the work-product protections of Fed.R.Civ.P.Rule 26(b)(3). Because the language of Rule 612 refers to writings being produced at the "hearing" in which the witness testifies, most courts have held that the Rule applies to materials used in refreshing memory in preparation for testimony at depositions as well as in preparation for trials.[4]

When a witness refreshes memory prior to testifying there is no automatic right of the adverse party to production of the materials used to refresh memory. Rule 612 requires disclosure only if, "the court in its discretion determines it is necessary in the interests of justice." Most courts have ordered disclosure when it is clear that the witness has used a document to refresh memory and that the document has had at least some effect in restoring the memory of the witness.[5] The precise manner by which a court determines that disclosure of Rule 612 material "is necessary in the interests of justice" is often not described in judicial opinions.[6]

When a witness uses materials protected by Rule 26(b)(3) of the Federal Rules of Civil Procedure or materials which are privileged to refresh memory prior to testifying at a trial or deposition, there are competing policies both for and against disclosure. The majority of courts have permitted disclosure—or at least identification—of privileged materials used to refresh memory prior to testimony.[7] Courts have used a balancing test to weigh the necessity of disclosure for effective cross-examination against the need to protect work-product

4. Sporck v. Peil, 759 F.2d 312, 317 (3d Cir.), *cert. denied,* 474 U.S. 903 (1985). Margaret Hall Foundation, Inc. v. Strong, 121 F.R.D. 141 (D.Mass., 1988); Barrer v. Women's National Bank, 96 F.R.D. 202 (D.D.C.1982); *but see* Omaha Public Power District v. Foster Wheeler Corp., 109 F.R.D. 615 (D.Neb.1986).

5. Sporck v. Peil, 759 F.2d 312 (3d Cir.), *cert. denied,* 474 U.S. 903 (1985). *See also* United States v. Larranga, 787 F.2d 489 (10th Cir.1986) (only the portion relied upon by the witness and other portions relating to the same subject matter need be disclosed).

6. *E.g.,* Cosden Oil & Chemical Co. v. Karl O. Helm Aktiengesellschaft, 736 F.2d 1064 (5th Cir.1984); Smith & Wesson v. United States, 782 F.2d 1074 (1st Cir.1986).

7. *See, e.g.,* Sporck v. Peil, 759 F.2d 312 (3d Cir.), *cert. denied,* 474 U.S. 903 (1985) (holding counsel-selected documents that were provided to an expert witness were protected from disclosure but permitting interrogation of the witness as to precisely which documents he reviewed); Gould Inc. v. Mitsui Mining & Smelting Co., 825 F.2d 676 (2d Cir.1987) (noting the narrowness of the *Sporck* holding as to non-disclosure and remanding for a determination whether documents should be disclosed); In re San Juan DuPont Plaza Hotel Fire Litig., 859 F.2d 1007 (1st Cir.1988) (distinguishing and disagreeing with *Sporck* on privilege holding); *see also* Barrer v. Women's National Bank, 96 F.R.D. 202 (D.D.C.1982).

and confidential communication.[8] In determining the needs of a party for disclosure, courts will consider whether other probative evidence is available to impeach the witness and whether undue hardship will result to the cross-examiner from denial of the materials.

In re Comair Air Disaster Litigation, 100 F.R.D. 350, 353 (E.D.Ky. 1983), suggested that rather than balancing conflicting policies with regard to work product, Rule 612 and Fed.R.Civ.P. 26(b)(3) should be read in harmony. If materials qualify as work product, they are discoverable only upon a showing that the party seeking discovery has substantial need of the materials in preparation of his case and that he is unable without undue hardship to obtain the substantial equivalent of the materials by other means. Fed.R.Civ.P. 26(b)(3). If a witness has used such materials to refresh his memory prior to testifying, Rule 612 weighs the balance in favor of finding such a substantial need because of the need for effective cross-examination.

Some courts have ordered disclosure of written material after finding that the act of using privileged material to refresh memory waives the privilege.[9] Any mechanical application of waiver principles, however, invites courts to avoid the balancing of important policies, and disregards the fact that the holder of a privilege may not be free to choose the materials that will be necessary to refresh memory.[10]

One court has indicated that the adverse party must make a stronger showing that disclosure of Rule 612 materials is "necessary in the interests of justice" when requested for use at a deposition than when sought for use at trial. Noting that Rule 612 is a rule of evidence, not a rule of discovery, the court noted that issues of credibility are best left until trial when issues are more clearly drawn and the court is in a better position to use the balancing test.[11]

8. *See, e.g., In re* Joint Eastern and Southern District Asbestos Litigation, 119 F.R.D. 4 (E.D.N.Y. and S.D.N.Y.1988).

9. *See* Eckert v. Fitzgerald, 119 F.R.D. 297, 299–300 (D.D.C., 1988); Margaret Hall Foundation, Inc. v. Strong, 121 F.R.D. 141 (D.Mass.1988).

10. Laxalt v. C.K. McClatchy Pub., 116 F.R.D. 438 (D.Nev.1987).

11. Derderian v. Polaroid Corp., 121 F.R.D. 13, 15–18 (D.Mass.1988).

RULE 613

I. TEXT OF RULE

RULE 613. Prior Statements of Witnesses

(a) Examining witness concerning prior statement. In examining a witness concerning a prior statement made by the witness, whether written or not, the statement need not be shown nor its contents disclosed to the witness at that time, but on request the same shall be shown or disclosed to opposing counsel.

(b) Extrinsic evidence of prior inconsistent statement of witness. Extrinsic evidence of prior inconsistent statement by a witness is not admissible unless the witness is afforded an opportunity to explain or deny the same and the opposite party is afforded an opportunity to interrogate the witness thereon, or the interests of justice otherwise require. This provision does not apply to admissions of a party-opponent as defined in Rule 801(d)(2).

II. DISCUSSION

This Rule has presented few problems in application. Although the Rule has worked well, however, there still exists confusion as to when the opportunity for the witness to explain or deny an inconsistent statement must be afforded. The legislative history indicates that it is permissible for a party to impeach a witness with an inconsistent statement and later to afford the witness the opportunity to explain or deny.[1] In some cases decided shortly after the Rules became effective, courts sometimes assumed that the more rigid "prior foundation" requirement of the common law was codified in rule 613.[2] In *United States v. Bonnett,*[3] the district court refused to allow defense counsel's use of one witness to impeach the testimony of witness on the stand. In affirming the lower court's decision, the Tenth Circuit held that Rule 613(b) required that a party be given an opportunity to deny or explain a prior inconsistent statement before it could be introduced. Subsequent cases have recognized, however, that the Rule provides more flexibility than the common law.[4]

The most difficult issues surrounding impeachment with prior inconsistent statements involve the relationship between Rule 607,

1. *See* 1 Saltzburg & Martin, *Federal Rules of Evidence Manual* 716–718 (5th ed. 1990). *See also* Wilmington Trust Co. v. Manufacturers Life Ins. Co., 749 F.2d 694 (11th Cir.1985) (court allowed prior inconsistent statement during rebuttal testimony because witness could explain it on surrebuttal).

2. *See, e.g.,* United States v. Harvey, 547 F.2d 720 (2d Cir.1976).

3. 877 F.2d 1450 (10th Cir.1989).

4. *See, e.g.,* United States v. Praetorious, 622 F.2d 1054 (2d Cir.1979), *cert. denied,* 449 U.S. 860 (1980); United States v. King, 560 F.2d 122 (2d Cir.), *cert. denied,* 434 U.S. 925.

which permits any party (including the calling party) to impeach a witness, Rule 801(d)(1)(A), which permits some prior inconsistent statements to be offered for their truth, and Rule 613, which confines itself to the impeachment use of inconsistent statements. The law has clearly developed that a party may not call a witness for the purpose of smuggling inconsistent statements into evidence under the guise of impeachment in the hope that they will be misused as substantive evidence.[5] It can be extremely important for the trial judge to determine whether a witness is being called in a good faith effort to elicit admissible testimony or in bad faith effort to put inconsistent statements of the witness before the trier of fact.

5. For a useful discussion of the cases, *see* 1 Saltzburg & Martin, *Federal Rules of Evidence Manual* 592–95 (5th ed. 1990).

RULE 614

I. TEXT OF RULE

RULE 614. Calling and Interrogation of Witnesses by Court

(a) Calling by court. The court may, on its own motion or at the suggestion of a party, call witnesses, and all parties are entitled to cross-examine witnesses thus called.

(b) Interrogation by court. The court may interrogate witnesses, whether called by itself or by a party.

(c) Objections. Objections to the calling of witnesses by the court or to interrogation by it may be made at the time or at the next available opportunity when the jury is not present.

II. DISCUSSION

Rule 614 has presented few problems in application. Judicial discretion in this context was traditionally broad in the federal courts and the Rule does not expand or contract the powers that federal judges had at common law. There is no indication that federal judges have taken the adoption of the Rule as an indication that they should ask more questions or call more witnesses than they traditionally have, and they are seldom reversed for calling or questioning,[1] or refusing to call or question witnesses.[2]

Much as is the case with the traditional prerogative of federal judges to summarize and comment upon the evidence at trial,[3] appel-

1. So long as the court does not stray from the appearance of impartiality, judicial questioning of witnesses called by the parties to clarify their testimony is entirely appropriate even where it is extensive. *See, e.g.,* Moore v. United States, 598 F.2d 439 (5th Cir.1979) (court questioned defendant as extensively as both sides together); United States v. Vega, 589 F.2d 1147 (2d Cir.1978) (court's questioning elicited key admission from defendant); United States v. Kidding, 560 F.2d 1303 (7th Cir.), *cert. denied,* 434 U.S. 872 (1977); United States v. Green, 544 F.2d 138 (3d Cir.1976), *cert. denied,* 430 U.S. 910 (1977) (judge allowed to question witnesses due to the complexity of the case).

2. The authorization contained in Rule 607 for parties to impeach their own witnesses as necessary removes much of the pressure upon the court to call witnesses merely to avoid the voucher rule. As a result, the refusal to call a witness under Rule 614(a) will not constitute an abuse of discretion. United States v. Herring, 602 F.2d 1220, 1226–1227 (5th Cir.1979), *cert. denied,* 444 U.S. 1046 (1980). Especially with the elimination of the voucher rule, however, a court's exercise of the authority to call witnesses in order to produce evidence which is essential to the government's prima facie case may constitute reversible error, at least where an explanation and cautionary instruction is not furnished to the jury. United States v. Karnes, 531 F.2d 214, 216–217 (4th Cir.1976) (court impermissibly called two witnesses whom the government had declined to call because they had earlier given conflicting statements; Rule 614 not yet in effect at the time of trial, but discussed in reversing conviction).

3. The judge must avoid intervening with comments in a manner likely to cause the jury to conclude that the judge believes, e.g., that a defendant is guilty. United States v. Victoria, 837 F.2d 50 (2d Cir.1988) (judge's questioning of the witness conveyed the opinion that the witness was not credible); *cf.,* United States v. Robinson, 635 F.2d 981,

late courts do apply some limits to the trial judges' discretion under Rule 614. A criminal conviction may be reversed where the circumstances of the judge's questioning reveal a likelihood of undue influence over the jury—for example, by "many and manifest interventions" usurping trial counsel's otherwise competent examinations of witnesses, coupled with prejudicial commenting upon the evidence.[4]

One of the difficult problems that lawyers face is how to object to questions asked by the court without running the risk that a jury will assume that they and the court are at odds with each other or that they are trying to interfere with the court's efforts to complete the record. One state has for that reason eliminated any requirement that an objection be made and simply presumes that one has been overruled.[5] The judgments that must be made by counsel when the judge is asking questions are subtle, and the arguments must be carefully offered. The judge, after all, must rule on the objections that are made to his or her questions, and it is unusual for the judge to be both interrogator and jurist at the same time.[6]

985 (2d Cir.1980), *cert. denied,* 451 U.S. 992 (1981) (judgment affirmed where defense counsel's misconduct provoked the challenged comments). The court will not be reversed for failing to marshall the evidence for the jury, even in complex cases.

4. United States v. Welliver, 601 F.2d 203, 208–209 (5th Cir.1980). *See also* United States v. Allsup, 566 F.2d 68, 72–73 (9th Cir.1977) (impermissible intervention to rehabilitate government witness who had been "seriously undermined" by cross-examination, by implying that sight of defendant had frightened her).

5. North Carolina. *See* 2 *Evidence in America* §§ 48.2–48.3.

6. Useful suggestions as to how objections can be put and a record made are found in Saltzburg, *The Unnecessarily Expanding Role of the American Trial Judge,* 64 Va.L.Rev. 1 (1978).

RULE 615

I. TEXT OF RULE

RULE 615. Exclusion of Witnesses

At the request of a party the court shall order witnesses excluded so that they cannot hear the testimony of other witnesses, and it may make the order of its own motion. This rule does not authorize the exclusion of (1) a party who is a natural person, or (2) an officer or employee of a party which is not a natural person designated as its representative by its attorney or (3) a person whose presence is shown by a party to be essential to the presentation of the party's cause.

II. DISCUSSION

Rule 615 is something of a rarity in that, under it, judicial discretion is more limited, rather than broader, than at common law. Previously, a party could ask for sequestration of witnesses, and the request was usually, but not always, granted. Under Rule 615, sequestration is a matter of right, except for the three categories of witnesses specified. It has worked well.

Rule 615 exempts three categories of witnesses from mandatory exclusion. The first category, parties who are natural persons, has provoked no real controversy and may be of constitutional dimension, even in civil cases. The second category, a non-natural party's designee, is most frequently applied in criminal cases to permit the government's case agent to assist the prosecution at trial.[1] The Fifth Circuit has dealt with the question of prejudice to defendants by noting the relationship between this exception and the court's power under Rule 611 to control the order of proof—for example, by requiring such a designee/witness to testify at an early stage.[2] Absent a request from the defendant to exercise such Rule 611 powers, however, the court has no obligation to interject itself into these matters *sua sponte.*[3]

The third category, persons necessary to a party's presentation of its cause, is most frequently applied to permit parties' retained experts, who also intend to testify, to remain in the courtroom throughout the trial to assist counsel.[4] However, exclusion of such witnesses remains

1. *E.g.,* United States v. Machor 879 F.2d 945 (1st Cir.1989), *cert. denied,* 110 S.Ct. 1138 (1990). *But see* United States v. Franham, 791 F.2d 331 (4th Cir.1986) (reversible error to allow two agents to remain in courtroom).

2. In re United States, 584 F.2d 666, 667 (5th Cir.1978).

3. United States v. Nix, 601 F.2d 214, 215 (5th Cir.), *cert. denied,* 444 U.S. 937 (1979).

4. *See, e.g.,* Morvant v. Construction Aggregates Corp., 570 F.2d 626, 629–630 (6th Cir. 1978), *cert. denied,* 439 U.S. 801 (1978).

within the court's discretion and such orders generally do not constitute reversible error.[5]

The developing law holds that only one person may be a designated representative under Rule 615.[6] This trend makes considerable sense. Individual parties are exempt from sequestration, but they cannot exempt family members, friends and witnesses. Organizational parties or governmental entities would be in a position to undermine Rule 615 if they had an unlimited right to exempt witnesses from sequestration by labeling them "essential representatives."

The largest problem arising under the Rule is the same problem that faced common law courts: how to devise appropriate sanctions or remedies for violations of exclusion orders. The sanctions available include (1) citing the witness for contempt, which does little to remedy any damage done by such witness' testimony; (2) permitting cross-examination and comment upon the violation by way of attacking the witness' credibility, which may result in a distorted perception of unaffected testimony; and (3) refusing to permit the testimony, which deprives the court of relevant evidence and is very invoked in a criminal context. This last option, the least often invoked,[7] has generated some controversy.

In civil cases, the Fifth Circuit has applied this strict sanction for violation of sequestration orders more often than other courts. In *Miller v. Universal City Studios, Inc.,*[8] a civil copyright action, the court upheld the exclusion of a proffered expert's testimony due to his having received and read daily transcript copy despite a Rule 615 order covering him. Similarly, in *Reeves v. International Tel. and Tel. Corp.,*[9] the court emphasized the flagrant violation and counsel's willful involvement in it, in upholding the prohibition of the violators' testimony.[10]

5. T.J. Stevenson & Co., Inc. v. 81,193 Bags of Flour, 629 F.2d 338, 384 (5th Cir.1980) (non-excluded expert permitted to testify as to general opinions as expert but not as to specific facts of case); Miller v. Universal City Studios, Inc., 650 F.2d 1365, 1374 (5th Cir. 1981).

6. *See, e.g.,* United States v. Franham, 791 F.2d 331 (4th Cir.1986).

7. Cases declining to preclude testimony despite witnesses' violations of Rule 615 exclusion orders include: Virgin Islands v. Edinborough, 625 F.2d 472, 474 (3d Cir.1980) (no showing of prejudice); United States v. Smith, 578 F.2d 1227, 1235 (8th Cir.1978); United States v. Oropeza, 564 F.2d 316, 326 (9th Cir.1977), *cert. denied,* 434 U.S. 1080 (1978); United States v. Lustig, 555 F.2d 737, 748 n. 14 (9th Cir.), *cert. denied,* 434 U.S. 1045 (1977).

8. 650 F.2d 1365, 1373 (5th Cir.1981).

9. 616 F.2d 1342, 1355 (5th Cir.1980), *cert. denied,* 449 U.S. 1077 (1981).

10. *See also* Calloway v. Blackburn, 612 F.2d 201, 204–205 (5th Cir.1980) (habeas corpus case upholding exclusion of testimony by violators of sequestration order where the proffer indicated it would have been cumulative). *Accord:* United States v. Avila–Macias, 577 F.2d 1384, 1389 (9th Cir.1978).

It is very important that parties ascertain what the trial judge intends the scope of sequestration to be. Questions may arise, for example, whether counsel may discuss a witness's testimony with someone who is sequestered and who has not testified, whether counsel may show daily transcript to a witness who has not testified, and whether counsel may discuss a non-party witness's testimony with that witness during a recess. Any doubts should be resolved by asking the court to rule as to scope before possible violations occur.

Finally, some question has arisen as to exclusion of witnesses from pre-trial proceedings. Although Rule 1101(d) expressly renders Rule 615 inapplicable to such hearings, many of the same considerations inherent in the drafters' decision to make exclusion mandatory (once requested by a party) apply with equal force to pretrial proceedings.[11] Additionally, Rule 615 has been held applicable to depositions, on the theory that it is incorporated by reference by Fed.R.Civ.P. 30(c).[12] It is not entirely clear that this result was intended by the drafters of either the civil or evidence rules.

11. *But see* United States v. West, 607 F.2d 300, 306 (9th Cir.1979) (applying discretionary standard in refusing to exclude police witnesses at pretrial hearing stage, without reference to Rule 1101). *Accord:* United States v. Warren, 578 F.2d 1058, 1076 (5th Cir. 1978), *cert. denied,* 446 U.S. 956 (1980) (suppression hearing).

12. Lumpkin v. Bi–Lo, Inc., 117 F.R.D. 451, 453 (M.D.Ga.1987); Solar Turbine, Inc. v. United States, 14 Cl.Ct. 551, 25 Fed.R.Evid.Serv. 381 (1988).

ARTICLE VII. OPINIONS AND EXPERT TESTIMONY

Introduction

Article VII concerns opinions and expert testimony and was intended to liberalize the rules governing admissibility. It appears to have done so without significant problems in application and has been well received by the courts.

Rule 701 removes the common law restraint barring laymen from testifying as to opinions or inferences. The Rule permits admission of lay opinion or inference if it is based on personal observation and helpful to the determination of an issue of fact. Rule 702 adopts a similar helpfulness standard for expert testimony. In addition, the qualifications requisite to the assumption of "expert" status have been broadened to include skill, experience or training.

Rule 703 permits an expert, in forming an opinion, to rely upon hearsay or other inadmissible evidence—"if [it is] of a type reasonably relied upon by experts in a particular field"—as well as on firsthand knowledge or facts presented at the trial. The Rule markedly widens the basis on which experts at common law could rest their opinions and was intended to reflect more realistically the practice of experts.

Rule 704 provides that experts and laymen may give opinions on the ultimate issues to be decided by the trier of fact. The Rule reflects the underlying helpfulness standard and the liberalizing tendency of Article VII.

Rule 705 concerns procedure. It removes the necessity of adducing the foundation for an expert opinion before that opinion may be admitted. The burden of testing the adequacy of an opinion's foundation is now placed on the opposing party's cross-examination.

Finally, Rule 706 sets forth the procedure for court appointment of expert witnesses.

RULE 701

I. TEXT OF RULE

RULE 701. Testimony by Lay Witnesses

If the witness is not testifying as an expert, the witness' testimony in the form of opinions or inferences is limited to those opinions or inferences which are (a) rationally based on the perception of the witness and (b) helpful to a clear understanding of the witness' testimony or the determination of a fact in issue.

II. DISCUSSION

Rule 701 changes the common law rule that lay witnesses cannot give opinion testimony. Even at common law, the rule was breached almost as frequently as it was honored. The line separating facts from opinions and inferences proved to be elusive, and trial judges were given wide latitude to expand the concept of a fact in order to permit testimony to develop.

The Advisory Committee Note to Rule 701 indicates that the Rule was intended to avoid the unrealistic restraint of limiting laymen to "facts." [1] The Rule itself imposes two limits on the use of opinions and inference by witnesses, however. First, opinions or inferences must be based upon the perception of the witness, a requirement that reinforces the personal knowledge requirement of Rule 602. Second, the opinion must be helpful to the trier of fact.

The trial court needs, and under the Rule has, discretion to determine whether proffered nonexpert opinions and inferences satisfy the Rule. Although the more difficult question usually is whether the opinion or inference is necessary, in some instances the judge must decide whether there is sufficient personal knowledge to support an opinion or inference. For example, in *Lubbock Feed Lots, Inc., v. Iowa Beef Processors,*[2] a witness's "understanding" that his business partner acted as defendant's agent in purchasing plaintiff's cattle was held properly admitted under Rule 701(a). The defendant had objected that the testimony was insufficiently grounded upon personal knowledge because it was based upon overheard telephone conversations and not direct knowledge of the business dealings. The appellate court stated that, although the evidence may have been "tenuous," the inference was based on observations and this was sufficient, if deemed helpful, to satisfy Rule 701(a) requirements.

While there is no clear rule that determines when an opinion or inference is helpful, courts appear anxious to see whether the opinion

1. 2 Saltzburg & Martin, *Federal Rules of Evidence Manual* 12 (5th ed. 1990).

2. 620 F.2d 250 (5th Cir.1980).

or inference adds to or clarifies the information that the witness is providing to the court.[3] If so, the testimony is likely to be permitted.

Bohannon v. Pegelow[4] illustrates the exercise of discretion under the helpfulness standard. The plaintiff's girlfriend was permitted to testify in a civil rights action that his arrest for pandering was motivated by racial prejudice. On appeal, the defendant police officer claimed that this testimony was merely a personal opinion regarding defendant's mental state. The appellate court upheld the decision on admissibility as within the discretion of the trial judge, observing that "[a]n appellate court is hardly in a position to reevaluate, based upon a cold record, the helpfulness of certain testimony or the subtle balancing of factors contained in Rule 403."[5]

Both *Lubbock* and *Bohannon* would have been decided differently at common law. These cases and others[6] reflect that Rule 701 has resulted in an increase in the admission of opinions of lay witnesses. Trial judges generally have exercised their discretion to expand the scope of lay testimony, and some appellate decisions reinforce this trend.

Thus, in *Teen–Ed, Inc. v. Kimball Int'l, Inc.*,[7] the court noted that testimony which an expert had been precluded from giving was admissible as a lay opinion. The plaintiff was unable to provide the testimony of its accountant or bookkeeper on lost profits because it had failed to comply with a pretrial order and was consequently awarded only nominal damages of one dollar. The appellate court held that, insofar as lost profits could be calculated based upon the accountant's or bookkeeper's knowledge of plaintiff's records, his was a lay opinion and should have been admitted. According to the court, the essential difference between expert and lay opinion testimony is that only experts can answer hypothetical questions.[8]

There appears to be no major problem in the implementation of the Rule. Thirty-one states have identical rules. Florida, Delaware and Tennessee have similar provisions, but have drafted their rules to

3. United States v. De Peri, 778 F.2d 963 (3d Cir.1985) (court allowed testimony of witness' understanding of a tape recording as being helpful to those listeners who otherwise might think the conversation was in code), *cert. denied,* 475 U.S. 1110 (1986).

4. 652 F.2d 729 (7th Cir.1981).

5. 652 F.2d at 732.

6. *See, e.g.,* United States v. Smith, 550 F.2d 277 (5th Cir.), *cert. denied,* 434 U.S. 841 (1977).

7. 620 F.2d 399 (3d Cir.1980).

8. Eisenberg v. Gagnon, 766 F.2d 770 (3d Cir) (defendant's law partner allowed to testify that information given to investors would not be adequate if he knew what defendants knew), *cert. denied,* 474 U.S. 946 (1985). *But see* United States v. Ranney, 719 F.2d 1183 (1st Cir.1983) (court allowed investors to answer hypothetical questions while recognizing they were not rendering expert opinions).

suggest somewhat more caution in receiving opinions where the witness is able to provide raw data to the court.[9]

The common law experience demonstrates the difficulty of distinguishing between facts and opinions. Few cases were reversed because a witness was permitted to offer an opinion that technically was improper. In using Rule 701, courts will continue to have some difficulty in deciding which opinions help the trier of fact and which do not. It will be the rare case in which the trial judge's exercise of discretion will be overturned on appeal.

Each of the cases described above in this discussion could have been decided the other way, and those decisions would not necessarily be less defensible than the decisions actually rendered. In *Lubbock Feed Lots, Inc.*, for example, the trial judge could have said that the witness could describe what he heard of the telephone conversations and no more. In *Bohannon*, the trial judge could have restricted the witness to a description of what the officers did and said and whether they treated other people differently from the way they treated the plaintiff. In *Teen–Ed, Inc.*, the court of appeals could have said that where a party planned to rely on any special expertise of a witness, that witness ought to be identified in the pretrial order.

These cases demonstrate that sound judgment requires a careful analysis of the testimony that a lay witness offers a court. Slight variations in a witness's opportunity to perceive events and in the nature of the opinion or inference the witness wishes to draw can be important. If a witness has not had an adequate opportunity to observe events firsthand, opinions may be excluded.[10] Where a witness attempts to characterize another's state of mind, some courts may hesitate to permit opinions to substitute for observations.[11] Rule 701 recognizes that an absolute ban on lay opinion is likely to deprive a court of helpful information, but it also recognizes that not all opinions or inferences lay witnesses are willing to offer are helpful. As a result, the Rule depends on the trial judge to exercise sound discretion. As long as the trial judge is careful in assessing lay opinion testimony, Rule 701 should generate no significant problems.

9. 2 *Evidence in America* §§ 50.2–50.4.

10. *See, e.g.,* Meder v. Everest & Jennings, Inc., 637 F.2d 1182 (8th Cir.1981) (police officer who investigated accident did not make personal observations).

11. *See, e.g.,* United States v. Phillips, 600 F.2d 535 (5th Cir.1979) (agent's opinion that defendant understood meaning of word "disability" might well be inadmissible).

RULE 702

I. TEXT OF RULE

RULE 702. Testimony by Experts

If scientific, technical, or other specialized knowledge will assist the trier of fact to understand the evidence or to determine a fact in issue, a witness qualified as an expert by knowledge, skill, experience, training, or education, may testify thereto in the form of an opinion or otherwise.

II. DISCUSSION

Under Rule 702, as under Rule 701 governing lay testimony, expert testimony is admissible if it is likely to help or assist the trier of fact. Expert testimony is admissible even where the issue is within the ordinary, unaided comprehension of the jury, as long as it will help the jury decide the case.

Rule 702 defines the qualifications of an expert in broad terms. A person may be an expert because of his experience rather than as a result of formal training.[1] In some cases, however, courts demand special expertise. In *Hartke v. McKelway,*[2] for example, the court required a showing of very specific expertise in a malpractice action alleging wrongful birth resulting from a relatively new obstetric technique and rejected the testimony of a family physician who had no experience with, or training in, that technique. In *Hughes v. Hemingway Transport, Inc.,*[3] the court similarly ruled that a person trained in tractor-trailer skid control, but who did not have a scientific or engineering background, was not sufficiently qualified as plaintiff's expert to testify whether defendant had used the appropriate technique for controlling a tractor-trailer skidding on ice in a personal injury case.

Under Rule 104(a), the trial judge decides when a person is sufficiently qualified to be an expert. Appellate courts indicate that they generally will defer to the decisions of trial judges. *See, e.g., Fernandez, supra.* There has been some concern expressed by appellate courts that trial judges ought not to exclude the testimony of experts who may be able to assist a jury even though they may not be the most qualified of all possible experts. The Third Circuit reversed a trial court's rejection of plaintiff's proffered testimony from an expert who had engineering training and experience with machine guards, but who had not designed elevators or examined the elevator in question in a design defect

1. *See, e.g.,* Fernandez v. Chios Shipping Co., Ltd., 542 F.2d 145 (2d Cir.1976) (witness permitted to testify about pallets that injured longshoremen); United States v. Kampiles, 609 F.2d 1233 (7th Cir.1979), *cert. denied,* 446 U.S. 954 (1980) (counterintelligence agent permitted to testify on Soviet recruiting procedures).

2. 526 F.Supp. 97 (D.D.C.1981).

3. 539 F.Supp. 130 (E.D.Pa.1982).

case involving unguarded elevator control buttons.[4] The same court expressed approval of the admission of expert testimony in *Hammond v. International Harvestor Co.,*[5] a wrongful death action arising out of the death of a farm laborer killed in a tractor turnover. The trial judge permitted a man experienced as an automobile and tractor salesman—who had taught high school auto repair and maintenance, but who had no engineering or other academic credentials—to testify.

United States v. Johnson,[6] illustrates how liberal some courts may be in interpreting Rule 702. The trial judge permitted a government witness whose only qualification was "the experience of being around a great deal [of marijuana] and smoking it" to testify on the origin of marijuana the government claimed was illegally imported from Colombia—even though a professor called by the defense stated that there was no way to determine from a physical inspection the origin of marijuana. Although the witness falls within the liberal "skilled witness" category of experts covered by the Rule, there is reason to question whether his qualifications actually supported the opinion he gave. There is no way of knowing with any high degree of certainty, and this helps to explain why appellate courts tend to defer to the rulings of trial judges. Cases like *Johnson* do serve as a reminder, however, of the importance of the foundational evidence offered to justify treatment of a person as an expert. Because the trial judge must decide whether a person may give expert testimony, the trial judge must carefully examine the foundation laid by the party relying on the witness.

A problem closely related to the determination of the expert's qualifications—and perhaps a part of the helpfulness consideration—is the question whether a novel form of expertise is sufficiently reliable to aid the jury in arriving at an accurate result. Prior to the adoption of the Rules, many courts used the test applied in *Frye v. United States,*[7] that the underlying scientific principle or discovery "must be sufficiently established to have gained general acceptance in the particular field in which it belongs"—a test that an early lie-detector failed.

The Advisory Committee Note to Rule 702 does not mention *Frye*'s general acceptance test, and the helpfulness standard may be thought to conflict with *Frye.* Courts have differed as to what standard to follow. For example, following an earlier decision applying the *Frye* test, the use of spectrographic voice identification was held inadmissible in *United States v. McDaniel.*[8] Conversely, in *United States v. Baller,*[9]

4. Knight v. Otis Elevator Co., 596 F.2d 84 (3d Cir.1979).

5. 691 F.2d 646 (3d Cir.1982).

6. 575 F.2d 1347 (5th Cir.1978), *cert. denied,* 440 U.S. 907 (1979).

7. 293 Fed. 1013, 1014 (D.C.Cir.1923).

8. 538 F.2d 408, 413 (D.C.Cir.1976).

9. 519 F.2d 463, 466 (4th Cir.), *cert. denied,* 423 U.S. 1019 (1975).

spectrographic voice identification was admitted, apparently notwithstanding the *Frye* standard, on the grounds that it was unlikely to mislead the jury or be prejudicial under Rule 403. Again, such evidence has been upheld as admissible under a Rule 403 balancing test and ruled admissible under the *Frye* test in *United States v. Williams.*[10]

The problems confronting the trial court in determining whether a novel scientific approach is admissible clearly confronted the court in *United States v. Transowski.*[11] The defendant was on trial for perjury for having provided a false alibi at his brother's criminal trial. He testified that he had taken a photograph of his brother and mother in the latter's backyard on the afternoon of May 12, 1974, at the time of the brother's alleged crime. The trial court, relying on Rule 702, had permitted an astronomer to testify for the government that, based upon the angle and altitude of the sun and the shadows in the photograph, the photograph must have been taken on either April 13 or August 31, 1974. The appeals court reversed the perjury conviction on the grounds that, as the procedure had never previously been used in this way nor adequately tested for this purpose, it was not sufficiently accepted in the field. The dissenting judge reasoned that the astronomer had simply made a new application of established principles and that errors and inaccuracies had been adequately accounted for.

The United States Court of Appeals for the Third Circuit has developed an approach to novel scientific evidence, in *United States v. Downing,*[12] which identifies such evidence as "evidence whose scientific fundaments are not suitable candidates for judicial notice." The court indicated that, in approaching such evidence, the trial judge should conduct a preliminary inquiry focusing on (1) the soundness and reliability of the technique used in generating the evidence, (2) the possibility that admitting the evidence would overwhelm, confuse, or mislead the jury, and (3) the proffered connection between the scientific research and test result to be presented, and particular disputed factual issues in the case. *Downing* was an eyewitness identification case, which resulted in a remand to the trial judge, who found *inter alia* an insufficient "fit" between various eyewitness studies and the issues in the case. The judge reinstated a conviction and was affirmed by the court of appeals.[13]

Although *Downing* has been utilized in various circumstances not involving eyewitness testimony,[14] the Third Circuit has been one of many courts that has had to differentiate a novel opinion from a novel

10. 443 F.Supp. 269 (S.D.N.Y.1977), *aff'd,* 583 F.2d 1194 (2d Cir.1978), *cert. denied,* 439 U.S. 1117 (1979).

11. 659 F.2d 750 (7th Cir.1981).

12. 753 F.2d 1224 (3d Cir.1985).

13. 609 F.Supp. 784 (E.D.Pa.), *aff'd* 780 F.2d 1017 (3d Cir.1985).

14. *E.g.,* United States v. Ferri, 778 F.2d 985 (3d Cir.1985), *cert. denied,* 106 S.Ct. 2896, 107 S.Ct. 117 (1986) (footprint analysis).

technique. If an expert relies upon standard techniques or accepted methodology and reaches an opinion that is shared by few, if any, other experts, that opinion is not necessarily inadmissible. A careful finding is required before a trial judge can conclude that an opinion cannot reasonably be based upon data developed according to standard methods. An opinion that runs against the weight of scientific opinion is not for that reason inadmissible.[15]

Federal and state courts have struggled to identify circumstances in which the use of standard data in an unusual way amounts to a novel methodology and to differentiate such circumstances from those in which one expert simply disagrees with the conclusion of others. In a series of cases involving the drug Bendectin, many courts concluded that expert testimony should not be admitted to support claims that the drug caused birth defects. In some cases, the courts have concluded that there is an inadequate foundation.[16] Other decisions are less clear.[17] The Third Circuit disagreed with the analysis in many of these cases.[18]

It is regrettable that the subject of scientific evidence received little, if any, consideration while the Rules were debated. Most states, in their discussions and commentaries, have chosen to ignore the topic also.[19] There clearly is a difference between courts that follow *Frye*[20] and courts that do not require such extensive proof of general acceptance before permitting evidence of new scientific techniques.[21] At some point a uniform approach would seem to be desirable.

Whether intended or not, it may be that the silence of the Rules on scientific evidence will provide a period of experimentation following which a generally applicable standard might be adopted. It is not clear that any standard would produce agreement at the moment. It is also unclear to what extent a *Frye* analysis will produce results different from a helpfulness or relevance analysis. It will be important for users of the Rules to monitor how federal courts handle novel questions of scientific evidence. Should it appear that a consensus is developing,

15. *See, e.g.,* In re Paoli R.R. Yard PCB Litig., 916 F.2d 829 (3d Cir.1990); DeLuca v. Merrell Dow Pharmaceuticals, Inc., 911 F.2d 941 (3d Cir.1990).

16. *See, e.g.,* Ealy v. Richardson–Merrell, Inc., 897 F.2d 1159 (D.C.Cir.), *cert. denied,* 111 S.Ct. 370 (1990).

17. E.g., Brock v. Merrell Dow Pharmaceuticals, Inc., 884 F.2d 167 (en banc) denying reh'g to 874 F.2d 307 (5th Cir.1989), *cert. denied,* 110 S.Ct. 1511 (1990).

18. *See* DeLuca v. Merrel Dow Pharmaceuticals, Inc., 911 F.2d 941 (3d Cir.1990).

19. *See* 2 *Evidence in America* § 51.5.

20. *See, e.g.,* United States v. Shorter, 809 F.2d 54 (D.C.Cir.) (court recognized that *Frye* was the standard to follow in that circuit), *cert. denied,* 484 U.S. 817 (1987).

21. *See, e.g.,* Clinchfield R.R. v. Lynch, 784 F.2d 545 (4th Cir.1986) (court reasoned that evidence shouldn't be excluded because of the mere fact that it's a novel theory). *See also* the Discussion in Rule 401, *supra.*

the time may come for a clear statement of that approach in Article VII.

The final words—"or otherwise"—in Rule 702 indicate that an expert need not offer an opinion when called to testify. Rather, the expert might provide factual data or give the jury background material in a technical area. By the same token, since the hypothetical question no longer is required, Rule 702 permits a party to use an expert in a way that is most likely to help the jury. Together with Rule 703, providing that an expert may rely on certain data that might not be independently admissible, and Rule 705, which permits an expert to offer an opinion before providing supporting data, Article VII offers litigants opportunities to make expert testimony as helpful as possible. The trial judge is endowed with authority, however, to require that a case proceed in a specific way if he determines that would be more helpful to the jury.

In the years to come it is likely that courts will be called upon to assess a number of challenges to expert opinion and to determine when an expert is helpful under Rule 702 and when he or she should be permitted to rely upon various data under Rule 703. In many instances, it is difficult to determine whether a challenge to expert testimony is more appropriately made under one rule or the other. Rule 702 challenges suggest that a person lacks expertise when offering opinions based upon analyses or data not relied upon by other experts in the field. Rule 703 challenges suggest that experts cannot reasonably rely upon certain data, even if some in the field have confidence in the data. More litigation and a flood of appellate opinions is to be expected in both state and federal courts.

RULE 703

I. TEXT OF RULE

RULE 703. Bases of Opinion Testimony by Experts

The facts or data in the particular case upon which an expert bases an opinion or inference may be those perceived by or made known to the expert at or before the hearing. If of a type reasonably relied upon by experts in the particular field in forming opinions or inferences upon the subject, the facts or data need not be admissible in evidence.

II. DISCUSSION

Rule 703 was a controversial rule when enacted, and it remains controversial. The source of controversy is that it permits experts to base their opinions on facts or data otherwise inadmissible if the data fall under the general rubric of being "of a type reasonably relied upon by experts in the particular field."

Rule 703 permits an expert to base his opinion upon information derived by three methods: (1) personal observation by the expert; (2) facts or data made known to him or her at or before the trial; and (3) facts or data reasonably relied upon by experts in the particular field in forming opinions, whether or not such information is admissible at trial.

The first method of forming an expert opinion is generally considered the most reliable; for example, the treating physician who observed the injured plaintiff's physical condition and thereafter renders an opinion as to prognosis and future treatment. The second method generally requires that the expert be present at trial to hear evidence or, more commonly, the expert is presented with a hypothetical question containing facts that are in evidence. The third method, unlike the first two, permits the expert to base an opinion upon facts or data that are not admissible in evidence, but may nevertheless be presented to the jury "if of a type reasonably relied upon by experts in the particular field."

The "facts" or "data" reasonably relied upon, may include a broad range of hearsay, from documents to oral statements. For instance, the Advisory Committee Notes indicate that physicians base their opinions on numerous sources, including statements by patients and relatives, reports and opinions from nurses, technicians and other doctors, hospital records, and x-rays. Allowing the physician to base an opinion upon this type of information brings Rule 703 into line with the realities of how the physician makes treatment decisions.

The application of the reasonable reliance standard has, however, proved somewhat problematic. First, there is at least the theoretical difficulty facing the judge, who is not likely to have expertise in any given expert's field, in determining whether similar facts or data are reasonably relied upon by other experts in the field. This is especially difficult where novel uses of technique or specialized knowledge are involved. Indeed, it may be that the reasonable reliance standard of Rule 703 implicitly involves *Frye*'s general acceptance test. Second, even where a type of information is generally relied upon in a field, the particular use of similar information in a particular case may be unreasonable. Note that because this lack of expertise, to the extent it is problematic, is not rule-caused, it is equally problematic at common law when the court is applying the *Frye* test.

In *Zenith Radio Corp. v. Matsushita Elec. Indus. Co., Ltd.,*[1] the district court took a restrictive view of what constitutes reasonable reliance. The court set forth six factors to be applied in determining reasonable reliance: (1) the extent to which the opinion is pervaded or dominated by reliance on materials judicially determined to be inadmissible on grounds of either relevance or trustworthiness; (2) the extent to which the opinion is dominated or pervaded by reliance upon other trustworthy materials; (3) the extent to which the expert's assumptions have been shown to be unsupported, speculative, or demonstrably incorrect; (4) the extent to which the materials on which the expert relied are within his immediate sphere of expertise, are of a kind customarily relied upon by experts in his field in forming opinions or inferences on that subject, and are not used only for litigation purposes; (5) the extent to which the expert acknowledges the questionable reliability of the underlying information, thus indicating that he has taken that factor into consideration in forming his opinion; and (6) the extent to which reliance on certain materials, even if otherwise reasonable, may be unreasonable in the peculiar circumstances of the case.[2]

The court eliminated a substantial number of the proffered opinions as based upon documents previously found to be unreliable hearsay, and granted summary judgment in favor of defendants.

On appeal, the Third Circuit determined that the district court took an unduly restrictive view of what constitutes reasonable reliance, and reversed the lower court.[3] The appellate court noted that the trial court's function is to make an initial inquiry to determine the data upon which experts in the field rely. The court concluded that once the trial court makes an initial determination that the data is of a type reasonably relied upon by experts in the field, further inquiry into the

1. 505 F.Supp. 1313 (E.D.Pa.1980).

2. *Id.* at 1330.

3. In re Japanese Elec. Prod. Antitrust Litig., 723 F.2d 238 (3d Cir.1983), *rev'g* Zenith Radio Corp. v. Matsushita Elec. Indus. Co., Ltd., 505 F.Supp. 1313 (E.D.Pa.1980), *rev'd on other grounds,* 475 U.S. 574 (1986) (Supreme Court in dictum agreed with district court's six-step analysis and findings).

expert's opinion should be reserved for cross-examination as is contemplated by Rule 705.[4]

The Third Circuit court's decision has been criticized by some writers.[5] The appellate court seemed to overlook the fact that an expert's reliance on a particular type of data is no guarantee of its accuracy. Through the trial court's six-step analysis, the judge attempted to determine whether data relied on for the purpose of litigation would also be relied on in other situations. While the Supreme Court did not decide the evidentiary rulings, in dictum it noted its agreement with the six-step analysis and findings. This appears to mean that later cases using the same six-step approach might be able to be more stringent when faced with expert testimony.

Data reasonably relied upon by an expert may come in many forms. For instance, the expert may base his opinion upon conversations he had with others. In *Lewis v. Rego Co.,*[6] the court held that it was error not to permit plaintiff's expert to disclose that his opinion was based, in part, upon discussions with another expert concerning the cause of a propane tank explosion. The court noted that experts may reasonably base their opinions upon discussions had with other experts.[7]

In *Stevens v. Cessna Aircraft Co.,*[8] an expert in an aviation products liability case was allowed to testify that his opinion that the plaintiff's decedent was under stress was based upon interviews with decedent's associates and friends. The court allowed the testimony because the expert testified that such interviews are normally relied upon by experts when evaluating a pilot's fitness.[9]

In *United States v. Lundy,*[10] the defendant was convicted of arson. The prosecution's expert rendered his opinion that the fire was caused by arson based, in part, upon interviews with witnesses at the scene. Lundy argued on appeal that the expert's testimony was inadmissible because based on hearsay statements and third party observations. The court agreed that it would be impermissible for the expert to simply summarize and testify to statements by third parties that Lundy was the person that torched the building. However, in this case the expert based his opinion upon observations and statements of witnesses that would reasonably be relied upon by experts. The court noted that the expert "presented uncontroverted evidence that interviews with

4. *See* Rule 705 *infra.*

5. *See, e.g.,* 2 Saltzburg & Martin, *Federal Rules of Evidence Manual* 75 (5th ed. 1990).

6. 757 F.2d 66 (3d Cir.1985).

7. *Id.* at 74.

8. 634 F.Supp. 137 (E.D.Pa.1986), *aff'd,* 806 F.2d 254 (3d Cir.1986).

9. *Id.* at 143.

10. 809 F.2d 392 (7th Cir.1987).

many witnesses to a fire are a standard investigatory technique in cause and origin [of fire] inquires." [11]

Lundy highlights the significance between a supposed expert who merely recites hearsay for the benefit of the jury and the expert that actually bases his opinion upon hearsay. The former type of testimony is an impermissible abuse of Rule 703.

Some courts have resorted to the more stringent "trustworthiness" test rejected by the Third Circuit Court in *In re Japanese Products, supra.* In *Ricciardi v. Children's Hosp. Medical Center,*[12] plaintiff brought a medical negligence action to recover for neurological injuries that allegedly resulted from negligence during an operation. Plaintiff's expert's opinion was based solely upon a handwritten note entered in his medical record two days after surgery by a neurology resident. The note was entered in a three page consultation report, and stated "during surgical episode of aortic cannula accidently out X 40–60 seconds." The resident did not have personal knowledge of the event nor did he know where he obtained the information. However, he assumed that he obtained the information from "professional people."

Based upon the above noted entry, the expert concluded that the cause of plaintiff's neurological injury was that the cannula came out during surgery. The court rejected the expert's opinion and in doing so noted that "the 'fact' or 'datum' on which [the expert] offered to base his opinion was not one which medical experts frequently encounter. [The expert] said never before had he seen such a statement in a hospital chart." [13]

The court in *Ricciardi* was arguably overly restrictive in applying Rule 704 and may possibly have confused Rule 703 with one of the rules providing an exception to the rule against hearsay. The court noted that "as an alternative basis for introducing [the resident's] note *to prove that the cannula came out during surgery,* Ricciardi sought to have an expert witness . . . rely on the statement to form an opinion that this occurred." [14] *Ricciardi* may more appropriately be looked at as a case where the plaintiff failed to meet his burden of proof. The expert's opinion, based upon a consultation report, probably could have been admitted subject to cross-examination.

In *Washington v. Armstrong World Industries, Inc.,*[15] plaintiff filed a wrongful death action claiming that her husband died as a result of exposure to asbestos. The court entered summary judgment in favor of the defendants. Plaintiff filed a motion for reconsideration on the basis of a newly submitted expert's affidavit. The expert concluded that the

11. *Id.* at 395–96.

12. 811 F.2d 18 (1st Cir.1987).

13. *Id.* at 25.

14. *Id.* at 24.

15. 839 F.2d 1121 (5th Cir.1988).

decedent died from asbestos exposure. His opinion was based upon decedent's 32 year exposure to asbestos and because there was a statistical relation between asbestos exposure and colon cancer. He concluded that the pathological tests performed on decedent may not have been sensitive enough to detect the presence of asbestos fibers.[16]

The district court concluded that the expert's opinion was "pure speculation and fundamentally unreliable." The court further noted that the opinion was unreliable because "it was based on possibilities that might exist as a result of [a] lack of certain tests [plaintiff's expert] could have performed on Mr. Washington while he was alive rather than specific findings or evaluations of test results that were available." [17]

The appellate court affirmed, noting that it was within the trial court's discretion to exclude the expert's testimony. The court found it significant that plaintiff's expert never examined the decedent and only relied upon examinations performed by other physicians who reached different conclusions.[18]

It is important to keep in mind that Rule 703 is not an exception to the rule against hearsay. Even though an expert may disclose to the jury the data he relied upon, the data will not be considered as substantive evidence for purposes of establishing a prima facie case.

In *Paddack v. Dave Christensen, Inc.*,[19] the trustees of an employee trust filed suit against defendant claiming its contributions to the trust were deficient. The plaintiffs retained an accounting firm to perform an audit of defendant's contributions. The audit disclosed a deficiency. During the trial, plaintiffs sought to admit the audit reports into evidence, as a basis of the expert's testimony under Rule 703, to establish that defendant did not adequately contribute to the trust fund. The trial court found the reports to be inadmissible hearsay. The appellate court affirmed and, in doing so, noted that "Rule 703 merely permits such hearsay, or other inadmissible evidence upon which an expert properly relies, to be admitted to explain the basis of the expert's opinion. It does not allow the admission of the reports to establish the truth of what they assert." [20]

In criminal prosecutions the defendant's constitutional right to confront and cross-examine adverse witnesses presents a concern not found in civil cases. In *United States v. Lawson*,[21] the defendant was convicted on one count of extortion and one count of assault. Defendant argued that his right to confront adverse witnesses was violated

16. *Id.* at 1122.

17. *Id.*

18. *Id.* at 1123–24.

19. 745 F.2d 1254 (9th Cir.1984).

20. *Id.* at 1261–62.

21. 653 F.2d 299 (7th Cir.1981), *cert. denied,* 454 U.S. 1150 (1982).

when the government's expert rendered an opinion that defendant was sane. The opinion was based solely on hearsay information obtained from other physicians and staff members, results of tests administered by the government and other reports from the F.B.I. and United States Attorney's Office. The court noted that in criminal cases, "inquiry under Rule 703 must go beyond finding that hearsay relied on by an expert [is of a type reasonably relied upon]. An expert's testimony that was based entirely on hearsay reports, while perhaps satisfying Rule 703, would nevertheless violate a defendant's constitutional right to confront adverse witnesses." [22]

The criminal defendant should certainly obtain a limiting instruction under Rule 105 with regard to hearsay information relied upon by a prosecution expert. However, the efficacy of such instructions may be questioned. Exclusion under Rule 403 should also be argued in the criminal case to exclude expert testimony whose inadmissible underlying basis may be unfairly prejudicial.

Without doubt, Rule 703 does provide opportunities for abuse. The trial judge is expected to control conduct under the Rule, however, and to keep abuses to a minimum. Thus far, the fears expressed about the Rule have not materialized, at least not in reported cases. One salutary aspect of practice under the Rule is that experts who used to rely on material that was inadmissible, but who testified only on the basis of the admissible data, now may reveal the entire basis of their opinions. As a result, the jury may have a more candid statement of the reasons supporting an expert's conclusions and an opposing party might have a greater opportunity to challenge the expert's approach.

22. *Id.* at 302.

RULE 704

I. TEXT OF RULE

RULE 704. Opinion on Ultimate Issue

(a) Except as provided in subdivision (b), testimony in the form of an opinion or inference otherwise admissible is not objectionable because it embraces an ultimate issue to be decided by the trier of fact.

(b) No expert witness testifying with respect to the mental state or condition of a defendant in a criminal case may state an opinion or inference as to whether the defendant did or did not have the mental state or condition constituting an element of the crime charged or of a defense thereto. Such ultimate issues are matters for the trier of fact alone.

II. DISCUSSION

According to the Advisory Committee Note, Rule 704 is an application of the basic "helpfulness" approach of Rules 701–702. If testimony is helpful to the trier of fact and otherwise satisfies the Rules, it should not be excluded simply because it embraces the ultimate issue in a case. Rule 704 applies to testimony of both expert and lay witnesses. However, the expert's opinion is still subject to the requirements of Rules 702 and 703, and the lay opinion must comply with Rule 701. Similarly, Rule 403 remains available to exclude the evidence if prejudicial, confusing or a waste of time.[1]

The most significant change in recent years to Rule 704 was the addition of subdivision (b), which precludes experts from rendering an opinion on mental state or condition if an element of the crime charged.[2] It has been held that Rule 704's bar against opinion testimony on the ultimate issue of insanity is not unconstitutional.[3] The change in Rule 704 merely leaves the ultimate issue of insanity for the jury to decide.[4]

The addition of subsection (b) may present some problems of interpretation and application. While that provision prohibits experts from offering an opinion on the defendant's mental state or condition constituting an element of the offense or a defense, it does not prohibit

1. *See generally,* 2 S. Saltzburg & M. Martin, *Federal Rules of Evidence Manual* at 99 (5th ed. 1990).

2. Subdivision (b) was made effective October 12, 1984.

3. *See, e.g.,* United States v. Freeman, 804 F.2d 1574 (11th Cir.1986).

4. The Insanity Defense Reform Act, 18 U.S.C.A. § 20, restricts the insanity defense only to the defendant who is "unable to appreciate the nature and quality or the wrongfulness of his acts" when the crime was committed. The Act also "prohibits experts for either the government or defendant from testifying as to the ultimate issue of the accused's sanity." United States v. Freeman, 804 F.2d 1574 (11th Cir.1986).

experts from offering testimony on mens rea or sanity.[5] Nor does the Rule bar an expert witness from providing data or facts which might be helpful to the jury in deciding for example, whether a defendant was sane at the time of the offense. The line is obviously very thin and trial judges are being called upon to make fine distinctions. In *United States v. Edwards,*[6] the court permitted an expert to testify in response to an insanity defense, noting that every fact concerning an accused's mental state is admissible. The court noted that Rule 704(b) only forbids the expert from offering an ultimate opinion on the defendant's state of mind. In *United States v. Windfelder,*[7] the court barred an IRS agent from testifying in a fraudulent tax case that the defendant intentionally misstated his income because that opinion testimony addressed an element of the offense.

Some confusion has resulted with respect to whether an expert may offer an opinion concerning a legal standard. For instance, in *Karns v. Emerson Electric Company,*[8] the plaintiff brought a products liability action to recover for an amputation to his arm which occurred when defendant's "weed eater" kicked back. The jury found in favor of plaintiff and the defendant appealed claiming it was an error to permit plaintiff's expert to testify that the product was "unreasonably dangerous beyond the expectation of the average user. . . ."[9]

The appellate court noted that it was within the trial court's discretion to admit or deny testimony addressing a legal standard. Legal standard testimony may, however, be excluded if it confuses or prejudices the jury. The court concluded that the most that could be said about the plaintiff's expert's opinion concerning the unreasonable danger of defendant's product was that it was not helpful since it merely told the jury what conclusion to reach. Any prejudice or confusion would have been alleviated because the expert disclosed the basis of his opinion and the jury was also instructed that they could entirely reject an expert's opinion if not properly supported by sound reasons.[10]

In *Ponder v. Warren Tool Corp.,*[11] the plaintiff was injured when a tire exploded while he was using defendant's tire bead seater. The trial court refused to admit testimony by plaintiff's expert concerning the cause of the explosion and that the defendant's warnings were inadequate. The trial court determined that such testimony was speculative

5. United States v. Edwards, 819 F.2d 262, 264–265 (11th Cir.1987). *See also* 2 Saltzburg & Martin, *Federal Rules of Evidence Manual* 100–101 (5th ed. 1990).

6. 819 F.2d 262 (11th Cir.1987).

7. 790 F.2d 576 (7th Cir.1986).

8. 817 F.2d 1452 (10th Cir.1987).

9. *Id.* at 1459.

10. *Id.* at 1459.

11. 834 F.2d 1553 (10th Cir.1987).

and took into account facts not in evidence. The appellate court held it was an error not to permit expert testimony on the cause of the accident. The court noted that a witness qualified with regard to technical matters may render an opinion encompassing his area of expertise even if it embraces an ultimate issue in the case.[12]

Courts have not hesitated to refuse testimony on an ultimate issue by lay persons. In essence, there has been a recognition that an ultimate issue opinion must assist the jury, such as in the case of expert opinions rendered on subjects beyond the knowledge of the average person. On the other hand, testimony by a lay person concerning an ultimate issue is simply of no value. In *Kostelecky v. NL Acme Tool Inc.,*[13] plaintiff brought an action to recover for personal injuries sustained as a result of defendant's negligence in supervising work on an oil rig. The trial court admitted into evidence an accident report containing a statement by plaintiff's co-employee expressing the opinion that plaintiff's injury was the result of his own conduct.[14]

Although recognizing that opinions by lay persons on ultimate issues are admissible, the opinion testimony is subject to Rule 701, that the witness must testify to facts within his knowledge. The appellate court stated that "evidence that merely tells the jury what result to reach is not sufficiently helpful to the trier of fact to be admissible." [15] For instance, testimony in an automobile accident that defendant was driving negligently would be inadmissible. However, testimony that defendant was driving in excess of the posted speed limit would be admissible to establish that he was negligent.

The problems that have arisen in connection with this rule are not serious. Most existed at common law. With the ban on ultimate issue testimony removed, courts are now authorized to admit helpful testimony while excluding testimony which is confusing to the jury or which usurps the functions of the judge.

12. *Id.* at 1557.

13. 837 F.2d 828 (8th Cir.1988).

14. *Id.* at 830.

15. *Id.*

RULE 705

I. TEXT OF RULE

RULE 705. Disclosure of Facts or Data Underlying Expert Opinion

The expert may testify in terms of opinion or inference and give reasons therefor without prior disclosure of the underlying facts or data, unless the court requires otherwise. The expert may in any event be required to disclose the underlying facts or data on cross-examination.

II. DISCUSSION

Prior to the adoption of the Federal Rules of Evidence, federal courts disagreed on whether the data used by the expert in formulating an opinion had to be brought out at trial by the party calling the expert as a condition precedent to admission of an expert opinion. Some courts required that the expert disclose on direct examination the sources used, while others assumed the credibility of the opinion without requiring such disclosure and left exploration of the sources for cross-examination.

With a promulgation of Rule 705, opinion testimony may be admitted by the expert without the prior disclosure of the facts or data underlying the opinion, unless the trial court requires otherwise. The Rule relies upon effective cross-examination to reveal the factual basis for an expert's opinion, which permits the fact finder to determine what weight to accord the testimony.

If the court believes that an opinion may be based on impermissible data, it may order the witness to reveal the data before offering an opinion. The last clause of the first sentence authorizes this procedure, since it is easier to avoid an objectionable opinion than to strike one from the memory of jurors who have heard it.[1]

Hypothetical questions setting forth the facts relied upon are no longer required. Hypothetical questions, however, are necessary where the expert would not otherwise satisfy the minimal foundation requirements of Rule 703. Thus, if an expert does not have any knowledge of the facts of the case or familiarity with the data that experts in field would reasonably rely upon, he will still have to be provided the facts to meet the fundamental requirements. This would occur, for instance, where an expert was used to draw a conclusion from a number of different more specialized experts' testimony.

Because Rule 705 underscores the importance of effective cross-examination, the availability of pre-trial discovery about the expert witness and his testimony is critical. This principle is displayed in

1. *See* Tabatchnick v. G.D. Searle & Co., 67 F.R.D. 49 (D.N.J.1975).

Smith v. Ford Motor Co.,[2] a diversity action arising out of an automobile collision, wherein the Tenth Circuit discussed the importance of pre-trial discovery to enable a party to prepare to cross-examine an expert, and reversed a plaintiff's verdict because of the failure to provide adequate information before trial about an expert and his proposed testimony. Perhaps no significant problem in this area has emerged because the expert's proponent is likely to provide the foundation for his expert's testimony for advocacy purposes because merely conclusory opinions are likely to carry little weight with a jury.

The Rule does permit the trial judge to compel a party to present facts before eliciting an opinion. In a case in which discovery has been resisted and the factual basis of an expert's opinion is unclear, a request may be made of the judge to bar the expert's opinion until the factual predicate has been laid. Should the facts appear insufficient to support the opinion, or of a type not reasonably relied upon, the opinion may then be rejected under Rule 703.

2. 626 F.2d 784 (10th Cir.1980), *cert. denied,* 450 U.S. 918 (1981).

RULE 706

I. TEXT OF RULE

RULE 706. Court Appointed Experts

(a) Appointment. The court may on its own motion or on the motion of any party enter an order to show cause why expert witnesses should not be appointed, and may request the parties to submit nominations. The court may appoint any expert witnesses agreed upon by the parties, and may appoint expert witnesses of its own selection. An expert witness shall not be appointed by the court unless the witness consents to act. A witness so appointed shall be informed of the witness' duties by the court in writing, a copy of which shall be filed with the clerk, or at a conference in which the parties shall have opportunity to participate. A witness so appointed shall advise the parties of the witness' findings, if any; the witness' deposition may be taken by any party; and the witness may be called to testify by the court or any party. The witness shall be subject to cross-examination by each party, including a party calling the witness.

(b) Compensation. Expert witnesses so appointed are entitled to reasonable compensation in whatever sum the court may allow. The compensation thus fixed is payable from funds which may be provided by law in criminal cases and civil actions and proceedings involving just compensation under the fifth amendment. In other civil actions and proceedings the compensation shall be paid by the parties in such proportion and at such time as the court directs, and thereafter charged in like manner as other costs.

(c) Disclosure of appointment. In the exercise of its discretion, the court may authorize disclosure to the jury of the fact that the court appointed the expert witness.

(d) Parties' experts of own selection. Nothing in this rule limits the parties in calling expert witnesses of their own selection.

II. DISCUSSION

In cases involving complicated or technical issues, parties often resort to hired experts who offer analyses favorable to the parties' positions in the case. As the Advisory Committee Notes to Rule 706 point out, "[t]he practice of shopping for experts, the venality of some experts, and the reluctance of many reputable experts to involve themselves in litigation, have been matters of deep concern." By making neutral experts more readily available to the court, Rule 706 exerts a "sobering effect" on the parties' experts, and perhaps its existence alone reduces the very need for court appointed experts.

While the use of court appointed experts is still the exception rather than the rule, increases in complex litigation will no doubt increase the frequency of courts' utilization of Rule 706.

Much has been written about the reluctance of parties and courts to use Rule 706 experts, with various theories offered as explanation. Trial judges may be hesitant to appoint their own experts sua sponte because of perceived risks to the traditional adversarial system; courts may wish to avoid interference with the parties' strategies and their ability to try the case as they see fit, or may believe that an expert's apparent association with, or sanction by, the court might cloak the witness with an undeserved aura of authority and persuasiveness that could unduly affect a jury's deliberations. Such an appointment could appear to cast a shadow on judicial objectivity, and some commentators fear that an appointed expert witness could in effect usurp the role of the factfinder, be it jury or judge. Clearly the appointment of an expert cannot be justified if the parties will be unable to pay his fees. Despite these and other speculations offered to explain why Rule 706 has been infrequently used, a recent Harris Poll survey of state and federal judges indicates that a substantial majority of judges would favor the use of independent expert witnesses in cases involving technical or scientific issues such as toxic torts, malpractice, or complex business cases.[1]

While considerations such as those mentioned above may have limited the use of appointed experts, complicated factual, scientific, or technical disputes in mass torts, antitrust, securities, and patent litigation (to name a few examples) can often develop into a "battle of experts," resulting in apparent deadlock or in widely divergent opinions. It is in these situations that an appointed expert can be most effectively utilized. In *Eastern Air Lines, Inc. v. McDonnell Douglas Corp.,*[2] the appellate court, in remanding the case, noted that the district court had the discretion to call its own expert witness who could provide objective insight into the over $24 million difference of opinion between the parties' experts' determination of damages due to lost profits. A similar recommendation was made in *Brown v. Ivarans Rederi A/S,*[3] when the appellate court remanded and suggested the use of a Rule 706 expert to resolve conflicting medical testimony presented by the parties' experts. Note, however, that a court appointed expert is not necessary to resolve divergent opinions.[4]

Although the courts have not often exercised their power of appointment under the rule, the procedures the Rule sets out are broadly drawn and adapted to minimizing difficulties. Rule 706(a) provides

1. *Judges' Opinions on Procedural Issues: A Survey of State and Federal Judges Who Spent at Least Half Their Time on General Civil Cases,* 69 B.U.L.Rev. 731, 741 (1989).

2. 532 F.2d 957, 1000 (5th Cir.1976).

3. 545 F.2d 854, 858 n. 6 (3d Cir.1976), *cert. denied,* 430 U.S. 969 (1977).

4. Georgia–Pacific Corp. v. United States, 640 F.2d 328, 334 (Ct.Cl.1980).

that either sua sponte or at the request of a party the court may issue an order to show cause why an expert should not be appointed. The court may obtain nominations from the parties. The appointed expert may be one suggested by the parties or one of the court's own choosing, or both. Once appointed, the expert is given instructions by the court and advises the parties of any findings. The parties may then depose the expert, who may be called by the court or the parties and is subject to cross-examination.

These procedures were followed in *Leesona Corp. v. Varta Batteries, Inc.,*[5] a bench-tried, complex patent case. The court directed the appointment of its own expert and sought nominations from the parties. One unquestionably qualified nominee appeared on both lists. The court communicated with him and provided him background materials, including each party's independent summary of its position which had been submitted to the court. After reviewing these materials, the expert agreed to serve and was appointed by consent order. Thereafter, at the court's request each side prepared technical questions which were forwarded to the expert. In response to these, a preliminary report was submitted to the court and provided to counsel, who then deposed the expert. The expert was called by the court at the trial; no final report was submitted. The court found the expert's testimony of an enormous help: he explained the technical issues and gave his opinion on the conflicting views of each side's own experts.

Rule 706(b) allows the court to fix compensation of appointed experts in civil cases and apportion it among the parties as it sees fit. In *Webster v. Sowders,*[6] the appellate court reversed the trial's apportionment of Rule 706(b) costs, for failure to make necessary findings of fact and conclusions of law justifying continuing employment of the experts.

Although Rule 706(c) leaves to the court's discretion whether to inform the jury that the expert is a court appointee, some concern has been expressed that a court-appointed expert will "usurp" the power of the jury to decide. As the court stated in *Kian v. Mirro Aluminum Co.,* "The presence of a court-sponsored witness, who would most certainly create a strong, if not overwhelming, impression of 'impartiality' and 'objectivity', could potentially transform a trial by jury into a trial by witness." [7]

A potential problem regarding Rule 706 concerns its scope and application; there may be occasional confusion about what a Rule 706 expert is and is not. For example, *Reilly v. United States* [8] makes it clear that Rule 706 does not circumscribe the court's power to call a

5. 522 F.Supp. 1304, 1312 (S.D.N.Y.1981).

6. 846 F.2d 1032, 1039 (6th Cir.1988).

7. 88 F.R.D. 351, 356 (E.D.Mich.1980).

8. 863 F.2d 149 (1st Cir.1988).

technical assistant or advisor. The court rejected the argument that its failure to comply with the provisions of Rule 706 was error, holding that the district court had inherent power to appoint an economist to assist the court in calculation of damages regarding the lost earning capacity of an infant girl born with brain damage.

In *Hemstreet v. Burroughs Corp.,*[9] a patent infringement case, the parties nominated and agreed on the appointment of an expert pursuant to Rule 706, to assist the judge and any jury with the complex technical matters upon which the parties' experts might disagree. Prior to trial, defendants moved for summary judgment. The court asked the expert to review the materials submitted in support of and opposition to the motion, and to assist the court in understanding the technical matters presented. He was not asked for and did not render any findings or opinions on the merits. The court granted defendants' motion for summary judgment. On a motion to reconsider the granting of summary judgment, plaintiff argued that summary judgment was improper because the court relied on the Rule 706 expert to resolve several genuine issues of material fact, and also that the court failed to comply with Rule 706 by not allowing plaintiff to depose or cross-examine the expert. The court emphasized that the expert wasn't asked to address the merits of any legal or factual issue, or to comment on or offer his opinion on the merits of such issues. The court further stated that there was no need for deposition or cross-examination of the expert because he had not rendered any "findings" within the meaning of Rule 706(a). Rather, the expert's function was to educate the court about the technology involved, and "to review the court's description of the circuitry described in this opinion to determine whether from a technical point of view it is accurately described." Thus, while he was originally appointed to serve as a Rule 706 expert witness, his function was actually more that of a technical advisor, making the plaintiff's challenges under Rule 706 misplaced.

In *Holland v. Commissioner,*[10] a taxpayer sought redetermination of an income tax deficiency, and offered photocopied documents as proof of his claimed deductions. The trial judge, concerned over a striking similarity in signatures, suggested that the government procure a handwriting expert to examine them. The appellate court rejected the argument that the trial court had failed to comply with Rule 706, holding that the trial court's more informal procedure substantially complied with Rule 614.

Other potential problems might arise from a blurring of the distinction between a Rule 706 expert witness and a special master appointed pursuant to Fed.R.Civ.P. 53. In *Students of California School for the Blind v. Honig,*[11] students sought to block the move of a state residen-

9. 666 F.Supp. 1096, 1124 (N.D.Ill.1987).

10. 835 F.2d 675 (6th Cir.1987).

11. 736 F.2d 538 (9th Cir.1984).

tial school for the blind, arguing among other things that the proposed site was earthquake-prone and dangerous. At trial there was much conflicting expert testimony. The court, unable to decide issues of seismic safety on the evidence presented at trial, reopened the case sua sponte and appointed its own neutral expert pursuant to Rule 706. On appeal, the circuit court found no abuse of discretion. The state also argued that the trial court treated the neutral expert not as a neutral expert but rather as a special master. The appellate court stated:

> Here, the district court first appointed Dr. Jahns expressly as a court-appointed neutral expert under Rule 706. He was not appointed a special master until later. After his testimony convinced the court to order additional testing, Dr. Jahns was appointed special master to oversee the court-ordered tests. The state defendants argue, however, that his role was akin to that of a special master throughout the proceeding, because the district court relied upon him so heavily. The argument is not persuasive. Even if Jahns is characterized as a special master from the time of his original appointment, the case is complex enough to fit the exceptional circumstances requirement of Rule 53(b).[12]

The court also held that when the trial judge appoints an expert under Rule 706 without the parties' consent, the issue of whether the expert is qualified rests in the trial court's discretion.

In *Board of Education, Yonkers City School District v. CNA Insurance Co.,*[13] the court created a potentially confusing blend of the functions of a special master and a Rule 706 expert by appointing one individual to serve in both capacities. A school board filed suit against its liability carrier seeking the expenses it incurred in defending a desegregation lawsuit. The trial court granted the board's motion for summary judgment, and on its own motion appointed "a Special Master pursuant to Fed.R.Civ.P. Rule 53" to serve "concurrently as a court-appointed expert pursuant to Fed.R.Evid. Rule 706." The court reasoned that a special master was necessary because the issues of attorney's services and defense costs were too complex and intricate and the evidence too voluminous for an otherwise unaided jury. The court reasoned that the purpose of expert testimony was to "assist the trier of the facts to understand, evaluate and decide the complex evidential materials in a case."

Another case indicating that the management of complex cases can blur the distinction between the role of a special master and a Rule 706 expert is *United States v. Michigan.*[14] There the United States brought an action against Michigan prison officials under the Civil Rights of Institutionalized Persons Act, 42 U.S.C. §§ 1977–1997j, challenging the

12. *Id.* at 549.

13. 113 F.R.D. 654 (S.D.N.Y.1987).

14. 680 F.Supp. 928 (W.D.Mich.1987).

totality of conditions in a Michigan prison. The trial judge filed various orders concerning compliance with a consent decree. The court appointed an independent expert under Rule 706 to help in evaluating a compliance plan proposed by the defendant. Subsequently, at the end of a compliance hearing, the court stated that it was going to "extend the authority of the Independent Expert." The United States argued that such an appointment was an abuse of discretion, and moved to terminate the expert's appointment, arguing that the expert had been appointed to study and report on the state's efforts to comply with the consent decree and had completed that task by producing his report and testifying at the compliance hearing. The United States further argued that, because it was fully capable of monitoring the state's compliance, there was no reasonable basis to continue the appointment, making it "unnecessary, redundant, and unduly costly." Finally, the United States asserted that continuation of the expert's appointment would convert him into a special master.

After reflecting on the role of the independent expert, and noting some merit to plaintiff's arguments, the court rejected the plaintiff's motion to terminate the expert's appointment. The court disagreed that the expert's task had been completed, stating that the appointment "was not . . . necessarily meant to be a 'one-shot' deal." The court stated "that there still exist mixed questions of fact and opinion regarding defendants' level of compliance," and that the expert was still needed to study and report on defendants' efforts. This ongoing need provided a reasonable basis for the continued appointment. Finally, the court noted that the expert's role was a limited one of supplying the court with an independent and informed view of the defendants' compliance, and that the expert's function did not constitute a significant intrusion on defendants' affairs nor constitute a delegation of the court's factfinding and interpretive powers. The court stated that the expert and his assistants were "empowered only to report on mixed questions of fact and opinion, that is to say, to give their professional view, as penologists, of defendants' efforts to comply with the requirements of the [consent decree]." The court stated that the expert was not empowered to conduct hearings or resolve factual disputes, and thus lacked the power and authority of a special master.

Martin v. Mabus [15] was a suit under the Voting Rights Act of 1965, 42 U.S.C. § 1973, challenging the method of electing judges in Mississippi. The trial court appointed an expert under Rule 706 "for the purpose of aiding the Court in drawing proposed subdistricts for election purposes of the districts found to be in violation . . ." The court wrote a partial draft opinion in an attempt to provide objective criteria and factors by which to draw redistricting plans, then directed the court-appointed expert to apply the criteria therein in formulating plans. The expert submitted his plans for the districts to the court,

15. 700 F.Supp. 327 (S.D.Miss.1988).

which provided copies to the parties and asked if they wished to depose the expert. The court filed the proposed plans and the draft opinion as exhibits for establishing a foundation for examining the expert and as a basis for objection to the plans.

Clearly, complex cases such as these may require that the court's need for both technical expertise and assistance in litigation management be met by outside experts whose function might not fall strictly within the confines of Rule 706. Rather, the unique circumstances of a case may require an independent expert to function as a hybrid or amalgam of technical advisor, expert witness, or special master.[16] Handling complex cases in a traditional judicial setting while avoiding the potential conflicts inherent in the blending of these diverse roles may present future challenges to courts attempting to utilize and define Rule 706.

Several states—Delaware, Florida, Montana, Nevada, New Hampshire, Ohio, Oklahoma, Oregon and Texas—did not adopt any version of Rule 706, generally on the theory that the rule is procedural, not evidentiary, in character. *See 2 Evidence in America* § 55.2.

16. *See generally* Brazil, *Special Masters in Complex Cases: Extending the Judiciary or Reshaping Adjudication?,* 53 U.Chi.L.Rev. 394, 414–419 (1986). *See also Manual for Complex Litigation (Second)* § 21.5 (1985) on the use of court appointed experts, special masters, and magistrates.

ARTICLE VIII. HEARSAY

Introduction

Article VIII codifies the hearsay rule and its various exceptions. It creates a system of class exceptions to the hearsay rule, supplemented by two open-ended "catch all," or residual, exceptions. In addition, some statements which have traditionally been admitted as hearsay exceptions, such as party admissions, are defined in Rule 801 as non-hearsay.

The Article consists of six rules. Rule 801 is the definitional section. Rule 802 articulates the general rule that hearsay is not admissible into evidence except as permitted by specific exceptions. Rules 803 and 804 prescribe the exceptions. The twenty-four exceptions enumerated in Rule 803, unlike those enumerated in Rule 804, are not premised upon the unavailability of the extrajudicial declarant as a witness at trial. The Rule 803 exceptions were believed by the Advisory Committee to reflect somewhat stronger guarantees of trustworthiness than the Rule 804 exceptions, thus accounting for the disparate treatment. Rule 805 deals in the conventional manner with the problem of multiple hearsay. Finally, Rule 806 authorizes introduction of evidence attacking or supporting the credibility of any extrajudicial declarant on the same terms as if he had appeared and testified at trial.

RULE 801

I. TEXT OF RULE

RULE 801. Definitions

The following definitions apply under this article:

(a) Statement. A "statement" is (1) an oral or written assertion of (2) nonverbal conduct of a person, if it is intended by the person as an assertion.

(b) Declarant. A "declarant" is a person who makes a statement.

(c) Hearsay. "Hearsay" is a statement, other than one made by the declarant while testifying at the trial or hearing, offered in evidence to prove the truth of the matter asserted.

(d) Statements which are not hearsay. A statement is not hearsay if—

(1) Prior statement by witness. The declarant testifies at the trial or hearing and is subject to cross-examination concerning the statement, and the statement is (A) inconsistent with the declarant's testimony, and was given under oath subject to the penalty of perjury at a trial, hearing, or other proceeding, or in a deposition, or (B) consistent with the declarant's testimony and is offered to rebut an express or implied charge against the declarant of recent fabrication or improper influence or motive, or (C) one of identification of a person made after perceiving the person; or

(2) Admission by party-opponent. The statement is offered against a party and is (A) the party's own statement, in either an individual or a representative capacity or (B) a statement of which the party has manifested an adoption or belief in its truth, or (C) a statement by a person authorized by the party to make a statement concerning the subject, or (D) a statement by the party's agent or servant concerning a matter within the scope of the agency or employment, made during the existence of the relationship, or (E) a statement by a co-conspirator of a party during the course and in furtherance of the conspiracy.

II. DISCUSSION

Rule 801(d)(1): Prior Statement by Witness

Rule 801(d)(1) defines certain prior statements of a witness as nonhearsay and, provided other nonhearsay rules of evidence do not bar the statement's receipt into evidence,[1] admissible as substantive

1. It is important to remember that Rules 801, 803, and 804 are not rules of admissibility; on the contrary, the rules merely provide that certain statements "are not

evidence. The Rule provides that three types of prior statements may be admissible as substantive evidence if the declarant testifies at the trial or hearing and is subject to cross-examination concerning the statement.

First, a prior statement of a witness is admissible if the statement is inconsistent with his trial testimony and was given under oath (Rule 801(d)(1)(A)) in a proceeding or deposition.

Second, a prior consistent statement is admissible to rebut an express or implied charge of recent fabrication or improper motive (Rule 801(d)(1)(B)). The prior consistent statement must, accordingly, have been made under circumstances that suggest that the prior statement negates the charge that the testimony is a fabrication or the product of a motive to falsify.

Third, Rule 801(d)(1)(C) defines as nonhearsay prior statements which identify a person.

The witness with memory problems presents a variety of difficulties under this Rule. First, to what extent is a witness who cannot remember the event or the prior statement "subject to cross-examination"? While it is certainly arguable that a witness who is unable to remember the event that was the subject of his prior statement is not "subject to cross-examination," [2] the concept of "lack of memory" has been complicated by the Supreme Court's holding in *United States v. Owens.*[3] *Owens* held that testimony of a witness to lack of recollection as to the underlying event satisfies both the Confrontation Clause of the Sixth Amendment and the requirement of Rule 801(d)(1)(C) that the declarant of the out of court statement by "subject to cross-examination concerning the statement." In *Owens,* the Court held that the Confrontation Clause of the Sixth Amendment—which guarantees only an *opportunity* for effective cross-examination, not cross-examination that is effective—is satisfied where the defendant has a full and fair opportunity to bring out the bad memory and other facts tending to discredit

excluded [from evidence] by the hearsay rule." Thus, other evidentiary rules may bar the introduction into evidence of statements that have overcome the hearsay hurdles of Article VIII. For example, an admission made in a settlement conference may satisfy Rule 801 but still be inadmissible because of Rule 408.

2. *Cf.,* 4 J. Weinstein & M. Berger, *Weinstein's Evidence* ¶ 801(d)(1)(A)[01] at 801–88 (Supp.1982) ("even apart from constitutional considerations [citing Douglas v. Alabama, 380 U.S. 415 (1965)] a prior inconsistent statement cannot be used if witness claims a privilege so that direct examination or effective cross-examination is thwarted").

3. 484 U.S. 554 (1988). The Supreme Court expressly reserved the issue of "[w]hether [a witness's] apparent lapse of memory so affected [the defendant's] right to cross-examine as to make a critical difference in the application of the Confrontation Clause" in California v. Green, 399 U.S. 149, 168–69 & N. 18 (1970). The Confrontation Clause issue was also noted, but not reached, by the Ninth Circuit in Vogel v. Percy, 691 F.2d 843 (7th Cir.1982). In Delaware v. Fensterer, 474 U.S. 15, 20 (1985) (per curiam), the Court determined that there was no confrontation clause violation when an expert witness testified as to what opinion he had formed, but could not recollect the basis on which he had formed it. *See* Annot., 99 A.L.R.3d 934, 942–944 (1980).

a witness's testimony as to the witness's current belief when the witness is unable to recollect the reason for that belief.

The Court in *Owens* rested its ruling on an interpretation of the language of Rules 801(d)(1)(C) and 802. The Court did not, however, provide an analysis of the problem of the witness who does not remember anything of the event or the statement. This problem must be evaluated by the trial court pursuant to Rule 403 and a determination must be made whether the jury can evaluate effectively the probative force of the statement. By eliminating the need to examine the effectiveness of the witness's cross-examination, the decision in *Owens* may lead courts to pay more attention to whether the prior statement was inconsistent with the in-court testimony. In a great number of cases, however, the question is rendered academic, and the prior statement admissible, by the "former testimony" exception of Rule 804(a)(3) and (b)(1), discussed below.

A second question—which the courts have addressed with some frequency—is whether a prior statement is "inconsistent with" the witness's trial testimony that he or she cannot recall either the subject matter of the statement, the statement itself, or both.[4] Certainly, some claims of lack of memory at trial are "inconsistent with" a prior statement. Thus, the courts have held that a prior statement is admissible under Rule 801(d)(1)(A) if the trial court finds that the witness "was fully aware of the content of his prior statement and was simply attempting [through claiming an inability to recall] to avoid implicating [the defendant]," [5] or that the witness has "falsifie[d] a lack of memory;" [6] that the trial judge could have found that the loss of memory was feigned,[7] that his claimed failure to collect is a mere "contrivance," [8] or "[w]hen a witness remembers events incompletely or with some equivocation at trial." [9]

On the other hand, the Third Circuit has recently cautioned that not all prior statements are necessarily inconsistent with a lack of memory at trial and therefore automatically admissible under Rule

4. Rule 801(d)(1)(A) contains no definition of inconsistency. The test of inconsistency applied with respect to impeachment by prior inconsistent statements should be employed. United States v. Morgan, 555 F.2d 238 (9th Cir.1977). *See* United States v. Williams, 737 F.2d 954, 606–10 (7th Cir.1984), *cert. denied,* 470 U.S. 1003 (1985) (to be inconsistent, statements need not be "diametrically opposed or logically incompatible"; inconsistency may be found in evasive answers, silence, a change in positions or even a purported change in memory). *See generally* Annot., 99 A.L.R.3d 934 (1980).

5. United States v. Rogers, 549 F.2d 490, 496 (8th Cir.1976), *cert. denied,* 431 U.S. 918 (1977).

6. United States v. Insana, 423 F.2d 1165, 1170 (2d Cir.), *cert. denied,* 400 U.S. 841 (1970).

7. United States v. Bigham, 812 F.2d 943 (5th Cir.1987).

8. United States v. Collins, 478 F.2d 837 (5th Cir.), *cert. denied,* 414 U.S. 1010 (1973).

9. United States v. Distler, 671 F.2d 954, 958 (6th Cir.), *cert. denied,* 454 U.S. 827 (1981).

801(d)(1)(A). In *United States v. Palumbo,*[10] the court held that the witness's claimed lack of memory at trial as to where she obtained cocaine was "not necessarily inconsistent with her prior statement that she had received cocaine from Palumbo." Essentially, the determination is a factual one left to the discretion of the trial judge, and the courts' exercise of this discretion has not proved particularly problematic.

It should be apparent that the drafting of the Rule is not responsible for the difficult issues that arise under it. The traditional common law approach to inconsistent statements—i.e., restricting them to impeachment use only—rendered it unnecessary to be quite as concerned about whether a statement was inconsistent with trial testimony and relatively unimportant whether the witness possessed much in the way of a current memory at trial. Any departure from that common law approach that permits the use of inconsistent statements as substantive evidence will require care in its implementation. Even if a trial judge believes that a witness is being evasive or feigning loss of memory concerning an inconsistent statement, so long as that witness will not cooperate, the party who is relying on the in-court testimony is largely disabled from examining him about the statement.

There may be nothing that the party can do to encourage or compel the witness to be forthcoming. Thus, courts will want to be cautious in admitting inconsistent statements of a witness when the party opposing them is able only in theory to examine the witness about the statements. At the same time, the court will not want to encourage a witness to pretend to have a memory problem in order to prevent the use of otherwise reliable inconsistent statements. Line drawing will require sensitivity to the interests of both sides. No rule change is likely to make this easier.

Rule 801(d)(1)(B) defines as nonhearsay prior consistent statements offered to rebut an express or implied charge of recent fabrication or improper influence or motive. Because the prior statement is only admissible in these limited circumstances, some circuits have held that "the proponent [of a 801(d)(1)(B) statement] must demonstrate that the prior consistent statement was made *prior to* the time that the supposed motive to falsify arose." [11]

10. 639 F.2d 123 (3d Cir.), *cert. denied,* 454 U.S. 819 (1981).

11. United States v. Quinto, 582 F.2d 224, 234 (2d Cir.1978) (emphasis added). *Accord* United States v. Vest, 842 F.2d 1319 (1st Cir.), *cert. denied,* 488 U.S. 812 (1988); United States v. Bowman, 798 F.2d 333, 338 (8th Cir.1986), *cert. denied,* 479 U.S. 1043 (1987); United States v. Stuart, 718 F.2d 931 (9th Cir.1983); United States v. Henderson, 717 F.2d 135 (4th Cir.1983), *cert. denied,* 465 U.S. 1009 (1984); United States v. Rohrer, 708 F.2d 429 (9th Cir.1983); United States v. Shulman, 624 F.2d 384, 392–93 (2d Cir.1980); United States v. McPartlin, 595 F.2d 1321 (7th Cir.), *cert. denied,* 444 U.S. 833 (1979). *But cf.* United States v. Doyle, 771 F.2d 250 (7th Cir.1985) (tape recorded conversation of witness admissible to rebut charge of fabrication, even though conversation took place after witness was aware of FBI investigation); United States v. Scholle, 553 F.2d 1109, 1122

Other courts, however, have expressly rejected any requirement that the prior consistent statement antedate the occurrence giving rise to the possibility of a fabrication or the existence of improper influence of motion.[12]

The significance of the date of, and circumstances surrounding, the prior consistent statement are illustrated in *United States v. Sampol,*[13] which involved a prosecution arising from the assassination of the former Chilean ambassador to the United States, Orlando Letelier. Pursuant to a plea bargain, Michael Townley, the organizer of the assassination, became the government's chief witness. In March 1978, while still in Chile, Townley made two statements to Chilean officials denying responsibility for the murder. In April, after extradition to the United States, Townley admitted his involvement to other Chilean officials.

At trial, the defendants impeached Townley's testimony with the two March 1978 prior inconsistent statements. The trial court then permitted the government to introduce the April prior consistent statement. The jury convicted. The court of appeals held that admission of the prior consistent statement was not error as, while Townley had a motive to lie to the Chilean officials in March in Chile, he had no such "improper motive" in April in the United States.[14] *Sampol,* thus, highlights the sometimes difficult threshold inquiry that Rule 801(d)(1)(B) requires the trial court to make—a determination whether the witness was under the "improper influence or motive" when he made the prior consistent statement.[15] The courts appear to be making that

(8th Cir.) (the court rejected the argument that the prior consistent statement must be made prior to the impeaching statement to be admissible, but did not consider whether the statements would be admissible if they had been made following the existence of a motive to fabricate), *cert. denied,* 434 U.S. 940 (1977).

12. *See e.g.,* United States v. Anderson, 782 F.2d 908 (11th Cir.1986); United States v. Hamilton, 689 F.2d 1262 (6th Cir.1982), *cert. denied,* 459 U.S. 1117 (1983); United States v. Parry, 649 F.2d 292 (5th Cir.1981); United States v. Rios, 611 F.2d 1335, 1349 (10th Cir. 1979), *cert. denied,* 452 U.S. 918 (1981). *See* United States v. Parodi, 703 F.2d 768 (4th Cir.1983), which purports to place the Fourth Circuit in the camp of those circuits permitting a prior consistent statement to be admitted even if made following the introduction of a motive to fabricate. *See* Annot., 47 A.L.R.Fed. 639, 655–59 (1980).

13. 636 F.2d 621 (D.C.Cir.1980).

14. *Id.* at 671–73.

15. The standards for deciding whether prior consistent statements can be admitted as substantive evidence under Rule 801(d)(1)(B) are not entirely clear. In United States v. Quinto, 582 F.2d 224, 233 (2d Cir.1978), the court held that they are precisely the same as the traditional standards for the situation in which rehabilitation through consistency would formerly have been allowed. But in United States v. Rubin, 609 F.2d 51, 61 (2d Cir.1979), *aff'd,* 449 U.S. 424 (1981), the same court left open the question of "[w]hether or not some lesser standard would be required if the prior statements had been offered merely to bolster [the witness's] credibility as a witness." Judge Friendly, concurring in *Rubin,* asserted that "the limitations [of Rule 801(d)(1)(B)] apply only to the use of prior consistent statements as *affirmative evidence* and are not controlling when such statements are used *only for rehabilitation.*" *Id.* at 66 (emphasis in original). In the latter

determination without any problems.[16]

The problem concerning the timing of prior consistent statements was not created by the Rules. The same problem faced common law courts. Because consistent statements are so easily manufactured, courts are suspicious of them. Clearly, statements made before an improper motive could have existed are likely to be most probative. Yet other circumstances may suggest that even later statements were made at a time when there was, in fact, no real likelihood of an improper motivation to fabricate or of undue influence. In such circumstances courts are unlikely to exclude evidence. The pattern that develops is similar to that found in common law decisions. Statements made before any improper motive existed are presumed admissible for rehabilitation while other statements require a showing of special circumstances before they are admitted.

Rule 801(d)(1)(C) has raised one major issue, and it does not seem to have arisen as a result of the drafting so much as a failure to pay close attention to the language of the Rule. Under Rule 801, a statement is not hearsay if the declarant testifies at trial, is subject to cross-examination concerning the statement, and the statement is one of identification of a person. Assume that W takes the stand and states that D identified the defendant in a criminal case as the person who robbed him. Also assume that D is not present to testify. Is W's testimony admissible? The answer should be "No." The declarant in this case is D, and D has not testified. The Rule is, therefore, not satisfied. If, however, D does testify, states that he made the identification, and one other witness proceeds to contradict D, then W should be able to say that W heard or saw D make the identification. W's

case, Judge Friendly contended that prior consistent statements should be admitted with greater liberality, with the jury clearly advised "that they are to be considered solely as breaking the force of the impeachment." *Id.* at 70.

At common law, statements consistent with trial testimony generally were excluded as easily manufactured and therefore not sufficiently probative to warrant admission unless (a) the credibility of the declarant/witness was attacked and (b) the statement was made under circumstances indicating that it was, and is, inconsistent with the attack. As Rule 801(d)(1)(B) appears to admit as substantive evidence virtually any statement that would have been admissible under common law decisions for rehabilitation, there are few cases where it is necessary to be concerned whether a consistent statement not fitting under rule 801 ought nonetheless be admitted.

16. What constitutes a "statement" was addressed in United States v. Moskowitz, 581 F.2d 14 (2d Cir.), *cert. denied,* 439 U.S. 871 (1978), which concerned the admissibility of a sketch. The majority concluded that, because the sketch was not a "statement" within the meaning of Rule 801(a), a hearsay exception was not necessary to admit the sketch into evidence. *Id.* at 20–21. Judge Friendly, in a concurring opinion, argued that the sketch was indeed a "statement," but that it was admissible as an "identification" under Rule 801(d)(1)(C). *Id.* at 22. The definition of "statement," as applied under Rule 801(d)(1), has not proved problematic. The role has also been interpreted to authorize testimony that the witness had made an out-of-court identification of a photograph of a person, rather than the person himself. *See, e.g.,* United States v. Fosher, 568 F.2d 207, 210 (1st Cir.1978).

testimony as to what he saw or heard would not be hearsay under the definition provided because it would not be offered for its truth but to rehabilitate D and prove that D, in fact, made the identification.

Prior to the adoption of the Rules, a number of courts admitted prior identifications of witnesses to bolster a witness's testimony or as substantive evidence. Rule 801(d)(1)(C) built upon these authorities and, in most instances, courts have read the Rule properly. The only problematic situation has been where one witness testifies as to another's identification, and that problem appears to be easily resolved under the current Rules.

In adopting Rule 801(d)(1), several states lifted the requirement that prior inconsistent statements have to be made under oath. In contrast, a number of other states limited the subdivision to require not only that the statement be under oath but also that it be offered in a criminal proceeding. Yet others chose to adhere to the traditional rule refusing to give prior consistent or inconsistent statements any substantive effect.[17]

Rule 801(d)(2): Admissions

Rule 801(d)(2) classifies as nonhearsay statements made by a party or his representative or agent and offered against that party. In contrast to the hearsay exceptions contained in Rules 803 and 804, which are excluded from the hearsay rule because of the statement's "circumstantial guarantees of trustworthiness," "no guarantee of trustworthiness is required in the case of an admission." [18] Instead, the Advisory Committee decided to exclude admissions by a party-opponent from the category of hearsay on the theory that their admissibility in evidence is the result of the adversary system.

The admissibility of admissions by "person[s] authorized" or by "agent[s] or servant[s]" under Rule 801(d)(2)(C) or (D) is frequently litigated. The provisions of the Rule expand the scope of admissions for authorized agents and employees. New issues have arisen and are only beginning to be resolved. One knotty question relates to the interaction between subdivisions (d)(2)(C), governing authorized statements, and (d)(2)(D), governing agents' or servants' statements. Any statement by an agent or servant made while employed concerning a matter within the scope of employment fits the broad language of Rule 801(d)(2)(D). The theory is that an agent or servant is unlikely to damage the principal while employed by making false statements that might harm the principal. The cases admitting agents' statements appear to be following the Rule as the drafters intended.

17. *See generally 2 Evidence in America* §§ 56.2–56.4.

18. *See* Advisory Committee Note to Rule 801(d)(2).

For example, relying on the Advisory Committee Note, the Fifth Circuit held in *Kingsley v. Baker/Beech-Nut Corp.*,[19] that Rule 801(d)(2)(C) includes statements made by an agent to his principal, as well as statements made by the agent to third parties.[20] In *Mahlandt v. Wild Canid Survival & Research Center, Inc.*,[21] the Eighth Circuit held that the same rationale applies to the statements of an agent made to his principal under 801(d)(2)(D). Similarly, in *B–W Acceptance Corp. v. Porter*,[22] the prior deposition of the plaintiff's branch manager was admissible since the plaintiff had authorized the manager to testify about what he knew.[23]

Even an expert employed by a party has been held to be a "person authorized . . . to make a statement" for his principal. In *Collins v. Wayne Corp.*,[24] the court held that the deposition testimony of the expert, employed by a bus manufacturer to investigate an accident, was admissible against the manufacturer because "[i]n giving his deposition he was performing the function that Wayne had employed him to perform."

One difficulty with this case is that it is not clear that an expert is an agent or servant in a continuing capacity for purposes of Rule 801(d)(2)(D). It is facially correct to say that an expert is a person authorized to make a statement, but it is equally correct that the expert is not speaking on behalf of, or with the authority to bind, the principal until the principal adopts the expert's statement. The conceptional problem with *Collins* is that, if extended, every time a party takes a statement from a witness, even one associated with an adverse party, the party could be said to authorize the witness to make the statement and it could be classified as an admission of the party taking the statement. The Advisory Committee apparently wanted to assure that statements made by corporate officers, or employees of other businesses, for the purpose of conveying information throughout the enterprise, ought to be considered as agents' statements, even if the communicator was speaking about activities of other personnel. *Collins* goes well beyond this and may require careful consideration in future cases.

19. 546 F.2d 1136, 1141 (5th Cir.1977).

20. *Accord* Reid Bros. Logging Co., v. Ketchikan Pulp Co., 699 F.2d 1292, 1306–07 n. 25 (9th Cir.), *cert. denied,* 464 U.S. 916 (1983).

21. 588 F.2d 626, 630 (8th Cir.1978).

22. 568 F.2d 1179, 1183 (5th Cir.1978).

23. *See also* United States v. Ojala, 544 F.2d 940, 945–46 (8th Cir.1976) (court appeared to rely on both 801(d)(2)(C) and (D) in holding that the statement of the defendant's attorney to IRS agents while in the defendant's presence was admissible against the defendant because the statement referred to a matter within the scope of the attorney's authority and the defendant had authorized his attorney to speak); United States v. Pilarinos, 864 F.2d 253 (2d Cir.1988) (court relied on 801(d)(2)(D) to find agency relationship).

24. 621 F.2d 777 (5th Cir.1980).

Another issue that has arisen is whether an agent-declarant must have personal knowledge of the facts underlying his vicarious admission in order for it to be admissible. In *Mahlandt v. Wild Canid Survival & Research Center, Inc.,*[25] the Eighth Circuit rejected any "implied condition" of personal knowledge in Rule 801(d)(2).[26] The Second Circuit has noted, but has expressly reserved, the "personal knowledge" issue.[27] Clarification of this issue would certainly be desirable.[28]

A third issue, and one that divides the courts, concerns whether the statement of a government agent is admissible against the government under Rule 801(d)(2)(C) or (D). In *United States v. Kampiles,*[29] the Seventh Circuit emphatically rejected any such interpretation of Rule 801(d)(2). Relying on a pre-Rules case, *United States v. Santos,*[30] the court held that the statements of a CIA employee could not be considered the statement of a government "agent" for purposes of Rule 801(d)(2)(D).

The *Kampiles* Court argued that the policies of the admission exception were not served because "agents of the government are supposedly disinterested in the outcome of the trial and are traditionally unable to bind the government,"[31] and attempted, with partial success, to distinguish the District of Columbia Circuit's opinion in *United States v. Morgan,*[32] In *Morgan,* the court held that statements

25. 588 F.2d 626 (8th Cir.1978).

26. *Accord* United States v. Southland Corp., 760 F.2d 1366, 1376–77 n. 4 (2d Cir.), *cert. denied,* 474 U.S. 825 (1985); United States v. Ammar, 714 F.2d 238 (3d Cir.), *cert. denied,* 464 U.S. 936 (1983); MCI Communications v. American Tel. & Tel. Co., 708 F.2d 1081 (7th Cir.), *cert. denied,* 464 U.S. 891 (1983).

27. Oreck Corp. v. Whirlpool Corp., 639 F.2d 75, 80 & n. 3 (2d Cir.1980), *cert. denied,* 454 U.S. 1083 (1981). *See also* Union Mut. Life Ins. Co. v. Chrysler Corp., 793 F.2d 1 (1st Cir.1986) (court suggested that had an objection been made that an accountant did not have sufficient information to give an opinion, the letter written by the accountant might still have been admitted given the accountant's employer's ability to explain its significance to the jury).

28. It should be noted that at least two courts of appeals have held that Rule 602's requirement that a witness have personal knowledge of the matters testified to precludes the admission, under Rule 804(b)(3), of statements against penal interest that are made without the declarant's personal knowledge. United States v. Lanci, 669 F.2d 391, 394 (6th Cir.), *cert. denied,* 457 U.S. 1134 (1982); United States v. Lang, 589 F.2d 92, 97–98 (2d Cir.1978). The Third Circuit has thought it to be "clear from the Advisory Committee Notes that the drafters intended that the personal knowledge foundation requirement of Rule 602 should apply to hearsay statements admissible as exceptions under Rules 803 and 804 but not to admissions (including co-conspirator statements) admissible under Rule 801(d)(2)." United States v. Ammar, 714 F.2d 238, 254 (3d Cir.), *cert. denied sub nom.* Stillman v. United States, 464 U.S. 936 (1983).

29. 609 F.2d 1233 (7th Cir.1979), *cert. denied,* 446 U.S. 954 (1980).

30. 372 F.2d 177 (2d Cir.1967).

31. 609 F.2d at 1233, n. 16.

32. 581 F.2d 933, 937–38 n. 11 (D.C.Cir.1978).

in a sworn government affidavit to a judicial officer were admissible as admissions against the government.[33] The case law in this area is flux and warrants clarification.

Although Fed.R.Evid. 104(a) requires that the court determine preliminary questions concerning the admissibility of evidence, the Rules do not define the standard of proof.[34] The threshold issue concerning the quantum of proof of the conspiracy that is required before the statement of an alleged co-conspirator may be admitted was, however, resolved in *Bourjaily v. United States.*[35]

In *Bourjaily,* the Court held that when the preliminary facts relevant to Rule 801(d)(2)(E)—the existence of a conspiracy and the non-offering party's involvement in it—are disputed, the offering party must prove them by a preponderance of the evidence, not some higher standard of proof. The Court also held that, in making a preliminary factual determination under Rule 801(d)(2)(E), the court may examine the hearsay statement sought to be admitted. In this regard, the Court found that there was no merit to petitioner's contention, which was based on the "bootstrapping rule" of *Glasser v. United States,* 315 U.S. 60 (1942), that a court, in determining the preliminary facts relevant to Rule 801(d)(2)(E), must look only to independent evidence other than the statement sought to be admitted. The Court, however, also held that it need not decide whether, under Rule 104(a), the courts below could have relied solely upon the hearsay statements to establish the preliminary facts for admissibility.

The decision in *Bourjaily* effectively overrules the majority of the circuits that have refused to permit the "bootstrapping" of the admissibility of a statement of a conspiracy that is, at least in part, preliminarily proven by that same statement.[36] The question, however, remains

33. *See also* Skaw v. United States, 740 F.2d 932 (Fed.Cir.1984) (letter from a Forest Service supervisor was admissible as an agent's admission); United States v. American Tel. & Tel., 498 F.Supp. 353, 356–58 (D.D.C.1980) (statements by three executive branch officials before the FCC admitted against the government in a civil antitrust suit). In United States v. Pena, 527 F.2d 1356, 1361 (5th Cir.), *cert. denied,* 426 U.S. 949 (1976), where the defendant sought to introduce the statement of a DEA agent against the government, the Fifth Circuit found it unnecessary to reach the issue of the applicability of Rule 801(d)(2) to government admissions because the declarant's relationship with the government had terminated by the time the statements were made.

34. Although there have been slight differences in decisions among the circuits, there is greater uniformity in the handling of the co-conspirator exception of Rule 801(d)(2)(E) than there was at common law. *See* Annot., 44 A.L.R.Fed. 627 (1978). It is clear that questions concerning the admissibility of a statement under Rule 801(d)(2)(E) are preliminary matters for the court to decide under Rule 104. *See, e.g.,* United States v. Jackson, 627 F.2d 1198, 1215 (D.C.Cir.1980); United States v. Bell, 573 F.2d 1040, 1043 (8th Cir. 1978); *cf.* United States v. Howard, 706 F.2d 267 (8th Cir.), *cert. denied,* 464 U.S. 934 (1983).

35. 483 U.S. 171 (1987).

36. *See, e.g.,* United States v. Patterson, 644 F.2d 890, 894 (1st Cir.1981); United States v. Alvarez–Porras, 643 F.2d 54, 57 (2d Cir.), *cert. denied,* 454 U.S. 839 (1981); United

whether independent evidence of the conspiracy is required, since that no circuit court has relied on the hearsay statements only.[37] Moreover, all courts must examine the contents of the hearsay statements to determine whether they were made in furtherance of the conspiracy.

Finally, must the conspiracy be proven before the hearsay statement is admitted, or can the statement be admitted conditionally, subject to later "connecting up"? In footnote 1 of its opinion, the Court in *Bourjaily* stated that "we do not express an opinion on the proper order of proof that trial courts should follow in concluding that the preponderance standard has been satisfied in an ongoing trial." The courts, however, agree that the "preferred" order of proof is that the conspiracy is proven prior to the admission of the statement.[38] However, this is not a constitutional or statutory requirement. Accordingly, if prior proof of the conspiracy is not "reasonably practical," the hearsay can be admitted subject to "connecting up." [39] Under this procedure, if, at the close of evidence, the court finds that a conspiracy has been demonstrated, the statement is admitted and the jury so instructed. If, however, the court finds insufficient evidence of the conspiracy, the jury is given a cautionary instruction or, if the court finds that to be inadequate to protect the defendant's rights, a mistrial must be declared.[40] A third alternative, suggested by the Sixth Circuit in *United States v. Vinson,*[41] is a "mini-hearing," outside the hearing of the jury, wherein the government is given the opportunity to establish the conspiracy. In any event, admissibility of co-conspirator statements subject to connecting up appears not to have presented the courts with any significant problems.[42]

States v. Gresko, 632 F.2d 1128 (4th Cir.1980); United States v. Jackson, 627 F.2d 1198, 1219–220 (D.C.Cir.1980); United States v. Petersen, 611 F.2d 1313, 1330 (10th Cir.1979), *cert. denied,* 447 U.S. 905 (1980); United States v. Dalzotto, 603 F.2d 642, 644 (7th Cir.), *cert. denied,* 444 U.S. 994 (1979); United States v. Watkins, 600 F.2d 201 (9th Cir.), *cert. denied,* 444 U.S. 871 (1979); United States v. James, 590 F.2d 575 (5th Cir.1978) (en banc), *cert. denied,* 442 U.S. 917 (1979); United States v. Bell, 573 F.2d 1040, 1043 (8th Cir.1978). *See* Annot., 39 A.L.R.Fed. 720, 725 (1978).

37. *See* United States v. Jaramillo–Montoya, 834 F.2d 276, 279 (2d Cir.1987) (the court, citing *Bourjaily,* concluded that statements considered with independent evidence were sufficient to establish a conspiracy), *cert. denied,* 486 U.S. 1023 (1988).

38. *See, e.g.,* United States v. Austin, 786 F.2d 986, 990 (10th Cir.1986); United States v. Manzella, 782 F.2d 533 (5th Cir.), *cert. denied,* 476 U.S. 1123 (1986).

39. United States v. Pinto, 838 F.2d 426, 433 (10th Cir.1988).

40. *See, e.g.,* United States v. Jackson, 627 F.2d 1198, 1215 (D.C.Cir.1980); United States v. Vinson, 606 F.2d 149 (6th Cir.1979), *cert. denied,* 444 U.S. 1074, 445 U.S. 904 (1980); United States v. Watkins, 600 F.2d 201 (9th Cir.), *cert. denied,* 444 U.S. 871 (1979); United States v. James, 590 F.2d 575, 581 (5th Cir.1978) (en banc), *cert. denied,* 442 U.S. 917 (1979).

41. 606 F.2d 149 (6th Cir.1979), *cert. denied,* 444 U.S. 1074.

42. *See* United States v. Holloway, 731 F.2d 378, 381–82 (6th Cir.), *cert. denied,* 469 U.S. 1021 (1984), for a further discussion of these options.

In its version of Rule 801(d)(2)(c)–(d), Maine excludes statements made by agents to their principals or employers. Florida, Michigan and Ohio reject *Bourjaily,* making explicit that a co-conspirator's statement is admissible only upon independent proof of the conspiracy. Delaware and Minnesota require that the court find that the conspiracy has just been established by the preponderance of the evidence, Minnesota explicitly providing that the statement alone is insufficient for this purpose.[43]

43. *See generally* 2 *Evidence in America* §§ 56.2–56.4.

RULE 802

I. TEXT OF RULE

RULE 802. Hearsay Rule

Hearsay is not admissible except as provided by these rules or by other rules prescribed by the Supreme Court pursuant to statutory authority or by Act of Congress.

II. DISCUSSION

This traditional statement of the hearsay rule has generated no difficulties for the courts. It is important to note that the Rule applies in bench trials as well as in jury trials. Some judges, however, continue to admit hearsay in bench trials subject to a ruling that is never made explicit on the record. Appellate courts generally assume that the trial judge has disregarded inadmissible hearsay unless there is some indication to the contrary in the record. This was true before Rule 802 was adopted and the Rule does not appear to have modified bench trials in any significant way.

RULE 803

I. TEXT OF RULE

RULE 803. Hearsay Exceptions; Availability of Declarant Immaterial

The following are not excluded by the hearsay rule, even though the declarant is available as a witness:

(1) Present Sense Impression. A statement describing or explaining an event or condition made while the declarant was perceiving the event or condition or immediately thereafter.

(2) Excited Utterance. A statement relating to a startling event or condition made while the declarant was under the stress of excitement caused by the event or condition.

(3) Then Existing Mental, Emotional, or Physical Condition. A statement of the declarant's then existing state of mind, emotional, sensation, or physical condition (such as intent, plan, motive, design, mental feeling, pain, and bodily health), but not including a statement of memory or belief to prove the fact remembered or believed unless it relates to the execution, revocation, identification, or terms of declarant's will.

(4) Statements for Purposes of Medical Diagnosis or Treatment. Statements made for purposes of medical diagnosis or treatment and describing medical history, or past or present symptoms, pain, or sensations, or the inception or general character of the cause or external source thereof insofar as reasonably pertinent to diagnosis or treatment.

(5) Recorded Recollection. A memorandum or record concerning a matter about which a witness once had knowledge but now has insufficient recollection to enable the witness to testify fully and accurately, shown to have been made or adopted by the witness when the matter was fresh in the witness' memory and to reflect that knowledge correctly. If admitted, the memorandum or record may be read into evidence but may not itself be received as an exhibit unless offered by an adverse party.

(6) Records of Regularly Conducted Activity. A memorandum, report, record, or data compilation, in any form, of acts, events, conditions, opinions, or diagnoses, made at or near the time by, or from information transmitted by, a person with knowledge, if kept in the course of a regularly conducted business activity, and if it was the regular practice of that business activity to make the memorandum, report, record, or data compilation, all as shown by the testimony of

the custodian or other qualified witness, unless the source of information or the method or circumstances of preparation indicate lack of trustworthiness. The term "business" as used in this paragraph includes business, institution, association, profession, occupation, and calling of every kind, whether or not conducted for profit.

(7) Absence of Entry in Records Kept in Accordance with the Provisions of Paragraph (6). Evidence that a matter is not included in the memoranda, reports, records, or data compilations, in any form, kept in accordance with the provisions of paragraph (6), to prove the nonoccurrence or nonexistence of the matter, if the matter was of a kind of which a memorandum, report, record, or data compilation was regularly made and preserved, unless the sources of information or other circumstances indicate lack of trustworthiness.

(8) Public Records and Reports. Records, reports, statements, or data compilations, in any form, of public offices or agencies, setting forth (A) the activities of the office or agency, or (B) matters observed pursuant to duty imposed by law as to which matters there was a duty to report, excluding, however, in criminal cases matters observed by police officers and other law enforcement personnel, or (C) in civil actions and proceedings and against the Government in criminal cases, factual findings resulting from an investigation made pursuant to authority granted by law, unless the sources of information or other circumstances indicate lack of trustworthiness.

(9) Records of Vital Statistics. Records or data compilations, in any form, of births, fetal deaths, deaths, or marriages, if the report thereof was made to a public office pursuant to requirements of law.

(10) Absence of Public Record or Entry. To prove the absence of a record, report, statement, or data compilation, in any form, or the nonoccurrence or nonexistence of a matter of which a record, report, statement, or data compilation, in any form, was regularly made and preserved by a public office or agency, evidence in the form of a certification in accordance with rule 902, or testimony, that diligent search failed to disclose the record, report, statement, or data compilation, or entry.

(11) Records of Religious Organizations. Statements of births, marriages, divorces, deaths, legitimacy, ancestry, relationship by blood or marriage, or other similar facts of personal or family history, contained in a regularly kept record of a religious organization.

(12) Marriage, Baptismal, and Similar Certificates. Statements of fact contained in a certificate that the maker performed a marriage or other ceremony or administered a sacrament, made by a clergyman, public official, or other person authorized by the rule or practices of a religious organization or by law to perform the act certified, and purporting to have been issued at the time of the act or within a reasonable time thereafter.

(13) Family Records. Statements of fact concerning personal or family history contained in family Bibles, genealogies, charts, engravings on rings, inscriptions on family portraits, engravings on urns, crypts, or tombstones, or the like.

(14) Records of Documents Affecting an Interest in Property. The record of a document purporting to establish or affect an interest in property, as proof of the content of the original recorded document and it execution and delivery by each person by whom it purports to have been executed, if the record is a record of a public office and an applicable statute authorizes the recording of documents of that kind in that office.

(15) Statements in Documents Affecting an Interest in Property. A statement contained in a document purporting to establish or affect an interest in property if the matter stated was relevant to the purpose of the document, unless dealings with the property since the document was made have been inconsistent with the truth of the statement or the purport of the document.

(16) Statements in Ancient Documents. Statements in a document in existence twenty years or more the authenticity of which is established.

(17) Market Reports, Commercial Publications. Market quotations, tabulations, lists, directories, or other published compilations, generally used and relied upon by the public or by persons in particular occupations.

(18) Learned Treatises. To the extent called to the attention of an expert witness upon cross-examination or relied upon by the expert witness in direct examination, statements contained in published treatises, periodicals, or pamphlets on a subject of history, medicine, or other science or art, established as a reliable authority by the testimony or admission of the witness or by other expert testimony or by judicial notice. If admitted, the statements may be read into evidence but may not be received as exhibits.

(19) Reputation Concerning Personal or Family History. Reputation among members of a person's family by blood,

adoption, or marriage, or among a person's associates, or in the community, concerning a person's birth, adoption, marriage, divorce, death, legitimacy, relationship by blood, adoption, or marriage, ancestry, or other similar fact of his personal or family history.

(20) Reputation Concerning Boundaries or General History. Reputation in a community, arising before the controversy, as to boundaries of or customs affecting lands in the community, and reputation as to events of general history important to the community or State or nation in which located.

(21) Reputation as to Character. Reputation of a person's character among associates or in the community.

(22) Judgment of Previous Conviction. Evidence of a final judgment, entered after a trial or upon a plea of guilty (but not upon a plea of nolo contendere), adjudging a person guilty of a crime punishable by death or imprisonment in excess of one year, to prove any fact essential to sustain the judgment, but not including, when offered by the Government in a criminal prosecution for purposes other than impeachment, judgments against persons other than the accused. The pendency of an appeal may be shown but does not affect admissibility.

(23) Judgment as to Personal, Family, or General History, or Boundaries. Judgments as proof of matters of personal, family, or general history, or boundaries, essential to the judgment, if the same would be provable by evidence of reputation.

(24) Other Exceptions. A statement not specifically covered by any of the foregoing exceptions but having equivalent circumstantial guarantees of trustworthiness, if the court determines that (A) the statement is offered as evidence of a material fact; (B) the statement is more probative on the point for which it is offered than any other evidence which the proponent can procure through reasonable efforts; and (C) the general purposes of these rules and the interests of justice will best be served by admission of the statement into evidence. However, a statement may not be admitted under this exception unless the proponent of it makes known to the adverse party sufficiently in advance of the trial or hearing to provide the adverse party with a fair opportunity to prepare to meet it, the proponent's intention to offer the statement and the particulars of it, including the name and address of the declarant.

II. DISCUSSION

Rule 803(1): Present Sense Impression and
Rule 803(2): Excited Utterance

In this Discussion, Rules 803(1) and (2) are considered together, a position consistent with the Advisory Committee's Notes and the approach of a number of commentators. Although there is considerable overlap between these two exceptions, they are based on different theories.

Rule 803(1), the exception for present sense impressions, modifies the common law which generally excluded such statements absent a state of excitement qualifying the statement as an excited utterance. The theory behind this exception is that "substantial contemporaneity of event and statement negative the likelihood of deliberate or conscious misrepresentation." [1]

If the declarant is a witness at trial, he or she can be questioned regarding the statement. If the declarant is not available at trial, the witness who testifies regarding the statement may be examined regarding the circumstances surrounding the making of the statement, to assist the trier of fact in evaluating it.[2] A statement meeting the requirements of Rule 803(1) is admissible even if, at trial, the declarant denies making the statement or denies the truth of facts contained in the alleged statement.[3]

The theory underlying Rule 803(2) is that the declarant's state of excitement "temporarily stills the capacity of reflection and produces utterances free of conscious fabrication." [4] This exception codifies the long-established exception to the hearsay rule. Commentators have noted that spontaneity resulting from a state of excitement may also produce error. However, statements are usually admitted.[5]

The permissible subject matter of a present sense impression is considerably narrower than that of an excited utterance. Subsection (1) is limited to statements "describing or explaining" the event or condition, while statements falling under subsection (2) need only be "relating to" a startling event or condition. The most significant difference between subsections (1) and (2) is the allowable length of time that may elapse between the event and the statement.

1. Advisory Committee Note to Rule 803(1).

2. *Id.*

3. Hilyer v. Howat Concrete Co., 578 F.2d 422 (D.C.Cir.1978).

4. Advisory Committee's Note to Rule 803(2).

5. *See, e.g.,* Hutchins and Slesinger, *Some Observations on the Law of Evidence: Spontaneous Exclamations,* 28 Colum.L.Rev. 432, 439 (1928) ("What the emotion gains by way of overcoming the desire to lie, it loses by impairing the declarant's power of observation."); Ladd, *The Hearsay We Admit,* 5 Okla.L.Rev. 271, 286 (1952) ("Spontaneous exclamations may emanate as much from the personality, prior experiences and personal attitudes of a person, as from a clear-cut accurate vision of the events perceived").

Subsection (1) recognizes that precise contemporaneity is not always possible. Some allowance must be made for the declarant to translate observations into speech. However, a substantial time interval between the event and the statement will not be allowed. The appropriate standard is whether a sufficient amount of time has lapsed since the event to have permitted reflective thought by the declarant.[6]

In *United States v. Cruz,*[7] for example, the court held that a statement was inadmissible where it was unclear how much time had passed between the event and the statement. The court reached a similar result in *United States v. Cain,*[8] holding that the declarant's distance from the scene of the event and the undetermined amount of time that had lapsed made it impossible to determine whether the statement was made immediately following the observation.

In *United States v. Blakey,*[9] the court allowed admission of a tape-recorded conversation involving the declarant that took place anywhere from several minutes to as long as twenty-three minutes after the event occurred. Other courts have excluded statements under circumstances similar to those present in *Blakey,* where the party offering the statement was unable to show the amount of time that passed between the event and the statement.

In *Blakey,* the court noted that the statement had been tape recorded and a number of other witnesses were available to testify to the surrounding circumstances. Other recorded statements also corroborated the statement in question. With these circumstantial guarantees of trustworthiness, it seems that the statement would have been more properly admitted under Rule 803(24).

In determining whether a statement is admissible as an excited utterance under Rule 803(2), the standard applied by the courts has been the duration of the state of excitement.[10] However, the lapse of time between the startling event and the declarant's statement is not dispositive under subsection (2). Other factors to be considered by the courts are the declarant's age, physical and mental state, the characteristics of the event, and the subject matter of the statements. In *Smith v. Fairman,*[11] for example, the court admitted as an excited utterance a statement identifying defendant as the murderer. While it was possible that the declarant, who was injured by the assailant, may have seen the body twice, the court stated that physical factors such as pain might

6. C. McCormick, *Evidence* 862 (Cleary ed. 1984); Hilyer v. Howat Concrete Co., 578 F.2d 422, 426 n. 7 (D.C.Cir.1978); Meder v. Everest & Jennings, Inc., 637 F.2d 1182 (8th Cir.1981); Wolfson v. Mutual Life Ins. Co., 455 F.Supp. 82 (M.D.Pa.), *aff'd,* 588 F.2d 825 (3d Cir.1978).

7. 765 F.2d 1020, 1024 (11th Cir.1985).

8. 587 F.2d 678, 681 (5th Cir.), *cert. denied,* 440 U.S. 975 (1979).

9. 607 F.2d 779, 786 (7th Cir.1979).

10. Graham, *Handbook of Federal Evidence* 813 (2d ed. 1986).

11. 862 F.2d 630, 636 (7th Cir.1988).

prolong the "excited utterance" period. In general, it must appear to the court that the declarant's statement was spontaneous, excited or impulsive, rather than the product of deliberation or reflection.[12]

However, the lapse of time is not irrelevant under Rule 803(2). In *David v. Pueblo Supermarket,*[13] the court permitted the plaintiff's husband to testify that after the plaintiff fell in a grocery store, the declarant stated that she had informed the store an hour and a half previously that there was a foreign substance on the floor. The court noted that the declarant had seen the eight-months-pregnant plaintiff fall directly on her stomach, and that the unsolicited statement was made within seconds after the fall. Without further explanation, the court noted that the trial judge had "reached a very outer bounds of his permissible discretion" in admitting the witness' statement under the excited utterance exception. 740 F.2d at 235.

The amount of elapsed time varies significantly in the cases. In *United States v. Bailey,*[14] the court affirmed admission of a Rule 803(2) statement made by the declarant approximately three minutes after the event, where another witness testified that at the time of the statement, the declarant appeared to be upset. In contrast, *Morgan v. Foretich,*[15] an action for child abuse by a four-year-old child and her mother, held that statements made within three hours of the child's return to the mother following a visit to the defendants should have been admitted as an excited utterance. Justice Powell, writing for the court, held that a child's out-of-court excited utterances are admissible regardless of whether the child would be competent to testify at trial.[16]

Sometimes a statement that is untimely under subsection (1) is nonetheless admissible under subsection (2). For example, in *Hilyer v. Howat Concrete Co.,*[17] the court held that a statement made between fifteen and forty-five minutes after an event was not admissible under Rule 803(1). However, the statement was admitted as an excited utterance under Rule 803(2).

A case that is more difficult to fit within the scope of subsection (2) is *United States v. Nick.*[18] In *Nick,* a three-year-old child made a statement concerning sexual abuse by the defendant. When the moth-

12. United States v. Iron Shell, 633 F.2d 77, 85–86 (8th Cir.1980), *cert. denied,* 450 U.S. 1001 (1981). *See also* United States v. Golden, 671 F.2d 369, 371 (10th Cir.), *cert. denied,* 456 U.S. 919 (1982). (court held that statement made by victim within fifteen minutes after an assault, after victim had driven twelve miles to his grandmother's house at over one hundred twenty miles per hour, was made under a state of excitement caused by the event).

13. 740 F.2d 230, 235 (3d Cir.1984).

14. 834 F.2d 218 (1st Cir.1987).

15. 846 F.2d 941, 950 (4th Cir.1988).

16. *See also* Annot., 15 A.L.R.4th 1043 (1982).

17. 578 F.2d 422 (D.C.Cir.1978).

18. 604 F.2d 1199, 1202 (9th Cir.1979).

er arrived at the defendant's home, the child was asleep. The mother then took the child home. Only after having been asked a question did the child make the statement. The court held that at the time of the statement, the child was still suffering distress from the assault. The court's analysis overlooks the fact that sufficient time for reflective thought had clearly transpired. As in *Blakey,* this statement would more properly be admitted under the residual exception if other circumstantial guarantees of the statement's trustworthiness were present.

Another problem considered by the courts under both subsection (1) and (2) is whether to admit the statement of an unidentified declarant. Nothing in the language of either subsection contains an identification requirement. On the contrary, each of the exceptions to the hearsay rule listed in Rule 803 specifies certain requirements that are considered to reflect circumstantial guarantees of trustworthiness sufficient to justify admission of evidence absent an opportunity to cross-examine the declarant at trial, even though he or she may be available.[19]

However, the courts have been hesitant to admit statements by unidentified declarants.[20] In *Miller v. Keating,*[21] for example, the court excluded a statement of an unidentified declarant under Rule 602, finding that the party offering the statement had failed to show the requisite spontaneity and personal knowledge on the part of the declarant required by Rule 803(2). In dictum, the court noted that in some instances, the statement itself might reveal perception and excitement on the part of the declarant; however, the burden of establishing those elements always rests with the statement's proponent. It might also be argued that a court could properly admit such statements under Rule 803(24) or 804(b)(5).

In contrast, the court held in *United States v. Boyd*[22] that statements made by unidentified persons to a police officer as the defendant ran from apartment to apartment with stolen mail were admissible as excited utterances. Similarly, in *McLaughlin v. Vinzant,*[23] the court held that it was permissible to draw an inference that the declarant had personal knowledge of the event from the force of the statement itself and the fact that the declarant had been with the defendant in the immediate vicinity of the event at the time of the event.

The unidentified declarant issue is related to the question whether corroboration of the statement is required. In *United States v.*

19. Advisory Committee's Note to Rule 803(1).

20. United States v. Medico, 557 F.2d 309, 315 (2d Cir.), *cert. denied,* 434 U.S. 986 (1977).

21. 754 F.2d 507 (3d Cir.1985).

22. 620 F.2d 129, 132 (6th Cir.), *cert. denied,* 449 U.S. 855 (1980).

23. 522 F.2d 448 (1st Cir.), *cert. denied,* 423 U.S. 1037 (1975).

Blakey,[24] the court held that Rule 803(1) contains no requirement that a witness to the actual event be available for cross examination. The court noted, however, that several witnesses could testify to all the events prior to and subsequent to the statement.

Commentators have noted that neither subsection (1) nor subsection (2) contains a requirement of corroboration.[25] The limits contained in those subsections as to time and subject matter appear virtually to assure that the witness who testifies regarding the statement must have either witnessed the event or observed circumstances strongly suggesting the event occurred. It has been suggested that problems of unidentified declarants and corroboration should go to the weight and sufficiency of the evidence, rather than imposing an additional, unwritten requirement for admissibility.

The hearsay exceptions listed under Rule 803 are phrased in terms of nonapplication of the hearsay rule, rather than in terms of positive admissibility of evidence meeting the specified requirements. Accordingly, evidence that might otherwise qualify for admission as an exception to the hearsay rule may still be excluded on other grounds, such as Rule 403 (Exclusion of Relevant Evidence on Grounds of Prejudice, Confusion or Waste of Time) or Rule 602 (Lack of Personal Knowledge).

Rule 803(3): Then Existing Mental, Emotional, or Physical Condition

The exception for present state of mind, emotional or physical condition is essentially a specialized application of the exception for present sense impressions.[26] This exception is most often applied in cases where a party seeks to admit a statement of intent by the declarant to infer that the intended act was done. Although state of mind may be proved by circumstantial evidence, the declarant's statements will often be the primary source of evidence.[27] The person whose state of mind is at issue may, of course, testify as to his or her own mental state.[28]

The theory behind this exception is that reliability is assured by the spontaneity and probable sincerity of the statement, since the statement must relate to a state of mind or emotion existing at the time the statement was made.[29] The Court noted in *Mutual Life Insurance Co. v. Hillmon* [30] that if the declarant were called to testify at trial, "his

24. 607 F.2d 779 (7th Cir.1979).

25. *See, e.g.,* C. McCormick, *Evidence* 862–63 (Cleary ed. 1984).

26. Advisory Committee Note to Rule 803(3).

27. C. McCormick, *Evidence* 843 (Cleary ed. 1984).

28. United States v. Dozier, 672 F.2d 531 (5th Cir.), *reh'g denied,* 677 F.2d 113, *cert. denied,* 459 U.S. 943 (1982).

29. C. McCormick, *Evidence* 844 (Cleary ed. 1984).

30. 145 U.S. 285, 295 (1982).

own memory of his state of mind at a former time is no more likely to be clear and true than a bystander's recollection of what he then said."

The primary difficulty that has arisen under this subsection is whether the declarant's statement of intent may be admitted to show what someone other than the declarant did. *Hillmon,* the leading case in this area, involved a suit on a life insurance policy by the insured's wife. The issue was whether a body that had been discovered was actually that of the plaintiff's husband or that of a man named Walters. The court held that a letter written by Walters to his sister had been erroneously excluded.

In that letter, Walters stated that he intended to leave Wichita with Hillmon shortly before the unidentified body was discovered. The letter tended to support the defendant's theory that the body that had been found was actually that of Walters. The court held that the letter was admissible, reasoning that the statement in Walters' letter that he intended to leave town with Hillmon made it more probable both that he did go and that he went with Hillmon, than if there had been no such statement.

The Advisory Committee's Note states that the rule of *Hillmon,* "allowing evidence of intention as tending to prove the doing of the act intended, is, of course, left undisturbed." The House Committee on the Judiciary stated in its report that it was intended that the rule of *Hillmon* be limited, "so as to render statements of intent by a declarant admissible only to prove his future conduct, not the future conduct of another person." Neither the Report of the Senate Committee on the Judiciary nor the Report of the House and Senate Conferees addressed the issue. Faced with an inconclusive legislative history, the courts have generally admitted such statements. A number of states directly address this issue in their codes, barring use of Rule 803(3) statement to prove the conduct of another.[31]

Admissibility has generally been based on two different theories. First, the statement is admitted to show what the declarant did, not what the other party did. The second theory is that declarations of intent are admissible against a person other than the declarant where there is independent evidence that corroborates the statement.[32]

31. 2 *Evidence in America* § 58.2 (Exception 3) (Alaska, Florida and Louisiana).

32. United States v. Cicale, 691 F.2d 95 (2d Cir.1982) (in a conspiracy case, the declarant's statement that he was going to meet with the defendant was held to be admissible against the defendant, where other witnesses testified the meeting actually took place), *cert. denied,* 460 U.S. 1082 (1983); United States v. Sperling, 726 F.2d 69 (2d Cir.) (following *Cicale*), *cert. denied,* 467 U.S. 1243 (1984); United States v. Badalamenti, 794 F.2d 821 (2d Cir.1986) (declarations of intent are admissible against a nondeclarant when they are linked with independent evidence of a connection between the declarant and a nondeclarant); United States v. Williams, 704 F.2d 315 (6th Cir.) (statement of defendant qualified for admission as statement of intent, but held inadmissible because not probative without corroborating evidence of the occurrence of either of two conditions qualifying the original statement), *cert. denied,* 464 U.S. 991 (1983); United States v.

Statements admitted under Rule 803(3) to show the declarant's state of mind may also contain assertions as to particular facts. In such instances, a limiting instruction under Rule 105 is proper to insure that those facts will be considered by the jury solely as bearing upon the declarant's state of mind, and not for the truth of the facts asserted. It has been suggested that a factor favoring admissibility of the statement is that, as a practical matter, it is unrealistic to expect a jury to consider the declarant's statement only as evidence of his or her own actions.[33]

In certain instances, where the danger that unfair prejudice to a party will result if the jury considers such a factual assertion in spite of a limiting instruction, and it substantially outweighs the probative value of the evidence, exclusion of the statement is proper under Rule 403.[34]

Rule 803(4): Statements for Purposes of Medical Diagnosis or Treatment

Statements of the declarant's present physical condition, medical history, past or present symptoms, pain, or the general cause of the declarant's condition are admissible under this exception "in view of the patient's strong motivation to be truthful." [35] These statements may be made in response to questions asked by the physician, and thus not totally spontaneous. However, such statements may be presumed to be reliable, since the declarant most likely believes that the effectiveness of the treatment received may depend in large part upon the accuracy of the information given to the physician.[36]

Statements offered under this exception may not be made only to a physician. They may be made to anyone associated with providing medical services, such as ambulance attendants, nurses or even family members. Such statements are limited to those made for purposes of medical diagnosis or treatment.[37] Accordingly, this subsection is somewhat less important in relation to statements of present physical condition. Those statements are admissible under Rule 803(3) regardless of the purpose for which the statements are made.

Astorga–Torres, 682 F.2d 1331 (9th Cir.), *cert. denied,* 459 U.S. 1040 (1982); *see also,* United States v. Pheaster, 544 F.2d 353, 379–80 (9th Cir.1976) (discussing Advisory Committee's Note and Report of the House Committee on the Judiciary), *cert. denied,* 429 U.S. 1099 (1977).

33. Graham, *Handbook of Federal Evidence* 823 n. 18 (2d ed. 1986).

34. *See, e.g.,* United States v. Brown, 490 F.2d 758, 774 (D.C.Cir.1973); *see also,* United States v. Jenkins, 579 F.2d 840 (4th Cir.), *cert. denied,* 439 U.S. 967 (1978) (Widener, J., dissenting).

35. Advisory Committee Note to Rule 803(4).

36. C. McCormick, *Evidence* 839 (Cleary ed. 1984).

37. 2 Saltzburg & Martin, *Federal Rules of Evidence Manual* 268–269 (5th ed. 1990).

One problem area has been whether statements of present pain or other symptoms are admissible when made to a physician who examined the declarant solely for the purpose of testifying at trial. Prior to adoption of the Federal Rules of Evidence, such statements were generally excluded on the ground that the declarant lacked the motive to be truthful.[38] The examining physician was limited to testifying to objective conditions that he or she observed.

The Senate Committee on the Judiciary stated in its report that statements made during examinations under Fed.R.Civ.P. 35 were those that would normally be admitted under this exception. However, if proof of the fact contained in the declarant's statements was independently put into evidence, the examining physician was permitted to state his opinion in response to a hypothetical question incorporating those facts with the physician's objective findings.[39]

The distinction between statements made to examining physicians and to treating physicians has been eliminated by Rule 803(4), although a few states have retained it in their evidence codes.[40] An examining physician may now testify regarding statements made for the purpose of medical diagnosis to the same extent as the treating physician, even though the only real purpose of the examination was to permit the physician to testify at trial.

The Advisory Committee Notes states that the reason for abolishing the limitation was that a jury would probably be unable to distinguish whether the statement was to be considered only as part of the basis of the examining physician's opinion or as substantive evidence. This position is also consistent with Rule 703, which states that the facts on which expert testimony is based need not be admissible in evidence themselves, if they are of a kind ordinarily relied on by experts in that field.[41]

In *O'Gee* the court considered, but did not decide, whether a patient's statement to his physician regarding another physician's opinion would be admissible. In dictum, the court suggested that the Rule was not intended to go that far. In *Bulthuis v. Rexall Corp.,*[42] the court reversed a summary judgment for the defendant, while holding that the declarant's testimony that her doctor told her she was being given a certain drug did not fall within the exception of Rule 803(4). The court stated that the statement was to, not by, the patient.

38. *E.g.,* Padgett v. Southern Ry. Co., 396 F.2d 303 (6th Cir.1968)

39. 2 Saltzburg & Martin, *Federal Rules of Evidence Manual* 389–390 (5th ed. 1990).

40. Louisiana, Michigan, Rhode Island and Tennessee. *See* 2 *Evidence in America* § 58.2 (Exception 4).

41. O'Gee v. Dobbs Houses, Inc., 570 F.2d 1084 (2d Cir.1978). Advisory Committee Note to Rule 803(4).

42. 789 F.2d 1315 (9th Cir.1985).

An interesting question is posed by the situation where, for example, a mother makes statements to a doctor about her child for the purpose of medical treatment. It has been suggested that that situation clearly falls within the scope of this Rule.[43] That issue was addressed by the Illinois appellate court in *Welter v. Bowman Dairy Co.,*[44] where the court held that such a statement was admissible.

Under subsection (4), statements as to the cause of the declarant's present medical condition are admissible only "insofar as reasonably pertinent to diagnosis or treatment." Another problem area under this subsection in determining has been just how far the courts will go in allowing statements explaining the cause of the declarant's medical condition.

Originally, all statements regarding causation were excluded, and some states have codified this result.[45] More recent decisions recognize that causation may be a factor in medical diagnosis or treatment. It appears that the courts will draw the line where the statement regarding causation enters the realm of fault. Then, the assurances of reliability are no longer present, and the statement should be excluded.[46]

In *United States v. Iron Shell,*[47] the court held that statements made by the victim of an assault to commit rape concerning the cause of her vaginal injury were sufficiently related to medical treatment to be admitted. The court proposed a two-part test for determining admissibility of statements under the exception. First, the declarant's motive must be consistent with the purposes of obtaining medical treatment. Second, the content of the statement must be such as is reasonably relied on by physicians in providing medical treatment or diagnosis.

A similar result was reached by the court in *United States v. Iron Thunder,*[48] where the court held that statements made by the victim to her physician that she had been raped were admissible. The court noted that the statements were made in response to questions by the physician. The statements did not specify the persons responsible for the declarant's condition or contain other fact unrelated to medical diagnosis and treatment.

Sometimes Rule 803(4) is used as a vehicle for a "tender years" exception to the hearsay rule. In *United States v. Nick,*[49] for example,

43. Graham, *Handbook of Federal Evidence* 827 n. 2 (2d ed. 1986).

44. 318 Ill.App. 305, 47 N.E.2d 739 (1943).

45. Idaho, Oklahoma and Vermont. 2 *Evidence in America* § 58.2 (Exception 4).

46. Advisory Committee Note to Rule 803(4); McCormick, *Evidence* 840 (Cleary ed. 1984).

47. 633 F.2d 77 (8th Cir.1980), *cert. denied,* 450 U.S. 1001 (1981).

48. 714 F.2d 765, 772 (8th Cir.1983).

49. 604 F.2d 1199, 1201–02 (9th Cir.1979).

statements made by the three-year-old victim of an assault to a physician were admissible where the identify of the alleged assailant was not revealed. A more expansive approach was taken by the court in *United States v. Renville.*[50] In *Renville,* the court held that statements made by a child to a physician regarding the identity of the person who abused her were admissible, where there was nothing to indicate a motive other than that of a patient responding to questions by a physician for purposes of medical treatment.[51]

There must be indicia of trustworthiness somewhere apparent before a statement will be admitted under this Rule. In *Cook v. Hoppin,*[52] the court held that statements as to the cause of the plaintiff's injuries contained in medical records should have been excluded where there was no showing in the records as to the source of the statement. The court further stated that the statement was not the kind of information generally relied upon by physicians in providing treatment. Finally, the court rejected an argument that the statements were admissible under Rule 803(24).

Where multiple statements are made, some but not others may be admitted. For example, in *United States v. Pollard,*[53] the court ruled that statements contained in medical records stating that the defendant reinjured his previously broken arm during an arrest should have been admitted as relevant to whether the defendant's confession had been voluntary. However, the court held that the portions of the records identifying the arresting officer as the person who twisted the defendant's arm were properly excluded as beyond the scope of Rule 803(4).

Rule 803(5): Recorded Recollection

Rule 803(5), which provides an exception to the hearsay rule for recorded recollection, has been the subject of relatively few decisions. The guarantee of trustworthiness underlying this exception is found in the inherent reliability of an accurate record that was made while facts were still fresh in the declarant's mind.

The language of subsection (5) requires that the witness have "insufficient recollection to enable the witness to testify fully and accurately." One question relating to this exception at common law

50. 779 F.2d 430, 438 (8th Cir.1985).

51. *Renville* was followed in United States v. DeNoyer, 811 F.2d 436, 438 (8thCir.1987) (statement by five-year-old boy that his father had sodomized him), and in United States v. Shaw, 824 F.2d 601, 608 (8th Cir.1987) ("statements of fault made to a physician by a child who has been sexually abused by a household member" are admissible), *cert. denied,* 484 U.S. 1068 (1988). Statements made by a five-year-old child to psychologist, in which she identified her alleged abusers, were held to be admissible in Morgan v. Foretich, 846 F.2d 941, 949–50 (4th Cir.1988).

52. 783 F.2d 684, 690 (7th Cir.1986).

53. 790 F.2d 1309, 1314 (7th Cir.1986), *vacated,* 830 F.2d 1382, 1393 (7th Cir.1987), *cert. denied,* 484 U.S. 1068 (1988) (overruled *Pollard* only to extent that Pollard forbade prosecutor to observe that the defense could produce a witness if it wished).

was whether the party offering the statement is required to make a preliminary showing of impaired memory on the part of the declarant.[54] It has been suggested that the absence of such a requirement would encourage the use of self-serving statements prepared solely for purposes of litigation.[55]

A determination whether the witness lacks sufficient present recollection to testify fully and accurately is made by the court under Rule 104(a). The most common method of demonstrating the declarant's lack of present recollection is by showing that the document or record fails to refresh the witness' recollection.[56] A witness may testify, for example, that he or she has completely forgotten the matter that the memorandum concerns, but believes that under the circumstances, he or she would not have made or adopted the memorandum unless it accurately reflected the witness' observations.[57]

The House Committee on the Judiciary amended the original text of the Rule in an attempt to make clear that a memorandum may be adopted by a witness, as well as made. Unfortunately, the language of subsection (5) is somewhat unclear on this point. The Report of the Senate Committee on the Judiciary indicates that Congress did not intend to narrow the scope of this subsection to preclude admissibility of evidence involving more than one participant. Accordingly, the phrase "by the witness" should be construed as modifying only the word "adopted," rather than the phrase "made or adopted." [58]

That interpretation makes clear that the witness may adopt a memorandum prepared by someone else, as long as the matter is fresh in the witness' memory at the time the memorandum was adopted. It is unclear at this time what is required to show adoption by the witness of a memorandum prepared by someone else.

The testimony of two or more witnesses may be required to lay a foundation for admission of a memorandum or record under this exception.[59] However, the original viewer's statement may be admissible under another exception to the hearsay rule, avoiding the need for that witness' testimony.[60]

54. Advisory Committee Note to Rule 803(5).

55. *E.g.,* C. McCormick, *Evidence* 866 (Cleary ed. 1984); *see also* United States v. Micke, 859 F.2d 473 (7th Cir.1988) (affidavit of witness was not admissible absent a showing that the witness could not recall the matters).

56. United States v. Senak, 527 F.2d 129, 137 (7th Cir.1975), *cert. denied,* 425 U.S. 907 (1976).

57. Putnam v. Moore, 119 F.2d 246 (5th Cir.1941) (memorandum in witness' own handwriting).

58. *See,* C. McCormick, *Evidence* 868–69 (3d ed. 1984).

59. *See, e.g.,* United States v. Civella, 666 F.2d 1122 (8th Cir.1981).

60. McGarry v. United States, 388 F.2d 862, 869 (1st Cir.1967), *cert. denied,* 394 U.S. 921 (1969); *see,* United States v. Steele, 685 F.2d 793 (3d Cir.), *cert. denied,* 459 U.S. 908 (1982).

Under Rule 803(5), because the memorandum or record is viewed as a substitute for oral testimony, the writing is normally read into evidence. Since the content of the writing is being proved, the Original Writing Rule, Rule 1002, applies to evidence admitted under this exception.[61]

Rule 803(6): Records of Regularly Conducted Activity

The exception for records of regularly conducted activity, Rule 803(6), has its origins in the common law rule known as the Shopbook Rule.[62] The Shopbook Rule can be traced to the practice in England which allowed a merchant to prove an account receivable upon which he brought suit. *Id.* Prior to the adoption of the Shopbook Rule in the United States, the offering party had to produce all participants in the process of gathering, transmitting and recording information in order to get a business record into evidence.[63]

Prior to the adoption of Federal Rule of Evidence 803(6), statutes such as the Commonwealth Fund Act and the Uniform Business Records As Evidence Act were enacted in order to overcome the unduly burdensome foundation requirements for admission of business records into evidence.[64] It was recognized that business entries relied heavily upon regularly kept records and, therefore, there was an incentive for business persons to be thorough and accurate.

Rule 803(6) is broadly written to include business institutions, associations, professions, occupations, and callings of every kind, regardless of whether it is conducted for profit, to be included in the definition of "business." Furthermore, memoranda, reports, records or data compilations of a business, in any form, of acts, events, conditions, opinions, or diagnoses may be admitted into evidence if the information taken from a person with knowledge was recorded in the regular practice of that business activity at or near the time it was transmitted. This must be shown by the testimony of the custodian of those records or other qualified witness.[65] It is not a requirement, however, that the custodian of the business records who is called to testify was the custodian of the records when they were made.[66] However, anyone

61. Jewett v. United States, 15 F.2d 955 (9th Cir.1926); *see* 4 J. Weinstein & M. Berger, *Weinstein's Evidence* ¶ 803(5)[02] at 803–169.

62. G. Lilly, *An Introduction to the Law of Evidence,* § 716 n. 2 (2d ed. 1987).

63. Graham, *Handbook of Federal Evidence,* § 803.6 (2d ed. 1986).

64. La Porte v. United States, 300 F.2d 878, 881 (9th Cir.1962); Stegemann v. Miami Beach Boat Slips, Inc., 213 F.2d 561, 563–64 (5th Cir.1954); United States v. Mortimer, 118 F.2d 266 (2d Cir.), *cert. denied,* 314 U.S. 616 (1941).

65. Fed.R.Evid. 803(6). *See* In re National Trust Group, Inc., 98 BR 90 (MD Fla.1989) (testimony of company president sufficient upon showing of personal knowledge of internal memorandum).

66. United States v. Scallion, 533 F.2d 903, 915 (5th Cir.1976), *cert. denied,* 429 U.S. 1079 (1977).

other than the custodian who participates in the initial furnishing of the information to be recorded must possess personal knowledge of matters. Thus, the records must be made by a person with knowledge or from information furnished by a person with personal knowledge.

Although the Federal Rule is ambiguous as to whether the recordkeeper or informer must have recorded the information pursuant to a business duty, courts have interpreted Rule 803(6) as having this requirement,[67] and some states have codified it.[68] Thus, if the supplier of the information is not acting in the regular course of business—that is, he is not acting pursuant to a business duty—the assurance of accuracy is not manifest as when one is acting in the regular course of business, and the profit should, therefore, be excluded.[69] Note, however, that if only one participant is acting under a business duty, the business record may still come into evidence if it is not hearsay or if it qualifies under another hearsay exception.[70] It is in the judge's discretion to determine whether business records will be admitted into evidence if the source of the information or the method or circumstances of preparation indicate a lack of trustworthiness.[71]

Prior to the enactment of the Federal Rules of Evidence, the federal courts drew a distinction between diagnoses involving "conjecture and opinion" and diagnoses upon which "competent physicians would not differ." [72] However, since the enactment of the Federal Rules of Evidence, opinions or diagnoses are specifically contained within the business record exception. A problem does arise, however, when a patient's medical record contains assertions as to the immediate cause of injury or assertions about fault. Generally, medical records which do contain these assertions are considered to be outside the scope of the entrant's business duty to record, and, therefore, are excluded.[73]

With the onslaught of the use of computers in business, the question arises as to the requirement of foundation testimony necessary before computer records of business activity can be introduced into

67. United States v. Baker, 693 F.2d 183, 188 (D.C.Cir.1982); United States v. Yates, 553 F.2d 518, 521 (6th Cir.1977); City of Cleveland v. Cleveland Elec. Illuminating Co., 538 F.Supp. 1257, 1269–71 (N.D.Ohio 1980).

68. 2 *Evidence in America* § 58.2 (Exception 6).

69. *See* Johnson v. Lutz, 253 N.Y. 124, 170 N.E. 517 (1930); United States v. Pfeiffer, 539 F.2d 668, 670–71 (8th Cir.1976).

70. United States v. Smith, 521 F.2d 957, 964 (D.C.Cir.1975).

71. Palmer v. Hoffman, 318 U.S. 109, *reh'g denied,* 318 U.S. 800 (1943); Hartzog v. United States, 217 F.2d 706 (4th Cir.1954).

72. J. Weinstein & M. Berger, *Weinstein's Evidence* ¶ 16.06[01][g] (1987); New York Life Ins. Co. v. Taylor, 147 F.2d 297, 300 (D.C.Cir.1945).

73. G. Lilly, *An Introduction to the Law of Evidence* § 7.17 (2d ed. 1987); Williams v. Alexander, 309 N.Y. 283, 129 N.E.2d 417 (1955); Lindstrom v. Yellow Taxi Co., 298 Minn. 224, 214 N.W.2d 672 (1974); Kelly v. Sheehan, 158 Conn. 281, 259 A.2d 605 (1969). *But see* Cestero v. Ferrara, 57 N.J. 497, 273 A.2d 761 (1971). *See also* the Discussion of Exception (4), *supra.*

evidence. Generally, in the trial judge's discretion, the introduction of computer business records may require a more comprehensive foundation to be layed before it will be admitted into evidence. Such "extra" requirements may include the production of evidence as to the method used to gather, store, and retrieve the information from the computer.[74]

Rule 803(6) is broadly written to include 803(8) public entities, *infra,* so that many recorded declarations may fit under both exceptions. There is some question whether, if a public record cannot meet the protective provisions in Rule 803(8), Rule 803(6) may be used to bypass Rule 803(8).[75] Some jurisdictions have found that government records and reports are exclusively governed by Rule 803(8) and are not within Rule 803(6).[76]

One of the major differences between Rule 803(6) and 803(8) is that, under the latter, investigative and police reports cannot be entered into evidence against an accused criminal defendant. The rationale for the exclusion of matters observed by police officers and law enforcement personnel rests on the theory that they are not as reliable as observations by public officials in other cases because the adversarial nature of the confrontation between the police and the defendant casts doubt on the objectivity of these entries.[77]

On the other hand, if evaluative reports are offered by the accused, then they should be admitted.[78] It should be noted, however, that although records of matters observed by law enforcement personnel are inadmissible when offered by the government against an accused, such matters may be presented orally by the observing officer and the records can be used to refresh memory.[79] Furthermore, it should be noted, that there has been a problem with defining who falls within the meaning of "law enforcement personnel" in Rule 803(8)(B).[80] Where that is in doubt, Rule 803(6) may be the preferred alternative.

74. United States v. Scholle, 553 F.2d 1109, 1125 (8th Cir.), *cert. denied,* 434 U.S. 940 (1977); United States v. DeGeorgia, 420 F.2d 889, 893 n. 11 (9th Cir.1969); *see also* G. Lilly, *An Introduction to the Law of Evidence* § 7.17 (2d ed. 1987); G. Joseph, *Modern Visual Evidence* §§ 7.02–7.03 (1984; Supp.1991).

75. *Compare* United States v. Cain, 615 F.2d 380, 382 (5th Cir.1980) (Rule 803(6) cannot be used as a back door for admitting evidence excluded by section (8)) *with* United States v. King, 613 F.2d 670, 673 (7th Cir.1980) (Rule 803(8) exclusion does not preclude admissibility under another rule, such as 803(6)). *See generally* the Discussion of Rule 803(8), *infra.*

76. *See* United States v. Orozco, 590 F.2d 789, 793 (9th Cir.), *cert. denied,* 442 U.S. 920 (1979); United States v. American Cyanamid Co., 427 F.Supp. 859, 867 (S.D.N.Y.1977).

77. G. Lilly, *An Introduction to the Law of Evidence* § 7.17 (2d ed. 1987); *see* Orozco, *supra* at 793. *But see* United States v. Dancy, 861 F.2d 77 (5th Cir.1988) (fingerprint records merely documenting unambiguous factual matters are admissible).

78. United States v. Smith, 521 F.2d 957, 968 n. 24 (D.C.Cir.1975).

79. G.Lilly, *An Introduction to the Law of Evidence* § 7.19 (2d ed. 1987).

80. United States v. Ruffin, 575 F.2d 346, 355–56 (2d Cir.1978) (IRS personnel gathering data for use in criminal prosecution are performing a law enforcement function);

Another difference between Rules 803(6) and 803(8) is that 803(8) public records are (under Rules 902 and 1005) frequently self-proving and, therefore, often do not require the testimony of a custodian of the records before they can be admitted into evidence. The theory upon which Rule 803(8) rests is the assumption that a public official or other person discharging the public's business will accurately maintain the public records because of the substantial reliance by their users and that it is unlikely that he will remember details independently of the record.[81] The record is that of the public body.[82] Rule 803(8) thus offers a simple route to admission if its criteria are satisfied.

Rule 803(7): Absence of Entry in Records Kept in Accordance With the Provisions of Paragraph (6)

Rule 803(7) is a counterpart to the business records exception in Rule 803(6) and indicates that evidence that a particular entry satisfying 803(6) does not exist is not hearsay. There are very few cases addressing this exception and those which have do not indicate any problems with the Rule.[83]

Rule 803(8): Public Records and Reports

Rule 803(8) creates an exception for certain public records and, as noted at the discussion of Rule 803(6), bears some resemblance to the business records exception. The exception addresses three types of public information: 803(8)(A) covers information about the activities of public offices or agencies; 803(8)(B) covers matters observed, except police reports in criminal cases; and 803(8)(C) addresses factual findings resulting from certain investigations.

Both subsections (B) and (C) of Rule 803(8) reflect Congressional judgments that certain governmental reports should not be admissible, as proof of their contents, against criminal accuseds. In the context of Rule 803(8)(C), the Advisory Committee made clear its concern that any such admission would present almost certain problems with an accused's confrontation rights. The debate on the House Floor concern-

United States v. Oates, 560 F.2d 45, 84 (2d Cir.1977) (Customs Service chemists qualified as "other law enforcement personnel"); *cf.* United States v. Hansen, 583 F.2d 325, 333 (7th Cir.) ("law enforcement personnel" does not include city building inspectors), *cert. denied,* 439 U.S. 912 (1978).

81. G. Lilly, *An Introduction to the Law of Evidence* § 7.18 (2d ed. 1987); Wong Wing Foo v. McGrath, 196 F.2d 120, 123 (9th Cir.1952); Chesapeake & Delaware Canal Co. v. United States, 250 U.S. 123 (1919).

82. *See* United States v. Torres, 733 F.2d 449, 455 n. 5 (7th Cir.), *cert. denied,* 469 U.S. 864 (1984); United States v. Regner, 677 F.2d 754, 763–64 (9th Cir.), *cert. denied,* 459 U.S. 911 (1982).

83. *See, e.g.,* United States v. Rich, 580 F.2d 929 (9th Cir.), *cert. denied,* 439 U.S. 935 (1978); United States v. Zeidman, 540 F.2d 314 (7th Cir.1976). *See also* 2 *Evidence in America* § 58.3 (Exception 7).

ing Rule 803(8)(B), moreover, reflects the same Congressional concern over potential admission of such reports against a criminal defendant.[84]

Rule 803(8) is not, however, a rule of exclusion. It is a rule of admissibility in certain defined circumstances. As a result, evidence not admissible under Rule 803(8) may, at least theoretically, be admissible under other provisions of the Rules. More specifically, the overlap between Rule 803(8) and Rules 803(5) and (6) has afforded a number of courts the opportunity to assess the admissibility of such governmental reports other than under Rule 803(8).

In *United States v. Oates,*[85] following an exhaustive review of the legislative history, the Second Circuit ruled that a government chemist's laboratory report of a heroin analysis was inadmissible under Rule 803(B) or (C) and that such inadmissibility foreclosed admissibility under any other hearsay exception, specifically including Rule 803(6) (business records) or 803(24) (residual exception).[86]

But in *United States v. Sawyer,*[87] the Seventh Circuit, distinguishing *Oates,* admitted an IRS agent's report of a telephone conversation with the defendant under Rule 803(5) (past recollection recorded). The *Sawyer* Court reasoned that, because the agent appeared and testified to making the record, he was confronted and cross-examined, thereby satisfying the prohibitions embodied in Rules 803(8)(B) and (C).[88] In fact, however, the agent was able to testify only as to the foundational facts, not the substance of the conversation. As to the latter, which comprised the matters in controversy, the defense was deprived of effective cross-examination and, arguably, confrontation.

Moreover, the breadth of prohibition against introduction of law enforcement reports against criminal accuseds is apparently not so unconditional as the language of Rule 803(8)(B) might suggest. Generally, it is clear, such reports may not be introduced in criminal cases to prove their contents.[89]

However, the Ninth Circuit has adopted the view that Congress, in its amendments to Rule 803(8), "did not intend to exclude records of

84. 120 Cong.Rec. 2387–2390 (Feb. 6, 1974).

85. 560 F.2d 45 (2d Cir.1977).

86. *See also* United States v. Cain, 615 F.2d 380 (5th Cir.1980); United States v. Orozco, 590 F.2d 789 (9th Cir.), *cert. denied,* 442 U.S. 920 (1979). *But see* United States v. Neff, 615 F.2d 1235 (9th Cir.), *cert. denied,* 447 U.S. 925 (1980) (absence of public record admissible under Rule 803(10).

87. 607 F.2d 1190 (7th Cir.1979), *cert. denied,* 445 U.S. 943 (1980).

88. *See also* United States v. King, 613 F.2d 670 (7th Cir.1980).

89. United States v. Cain, 615 F.2d 380, 382 (5th Cir.1980) (report of an escape from a federal correctional institution not admissible to prove the details of the information set forth therein (other than the simple fact of escape)); United States v. Davis, 571 F.2d 1354 (5th Cir.1978).

routine, nonadversarial matters. . . ." [90] Moreover, in *United States v. Barrentine,*[91] the Fifth Circuit permitted the government to introduce police reports, not for substantive purposes, but for the purpose of rehabilitating a government witness whom the defense had attempted to impeach with incomplete information concerning the matters covered in the reports.

In light of the conflict among the circuits, it would be desirable to clarify whether, or in what circumstances, matters excluded by Rules 803(B) and (C) may be admitted against criminal accuseds under other exceptions to the hearsay rule.

The extent to which Rule 803(8)(C) "factual findings" embrace opinions contained in investigative reports was initially unclear.[92] The Supreme Court ultimately concluded in *Beech Aircraft Corp. v. Rainey* [93] that statements in the form of conclusions or opinions are not by that fact excluded from coverage under 803(8)(C).

The admissibility under Rule 803(8)(C) of administrative findings in subsequent civil suits seems to depend in large part on the nature of the antecedent administrative action or proceedings. In *Chandler v. Roudebush* [94] the Supreme Court endorsed the admissibility of an administrative adjudicatory finding in a subsequent civil proceeding involving the same substantive matters. With respect to adjudicatory findings, the courts of appeals have uniformly followed *Chandler*'s lead.[95]

90. United States v. Orozco, 590 F.2d 789, 793 (9th Cir.), *cert. denied,* 442 U.S. 920 (1979) (affirming prosecution's introduction of Treasury Enforcement Communication System computer data cards to prove that a drug-possession defendant's auto crossed a border on the night of the defendant's arrest). *See also* United States v. Hernandez–Rojas, 617 F.2d 533 (9th Cir.), *cert. denied,* 449 U.S. 864 (1980). *Cf.* United States v. Grady, 544 F.2d 598 (2d Cir.1976) (foreign police report admitted for contents; live testimony as to reported facts also introduced, thereby rendering any conceivable error harmless.

91. 591 F.2d 1069 (5th Cir.), *cert. denied,* 444 U.S. 990 (1979).

92. *Compare, e.g.,* Baker v. Elcona Homes Corp., 588 F.2d 551 (6th Cir.1978), *cert. denied,* 441 U.S. 933 (1979) (liberal interpretation including opinions) and Lloyd v. American Export Lines, 580 F.2d 1179 (3d Cir., *cert. denied,* 439 U.S. 969 (1978) (same) with Smith v. Ithaco Corp., 612 F.2d 215, 220–223 (5th Cir.1980) (more moderate interpretation, reserving right to exclude certain opinions) and Dallas & Mavis Forwarding Co. v. Stegall, 659 F.2d 721, 722 (6th Cir.1981) (opinions excluded where predicate facts omitted from report.

93. 488 U.S. 153 (1988).

94. 425 U.S. 840, 863 n. 39 (1976).

95. *See, e.g.,* Nulf v. International Paper Co., 656 F.2d 553, 563 (10th Cir.1981); Bradshaw v. Zoological Society of San Diego, 569 F.2d 1066, 1068 (9th Cir.1978); In re Plywood Antitrust Litigation, 655 F.2d 627, 637 (5th Cir.1981), *cert. dismissed,* 462 U.S. 1125 (1983); United States v. School District of Ferndale, 577 F.2d 1339, 1354–1355 (6th Cir.1978).

In contrast, nonadjudicatory administrative findings have not uniformly been admitted. In *Robbins v. Whalen,*[96] the First Circuit held it reversible error to exclude an agency report compiled from objective technical analytical data supplied to the government by auto manufacturers as required by law. The *Robbins* Court ruled that the agency need only have firsthand knowledge of the method or investigation by which the facts were accumulated and need not itself have produced or verified the data.[97]

The same court, however, like the Third Circuit, has barred introduction of nonadjudicatory agency findings based on subjective commentary from interviewees who witnessed particular acts. Such witness commentary and, therefore, the findings predicated thereon were viewed as lacking any objective guarantees of trustworthiness.[98]

The Fifth Circuit, though, has affirmed introduction of an agency's letter determination that, upon investigation, it found no evidence to support a complaint's position.[99] However, in *Denny v. Hutchinson Sales Corp.*[100] the Tenth Circuit affirmed the exclusion of the findings of an informal, ex parte agency proceeding.

Succinctly put, the admissibility of nonadjudicatory agency findings appears to be contingent upon judicial satisfaction with the fact-gathering process—the trustworthiness of the facts—underlying the findings.

Rule 803(8)(C) represents a tremendous expansion of the typical public records exception. It has imposed burdens on federal courts that the drafters of the Rule may not have fully contemplated. Agency findings can be lengthy and complex. The data relied upon to support those findings may be complicated and extensive. When a claim that a finding is untrustworthy is made, a federal judge may find that reviewing the agency's work is an arduous task. If the report is offered, impeachment and rebuttal evidence may protract litigation. A number of state courts opted for a more restricted version of the public records exception.[101] It should be interesting as more cases are decided to compare the results of the Federal Rule with those of these states to see whether the liberal approach of the Federal Rule, combined with its

96. 653 F.2d 47 (1st Cir.), *cert. denied,* 454 U.S. 1123 (1981).

97. *But see* City of New York v. Pullman Co., 662 F.2d 910, 914–915 (2d Cir.1981), *cert. denied,* 454 U.S. 1164 (1982), in which the Second Circuit barred introduction of an "interim" staff report containing the "tentative results of an incomplete staff investigation" because, *inter alia,* it constituted merely staff recommendations to an agency head and it simply incorporated various "handouts" from the parties, rather than an independent agency analysis.

98. McKinnon v. Skil Corp., 638 F.2d 270, 278–279 (1st Cir.1981); John McShain, Inc. v. Cessna Aircraft Co., 563 F.2d 632, 635–636 (3d Cir.1977). *See also* Fowler v. Firestone Tire & Rubber Co., 92 F.R.D. 1, 2 (N.D.Miss.1980).

99. Local No. 59, IBEW v. Namco Elec., Inc., 653 F.2d 143, 145 (5th Cir.1981).

100. 649 F.2d 816 (10th Cir.1981).

101. *See* 2 *Evidence in America* §§ 58.2–58.3 (Exception 8).

provision that untrustworthy records may be excluded, provides for more efficient litigation than narrower state rules.

Rule 803(9): Records of Vital Statistics

Rule 803(9) concerns the exception allowed for records reporting births, deaths, or marriages which were made to a public office pursuant to law. While the standard of trustworthiness is met in such documents with respect to facts concerning date of birth or death and similar matters, such reports may contain other evaluative or explanatory materials where the issue of trustworthiness is not so apparent. Most often this arises in connection with statements in death certificates concerning cause of death or circumstances leading to death. Although such statements have been attacked as "hearsay within hearsay" or being made "without personal knowledge," courts considering this issue have admitted such documents as being covered by this Rule.[102] State courts construing this Rule have been more conservative.[103]

Rule 803(10): Absence of Public Record or Entry

Rule 803(10) addresses the problem of proving the "non-occurrence of an event by evidence of the absence of a record which would regularly be made of its occurrence." [104] Under this Rule, evidence in the form of testimony or certification pursuant to Rule 902 that "diligent search failed to disclose" the record or entry is not included within the hearsay rule.

Despite the implication from the Rule's title, Rule 803(10) is not simply the reverse side of Rule 803(8), Public Records and Reports. While Rule 803(8) excludes from the hearsay rule records, reports, statements, or data compilations of public offices or agencies, the Rule does not apply to law enforcement reports or investigative reports offered against defendants in criminal trials. On the other hand, Rule 803(10) does not contain such exclusionary language. Accordingly, a search made of public records and reports revealing the absence of a report or entry which was done by law enforcement personnel or pursuant to an authorized investigation is not excluded as hearsay under Rule 803(10).[105]

102. *See* Kromnick v. State Farm Mutual Automobile Insurance Co., Civ.A. No. 85–5824, 1990 WL 1407 (ED.Pa.1990), (certificate stating cause of death as automobile accident was admitted). *See also* Shell v. Parrish, 448 F.2d 528, 530–31 (6th Cir.1971) (death certificate reciting circumstances of accident was prima facie proof of the facts stated therein).

103. *See* 2 *Evidence in America* § 58.3 (Exception 9).

104. Advisory Committee Note to Rule 803 (Exception 10).

105. United States v. Yakobov, 712 F.2d 20, 24–27 (2d Cir.1983); United States v. Metzger, 778 F.2d 1195, 1200–1202 (6th Cir.1985), *cert. denied,* 477 U.S. 906 (1986).

By its terms, Rule 803(10) requires evidence that a thorough, diligent search of the public records was undertaken. A casual or partial search is not sufficient, nor will a statement that there has been a "diligent search" suffice if the circumstances indicate otherwise.[106]

While there has been some challenge as to the admissibility of evidence under this Rule as being violative of the Confrontation Clause of the Sixth Amendment, such challenges have been rejected.[107]

The applicability of Rule 803(10), and whether its phrase "public office or agency" extends to foreign or international agencies, was addressed in *United States v. M'Biye.*[108] In *M'Biye,* the Rule was interpreted to include supranational agencies such as the United Nations, rejecting the contention that the Rule was limited to the "domestic" agencies listed in Rule 902(1).

Similarly, in *United States v. Regner,*[109] the majority of the court rejected defendant's argument that the admission of certain Hungarian documents certifying the absence of entries in "official" Hungarian records violated defendant's rights under the Confrontation Clause of the Sixth Amendment. However, the majority did not deal with the nature of the documents themselves. A dissenting opinion objected to the expansion of Rule 803(10) to encompass foreign documents without considering the nature of the documents as "official," "proprietary," or "business" records. This dissenting view in *Regner* was apparently relied upon by the defendant in *United States v. Cahill,*[110] where the defendant attempted to exclude certain Mexican documents such as telephone books and letters written by public registrars and agency representatives. The district court held that the *Regner* dissent was not controlling and admitted the documents.

As the dissent in *Regner* correctly observes, documents which may be considered "official" in foreign countries may not be considered such in the United States. Accordingly, applicability of Rule 803(10) to searches of foreign "official" records should not be unquestioned. Rule 803(10), along with the other subsections of Rule 803, excludes certain statements from the general hearsay rule on the theory that such statements "possess circumstantial guarantees of trustworthiness."[111] It is significant that Rule 803(8), which also concerns records or reports prepared by "public offices or agencies," recognizes that lack of trust-

106. United States v. Yakabov, 712 F.2d 20, 23–24 (2d Cir.1983).

107. United States v. Metzger, 778 F.2d 1195, 1202 (6th Cir.1985), *cert. denied,* 477 U.S. 906 (1986). *See also* United States v. Herrera–Britto, 739 F.2d 551, 552 (11th Cir. 1984) (admission of defendant's statements did not violate *Miranda*); United States v. Lee, 589 F.2d 980, 988–89 (9th Cir.) (admission of CIA affidavits did not violate Confrontation Clause), *cert. denied,* 444 U.S. 969 (1979).

108. 655 F.2d 1240, 1242 (D.C.Cir.1981) (per curiam).

109. 677 F.2d 754, 758–59 (9th Cir.), *cert. denied,* 459 U.S. 911 (1982).

110. No. 85 CR 773 1988 WL 71239 (N.D.Ill.1988).

111. Advisory Committee Note to Rule 803 (Exception 10).

worthiness may result in the exclusion of records or reports. This strongly suggests that trustworthiness of the documents being searched is still an important factor under Rule 803(10). Dealing with this problem should be on a case-by-case basis.

Rule 803(11): Records of Religious Organizations

Rule 803(11) provides an exception to the hearsay rule for records of religious organizations. The Rule has been primarily invoked by taxpayers trying to use records of religious organizations to prove a bona fide tax deduction for a contribution made to the religious organization. However, the courts have uniformly rejected these efforts. In *Hall v. Commissioner,*[112] the Second Circuit held "[t]he exception for records of personal and family history kept by religious organizations, Fed.R.Evid. 803(11), is clearly inapplicable to receipts of this kind."

The only reported federal case which suggested the exception might be applicable is *McMorrow v. Schweiker.*[113] In *McMorrow,* suit was brought against the Secretary of Health and Human Services in which the plaintiff claimed entitlement to widow's insurance benefits under Title II of the Social Security Act. The critical issue was whether the plaintiff could prove she had been married to the decedent at the time of his death. While the district court allowed as to how records of religious organizations could be introduced in spite of their hearsay nature, and cited Rule 803(11) as authority for that proposition, the plaintiff was denied benefits because she could not introduce any records from the church where she was purportedly married.

Rule 803(12): Marriage, Baptismal, and Similar Certificates

Rule 803(12) excepts from the hearsay rule a statement of fact contained in a certificate which evidences the fact a marriage or other ceremony has taken place or which shows that a clergy member has administered a sacrament. In order to qualify for the exception, the person making the certificate must be authorized by either the rules or practices of a religious organization or by law to perform the act certified. In addition, the certificate must have been issued "at the time of the act or within a reasonable time thereafter." This Rule "is a duplication to the extent that it deals with a certificate by a public official, as in the case of a judge who performs a marriage ceremony. The area covered by the rule is, however, substantially larger and extends the certification procedure to clergymen and the like who perform marriages and other ceremonies or administer sacraments. Thus certificates of such matters as baptism or confirmation, as well as marriage, are included." [114]

112. 774 F.2d 61, 63 (2d Cir.1985).

113. 561 F.Supp. 584 (D.N.J.1982). *See also* the discussion of *McMorrow* under Rules 803(12) and 803(13).

114. Advisory Committee Note to Rule 803 (Exception 12).

The Rule has seen little application. The only federal case in which it is cited is *McMorrow v. Schweiker.*[115] *McMorrow* involved a woman seeking widow's insurance benefits under Title II of the Social Security Act. While the widow lacked any tangible proof of marriage and was denied benefits, the district court cited Rule 803(12) for the following proposition:

> The most common mode of proof of a ceremonial marriage, oddly enough, is by hearsay, namely the marriage certificate issued by the performing official, and such hearsay is regularly received despite the availability of the declarant. *See,* 5 Wigmore, "Evidence," I 1644, 1645 (Chadbourn rev. 1974); Fed.Ev.Rule 803(12); N.J.Ev.Rule 63(18); Belazinski v. Lebid, 65 N.J.Super. 483, 168 A.2d 209 (App.1961).

561 F.Supp. at 589. The Rule has seen little more activity in the states.[116]

Rule 803(13): Family Records

Rule 803(13) establishes an exception to the rule against hearsay for records containing statements of fact regarding personal or family history. The Rule is expansive in that it provides an exception for statements of fact contained in "family Bibles, genealogies, charts, engravings on rings, inscriptions on family portraits, engravings on urns, crypts, or tombstones, or the like." [117]

The rule has been cited in two federal decisions. The first, *McMorrow v. Schweiker,*[118] involved a widow trying to obtain insurance benefits under the Social Security Act. While the court denied the plaintiff's claim because she failed to prove she had been married to the decedent, the court indicated the plaintiff could have proved her case through statements of fact contained in a family Bible or the like.

The second case is *United States v. Sheets.*[119] *Sheets* was a criminal prosecution for securities violations brought by the federal government. In advance of trial, the government filed a motion in limine to determine if it would be allowed to introduce at trial portions of a diary of the deceased former wife of the defendant. After analyzing the diary, the magistrate found that the catch-all hearsay exception under Fed. Rule Evid. 803(24) allowed the introduction of the diary. However, in *dicta,* the magistrate also found the evidence "akin to other recognized exceptions to the hearsay rule expressly provided for in the F.R.E.

115. 561 F.Supp. 584 (D.C.N.J.1982). *See also* the discussion of *McMorrow* under Rules 803(11) and 803(13).

116. 2 *Evidence in America* § 58.3 (Exception 12).

117. Fed.Ev.Rule 803(13) (emphasis added).

118. 561 F.Supp. 584 (D.C.N.J.1982). *See also* the discussion of *McMorrow* under Rules 803(11) and 803(12).

119. 125 F.R.D. 172 (D.Utah 1989).

. . ." and specifically identified Rule 803(13) as being analogous. 125 F.R.D. at 177.

The Rule has proved equally unproblematic in the state courts.[120]

Rule 803(14): Records of Documents Affecting an Interest in Property

Rule 803(14) carves out an exception to the hearsay rule for records purporting to establish or affect an interest in property. The Rule allows the document to be used as proof of the execution and delivery of the document if the record is a record of a public office and the recording of such a document is authorized by an applicable statute. Rule 803(14) goes beyond the public records exception, in that it allows a recorded document to prove execution and delivery of that document.

The Rule is infrequently invoked and not problematic in application. For example, a case which applied Rule 803(14) is *United States v. Ruffin,*[121] in which the United States obtained convictions against defendant William Ruffin (Ruffin) on charges of income tax evasion on his personal income tax return and those of a wholly-owned corporation, Rugore Associates (Rugore). The case arose in early 1975, when a special grand jury subpoenaed Ruffin to produce records of a lease he or Rugore had with the Bedford–Stuyvesant Community Corporation and Mothers' Program. Under questioning, Ruffin revealed that the property which was the subject of the lease, generated rental income of roughly $30,000 annually and that neither he nor Rugore had recognized the income as required by federal law. Ruffin was indicted and tried on eleven counts of tax evasion. During the rebuttal stage of the trial, the government offered testimony to the effect that expenditures of Rugore money was used to buy a $26,000 mortgage for Ruffin. The testimony was elicited through an expert who had reviewed certain documents in the county clerk's office regarding Ruffin's transactions. The trial court allowed the expert to testify regarding what he had read in the county clerk's records. The jury convicted Ruffin on three of the eleven counts. Ruffin appealed. On appeal, the Second Circuit found the district court erred in allowing the expert to testify in regard to the records contained in the county clerk's office.

In reversing the conviction, the Second Circuit wrote:

> On the initial level the mortgage which Ruffin allegedly purchased in his own name by use of Rugore corporate funds would itself satisfy Fed.R.Evid. 803(14), the hearsay exception for "[r]ecords of documents affecting an interest in property" but Hamel's recitation of the contents of the documents, if offered, as it was here, to prove the truth of the matters asserted in the mort-

120. 2 *Evidence in America* § 58.3 (Exception 13).

121. 575 F.2d 346 (2d Cir.1978).

> gage, cannot satisfy any hearsay exception set forth in Fed.R.Evid. 803 or 804.

575 F.2d at 357. Had the government sought to introduce into evidence the records themselves, and assuming it could have proved their authenticity, the problem very likely could have been avoided.[122]

Rule 803(14) has proved equally uncontroversial in the state courts.[123]

Rule 803(15): Statements in Documents Affecting an Interest in Property

Rule 803(15) exempts from hearsay recitals of fact contained in deeds. "The circumstances under which dispositive documents are executed and the requirement that the recital be germane to the purpose of the document are believed to be adequate guarantees of trustworthiness, particularly in view of the nonapplicability of the rule if dealings with the property have been inconsistent with the document." [124]

The Rule has not presented many difficulties, as illustrated by *Compton v. Davis Oil Company.*[125] In *Compton* the district court found that recitals in two warranty deeds proved the fact that Dave and Nettie Lewis were husband and wife. In interpreting the Rule, the court held "the exception to the hearsay rule Rule 803[15] concerning records and instruments affecting interests in property is based upon the reliability of such documents." The court also found that the documents affecting an interest in property carried with them a "presumption of reliability" which could be undermined if subsequent dealings were inconsistent with the "statements or purport of the document. . . ." [126]

Rule 803(16): Statements in Ancient Documents

The ancient document hearsay exception permits admission of authentic documents that are over twenty years old. It is frequently used to permit the admission of newspaper articles concerning events

122. Other cases which have cited Rule 803(14) are: Greycas, Inc. v. Proud, 826 F.2d 1560, 1567 (7th Cir.1987), *cert. denied,* 484 U.S. 1043 (1988); Compton v. Davis Oil Co., 607 F.Supp. 1221, 1228 (D.Wyo.1985); S.S. Enterprises v. India Sari Palace, 1983 WL 1129, (S.D.N.Y.1983); McMorrow v. Schweiker, 561 F.Supp. 584, 589 (D.N.J.1982); and Amoco Production Co. v. United States, 455 F.Supp. 46, 49 (D.Utah 1977), *rev'd,* 619 F.2d 1383 (10th Cir.1980) discussed in conjunction with Rule 1005, *infra.*

123. 2 *Evidence in America* § 58.3 (Exception 14).

124. Advisory Committee Note to Rule 803 (Exception 15).

125. 607 F.Supp. 1221 (D.Wyo.1985).

126. *Id.* at 1229.

long ago, and is not controversial.[127] Most of the states have adopted the Federal Rule verbatim, with only nonsubstantive differences, or by requiring that the document be over thirty years old instead of twenty.[128]

The theory behind this exception is statements that would otherwise be hearsay were made well before the action was instituted and thus could not have been distorted or planted by the litigants.[129] An unusual use of the exception is presented in *Dartez v. Fibreboard Corp.,*[130] a products liability case in which plaintiff sought to prove that the dangers of exposure to asbestos fibers were or could have been known at the time of his exposure decades before. Plaintiff sought to introduce forty year old trade association meeting minutes in which the relative health dangers of fiberglass and asbestos insulation were discussed, in order to demonstrate that the insulation industry was aware of the dangers at that time. The documents were not admitted, not because of the hearsay exception, but because they had not been properly authenticated. Rule 803(16) explicitly refers to the need to authenticate ancient documents, and Rule 901(b)(8) describes a proper mode of authentication.

Rule 803(17): Market Reports, Commercial Publications

The market reports exception has not been widely interpreted, resulting in few published cases. The list of statements that can be admitted using the exception is not particularly clear, including "market quotations, tabulations, lists, directories, or other published compilations." Thus, the cases interpreting the rule focus on whether a particular type of document is intended to be included in the exception. For example, *White Indus., Inc. v. Cessna Aircraft Co.,*[131] resolved several evidentiary issues that had arisen during the liability phase in the bifurcated bench trial of a Robinson–Patman Act claim. Among the disputed documents sought to be admitted were documents filed with the Securities and Exchange Commission by a distributor—10–K forms and a prospectus. *Id.* at 1068. The district court held that the documents did not qualify as market reports or commercial publications because they were not "published" as the text of the Rule appears to require, and because the kinds of publications encompassed by the Rule dealt with "compilations of relatively straightforward *objective facts,*" not with the kind of subjective analysis of information contained

127. *E.g.,* Ammons v. Dade City, 594 F.Supp. 1274 (M.D.Fla.1984) (newspaper articles over twenty years old used to prove discrimination by municipality in providing services such as street paving), *aff'd,* 783 F.2d 982 (11th Cir.1986).

128. *See* 2 *Evidence in America* § 58.2.

129. *See* C. McCormick, *Evidence* § 323 (Cleary ed. 1984).

130. 765 F.2d 456 (5th Cir.1985).

131. 611 F.Supp. 1049 (W.D.Mo.1985).

in prospectuses and 10–K forms.[132] The gist of the cases is that judges will not apply the exception in ambiguous situations where the statements sought to be admitted are central to the litigation or where the court has any doubt as to the reliability of the statements.

While hearsay exceptions usually only provide relief from one level of hearsay, the market reports exception has been interpreted to overcome multiple hearsay problems. In *Ellis v. International Playtex, Inc.,*[133] the court held that the exception permitted evidence of findings by the Center for Disease Control concerning toxic shock syndrome, even though the findings were based on reports from doctors who interviewed patients.[134] The rationale given for permitting the exception to cover multiple levels of hearsay was the inherent reliability of the underlying statements and the impossibility of calling each of the patients whose comments contributed to the study.

Rule 803(18): Learned Treatises

The learned treatise exception is premised upon the "high standard of accuracy [which] is engendered by various factors: the treatise is written primarily and impartially for professionals, subject to scrutiny and exposure for inaccuracy, with the reputation of the writer at stake." [135] To avoid the danger of misapplication and misunderstanding of the treatise by the jury, the drafters of Rule 803(18) limited use of treatises as substantive evidence to "situations in which an expert is on the stand and available to explain and assist." [136] In such circumstances, the exclusion of treatises has been held reversible error.[137]

One situation possibly overlooked by the drafters of the last sentence of Rule 803(18) is the learned treatise excerpt in chart form. In *United States v. Mangan,*[138] a handwriting expert was cross-examined with a chart extracted from a learned treatise. The Second Circuit noted that it is "not clear that a chart can be 'read into evidence' " but that "good sense would seem to favor its admission."

The exception appears to have worked well. It has avoided the complicated problems concerning when a treatise may be used to impeach an expert, an issue on which common law courts were divided.

132. *Id.* at 1069. *See also* In re Richardson–Merrell, Inc. Bendectin Products Liability Litigation, 624 F.Supp. 1212, 1231 (S.D.Ohio 1985) (Rugin, J.) (holding that excerpts from the Physicians Desk Reference were not admissible under Rule 803(17) to show side effects of drugs similar to Bendectin), *aff'd,* 857 F.2d 290 (6th Cir.1988), *cert. denied,* 488 U.S. 1006 (1989).

133. 745 F.2d 292 (4th Cir.1984).

134. *Id.* at 303 n. 10 (and authorities cited).

135. Advisory Committee Note to Rule 803(18).

136. *Id.*

137. *See* Johnson v. William C. Ellis & Sons Iron Works, Inc., 609 F.2d 820 (5th Cir. 1980) (safety codes).

138. 575 F.2d 32, 48 (2d Cir.), *cert. denied,* 439 U.S. 931 (1978).

If there is any disappointment in the operation of the exception, it is that many lawyers have failed to appreciate the significance of this provision.

In adopting Rule 803(18), Maine conditioned admissibility upon the use of the learned treatise during cross-examination; so, too, did Louisiana in criminal cases—both states thus precluding reliance upon the treatise during direct examination. Colorado, Idaho, Louisiana, Nevada, New Hampshire and Wisconsin permit the treatise to be admitted as an exhibit in the trial court's discretion. Florida, Nebraska, Ohio, Oregon and Tennessee declined to enact any provision comparable to Rule 803(18).[139]

Rule 803(19): Reputation Concerning Personal or Family History

This exception is thoroughly noncontroversial, having been adopted in virtually all the states without substantive change and generating virtually no case law addressing its applicability. Those cases which do cite the rule usually apply it as secondary authority for a proposition.[140]

Rule 803(20): Reputation in the Community as to Boundaries and Events of General History

This exception permits testimony concerning reputation in the community as to boundaries or customs affecting lands in the community, as well as reputation of events of general history that are "important to the community or State or nation in which located." The exception has been adopted without substantive change in almost every state.[141] It is the least-cited exception to the hearsay rule, demonstrating its noncontroversiality as well as its infrequent usefulness.

For example, in *People v. Ocean Club, Inc.*,[142] plaintiffs were suing a swim club on the grounds that it discriminated against Jews. The club denied that it had such a practice or policy. The plaintiffs unsuccessfully attempted to introduce evidence concerning the club's reputation for discrimination against Jewish applicants or guests to prove the alleged discriminatory practice. The district court noted that the exception only applied to ancient matters or those as to which living witnesses would be unlikely to be able to testify about. However, the Advisory Committee Note concerning this exception states that the

139. *See generally* 2 *Evidence in America* §§ 58.2–58.3 (Exception 17.)

140. *See* Government of the Virgin Islands v. Joseph, 765 F.2d 394, 397 n. 5 (3d Cir. 1985) (testimony by victim as to her age, in statutory rape case, held admissible); Brown v. Bowen, 668 F.Supp. 146, 150 (E.D.N.Y.1987) (noting that hearsay is admissible in administrative hearings and citing Rule 803(19) as additional authority; Lazovick v. Sun Life Insurance Co., 586 F.Supp. 918 (E.D.Pa.1984) (parent's admission that son committed suicide binding because it was an admission, Rule 803(19) cited as additional support). For the states' experience, *see* 2 *Evidence in America* § 58.3 (Exception 19).

141. *See* 2 *Evidence in America* § 58.3 (Exception 20).

142. 602 F.Supp. 489, 491 (E.D.N.Y.1984).

reputation evidence sought to be admitted need not be ancient.[143] The court clearly and understandably was reluctant to permit hearsay evidence to be used to prove the central factual contention of plaintiff's case, particularly when other proof was available on the issue.

Rule 803(21): Reputation as to Character

The exception for testimony concerning a person's character reputation is noncontroversial, but frequently used. Such testimony is by its nature hearsay. This exception must be read in conjunction with Rules 404, 405, and 608, which provide the principal limitations on testimony concerning character. Reported cases dealing with admissibility of character evidence usually deal with the application of these Rules rather than the hearsay exception.[144]

Rule 803(22): Judgment of Previous Conviction

Rule 803(22) provides a specific hearsay exception for evidence in criminal trials of certain criminal convictions. The exception applies only to convictions for crimes "punishable by death or imprisonment in excess of one year" (usually felonies) and only to convictions after trial or upon the entry of a guilty plea. Rule 803(22) does not apply to *nolo contendere* pleas or convictions of persons other than the accused if offered for purposes other than impeachment.[145] Uniform Rule 803(22), as well as several states, versions, include *nolo* pleas or their substantive equivalents, such as pleas of no contest, in this exception.[146]

Courts are usually careful in deciding whether to admit evidence of convictions because of the great weight such evidence carries with a jury.[147] The main issue that has arisen in connection with this exception is admissibility of criminal verdicts that are not included in the exception—misdemeanor convictions. The Advisory Committee excluded misdemeanor convictions because "motivation to defend at this level is often minimal or nonexistent." [148] Most courts find that guilty pleas are admissible, even if they are for crimes less serious than those excepted by Rule 803(22), since the plea usually qualifies as an admission or a statement against interest under Rules 801(d)(2)(A) or 804(b)

143. 56 F.R.D. 183, 318 (1975).

144. *See, e.g.,* United States v. Logan, 717 F.2d 84 (3d Cir.1983) (discussing the rationale and limitations on admissibility of character evidence).

145. *See* In re Raiford, 695 F.2d 521, 523 (11th Cir.1983) (defendant who wishes to avoid subsequent admissibility of guilty plea can request permission to plead *nolo contendere.*

146. *See* 2 *Evidence in America* §§ 58.1–58.2 (Exception 22).

147. *See* Index Fund, Inc. v. Hagopian, 677 F.Supp. 710, 720 (S.D.N.Y.1987) (guilty pleas of alleged co-conspirators inadmissible because not specifically related to the alleged conspiracy).

148. 56 F.R.D. 183, 319 (1975).

(3).[149] While Judge Weinstein has argued that non-felony guilty pleas should not be admitted, his view has not received support in the courts.[150]

Evidence of acquittals are routinely excluded on relevance grounds "because [they] do not prove innocence but rather merely indicate[ ] that the prior prosecution failed to meet its burden of proving beyond a reasonable doubt at least one element of the crime."[151]

Rule 803(23): Judgments as to Personal, Family or General History, or Boundaries

This exception is so noncontroversial that it has resulted in no reported cases applying it, let alone perceiving problems with it.

Rule 803(24): Other Exceptions

In 1983, the Litigation Section's first edition of this study pointed out that the residual exceptions "have been the focal point of considerable judicial activism. . . ." This trend has continued unabated, with the exceptions generating some 50 reported decisions each year. For the most part, courts refer to 803(24) and 804(b)(5) interchangeably, without analyzing whether there are differences in application.

A few circuits claim to invoke the residual clause sparingly or only in exceptional circumstances.[152] The Third Circuit has given the exceptions a "narrow focus."[153] However, such language is often saved for the cases in which the court refuses to admit the hearsay pursuant to the residual clauses, and is conveniently absent from the numerous cases applying the exceptions. A court may even preface its remarks by indicating that 803(24) should be used "stintingly," and then hold that its requirements were met on this occasion.[154] The current judicial view of the residual clause is reflected by *United States v. Cowley,*[155] which aptly referred to 803(24) as the "expanding exception."

Courts have encouraged the use of the residual clause by gratuitous comments about its applicability in situations where it is unclear

149. *See* United States v. Gotti, 641 F.Supp. 283, 289–90 (E.D.N.Y.1986) (misdemeanor guilty plea admissible in criminal proceedings); Hinshaw v. Keith, 645 F.Supp. 180, 182–83 (D.Maine 1986) (misdemeanor guilty plea admissible in civil litigation).

150. J. Weinstein & M. Berger, *Weinstein's Evidence* ¶ 803(22)[01], at 803–355 (1985).

151. United States v. Kerley, 643 F.2d 299, 300–01 (5th Cir.1981). *See also* United States v. Jones, 808 F.2d 561, 566 (7th Cir.1986), *cert. denied,* 481 U.S. 1006 (1987).

152. *See e.g.,* In re Corrugated Container Antitrust Litig., 756 F.2d 411, 414–15 (5th Cir.1985); United States v. Heyward, 729 F.2d 297, 299–300 (4th Cir.1984), *cert. denied,* 469 U.S. 1105 (1985).

153. In re Japanese Elec. Products Antitrust Litig., 723 F.2d 238, 301 (3d Cir.1983), *rev'd on other grounds,* 475 U.S. 574 (1986).

154. *See* United States v. Nivica, 887 F.2d 1110, 1127 (1st Cir.1989), *cert. denied,* 110 S.Ct. 1300 (1990).

155. 720 F.2d 1037, 1045 (9th Cir.1983), *cert. denied,* 465 U.S. 1029 (1984).

whether the parties raised the issue.[156] For example, the appeal in *U.S. v. Furst,*[157] focused on the residual clause although it had only been mentioned in passing below. In *United States v. Nivica,*[158] the appellate court even upheld the introduction of hearsay under the residual clause which the trial court had incorrectly admitted under 803(6). However, due to the residual clause notice requirements, *Nivica* should be limited to those cases in which the exception was properly raised in the trial court. The popularity of the residual clause is so great that it is not surprising to find it invoked in complex or controversial cases. For example, Oliver North's attorneys argued, *albeit* unsuccessfully, that excerpts of videotaped testimony should be admitted under 803(24).[159]

Near Misses

The expansive treatment of the residual clauses has been accelerated by the rejection of the "near miss" theory proposed by Judge Becker in *Zenith Radio Corp. v. Matsushita Elec. Indus. Co.*[160] Judge Becker had separated the specific hearsay exceptions into well defined categories and amorphous categories for purposes of determining whether a near miss could be admitted under the residual clause.[161] He rejected the admission of near misses of specific categories such as former testimony, but permitted near misses of amorphous exceptions such as business records and present sense impressions. However, the Third Circuit in later reversing Judge Becker on evidentiary points, noted that this "theory puts the federal evidence rules back into the straightjacket from which the residual exceptions were intended to free them." [162] Recently, in *U.S. v. Furst,*[163] the Third Circuit explicitly held that 803(24) is available when the proponent fails to meet the standards set forth in the other exceptions.

Most cases which discuss the near miss exception reach the same result.[164] Most courts simply ignore the near miss issue when they

156. *See e.g.,* Driscoll v. Schuttler, 697 F.Supp. 1195, 1199 n. 1 (N.D.Ga.1988).

157. 886 F.2d 558, 573–74 (3d Cir.1989), *cert. denied,* 110 S.Ct. 878 (1990).

158. 887 F.2d 1110, 1127 (1st Cir.1989), *cert. denied,* 110 S.Ct. 1300 (1990).

159. United States v. North, 713 F.Supp. 1450, 1451 (D.D.C.1989).

160. 505 F.Supp. 1190, 1262–63 (E.D.Pa.1980).

161. *Id.* at 1264.

162. In re Japanese Elec. Products Antitrust Litig., 723 F.2d 238, 302 (3d Cir.1983), *rev'd on other grounds,* 475 U.S. 574 (1986).

163. 886 F.2d 558, 573 (3d Cir.1989), *cert. denied,* 110 S.Ct. 878 (1990).

164. For example, in United States v. Gotti, 641 F.Supp. 283, 289 (E.D.N.Y.1986), the judge found no reason in principle why a misdemeanor conviction not admissible under 803(22) should not be admitted under the residual clause. Similarly, United States v. Popenas, 780 F.2d 545, 547 (6th Cir.1985), specifically rejected the near miss reasoning concerning introduction of a prior inconsistent statement under the residual clause, because "we feel the district court's approach would render it (the exception) a nullity." United States v. Frazier, 678 F.Supp. 499, 503 (E.D.Pa.), *aff'd,* 806 F.2d 255 (3d Cir.1986),

admit hearsay ranging from grand jury testimony to not quite business or public records. On occasion, even the rare case which appears to approve the near miss theory can be otherwise explained. For example, in *United States v. York,*[165] the court stated that it would not admit a statement under 804(b)(5) if it did not meet 804(b)(3). Rather than approving a near miss theory, the court simply recognized that a statement which was not trustworthy enough be a declaration against penal interest, would also not meet the trustworthiness requirement of the residual clause.

Regardless of whether one believes that Judge Becker's theory of near misses fits more closely with the Rule's intention than present practice, it is clear that courts are almost uniformly applying the residual clause to near misses. Thus, it presently does not matter if a category of hearsay was specifically rejected as an exception when considering its admissibility under the catch-all provision. Indeed, it has been suggested that being a near miss may be a positive factor in evaluating trustworthiness.[166] It is unlikely that this approach will change unless the Rule is modified or its use is limited by the Supreme Court.

The Requirement of Trustworthiness

The Supreme Court's recent decision in *Idaho v. Wright,*[167] pinpoints a problem in analyzing trustworthiness under the residual clause. *Wright* held that admission of a statement by a child to her pediatrician concerning the identity of the person who sexually abused her violated the defendant's right to confrontation where the child did not testify at trial. The statement had been admitted pursuant to Idaho's residual clause which mirrors the federal rule. While the Court did not evaluate the correctness of Idaho's evidentiary decision, its confrontation approach places practical limitations on the use of the residual clause in criminal cases, because it focuses on trustworthiness at the time the statement was made, rather than on other circumstances corroborating the statement.

Initially, *Wright* requires that statements admitted under the residual clause have particularized guarantees of trustworthiness, because the exception is not firmly rooted.[168] Indeed, the Court notes that there is a presumption of inadmissibility and unreliability of such

rejected the near miss approach in assessing the admissibility of a statement of a child who was the alleged victim of sexual abuse.

165. 1989 WL 65167 n. 8 (N.D.Ill.1989).

166. Comment, *Admitting "Near Misses" Under the Residual Hearsay Exceptions,* 66 Ore.L.Rev. 599, 613–19 (1987).

167. 110 S.Ct. 3139 (1990).

168. 110 S.Ct. at 3147.

statements for confrontation purposes.[169] Generally, courts have been utilizing a separate confrontation analysis when considering evidence admitted pursuant to the residual hearsay exception, but often repeat the factors which support trustworthiness for purposes of the exception as meeting the confrontation clause concerns. However, *Wright* has now held that corroboration of hearsay is not relevant in deciding whether it is sufficiently trustworthy to be admitted. In other words, while indicia of reliability can be shown from the totality of the circumstances, the relevant circumstances include only those that surround the making of the statement and that render the declarant particularly worthy of belief.[170]

This approach is contrary to the position taken by the vast majority of cases which routinely rely on corroboration in analyzing trustworthiness for purposes of both the residual exception and the confrontation clause.[171] For example, when grand jury testimony is admitted pursuant to the residual clause, corroboration typically focuses on testimony from other witnesses and tangible evidence rather than looking solely or even primarily at the declarant's motivation to be truthful.[172] If trial courts had to exclude corroboration, undoubtedly some of these decisions would prohibit such hearsay as being violative of the defendant's right to confront witnesses. Ultimately, *Wright* renders reliance on corroboration for the residual exception purposes counterproductive in criminal cases, since the court would first consider the corroboration in its evidentiary analysis, and then exclude it when determining the confrontation challenge. In other words, courts would have to engage in a futile exercise which determines evidentiary admissibility based on corroboration for hearsay which would clearly offend the confrontation clause when such corroboration is excluded.

The approach adopted by *Wright,* which excluded after-the-fact corroboration from the trustworthiness analysis, is not new in the residual clause context. *Wright* favorably cites *Huff v. White Motor Corp.,*[173] which held that equivalent circumstances of trustworthiness for purposes of the residual clause can only logically be evaluated by looking at the statement when it was made. Courts have rejected *Huff* mainly because they focus on trustworthiness as a reliability concept whereas *Huff* emphasized that "equivalent circumstantial guarantees of trustworthiness" relate to the justifications underlying the specific hearsay exceptions. Similarly, *Wright* views the justification for hearsay exceptions as being whether the statement's truthfulness is so clear

169. *Id.*

170. *Id.* at 3148.

171. *See, e.g.,* United States v. Roberts, 844 F.2d 537, 546–47 (1988), *cert. denied,* 109 S.Ct. 172 (1990).

172. *See, e.g.,* United States v. Marchini, 797 F.2d 759, 763 (9th Cir.1986); United States v. Barlow, 693 F.2d 954, 962–63 (6th Cir.1982); *cert. denied,* 461 U.S. 945 (1983).

173. 609 F.2d 286, 292 (1979).

from the surrounding circumstances that the test of cross examination would be of marginal utility.

While *Wright* focused on the suggestiveness of the interview in its confrontation analysis, it did not require any particular procedural safeguards. However, it identified the following factors as bearing on reliability of a child's statements: spontaneity and consistent repetition; mental state of the declarant; use of terminology unexpected of a child of similar age; and lack of motive to fabricate. The Court noted that spontaneity was not always significant where there has been prior interrogation, prompting or manipulation by adults.

If hearsay is improperly admitted at trial, *Wright* permits corroboration to be used in analyzing whether the error was harmless.[174] However, no specific guidance was given on this issue because the state did not challenge the Idaho Supreme Court's finding that the error was harmful.

Wright did not determine what, if any, type of unavailability of the declarant is required for purposes of confrontation since the child in question, who was 2½ when she made the statement and 3 at the time of trial, was found by the judge to be incapable of communicating with the jury. The Court noted that it assumed she was unavailable.[175] Therefore, some statements of children who do not testify which are admitted pursuant to the residual clause may still run afoul of the confrontation clause. In *Maryland v. Craig,*[176] decided the same day as *Wright,* the Court upheld the testimony of a child given outside the presence of the defendant by one-way closed circuit television, where the judge made a finding of individualized trauma. The key will be an individual analysis of the child's unavailability rather than a blanket legislatively imposed presumption of trauma.[177]

174. *Id.* at 3150–51.

175. 110 S.Ct. at 3147.

176. 110 S.Ct. 3157 (1990).

177. *See* Coy v. Iowa, 487 U.S. 1012, 1021 (1988).

RULE 804

I. TEXT OF RULE

RULE 804. Hearsay Exceptions; Declarant Unavailable

(a) Definition of unavailability. "Unavail-ability as a witness" includes situations in which the declarant:

(1) is exempted by ruling of the court on the ground of privilege from testifying concerning the subject matter of the declarant's statement; or

(2) persists in refusing to testify concerning the subject matter of the declarant's statement despite an order of the court to do so; or

(3) testifies to a lack of memory of the subject matter of the declarant's statement; or

(4) is unable to be present or to testify at the hearing because of death or then existing physical or mental illness or infirmity; or

(5) is absent from the hearing and the proponent of the declarant's statement has been unable to procure the declarant's attendance (or in the case of a hearsay exception under subdivision (b)(2), (3), or (4), the declarant's attendance or testimony) by process or other reasonable means.

A declarant is not unavailable as a witness if the exemption, refusal, claim or lack of memory, inability, or absence is due to the procurement or wrongdoing of the proponent of a statement for the purpose of preventing the witness from attending or testifying.

(b) Hearsay exceptions. The following are not excluded by the hearsay rule if the declarant is unavailable as a witness:

(1) Former testimony. Testimony given as a witness at another hearing of the same or a different proceeding, or in a deposition taken in compliance with law in the course of the same or another proceeding, if the party against whom the testimony is now offered, or, in a civil action or proceeding, a predecessor in interest, had an opportunity and similar motive to develop the testimony by direct, cross, or redirect examination.

(2) Statement under belief of impending death. In a prosecution for homicide or in a civil action or proceeding, a statement made by a declarant while believing that the declarant's death was imminent, concerning the cause or circumstances of what the declarant believed to be impending death.

(3) Statement against interest. A statement which was at the time of its making so far contrary to the declarant's pecuniary or proprietary interest, or so far tended to subject the declarant to civil or criminal liability, or to render invalid a claim by the declarant against another, that a reasonable person in the declarant's position would not have made the statement unless believing it to be true. A statement tending to expose the declarant to criminal liability and offered to exculpate the accused is not admissible unless corroborating circumstances clearly indicate the trustworthiness of the statement.

(4) Statement of personal or family history. (A) A statement concerning the declarant's own birth, adoption, marriage, divorce, legitimacy, relationship by blood, adoption, or marriage, ancestry, or other similar fact of personal or family history, even though declarant had no means of acquiring personal knowledge of the matter stated; or (B) a statement concerning the foregoing matters, and death also, of another person, if the declarant was related to the other by blood, adoption, or marriage or was so intimately associated with the other's family as to be likely to have accurate information concerning the matter declared.

(5) Other exceptions. A statement not specifically covered by any of the foregoing exceptions but having equivalent circumstantial guarantees of trustworthiness, if the court determines that (A) the statement is offered as evidence of a material fact; (B) the statement is more probative on the point for which it is offered than any other evidence which the proponent can procure through reasonable efforts; and (C) the general purposes of these rules and the interests of justice will best be served by admission of the statement into evidence. However, a statement may not be admitted under this exception unless the proponent of it makes known to the adverse party sufficiently in advance of the trial or hearing to provide the adverse party with a fair opportunity to prepare to meet it, the proponent's intention to offer the statement and the particulars of it, including the name and address of the declarant.

II. DISCUSSION

Rule 804(a): Definition of Unavailability

Rule 804(a) provides the framework within which to determine a declarant's unavailability. These situations are mainly grounded in the common law and there have not been many changes from common law jurisdictions. One area which raises questions is the testimony concerning a lack of memory of the subject matter. There is a possibility of one feigning memory loss to avoid testifying. In this case, some commentators believe the court should order a witness to testify and only after the person's refusal should the declarant be deemed unavailable.[1] In *North Miss. Communications, Inc. v. Jones,*[2] the court determined the witness was unavailable because of the lack of memory of certain details although the witness remembered the subject matter in general. There have been no other problems of interpretation of Rule 804(a).

Rule 804(b)(1): Former Testimony

The "former testimony" exception permits the introduction of the deposition or hearing testimony of an "unavailable" witness if the party against whom the testimony is offered—or, in a civil case only, the party's "predecessor in interest"—had both an opportunity and a similar motive to cross-examine the witness.

Who is a "predecessor in interest"? As promulgated by the Supreme Court, Rule 804(b)(1) did not contain the predecessor in interest limitation. The original rule would have admitted prior testimony of an unavailable witness so long as a person "with motive or similar interest" to the party had an opportunity to examine the witness. The House Judiciary Committee, however, decided that it would be generally unfair to impose upon a party the responsibility for another's examination of a witness and, accordingly, limited the prior testimony exception to situations in which a party or that party's "predecessor in interest" had an opportunity to examine the witness.[3] The parameters of the quoted phrase remain somewhat uncertain.

Lloyd v. American Export Lines, Inc.,[4] apparently the first case to construe the "predecessor in interest" requirement of 804(b)(1), gave it an expansive interpretation. In *Lloyd,* the Third Circuit held that the "predecessor in interest" language required only that "it appears that in the former suit a party having a like motive to cross-examine about the same matters as the present party would have, was accorded an adequate opportunity for such examination. . . ."[5] Under that test, the court found there to be sufficient "community of interest" between the plaintiff, an injured crewman suing a shipowner for an assault committed upon him by another crewman, and the United States Coast Guard, which had conducted a prior administrative proceeding against the assaulting crewman to authorize introduction of administrative testimony. The court reasoned that "the basic interest advanced by both [the plaintiff and the Coast Guard] was that of determining

1. 2 Saltzburg & Martin, *Federal Rules of Evidence Manual* 398 (5th ed. 1990).

2. 792 F.2d 1330 (5th Cir.1986).

3. *See* 4 J. Weinstein & M. Berger, *Weinstein's Evidence* ¶ 804(b)(1)[04] at 804–67 (Supp.1990).

4. 580 F.2d 1179 (3d Cir.), *cert. denied,* 439 U.S. 969 (1978).

5. *Id.* at 1187, *quoting* C. McCormick, *Evidence* § 256 at 619–620 (Cleary ed. 1984).

culpability and, if appropriate, exacting a penalty for the same condemned behavior thought to have occurred."

Judge Stern, in a concurring opinion, observed that if, as the *Lloyd* majority contended, "predecessor in interest" means only "similarity in motive," then the "predecessor in interest" language of Rule 804(b)(1) was meaningless. Although the requirements of Rule 804(b)(1) were in his judgment not satisfied, Judge Stern would have nevertheless admitted the prior testimony under the residual exception of Rule 804(b)(5).

After *Lloyd,* in *Carpenter v. Dizio,*[6] the district court admitted, in a civil rights and malicious prosecution action arising from an alleged beating of the plaintiff during his arrest, the testimony given by plaintiff's witness in the earlier criminal prosecution. The court found that the district attorney in the criminal proceeding and the City Solicitor in the civil rights action shared the *Lloyd* "community of interest"—to try to discredit the plaintiff's self-defense claim and his witness' testimony.

In contrast, in *Zenith Radio Corp. v. Matsushita Elec. Ind. Co.,*[7] the district court distinguished *Lloyd* and refused to admit against defendant A the testimony given in a prior Japanese Fair Trade Commission (JFTC) proceeding to which defendants B, C and D, but not A, were parties. The court found that the testimony was inadmissible because the JFTC defendants did not share a "like motive to develop testimony" with defendant A. In contrast to the Coast Guard investigator in *Lloyd,* who was "presumably impartial," a "representative of the public" and who had no role in the subsequent civil action brought against the shipowner, the defendants in *Zenith* had potentially conflicting interests and litigation strategies. In the court's view it would be unfair to admit the prior testimony of a witness against defendant A, on the basis of cross-examination undertaken by the JFTC defendants "merely because the plaintiffs have joined them [all in this action]. . . ."[8]

With the above cases compare *In re Master Key Antitrust Litigation,*[9] in which the prior testimony of witnesses in an antitrust action brought by the Government was admitted in a subsequent private

6. 506 F.Supp. 1117, 1124 (E.D.Pa.), *aff'd mem.,* 673 F.2d 1298 (3d Cir.1981).

7. 505 F.Supp. 1190, 1252–55 (E.D.Pa.1980). *Zenith* was reversed on several grounds, but not this issue.

8. *See also* In re Screws Antitrust Litigation, 526 F.Supp. 1316, 1319 (D.Mass.1981) (court declined to admit against the defendants in a civil antitrust action testimony taken in a prior criminal antitrust prosecution against different defendants but nevertheless admitted the prior testimony under Rule 804(b)(5)); In re IBM Peripheral EDP Devices Antitrust Litigation, 444 F.Supp. 110 (N.D.Cal.1978) (court refused to admit former testimony given in antitrust cases, an administrative (SEC) investigation and another case, against Memorex, which was not a party to any of the prior proceedings noting that a "common motive" was not an accurate test and further rejected admittance under Rule 804(b)(5)).

9. 72 F.R.D. 108 (D.Conn.1976).

antitrust class action. While the court read the relevant legislative history as suggesting that Rule 804(b)(1) be "narrowly construed," it focused upon the "special circumstances" of antitrust litigation and the "unique relationship between the government's antitrust enforcement suits and the private actions," "which weigh in favor of holding that the United States was a predecessor in interest of present plaintiffs."

The problems that the courts face in defining the term "predecessor in interest" is attributable in no small part to the absence of a clear definition in the legislative history. Thus far, most courts—the *Lloyd* majority being the exception—have attempted to make the term mean something more than the similar motive approach rejected by the Congress. Case-by-case definition has been slow because few cases have considered the definitional problem. To date, the decisions do not appear to present major problems.

Nine states adopted versions of Rule 804(b)(1) similar to that originally proposed by the Supreme Court, expanding the exception to include all former testimony elicited by or against a party with a similar motive and opportunity for examination.[10]

Puerto Rico has no "predecessor in interest" provision, requiring actual identity of party in both proceedings. P.R.R.Evid. 64(B)(1).

Rule 804(b)(2): Statement Under Belief of Impending Death

There have been no problems in the application of this Rule. It is only necessary to reiterate that not all statements made under belief of impending death are allowed, but rather only those statements as to the cause of death. Thus, in *United States v. Fernandez,*[11] the court reversed defendants' convictions of conspiracy to illegally influence a benefit plan noting that a witness' testimony before the grand jury could not be admitted under Rule 804(b)(2) because he was not testifying as to the cause of his impending death. Many states have expanded the exception to apply to all civil and criminal cases, not just homicide prosecutions and civil actions.[12]

Rule 804(b)(3): Statements Against Interest

"The circumstantial guarantee of reliability for declarations against interest is the assumption that persons do not make statements which are damaging to themselves unless satisfied for good reason that they are true." [13] Rule 804(b)(3) enumerates four categories of declarations against interest which are admissible if "a reasonable man in [the position of the declarant] would not have made the statement unless he

10. *See* 2 *Evidence in America* §§ 59.2–59.4 (Hawaii, Louisiana, Minnesota, Montana, Nebraska, Rhode Island, Tennessee, Texas and Wisconsin).

11. 892 F.2d 976 (11th Cir.1989, amended 1990), *cert. dismissed,* 110 S.Ct. 2201 (1990).

12. 2 *Evidence in America* § 59.2.

13. Advisory Committee Note to Rule 804(b)(3).

believed it to be true." Of the four, declarations against penal interest have presented the greatest difficulty.[14]

Perhaps the most troublesome aspect of statements against penal interest are those which inculpate the criminal defendant as well as the declarant. The drafters of the Rule expressly contemplated that an 804(b)(3) declaration against penal interest "may include statements implicating the [defendant, which would be admissible] under the general theory of declarations against interest." [15] At the same time, the drafters acknowledged that, under certain circumstances, admission of inculpatory declarations against the accused could raise serious Confrontation Clause problems.[16]

While Rule 804(b)(3) provides that "a statement tending to expose the declarant to criminal liability and offered to exculpate the accused is not admissible unless corroborating circumstances thereby indicate the trustworthiness of the statement," the Rule has no similar requirement for inculpatory declarations offered by the prosecution. Several circuits, however, have judicially imposed a requirement that inculpatory declarations be similarly corroborated by other "indicia of reliability." [17] It has been held that the Confrontation Clause of the Constitution requires no less.[18]

14. A fifth category—statements that tended to make the declarant "an object of hatred, ridicule or disgrace" ("statements against social interest")—was included in Rule 804(b)(3) as proposed by the Supreme Court, but deleted by Congress. *See* 4 J. Weinstein & M. Berger, *Weinstein's Evidence* ¶ 804(b)(3)[01] at 804–93 to 804–94 (Supp.1982). Several states and the Uniform Rule also include an exception for statements against social interest. 2 *Evidence in America* §§ 59.2–59.3.

15. Advisory Committee Note to Rule 804(b)(3).

16. As originally drafted by the Advisory Committee, Rule 804(b)(3) flatly prohibited the admission of inculpatory statements. The Supreme Court deleted this exclusion when it promulgated the official draft of the Federal Rules, but the House Committee reinserted it. The Senate Committee rejected the House's express prohibition of inculpatory statements, and the Senate's position prevailed in the Conference Committee. *See* United States v. Palumbo, 639 F.2d 123, 129–30 (3d Cir.) (Adams, J., concurring), *cert. denied,* 454 U.S. 819 (1981).

17. United States v. Riley, 657 F.2d 1377, 1383 (8th Cir.1981), *cert. denied,* 495 U.S. 1111 (1983); United States v. Palumbo, 639 F.2d 123, 131 (3d Cir.) (Adams, J., concurring), *cert. denied,* 454 U.S. 819 (1981); United States v. Oliver, 626 F.2d 254, 260 (2d Cir.1980); United States v. Alvarez, 584 F.2d 694, 700–701 (5th Cir.1978).

18. *See* United States v. Sarmiento–Perez, 633 F.2d 1092, 1099–1100 (5th Cir.1980), *cert. denied,* 459 U.S. 834 (1982). The "indicia of reliability" required by the Confrontation Clause before an extrajudicial statement of an unavailable declarant may be admitted against the accused have been articulated by the Supreme Court in a series of opinions. *See* Ohio v. Roberts, 448 U.S. 56 (1980); Chambers v. Mississippi, 410 U.S. 284 (1973); Dutton v. Evans, 400 U.S. 74 (1970); Bruton v. United States, 391 U.S. 123 (1968), *cert. denied,* 397 U.S. 1014 (1970); 4 J. Weinstein & M. Berger, *Weinstein's Evidence* ¶ 804(b)(3)[03] at 804–110 to 804–111 (Supp.1981). Additionally, the Second Circuit has held that a declarant's nodding in response to a question about defendant's hiring him to commit arson was an acceptable and reliable statement against interest because the declarant died before trial and there was no reason to believe that he gained anything.

As judicially supplemented, then, an inculpatory statement against penal interest is admissible against the defendant if: (1) the declarant is unavailable; (2) the statement is so far contrary to the declarant's penal interest that a reasonable person in his position would not have made the statement unless he believed it to be true; and (3) corroborating circumstances clearly indicate the statement's trustworthiness. In practice, the second and third requirements frequently merge into one—was the declarant's statement, under all the circumstances, in fact against his penal interest?

Several courts have recognized that an inculpatory declaration made while the declarant is in custody and charged with a crime is very likely no more than an attempt to curry favor with the police and prosecution and alleviate his culpability by implicating an accomplice. For this reason, a custodial inculpatory statement—and particularly one made after the declarant has been implicitly or expressly offered a plea bargain in exchange for this confession—has been held inadmissible under Rule 804(b)(3) as a declaration against penal interest.[19] Conversely, courts have cited the noncustodial nature of the inculpatory declaration as a factor supporting the trustworthiness of the statement.[20]

United States v. Katsougrakis, 715 F.2d 769 (2d Cir.1983), *cert. denied,* 464 U.S. 1040 (1984).

19. *See, e.g.,* United States v. Sarmiento–Perez, 633 F.2d 1092–1104 (5th Cir.1980), *cert. denied,* 459 U.S. 834 (1982) (custodial confession by a non-testifying, separately tried co-defendant which implicates the accused is "not sufficiently contrary to [the defendant's] penal interest," since due the "obvious motives for falsification . . . a reasonable person [in the declarant's position] might well have viewed the statement as a whole . . . to be in his interest rather than against it;" such a custodial confession also lacks sufficient "indicia of reliability"); United States v. Boyce, 849 F.2d 833 (3d Cir.1988) (co-defendant's statement made while in custody was not a declaration against interest and there was nothing to show that this wasn't an attempt to curry favor); United States v. Oliver, 626 F.2d 254, 261 (2d Cir.1980) (custodial confession not trustworthy when declarant under arrest, facing probable long prison term and told that if he cooperates, the police will suggest leniency to the U.S. Attorney); United States v. Palumbo, 639 F.2d 123, 127–28 (3d Cir.), *cert. denied,* 454 U.S. 819 (1981) (viewed against the totality of circumstances, statement not against penal interest when, *inter alia,* it was given while declarant in custody, in response to police questioning and for likely purpose of currying favor with police); United States v. Riley, 657 F.2d 1377, 1384 (8th Cir.1981), *cert. denied,* 459 U.S. 1111 (1983) (inculpatory statement "not in fact against [declarant's] interest" when given while in custody, in response to police questioning, and after declarant has been told that a prostitution conviction could jeopardize her custody of her child); United States v. McClendon, 454 F.Supp. 960, 962 (W.D.Pa.1978), *aff'd mem.,* 601 F.2d 577 (3d Cir.), *cert. denied,* 444 U.S. 952 (1979) (in "the case of a declarant who is under arrest and offered a lesser sentence if he implicates another . . . one can almost surely say the statement is self-serving") (*dicta*).

20. United States v. Robinson, 635 F.2d 363 (5th Cir.) (per curiam), *cert. denied,* 452 U.S. 916 (1981); United States v. White, 553 F.2d 310, 313 (2d Cir.), *cert. denied,* 431 U.S. 972 (1977).

While the Fifth Circuit, in *United States v. Sarmiento–Perez,*[21] appeared to establish a *per se* rule prohibiting the admissibility of custodial confessions under Rule 804(b)(3), the Second Circuit held such a custodial inculpatory declaration admissible as a declaration against penal interest in *United States v. Garris.*[22] The Second Circuit ruled that the declarant's statement to an FBI agent that her brother said to her that no one had seen him while he robbed the bank was admissible against the brother under 804(b)(3). The statement was reasoned to be a declaration against penal interest because it "would be probative in a trial [of the declarant] for acting as an accessory after the fact [of robbery] for it shows that with knowledge of her brother's offense she concealed from the FBI that she knew how to contact him." [23] That the statement was made while the declarant was in custody was held not determinative because at the time of the statement no plea bargaining had occurred, there were no threats or promises of leniency, and the declarant had been apprised of her *Miranda* rights. Moreover, "other circumstances support[ed] the trustworthiness of the statement." [24] However, *United States v. Winley,*[25] decided less than one year after *Garris* by a different panel of the Second Circuit, expressly reserved decision on the issue of whether "an admission made in police custody can be considered against penal interest . . . if, at the time it is made, the declarant also implicates the defendant."

Of course, an essential prerequisite of admissibility under Rule 804(b)(3) is that the declarant is in fact subject to criminal liability at the time the statement is made. Thus, an inculpatory statement made after the declarant has been granted immunity is not admissible under Rule 804(b)(3).[26] In *United States v. Love,*[27] the court held that the declarant's statement that "[the defendant] had previously told me [that] I had to earn $1500 prostituting myself and that I was to turn over all of the money I made to him" was not admissible as a declaration against penal interest because, *inter alia,* at the time the statement was made all charges of prostitution had been dropped and the defendant was immune from federal prosecution under the Mann Act. Finally, the courts have uniformly rejected the contention that an inculpatory statement is not against the declarant's penal interest if made to a friend, confederate or relative of the declarant because,

21. 633 F.2d 1092, 1104 (5th Cir.1980), *cert. denied,* 459 U.S. 834 (1982).

22. 616 F.2d 626 (2d Cir.), *cert. denied,* 447 U.S. 926 (1980).

23. *Id.* at 630.

24. *Id.* at 632.

25. 638 F.2d 560, 562 n. 2 (2d Cir.1981), *cert. denied,* 455 U.S. 959 (1982).

26. United States v. Gonzalez, 559 F.2d 1271, 1273 (5th Cir.1977) (after immunity has been granted "whether [the declarant] told the truth or not was incidental to what would happen to him if he did not say *something*").

27. 592 F.2d 1022 (8th Cir.1979).

under those circumstances the declarant is not tending to subject himself to criminal liability.[28]

The nature of the inquiry into whether a declaration against penal interest—as against any other interest—is necessarily factual. The courts are developing benchmarks to facilitate this determination, but no modification of the Rule itself appears warranted.

Rule 804(b)(4): Statements of Personal or Family History

Not surprisingly, this exception has been infrequently litigated in federal courts. Will contests, family disputes and similar cases are not likely to be heard in federal tribunals, although they are the staple of both general and special jurisdiction state courts. Thus far, courts have resisted attempts to read the exception broadly.[29]

Rule 804(b)(5): Other Exceptions

This Rule is discussed above in conjunction with Rule 803(24).

28. *See, e.g.,* United States v. Goins, 593 F.2d 88, 91 (9th Cir.), *cert. denied,* 444 U.S. 827 (1979) (declarant's acknowledgment to her daughter and friend that she committed perjury before the grand jury satisfies 804(b)(3); "acknowledgment of criminal activity is generally made only to confederates and to persons in whom the declarant imposes trust"); United States v. Mock, 640 F.2d 629, 631–32 (5th Cir.1981) (inculpatory statement to declarant's ex-wife); United States v. Lang, 589 F.2d 92, 97 (2d Cir.1978) (statement to declarant's confederate qualifies under 804(b)(3) since the declarant need not be aware that the incriminating statement subjects him to immediate criminal liability).

29. *See generally* cases cited in 2 Saltzburg & Martin, *Federal Rules of Evidence Manual* 436 (5th ed. 1990); *see also* 2 *Evidence in America* §§ 59.2–59.3.

RULE 805

I. TEXT OF RULE

RULE 805. Hearsay Within Hearsay

Hearsay included within hearsay is not excluded under the hearsay rule if each part of the combined statements conforms with an exception to the hearsay rule provided in these rules.

II. DISCUSSION

Sometimes referred to as the "double hearsay" rule, Rule 805 applies to situations in which one hearsay statement falls within another hearsay statement. Where this occurs, each part of the statement must satisfy a hearsay exception before it may be admitted. While there may be an exception for each portion of the multiple hearsay statement, some commentators recognize that the trial judge may still exclude it as "dangerous evidence" if it is believed that the prejudicial effect of the multiple hearsay substantially outweighs the probative value.[1] Other concerns addressed by courts involve evidence in which only one of the two parts is hearsay. One approach may be to apply a Rule 805 test merely to the hearsay portion.

In addition, one commentary points out:

> [A]dmissions under Rule 801(d)(2) and certain prior statements of available witnesses under Rule 801(d)(1) are not actually hearsay. So Rule 805 technically does not apply to situations in which these statements are included within another statement that is hearsay. But the result is the same. A statement admissible under 801(d) can be admitted when included in another hearsay statement if the other hearsay statement qualifies as an exception.[2]

This view is correct as a matter of logic and as a matter of practice. When courts are confronted with an 801(d) non-hearsay statement contained within a hearsay statement, they consistently consider each component statement separately applying a Rule 805–type of analysis.[3]

However, a review of recent United States court of appeals decisions indicates that there may be some confusion as to how, or whether, Rule 805 applies in the reverse situation, i.e., where there is a hearsay statement contained within a non-hearsay statement. Most courts have subjected such multiple statements to Rule 805 analysis and, if

1. 2 Saltzburg & Martin, *The Federal Rules of Evidence Manual* 460 (5th ed. 1990).

2. *Id.*

3. *See* United States v. Dotson, 821 F.2d 1034, 1035 (5th Cir.1987) (applying Rule 805, the court excluded an 801(d)(2)(B) prior consistent statement because it was contained within an inadmissible hearsay statement). *See also* Williams v. Tri–County Growers, Inc., 747 F.2d 121, 133 (3d Cir.1984) (the court admitted an 801(d)(2)(D) admission contained within a hearsay statement because the encompassing hearsay was admissible under Rules 803(8)(B) and (C)).

any component is deemed inadmissible, the combined statement is excluded.[4]

The decisions of at least two circuit courts, however, can be interpreted as posing the proposition that, because an admission of a party opponent is technically non-hearsay under Rule 801(d), Rule 805 does not apply to the Rule 801(d) statement at all. Under this approach, any hearsay statements contained within a non-hearsay statement would not be scrutinized and would be admitted as part of (and as if cleansed by) the non-hearsay.

In *State v. Hendrickson Brothers, Inc.*,[5] although the court found it unnecessary to determine whether Rule 805 applied to a hearsay statement within a Rule 801(d)(2)(E) co-conspirator's statement, it appeared to indicate that this was an open question:

> We find no merit in the contention that the court should have excluded Farino's statements pursuant to Fed.R.Evid. 805 because they themselves contained hearsay statements by other unidentified declarants. Rule 805 provides for the exclusion of "[h]earsay included within hearsay" unless the included statement, as well as the encompassing statement, is covered by some exception to the hearsay rule. Whether or not Rule 805 is applicable when the encompassing statement is defined as nonhearsay, as is true of co-conspirator statements, and the only hearsay is a statement contained in the nonhearsay statement, *compare Cedeck v. Hamiltonian Federal Savings & Loan Ass'n,* 551 F.2d 1136, 1138 (8th Cir. 1977) (hearsay within co-conspirator statement excludable unless it meets a hearsay exception), with *United States v. McLernon,* 746 F.2d 1098, 1106 (6th Cir.1984) (upholding admissibility without reference to such exceptions), we reject appellants' contention because the challenged contents of Farino's statements were not themselves hearsay.[6]

The case cited in *Hendrickson* for the proposition that Rule 805 does not apply to hearsay within a non-hearsay statement, *United States v. McLernon,*[7] likewise does not directly confront the issue. The *McLernon* decision concerned testimony of a government agent concerning what one of the defendant co-conspirators Valdez, had told him about the other two defendant co-conspirators. At trial, the defendants objected to this testimony because, among other reasons, it contained double hearsay. It is not discernable from the opinion what the alleged hearsay within hearsay statements were. The relevant part of the

4. *See* Carden v. Westinghouse Elec. Corp., 850 F.2d 996, 1003 (3d Cir.1988) (applying Rule 805, the court excluded an otherwise admissible 801(d)(2)(D) statement because it encompassed an inadmissible hearsay statement). *See also* Cedeck v. Hamiltonian Fed. Sav. & Loan Ass'n, 551 F.2d 1136 (8th Cir.1977) (discussed *infra*).

5. 840 F.2d 1065 (2d Cir.), *cert. denied,* 488 U.S. 848 (1988).

6. *Id.* at 1074, 1075.

7. 746 F.2d 1098 (6th Cir.1984).

decision for our purposes (and the reason it was cited by the Second Circuit in *Hendrickson*) is that the court appeared to ignore any Rule 805 double hearsay analysis because the encompassing statement constituted non-hearsay.[8]

It is possible that the court was merely condensing its Rule 805 analysis into a one-step determination that all of the defendants' statements, whether to each other or to undercover agents, constituted co-conspirator's statements and were thus admissible. As reported, however, it is difficult to determine the proposition for which *McLernon* stands.

Cedeck v. Hamiltonian Fed. Sav. & Loan Ass'n [9] is the case cited by the Second Circuit in *Hendrickson* for the proposition that Rule 805 does apply to a hearsay statement encompassed by a non-hearsay statement. In *Cedeck,* the appellant/employee sought to introduce as an 801(d)(2)(D) admission a statement by her superior, Murphy, regarding her prospects for promotion. The Court excluded the proffered statement because it encompassed an inadmissible hearsay statement:

> Appellant argues that Murphy's statement was admissible as an admission by party-opponent under Fed.R.Evid. 801(d)(2)(D). An argument for admission of the statement under this rule could be made had Murphy stated in effect to Cedeck that she was qualified except for the fact that she was not a male. Part of Murphy's statement, however, contained a reiteration of what someone told him. Therefore, Murphy's statement to Cedeck is hearsay within hearsay. . . . That part of Murphy's statement which contains a reiteration of what someone told him is not admissible as an admission by party-opponent [sic] since the author of the statement is unknown. Furthermore, we do not believe it falls within any of the exceptions to the hearsay rule. Therefore, under Rule 805, the statement is not admissible.[10]

It is unclear whether the circuit courts are at odds over whether, or how, Rule 805 applies to hearsay statements encompassed by non-hearsay statements. It really should not matter whether Rule 805 applies to such combined statements. The proper analytical approach to any proffered statement containing one or more additional statements should be to treat each component statement individually under the Rules.

8. "Appellants Farrell and McLernon further contend that Valdez's statements concerning them constituted double hearsay. Rule 801(d)(2)(E), however, specifically exempts co-conspirator's statements from the hearsay rule. The requirement that the declarant have personal knowledge of his statements in such a case is waived. *See e.g.,* U.S. v. Ammar, 714 F.2d 238 (3d Cir.), *cert. denied,* 464 U.S. 936 (1983). We find, therefore, that the hearsay rules do not preclude the admission into evidence of Valdez's pre-arrest statements." 746 F.2d at 1106.

9. 551 F.2d 1136 (8th Cir.1977).

10. *Id.* at 1138.

RULE 806

I. TEXT OF RULE

RULE 806. Attacking and Supporting Credibility of Declarant

When a hearsay statement, or a statement defined in rule 801(d)(2), (C), (D), or (E), has been admitted in evidence, the credibility of the declarant may be attacked, and if attacked may be supported, by any evidence which would be admissible for those purposes if declarant had testified as a witness. Evidence of a statement or conduct by the declarant at any time, inconsistent with the declarant's hearsay statement, is not subject to any requirement that the declarant may have been afforded an opportunity to deny or explain. If the party against whom a hearsay statement has been admitted calls the declarant as a witness, the party is entitled to examine the declarant on the statement as if under cross-examination.

II. DISCUSSION

Rule 806 allows the credibility of a hearsay declarant to be impeached as if the declarant had taken the stand to testify.[1] Thus, for impeachment purposes, the physical location of the testifying declarant is legally insignificant.[2] Impeachment may be made through the use of prior inconsistent statements under Rule 613,[3] reputation testimony under Rule 608,[4] or through prior convictions under Rule 609.[5]

This rule has been cited in only a relatively few cases and shows few difficulties in application. In *United States v. Moody,*[6] for example, the defendant trustee was charged with seventeen counts of fraud arising out of the misuse of funds in the Moody Foundation. The government offered statements by the defendant's co-conspirators pursuant to Rule 801(d)(2)(E) against the defendant.[7] When the defense tried to impeach the out-of-court declarants, the prosecution objected on the grounds of their unavailability, and was sustained. In reversing the conviction, the Fifth Circuit noted that the government as well as the trial court were mistaken in their belief that unavailable declarants

1. Advisory Committee Note, Rule 806.

2. *See* United States v. Moody, 903 F.2d 321, 329 (5th Cir.1990).

3. *See* United States v. Graham, 858 F.2d 986 (5th Cir.1988), *cert. denied,* 489 U.S. 1020 (1989).

4. *See* United States v. Katsougrakis, 715 F.2d 769 (2d Cir.1983) (trial court erred by not allowing reputation evidence about declarant), *cert. denied,* 464 U.S. 1040 (1984).

5. *E.g.,* United States v. Bovain, 708 F.2d 606 (11th Cir.), *cert. denied,* 464 U.S. 898 (1983).

6. 903 F.2d 321 (5th Cir.1990).

7. *Id.* at 327.

could not be impeached.[8] Indeed the appellate court was surprised that Rule 806 had not even been cited by the parties.[9] Citing *Delaware v. Van Arsdall,*[10] the court concluded that the Sixth Amendment's guarantee included a right to cross-examination and could not be defeated merely because the declarant is unavailable.[11] This reversal reflects the linkage between the evidentiary rule and constitutional prescriptions.

There is little doubt that Rule 806 is underutilized. When lawyers learn how important it can be, it is likely that trial judges will have some difficult decisions to make. Consider the typical federal criminal trial in which there are multiple defendants. Any statement offered by the government as a co-conspirator statement entitles the defendant to impeach the declarant under Rule 806. Yet, such impeachment may result in the introduction of prior convictions which would not be admitted under Rule 404 and cannot be admitted under Rule 609 if the declarant-defendant does not testify and might not be admitted even if he does. Striking a balance between the rights of one defendant to impeach a declarant and another defendant to be free from prejudicial use of prior convictions might prove difficult. The fact that each defendant has a confrontation right to impeach any witness or declarant upon whom the government relies will complicate the trial judge's ruling. There are cases in which the balance has been struck against impeachment and in favor of protecting the declarant-defendant from prejudice.[12] There are cases in which the balance has been struck in favor of impeachment.[13] And some decisions strongly suggest that a defendant's right to attack the hearsay offered by the government is important.[14] The cases are likely to multiply, and defense counsel are likely to make additional motions for severance in order to make it difficult for the prosecutor to argue, after choosing to join defendants for purposes of trial, that impeachment opportunities should be denied to some defendants who could have impeached hearsay declarants had they been tried alone.

8. *Id.* at 328.

9. *Id.* at 329.

10. 475 U.S. 673, 678–79 (1986).

11. *Id.*

12. *E.g.,* United States v. Robinson, 783 F.2d 64 (7th Cir.1986).

13. *E.g.,* United States v. Bovain, 708 F.2d 606 (11th Cir.), *cert. denied,* 464 U.S. 898, 1018 (1983).

14. *E.g.,* United States v. Wali, 860 F.2d 588 (3d Cir.1988) (reversing a defendant's drug-related convictions because he was denied impeachment of a conspirator-declarant); United States v. Moody, 903 F.2d 321 (5th Cir.1990) (reversing a defendant's fraud convictions because he was not permitted to show that co-conspirators whose statements were admitted had bad reputations for truthfulness).

ARTICLE IX. AUTHENTICATION AND IDENTIFICATION

Introduction

Article IX covers authentication of evidence. It has generally relaxed common law authentication requirements, and this relaxation of foundation requirements has produced few problems in practice. Rule 901 states a liberal general definition of the authentication requirement and provides ten illustrations of acceptable authentication. Rule 902 identifies another ten categories of evidence which are "self-authenticati[ng]" and require no extrinsic evidence of authenticity to be admissible. Rule 903 dispenses with the necessity of subscribing witnesses' testimony unless it is otherwise required by law.

RULE 901

I. TEXT OF RULE

RULE 901. Requirement of Authentication or Identification

(a) General provision. The requirement of authentication or identification as a condition precedent to admissibility is satisfied by evidence sufficient to support a finding that the matter in question is what is proponent claims.

(b) Illustrations. By way of illustration only, and not by way of limitation, the following are examples of authentication or identification conforming with the requirements of this rule:

(1) Testimony of witness with knowledge. Testimony that a matter is what it is claimed to be.

(2) Nonexpert opinion on handwriting. Nonexpert opinion as to the genuineness of handwriting, based upon familiarity not acquired for purposes of the litigation.

(3) Comparison by trier or expert witness. Comparison by the trier of fact or by expert witnesses with specimens which have been authenticated.

(4) Distinctive characteristics and the like. Appearance, contents, substance, internal patterns, or other distinctive characteristics, taken in conjunction with circumstances.

(5) Voice identification. Identification of a voice, whether heard firsthand or through mechanical or electronic transmission or recording, by opinion based upon hearing the voice at any time under circumstances connecting it with the alleged speaker.

(6) Telephone conversations. Telephone conversations, by evidence that a call was made to the number assigned at the time by the telephone company to a particular person or business, if (A) in the case of a person, circumstances, including self-identification, show the person answering to be the one called, or (B) in the case of a business, the call was made to a place of business and the conversation related to business reasonably transacted over the telephone.

(7) Public records or reports. Evidence that a writing authorized by law to be recorded or filed and in fact recorded or filed in a public office, or a purported public record, report, statement, or data compilation, in any form, is from the public office where items of this nature are kept.

(8) Ancient documents or data compilation. Evidence that a document or data compilation, in any form, (A) is in such condition as to create no suspicion concerning its authenticity, (B) was in a place where it, if authentic, would

likely be, and (C) has been in existence 20 years or more at the time it is offered.

(9) Process or system. Evidence describing a process or system used to produce a result and showing that the process or system produces an accurate result.

(10) Methods provided by statute or rule. Any method of authentication or identification provided by Act of Congress or by other rules prescribed by the Supreme Court pursuant to statutory authority.

II. DISCUSSION

Courts and commentators alike have had difficulty reconciling the permissive nature of Rule 901(a) authentication requirements with the more traditional approach reflected in the 901(b) illustrations. This difficulty appears to stem from a conflicting approach to authentication reflected in 901(a) and 901(b). The Advisory Committee Notes for 901(a) describe the common law approach to authentication as one which "departs sharply from men's customs in ordinary affairs." [1] However, the illustrations in subdivision (b) are said to be drawn in part "upon the experience embodied in the common law." [2] The philosophy underlying subdivision (a) is to base authentication on principles which resemble customs in ordinary affairs. However, the subdivision (b) illustrations drawn from the common law experience require a more demanding standard for authentication and identification issues. This conflict is noted in the writings of several commentators.[3]

In practice, courts have generally adopted the more relaxed standard set forth in 901(a), which merely requires that the court make a prima facie determination based on "evidence sufficient to support a finding that that matter in question is what its proponent claims." [4] This is "essentially a reasonableness test based on the totality of circumstances." [5]

1. Advisory Committee Note to Rule 901(a).

2. Advisory Committee Note to Rule 901(b).

3. "We begin with the premise that the confusion found in Rule 901 derives from the confusion that exists even in common law jurisdictions over whether authentication is a problem involving a question of 'competency' which must be resolved by preliminary fact-finding and decision-making by the Trial Judge, or whether it involves a question of conditional relevancy which requires that the Judge only insure that a *prima facie* case is made before leaving the matter to the jury to resolve." 2 S. Saltzburg & M. Martin, *Federal Rules of Evidence Manual* 478 (5th ed. 1990).

See also The ABA Criminal Justice Section's Committee on Rules of Criminal Procedure and Evidence, Proposed Rules, 120 F.R.D. 299 and 2 *Evidence in America* § 62.3 (1988).

4. Fed.R.Evid. 901(a) Advisory Committee's Note.

5. 2 *Evidence in America* § 62.3.

It would appear that the widespread use of civil discovery and pretrial procedures has reduced the number and difficulty of authentication issues presented to courts in recent years. However, as the Advisory Committee Note to Rule 901(a) observes, in criminal cases difficult authentication issues may persist. This is true both on a policy and constitutional level. The lack of certainty in the Rule regarding the appropriate authentication standards has prompted the ABA Criminal Justice Section's Committee on Rules of Criminal Evidence to state its disapproval of certain court decisions where the relaxed authentication standards were improperly applied.[6]

Certainly, admissions gained in civil discovery obviate the need for courtroom authentication in many instances, where the issue is the genuineness of a document, the identity of the speaker on a recording or the author of a writing. However, authenticity will still be contested in certain instances where the trustworthiness of evidence to be authenticated is questioned or where its creation or acquisition is clouded by circumstances which are not free of suspicion.

A common example of this kind of challenge to authenticity may be found in cases involving fungible physical evidence (contraband) under Rule 901(b)(4) and (5). The court has three standards from which to choose: (1) the traditional standards as relaxed by the 901(a) standard,[7] (2) references to 901(b)(4) and (5) standards as relaxed by the 901(a) standard,[8] and (3) 901(b)(4) and (5) standards based upon traditional common law chain of custody foundations.[9] The fact that the courts' interpretations of the requirements of Rule 901 are so varied lends credence to the concern that the rulings on authentication are "outcome determinative." [10]

Perhaps the Rule or the comments should provide more guidance as to the intent of the drafters. With regard to Rule 901, one commentator has observed:

> This rule does not ignore or repudiate the policy justifications for the authentication requirement. It simply recognizes that

6. "The true rule should be that something more than would justify an ordinary reasonable person in daily life to make the inference should be required. This was the thrust of the common law. In litigation there are special motivations to falsify that are not found in daily life. For these reasons the ABA Criminal Justice Section's Committee on Rules of Criminal Procedure and Evidence disapproves the stated grounds of decision in cases (citations omitted) . . . [where] the court seems to accept as authentication circumstantial indicators of authenticity that are scarcely more than would be provided by a more authenticated signature and as easily faked." 120 F.R.D. at 299.

7. United States v. Jardina, 747 F.2d 945 (5th Cir.1984), *cert. denied,* 470 U.S. 1058 (1985).

8. United States v. Jefferson, 714 F.2d 689 (7th Cir.1983), *vacated and remanded on other grounds,* 474 U.S. 806 (1985).

9. United States v. McMillan, 508 F.2d 101, 104 (5th Cir.1974), *cert. denied,* 421 U.S. 916 (1975).

10. 2 *Evidence in America* § 62.3. *See also* 120 F.R.D. at 299.

> where the question is one of probative force or credibility—as it necessarily always is with questions of authenticity and identity—the jury is as competent as the Court.[11]

The Rule and Advisory Committee Notes may not make clear what the judge's role is when the issue is whether the evidence is genuine or trustworthy.

As a matter of policy, is it acceptable for the court to "err" on the side of relaxed authentication because the factfinder ultimately must re-evaluate the genuineness of the evidence anyway? Even if one assumes that the factfinder's evaluation of the weight and credibility of the evidence subsumes authenticity and has a corrective effect on erroneous or marginal authentication findings by the court, there are problems which may contaminate the proceedings when the judge's preliminary finding is made without a concern for trustworthiness, in the belief that the jury can sort it out.[12]

In a criminal case, the willingness of a court to adopt a Rule 901(a) approach to authentication and overlook gaps in the authentication foundation may have the effect of shifting the burden to challenge authentication to the defendant. The defendant may be required to put on affirmative evidence challenging the authenticity of evidence which would not be deemed authenticated were the court to require an unbroken chain of authentication.[13] It must be assumed that any gaps in the chain are real and not merely the failure of the foundation evidence available to him.[14] The text of the Rule and Advisory Committee Notes do not provide courts with sufficient guidance concerning instances where a mere Rule 901(a) foundation instead of a traditional common law foundation may be prejudicial to the party wishing to exclude the evidence.[15]

In a civil setting, the efficacy of modern discovery used to streamline authentication can pose a problem for the individual litigant with limited resources involved in litigation with the government or a well-financed corporation. The effect of the civil discovery rules can shift the burden from one seeking authentication to one challenging authentication and can make it both burdensome and expensive to undertake such challenges to authentication through discovery.[16] The text of the Rule and the Advisory Committee Notes do not address this situation.

11. 5 J. Weinstein & M. Berger, *Weinstein's Evidence* ¶ 901(9)[02].

12. Ballou v. Henri Studios, Inc., 656 F.2d 1147 (5th Cir.1981).

13. Shmukler, *Voice Identification in Criminal Cases Under Article IX of the Federal Rules of Evidence,* 49 Temple L.Q. 867, 874 (1976).

14. 2 *Evidence in America* § 62.3.

15. The Advisory Committee Notes may be amended to include citations to leading cases which set forth appropriate foundations under certain circumstances. *See* 2 S. Saltzburg & M. Martin, *Federal Rules of Evidence Manual* 480 (5th ed. 1990).

16. P. Rothstein, *Federal Rules of Evidence for the United States Courts* 447 (2d ed. 1987).

Another internal inconsistency in the Rule concerns the standard for authentication by a nonexpert under Rule 901(b)(2) (handwriting) and Rule 901(b)(5) (voice identification). Several commentators have pointed out that a nonexpert may authenticate the voice identification based on familiarity with the voice gained at any time, whereas a nonexpert authenticating handwriting must have gained his familiarity with the handwriting, not for purposes of litigation.[17] But if authentication is a matter of conditional relevancy to be guided by the procedures in Rule 104(b), what difference does it make when the nonexpert acquires his familiarity with the handwriting? [18] This dichotomy is especially perplexing given the scientific data available on the unreliability of voice identification.[19]

An omission in the Rule has been revealed by one commentator who notes that the authentication requirements for Rule 901 do not provide explicit guidance for the authentication of demonstrative or real evidence.[20] Some clarification of this seeming omission is in order.

Most of the states which have adopted Rules of Evidence have made only minor changes to the text of Rule 901. However, two of the states which have adopted Rules of Evidence, Alaska and Florida, have not adopted the 901(b) illustrations as part of the Rule, but have provided them merely as commentary. Alaska, however, has added chain of custody requirements for 901(a) under certain circumstances. Maine, Mississippi, Texas and Washington interpose the judge in the authentication process in ways elsewhere left to the jury. Rule 901 has operated unproblematically in the states.[21]

17. 2 S. Saltzburg & M. Martin, *Federal Rules of Evidence Manual* 479 (5th ed. 1990); 2 *Evidence in America* § 62.3.

18. 2 S. Saltzburg & M. Martin, *Federal Rules of Evidence Manual* 479 (5th ed. 1990).

19. Shmukler, *supra,* n. 13 at 873.

20. 2 S. Saltzburg & M. Martin, *Federal Rules of Evidence Manual* 481 (5th ed. 1990).

21. 2 *Evidence in America* §§ 62.2–62.3.

RULE 902

I. TEXT OF RULE

RULE 902. Self-Authentication

Extrinsic evidence of authenticity as a condition precedent to admissibility is not required with respect to the following:

(1) Domestic public documents under seal. A document bearing a seal purporting to be that of the United States, or of any State, district, Commonwealth, territory, or insular possession thereof, or the Panama Canal Zone, or the Trust Territory of the Pacific Islands, or of a political subdivision, department, officer, or agency thereof, and a signature purporting to be an attestation or execution.

(2) Domestic public documents not under seal. A document purporting to bear the signature in the official capacity of an officer or employee of any entity included in paragraph (1) hereof, having no seal, if a public officer having a seal and having official duties in the district or political subdivision of the officer or employee certifies under seal that the signer has the official capacity and that the signature is genuine.

(3) Foreign public documents. A document purporting to be executed or attested in an official capacity by a person authorized by the laws of a foreign country to make the execution or attestation, and accompanied by a final certification as to the genuineness of the signature and official position (A) of the executing or attesting person, or (B) of any foreign official whose certificate of genuineness of signature and official position relating to the execution or attestation. A final certification may be made by a secretary of embassy or legation, consul general, consul, vice consul, or consul agent of the United States, or a diplomatic or consular official of the foreign country assigned or accredited to the United States. If reasonable opportunity has been given to all parties to investigate the authenticity and accuracy of official documents, the court may, for good cause shown, order that they be treated as presumptively authentic without final certification or permit them to be evidenced by an attested summary with or without final certification.

(4) Certified copies of public records. A copy of an official record or report or entry therein, or of a document authorized by law to be recorded or filed and actually recorded or filed in a public office, including data compilations in any form, certified as correct by the custodian or other person authorized to make the certification, by certificate complying with paragraph (1), (2), or (3), of this rule or complying with

any Act of Congress or rule prescribed by the Supreme Court pursuant to statutory authority.

(5) Official publications. Books, pamphlets, or other publications purporting to be issued by public authority.

(6) Newspapers and periodicals. Printed materials purporting to be newspapers and periodicals.

(7) Trade inscriptions and the like. Inscriptions, signs, tags, or labels purporting to have been affixed in the course of business and indicating ownership, control, or origin.

(8) Acknowledged documents. Documents accompanied by a certificate of acknowledgment executed in the manner provided by law by a notary public or other officer authorized by law to take acknowledgments.

(9) Commercial paper and related documents. Commercial paper, signatures thereon, and documents relating thereto to the extent provided by general commercial law.

(10) Presumptions under Acts of Congress. Any signature, document or other matter declared by Act of Congress to be presumptively or prima facie genuine or authentic.

II. DISCUSSION

Rule 902 has not presented any major difficulties for the courts. It appears to have accomplished what it was designed to do: to eliminate the need to call witnesses to lay foundations for evidence that is so likely to be authentic that such testimony would unnecessarily consume judicial time and litigants' resources.[1] In fact, experience with Rule 902 has lead to suggestions that the self-authentication provisions be extended to all documents that have been produced in discovery or that are connected with the party against whom they are offered unless there is a specific disclaimer of genuineness.[2]

In determining whether a public document under Rule 902 is self-authenticating, commentators have disagreed as to whether this subsection applies to photocopies. One view is that Rule 902(1) only applies to original documents.[3] Other writers assert that copies of public docu-

1. A party who wishes to challenge the authenticity of self-authenticating evidence may, of course, do so. While self-authentication satisfies Article IX, it is not necessarily conclusive.

2. *See* C. McCormick, *Evidence* § 228 (Cleary ed. 1984); Weissenberger's Federal Evidence § 902.19.

3. Wellborn, *Authentication and Identification Under Article IX of the Texas Rules of Evidence,* 16 St. Mary's L.J. 371, 390 (1985).

ments should be self-authenticating unless "circumstances exist which question the genuineness of the document." [4]

Courts have not yet resolved this conflict. In *United States v. Hitsman,*[5] the court held that a copy of defendant's college transcript was self-authenticating because it bore indicia of reliability where it had the university seal above the name of the registrar. Similarly in *AMFAC Distribution Corp. v. Harrelson,*[6] a copy of a state court judgment was admissible because a stamp found on the back of the judgment, satisfied the requirement that it bear a seal and a signature purporting to be that of custodian of the original judgment. In the case of public documents without seals the court in *In re Leifheit,*[7] held a copy of an accident report was not self-authenticating and therefore inadmissible under Rule 902(2).

Rule 902(4) has been interpreted as rendering officially certified computer data compilations of public offices and governmental agencies self-authenticating.[8] This Rule, in conjunction with Rules 803(6) and (8), which generally except such data compilations from exclusion under the hearsay rule, effectively renders such documents virtually admissible per se. To the extent that this permits the unimpeded introduction of computerized summaries or calculations absent the foundation required under Rule 1006, or the limited protections afforded to adversaries under that Rule, unfairness could result.

States have included a variety of unique provisions into their versions of Rule 902. Two of the most noteworthy are (1) Wisconsin's subdivision (11), under which hospital records filed with the court pursuant to a special hearsay exception, are self-authenticating, and (2) Texas' subdivision (10), which provides for self-authentication of business records by affidavit in a manner paralleling Unif.R.Evid. 803(11) and 18 U.S.C. § 3505.[9]

4. S. Saltzburg & M. Martin, *Federal Rules of Evidence Manual* 507 (5th ed. 1990). *See also,* H. Wendorf & D. Schlueter, *Texas Rules of Evidence Manual* 392 (2d ed. 1988) (expressing the opinion that 902(1) applies to copies).

5. 604 F.2d 443 (5th Cir.1979).

6. 841 F.2d 304 (11th Cir.1988).

7. 53 B.R. 271 (Bkrtcy.S.D.Ohio 1985).

8. United States v. Farris, 517 F.2d 226 (7th Cir.), *cert. denied,* 423 U.S. 892 (1975) (interpreting identical final draft version of Rule 902(4)); United States v. Hart, 673 F.Supp. 932 (N.D.Ind.1987) (applying Rule 902(4)). *See also* United States v. Hays, 525 F.2d 455 (7th Cir.1975).

9. 2 *Evidence in America* §§ 63.2–63.3.

RULE 903

I. TEXT OF RULE

RULE 903. Subscribing Witness' Testimony Unnecessary

The testimony of a subscribing witness is not necessary to authenticate a writing unless required by the laws of the jurisdiction whose laws govern the validity of the writing.

II. DISCUSSION

Rule 903 provides that it is not necessary to call a subscribing witness to authenticate a writing except in the case of a writing invalid unless so witnessed. Thus, even though a writing has been attested, unless its validity under the applicable substantive law depends upon a subscribing witness, it may be authenticated in the same way as that of an unattested writing.[1]

Since no federal statute requires subscribing witnesses to a writing to be called, and very few state laws so require, Rule 903 is rarely encountered in litigation. When it is applicable, the Rule has presented no problem in application.

1. Zenith Radio Corp. v. Matsushita Elec. Ind. Co., 505 F.Supp. 1190 (E.D.Pa.1980) (absence of subscribing witness not fatal to authentication).

ARTICLE X. CONTENTS OF WRITING, RECORDINGS AND PHOTOGRAPHS

Introduction

Article X deals with what at common law was termed the "best evidence rule," but should, more accurately, be called the "original document rule." Rule 1002 sets forth a classical statement of the rule, ostensibly preserving the common law requirement that the original be produced to prove the contents of any writing, recording or photograph. Moreover, the breadth of the definitions contained in Rule 1001 seemingly expands the coverage of the Rule beyond simple documents to all writings, recordings, and photographs, including virtually all methods of data storage. Rules 1003–1007, however, provide a series of exceptions which largely envelop the common law rule. Finally, Rule 1008 defines the respective roles of court and jury with respect to Article X issues, carving out a substantial role for the jury in resolving disputed fact questions.

RULE 1001

I. TEXT OF RULE

RULE 1001. Definitions

For purposes of this article the following definitions are applicable:

(1) Writings and recordings. "Writings" and "recordings" consist of letters, words, or numbers, or their equivalent, set down by handwriting, typewriting, printing, photostating, photographing, magnetic impulse, mechanical or electronic recording, or other form of data compilation.

(2) Photographs. "Photographs" include still photographs, X–ray films, video tapes, and motion pictures.

(3) Original. An "original" of a writing or recording is the writing or recording itself or any counterpart intended to have the same effect by a person executing or issuing it. An "original" of a photograph includes the negative or any print therefrom. If data are stored in a computer or similar device, any printout or other output readable by sight, shown to reflect the data accurately, is an "original."

(4) Duplicate. A "duplicate" is a counterpart produced by the same impression as the original, or from the same matrix, or by means of photography, including enlargements and miniatures, or by mechanical or electronic re-recording, or by chemical reproduction, or by other equivalent techniques which accurately reproduces the original.

II. DISCUSSION

This Rule has presented few problems in application, but the breadth of Rule 1001(1)'s definition of "writings and recordings" is at least potentially problematic in that, literally applied, the rule comprehends inscribed chattels.[1] Historically, the courts have never rigorously applied the original document rule in inscribed chattel cases,[2] due to the fact that the reasons underlying the Rule are less, if at all, applicable in such cases. The loss of fine detail through mistransmission ordinarily does not import a substantial risk in cases of inscribed chattels, as opposed to documents, either because no legally consequential detail exists (e.g., handwriting or erasures) or because it is strictly

1. Inscribed chattels are non-documentary chattels, other than recordings or photographs, which bear letters, words or number. Common examples include revolvers, automobiles, police badges, license plates, money, billboards and tombstones.

2. 4 J. Wigmore, *Evidence* § 1182 at 421 (Chadbourn rev. 1972). *Accord* 5 J. Weinstein & M. Berger, *Weinstein's Evidence* ¶ 1001(1)[01] at pp. 1001–11 (1989).

limited in quantity.[3] As a result, whether, or to what extent, to apply the original document rule to inscribed chattels has traditionally been a matter committed to the sound discretion of the trial judge.[4]

In determining whether to apply the original document rule to inscribed chattels or whether a particular item constitutes the "equivalent" of "letters, words or numbers," courts have, laudably, looked to the Rule's purposes: preventing fraud and reducing the hazards of mistransmission or misrecollection. Thus, one court, in a prosecution for the sale of watches bearing counterfeit trademarks, rejected the contention that the watches themselves must be introduced.[5] In contrast, in a copyright infringement case, another court applied the rule to "reconstructions" of lost original drawings of science fiction characters that the plaintiff-artist alleged had been infringed by characters appearing in a feature film, *The Empire Strikes Back.*[6] Though the first court found the original document rule inapplicable because the trademarks were "more like a picture or a symbol than a written document," 868 F.2d at 134, and the latter court found the Rule applicable to the drawings because "[j]ust as a contract objectively manifests the subjective intent of the makers, so [plaintiff's] drawings are objective manifestations of the creative mind," 797 F.2d at 1508, their results seem consistent with each other and with the language and purposes of the Rule.

It should be noted that one reason why inscribed chattels have probably presented few problems for federal courts is that often the contents of such chattels relate to collateral matters within Rule 1004(4). When this is the case, secondary evidence is permitted. The

3. 4 J. Wigmore, *Evidence* §§ 1181–1182 (Chadbourn rev. 1972); C. McCormick, *Evidence* § 232 (Cleary ed. 1984).

4. United States v. Yamin, 868 F.2d 130, 134 (5th Cir.), *cert. denied,* 492 U.S. 924 (1989).

5. United States v. Yamin, 868 F.2d 130, 134 (5th Cir.) ("The purpose of the best evidence rule, however, is to prevent inaccuracy and fraud when attempting to prove the contents of a writing. Neither of those purposes was violated here. The viewing of a simple and recognized trademark is not likely to be inaccurately remembered."), *cert. denied,* 492 U.S. 924 (1989). *Cf.* United States v. Bueno–Risquet, 799 F.2d 804 (2d Cir. 1986) (applying rule to skull-and-crossbones markings on bags of heroin).

6. Seiler v. Lucasfilm, Ltd., 797 F.2d 1504, 1508–09 (9th Cir.), *aff'd* 808 F.2d 1316 (9th Cir.1986), *cert. denied,* 484 U.S. 826 (1987):

> The dangers of fraud in this situation are clear. The rule would ensure that proof of the infringement claim consists of the works alleged to be infringed. Otherwise, "reconstructions" which might have no resemblance to the purported original would suffice as proof for infringement of the original. . . .
>
> Our holding is also supported by the policy served by the best evidence rule in protecting against faulty memory. [Plaintiff's] reconstructions were made four to seven years after the alleged originals; his memory as to specifications and dimensions may have dimmed significantly. Furthermore, reconstructions made after the release of The Empire Strikes Back may be tainted, even if unintentionally, by exposure to the movie.

more central the inscription on a chattel is to the merits of a case, the more likely a court is to insist upon production of the chattel unless Rule 1004 provides some excuse for nonproduction. Also, it may be helpful to recall that the definition of a duplicate in Rule 1001(4) includes a photograph. Often, the evidence offered as a substitute for a chattel will be a photo. When this evidence is offered, it is presumptively admissible under Rule 1003, and the original (i.e., the chattel) will not be required unless special circumstances are present.

Apart from the inscribed chattel issue, it deserves mention that Montana, in promulgating Rule 1001, believed it necessary to add a section entitled "Copies of entries in the regular course of business" to cover business records copied from other business records. Some commentators have expressed the view that such provision is unnecessary because each business record may be an original under the rule.[7] In any event the issue does not appear to have caused problems for federal courts, nor has Montana's lead been followed by any other jurisdiction adopting the Rules.[8]

7. 2 S. Saltzburg & M. Martin, *Federal Rules of Evidence Manual* 525 (5th ed. 1990).

8. *See generally* 2 *Evidence in America* §§ 65.2–65.4.

RULE 1002

I. TEXT OF RULE

RULE 1002. Requirement of Original

To prove the content of a writing, recording, or photograph, the original writing, recording, or photograph is required, except as otherwise provided in these rules or by Act of Congress.

II. DISCUSSION

This Rule has presented no novel problems in application. The difficulties associated with it are the same difficulties lawyers encountered at common law. Usually, the problem lies in determining when a writing or recording is offered to prove its contents and when it is offered for another reason.[1]

Some lawyers, though apparently not judges, appear to still be confused by the persistence of the "best evidence" nomenclature, and continue to argue that oral testimony should be inadmissible where the same facts could be proven by "better evidence," i.e., documents or recordings. Such argument is uniformly, and rightly, rejected.[2]

Many original document rule problems are resolved in pre-trial proceedings. This is especially true in civil cases. In complicated civil litigation, some courts have developed forms or pretrial statements that require parties to state whether they have authentication or best evidence objections and, if so, to raise them. Virtually all such objections are resolved before trial begins. Criminal proceedings may cause more problems because the government, and the defendant as well, can choose not to disclose written statements or copies thereof until after its witnesses testify on direct examination. Such choices are permitted by the Jencks Act, 18 U.S.C. § 3500, and Fed.R.Crim.P. 26.2. Where the parties are willing to afford discovery, pretrial resolution of best evidence questions is accomplished as easily in criminal as in civil cases. Where discovery is restricted, original document rule questions may arise for the first time during trial.

1. *Compare, for example,* United States v. Levine, 546 F.2d 658, 668 (5th Cir.1977) (stating that, in an obscenity case, the contents of films were sought to be proved so that the Rule applied) with United States v. Rose, 590 F.2d 232, 236–37 (7th Cir.1978), (tape recording of telephone conversation need not be offered to prove contents of conversation), *cert. denied,* 442 U.S. 929 (1979); United States v. Boley, 730 F.2d 1326, 1332–33 (10th Cir.1984) (tape recording used only to prove contents of conversation). For the states' experience, *see generally* 2 *Evidence in America* §§ 66.2–66.4.

2. *See, e.g.,* R & R Associates, Inc. v. Visual Scene, Inc., 726 F.2d 36, 38 (1st Cir.1984) ("Rule 1002 applies not when a piece of evidence sought to be introduced has been somewhere recorded in writing but when it is that written record itself that the party seeks to prove"). One commentator, however, has argued that the original document rule is limited example of a more general "best evidence" principle that can be found in the law of evidence and should be expanded. *See* Nance, *The Best Evidence Principle,* 73 Iowa L.Rev. 227 (1988).

RULE 1003

I. TEXT OF RULE

RULE 1003. Admissibility of Duplicates

A duplicate is admissible to the same extent as an original unless (1) a genuine question is raised as to the authenticity of the original or (2) in the circumstances it would be unfair to admit the duplicate in lieu of the original.

II. DISCUSSION

This Rule has presented no problems in application. It has been adopted, verbatim or in substance, by every jurisdiction which has promulgated or enacted the Rules, except Maine, which declined to depart from the common law rule.[1]

As the Introduction to this section states, Rules 1003–1007 largely supersede the application of Rule 1002. Rule 1003 is probably the most significant Rule in this respect because it permits duplicates (defined by Rule 1001(4)) to be admitted without accounting for nonproduction of the original absent special circumstances. Duplicates at common law would not have been so readily admitted.

The most important decision that a court is called upon to make is when to call for the original or an explanation for its nonproduction. Because Rule 1001 covers tape recordings as well as writings, it is not surprising that tapes that have been re-recorded with some editing or erased may trigger special concern. For example, in *United States v. Balzano,*[2] where the government erased an original tape in the course of re-recording it, the trial judge admitted the re-recording only after hearing testimony concerning the government's procedure and assuring itself that the defense had no real claim that the re-recording was inaccurate. Given the accuracy and ubiquity of contemporary duplicating techniques, courts rarely reject duplicates.[3]

1. 2 *Evidence in America* §§ 67.2–67.4.

2. 687 F.2d 6 (1st Cir.1982).

3. *See, e.g.,* United States v. Leight, 818 F.2d 1297 (7th Cir.), *cert. denied,* 484 U.S. 958 (1987) (not error to admit "diagnostic-quality" copy of x-ray where original was accidentally destroyed by government). *But see* Ruberto v. Commissioner, 774 F.2d 61 (2d Cir. 1985) (tax court did not err in refusing to admit photocopies of cancelled checks, since problems in matching the copies of the backs of the checks with copies of the fronts made them somewhat suspect).

RULE 1004

I. TEXT OF RULE

RULE 1004. Admissibility of Other Evidence of Contents

The original is not required, and other evidence of the contents of a writing, recording, or photograph is admissible if—

> **(1) Originals lost or destroyed. All originals are lost or have been destroyed, unless the proponent lost or destroyed them in bad faith; or**
>
> **(2) Original not obtainable. No original can be obtained by any available judicial process or procedure; or**
>
> **(3) Original in possession of opponent. At a time when an original was under the control of the party against whom offered, that party was put on notice, by the pleadings or otherwise, that the contents would be a subject of proof at the hearing, and he does not produce the original at the hearing; or**
>
> **(4) Collateral matters. The writing, recording, or photograph is not closely related to a controlling issue.**

II. DISCUSSION

By its terms, Rule 1004(2) provides that "other evidence" may be offered to prove the contents of the original writing, recording or photograph only if "[n]o original *can* be obtained by *any* available judicial process or procedure" (emphasis added). This language suggests an imperative which is not recognized in practice; the terms of the Rule are not so strictly construed.

> While the rule is written in absolute terms, the courts are afforded a good deal of discretion to use common sense. . . . [I]t would be ludicrous to force a litigant to expend thousands of dollars to obtain a document abroad when $10,000 or so is at stake. The phrase "to the extent practicable and reasonable should be read into the rule." [1]

Idaho and Louisiana have adopted this suggestion and permit introduction of a duplicate where no original can be obtained practicably.[2]

It is clear that pointless process need not be issued. Thus, in a bank robbery prosecution, oral proof was admitted as to the serial numbers on marked bills which had been seen by police at the defendants' residence, even though no subpoena had been issued for the bills. Fifth Amendment issues aside, the court ruled it unnecessary for the government to "go through the motion of having a subpoena issued,

1. 5 J. Weinstein & M. Berger, *Weinstein's Evidence,* ¶ 1004(2)[01] at pp. 1004–23 (1989).

2. *See* 2 *Evidence in America* § 68.2.

served [upon defendants] and returned unexecuted in order to establish, under section (2), that the bills were not obtainable." [3]

There exists, however, some dispute concerning the reach of the requirement to resort to "any available" process. The Advisory Committee Note recites that, for Rule 1004(2) purposes, "[j]udicial procedure includes subpoena[e] duces tecum as an incident to the taking of a deposition in another jurisdiction." [4] In contrast, the select committee of the Colorado Bar Association, which adopted and urged promulgation of Rule 1004(2) in Colorado, expressly took issue with the Federal Advisory Committee's position, stating that "such time and expense would often appear to be unjustified, and should in part be taken care of by . . . pre-trial procedures.[5] Moreover, the Oklahoma Evidence Subcommittee's Note to the identical Oklahoma Rule 1004(2), refers with approval to a venerable Oklahoma precedent holding that secondary evidence is admissible where the original is in the possession of a third party in another state and he refuses to deliver the document.[6]

It would be desirable to clarify that the efforts made to secure the original need only be reasonable in the circumstances to permit introduction of "other evidence" under Rule 1004.

Rule 1004 largely codifies the common law. The Rule does not specify what kind of showing must be made that, when an original was lost, there was no bad faith involved. It is likely that courts will employ the same kind of reasoning that they used at common law.[7] Courts have consistently applied a subjective test of bad faith, allowing "other evidence" where, for example, originals were stolen by an Assistant United States Attorney for his personal use,[8] where the government negligently destroyed originals,[9] where the government

3. United States v. Marcantoni, 590 F.2d 1324, 1330 (5th Cir.), *cert. denied,* 441 U.S. 937 (1979).

4. It has even been suggested that the Hague Convention on the Taking of Evidence Abroad, 23 UST 2555, TIAS 7444, entered into by various signatory nations including the United States, may have implications on what is "available" within Rule 1004(2). *See* Schmertz, 5 *Fed.R.Evid.News* 80–132 (1980).

5. 7B Colo.Rev.Stat.Ann., 1981 Supp. at p. 300. With respect to the role of pretrial procedure in resolving Article X issues, the Colorado committee specifically "note[d] the desirability of requiring, in pretrial procedures, that any genuine questions as to the authenticity . . . or of the circumstances . . . be raised so that the offering party may take appropriate steps under R. 1004 to obtain the original." *Id.* at p. 299 (Comment to Rule 1003).

6. 12 Okla.Stat.Ann. at p. 525 (foll. § 3004), *citing* Pringey v. Guss, 16 Okla. 82, 86 P. 292 (1905).

7. *E.g.,* Wright v. Farmers Co-op, 681 F.2d 549, 553 (8th Cir.1982) (court suggests that where a tape of a statement was destroyed and a transcript of the statement was offered instead, some careful examination of the circumstances of the destruction may be required).

8. United States v. Bueno–Risquet, 799 F.2d 804 (2d Cir.1986).

9. Estate of Gryder v. Commissioner, 705 F.2d 336 (8th Cir), *cert. denied,* 464 U.S. 1008 (1983).

destroyed originals in violation of both statute and regulation,[10] and where a private party destroyed records in violation of a specific court order of which he was unaware.[11]

The burden of proving the absence of bad faith by a preponderance of the evidence is on the proponent, and a court may impute bad faith in the absence of a satisfactory explanation for the loss or destruction of originals.[12]

In two recent cases, parties have sought to introduce "reconstructions" of lost original documents as "other evidence" of their content.[13] Although both panels of the Ninth Circuit upheld exclusion of the "reconstructions" under conventional Rule 1004 analyses, both were also clearly troubled by this particular approach to proving the contents of missing documents. It may be helpful to clarify that "other evidence," even if permissible under Rule 1004, is subject to all other rules of evidence, including Rule 403 and Rule 901, either of which might call for exclusion of document "reconstructions" in a given case.

10. Murray v. District of Columbia Board of Education, 13 Fed.R.Evid.Serv. 554 (D.D.C.1983).

11. White Industries, Inc. v. The Cessna Aircraft Co., 611 F.Supp. 1049, 1079.

12. *See, e.g.,* Seiler v. Lucasfilm, Ltd., 613 F.Supp. 1253 (N.D.Cal.1984) (finding bad faith where proponent's testimony regarding destruction by flood was "inherently unbelievable and disturbingly contradictory"), *aff'd,* 797 F.2d 1504 (9th Cir.1986).

13. *See* Seiler v. Lucasfilm, Ltd., 797 F.2d 1504 (9th Cir.), *aff'd,* 808 F.2d 1316 (9th Cir. 1986), *cert. denied,* 484 U.S. 826 (1987); United States v. Feldman, 788 F.2d 544 (9th Cir. 1986), *cert. denied,* 479 U.S. 1067 (1987).

RULE 1005

I. TEXT OF RULE

RULE 1005. Public Records

The contents of an official record, or of a document authorized to be recorded or filed and actually recorded or filed, including data compilations in any form, if otherwise admissible, may be proved by copy, certified as correct in accordance with Rule 902 or testified to be correct by a witness who has compared it with the original. If a copy which complies with the foregoing cannot be obtained by the exercise of reasonable diligence, then other evidence of the contents may be given.

II. DISCUSSION

Rule 1005 is predicated on the theory that "[p]ublic records call for somewhat different treatment" than other documents in order to avoid the disruption entailed by removing originals for evidentiary use. The Rule therefore creates a separate hierarchy of evidence admissible to prove the contents of a public record. First, Rule 1005 deletes the Rule 1002 requirement that an original be offered. Second, Rule 1005 expressly gives "preference [to] certified or compared copies" even though such "[r]ecognition of degrees of secondary evidence" stands at odds with the philosophy reflected in Rules 1003–1004.[1]

Neither the courts nor the commentators, however, are in agreement as to the ramifications of Rule 1005's evidentiary hierarchy. The commentators differ as to the admissibility of "other evidence" in the absence of a certified or compared copy of the public record at issue. Some commentators assert that when neither a certified nor compared copy can be obtained by the exercise of reasonable diligence, then any other probative evidence is admissible since the "other evidence" clause at the end of the Rule "signifies that no hierarchy of preferences is created, an approach that is consistent with Rule 1004 but is a change from the common law." [2] Others, however, contend that: "Only if *both the original and a Rule 1005 copy* are unavailable may other evidence be used." [3]

While this dispute, as such, does not merit rule-changing attention,[4] it reflects uncertainty in the case law which extends even to cases

1. *See* Advisory Committee Note to Rule 1005.

2. 2 S. Saltzburg and M. Martin, *Federal Rules of Evidence Manual* 542 (5th ed. 1990).

3. 5 J. Weinstein & M. Berger, *Weinstein's Evidence* ¶ 1005[06] at 1005–11 (1989) (emphasis added).

4. No reported decision has found this issue problematic. Moreover, given that Rule 1005 expressly authorizes introduction of other evidence "[i]f a copy which does not comply with the foregoing cannot be obtained . . .," and in view of advocates' desire to proffer the most persuasive evidence, the original would most likely be subpoenaed (or sought) if certified/compared copies were for some reason unobtainable. However,

in which Rule 1005 copies do exist and are in evidence. In *Amoco Production Co. v. United States,*[5] a quiet title action, the pivotal issue was whether a 1942 deed from defendant to plaintiffs contained a reservation of oil, gas and mineral rights. The original deed was lost; however, it had been manually recorded—a copy typed by county personnel—in the county recorder's office. Because plaintiffs had obtained and offered (1) a certified copy of the recorded version (containing no such reservation of rights), which the court admitted into evidence, the court excluded defendants' proffer of (2) evidence of defendants' routine practice, in 1942, of including such clauses and (3) a photocopy of a conformed file copy maintained by defendants. The district court reasoned that, because a Rule 1005 copy was available, all "other evidence" was barred.

On appeal, the Tenth Circuit reversed the exclusion of (2) routine practice and remanded for reconsideration of the exclusion of (3) the conformed file copy.[6] The court of appeals reasoned that

> [t]he purpose of the rule is to eliminate the necessity of the custodian of public records producing the originals in court [, and that] purpose is not furthered by extending the rule to encompass documents not filed and stored in public offices. . . . [I]t is the actual record maintained by the public office which is the object of Rule 1005, not the original deed for which the record is made. If the original deed is returned to the parties after it is recorded, it is not a public record as contemplated by Rule 1005.[7]

Accordingly, the court of appeals ruled that Rule 1004(1), not Rule 1005, governed admissibility of the "other evidence" proffered, but improperly excluded, below.

The Tenth Circuit added, however, that not every document "filed and stored in public offices" constitutes a "public record" for Rule 1005 purposes. Thus, with respect to (3) the proffered photocopy of a conformed file copy, the court of appeals declared:

> [T]he mere fact that a document is kept in a working file of a governmental agency does not automatically qualify it as a public record for purposes of authentication or hearsay. Although the recorded version of a deed is public record, a copy of a deed deposited in a working file of the [government] is not, by that fact alone, a public record.[8]

expressly to compel production of the original in these circumstances—which the current Rule does not—seems to run counter to the thrust of the Rules' deletion of the original requirement *ab initio.* The Rule should, therefore, remain intact.

5. 455 F.Supp. 46 (D.Utah 1977).

6. Amoco Production Co. v. United States, 619 F.2d 1383, 1390–1391 (10th Cir.1980).

7. *Id.* at 1390.

8. *Id.* at 1391 n. 7.

It is arguable that, while reaching perhaps a felicitous result, the Tenth Circuit's decision does violence to the Rule's express creation of a hierarchy of secondary evidence for the purposes of proving "[t]he contents . . . of a document authorized to be recorded and actually recorded. . . ." On the other hand, the document ultimately at issue at *Amoco* was not the recorded version of the deed but the original unfiled document. Applying the strictures of Rule 1005 to the latter does not further the Rule's purposes, as the Tenth Circuit aptly observed. Further, because the actual contents of the original deed were in dispute, the question whether evidence other than the recorded version "correctly reflect[ed] the contents" was properly admissible under Rule 1008.

Zenith Radio Corp. v. Matuhita Elec. Ind. Co.[9] serves as another reminder that it may be important to decide whether a document is a public record. If it is, then one of the two forms of proof required by Rule 1005, if available, will have to be supplied. If it is not, then any duplicate will be admissible under Rule 1003.

Consequently, it would be desirable to clarify the distinction between (1) an original in official custody, whether that original be the document ultimately at issue or a copy thereof, and (2) an original not in official custody, a distinction not now apparent in the Rule. This could be achieved either by judicial decision or by rule amendment. It might be noted that one state, in adopting Article X, promulgated a definition of "official record." [10] Such a definition, carefully drafted, could serve to obviate the apparent dilemma presented by *Amoco Production.*[11]

9. 505 F.Supp. 1190 (E.D.Pa.1980).

10. Hawaii R.Evid. 1001(5). *See generally* the states' experience as reported in 2 *Evidence in America* §§ 69.2–69.4.

11. Note that the Hawaii definition would not accomplish this result. Because it encompasses, *inter alia,* every "writing . . . book or paper . . . in the custody of any department or agency of government," the Hawaii definition does not make the suggested distinction and runs afoul of the Tenth Circuit's admonition that not every paper in a bureaucratic file is an "official record" for Fed.R.Evid. 1005 purposes.

RULE 1006

I. TEXT OF RULE

RULE 1006. Summaries

The contents of voluminous writings, recordings, or photographs which cannot conveniently be examined in court may be presented in the form of a chart, summary, or calculation. The originals, or duplicates, shall be made available for examination or copying, or both, by other parties at reasonable time and place. The court may order that they be produced in court.

II. DISCUSSION

Pretrial review of summaries. The absence of any right of pretrial review of written charts, summaries and calculations ("summaries") by adversaries may in certain cases create an unnecessary risk of unfairness, prejudice or confusion as well as needless prolongation of trial.

The use of summaries has become an integral part of complex litigation. Yet, in such cases, summaries rarely "summarize" in a neutral fashion. Within the frequently complicated calculations which may underlie them, such summaries are often replete with assumptions (and, commonly, arguments) concerning factual or legal matters which are the subject of vigorous dispute. Due to the sophistication and expertise of the preparers, moreover, such assumptions (or arguments) may well be unascertainable except upon very close scrutiny.[1]

Cross-examination does not, moreover, uniformly afford an adequate opportunity to reveal internal inconsistencies, unsupported assumptions or argumentative premises. The short time frame aside, courts have facilitated the authentication process by allowing supervisory personnel to attest to the authenticity and accuracy of charts [2] and such personnel need not be—often are not—intimately familiar with all

1. For example, in a case in which the plaintiff asserted approximately two dozen antitrust, contract, fiduciary-duty and other claims against the defendant, plaintiff proffered some two dozen summaries among hundreds of other exhibits. The summaries in many cases consisted of one or two pages of figures which had been derived by sophisticated calculations, many of which assumed matters of fact and not law immediately apparent from the face of the summary. Due to the strictures of local practice, all exhibits, including the summaries, were exchanged between counsel prior to trial. As a result, defense counsel had the opportunity to scrutinize plaintiff's summaries in detail, ascertain the factual and legal assumptions upon which each was predicated and discern internal inconsistencies among them. Consequently, many of the summaries were the subject of successful objections and were kept from the jury's consideration. Brierwood Shoe Corp. v. Sears Roebuck and Co., No. 79 Civ. 2832 (S.D.N.Y.1980). In complicated cases, some judges have developed document identification forms that are especially helpful in identifying disputed issues surrounding documents of all sorts and in resolving them before trial. *See, e.g.,* Zenith Radio Corp. v. Matsushita Elec. Ind. Co., 505 F.Supp. 1125, 1189–1190 (E.D.Pa.1980).

2. 5 J. Weinstein & M. Berger, *Weinstein's Evidence* ¶ 1006[06] at 1006–13 (1989).

of the minutiae relating to summaries' composition. The opportunity for cross-examination may be meaningless where a summary is first presented at trial and the underlying documents are in a remote location.[3]

Further, the availability to both sides of the raw data from which the summaries have been compiled may be entirely inadequate to permit brief and cogent cross-examination as to matters buried beneath a simple entry on a chart, due to the permutation and combination of those data in the calculation/summarization process.

Finally, there is a danger of substantial prejudice whenever argumentative matter goes before a jury in the guise of a "summary." [4]

Some authorities have expressly recognized the desirability of pretrial resolution of "summary" questions. In addition to varying local practices, under which the exchange of all exhibits (including summaries) may be routine, it has been noted that "the framers of the Rule clearly contemplated a pre-trial resolution of any issues that may be raised concerning the use of summaries." [5] Florida, moreover, in enacting its version of Rule 1006, incorporated a requirement that "the party intending to sue such a summary must give timely written notice of his intention to sue the summary, proof of which shall be filed with the court, and shall make the summary and the originals or duplicates of the data from which the summary is compiled available for examination or copying, or both, by other parties at a reasonable time and place.[6] Nebraska so construes its version of Rule 1006.[7] However, the federal courts have generally enforced Rule 1006 as written and have not required pre-trial review of summaries by adversaries in the absence of authority in the Rule or otherwise.[8]

Serious consideration should be given to requiring pre-trial exchange of summaries, at least in civil cases. Conceivably such a requirement could be subject to abuse—e.g., disclosure delayed until the eve of trial or claims of mid-trial summary preparation. Whether the possibility of such abuse, and possible attendant litigation over the admissibility of summaries in such circumstances, outweighs the desirability of a general disclosure requirement should be considered.

3. White Industries, Inc. v. The Cessna Aircraft Co., 611 F.Supp. 1049, 1078 (W.D.Mo. 1985) (assuming without deciding, that Rule 1006 could apply to an *oral* summary).

4. *See, e.g.,* United States v. Smyth, 556 F.2d 1179, 1184 and n. 12 (5th Cir.), *cert. denied,* 434 U.S. 862 (1977); United States v. Scales, 594 F.2d 558, 564 (6th Cir.), *cert. denied,* 441 U.S. 946 (1979).

5. United States v. Smyth, *supra* 556 F.2d at 1184 n. 12. Commentators view this as desirable. 5 J. Weinstein & M. Berger, *Weinstein's Evidence* ¶ 1006[06] at 1006–13 (1989); *cf.,* the discussion concerning Rule 1004(2), *supra.*

6. Fla.Stat.Ann. § 90.956.

7. *See generally,* 2 *Evidence in America* §§ 70.2–70.4.

8. *See* United States v. Foley, 598 F.2d 1323, 1338 (4th Cir.1979), *cert. denied,* 444 U.S. 1043 (1980).

Admissibility of summary. One treatise admonishes that "[c]are should be taken to distinguish between the use of summaries or charts *as evidence* pursuant to Rule 1006, and the use of summaries, charts or other aids *as pedagogical devices* to summarize or organize testimony or documents which have themselves been admitted in evidence," and that the latter should not be permitted to go to the jury room absent consent.[9] Most courts, however, hold that summaries may be admitted into evidence under Rule 1006 and may go to the jury room even where the underlying documentation has also been admitted into evidence.[10] Where both a Rule 1006 summary and the underlying documentation are in evidence, some courts make it a practice to instruct the jury, somewhat paradoxically, that "the summary charts [do] not constitute evidence in the case, the real evidence [is] the underlying documents."[11] A better approach, exemplified by *United States v. Pinto,*[12] is to instruct the jurors that it is "their responsibility to determine whether the charts accurately [reflect] the evidence presented."

9. 5 J. Weinstein & M. Berger, *Weinstein's Evidence* ¶ 1006[07] at 1006–15 (1989).

10. United States v. Campbell, 845 F.2d 1374, 1381 (6th Cir.), *cert. denied,* 488 U.S. 908, 109 S.Ct. 259 (1988).

11. United States v. Stephens, 779 F.2d 232, 238 (5th Cir.1985). *See also* United States v. Lewis, 759 F.2d 1316, 1329 n. 6 (8th Cir.) (summary exhibits solely for convenience and not evidence themselves), *cert. denied,* 474 U.S. 994 (1985).

12. 850 F.2d 927, 935 (2d Cir.), *cert. denied,* 488 U.S. 867 (1988).

RULE 1007

I. TEXT OF RULE

RULE 1007. Testimony of Written Admission of Party

Contents of writings, recordings, or photographs may be proved by the testimony or deposition of the party against whom offered or by that party's written admission, without accounting for the nonproduction of the original.

II. DISCUSSION

No problems have been presented by this Rule. State experience is reported in 2 *Evidence in America* §§ 71.2–71.4.

RULE 1008

I. TEXT OF RULE

RULE 1008. Functions of Court and Jury

When the admissibility of other evidence of contents of writings, recordings, or photographs under these rules depends upon the fulfillment of a condition of fact, the question whether the condition has been fulfilled is ordinarily for the court to determine in accordance with the provisions of Rule 104. However, when an issue is raised (a) whether the asserted writing ever existed, or (b) whether another writing, recording, or photograph produced at the trial is the original, or (c) whether other evidence of contents correctly reflects the contents, the issue is for the trier of fact to determine as in the case of other issues of fact.

II. DISCUSSION

No problems have been presented by this Rule. State experience is reported in 2 *Evidence in America* §§ 72.2–72.4.

APPENDIX I

ARTICLE XI. GENERAL PROVISIONS

Introduction

Like the rules found in Article I, the three rules of Article XI provide criteria for using the rules set forth in Articles II–X, which govern admissibility and exclusion of evidence. Rule 1101 specifies the courts and actions to which the Rules apply. Rule 1102 provides that amendments to the Rules are governed by 28 U.S.C. § 2076. Rule 1103 denominates the Rules "the Federal Rules of Evidence."

RULE 1101

I. TEXT OF RULE

RULE 1101. Applicability of Rules

(a) Courts and magistrates. These rules apply to the United States district courts, the district Court of Guam, the District Court of the Virgin Islands, and District Court for the Northern Mariana Islands, the United States Courts of Appeals, the United States Claims Court, and to United States bankruptcy judges and United States magistrates, in the actions, cases, and proceedings and to the extent hereinafter set forth. The terms "judge" and "court" in these rules include United States bankruptcy judges and United States magistrates.

(b) Proceedings generally. These rules apply generally to civil actions and proceedings, including admiralty and maritime cases, to criminal cases and proceedings, to contempt proceedings except those in which the court may act summarily, and to proceedings and cases under Title 11, United States Code.

(c) Rule of privilege. The rule with respect to privileges applies at all stages of all actions, cases, and proceedings.

(d) Rules inapplicable. The rules (other than with respect to privileges) do not apply in the following situations:

(1) Preliminary questions of fact. The determination of questions of fact preliminary to admissibility of evidence when the issue is to be determined by the court under Rule 104.

(2) Grand jury. Proceedings before grand juries.

(3) Miscellaneous proceedings. Proceedings for extradition or rendition; preliminary examinations in criminal cases; sentencing, or granting or revoking probation; issuance of warrants for arrest, criminal summonses, and search warrants; and proceedings with respect to release on bail or otherwise.

(e) Rules applicable in part. In the following proceedings these rules apply to the extent that matters of evidence are not provided for in the statutes which govern procedure therein or in other rules prescribed by the Supreme Court pursuant to statutory authority: the trial of minor and petty offenses by United States magistrates; review of agency actions when the facts are subject to trial de novo under section 706(2)(F) of title 5, United States Code; review of orders of the Secretary of Agriculture under section 2 of the Act entitled "An Act to authorize association of producers of agricultural products" approved February 18, 1922 (7 U.S.C. 292), and under sections 6 and 7(c) of the Perishable

Agricultural Commodities Act, 1930 (7 U.S.C. 499f, 499g(c); naturalization and revocation of naturalization under sections 310–318 of the Immigration and Nationality Act (8 U.S.C. 1421–1429); prize proceedings in admiralty under sections 7651–7681 of title 10, United States Code; review of orders of the Secretary of the Interior under section 2 of the Act entitled "an Act authorizing associations of producers of aquatic products" approved June 25, 1934 (15 U.S.C. 522); review of orders of petroleum control boards under section 5 of the Act entitled "An Act to regulate interstate and foreign commerce in petroleum and its products by prohibiting the shipment in such commerce of petroleum and its products produced in violation of State law, and for other purposes," approved February 22, 1935 (15 U.S.C. 715d); actions for fines, penalties, or forfeitures under part V of title IV of the Tariff Act of 1930 (19 U.S.C. 1581–1624), or under the Anti-Smuggling Act (19 U.S.C. 1701–1711); criminal libel for condemnation, exclusion of imports, or other proceedings under the Federal Food, Drug, and Cosmetic Act (21 U.S.C. 301–392); disputes between seamen under sections 4079, 4080, and 4081 of the Revised Statutes (22 U.S.C. 256–258); habeas corpus under sections 2241–2254 of title 28, United States Code; motions to vacate, set aside or correct sentence under section 2255 of title 28, United States Code; actions for penalties for refusal to transport destitute seamen under section 4578 of the Revised Statutes (46 U.S.C. 679); actions against the United States under the Act entitled "An Act authorizing suits against the United States in admiralty for damage caused by the salvage service rendered to public vessels belonging to the United States, and for other purposes," approved March 3, 1925 (46 U.S.C. 781–790), as implemented by section 7730 of title 10, United States Code.

II. DISCUSSION

Rule 1101 is undoubtedly the most important of the Article XI Rules. It provides the specifics lacking in Rule 101 and identifies the courts, actions and stages of proceedings in which the Rules are applicable. As noted in the discussion accompanying Rule 101, the Rules govern in all United States district courts and courts of appeals. The Rules are applicable to the trial of civil actions and criminal cases, at least when the merits of a dispute are at issue. They are also applicable to the various other courts specified in Rule 1101(a), including the bankruptcy courts.[1] Further, they apply whether a case is tried before an Article III judge, a magistrate, or a bankruptcy judge.

The most important subdivision of Rule 1101 may be (d), which provides that, in certain stages of civil and criminal actions, the Rules

1. *See* Advisory Committee Note to Rule 1101(a). In 1987, Rule 1101(a) was amended to include "the United States bankruptcy courts" by name.

are inapplicable—except for privilege rules, which under subdivision (c) apply to all stages of all cases. Subdivision (e) makes the Rules applicable to certain types of cases, unless a statute or rule adopted by the Supreme Court provides otherwise.

Rule 1101 does not appear to have caused many problems, but the approach taken by the Rule can be criticized. Some states, for example, have placed limits on the use of hearsay evidence before grand juries, an approach which has received support from prestigious sources.[2] Other commentators have suggested more elaborate preliminary hearings.[3] In addition, some writers have expressed concern about the informality and possible unfairness of fact finding in sentencing.[4] However, criticisms of Rule 1101 on such grounds represent policy disagreements that are outside the purview of this Report.

The coverage of Rule 1101 would not be surprising if the Rules had been approved by the Supreme Court and only tacitly approved by Congress pursuant to the Rules Enabling Acts.[5] But, as described in Appendix A, Congress actually debated and considerably changed the Rules approved by the Supreme Court. In the process, Congress, not constrained by the enabling acts, could have incorporated into Rule 1101 the various statutory provisions that govern Article I courts and federal agencies. Many of these provisions require that the Rules be used insofar as practicable.[6] Locating all provisions regarding rules of evidence for federal tribunals in one place would have been helpful, but it is a task that Congress did not contemplate or undertake as it considered the Rules.

It should be noted that nothing in Rule 1101 is intended to override decisions of the federal courts that certain procedures are constitutionally required.[7] Consequently, counsel must be aware that, even if the Rules are not necessarily applicable in a certain proceeding under Rule 1101, the due process clauses of the Fifth and Fourteenth Amendments, and the confrontation and compulsory process clauses of the Sixth Amendment, may produce results similar to those obtained under the Rules.[8]

2. *See, e.g.,* ALI Model Code of Pre–Arraignment Procedure, § 340.5, Commentary at 606–607 (Proposed Official Draft 1975). State versions of Rule 1101 are analyzed at 2 *Evidence in America* §§ 73.2–73.4.

3. *See, e.g.,* Arenella, *Reforming the Federal Grand Jury and the State Preliminary Hearing to Prevent Conviction Without Adjudication,* 78 Mich.L.Rev. 463 (1980).

4. *See, e.g.,* Schulhofer, *Due Process of Sentencing,* 128 U.P.L.Rev. 733 (1980).

5. 18 U.S.C. §§ 3771, 3772, 3402; 28 U.S.C. §§ 2072, 2075.

6. *See, e.g.,* § 10(b) of the National Labor Relations Act, discussed in NLRB v. Stark, 525 F.2d 422 (2d Cir.1975), *cert. denied,* 424 U.S. 967 (1976), and Beth Israel Hosp. & Ger. Ctr. v. NLRB, 688 F.2d 697 (10th Cir.1982).

7. *See, e.g.,* Morrissey v. Brewer, 408 U.S. 471 (1972).

8. *See generally* United States v. Fatico, 441 F.Supp. 1285 (E.D.N.Y.1977), *rev'd,* 579 F.2d 707 (2d Cir.1978), *cert. denied,* 444 U.S. 1073 (1980).

Finally, Rule 1101 should put to rest most debate about the applicability of the Rules in diversity cases. Under Rule 1101, the Rules apply in diversity cases as well as in federal questions cases. Of course, three of the Rules—302, 501, and 601—expressly defer to state law in some circumstances. And in certain instances rules of evidence may be so intertwined with substantive state law that a federal court would defer to state law, not because the Rules do not apply to the action, but because an evidence issue is more substantive than procedural.[9]

9. *See generally* Wellborn, *The Federal Rules of Evidence and the Application of State Law in the Federal Courts,* 55 Tex.L.Rev. 371 (1977).

RULE 1102

I. TEXT OF RULE

RULE 1102. Amendments

Amendments to the Federal Rules of Evidence may be made as provided in section 2076 of title 28 of the United States Code.

II. DISCUSSION

This Rule adds nothing to 28 U.S.C. § 2076, which provides:

> The Supreme Court of the United States shall have the power to prescribe amendments to the Federal Rules of Evidence. Such amendments shall not take effect until they have been reported to Congress by the Chief Justice at or after the beginning of a regular session of Congress but not later than the first day of May, and until the expiration of one hundred and eighty days after they have been so reported; but if either House of Congress within that time shall by resolution disapprove any amendment so reported it shall not take effect. The effective date of any amendment so reported may be deferred by either House of Congress to a later date or until approved by Act of Congress. Any rule whether proposed or in force may be amended by Act of Congress. Any provision of law in force at the expiration of such time and in conflict with such amendment not disapproved shall be of no further force and effect after such amendment has taken effect. Any such amendment creating, abolishing, or modifying a privilege shall have no force or effect unless it shall be approved by Act of Congress.

This statute governs amendments to the Rules. Rule 1102 serves simply as a reminder of the statute.

It should be noted that amendments to the Rules are more tightly controlled than amendments to the Federal Rules of Civil or Criminal Procedure.[1] This is especially true of amendments to the privilege rules. Without affirmative Congressional action, Article V, which contains only one rule, cannot be changed and no additions may be made to it. However, section 2076 has been held by the Supreme Court not to bar changes in traditional approaches to privileges through adjudication. The Court has thus rendered several important decisions that change or arguably change the law on privileges.[2]

1. Both the House and Senate Judiciary Committees viewed the Federal Rules of Evidence as sufficiently important to require a greater Congressional role in their consideration. *See* 2 S. Saltzburg & M. Martin, *Federal Rules of Evidence Manual* 580–581 (5th ed. 1990).

2. *See, e.g.,* Upjohn Co. v. United States, 449 U.S. 383 (1981) (attorney-client); Trammel v. United States, 445 U.S. 40 (1980) (marital); United States v. Helstoski, 442 U.S. 477 (1978) (legislative vote).

Thus far, it does not appear that the increased Congressional role in connection with amendments of the Rules has caused problems. Rule 410 has been amended twice. Rule 412 was added to the Rules by Congress. Rule 801 and Rule 1101 also have been amended.[3] And in 1987, a number of technical amendments were made in order to make the Rules gender neutral.

3. Subdivision 801(d)(1)(C) was added after the Rules were adopted and, in Rule 1101, references to the United States Claims Court and certain other matters have been changed. Additionally, amendments to Rule 609, as noted *supra*, have been submitted to Congress.

RULE 1103

I. TEXT OF RULE

RULE 1103. Title

These rules may be known and cited as the Federal Rules of Evidence.

II. DISCUSSION

This Rule warrants no discussions.

APPENDIX I

APPENDIX A

A THUMBNAIL HISTORY OF THE FEDERAL RULES OF EVIDENCE

The movement toward codification of procedure and evidence rules can be traced to the latter part of the nineteenth century, when it proved unsuccessful. Part of the movement involved attempts to have the Congress give the Supreme Court rulemaking power over procedural issues. At long last in 1934 Congress enacted the Rules Enabling Act that provided the authority for the adoption of the Federal Rules of Civil Procedure in the late 1930's. The Chairman of the Advisory Committee on the civil procedure rules, Attorney General William Mitchell, observed that many people pressured the committee to recommend rules of evidence and that the committee recognized that it did not meet that need for reform. The suggestion was therefore made that some other advisory committee should tackle the task of codifying evidence rules.

The reluctance of the civil procedure committee to take up evidence rules is understandable. The background of the 1934 Rules Enabling Act suggests that influential members of Congress believed evidence rules to be more substantive than other rules of practice and procedure and opposed their being left to the courts alone.

The American Law Institute responded to Attorney General Mitchell by promulgating the Model Code of Evidence in 1942 under the direction of its Reporter, Edmund Morgan of the Harvard Law School. That Code stimulated academic discussion of evidence issues but proved unacceptable to virtually all American jurisdictions. Subsequently, the American Bar Association enlisted the help of the National Conference of Commissioners of Uniform State Laws in an effort to codify evidence rules. In 1953, the Uniform Rules of Evidence were approved and ultimately adopted by a handful of jurisdictions.

In 1961, the Judicial Conference of the United States, approved a proposal of the Standing Committee on Rules of Practice and Procedure that called for the development of Federal Rules of Evidence. The Chief Justice appointed Yale Law School Professor James William Moore to head a committee to inquire into the appropriateness of an evidence code for federal courts. The committee submitted its report, *A Preliminary Report on the Advisability and Feasibility of Developing Uniform Rules of Evidence for the United States District Courts,* the same year. The committee found that rules of evidence were both advisable and feasible. The following year that report was circulated to the bench and bar for comment. In 1965 the Chief Justice appointed an Advisory Committee on Rules of Evidence.

That committee transmitted to the Standing Committee its first draft of rules on January 30, 1969. Shortly thereafter, the Standing

Committee circulated the draft to the bench and bar for comments. The Standing Committee approved a revised draft in 1970 and submitted it to the Judicial Conference, which approved the draft and sent it to the Supreme Court. The Court concluded that the new draft should again be circulated. It was, in March 1971.

Comments were received and the Advisory Committee reworked its draft. The draft was resubmitted to the Standing Committee, which made further revisions and submitted the draft to the Judicial Conference. Again, the Conference approved the draft and sent the proposed rules to the Supreme Court. The Court received further comments, including some from the Justice Department, and it requested consideration of these comments by the Advisory and Standing Committees. Finally, on November 20, 1972, the Court promulgated the Federal Rules of Evidence.

The Chief Justice transmitted the rules to Congress in February 1973. Criticism surfaced even before the rules had been transmitted, however, because the comments received by the Supreme Court never were made public. The 93rd Congress, like previous Congresses that had expressed concern about conferring too much power on the Court to make "substantive decisions," decided to scrutinize the evidence rules closely. Early in 1973, Congress enacted a statute that nullified the Rules Enabling Act with respect to the evidence rules and provided that those rules would not take effect until Congress expressly approved them.

Hearings commenced before the House Subcommittee on Criminal Justice. That committee circulated its own draft of the rules. After receiving comments, it circulated a second draft. The House Judiciary Committee debated the bill, made further revisions and reported it to the full House. The House made further changes before passing a bill on February 6, 1974. A Senate Committee held hearings and ultimately the Senate passed a bill adopting evidence rules on November 22, 1974. Close to the end of the session, a conference committee reconciled differences and both Houses of Congress agreed on a bill in mid-December 1974. President Ford signed the bill into law on January 2, 1975.

Both before and after the Federal Rules of Evidence became effective on July 1, 1975, states were looking to and benefitting from the work done by the drafters of the Rules. Almost half of the states today have codes that owe much to the Rules.

The process that led to the enactment of the Rules involved bar associations, trial and appellate judges, law professors, the Supreme Court and the Congress. The Rules received closer scrutiny than is typical of proposals made by the Supreme Court under Rules Enabling Acts. As a result of what transpired in Congress, especially during the effort to reconcile the House and Senate bills, the Federal Rules of Evidence came into being with a history more complicated than is typical of rules governing federal practice and procedure. Some of the drafting compromises or oversights are responsible for problems identified in this Report.

From the first proposals for rules of evidence, it has been apparent that lawyers and lawmakers have regarded the rules used by their courts to decide disputes are tremendously important. It is out of respect for this judgment that this study has been undertaken.

APPENDIX B

PROPOSED RULES 501–513 (PRIVILEGE) REJECTED BY CONGRESS

RULE 501. Privileges Recognized Only as Provided

Except as otherwise required by the Constitution of the United States or provided by Act of Congress, and except as provided in these rules or in other rules adopted by the Supreme Court, no person has a privilege to:

(1) Refuse to be a witness; or

(2) Refuse to disclose any matter; or

(3) Refuse to produce any object or writing; or

(4) Prevent another from being a witness or disclosing any matter or producing any object or writing.

RULE 502. Required Reports Privileged by Statute

A person, corporation, association, or other organization or entity, either public or private, making a return or report required by law to be made has a privilege to refuse to disclose and to prevent any other person from disclosing the return or report, if the law requiring it to be made so provides. A public officer or agency to whom a return or report is required by law to be made has a privilege to refuse to disclose the return or report if the law requiring it to be made so provides. No privilege exists under this rule in actions involving perjury, false statements, fraud in the return or report, or other failure to comply with the law in question.

RULE 503. Lawyer–Client Privilege

(a) Definitions. As used in this rule:

(1) A "client" is a person, public officer or corporation, association, or other organization or entity, either public or private, who is rendered professional legal services by a lawyer, or who consults a lawyer with a view to obtaining professional legal services from him.

(2) A "lawyer" is a person authorized, or reasonably believed by the client to be authorized, to practice law in any state or nation.

(3) A "representative of the lawyer" is one employed to assist the lawyer in the rendition of professional legal services.

(4) A communication is "confidential" if not intended to be disclosed to third persons other than those to whom disclosure is in furtherance of the rendition of professional legal services to the client or those reasonably necessary for the transmission of the communication.

(b) General rule of privilege. A client has a privilege to refuse to disclose and to prevent any other person from disclosing confidential communications made for the purpose of facilitating the rendition of professional legal services to the client, (1) between himself or his representative and his lawyer or his lawyer's representative, or (2) between his lawyer and the lawyer's representative, or (3) by him or his lawyer to a lawyer representing another in a matter of common interest, or (4) between representatives of the client or between the client and a representative of the client, or (5) between lawyers representing the client.

(c) Who may claim the privilege. The privilege may be claimed by the client, his guardian or conservator, the personal representative of a deceased client, or the successor, trustee, or similar representative of a corporation, association or other organization, whether or not in existence. The person who was the lawyer at the time of the communication may claim the privilege but only on behalf of the client. His authority to do so is presumed in the absence of evidence to the contrary.

(d) Exceptions. There is no privilege under this rule:

(1) Furtherance of crime or fraud. If the services of the lawyer were sought or obtained to enable or aid anyone to commit or plan to commit what the client knew or reasonably should have known to be a crime or fraud; or

(2) Claimants through same deceased client. As to a communication relevant to an issue between parties who claim through the same deceased client, regardless of whether the claims are by testate or intestate succession or by *inter vivos* transaction; or

(3) Breach of duty by lawyer or client. As to a communication relevant to an issue of breach by the lawyer to his client or by the client to his lawyer; or

(4) Document attested by lawyer. As to a communication relevant to an issue concerning an attested document to which the lawyer is an attesting witness; or

(5) Joint clients. As to a communication relevant to a matter of common interest between two or more clients if the communication was made by any of them to a lawyer retained or consulted in common, when offered in an action between any of the clients.

RULE 504. Psychotherapist–Patient Privilege

(a) Definitions.

(1) A "patient" is a person who consults or is examined or interviewed by a psychotherapist.

(2) A "psychotherapist" is (A) a person authorized to practice medicine in any state or nation, or reasonably believed by the patient so to be, while engaged in the diagnosis or treatment of a

mental or emotional condition, including drug addiction, or (B) a person licensed or certified as a psychologist under the laws of any state or nation, while similarly engaged.

(3) A communication is "confidential" if not intended to be disclosed to third persons other than those present to further the interest of the patient in the consultation, examination, or interview, or persons reasonably necessary for the transmission of the communication, or persons who are participating in the diagnosis and treatment under the direction of the psychotherapist, including members of the patient's family.

(b) General rule of privilege. A patient has a privilege to refuse to disclose and to prevent any other person from disclosing confidential communications made for the purposes of diagnosis or treatment of his mental or emotional condition, including drug addiction, among himself, his psychotherapist, or persons who are participating in the diagnosis or treatment under the direction of the psychotherapist, including members of the patient's family.

(c) Who may claim the privilege. The privilege may be claimed by the patient, by his guardian or conservator, or by the personal representative of a deceased patient. The person who was the psychotherapist may claim the privilege but only on behalf of the patient. His authority so to do is presumed in the absence of evidence to the contrary.

(d) Exceptions.

(1) Proceedings for hospitalization. There is no privilege under this rule for communications relevant to an issue in proceedings to hospitalize the patient for mental illness, if the psychotherapist in the course of diagnosis or treatment has determined that the patient is in need of hospitalization.

(2) Examination by order of judge. If the judge orders an examination of the mental or emotional condition of the patient, communications made in the course thereof are not privileged under this rule with respect to the particular purpose for which the examination is ordered unless the judge orders otherwise.

(3) Condition an element of claim or defense. There is no privilege under this rule as to communications relevant to an issue of the mental or emotional condition of the patient in any proceeding in which he relies upon the condition as an element of his claim or defense, or, after the patient's death, in any proceeding in which any party relies upon the condition as an element of his claim or defense.

RULE 505. Husband–Wife Privilege

General rule of privilege. An accused in a criminal proceeding has a privilege to prevent his spouse from testifying against him.

RULE 508. Trade Secrets

A person has a privilege, which may be claimed by him or his agent or employee, to refuse to disclose and to prevent other persons from disclosing a trade secret owned by him, if the allowance of the privilege will not tend to conceal fraud or otherwise work injustice. When disclosure is directed, the judge shall take such protective measure as the interests of the holder of the privilege and of the parties and the furtherance of justice may require.

RULE 509. Secrets of State and Other Official Information

(a) Definitions.

(1) Secret of state. A "secret of state" is a governmental secret relating to the national defense or the international relations of the United States.

(2) Official information. "Official information" is information within the custody or control of a department or agency of the government the disclosure of which is shown to be contrary to the public interest and which consists of: (A) intragovernmental opinions or recommendations submitted for consideration in the performance of decisional or policymaking functions, or (B) subject to the provisions of 18 U.S.C. § 3500, investigatory files complied for law enforcement purposes and not otherwise available, or (C) information within the custody or control of a governmental department or agency whether initiated within the department or agency or acquired by it in its exercise of its official responsibilities and not otherwise available to the public pursuant to 5 U.S.C. § 552.

(b) General rule of privilege. The government has a privilege to refuse to give evidence and to prevent any person to refuse to give evidence upon a showing of reasonable likelihood of danger that the evidence will disclose a secret of state or official information, as defined in this rule.

(c) Procedures. The privilege for secrets of state may be claimed only by the chief officer of the government agency or department administering the subject matter which the secret information sought concerns, but the privilege for official information may be asserted by any attorney representing the government. The required showing may be made in whole or in part in the form of a written statement. The judge may hear the matter in chambers, but all counsel are entitled to inspect the claim and showing and to be heard thereon, except that, in the case of secrets of state, the judge upon motion of the government, may permit the government to make the required showing in the above form *in camera.* If the judge sustains the privilege upon a showing *in camera,* the entire text of the government's statements shall be sealed and preserved in the court's records in the event of appeal. In the case of privilege claimed for official information the court may require examination *in camera* of the information itself. The judge may take any protective measure which the interests of the government and the furtherance of justice may require.

(d) Notice to government. If the circumstances of the case indicate a substantial possibility that a claim of privilege would be appropriate but has not been made because of oversight or lack of knowledge, the judge shall give or cause notice to be given to the officer entitled to claim the privilege and shall stay further proceedings a reasonable time to afford opportunity to assert a claim of privilege.

(e) Effect of sustaining claim. If a claim of privilege is sustained in a proceeding to which the government is a party and it appears that another party is thereby deprived of material evidence, the judge shall make any further orders which the interests of justice require, including striking the testimony of a witness, declaring a mistrial, finding against the government upon an issue as to which the evidence is relevant, or dismissing the action.

RULE 510. Identity of Informer

(a) Rule of privilege. The government or a state or subdivision thereof has a privilege to refuse to disclose the identity of a person who has furnished information relating to or assisting in an investigation of a possible violation of law to a law enforcement officer or member of a legislative committee or its staff conducting an investigation.

(b) Who may claim. The privilege may be claimed by an appropriate representative of the government, regardless of whether the information was furnished to an officer of the government or of a state or subdivision thereof. The privilege may be claimed by an appropriate representative of a state or subdivision if the information was furnished to an officer thereof, except that in criminal cases the privilege shall not be allowed if the government objects.

(c) Exceptions.

(1) Voluntary disclosure; informer a witness. No privilege exists under this rule if the identity of the informer or his interest in the subject matter of his communication has been disclosed to those who would have cause to resent the communication by a holder of the privilege or by the informer's own action, or if the informer appears as a witness for the government.

(2) Testimony on merits. If it appears from the evidence in the case or from other showing by a party that an informer may be able to give testimony necessary to a fair determination of the issue of guilt or innocence in a criminal case or of a material issue on the merits in a civil case to which the government is a party, and the government invokes the privilege, the judge shall give the government an opportunity to show *in camera* facts relevant to determining whether the informer can, in fact, supply that testimony. The showing will ordinarily be in the form of affidavits, but the judge

may direct that testimony be taken if he finds that the matter cannot be resolved satisfactorily upon affidavit. If the judge finds that there is a reasonable probability that the informer can give the testimony, and the government elects not to disclose his identity, the judge on motion of the defendant in a criminal case shall dismiss the charges to which the testimony would relate, and the judge may do so on his own motion. In civil cases, he may make any order that justice requires. Evidence submitted to the judge shall be sealed and preserved to be made available to the appellate court in the event of an appeal, and the contents shall not otherwise be revealed without consent of the government. All counsel and parties shall be permitted to be present at every stage of proceedings under this subdivision except a showing *in camera*, at which no counsel or party shall be permitted to be present.

(3) Legality of obtaining evidence. If information from an informer is relied upon to establish the legality of the means by which evidence was obtained and the judge is not satisfied that the information was received from an informer reasonably believed to be reliable or credible, he may require the identity of the informer to be disclosed. The judge shall, on request of the government, direct that the disclosure be made *in camera*. All counsel and parties concerned with the issue of legality shall be permitted to be present. If disclosure of the identity of the informer is made *in camera*, the record thereof shall be sealed and preserved to be made available to the appellate court in the event of an appeal, and the contents shall not otherwise be revealed without consent of the government.

RULE 511. Waiver of Privilege by Voluntary Disclosure

A person upon whom these rules confer a privilege against disclosure of the confidential matter of communication waives the privilege if he or his predecessor while holder of the privilege voluntarily discloses or consents to disclosure of any significant part of the matter of communication. This rule does not apply if the disclosure is itself a privileged communication.

RULE 512. Privileged Matter Disclosed Under Compulsion or Without Opportunity to Claim Privilege

Evidence of a statement or other disclosure of privileged matter is not admissible against the holder of the privilege if the disclosure was (a) compelled erroneously or (b) made without opportunity to claim the privilege.

RULE 513. Comment Upon or Inference From Claim of Privilege; Instruction

(a) Comment or inference not permitted. The claim of a privilege, whether in the present proceeding or upon a prior occasion, is not a proper subject of comment by judge or counsel. No inference may be drawn therefrom.

(b) Claiming privilege without knowledge of jury. In jury cases, proceedings shall be conducted, to the extent practicable, so as to facilitate the making of claims of privilege without the knowledge of the jury.

(c) Jury instruction. Upon request, any party against whom the jury might draw an adverse inference from a claim of privilege is entitled to an instruction that no inference may be drawn therefrom.

*

Appendix II

A FLOW CHART OF THE FEDERAL RULES OF EVIDENCE

David L. Faigman

University of California
Hastings College of the Law

Preface

I designed the flow chart of the Federal Rules of Evidence to provide a helpful guide for those who find themselves lost in the seemingly seamless web of the Federal Rules. In my experience, the most difficult task confronting users of the Federal Rules involves integrating the details of individual rules into the greater structure of the Code. I started using the flow chart in my evidence classes to meet this difficulty and now hope that a wider audience will find them useful. I have endeavored to make plain the details *within* particular Rules and, moreover, to illustrate the connections *between* certain Rules.

The flow chart is couched almost entirely in the language of the Rules. I chose this format in order to avoid the appearance that the flow chart constitutes a delphic oracle for evidentiary queries. Contrary to its appearance, perhaps, the flow chart does not provide "answers" to the countless inquiries that might arise under the Rules. Instead, it arranges the questions that the user must scrutinize in order to reach satisfactory answers.

In the first instance, the flow chart provides a detailed rendering of the most often studied Rules. All of the Rules, to varying degrees, contain multiple components that can sometimes be quite confusing. Hence, the flow chart offers step-by-step guidance through the details *within* particular Rules.

Of greater importance, the flow chart also offers a schematic of the relations *between* certain Rules. Many perceive the subject of evidence as a series of discrete areas, such as hearsay, character, expert testimony and so on, without appreciating how they relate to one another. The Rules, however, were intended to provide a comprehensive scheme to resolve questions of admissibility. Evidence does not come neatly divided into discrete packages, labeled "hearsay," "character," or some other designation. A single item of evidence might raise an assortment of evidence problems spanning the spectrum of the Rules. The real challenge comes from the difficulty in recognizing the range of possible objections posed by a particular form of evidence.

APPENDIX II

The flow chart provides an elementary attempt to illustrate some of the more important connections between particular Rules. Of course, the innumerable interactions among the many Federal Rules could never be fully captured in a flow chart. The flow chart, therefore, provides only a rough and rather incomplete guide to the Rules and cannot substitute for the personal exploration of the terrain necessary to fully understand its complexity. The flow chart is merely a beginning point; it is the user who must invest the time before meaningful discovery can occur.

Finally, I would like to thank the many evidence students who commented on various parts of the flow chart and who enthusiastically encouraged the enterprise. In particular, I owe a debt of gratitude to my research assistants Deborah Brown, Jordonna Sabih and Elizabeth C. Johnsen for their careful proofreading of the flow chart. Also, thanks go to my colleagues Eileen Scallen and Mary Kay Kane for their valuable assistance and support. As is the tradition, however much I might wish to depart from it, any errors remain my own.

A FLOW CHART OF *THE FEDERAL RULES OF EVIDENCE*

David L. Faigman*

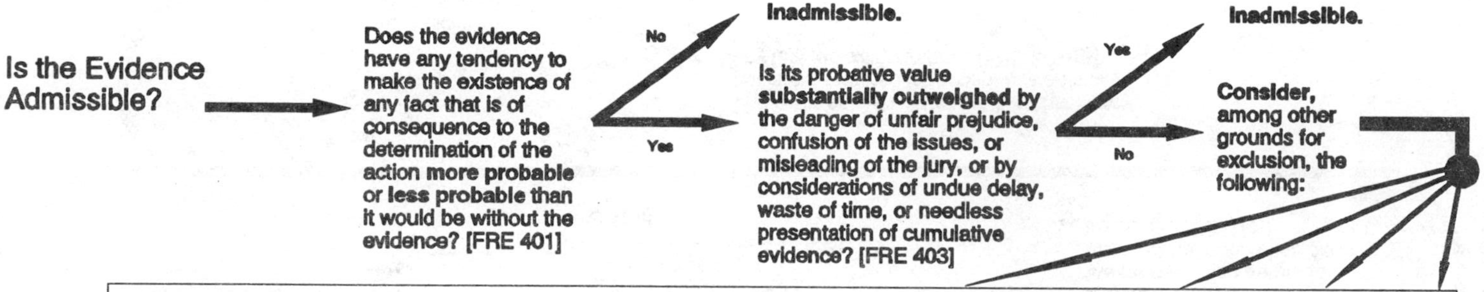
Is the Evidence Admissible?
Does the evidence have any tendency to make the existence of any fact that is of consequence to the determination of the action more probable or less probable than it would be without the evidence? [FRE 401]
No
Yes
Inadmissible.
Is its probative value substantially outweighed by the danger of unfair prejudice, confusion of the issues, or misleading of the jury, or by considerations of undue delay, waste of time, or needless presentation of cumulative evidence? [FRE 403]
Yes
No
Inadmissible.
Consider, among other grounds for exclusion, the following:

[G10358]

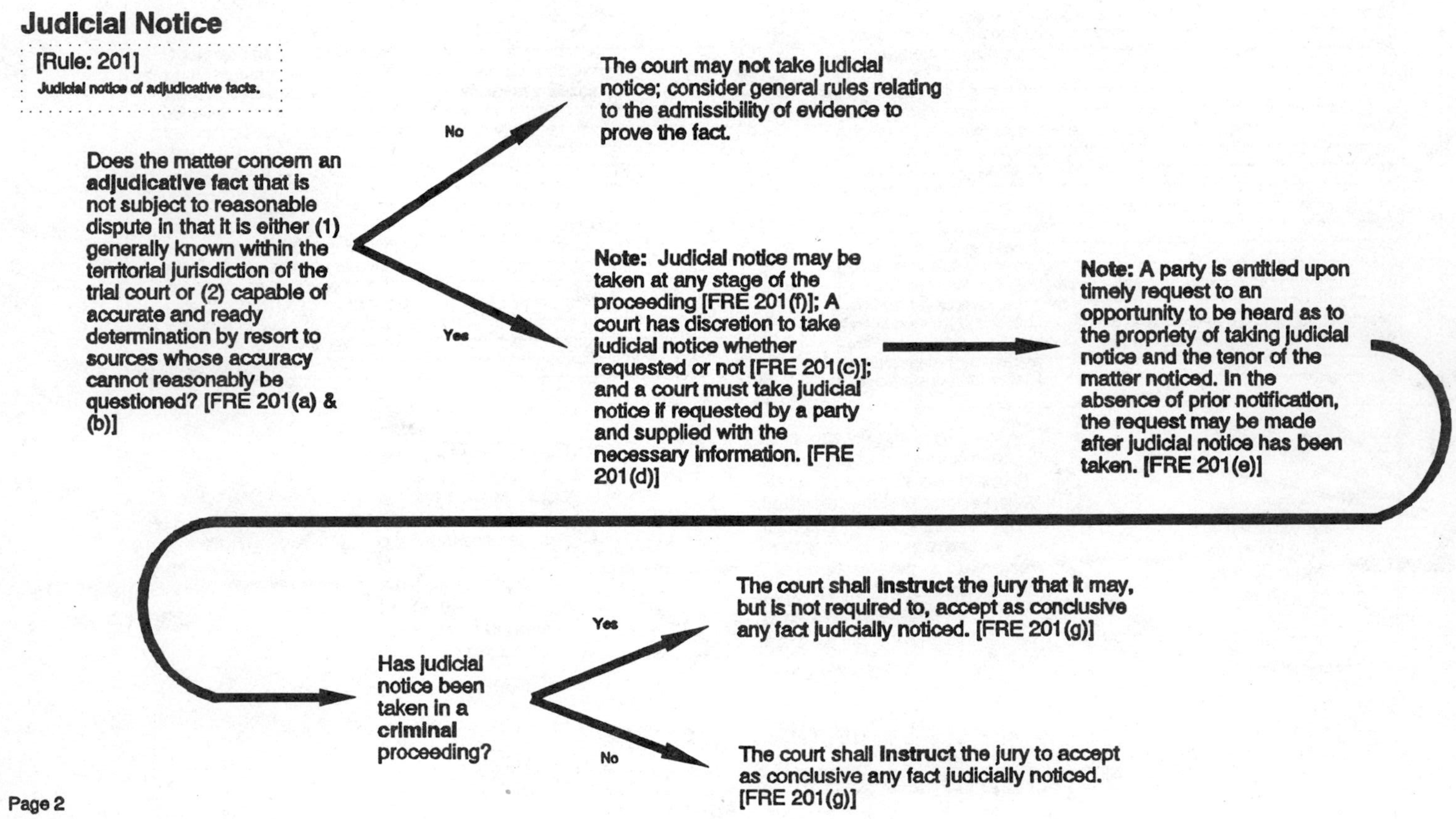
Judicial Notice
[Rule: 201]
Judicial notice of adjudicative facts.
Does the matter concern an adjudicative fact that is not subject to reasonable dispute in that it is either (1) generally known within the territorial jurisdiction of the trial court or (2) capable of accurate and ready determination by resort to sources whose accuracy cannot reasonably be questioned? [FRE 201(a) & (b)]
No
The court may not take judicial notice; consider general rules relating to the admissibility of evidence to prove the fact.
Yes
Note: Judicial notice may be taken at any stage of the proceeding [FRE 201(f)]; A court has discretion to take judicial notice whether requested or not [FRE 201(c)]; and a court must take judicial notice if requested by a party and supplied with the necessary information. [FRE 201(d)]
Note: A party is entitled upon timely request to an opportunity to be heard as to the propriety of taking judicial notice and the tenor of the matter noticed. In the absence of prior notification, the request may be made after judicial notice has been taken. [FRE 201(e)]
Has judicial notice been taken in a criminal proceeding?
Yes
The court shall instruct the jury that it may, but is not required to, accept as conclusive any fact judicially noticed. [FRE 201(g)]
No
The court shall instruct the jury to accept as conclusive any fact judicially noticed. [FRE 201(g)]
Page 2

[G10359]

FLOW CHART

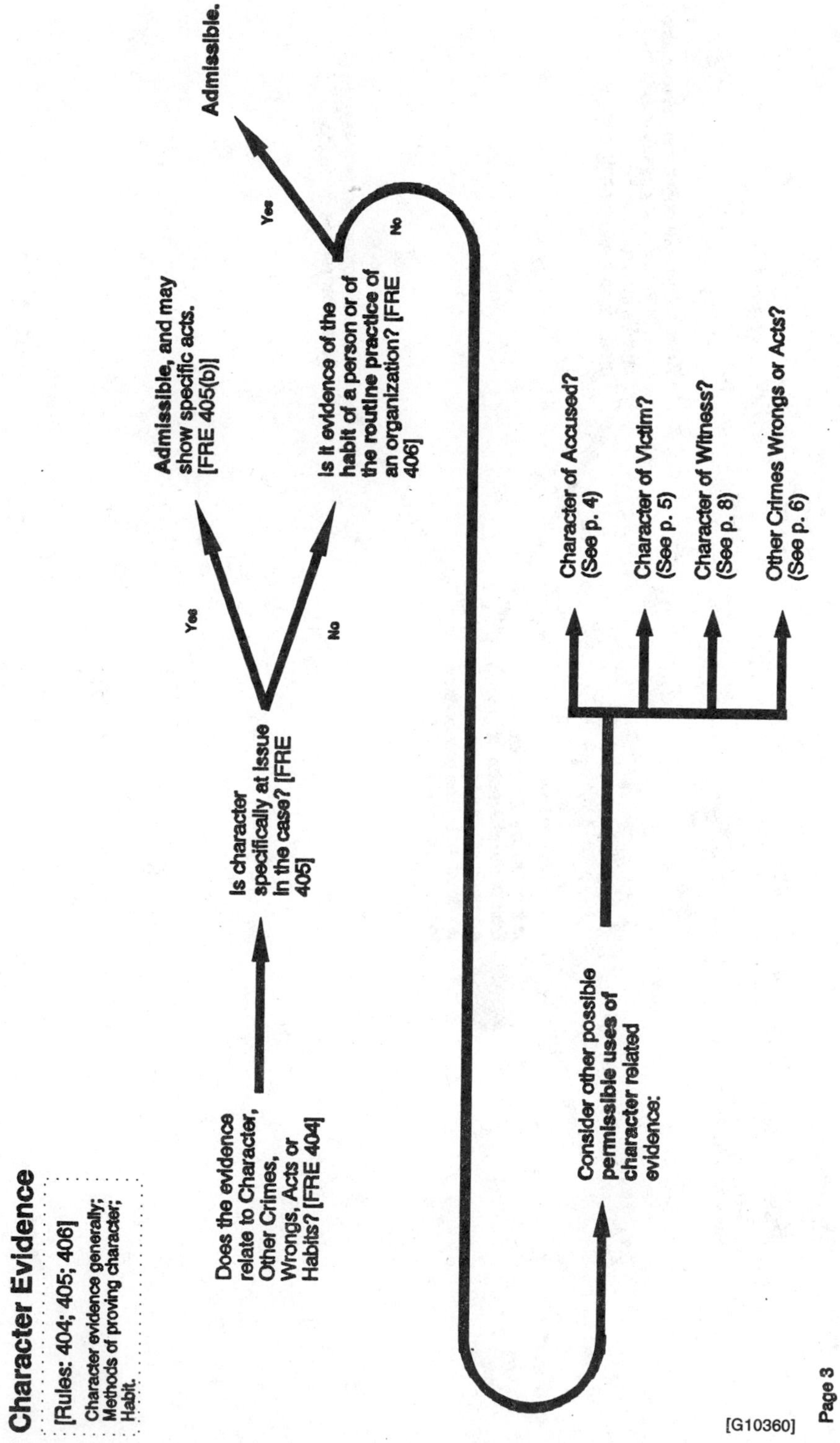

Character Evidence
[Rules: 404; 405; 406]
Character evidence generally; Methods of proving character; Habit.
Does the evidence relate to Character, Other Crimes, Wrongs, Acts or Habits? [FRE 404]
Is character specifically at issue in the case? [FRE 405]
Yes
Admissible, and may show specific acts. [FRE 405(b)]
No
Is it evidence of the habit of a person or of the routine practice of an organization? [FRE 406]
Yes
Admissible.
No
Consider other possible permissible uses of character related evidence:
Character of Accused? (See p. 4)
Character of Victim? (See p. 5)
Character of Witness? (See p. 8)
Other Crimes Wrongs or Acts? (See p. 6)
[G10360]
Page 3

Character, cont.

[Rules: 404(a)(1); 405(a)]

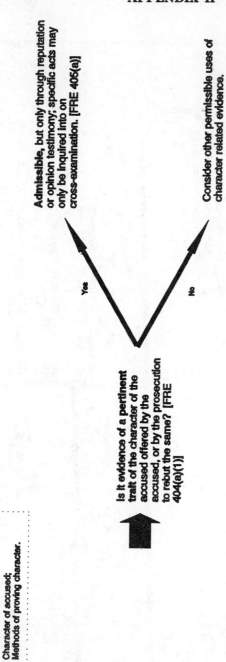

Character of accused;
Methods of proving character.

➡ **Is it evidence of a pertinent trait of the character of the accused offered by the accused, or by the prosecution to rebut the same? [FRE 404(a)(1)]**

- Yes → **Admissible, but only through reputation or opinion testimony; specific acts may only be inquired into on cross-examination. [FRE 405(a)]**
- No → **Consider other permissible uses of character related evidence.**

[G10361]

Page 4

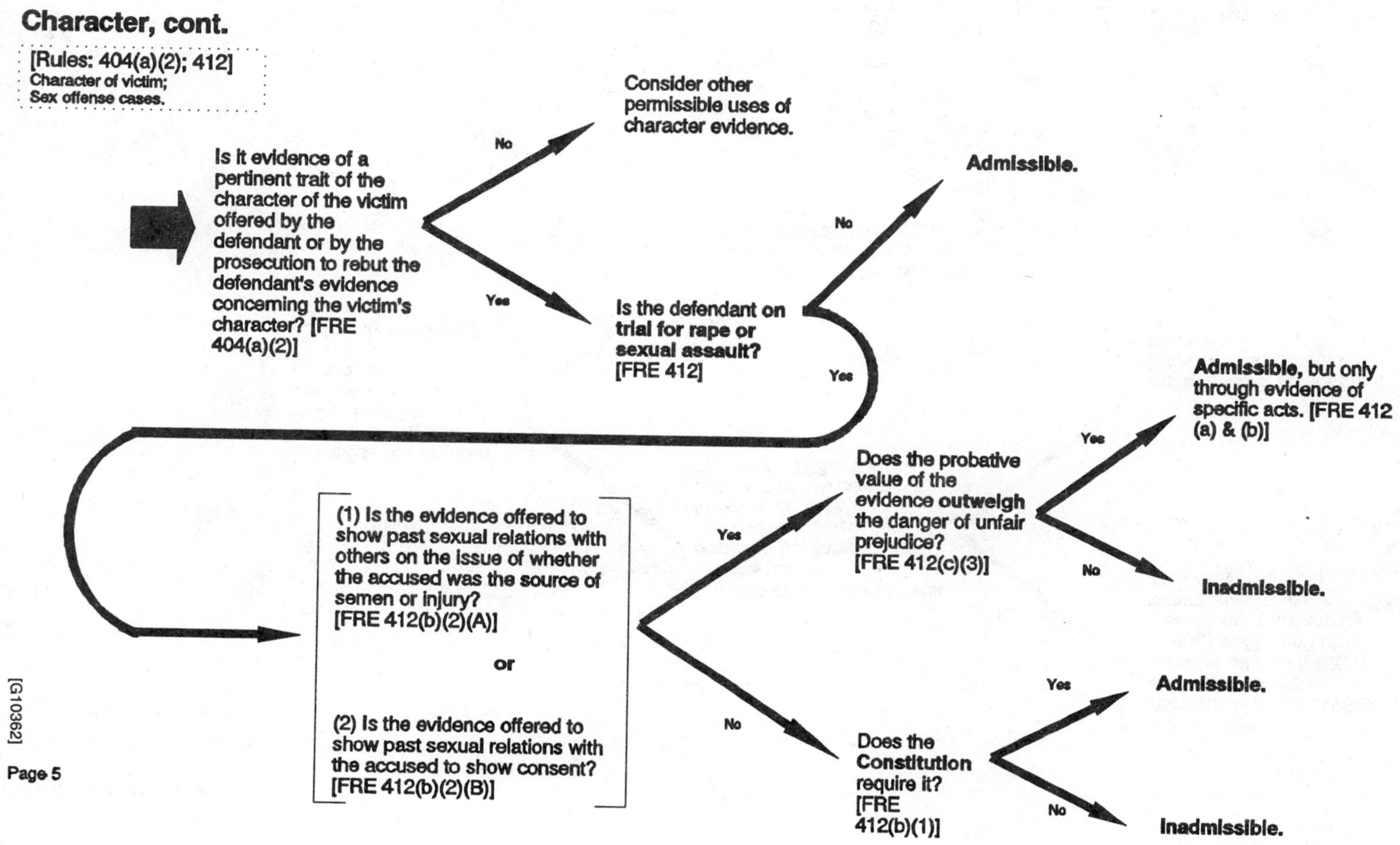
Character, cont.
[Rules: 404(a)(2); 412]
Character of victim;
Sex offense cases.
Is it evidence of a pertinent trait of the character of the victim offered by the defendant or by the prosecution to rebut the defendant's evidence concerning the victim's character? [FRE 404(a)(2)]
No
Consider other permissible uses of character evidence.
Yes
Is the defendant on trial for rape or sexual assault? [FRE 412]
No
Admissible.
Yes
(1) Is the evidence offered to show past sexual relations with others on the issue of whether the accused was the source of semen or injury? [FRE 412(b)(2)(A)]
or
(2) Is the evidence offered to show past sexual relations with the accused to show consent? [FRE 412(b)(2)(B)]
Yes
Does the probative value of the evidence outweigh the danger of unfair prejudice? [FRE 412(c)(3)]
Yes
Admissible, but only through evidence of specific acts. [FRE 412 (a) & (b)]
No
Inadmissible.
No
Does the Constitution require it? [FRE 412(b)(1)]
Yes
Admissible.
No
Inadmissible.
[G10362]
Page 5

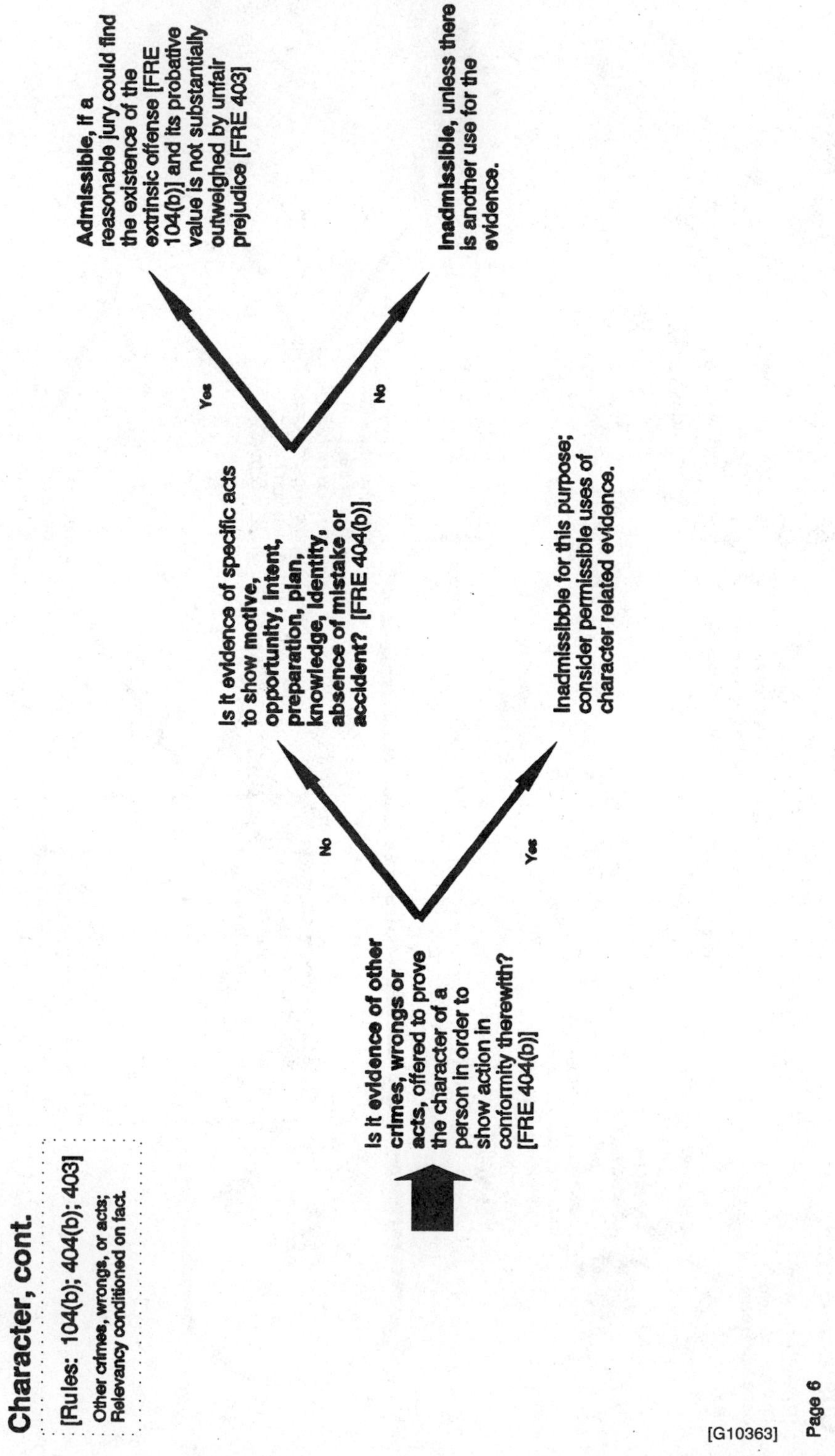
Character, cont.
[Rules: 104(b); 404(b); 403]
Other crimes, wrongs, or acts; Relevancy conditioned on fact.
Is it evidence of other crimes, wrongs or acts, offered to prove the character of a person in order to show action in conformity therewith? [FRE 404(b)]
No
Yes
Is it evidence of specific acts to show motive, opportunity, intent, preparation, plan, knowledge, identity, absence of mistake or accident? [FRE 404(b)]
Inadmissible for this purpose; consider permissible uses of character related evidence.
Yes
No
Admissible, if a reasonable jury could find the existence of the extrinsic offense [FRE 104(b)] and its probative value is not substantially outweighed by unfair prejudice [FRE 403]
Inadmissible, unless there is another use for the evidence.
[G10363]
Page 6

Subsequent Remedial Measures

[Rule: 407]
Subsequent remedial measures.

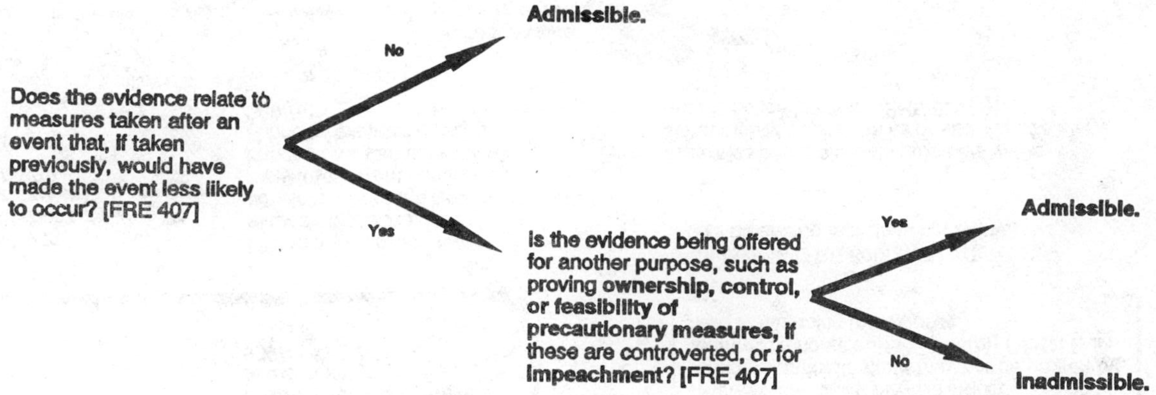
Does the evidence relate to measures taken after an event that, if taken previously, would have made the event less likely to occur? [FRE 407]
No
Admissible.
Yes
Is the evidence being offered for another purpose, such as proving ownership, control, or feasibility of precautionary measures, if these are controverted, or for impeachment? [FRE 407]
Yes
Admissible.
No
Inadmissible.

[G10364]

Page 7

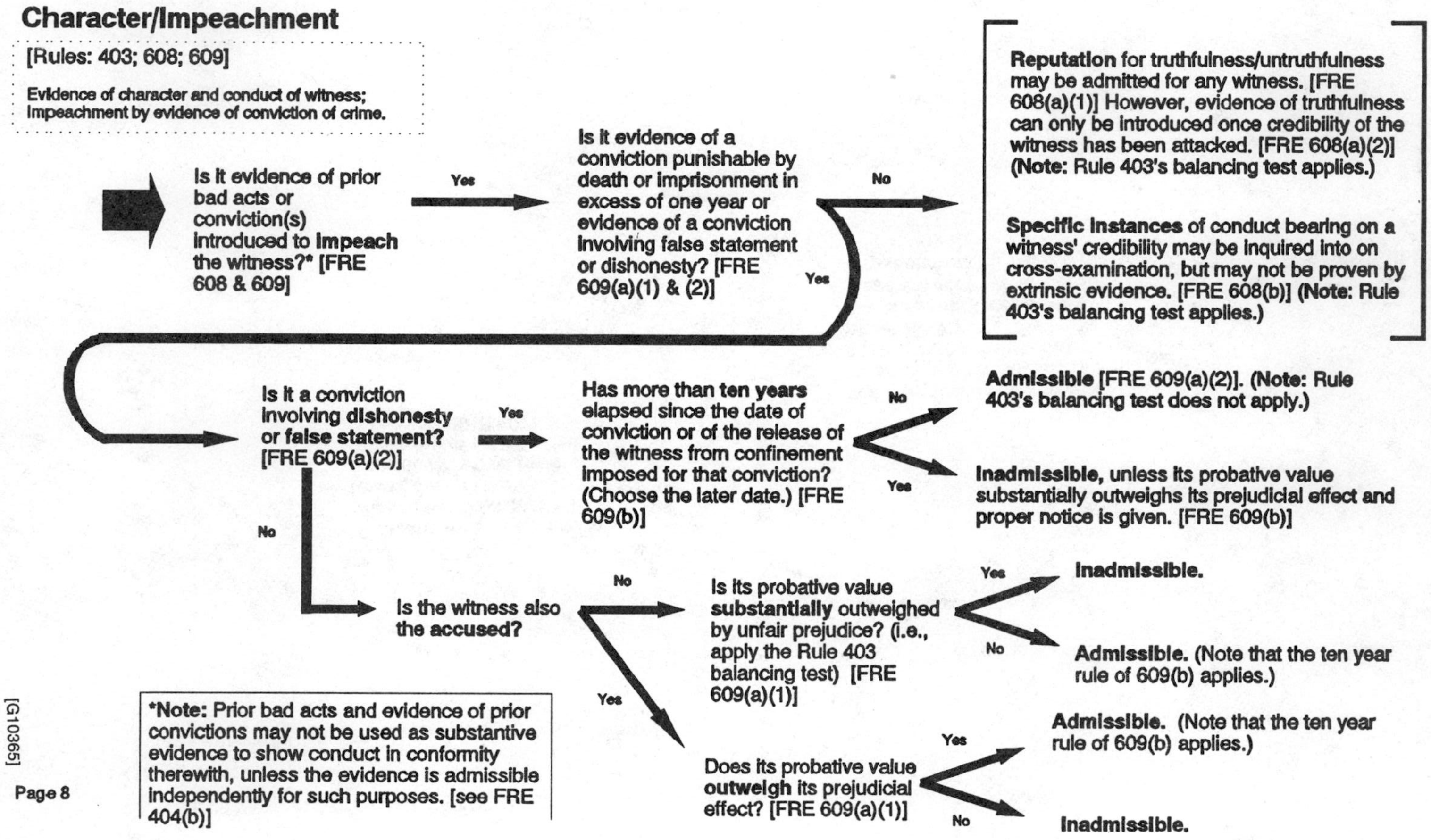
Character/Impeachment
[Rules: 403; 608; 609]
Evidence of character and conduct of witness; Impeachment by evidence of conviction of crime.
Is it evidence of prior bad acts or conviction(s) introduced to **impeach** the witness?* [FRE 608 & 609]
Yes
Is it evidence of a conviction punishable by death or imprisonment in excess of one year or evidence of a conviction involving false statement or dishonesty? [FRE 609(a)(1) & (2)]
No
Yes
Reputation for truthfulness/untruthfulness may be admitted for any witness. [FRE 608(a)(1)] However, evidence of truthfulness can only be introduced once credibility of the witness has been attacked. [FRE 608(a)(2)] (Note: Rule 403's balancing test applies.)
Specific instances of conduct bearing on a witness' credibility may be inquired into on cross-examination, but may not be proven by extrinsic evidence. [FRE 608(b)] (Note: Rule 403's balancing test applies.)
Is it a conviction involving **dishonesty** or **false statement?** [FRE 609(a)(2)]
Yes
No
Has more than **ten years** elapsed since the date of conviction or of the release of the witness from confinement imposed for that conviction? (Choose the later date.) [FRE 609(b)]
No
Yes
Admissible [FRE 609(a)(2)]. (Note: Rule 403's balancing test does not apply.)
Inadmissible, unless its probative value substantially outweighs its prejudicial effect and proper notice is given. [FRE 609(b)]
Is the witness also the **accused?**
No
Yes
Is its probative value **substantially** outweighed by unfair prejudice? (i.e., apply the Rule 403 balancing test) [FRE 609(a)(1)]
Yes
No
Inadmissible.
Admissible. (Note that the ten year rule of 609(b) applies.)
Does its probative value **outweigh** its prejudicial effect? [FRE 609(a)(1)]
Yes
No
Admissible. (Note that the ten year rule of 609(b) applies.)
Inadmissible.
*Note: Prior bad acts and evidence of prior convictions may not be used as substantive evidence to show conduct in conformity therewith, unless the evidence is admissible independently for such purposes. [see FRE 404(b)]
[G10365]
Page 8

Opinion, Expert Testimony

[Rules: 701; 702; 703; 704]
Opinion testimony by lay witnesses;
Testimony by experts;
Bases of opinion testimony by experts;
Opinion on ultimate issue.

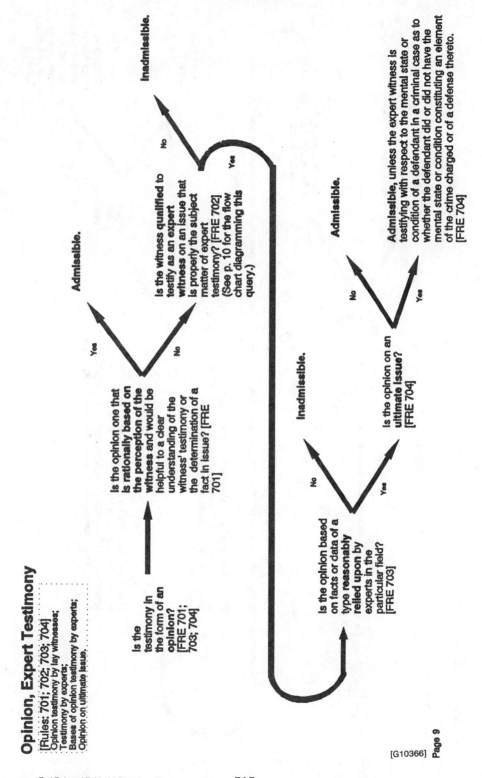

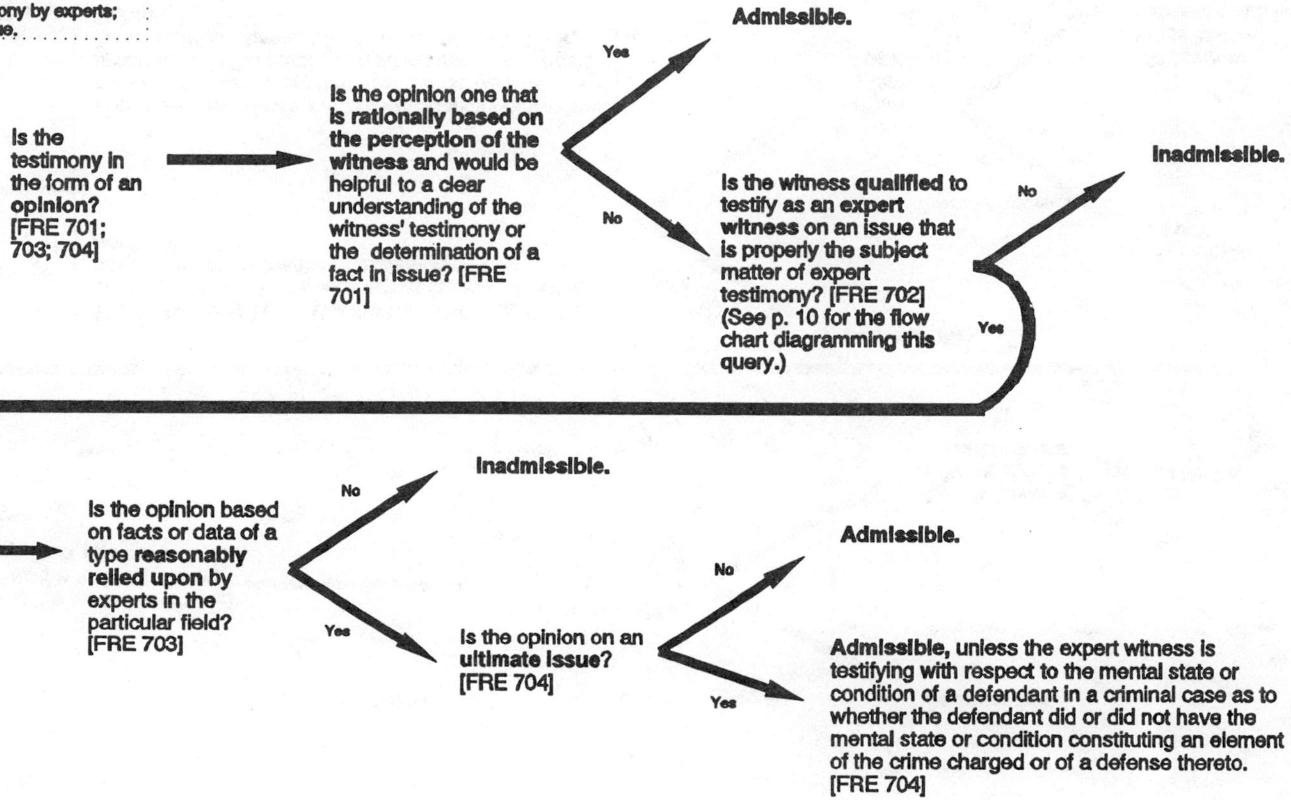

Is the testimony in the form of an opinion? [FRE 701; 703; 704]
Is the opinion one that is rationally based on the perception of the witness and would be helpful to a clear understanding of the witness' testimony or the determination of a fact in issue? [FRE 701]
Yes
Admissible.
No
Is the witness qualified to testify as an expert witness on an issue that is properly the subject matter of expert testimony? [FRE 702] (See p. 10 for the flow chart diagramming this query.)
No
Inadmissible.
Yes
Is the opinion based on facts or data of a type reasonably relied upon by experts in the particular field? [FRE 703]
No
Inadmissible.
Yes
Is the opinion on an ultimate issue? [FRE 704]
No
Admissible.
Yes
Admissible, unless the expert witness is testifying with respect to the mental state or condition of a defendant in a criminal case as to whether the defendant did or did not have the mental state or condition constituting an element of the crime charged or of a defense thereto. [FRE 704]

[G10366]
Page 9

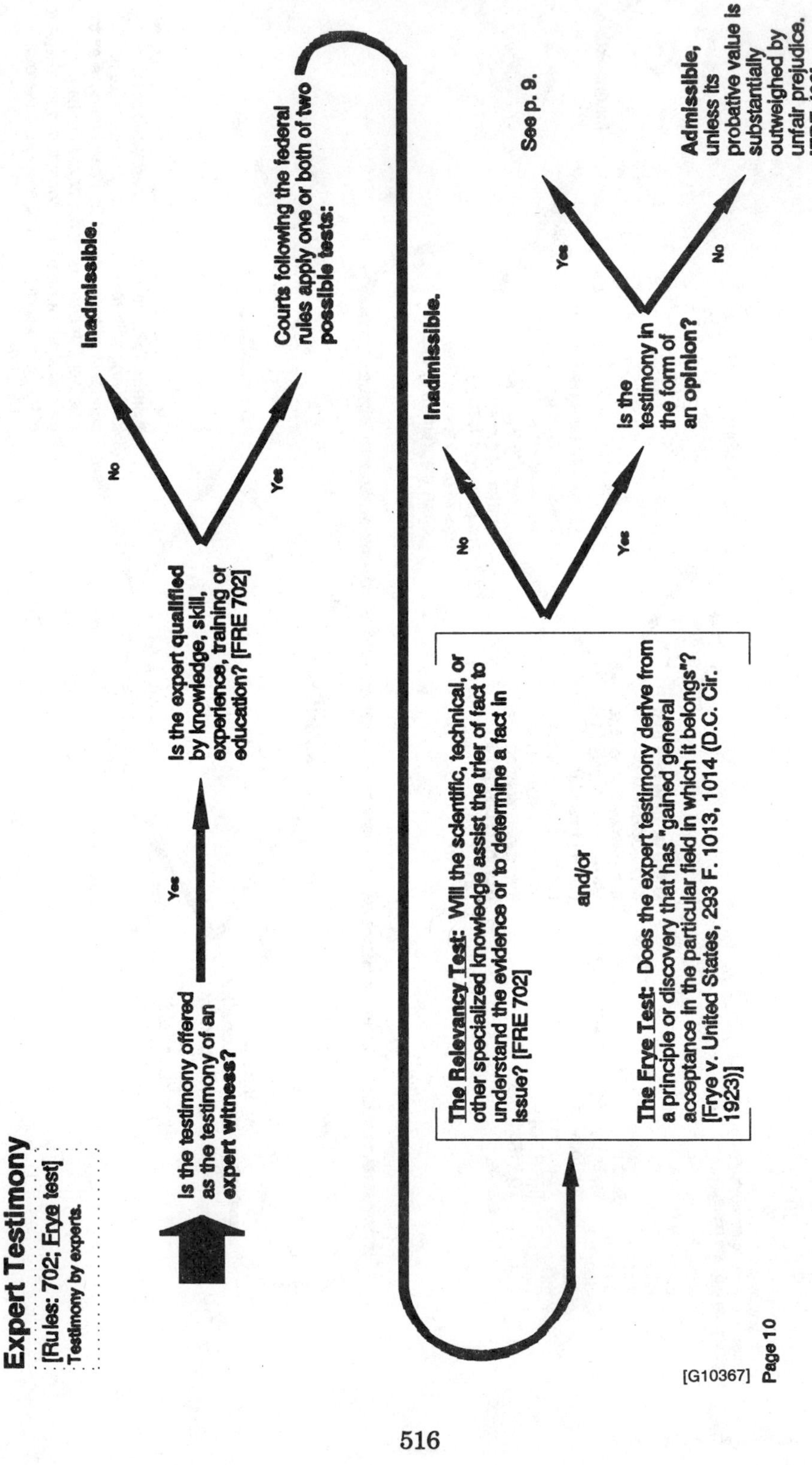
Expert Testimony
[Rules: 702; Frye test]
Testimony by experts.
Is the testimony offered as the testimony of an expert witness?
Yes
Is the expert qualified by knowledge, skill, experience, training or education? [FRE 702]
No
Inadmissible.
Yes
Courts following the federal rules apply one or both of two possible tests:
The Relevancy Test: Will the scientific, technical, or other specialized knowledge assist the trier of fact to understand the evidence or to determine a fact in issue? [FRE 702]
and/or
The Frye Test: Does the expert testimony derive from a principle or discovery that has "gained general acceptance in the particular field in which it belongs"? [Frye v. United States, 293 F. 1013, 1014 (D.C. Cir. 1923)]
No
Inadmissible.
Yes
Is the testimony in the form of an opinion?
Yes
See p. 9.
No
Admissible, unless its probative value is substantially outweighed by unfair prejudice. [FRE 403]
[G10367] Page 10

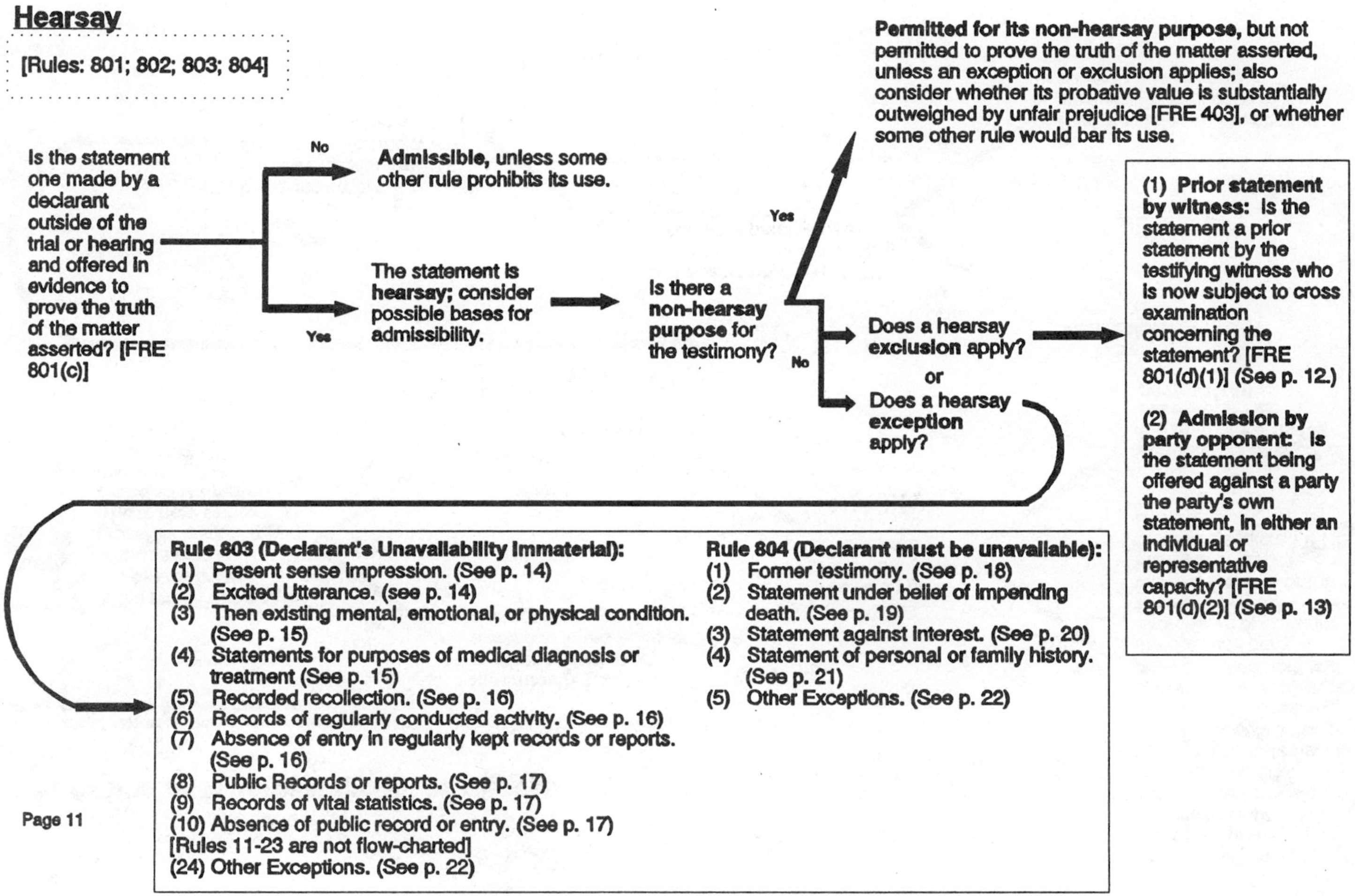
Hearsay
[Rules: 801; 802; 803; 804]
Is the statement one made by a declarant outside of the trial or hearing and offered in evidence to prove the truth of the matter asserted? [FRE 801(c)]
No
Admissible, unless some other rule prohibits its use.
Yes
The statement is hearsay; consider possible bases for admissibility.
Is there a non-hearsay purpose for the testimony?
Yes
Permitted for its non-hearsay purpose, but not permitted to prove the truth of the matter asserted, unless an exception or exclusion applies; also consider whether its probative value is substantially outweighed by unfair prejudice [FRE 403], or whether some other rule would bar its use.
No
Does a hearsay exclusion apply?
or
Does a hearsay exception apply?
(1) Prior statement by witness: Is the statement a prior statement by the testifying witness who is now subject to cross examination concerning the statement? [FRE 801(d)(1)] (See p. 12.)
(2) Admission by party opponent: Is the statement being offered against a party the party's own statement, in either an individual or representative capacity? [FRE 801(d)(2)] (See p. 13)
Rule 803 (Declarant's Unavailability Immaterial):
(1) Present sense impression. (See p. 14)
(2) Excited Utterance. (see p. 14)
(3) Then existing mental, emotional, or physical condition. (See p. 15)
(4) Statements for purposes of medical diagnosis or treatment (See p. 15)
(5) Recorded recollection. (See p. 16)
(6) Records of regularly conducted activity. (See p. 16)
(7) Absence of entry in regularly kept records or reports. (See p. 16)
(8) Public Records or reports. (See p. 17)
(9) Records of vital statistics. (See p. 17)
(10) Absence of public record or entry. (See p. 17)
[Rules 11-23 are not flow-charted]
(24) Other Exceptions. (See p. 22)
Rule 804 (Declarant must be unavailable):
(1) Former testimony. (See p. 18)
(2) Statement under belief of impending death. (See p. 19)
(3) Statement against interest. (See p. 20)
(4) Statement of personal or family history. (See p. 21)
(5) Other Exceptions. (See p. 22)
Page 11

[G10368]

Hearsay exclusions; Impeachment of witness

[Rule: 613; 801(d)(1)]

Prior statements of witnesses (Impeachment purposes);
Prior statement of witness (Hearsay exclusion).

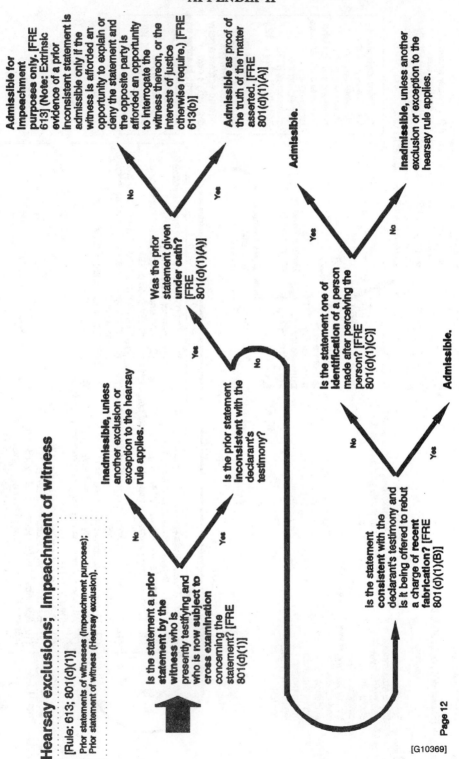

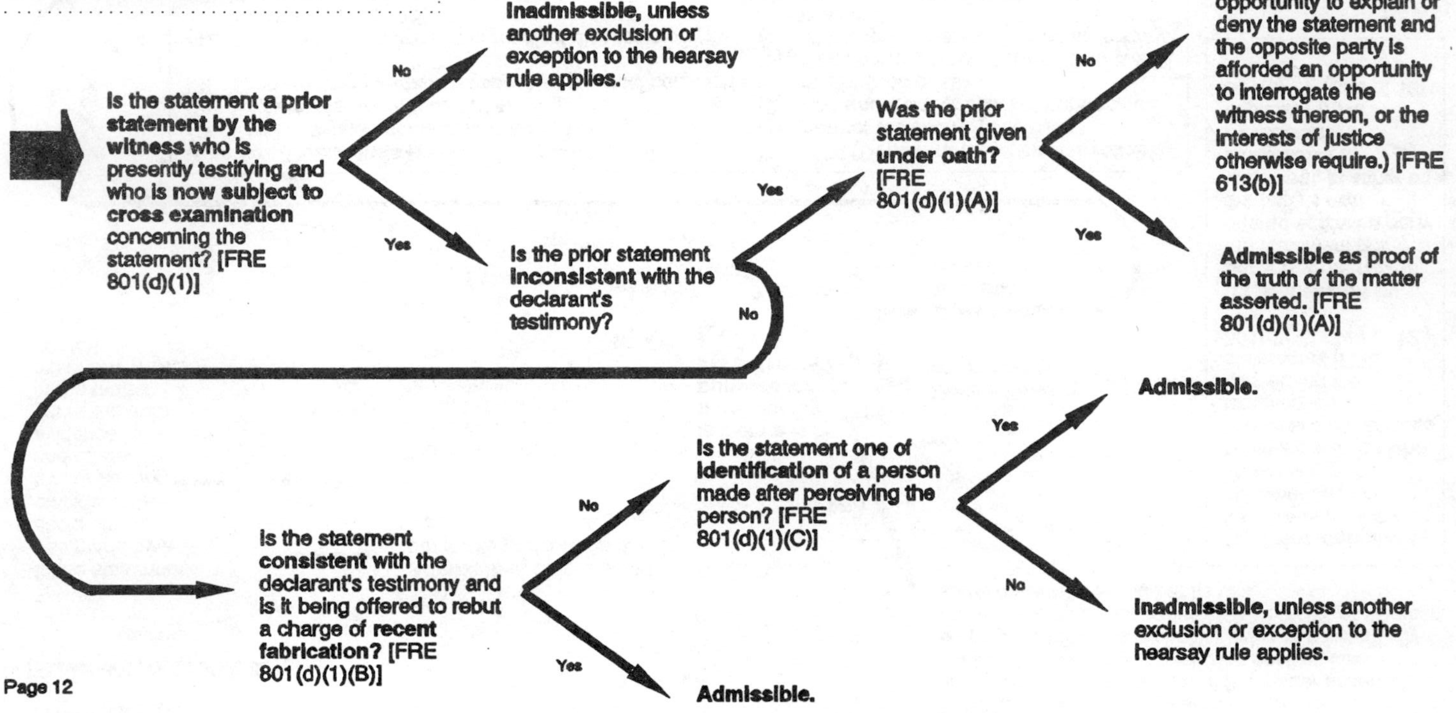
Is the statement a prior statement by the witness who is presently testifying and who is now subject to cross examination concerning the statement? [FRE 801(d)(1)]
No
Inadmissible, unless another exclusion or exception to the hearsay rule applies.
Yes
Is the prior statement inconsistent with the declarant's testimony?
Yes
Was the prior statement given under oath? [FRE 801(d)(1)(A)]
No
Admissible for impeachment purposes only. [FRE 613] (Note: Extrinsic evidence of a prior inconsistent statement is admissible only if the witness is afforded an opportunity to explain or deny the statement and the opposite party is afforded an opportunity to interrogate the witness thereon, or the interests of justice otherwise require.) [FRE 613(b)]
Yes
Admissible as proof of the truth of the matter asserted. [FRE 801(d)(1)(A)]
No
Is the statement consistent with the declarant's testimony and is it being offered to rebut a charge of recent fabrication? [FRE 801(d)(1)(B)]
Yes
Admissible.
No
Is the statement one of identification of a person made after perceiving the person? [FRE 801(d)(1)(C)]
Yes
Admissible.
No
Inadmissible, unless another exclusion or exception to the hearsay rule applies.

Page 12

[G10369]

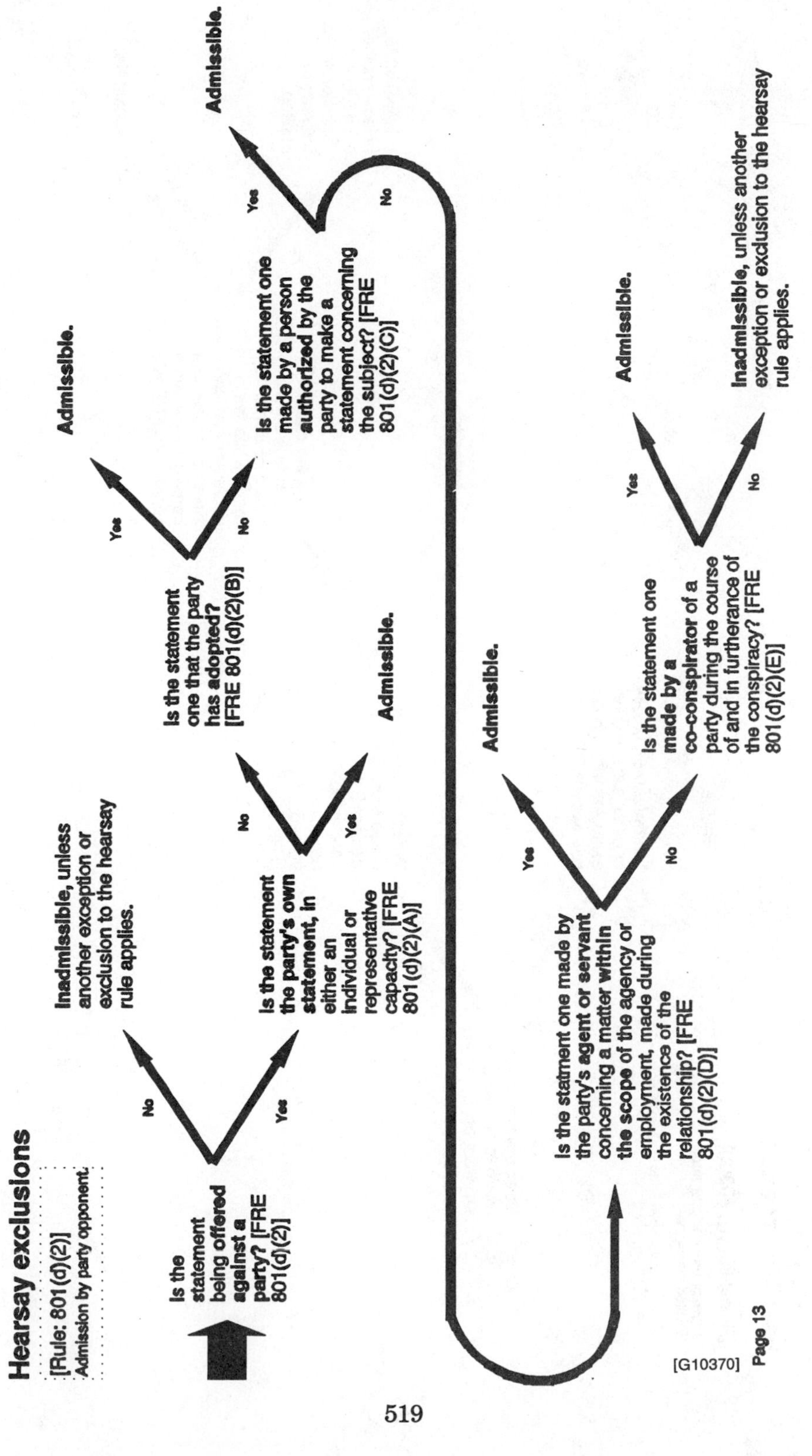
Hearsay exclusions
[Rule: 801(d)(2)]
Admission by party opponent.
Is the statement being offered against a party? [FRE 801(d)(2)]
No
Inadmissible, unless another exception or exclusion to the hearsay rule applies.
Yes
Is the statement the party's own statement, in either an individual or representative capacity? [FRE 801(d)(2)(A)]
Yes
Admissible.
No
Is the statement one that the party has adopted? [FRE 801(d)(2)(B)]
Yes
Admissible.
No
Is the statement one made by a person authorized by the party to make a statement concerning the subject? [FRE 801(d)(2)(C)]
Yes
Admissible.
No
Is the statment one made by the party's agent or servant concerning a matter within the scope of the agency or employment, made during the existence of the relationship? [FRE 801(d)(2)(D)]
Yes
Admissible.
No
Is the statement one made by a co-conspirator of a party during the course of and in furtherance of the conspiracy? [FRE 801(d)(2)(E)]
Yes
Admissible.
No
Inadmissible, unless another exception or exclusion to the hearsay rule applies.
[G10370]
Page 13

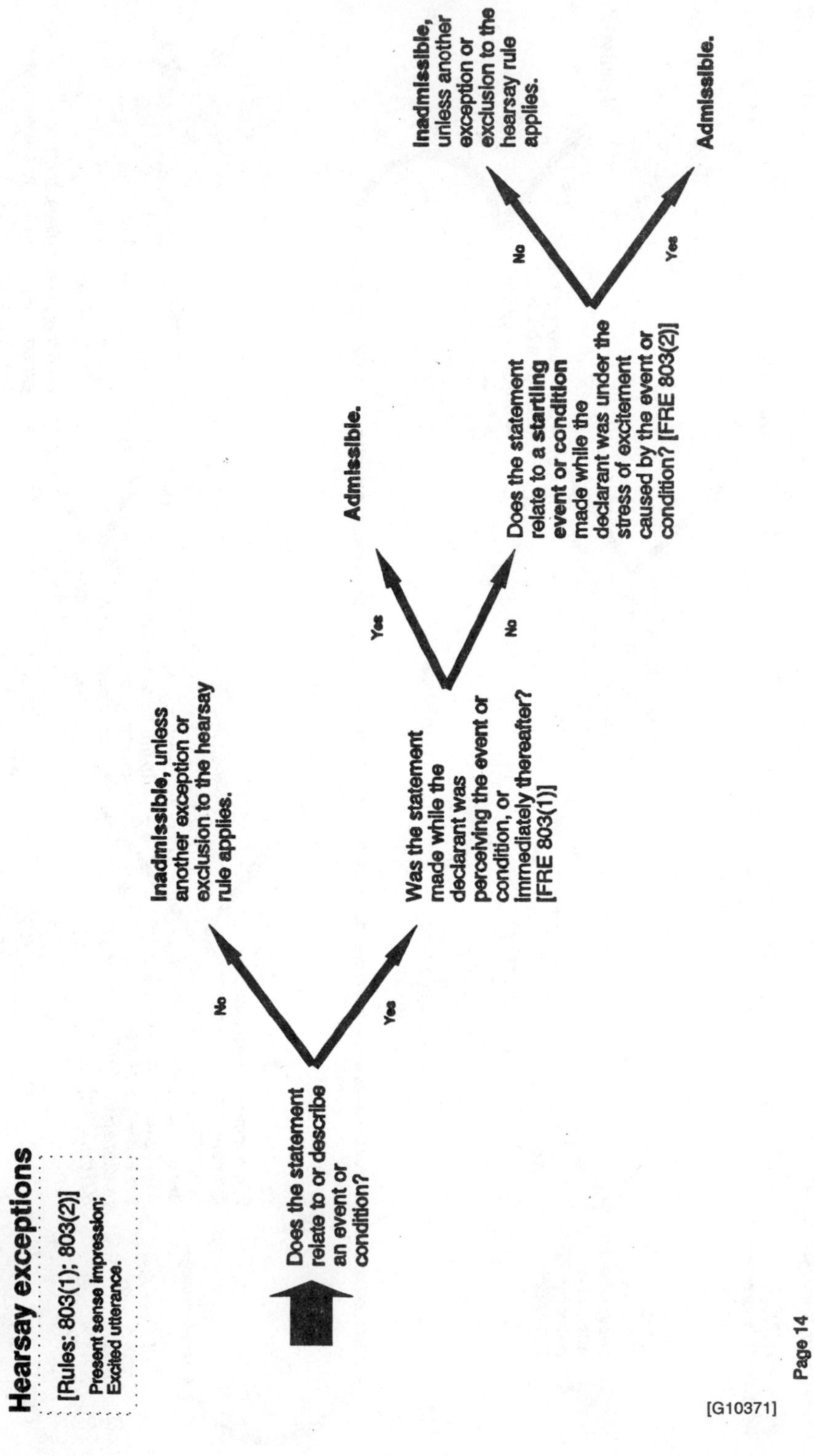
Hearsay exceptions
[Rules: 803(1); 803(2)]
Present sense impression; Excited utterance.
Does the statement relate to or describe an event or condition?
No
Inadmissible, unless another exception or exclusion to the hearsay rule applies.
Yes
Was the statement made while the declarant was perceiving the event or condition, or immediately thereafter? [FRE 803(1)]
Yes
Admissible.
No
Does the statement relate to a startling event or condition made while the declarant was under the stress of excitement caused by the event or condition? [FRE 803(2)]
No
Inadmissible, unless another exception or exclusion to the hearsay rule applies.
Yes
Admissible.
[G10371]
Page 14

Hearsay exceptions

[Rules: 803(3); 803(4)]

Then existing mental, emotional, or physical condition;
Statements for purposes of medical diagnosis or treatments.

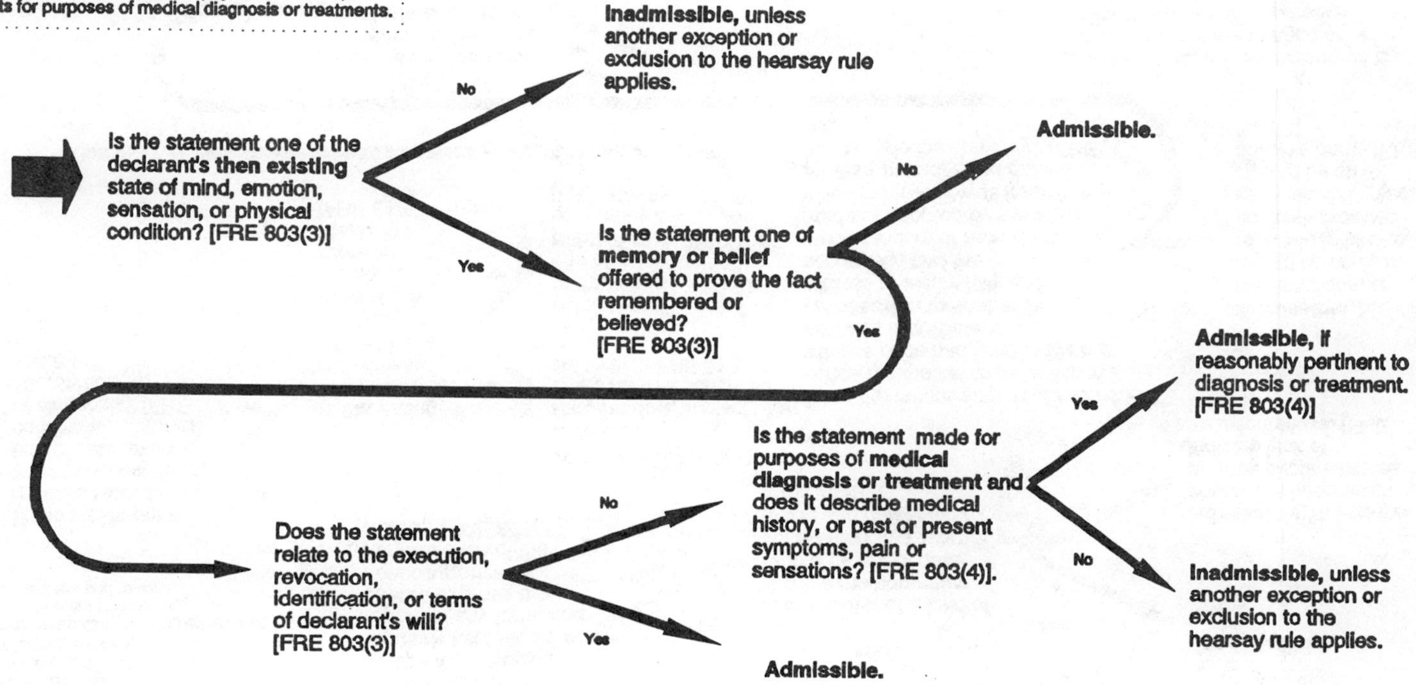
Is the statement one of the declarant's then existing state of mind, emotion, sensation, or physical condition? [FRE 803(3)]
No
Inadmissible, unless another exception or exclusion to the hearsay rule applies.
Yes
Is the statement one of memory or belief offered to prove the fact remembered or believed? [FRE 803(3)]
No
Admissible.
Yes
Does the statement relate to the execution, revocation, identification, or terms of declarant's will? [FRE 803(3)]
Yes
Admissible.
No
Is the statement made for purposes of medical diagnosis or treatment and does it describe medical history, or past or present symptoms, pain or sensations? [FRE 803(4)].
Yes
Admissible, if reasonably pertinent to diagnosis or treatment. [FRE 803(4)]
No
Inadmissible, unless another exception or exclusion to the hearsay rule applies.

Page 15

[G10372]

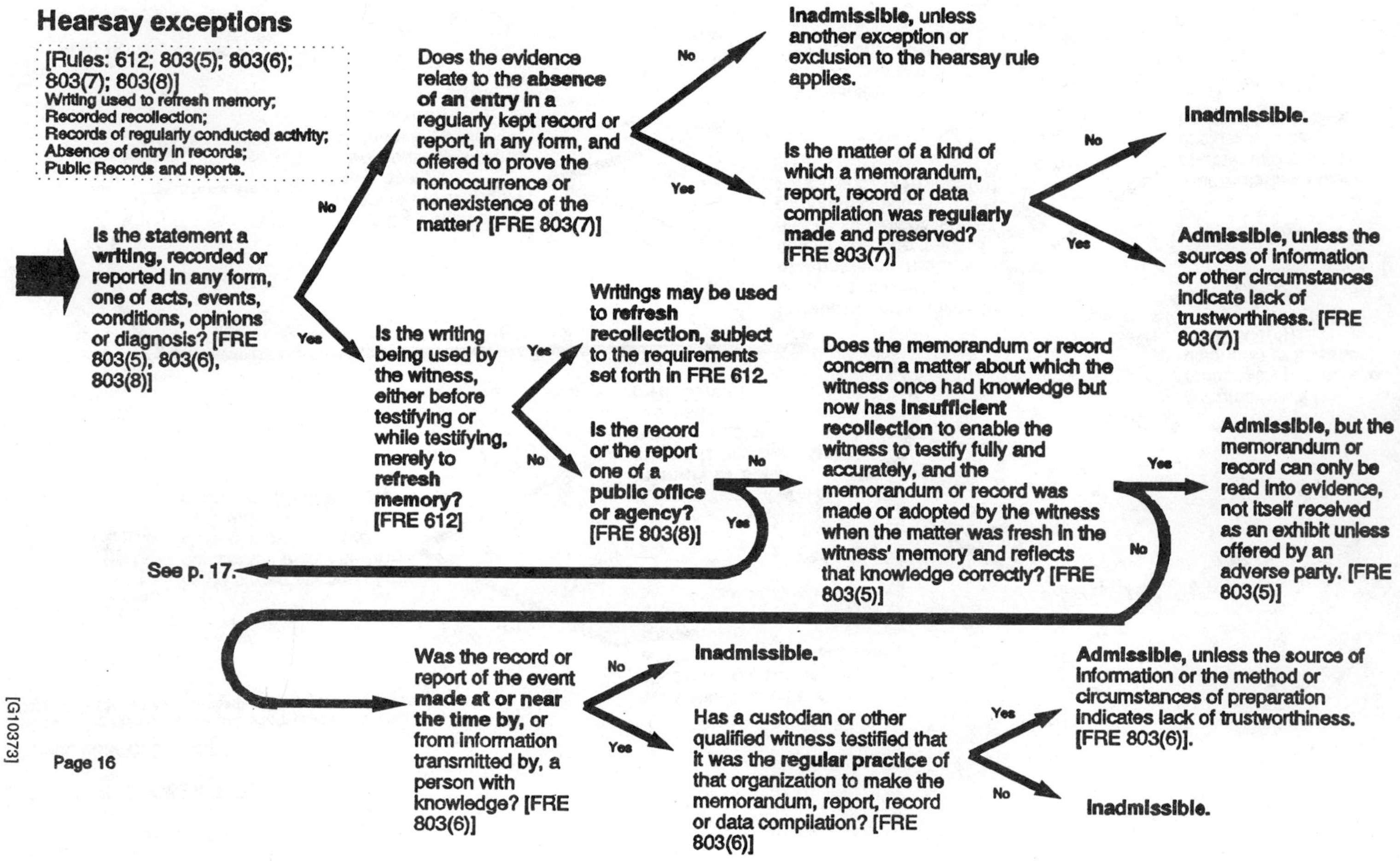
Hearsay exceptions
[Rules: 612; 803(5); 803(6); 803(7); 803(8)]
Writing used to refresh memory;
Recorded recollection;
Records of regularly conducted activity;
Absence of entry in records;
Public Records and reports.
Is the statement a writing, recorded or reported in any form, one of acts, events, conditions, opinions or diagnosis? [FRE 803(5), 803(6), 803(8)]
No
Yes
Does the evidence relate to the absence of an entry in a regularly kept record or report, in any form, and offered to prove the nonoccurrence or nonexistence of the matter? [FRE 803(7)]
No
Yes
Inadmissible, unless another exception or exclusion to the hearsay rule applies.
Is the matter of a kind of which a memorandum, report, record or data compilation was regularly made and preserved? [FRE 803(7)]
No
Yes
Inadmissible.
Admissible, unless the sources of information or other circumstances indicate lack of trustworthiness. [FRE 803(7)]
Is the writing being used by the witness, either before testifying or while testifying, merely to refresh memory? [FRE 612]
Yes
No
Writings may be used to refresh recollection, subject to the requirements set forth in FRE 612.
Is the record or the report one of a public office or agency? [FRE 803(8)]
No
Yes
See p. 17.
Does the memorandum or record concern a matter about which the witness once had knowledge but now has insufficient recollection to enable the witness to testify fully and accurately, and the memorandum or record was made or adopted by the witness when the matter was fresh in the witness' memory and reflects that knowledge correctly? [FRE 803(5)]
Yes
No
Admissible, but the memorandum or record can only be read into evidence, not itself received as an exhibit unless offered by an adverse party. [FRE 803(5)]
Was the record or report of the event made at or near the time by, or from information transmitted by, a person with knowledge? [FRE 803(6)]
No
Yes
Inadmissible.
Has a custodian or other qualified witness testified that it was the regular practice of that organization to make the memorandum, report, record or data compilation? [FRE 803(6)]
Yes
No
Admissible, unless the source of information or the method or circumstances of preparation indicates lack of trustworthiness. [FRE 803(6)].
Inadmissible.
Page 16
[G10373]

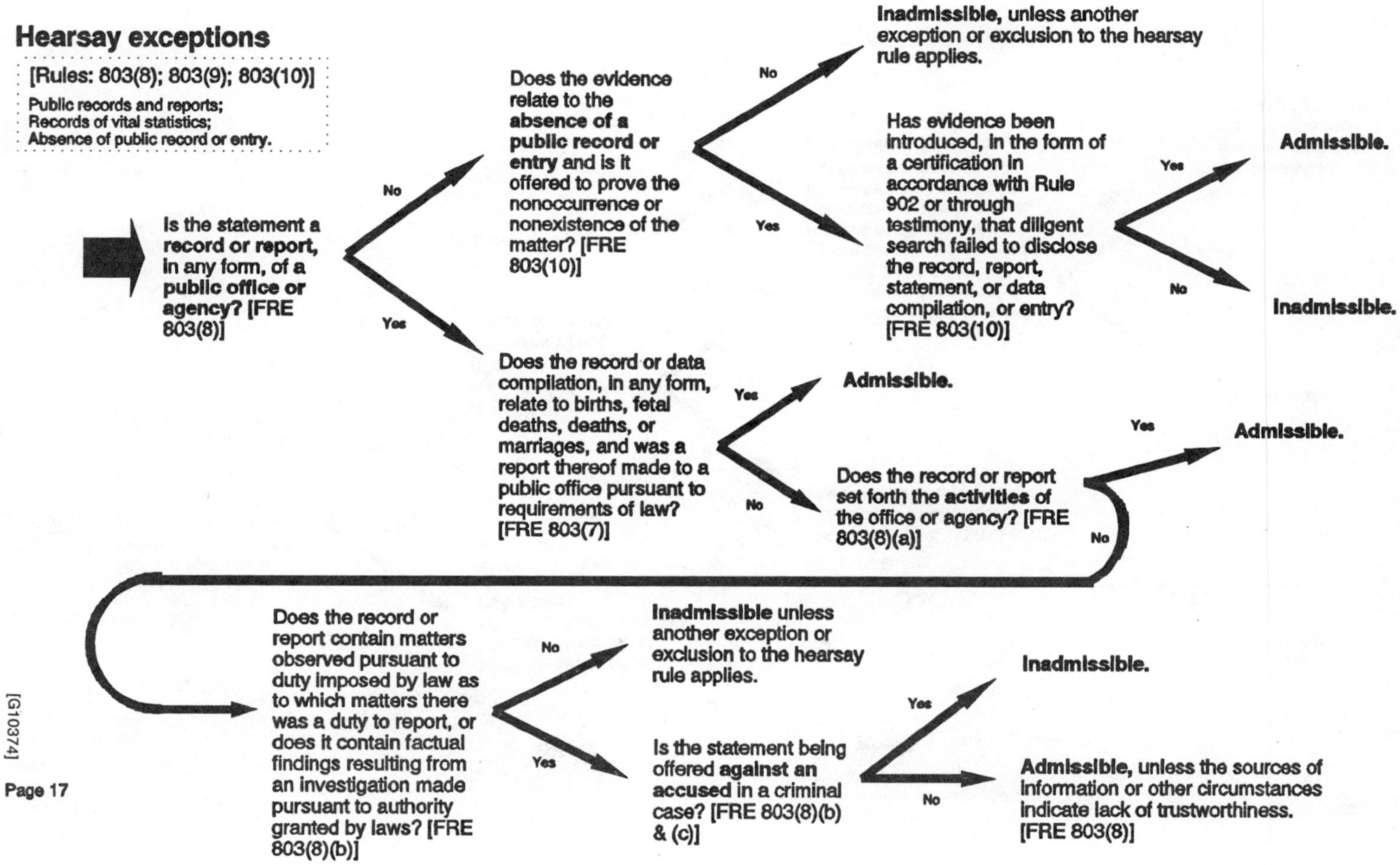
Hearsay exceptions
[Rules: 803(8); 803(9); 803(10)]
Public records and reports;
Records of vital statistics;
Absence of public record or entry.
Is the statement a record or report, in any form, of a public office or agency? [FRE 803(8)]
No
Yes
Does the evidence relate to the absence of a public record or entry and is it offered to prove the nonoccurrence or nonexistence of the matter? [FRE 803(10)]
No
Inadmissible, unless another exception or exclusion to the hearsay rule applies.
Yes
Has evidence been introduced, in the form of a certification in accordance with Rule 902 or through testimony, that diligent search failed to disclose the record, report, statement, or data compilation, or entry? [FRE 803(10)]
Yes
Admissible.
No
Inadmissible.
Does the record or data compilation, in any form, relate to births, fetal deaths, deaths, or marriages, and was a report thereof made to a public office pursuant to requirements of law? [FRE 803(7)]
Yes
Admissible.
No
Does the record or report set forth the activities of the office or agency? [FRE 803(8)(a)]
Yes
Admissible.
No
Does the record or report contain matters observed pursuant to duty imposed by law as to which matters there was a duty to report, or does it contain factual findings resulting from an investigation made pursuant to authority granted by laws? [FRE 803(8)(b)]
No
Inadmissible unless another exception or exclusion to the hearsay rule applies.
Yes
Is the statement being offered against an accused in a criminal case? [FRE 803(8)(b) & (c)]
Yes
Inadmissible.
No
Admissible, unless the sources of information or other circumstances indicate lack of trustworthiness. [FRE 803(8)]

[G10374]

Page 17

Hearsay exceptions

[Rules: 804(a); 804(b)(1)]

Former testimony.

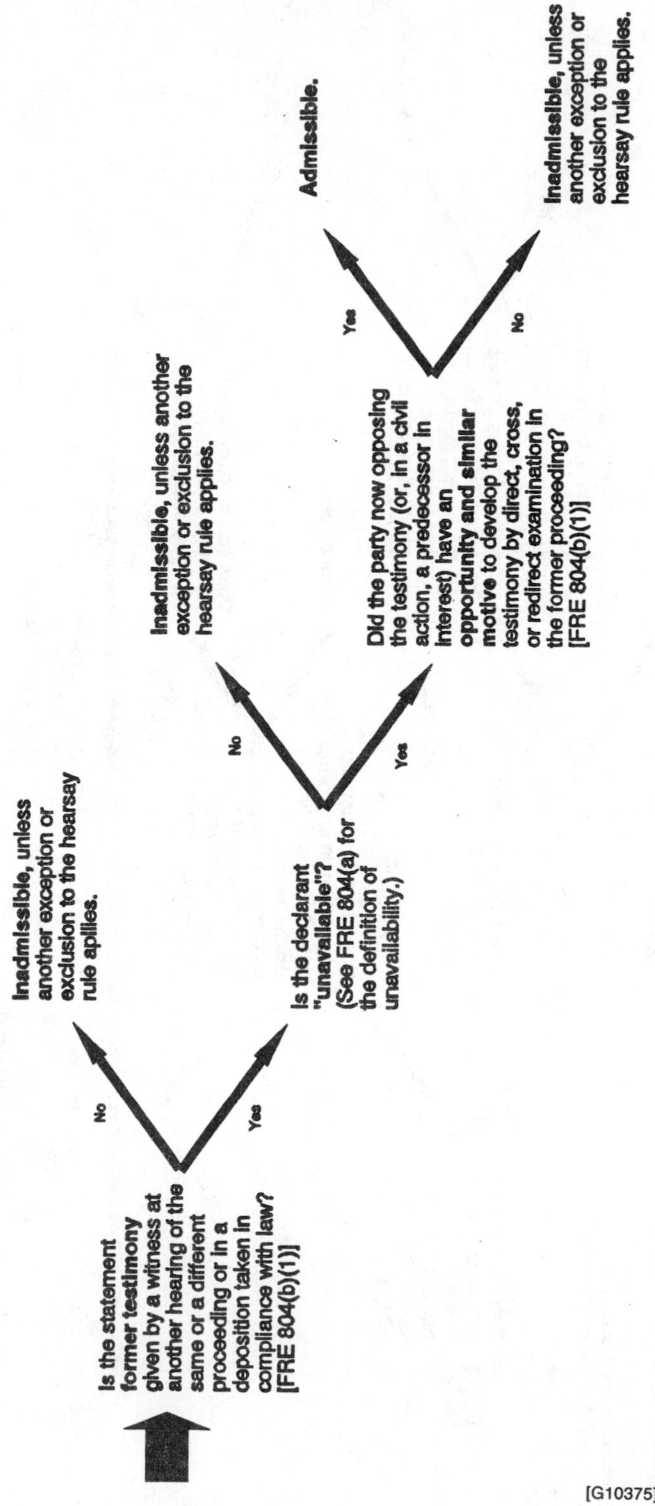
Is the statement former testimony given by a witness at another hearing of the same or a different proceeding or in a deposition taken in compliance with law? [FRE 804(b)(1)]
No
Inadmissible, unless another exception or exclusion to the hearsay rule aplies.
Yes
Is the declarant "unavailable"? (See FRE 804(a) for the definition of unavailability.)
No
Inadmissible, unless another exception or exclusion to the hearsay rule applies.
Yes
Did the party now opposing the testimony (or, in a civil action, a predecessor in interest) have an opportunity and similar motive to develop the testimony by direct, cross, or redirect examination in the former proceeding? [FRE 804(b)(1)]
Yes
Admissible.
No
Inadmissible, unless another exception or exclusion to the hearsay rule applies.

[G10375] Page 18

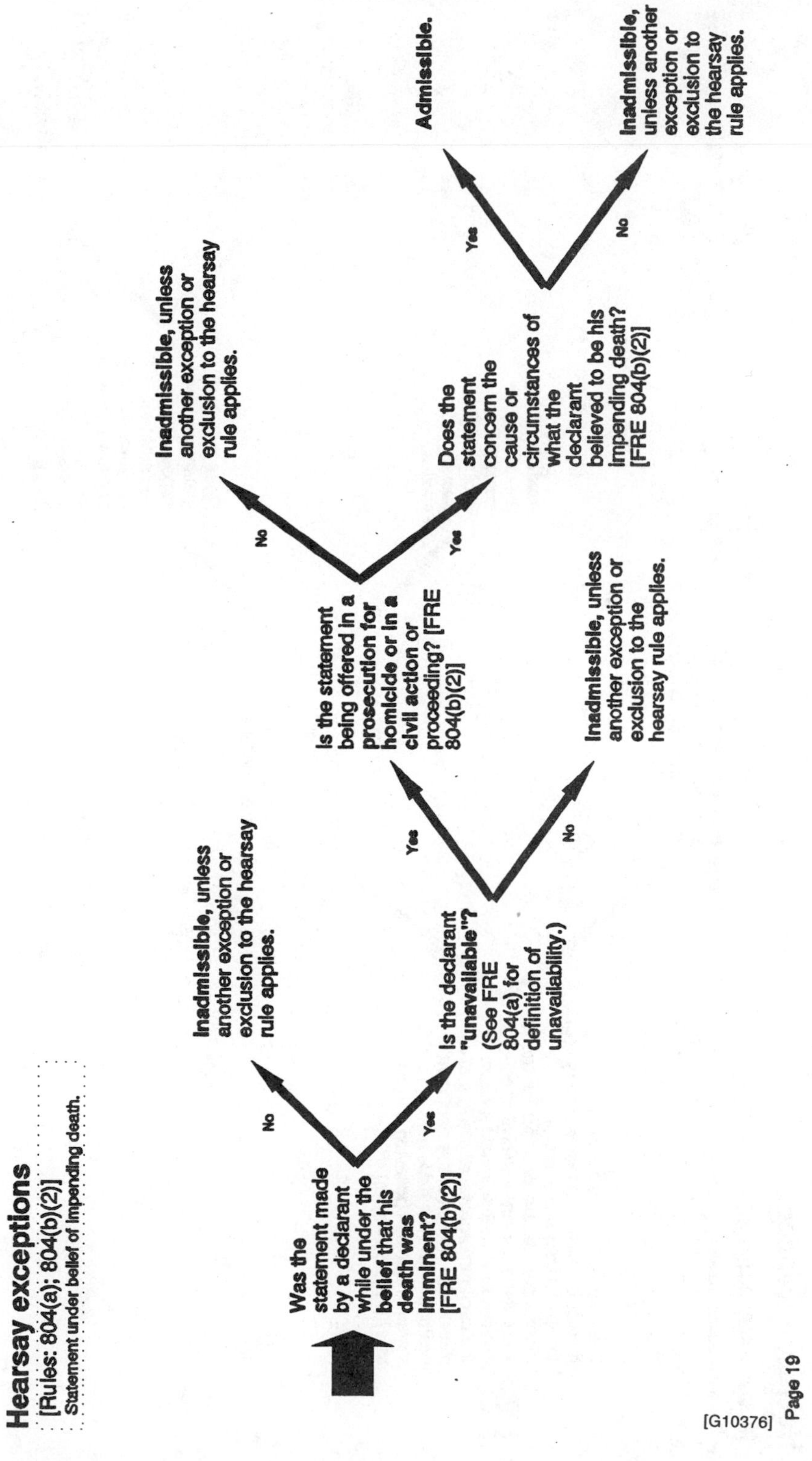
Hearsay exceptions
[Rules: 804(a); 804(b)(2)]
Statement under belief of impending death.
Was the statement made by a declarant while under the belief that his death was imminent? [FRE 804(b)(2)]
No
Inadmissible, unless another exception or exclusion to the hearsay rule applies.
Yes
Is the declarant "unavailable"? (See FRE 804(a) for definition of unavailability.)
No
Inadmissible, unless another exception or exclusion to the hearsay rule applies.
Yes
Is the statement being offered in a prosecution for homicide or in a civil action or proceeding? [FRE 804(b)(2)]
No
Inadmissible, unless another exception or exclusion to the hearsay rule applies.
Yes
Does the statement concern the cause or circumstances of what the declarant believed to be his impending death? [FRE 804(b)(2)]
Yes
Admissible.
No
Inadmissible, unless another exception or exclusion to the hearsay rule applies.
[G10376]
Page 19

Hearsay exceptions

[Rules: 804(a); 804(b)(3)]

Statement against interest.

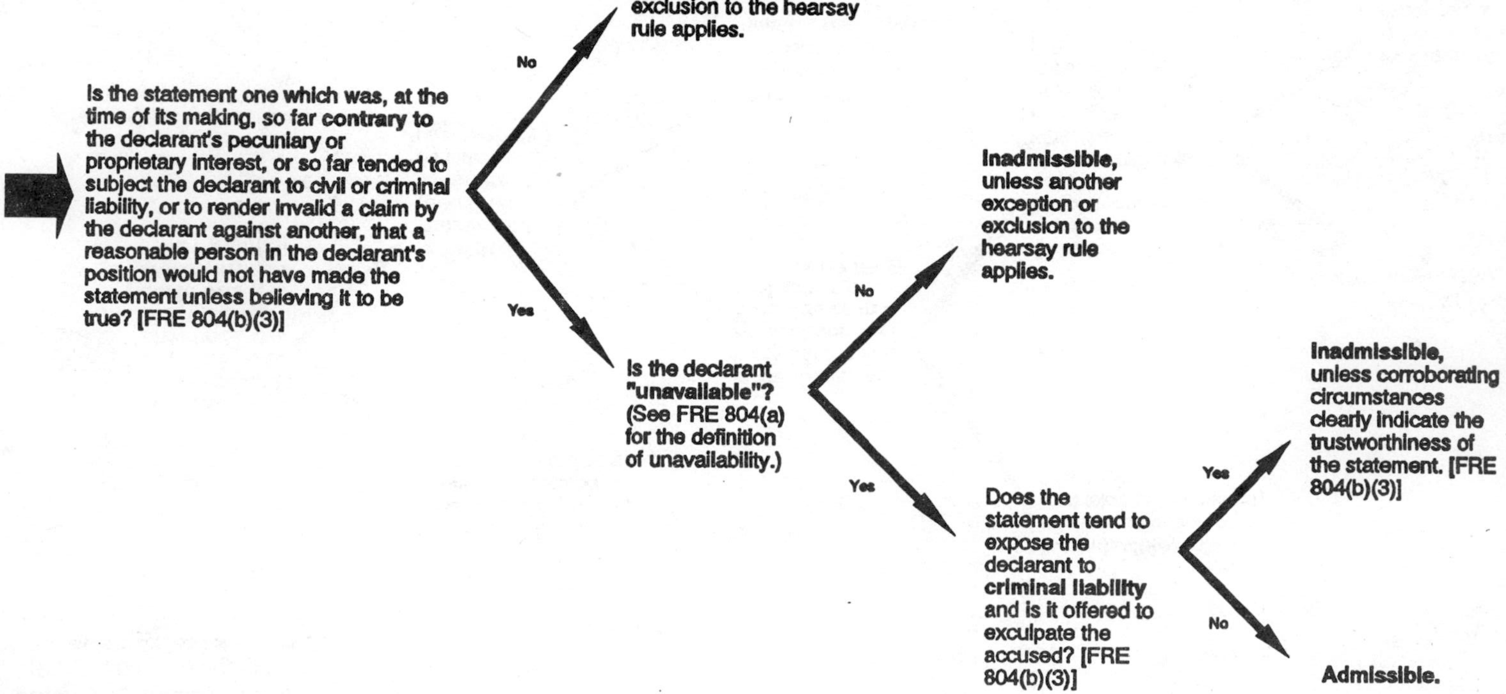
Is the statement one which was, at the time of its making, so far contrary to the declarant's pecuniary or proprietary interest, or so far tended to subject the declarant to civil or criminal liability, or to render invalid a claim by the declarant against another, that a reasonable person in the declarant's position would not have made the statement unless believing it to be true? [FRE 804(b)(3)]
No
Inadmissible, unless another exception or exclusion to the hearsay rule applies.
Yes
Is the declarant "unavailable"? (See FRE 804(a) for the definition of unavailability.)
No
Inadmissible, unless another exception or exclusion to the hearsay rule applies.
Yes
Does the statement tend to expose the declarant to criminal liability and is it offered to exculpate the accused? [FRE 804(b)(3)]
Yes
Inadmissible, unless corroborating circumstances clearly indicate the trustworthiness of the statement. [FRE 804(b)(3)]
No
Admissible.

[G10377]

Page 20

Hearsay exceptions

[Rules: 804(a); 804(b)(4)]

Statement of personal or family history.

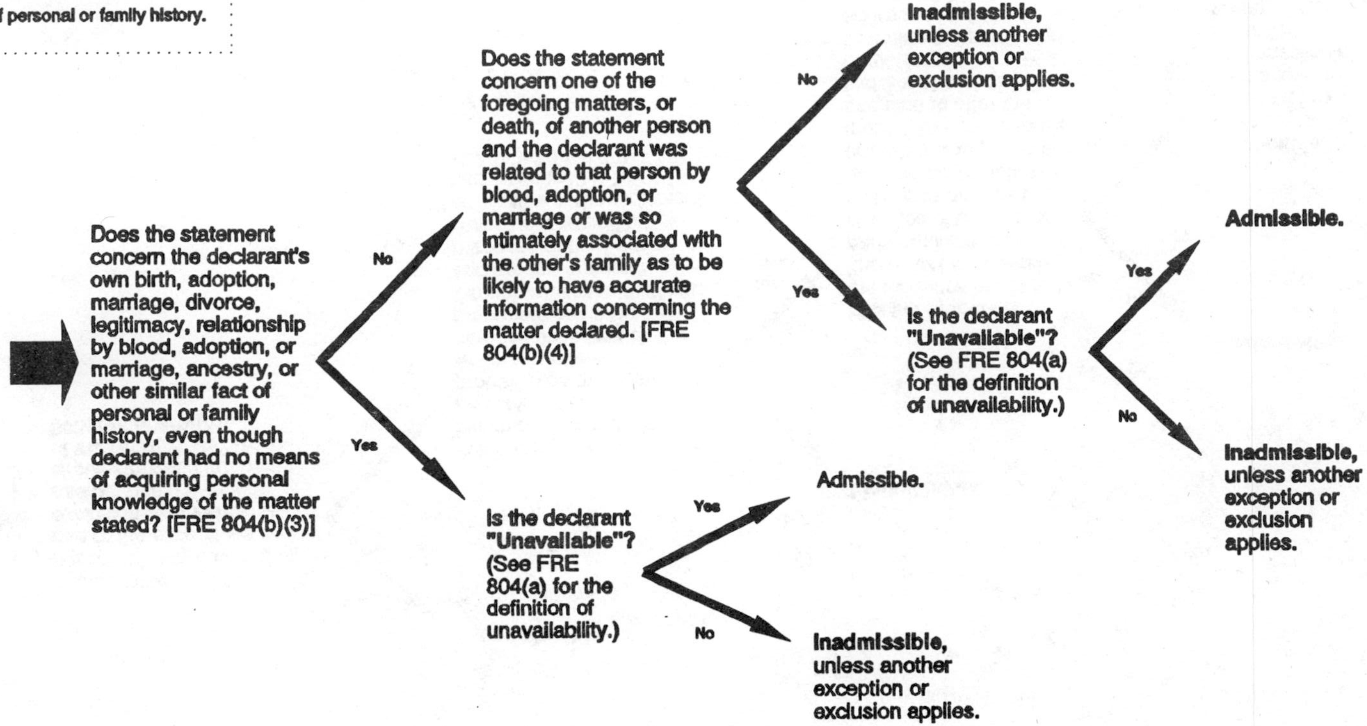
Does the statement concern the declarant's own birth, adoption, marriage, divorce, legitimacy, relationship by blood, adoption, or marriage, ancestry, or other similar fact of personal or family history, even though declarant had no means of acquiring personal knowledge of the matter stated? [FRE 804(b)(3)]
No
Yes
Does the statement concern one of the foregoing matters, or death, of another person and the declarant was related to that person by blood, adoption, or marriage or was so intimately associated with the other's family as to be likely to have accurate information concerning the matter declared. [FRE 804(b)(4)]
No
Inadmissible, unless another exception or exclusion applies.
Yes
Is the declarant "Unavailable"? (See FRE 804(a) for the definition of unavailability.)
Yes
Admissible.
No
Inadmissible, unless another exception or exclusion applies.
Is the declarant "Unavailable"? (See FRE 804(a) for the definition of unavailability.)
Yes
Admissible.
No
Inadmissible, unless another exception or exclusion applies.

[G10378]

Page 21

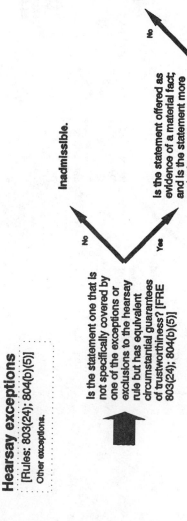

Hearsay exceptions

[Rules: 803(24); 804(b)(5)]
Other exceptions.

Is the statement one that is not specifically covered by one of the exceptions or exclusions to the hearsay rule but has equivalent circumstantial guarantees of trustworthiness? [FRE 803(24); 804(b)(5)]

- No → **Inadmissible.**
- Yes → Is the statement offered as evidence of a material fact; and is the statement more probative on the point for which it is offered than any other evidence which the proponent can procure through reasonable efforts; and are the general purposes of the Federal Rules best served by admission of the statement into evidence? [FRE 803(24); 804(b)(5)]
  - No → **Inadmissible.**
  - Yes → Has the proponent of the evidence made it known to the adverse party sufficiently in advance of the trial or hearing to provide the adverse party with a fair opportunity to prepare to meet it, the proponent's intention to offer the statement and the particulars of it, including the name and address of the declarant? [FRE 803(24); 804(b)(5)]
    - No → **Inadmissible.**
    - Yes → **Admissible.** (Note that if the declarant has been shown to be "unavailable" under FRE 804(a), FRE 804(b)(5) applies; if not, 803(24) applies.)

[G10379] Page 22

FLOW CHART

Best Evidence Rule

[Rules: 1001; 1002; 1003; 1004]
Definitions;
Requirement of original;
Admissibility of duplicates;
Admissibility of other evidence of contents.

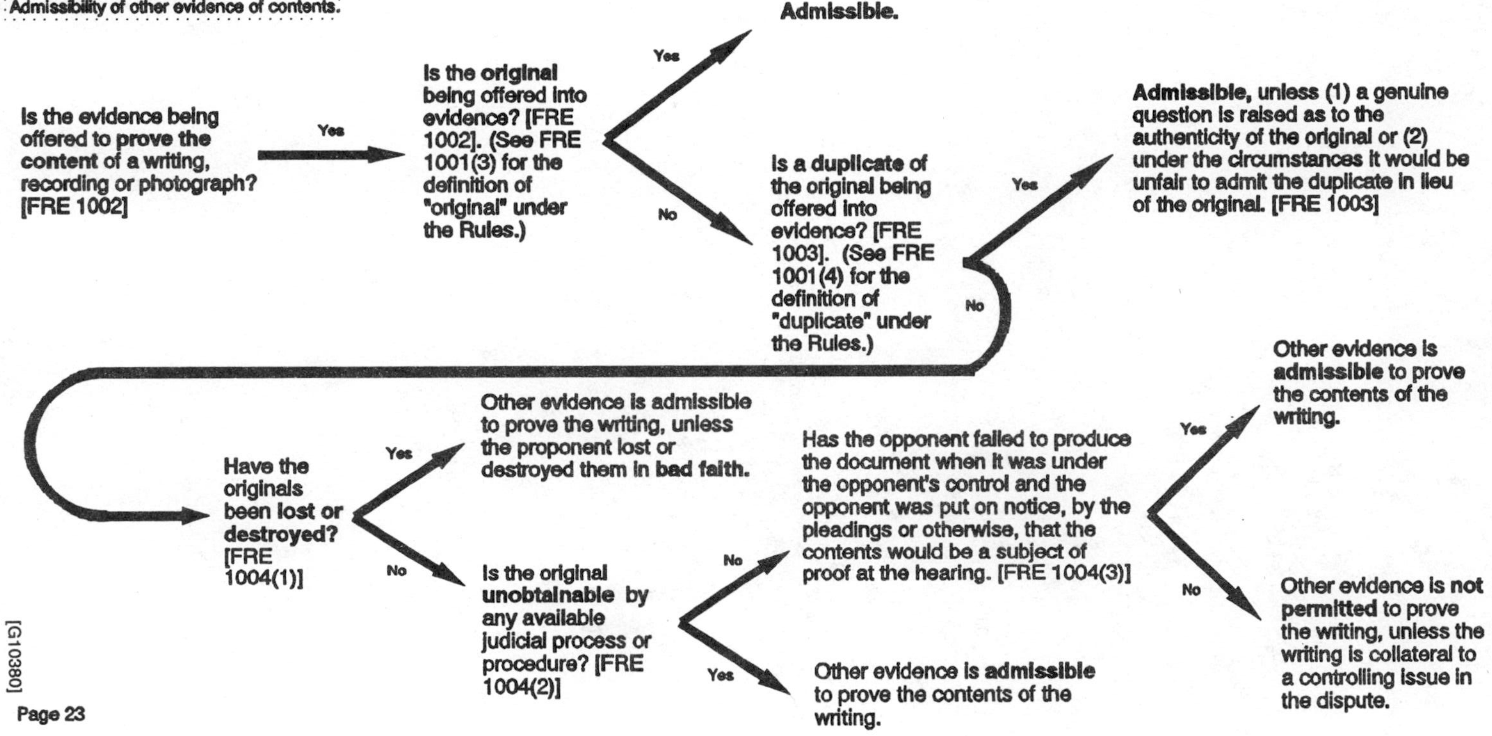
Is the evidence being offered to **prove the content of a writing**, recording or photograph? [FRE 1002]
Yes
Is the **original** being offered into evidence? [FRE 1002]. (See FRE 1001(3) for the definition of "original" under the Rules.)
Yes
No
Admissible.
Is a **duplicate** of the original being offered into evidence? [FRE 1003]. (See FRE 1001(4) for the definition of "duplicate" under the Rules.)
Yes
No
Admissible, unless (1) a genuine question is raised as to the authenticity of the original or (2) under the circumstances it would be unfair to admit the duplicate in lieu of the original. [FRE 1003]
Have the originals been **lost or destroyed?** [FRE 1004(1)]
Yes
No
Other evidence is admissible to prove the writing, unless the proponent lost or destroyed them in **bad faith.**
Is the original **unobtainable** by any available judicial process or procedure? [FRE 1004(2)]
No
Yes
Has the opponent failed to produce the document when it was under the opponent's control and the opponent was put on notice, by the pleadings or otherwise, that the contents would be a subject of proof at the hearing. [FRE 1004(3)]
Other evidence is **admissible** to prove the contents of the writing.
Yes
No
Other evidence is **admissible** to prove the contents of the writing.
Other evidence is **not permitted** to prove the writing, unless the writing is collateral to a controlling issue in the dispute.

[G10380]
Page 23

Appendix III
ELECTRONIC RESEARCH IN EVIDENCE

Analysis

Section 1. Introduction

Analyzing an evidence problem can be a complex task, calling for the examination of case law, statutes, court rules and orders, administrative pronouncements and commentary. WESTLAW is an efficient vehicle for such extended research.

WESTLAW evidence databases contain rules, commentaries, statutes, cases and administrative materials. Each database is assigned an identifier, which you use to access the database. You can find identifiers for all WESTLAW databases in the WESTLAW Directory and in the *WESTLAW Database List.* When you need to know more detailed information about a database, use the SCOPE command. SCOPE displays unique commands and related databases for each WESTLAW database and service.

You can retrieve documents on WESTLAW by accessing a database and entering a query; by using FIND, a one-step document retrieval service; or by using such services as Insta–Cite ®, Shepard's Citations ®, Shepard's PreView ™ and Quick*Cite* ™. You can also use West's menu-driven research system, EZ ACCESS ™, for additional help.

APPENDIX III

Additional Resources

If you have not used WESTLAW or have questions not addressed in this appendix, see the *WESTLAW Reference Manual* or contact the West Reference Attorneys at 1-800-688-6363.

Section 2. Evidence Law Databases

Because new information is continually being added to WESTLAW, you should check the WESTLAW Directory for any new database information.

Database Description	Database Identifier	Coverage
Federal Databases		
U.S. Supreme Court Cases	SCT	From 1945 (1)
U.S. Courts of Appeals Cases	CTA	From 1945 (1)
Individual Courts of Appeals	CTA1–CTA11 CTADC CTAF	See SCOPE for the specific court.
U.S. District Courts Cases (2)	DCT	See SCOPE for the specific court.
U.S. Code Annotated	USCA	Current
U.S. Public Laws	US–PL	Current (3)
Federal Rules	US–RULES	Current
Federal Orders	US–ORDERS	Current
Federal Register	FR	From July 1980
Code of Federal Regulations	CFR	Current (3)
State Databases		
Case Law from all 50 states and the District of Columbia	ALLSTATES	From 1945 (1)
Individual State Cases (3)	XX–CS	See SCOPE for the specific state.
State Statutes—Annotated Statutes and annotations from all available states, the District of Columbia, Puerto Rico and the Virgin Islands	ST–ANN–ALL	See SCOPE for the specific state.
State Statutes—Unannotated Unannotated statutes from all available states, the District of Columbia, Puerto Rico and the Virgin Islands	STAT–ALL	See SCOPE for the specific state.

Database Description	Database Identifier	Coverage
State Databases		
Individual State Statutes—Annotated (4)	XX–ST–ANN	See SCOPE for the specific state.
Individual State Statutes—Unannotated (4)	XX–ST	See SCOPE for the specific state.
Multistate Legislative Service Documents passed by the legislative bodies from all available states, the District of Columbia, Puerto Rico and the Virgin Islands	LEGIS–ALL	See SCOPE for the specific state.
Individual State Legislative Service (3) Documents passed by the legislative bodies of each state, district or territory	XX–LEGIS	See SCOPE for the specific state.
Individual State Statutes (3) General index references for the statutes and constitutions of all available states and the District of Columbia	XX–ST–IDX	See SCOPE for the specific state.
Individual State Attorney General Opinions (3) Attorney general opinions from 49 states	XX–AG	See SCOPE for the specific state.
Individual State Court Rules (4) State court rules from all available states, Puerto Rico and the Virgin Islands	XX–RULES	See SCOPE for the specific state.
Individual State Court Orders (4) State court orders from all available states	XX–ORDERS	See SCOPE for the specific state.
Specialized Materials		
Federal Military Law—Manual for Courts–Martial	FMIL–MCM	From 1941
Military Criminal Law Evidence	MCLE	From July 1987
WESTLAW Topical Highlights—Federal Practice and Procedure	WTH–FPP	Current
Texts & Treatises		
Federal Rules Decisions (5) (articles)	FEDRDTP	From 1986

(1) Cases dated before 1945 are contained in databases whose identifiers end with the suffix—OLD. For example, the identifier for the U.S. Supreme Court Cases—Before 1945 database is SCT–OLD. Coverage for federal databases whose identifiers end with the suffix—OLD is 1789–1944. Coverage for the ALLSTATES–OLD database varies by state.

(2) Case law from the *Federal Rules Decisions* ® reporter can be found in the U.S. District Courts Cases database (DCT).

(3) To search for historical versions of the C.F.R. or U.S. Public Laws, access the appropriate database by typing **db cfrxx** or **db us-plxx**, where xx is the last two digits of a year. For example, to access the C.F.R. as it existed in 1986, type **db cfr86**. To access U.S. Public Laws for 1990, type **db us-pl90**.

(4) XX is a state's two-letter postal abbreviation.

(5) Case law from the *Federal Rules Decisions* reporter can be found in the U.S. District Courts Cases database (DCT), articles from the *Federal Rules Decisions* reporter can be found in the Federal Rules Decisions database (FEDRDTP).

Section 3. EZ ACCESS ™

EZ ACCESS is West Publishing company's menu-driven research system. It is ideal for new or infrequent WESTLAW users because it requires no experience or training on WESTLAW.

EZ ACCESS assists you in performing the following research tasks on WESTLAW:

1. Retrieving a document using its citation or title
2. Retrieving cases using a West topic or key number
3. Retrieving documents using significant words
4. Retrieving references to a document using Insta–Cite ®, Shepard's Citations ®, Shepard's PreView ™ and WESTLAW as a citator.

To access EZ ACCESS, type **ez.** Whenever you are unsure of the next step, or if the choice you want is not listed, simply type **ez**; additional choices will be displayed. Once you retrieve documents with EZ ACCESS, use standard WESTLAW commands to browse your documents. For more information on EZ ACCESS, see the *Guide to EZ ACCESS.* For more information on browsing documents, see the browsing commands listed later in this appendix or Section 9 of the *WESTLAW Reference Manual.*

Section 4. FIND

Overview: FIND is a WESTLAW service that allows you to retrieve a document by entering its citation. FIND allows you to retrieve documents from anywhere in WESTLAW without accessing or changing databases or losing your search result. FIND is available for many documents including federal court rules, case law (federal and state), state statutes, *United States Code Annotated ®*, *Code of Federal Regulations* and *Federal Register* materials, and state and federal public laws.

- ☐ To use FIND, type **fi** followed by the document citation.
- ☐ When you are finished using FIND, you have several options. You can access other services, such as Insta-Cite, Shepard's Citations, Shepard's PreView or Quick*Cite* ™. You can also return to the last database or service accessed before using FIND by typing **gb** or **map**.

To FIND This Document	Type
Jones v. Goodyear Tire & Rubber Co., 1991 WL 128474	**fi 1991 wl 128474**
Wardwell v. United States, 758 F.Supp. 769	**fi 758 fsupp 769**
United States Public Law ** 102–40	**fi us pl 102–40**
Federal Rules of Evidence Rule 803	**fi fre rule 803**
137 Cong.Rec. S8486 (daily ed. June 24, 1991) (statement of Sen. Grassley)	**fi 137 cr s8486**

Section 5. Query Formulation

Overview: A query is a request you make to WESTLAW specifying the information you wish to retrieve. The terms in a query are words or numbers that you include in your request so that WESTLAW will retrieve documents containing those words or numbers. These terms are linked together by connectors, which specify the relationship in which the terms must appear.

5.1 Terms

Plurals and Possessives: Plurals are automatically retrieved when you enter the singular form of a term. This is true for both regular and irregular plurals (e.g., **child** retrieves *children*). If you do not want to retrieve the plural form, you can turn off the automatic pluralizer by typing the # symbol in front of the singular form. If you enter the plural form of a term, you will not retrieve the signular form.

If you enter the non-possessive form of a term, WESTLAW automatically retrieves the possessive form as well. However, if you enter the possessive form, only the possessive form is retrieved.

** FIND retrieves public laws from the current congressional session. To search for historical versions of U.S. public laws, access the appropriate database by typing **db us-plxx,** where xx is the last two digits of a year. For example, to access the United States Public Laws—1990 database (US–PL90), type **db us-pl90**.

Automatic Equivalencies: Some terms have alternative forms or equivalencies; for example, *5* and *five* are equivalent terms. WESTLAW automatically retrieves equivalent terms.

Compound Words and Acronyms: When a compound word is one of your search terms, use a hyphen to retrieve all forms of the word. For example, the term **cross-examination** retrieves *cross-examination, cross examination* and *crossexamination.*

When using an acronym as a search term, place a period after each of the letters in the acronym to retrieve any of its forms. For example, the term **a.p.a.** retrieves *apa, a.p.a., a p a* and *a. p. a.*

Root Expander and Universal Character: Placing a root expander (!) at the end of a root term generates ALL other terms with that root. For example, adding the ! symbol to the root *confess* in the query

confess! /s miranda

instructs WESTLAW to retrieve such words as *confess, confesses, confessed, confessing, confession,* and *confessions.*

The universal character (*) stands for one character and can be inserted in the middle or at the end of a term. For example, the term

withdr*w

will retrieve *withdraw* and *withdrew.* More than one universal character can be used in a term. But adding only two asterisks to the root *jur* in the query

jur**

instructs WESTLAW to retrieve all forms of the root with up to two additional characters. Terms like *jury* or *juror* are retrieved by this query. However, terms with more than two letters following the root, such as *jurisdiction,* are not retrieved. Plurals are always retrieved, even if more than two letters follow the root.

Phrase Searching: To search for a phrase on WESTLAW, place it within quotation marks. For example, to search for references to the doctrine of *res gestae,* type **"res gestae"**. You should use phrase searching only when you are certain that the phrase will not appear in any other form.

5.2 Alternative Terms

After selecting the terms for your query, consider which alternative terms are necessary. For example, if you are searching for the term *custody,* you might also want to search for the terms *detain!* and *detention.* You should consider both synonyms and antonyms as alternative terms.

5.3 Connectors

After selecting terms and alternative terms for your query, use connectors to specify the relationship that should exist between search terms in your retrieved documents. The connectors you can use are described below:

Connector	Meaning	Example
or (space)	Retrieves documents containing either term or both terms.	**coerc! force***
& (and)	Retrieves documents containing both terms.	**waiver & privilege**
/p	Retrieves documents containing both terms in the same paragraph.	**withdr*w /p plea**
/s	Retrieves documents containing both terms in the same sentence.	**refresh! /s recollection**
+s	Retrieves documents in which the first term precedes the second within the same sentence.	**marital +s privilege**
/n	Retrieves documents in which terms are within a specified number of terms of each other.	**business /3 record**
+n	Retrieves documents in which the first term precedes the second by no more than the specified number of terms.	**parol +2 evidence**
% (but not)	Excludes all documents containing the term(s) following the % symbol.	**los* /3 evidence % to (110)**

5.4 Restricting Your Search by Field

Documents in each WESTLAW database consist of several segments, or fields. One field may contain the citation, another the title, another the synopsis, and so forth. A query can be formulated to retrieve only those documents that contain search terms in a specified field. Not all databases contain the same fields. Also, depending on the database, fields of the same name may contain different types of information.

To view the fields and field content for a specific database, type **f** while in the database. Note that in some databases, not every field is available for every document. To restrict your search to a specific field, type the field name or its two-letter abbreviation followed by search terms enclosed in parentheses.

The following fields are available in some WESTLAW databases you might use for evidence law research:

Digest and Synopsis Fields: The digest and synopsis fields, available in cases published by West Publishing Company, summarize the main points of a case. A search in these fields is useful because it retrieves only cases in which a search term was significant enough to be included in a summary.

Consider restricting your search to one or both of these fields if

- ☐ you are searching for common terms or terms with more than one meaning, and you need to narrow your search; or
- ☐ you cannot narrow your search by moving to a smaller database.

For example, suppose you want to retrieve cases that discuss whether parol evidence is admissible in a contract dispute to explain ambiguity in the contract. Access an appropriate database, such as the Connecticut Cases database (CT–CS) and type a query like the following:

sy,di(parol extrinsic /p ambigui! /s contract agreement)

Headnote Field: You can also restrict your search to the headnote field. The headnote field, which is part of the digest field, does not include the topic number, the key number, the citation or the title. A headnote field search is useful when you are searching for references to specific code sections or rule numbers.

For example, to retrieve cases that discuss rule 803(24) of the Federal Rules of Evidence, access a database such as the U.S. Court of Appeals for the Fifth Circuit Cases database (CTA5), and type a query like the following:

he(803(24))

Topic Field: The topic field includes the West digest topic number, topic name, key number and text of the key line for each key number. You should restrict your search to the topic field in a case law database if

- ☐ a digest field search retrieves too many documents; or
- ☐ you want to retrieve cases with digest paragraphs classified under more than one topic.

For example, the topic *Evidence* has the topic number 157. To retrieve Illinois cases that discuss the work product doctrine, access the Illinois Cases database (IL–CS) and type a query like the following:

to(157) /p work-product

To retrieve West headnotes classified under more than one topic, search for the topic name in the topic field.

For example, to search for Illinois cases that discuss privilege and the work product doctrine, access the Illinois Cases database (IL–CS) and type a query like the following:

to(privilege!) /p work-product

Be aware that cases from slip opinions and looseleaf services do not contain the digest, synopsis, headnote or topic fields.

Prelim and Caption Fields: Restrict your search to the prelim and caption fields in a database containing statutes, rules or regulations to retrieve documents where your terms are important enough to appear in the heading or name of a statute or rule.

For example, to retrieve the federal rules of evidence discussing character evidence, access the Federal Rules database (US–RULES) and type

pr,ca(character & evidence)

☐ To look at sections surrounding those your query retrieved, use the DOCUMENTS IN SEQUENCE command. When you are viewing rule 404 you can retrieve the section preceding it by typing **d-**. To retrieve the section immediately following a retrieved document, type **d.** To cancel this command and return to your original search result, type **xd.**

☐ To see if a rule has been amended or repealed, use the UPDATE service. Simply type **update** while viewing the rule to display any court order that amends or repeals the rule.

5.5 Restricting Your Search by Date

You can instruct WESTLAW to retrieve documents decided or issued before, after, or on a specified date, as well as within a range of dates. The following are examples of queries that contain date restrictions:

da(bef 1991 & aft 1986) & los* /3 evidence

da(1990) & los* /3 evidence

da(1988 1989) & los* /3 evidence

da(4/26/90) & los* /3 evidence

da(april 26, 1990) & los* /3 evidence

da(aft 1–1–89) & los* /3 evidence

You can also instruct WESTLAW to retrieve documents added to a database on or after a specified date, as well as within a range of dates. The following are examples of queries that contain added date restrictions:

ad(5–10–91) & los* /3 evidence

ad(aft 1–1–89) & los* /3 evidence

ad(aft 2–1–91 & bef 3–1–91) & los* /3 evidence

Section 6. Insta–Cite ®

Overview: Insta–Cite is West Publishing Company's case history and citation verification service. It is the most current case history service available. Insta–Cite provides the following types of information about a citation:

Direct History: In addition to reversals and affirmances, Insta–Cite gives you the complete reported history of a litigated matter including any related cases. Insta–Cite provides direct history for federal cases from 1754 and for state cases from 1879.

Related References: Related references are cases that involve the same parties and facts as your case, but deal with different legal issues. Insta–Cite provides related references from 1983 to date.

Negative Indirect History: Insta–Cite lists subsequent cases that have a substantial negative impact on your case, including cases overruling your case or calling it into question. Cases affected by decisions from 1972 to date will be displayed on Insta–Cite. To retrieve negative indirect history prior to 1972, use Shepard's Citations (discussed in Section 7).

Secondary Source References: Insta–Cite also provides references to secondary sources that cite your case. These secondary sources presently include legal encyclopedias such as *Corpus Juris Secundum* ®.

Parallel Citations: Insta–Cite provides parallel citations for cases including citations to *Callaghan's Federal Rules Service, Federal Rules Decisions* (cases only), and many other looseleaf reporters.

Citation Verification: Insta–Cite confirms that you have the correct volume and page number for a case. Citation verification information is available from 1754 for federal cases and from 1920 for state cases.

Commands

The following commands can be used in Insta–Cite:

ic xxx or **ic** — Retrieves an Insta–Cite result when followed by a case citation (where xxx is the citation), or when entered from a displayed case, Shepard's result or Shepard's PreView result.

pubs — Displays a list of publications and publication abbreviations available in Insta–Cite.

sc — Displays the scope of Insta–Cite coverage.

expand — Displays the Insta–Cite result with chronological case history. (LOCATE is not available in an expanded Insta–Cite result.)

Loc xxx Restricts an Insta-Cite result to direct or indirect history or to secondary source references when followed by the appropriate code. For example, **Loc dir** restricts the Insta-Cite result to direct history, including related references.

xLoc Cancels your LOCATE request.

Loc auto xxx Automatically restricts subsequent Insta-Cite results according to your LOCATE request (where **XXX** is a LOCATE request).

xLoc auto Cancels your LOCATE AUTO request.

gb or **map2** Returns you to your previous service or search result, if one exists.

Section 7. Shepard's Citations ®

Overview: Shepard's provides a comprehensive list of cases and publications that have cited a particular case. Shepard's also includes explanatory analysis to indicate how the citing cases have treated the case, e.g., "followed," "explained."

In addition to citations from federal, state, and regional citators, Shepard's on WESTLAW includes citations from specialized citators, such as *Civil Procedure Reports, Federal Rules Decisions* (cases only), and many other looseleaf reporters.

Commands

The following commands can be used in Shepard's:

sh xxx or **sh** Retrieves a Shepard's result when followed by a case citation (where xxx is the citation), or when entered from a displayed case, Insta-Cite result or Shepard's PreView result.

pubs Displays a list of publications that can be Shepardized ® and their publication abbreviations.

sc xxx Displays the scope of coverage for a specific publication in Shepard's, where xxx is the publication abbreviation (e.g., **sc civ. proc. n.s.**).

cmds Displays a list of Shepard's commands.

Loc Restricts a Shepard's result to a specific category when followed by the analysis code, headnote number, or state/circuit or publication abbreviation to which you want the display restricted. For example, **Loc 5** restricts the Shepard's result to cases discussing the point of law contained in headnote number five of the cited case. Type **xLoc** to cancel LOCATE.

gb or **map2** Leaves Shepard's and returns you to your previous service or search result, if one exists.

Section 8. Shepard's PreView ™

Overview: Shepard's PreView gives you a preview of citing references from West's National Reporter System ® that will appear in Shepard's Citations. Depending on the citation, Shepard's PreView provides citing information days, weeks or even months before the same information appears in Shepard's online. Use Shepard's PreView to update your Shepard's results.

Commands

The following commands can be used in Shepard's PreView:

sp xxx or **sp** Retrieves a Shepard's PreView result when followed by a case citation (where xxx is the citation), or when entered from a displayed case, Insta–Cite result or Shepard's result.

pubs Displays a list of publications and publication abbreviations that are available in Shepard's PreView.

sc xxx Displays the scope of citing references.

cmds Displays a list of Shepard's PreView commands.

Loc xxx Restricts a Shepard's PreView result by date, publication or jurisdiction, where xxx is the abbreviation.

gb or **map2** Leaves Shepard's PreView and returns you to your previous service or search result, if one exists.

Section 9. Quick*Cite* ™

Overview: Quick*Cite* is a citator service on WESTLAW that enables you to retrieve the most recent citing cases, including slip opinions, automatically.

There is a four- to six-week gap between citing cases listed in Shepard's PreView and the most recent citing cases available on WESTLAW. This gap occurs because cases go through an editorial process at West before they are added to Shepard's PreView. To retrieve the most recent citing cases, therefore, you need to search case law databases on WESTLAW for references to your case; this search technique is known as using WESTLAW as a citator. Quick*Cite* makes using WESTLAW as a citator automatic.

After you've checked your case in the other citator services on WESTLAW, type **qc** to display the Quick*Cite* screen. From this screen, you can press **ENTER** to retrieve the most recent citing cases on WESTLAW, including slip opinions. You can also type **qc** and the citation to display the Quick*Cite* screen, e.g., **qc 96 sct 1569.**

Quick*Cite* formulates a query using the title, the case citation(s), and an added date restriction to retrieve cases more recent than those listed in Shepard's PreView. Quick*Cite* then accesses the appropriate database, either ALLSTATES or ALLFEDS, and runs the query for you.

Quick*Cite* also allows you to choose a different date range and database for your query so you can tailor it to your specific research needs.

Commands

The following commands can be used in Quick *Cite:*

qc xxx or **qc**	Retrieves a Quick*Cite* result when followed by a case citation (where xxx is the citation), or when entered from a displayed case, Insta–Cite result, Shepard's result or Shepard's PreView result.
scope	Displays the scope of Quick*Cite* coverage.
Press ENTER	Updates Shepard's and Shepard's PreView by retrieving documents added to ALLFEDS within the last three months that cite this decision.
all	Retrieves all ALLFEDS documents that cite this decision.
Database Identifier	Retrieves documents added to WESTLAW within the last three months that cite this decision in the selected database.
q	Displays the Quick*Cite* query for editing in ALLFEDS.
map1	Leaves your Quick*Cite* result and returns you to the WESTLAW Directory.

Quick*Cite* is designed to retrieve documents that cite cases. To retrieve citing references to other documents, such as statutes and law review articles, use WESTLAW as a citator.

Section 10. WESTLAW as a Citator

Using WESTLAW as a citator, you can search for documents citing a specific statute, regulation, rule or agency decision. To retrieve documents citing Miss.R.Evid. 804(b), *Hearsay exceptions,* access the Mississippi Cases database (MS–CS) and search for the citation alone:

804(b)

If the citation is not a unique term, add descriptive terms. For example, to retrieve documents citing Miss.R.Evid. 404, discussing character evidence, type a query like the following:

404 /p character /3 evidence

Section 11. Research Examples

1. A colleague refers you to a periodical article surveying the federal law of privileges. How can you retrieve the article on WESTLAW?

Solutions

☐ If you know the publication in which the article appeared, in this case, *Litigation,* check the WESTLAW Directory to see if the publication is online and find the database identifier. Access the database by typing **db litig.** At the Enter Query screen, type a query like the following:

evidence /p privilege

☐ If you know that the title of the article is *The Federal Law of Privileges,* but you don't know the journal in which it appears, access the Journals & Law Reviews database (JLR). Search for key terms in the title field:

ti(federal /s law /s privilege)

☐ If you know that the article citation is 16 Litigation 32 (1989), access the Litigation database (LITIG). Search for terms from the citation in the citation field:

ci(16 +5 32)

2. Your client, who lives in Oregon, is charged with a sex crime against a child. You need to retrieve court rules governing the competency of children as witnesses.

Solution

☐ Access the Oregon Rules database (OR–RULES) and type a query like the following:

child /p witness /p competen!

☐ To see if a rule has been amended or repealed, use the UPDATE service. Simply type **update** while viewing the rule to display any court orders that amend or repeal the rule.

To run your original query in the Oregon Criminal Justice Cases database (ORCJ–CS), type **sdb orcj-cs.**

3. Your client is injured in an automobile accident with an out of state driver. You have brought the action in federal court because of diversity of parties. The defendant has indicated that pursuant to Fed.R.Evid. 609, he intends to impeach the plaintiff by introducing evidence of the plaintiff's past conviction for issuing a bad check with the intent to defraud.

☐ When you know the citation for a specific rule, use FIND to retrieve it. For example, to retrieve Fed.R.Evid. 609, *Impeachment by Evidence of Conviction of Crime,* type the following:

fi fre 609

☐ To view preceding and subsequent rules, use the DOCUMENTS IN SEQUENCE command. To view Fed.R.Evid. 608, type **d-.** To view Rule 610, type **d.**

☐ To see if a rule has been amended or repealed, use the UPDATE service. Simply type **update** while viewing the rule to display any court orders that amend or repeal the rule.

When you retrieve Fre.R.Evid. 609, you also retrieve historical and statutory notes, advisory committee notes, cross references, references to law review commentaries and notes of decisions. Use the LOCATE command to quickly zero in on any annotations in Fed.R. Evid. 609 that discuss bad checks. Type Loc and your query, e.g., **Loc check.**

One of the cases noted is *Petty v. Ideco, Div. of Dresser Industries, Inc.,* 761 F.2d 1146 (5th Cir.1985). Use FIND to retrieve this case by typing **fi 761 f2d 1146.**

You wish to see if this case is still good law and if other cases have cited this case.

Solution

☐ Use Insta-Cite to retrieve the direct and negative indirect history of *Petty*. While viewing the case, type **ic.**

☐ You want to Shepardize ® *Petty*. Type **sh.**

Limit your Shepard's result to decisions containing a reference to a specific headnote, such as headnote 12. Type **Loc 12.**

☐ Check Shepard's PreView for more current cases citing *Petty*. Type **sp.**

☐ Check QuickCite for the most current cases citing *Petty*. Type **qc** and follow the online instructions.

4. In a personal injury action, you want to introduce thermographic evidence to substantiate your client's chiropractor's diagnosis and treatment. You have not found any cases on this subject. How can you retrieve cases discussing the admissibility of thermographic evidence?

Solution

☐ Access the ALLSTATES database and type a query like the following:

thermogra! /p admiss! admit! inadmissib!

5. Your client is chemically dependent and at times forgets to feed her children and clean the house. She went to a social worker for family therapy. Her ex-spouse has commenced an action for change in custody and intends to call the social worker to testify about your client's problems. There are physician-patient and psychotherapist privileges in New York, but you are unsure if these privileges cover social workers or other mental health therapists and counselors engaged in marriage and family therapy.

Solution

☐ Access the New York Cases database (NY-CS), and type a query like the following:

sy,di(privilege* /p social mental family /3 worker counselor therapist)

6. With the advent of computer simulations, it is now possible to display the movement of a car under specified conditions and in compliance with the laws of physics based on mathematical calculations.

While driving in her car, your client's spouse was hit and run over by a semi-truck, killing her instantly. The truck apparently was forced into the spouse's lane when the road narrowed and a red Corvette passed the truck on the right.

Your accident reconstruction expert has a computer-generated simulation that graphically demonstrates, based on the skid marks and the speed of the vehicles, that the truck driver lost control of his vehicle and literally ran over your client's car. How can you get this simulation admitted into evidence?

Solution

☐ Access the Pennsylvania Cases database (PA–CS), and type a query like the following:

computer! /s animat! simulat! /p evidence admiss! admit! inadmissib!

☐ If you don't retrieve any cases in your jurisdiction, you will want to run the same query in the ALLSTATES database by typing **sdb allstates**.

☐ Run the same query in the Journals & Law Reviews database (JLR) by typing **sdb jlr**. The JLR database contains articles from law reviews, Continuing Legal Education course handbooks and bar journals.

7. As a new associate in the firm, you are expected to keep up with and summarize recent legal developments in the area of evidence. How can you monitor developments in evidence efficiently?

Solution

☐ One of the easiest ways to stay abreast of recent developments in evidence is by regularly accessing the WESTLAW Topical Highlights—Federal Practice and Procedure database (WTH–FPP). The WTH–FPP database summarizes recent legal developments, including court decisions, legislation and materials released by administrative agencies that pertain to the issues of jurisdiction, evidence, the rules of civil and appellate procedure, limitations and the mechanics of practicing law in the federal courts.

☐ To access the database, type **db wth-fpp**. You automatically retrieve a list of documents added to the database in the last two weeks. To read a summary of a document listed, type its corresponding number.

☐ You can also search this database. To display the Enter Query screen, type **s** from anywhere in the database. At the Enter

Query screen, type your query. For example, to retrieve references discussing evidence and discovery of business records, type a query like the following:

business /3 record file

Section 12. WESTLAW Commands

General Commands

ez	Accesses the EZ ACCESS system; when entered from EZ ACCESS, displays additional choices.
help	Displays explanatory messages.
scope	Displays a database description when followed by a database identifier or when entered from a database; displays the scope of coverage when entered from a service, such as Insta-Cite.
time	Displays the amount of chargeable time used in your research session.
off	Signs off WESTLAW.
pr	Displays the Offline Printing and Downloading Menu.
opd	Displays the Offline Print Directory.
client	Allows you to change your client identifier.
options	Displays the WESTLAW Options Directory.

Search Commands

s	New search—displays the Enter Query screen.
q	Edit query—displays the last query for editing.
x	Cancels a search in progress.
db	Returns to the WESTLAW Directory from a database; accesses a database when followed by a database identifier: **db sct**.
sdb xxx	Runs the same query in a different database, where **xxx** is the database identifier: **sdb allfeds**.
qdb xxx	Displays the query for editing in a different database, where **xxx** is the database identifier: **qdb allstates**.
read	In selected databases, retrieves the most recent documents when entered at the Enter Query screen.
List	In selected databases, retrieves a list of the most recent documents when entered at the Enter Query screen.

Browsing Commands

t	Term mode—displays the next page containing the terms in the requested relationship; **t-** displays the previous page containing the terms in the requested relationship.

p	Page mode—displays the next page of a document; **p-** displays the previous page of a document. To display a specific page, type **p** followed by the page number: **p5**.
Loc	LOCATE—locates selected terms in retrieved documents; also restricts a Shepard's display to selected categories, such as history and treatment codes, headnote numbers and citing publications.
LLoc	Retrieves a citations list of LOCATE documents.
xLoc	Cancels a LOCATE command.
r	Displays the next ranked document; displays a specific document when followed by the document's rank number: **r3**.
L	Displays a citations list.
Lr#	Displays a citations list beginning with a specific rank number: **Lr8**.
g	Search summary—displays the query and the number of documents retrieved by it.
h+	Advances one half page in a document.
h−	Moves back one half page in a document.
d	DOCUMENTS IN SEQUENCE—displays sections preceding or following the retrieved document: **d+#, d−#**.
xd	Cancels DOCUMENTS IN SEQUENCE and displays the document you were viewing when you entered the DOCUMENTS IN SEQUENCE command.
f	Displays a list of fields in a database; restricts your display to a selected field or fields when followed by the field name: **f opinion**.
xf	Cancels your command to restrict your display by field.

Service Commands

fi	FIND—retrieves a document when followed by its citation: **fi 93 sct 2357**.
ic	Retrieves an Insta-Cite result when followed by the case citation, **ic 93 sct 2357**, or when entered from a displayed case, Shepard's result or Shepard's PreView result.
sh	Retrieves a Shepard's result when followed by the case citation, **sh 93 sct 2357**, or when entered from a displayed case, Insta-Cite result or Shepard's PreView result.

sp	Retrieves a Shepard's PreView result when followed by the case citation, **sp 93 sct 2357**, or when entered from a displayed case, Insta–Cite result or Shepard's result.
qc	Retrieves a QuickCite result when followed by the case citation, **qc 93 sct 2357**, or when entered from a displayed case, Insta–Cite result, Shepard's result or Shepard's PreView result.
pdq	Personal Directory of Queries—displays a list of saved queries for selection and update.
di	Enters the Black's Law Dictionary ® service or displays a definition when followed by the word or phrase: **di presumption**.
update	Displays any document amending or repealing the statute, rule or regulation you are viewing.
rm	Displays the Related Materials Directory for a statute, legislative service document, rule or order.
gm	Displays General Materials, which are references and tables applicable to the entire title, chapter and subchapter containing the displayed statute.
annos	Displays annotations (Notes of Decisions) for the displayed statute.
refs	Displays references to the unannotated statutory document you are viewing.
st-ann	Displays the annotated statute(s) amended or repealed by the displayed document.
stat	Displays the unannotated statute(s) amended or repealed by the displayed document.
rules	Displays the court rule(s) affected by the displayed court order.
gb	GO BACK—returns to a previous location in WESTLAW from a service, e.g., Insta–Cite, Shepard's, FIND.
map	Displays a list containing the most recent database and services accessed and allows you to return to them.
map1	Returns to the WESTLAW Directory.
map2	Returns to your search result, if one exists.

†